THE CAMBRIDGE WORLD HISTORY

*

VOLUME VII

Since 1750, the world has become ever more connected, with processes of production and destruction no longer limited by land- or water-based modes of transport and communication. Volume VII of the *Cambridge World History* series, divided into two books, offers a variety of angles of vision on the increasingly interconnected history of humankind. The first book examines structures, spaces, and processes within which and through which the modern world was created, including the environment, energy, technology, population, disease, law, industrialization, imperialism, decolonization, nationalism, and socialism, along with key world regions. The second book questions the extent to which the transformations of the modern world have been shared, focusing on social developments such as urbanization, migration, and changes in family and sexuality; cultural connections through religion, science, music, and sport; ligaments of globalization including rubber, drugs, and the automobile; and moments of particular importance from the Atlantic revolutions to 1989.

J. R. McNeill is a Professor of History and University Professor at Georgetown University. His books include *The Atlantic Empires of France and Spain, 1700–1763, The Mountains of the Mediterranean World* (Cambridge University Press, 1992), *Something New Under the Sun: An Environmental History of the Twentieth-century World, The Human Web: A Bird's-eye View of World History*, and *Mosquito Empires: Ecology and War in the Greater Caribbean, 1620–1914* (Cambridge University Press, 2010).

Kenneth Pomeranz is a University Professor of History and in the College at the University of Chicago. His publications include *The Great Divergence: China, Europe, and the Making of the Modern World Economy, The Making of a Hinterland: State, Society and Economy in Inland North China, 1853–1937*, and *The World that Trade Created.*

THE CAMBRIDGE WORLD HISTORY

The Cambridge World History is an authoritative new overview of the dynamic field of world history. It covers the whole of human history, not simply history since the development of written records, in an expanded time frame that represents the latest thinking in world and global history. With over two hundred essays, it is the most comprehensive account yet of the human past, and it draws on a broad international pool of leading academics from a wide range of scholarly disciplines. Reflecting the increasing awareness that world history can be examined through many different approaches and at varying geographic and chronological scales, each volume offers regional, topical, and comparative essays alongside case studies that provide depth of coverage to go with the breadth of vision that is the distinguishing characteristic of world history.

THE CAMBRIDGE WORLD HISTORY

*

VOLUME VII

Production, Destruction, and Connection, 1750–Present
Part 2: Shared Transformations?

*

Edited by
J. R. MCNEILL
Georgetown University
and
KENNETH POMERANZ
University of Chicago

CAMBRIDGE
UNIVERSITY PRESS

University Printing House, Cambridge CB2 8BS, United Kingdom

Cambridge University Press is part of the University of Cambridge.

It furthers the University's mission by disseminating knowledge in the pursuit of education, learning and research at the highest international levels of excellence.

www.cambridge.org
Information on this title: www.cambridge.org/9780521199643

First published 2015

Printed in the United Kingdom by TJ International Ltd. Padstow Cornwall

A catalog record for this publication is available from the British Library

ISBN 978-0-521-19964-3 Hardback

Contents

PART IV: LIGAMENTS OF GLOBALIZATION

Figures

Maps

Tables

Contributors

SUSAN BROWNELL, University of Missouri-St. Louis
CAROLE FINK, Ohio State University
ANTONIA FINNANE, University of Melbourne
LALITHA GOPALAN, University of Texas
DANIEL HEADRICK, Roosevelt University
DIRK HOERDER, University of Arizona
LYNN HOLLEN LEES, University of Pennsylvania
WILLIAM MCALLISTER, Georgetown University
JAMES E. MCCLELLAN III, Stevens Institute of Technology
JÜRGEN OSTERHAMMEL, University of Konstanz
RICHARD OVERY, University of Exeter
JULIE PEAKMAN, University of London
NICOLE REBEC, University of California, Irvine
BERNHARD RIEGER, University College London
JAIME RODRÍGUEZ, University of California, Irvine
DANIEL SARGENT, University of California, Berkeley
ALESSANDRO STANZIANI, Ecole des Hautes Etudes en Sciences Sociales and Centre National des Recherches Scientifique
PETER STEARNS, George Mason University
TIMOTHY D. TAYLOR, University of California, Los Angeles
RICHARD TUCKER, University of Michigan and Oakland University
PETER VAN DER VEER, Max Planck Institute
JEFFREY WASSERSTROM, University of California, Irvine
THOMAS W. ZEILER, University of Colorado, Boulder

Preface

The Cambridge Histories have long presented authoritative multi-volume overviews of historical topics, with chapters written by specialists. The first of these, the *Cambridge Modern History*, planned by Lord Acton and appearing after his death from 1902 to 1912, had fourteen volumes and served as the model for those that followed, which included the seven-volume *Cambridge Medieval History* (1911–1936), the twelve-volume *Cambridge Ancient History* (1924–1939), the thirteen-volume *Cambridge History of China* (1978–2009), and more specialized multi-volume works on countries, religions, regions, events, themes, and genres. These works are designed, as the *Cambridge History of China* puts it, to be the "largest and most comprehensive" history in the English language of their topic, and, as the *Cambridge History of Political Thought* asserts, to cover "every major theme."

The *Cambridge World History* both follows and breaks with the model set by its august predecessors. Presenting the "largest and most comprehensive" history of the world would take at least three hundred volumes – and a hundred years – as would covering "every major theme." Instead the series provides an overview of the dynamic field of world history in seven volumes over nine books. It covers all of human history, not simply that since the development of written records, in an expanded time frame that represents the newest thinking in world history. This broad time frame blurs the line between archaeology and history, and presents both as complementary approaches to the human past. The volume editors include archaeologists as well as historians, and have positions at universities in the United States, Britain, France, Australia, and Israel. The essays similarly draw on a broad author pool of historians, art historians, anthropologists, classicists, archaeologists, economists, linguists, sociologists, biologists, geographers, and area studies specialists, who come from universities in Australia, Britain, Canada, China, Estonia, France, Germany, India, Israel, Italy, Japan, the Netherlands, New Zealand, Poland, Portugal, Singapore, Sweden, Switzerland, and the United States. They include very senior scholars whose works have helped to form the field, and also mid-career and younger scholars whose research will continue to shape it in the future. Some of the authors are closely associated with the rise of world history as a distinct research and teaching field, while others describe what they do primarily as global history, transnational history, international history, or comparative history. (Several of the essays in Volume I trace the development of these overlapping, entangled, and at times competing fields.) Many authors are simply specialists on their topic who the editors thought could best explain this to a broader audience or reach beyond their comfort zones into territory that was new.

Reflecting the increasing awareness that world history can be examined through many different approaches and at varying geographic and chronological scales, each volume offers several types of essays, including regional, topical, and comparative ones, along with case studies that provide depth to go with the breadth of vision that is the distinguishing characteristic of world history. Volume 1 introduces key frames of analysis that shape the making of world history across time periods, with essays on overarching approaches, methods, and themes. It then includes a group of essays on the Paleolithic, covering the 95 percent of human history up to 10,000 BCE. From that point on, each volume covers a shorter time period than its predecessor, with slightly overlapping chronologies volume to volume to reflect the complex periodization of a truly global history. The editors chose the overlapping chronologies, and stayed away from traditional period titles (e.g. "classical" or "early modern") intentionally to challenge standard periodization to some degree. The overlapping chronologies also allow each volume to highlight geographic disjunctures and imbalances, and the ways in which various areas influenced one another. Each of the volumes centers on a key theme or cluster of themes that the editors view as central to the period covered in the volume and also as essential to an understanding of world history as a whole.

Volume 2 (A World with Agriculture, 12,000 BCE–500 CE) begins with the Neolithic, but continues into later periods to explore the origins of agriculture and agricultural communities in various regions of the world, as well as to discuss issues associated with pastoralism and hunter-fisher-gatherer economies. It traces common developments in the more complex social structures and cultural forms that agriculture enabled, and then presents a series of regional overviews accompanied by detailed case studies from many different parts of the world.

Volume 3 (Early Cities and Comparative History, 4000 BCE–1200 CE) focuses on early cities as motors of change in human society. Through case studies of cities and comparative chapters that address common issues, it traces the creation and transmission of administrative and information technologies, the performance of rituals, the distribution of power, and the relationship of cities with their hinterlands. It has a broad and flexible chronology to capture the development of cities in various regions of the world and the transformation of some cities into imperial capitals.

Volume 4 (A World with States, Empires, and Networks, 1200 BCE–900 CE) continues the analysis of processes associated with the creation of larger-scale political entities and networks of exchange, including those generally featured in accounts of the rise of "classical civilizations," but with an expanded time frame that allows the inclusion of more areas of the world. It analyzes common social, economic, cultural, political, and technological developments, and includes chapters on slavery, religion, science, art, and gender. It then presents a series of regional overviews, each accompanied by a case study or two examining one smaller geographic area or topic within that region in greater depth.

Volume 5 (Expanding Webs of Exchange and Conquest, 500 CE–1500 CE) highlights the growing networks of trade and cross-cultural interaction that were a hallmark of the millennium covered in the volume, including the expansion of text-based religions and the transmission of science, philosophy, and technology. It explores social structures, cultural institutions, and significant themes such as the environment, warfare, education, the family, and courtly cultures on both a global and Eurasian scale, and continues the examination of state formation begun in Volume 4 with chapters on polities and empires in Asia, Africa, Europe, and the Americas.

The first five volumes each appear in a single book, but the last two are double volumes covering the periods conventionally known as the early modern and modern, an organization signaling the increasing complexity of an ever more globalized world in the last half millennium, as well as the expanding base of source materials and existing historical analyses for these more recent eras. Volume 6 (The Construction of a Global World, 1400–1800 CE) traces the increasing biological, commercial, and cultural exchanges of the period, and explores regional and transregional political, cultural and intellectual developments. The first book within this volume, "Foundations," focuses on global matrices that allowed this increasingly interdependent world to be created, including the environment, technology, and disease; crossroads and macro-regions such as the Caribbean, the Indian Ocean, and Southeast Asia in which connections were especially intense; and large-scale political formations, particularly maritime and land-based empires such as Russia, the Islamic Empires, and the Iberian Empires that stretched across continents and seas. The second book within this volume, "Patterns of Change," examines global and regional migrations and encounters, and the economic, social, cultural, and institutional structures that both shaped and were shaped by these, including trade networks, law, commodity flows, production processes, and religious systems.

Volume 7 (Production, Destruction, and Connection, 1750-Present) examines the uneven transition to a world with fossil fuels and an exploding human population that has grown ever more interactive through processes of globalization. The first book within this double volume, "Structures, Spaces, and Boundary Making," discusses the material situations within which our crowded world has developed, including the environment, agriculture, technology, energy, and disease; the political movements that have shaped it, such as nationalism, imperialism, decolonization, and communism; and some of its key regions. The second book, "Shared Transformations?" explores topics that have been considered in earlier volumes, including the family, urbanization, migration, religion, and science, along with some that only emerge as global phenomena in this era, such as sports, music, and the automobile, as well as specific moments of transition, including the Cold War and 1989.

Taken together, the volumes contain about two hundred essays, which means the *Cambridge World History* is comprehensive, but certainly not exhaustive. Each volume editor has made difficult choices about what to include and what to leave out, a problem for all world histories since those of Herodotus and Sima Qian more than two millennia ago. Each volume is arranged in the way that the volume editor or editors decided is most appropriate for the period, so that organizational schema differ slightly from volume to volume. Given the overlapping chronologies, certain topics are covered in several different volumes because they are important for understanding the historical processes at the heart of each of these, and because we as editors decided that viewing key developments from multiple perspectives is particularly appropriate for world history. As with other

Cambridge Histories, the essays are relatively lightly footnoted, and include a short list of further readings, the first step for readers who want to delve deeper into the field. In contrast to other Cambridge Histories, all volumes are being published at the same time, for the leisurely pace of the print world that allowed publication over several decades does not fit with twenty-first-century digital demands.

In other ways as well, the *Cambridge World History* reflects the time in which it has been conceptualized and produced, just as the *Cambridge Modern History* did. Lord Acton envisioned his work, and Cambridge University Press described it, as "a history of the world," although in only a handful of chapters out of several hundred were the principal actors individuals, groups, or polities outside of Europe and North America. This is not surprising, although the identical self-description of the *New Cambridge Modern History* (1957–1979), with a similar balance of topics, might be a bit more so. The fact that in 1957 – and even in 1979, when the last volume of the series appeared – Europe would be understood as "the world" and as the source of all that was modern highlights the power and longevity of the perspective we have since come to call "Eurocentric." (In other languages, there are perspectives on world history that are similarly centered on the regions in which they have been produced.) The continued focus on Europe in the mid-twentieth century also highlights the youth of the fields of world and global history, in which the conferences, professional societies, journals, and other markers of an up-and-coming field have primarily emerged since the 1980s, and some only within the last decade. The *Journal of World History*, for example, was first published in 1990, the *Journal of Global History* in 2005, and *New Global Studies* in 2007.

World and global history have developed in an era of intense self-reflection in all academic disciplines, when no term can be used unselfconsciously and every category must be complicated. Worries about inclusion and exclusion, about diversity and multivocality, are standard practice in sub-fields of history and related disciplines that have grown up in this atmosphere. Thus as we editors sought topics that would give us a balance between the traditional focus in world history on large-scale political and economic processes carried out by governments and commercial elites and newer concerns with cultural forms, representation, and meaning, we also sought to include topics that have been important in different national historiographies. We also attempted to find authors who would provide geographic balance along with a balance between older and younger voices. Although the author pool is decidedly broader geographically – and more balanced in terms of gender – than it was in either of the Cambridge Modern Histories, it is not as global as we had hoped. Contemporary world and global history is overwhelmingly Anglophone, and, given the scholarly diaspora, disproportionately institutionally situated in the United States and the United Kingdom. Along with other disparities in our contemporary world, this disproportion is, of course, the result of the developments traced in this series, though the authors might disagree about which volume holds the key to its origins, or whether one should spend much time searching for origins at all.

My hopes for the series are not as sweeping as Lord Acton's were for his, but fit with those of Tapan Raychaudhuri and Irfan Habib, the editors of the two-volume Cambridge Economic History of India (1982). In the preface to their work, they comment: "We only dare to hope that our collaborative effort will stimulate discussion and help create new knowledge which may replace before many years the information and analysis offered in this volume." In a field as vibrant as world and global history, I have no doubts that such new transformative knowledge will emerge quickly, but hope this series will provide an entrée to the field, and a useful overview of its state in the early twenty-first century.

MERRY E. WIESNER-HANKS

PART I

⋆

SOCIAL DEVELOPMENTS

1

Migrations

DIRK HOERDER

Human mobility balances the supply of and demand for human capital over small and large distances connected by information flows and means of transportation. Migration involves costs, so people who move are generally seeking options, not necessarily "unlimited opportunities." Regions and societies of departure lost (and, in the present, lose) human capital – the capabilities of young working-age men and women into whom families and states had invested training and education – while societies and economies of destination gained (and gain) productive and tax-paying input. Although scholars and political leaders generally pay more attention to long-distance migration, usually undercounting women and thus providing a skewed data set, much migration is short- or medium-distance. Migration internal to empires and countries is far more extensive than is migration that crosses international boundaries. Migration systems are empirically observable patterns of large-scale movement over extended periods of time. They may be region-specific or they may be transcontinental or transoceanic. Analysis of patterns requires an integrated perspective on short- and long-distance, men's and women's, single and family migrations. It requires distinguishing among types of migration – temporary labor, permanent urban, permanent rural settlement, refugee or deportation – but also being aware that the types may intermesh. Finally, it requires combining attention to economic frames in the societies of departure and arrival and state-imposed legal frames with consideration of migrants' life-course perspectives and actual decision-making.[1]

1 This chapter is based on Dirk Hoerder, *Cultures in Contact: World Migrations in the Second Millennium* (Durham: Duke University Press, 2002), and Christiane Harzig, Dirk Hoerder, Donna Gabaccia, *What is Migration History?* (Cambridge: Polity, 2009). Quantitative data are mainly from Adam M. McKeown, "Global Migration, 1846–1940," *Journal of World History* 15.2 (2005), 155–189, José C. Moya, "A Continent of Immigrants: Postcolonial Shifts in the Western Hemisphere," *Hispanic American Historical Review* 86/1 (2006), 1–28, and Moya and McKeown, "World migration in the long twentieth century," in Michael Adas (ed.), *Essays on Twentieth-Century History* (Philadelphia: Temple University Press, 2010), pp. 9–52.

Patterns and directions of migrations changed, and during this era there were four distinct periods: from the 1770s to the 1830s, from the 1830s to the 1930s, from the early 1950s to the 1990s, and finally the beginning of the twenty-first century. Region-specific political and economic developments, changing borders and power hierarchies between empires and states, shifting relative importance of medium or small economic regions, and war, revolution, or natural disasters all impacted individuals' and families' migration decisions. Aware of the local problems in eking out bare subsistence in rural or urban economies and having information about better working and living conditions elsewhere, individuals and families decided in the context of systems of norms and values – Confucianism, Islam, Christianity, or other. Migration in turn had an impact on families, gender relations, intergenerational hierarchies and on society-wide economic and social relations. Quantitatively, those making decisions – the world population – grew from just under 1 billion in 1800 to around 7 billion in 2010. Accordingly, in absolute terms the number of migrants grew, but relatively – number of migrants per 1000 population – the ratio depended on socio-economic factors. Increasing nearby options with relatively low costs for a move, like urban development and industrialization, increased mobility. So did imperial expansion – the ratio of mobility among the Dutch, for example, was highest during the country's seventeenth-century colonizing expansion. Quantitative data about actual migrations are often lacking or skewed, since assumptions about the sedentariness of "common" people initially prevented an interest in data collection, and when data began to be collected in the nineteenth century, the emphasis on the state and nation meant they were collected only at interstate borders, and then in a gendered mental framework that relegated women and children to "associational" status to male migrants.

In the first of the four periods, the 1770s to the 1830s, macro-regionally distinct patterns of migrations were connected, in that a small number of heavily armed and powerful colonizer migrants imposed their rule and established export economies in many places. But, as yet, vast regions like China remained practically untouched. From the 1830s to the 1930s hemispheric migration systems may be discerned: the continued forced migrations of the Africa–Plantation Belt-Americas slave regime; the massive expansion of the transatlantic migration system and of the Russian–Siberian one; the imposition of a British India and Southern China Plantation Belt system of indentured servitude (replacing the usage of African slave labor); and late in the nineteenth century a North China-to-Manchuria system. After a kind of intermission due to the Global

Depression of the 1930s and World War II, new macro-regional systems developed in the early 1950s that lasted until the 1990s. These were changed in the early twenty-first century with the emergence of new, powerful economies in some of the formerly colonized societies, although this new pattern was interrupted by the financial crisis of 2008.

Migrations from the 1770s to the 1830s

In the so-called Age of Revolution in the Atlantic World, British and continental European anti-revolutionary warfare made migration perilous. Although vast numbers of hired or drafted soldiers were moved, and refugees, uprooted people, and return migrants crisscrossed zones of fighting, survivors were often left stranded somewhere. In the hinge region of the Mediterranean-European and Indian Ocean-Asian Worlds the power struggle of the Tsarist and Habsburg Empires against the Ottoman Empire sent soldiers moving and Muslim peasant families fleeing. Thus vast territories north of the Black Sea were opened for resettlement by immigrant peasant families of other faiths, mostly from the smaller states of southwestern Germany. In the Balkans, the Habsburgs' re-imposition of feudal exactions, like their earlier re-catholicization in Hungary, increased out-migration. In the process the ethno-culturally and religiously pluralist structures of the Ottoman Empire – a model for Europe at the time – weakened. In the Tsarist Empire, the administration made Siberia's climatically harsh regions (long part of the global fur trade economy) a destination for political and criminal deportees, but unauthorized peasant migrants who lacked land and who preferred distance to state control and government tax collectors made its fertile southern belt their destination in the eighteenth century. In the Chinese Empire, economic growth and innovation in specific economic sectors drew migrants in search of better investment options for their human capital. Imperial expansion involved uprooting, a change of culture, and resettlement migrations. As regards the global plantation belt, which had developed with the Iberian powers' acquisition of the Caribbean in the early sixteenth century and the accompanying forced slave migrations, human rights concepts and economic change brought an outlawing of the slave trade in 1807/1808 in areas controlled by signatories to the Vienna Congress, but not in Brazil for example. In defiance of their countries' laws, however, slavers from Europe and the Americas continued the trade to the 1870s. In Latin America as in the emerging USA, trans-European warfare with its transatlantic corollaries from the 1760s to 1815 resulted in a decline of colonizer power and the emergence of independent states by the 1820s. Involuntary mobility was part of the warfare as soldiers, slaves, and refugees moved, as was voluntary mobility with the flight of Spanish-Creole elites. In contrast to North America, no immigrant-attracting economies developed in Latin America in the first half of the nineteenth century.

Internal migrations and hemispheric migration systems from the 1830s to the 1930s

The nineteenth century saw the development of systemic frames of mobility: the gradual abolition of the slave trade and slavery in the global plantation belt and mining regions as well as imposition of colonizers' forced labor regimes in Asia and Africa; stepwise state-by-state ending of servitude in Europe; and migration of rural surplus populations into fertile regions (thinly) inhabited by other peoples and to industrial wage work in all segments of the globe. At the same time imperial penetration extended into China, Japan, and sub-Saharan Africa's interior. With the expansion of rail networks from the 1830s and the introduction of steamships on transoceanic routes from the 1870s, mobility increased and transport costs plummeted. Products from the colonies, too, could be transported more cheaply, demand increased, and the plantation and extraction system relying on local forced and free migratory labor expanded.

Within this global frame, hemisphere-wide migrations systems emerged of men and women moving independently, in family units, or sequentially as families or siblings. Best-known is the Atlantic one, resuming after 1815, mainly to North America but including South America from the second half of the nineteenth century (55–58 million) and, in small numbers of almost exclusively men, to the European powers' worldwide colonized realm (1 million). This included the forced migrations of enslaved African men and women, profitable to African slave-catching states, White trading and shipping interests, and White and Métis plantation owners, which involved about 2 million in the nineteenth century, ending in the 1870s. A second was the Indian Ocean–Southeast Asian–South China system developed from the 1830s, continuing earlier patterns but influenced by European colonizer interests. It extended to the Caribbean, Brazil, and – during World War I – to Europe (48–52 million). A third was a North China-to-Manchuria System from the 1880s, in which impoverished rural residents headed for agricultural and industrial frontier regions (*c.* 40 million). A fourth was the Russian–Siberian System, in which an estimated 10–12 million men and women moved

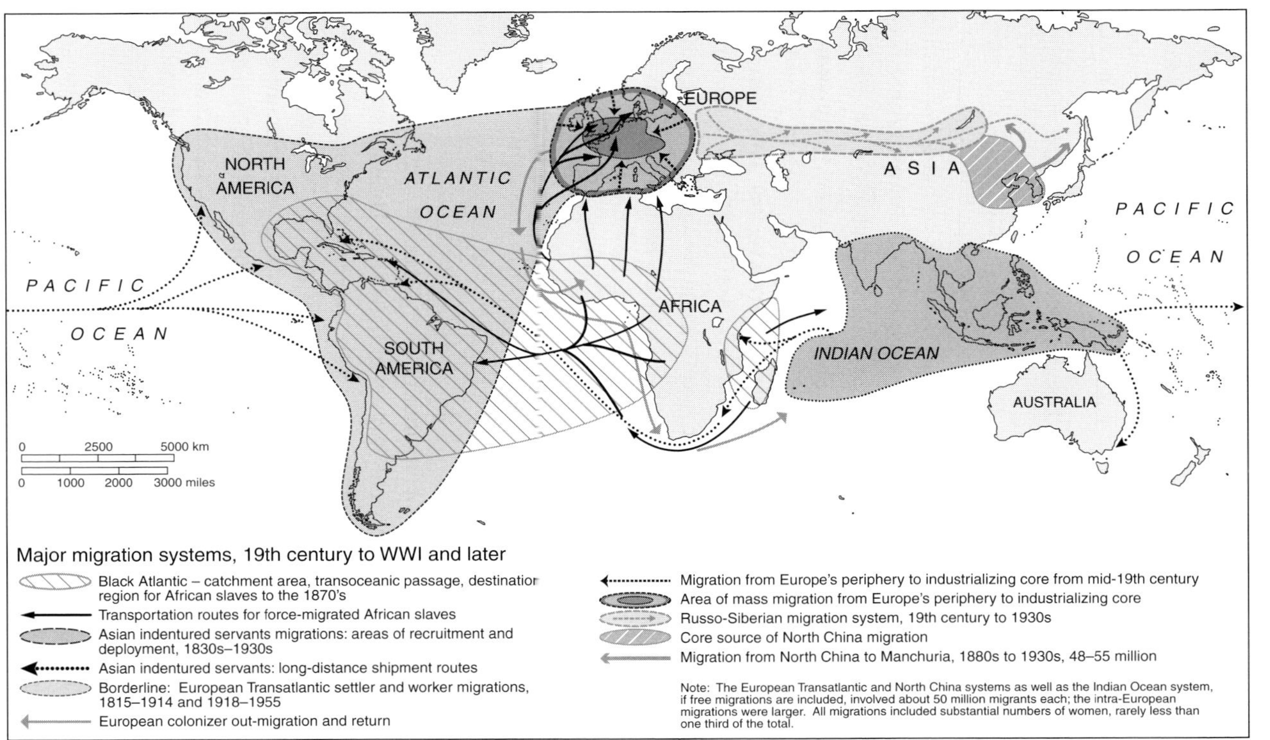
EUROPE
NORTH AMERICA
ATLANTIC OCEAN
ASIA
PACIFIC OCEAN
AFRICA
SOUTH AMERICA
INDIAN OCEAN
AUSTRALIA
PACIFIC OCEAN
0 2500 5000 km
0 1000 2000 3000 miles
Major migration systems, 19th century to WWI and later
Black Atlantic – catchment area, transoceanic passage, destination region for African slaves to the 1870's
Transportation routes for force-migrated African slaves
Asian indentured servants migrations: areas of recruitment and deployment, 1830s–1930s
Asian indentured servants: long-distance shipment routes
Borderline: European Transatlantic settler and worker migrations, 1815–1914 and 1918–1955
European colonizer out-migration and return
Migration from Europe's periphery to industrializing core from mid-19th century
Area of mass migration from Europe's periphery to industrializing core
Russo-Siberian migration system, 19th century to 1930s
Core source of North China migration
Migration from North China to Manchuria, 1880s to 1930s, 48–55 million
Note: The European Transatlantic and North China systems as well as the Indian Ocean system, if free migrations are included, involved about 50 million migrants each; the intra-European migrations were larger. All migrations included substantial numbers of women, rarely less than one third of the total.

Map 1.1 Major migration systems

east to southern Siberia's fertile lands as far as the Amur River. In South America's newly independent societies numerous regional patterns of migration developed. In North Africa from the 1830s and sub-Saharan Africa from the 1880s massive military colonization of European powers caused refugee movements, regional forced labor migrations, and other migrations in which individuals or families themselves made the decision to move. Earlier Eurocentric scholarship on migration has ignored some of these, however, such as the North China–Manchuria ones, and reduced others to racialized clichés, such as free (white) versus bound (brown and yellow) "coolie" migrations, or free transatlantic migrations versus absolutist bureaucracy-imposed Siberian exile.

Abolition of serfdom in Europe and of slavery in the Plantation Belt and the Americas should have increased self-directed mobility, but those emancipated in many cases had to compensate their former owners for the loss of property rather than being compensated for their unpaid labor. Resulting further impoverishment might force people to move, but new restraints might also impose further immobility. Where demand for labor remained high, official structural violence of new laws or private lynch violence regimes (as in the US South) prevented freed Black men and women from gaining liberty of movement. In other sections of the Plantation Belt, Haiti and Brazil for example, those liberated from bondage migrated to wage labor or to marginal regions where they engaged in independent subsistence farming. In Europe, liberated serfs escaped from extreme constraints, but they were not completely "free" migrants as their destination was often not self-willed.

In India, South China, and some South East Asian islands, indenture or "second slavery" bound men and women for five years. Reasons for indentures included individual shortcomings, poverty, and unfortunate circumstances, and also the new British – as well as Dutch and French – tax and labor impositions. Coercion to purchase food in plantation stores and employer refusal to pay return fare could result in forced re-indenture or permanent enslavement. All systems of bondage involved forced mobilization and, at the destination, forced immobilization. However, when the location of production changed, secondary forced migrations ensued, as with exhaustion of soils or shifts to new crops in the USA and Brazil.

Gender ideologies "bound" women and sometimes reduced their mobility. In China, for example, Confucian prescripts of women as dependent, even servant-like members of families severely restrained their options to migrate. The traditional equation of migrants with men, however, is as

Figure 1.1 Plantation workers on arrival from India, mustered at Depot, *c.*1891 (Royal Commonwealth Society, London, UK / Bridgeman Images)

wrong as the data collected by male-staffed state bureaucracies was. In nineteenth-century intra-European migrations about 50 percent of the migrants were women, and in the transatlantic ones 40 percent, although this varied by group and stage of a migration process. Under indentured servitude about 20–35 percent of the migrants were women. Without presence of women neither community formation nor inter-generational continuity was possible.[2] Women often migrated (and migrate) to service positions, but rather than remaining in "their" sphere they crossed two borders: that between rural and urban lifeways and that between the laboring and employing classes. In some places gender systems actually increased women's mobility in comparison with men's. In Africa, for example, regional forms of rights-in-person dependency of debtors to creditors were feminized,

2 Hoerder and Amarjit Kaur, eds., *Proletarian and Gendered Mass Migrations: A Global Perspective on Continuities and Discontinuities from the 19th to the 21st Century* (Leiden: Brill, 2013); Linda Bryder, "Sex, race, and colonialism: an historiographic review," *International History Review* 20 (1998), 806–822; Clare Midgley, ed., *Gender and Imperialism* (Manchester University Press, 1998).

and mainly women and children migrated short-distance to serve or work for creditors.

Globally, with fast population growth, in all rural regions with family subsistence plots all but the first two surviving children had to out-migrate. Destinations involved (and involve) thinly settled rural areas (from New England to the Ohio Valley, from the Yangzi's plains to ever steeper hillsides), labor markets in infra-structural, usually earth-moving tasks such as the building of canals, roads, railroads, and urban labor markets. At the peak of transatlantic emigration from the Habsburg Empire around 1910, 95 per cent of those leaving their land or small towns migrated internally, so absolute numbers and ratios have to be reconstructed from local vital records. Given the high mortality in all cities with poor sanitation systems, even maintenance of population levels depended on continuous in-migration. Ritual washing, prescribed in Islamic societies, improved public hygiene. Traditionally, people in some rural regions generated non-agricultural income by gendered specialized craftwork in the home, such as cloth in most regions of the world, pottery in some regions of China and among West African Mande, cutlery in the German Palatinate, or lace in Swiss mountain valleys. Nineteenth-century concentration of production in manufactorics and, subsequently, machine-driven ones, as well as railway-mediated import of mass-produced goods, reduced such local sources of income and forced single young men and women or whole families to depart. Studies of village as well as pastoral populations indicate high mobility and contradict the imagery of immobile countrysides. People were aware that urban agglomerations provided and provide more job and training options as well as recreational and marriage choices. From the 1880s to World War One, patterns of migration changed because of regionally specific job-providing industrialization and option-increasing urbanization.

The Atlantic migration system

While in the nineteenth century the world's population grew by about 60 per cent, Europe's doubled, which contributed to the development of an Atlantic migration system. Moves in this system, often called a "proletarian mass migration," were proletarianizing ones for rural migrants from Eastern and Southern Europe: skilled agriculturalists became unskilled factory workers. Migration accelerated in Britain and Ireland under the concentration of landholding, early industrialization, and colonialism; in post-revolutionary continental Europe when the reactionary trans-European regime at the Congress of Vienna in 1815 re-imposed high taxes and tithes, rigorous social hierarchies, and the oppression of the underclasses; and with slow industrial growth everywhere with the exceptions of England and Saxony. The seventeenth- and eighteenth-century system of poor people's self-indenture for three to seven years to defray the cross-Atlantic cost of passage ended in the 1820s, as did migrations from southwestern Germany via the Danube to the South Russian Plains opened by Catherine II in 1763. In addition to the vast intra-European movements, transatlantic migration became the choice of western, then northern, and finally eastern and southern Europeans. Far fewer targeted agricultural colonies elsewhere like Algeria (French from 1830), South Africa (Dutch and English), Kenya, and Australia and even smaller numbers went to plantation colonies in the subtropics and tropics.

About 35 million selected the North Atlantic route. After 1776, the new rulers had expelled Native peoples and (white) settler advance caused (red) refugee migrations. By the 1830s, the lands east of the Mississippi were almost "clean" of Natives – a term not used at the time, but developed in the twentieth century for the deporting of racially or ethnically unwanted

Figure 1.2 An Irish immigrant sits on a chair and waits next to an Italian immigrant and her children, Ellis Island, early twentieth century
(FPG/Getty Images)

peoples (*judenrein*, ethnic cleansing). In the 1840s about one third of the Europeans who came to the USA settled farm lands, and two thirds became urban workers; from the 1890s 95 percent worked in industries. Without their labor the fast transition to urban-industrial production could not have been achieved, nor could they have found jobs without the simplification of production processes generally known as "Taylorization." Millions moved to Canada, and a few to Mexico. In the latter the liberalist government of the 1850s had deprived "Indios" of their land and thus forced them to migrate internally. Eight million romance-language speakers from the Iberian and Italian peninsulas moved to South America's frontier societies, Brazil and Argentina in particular. Most became plantation or urban laborers. By the 1890s, migrating Italians integrated the southern and northern transatlantic routes by choosing destinations from Buenos Aires to Montreal.

Labeled "immigrants," about one third to one half of the migrants, sojourners, or "guest workers" returned to Europe. Rural Italian laborers even seasonally circulated intercontinentally to earn their livelihood in the northern and southern hemispheres' harvests. At the same time, working men and women migrated from Europe's periphery, Ireland–Scandinavia–Eastern Europe–Mediterranean Europe, to its industrializing core, Great Britain–France–Germany–Switzerland–Bohemia–Lower Austria. In the 1880s most of the core's city population consisted of more than 50 percent of in-migrants often speaking the same language but in a different dialect. Residents and migrants could often not understand each other.[3]

The "Black Atlantic" was complementary as well as juxtaposed to the "White Atlantic." The labor of Africans who had been forcibly migrated in the "factories in fields" produced sugar, cotton, and other crops for export to the colonizers' markets. To the 1830s, more African than European men and women reached the Americas. However, the African-origin share of the population hardly increased. In what has been called a "second genocide" – after the deaths during capture, march to the coast, and Middle Passage – many were worked to death, and most prevented from having children. Re-creation of culture and political agency varied widely. In Brazil, where enslaved men and women shared cultures, vibrant African-background everyday practices emerged. In the Caribbean, slaves in Haiti joined the Atlantic World's revolutions but on the other islands they

3 Walter Nugent, *Crossings: The Great Transatlantic Migrations, 1870–1914* (Bloomington: Indiana University Press, 1992); Moya, "A continent of immigrants."

remained bound to – mainly – Creole elites. In the US South – in terms of economy and race hierarchies closer to the circum-Caribbean societies than to New York or Boston – migration via a "breaking-in" period in the Caribbean and rigorous planter control reduced cultural re-creation but encouraged procreation – though not family stability – to ensure successive generations of slave labor. Slavery was abolished in the Republican US in 1863/65, later than serfdom in Tsarist Russia, and, by 1888, ended in Brazil and Cuba as well.[4]

The Indian Ocean–Southeast Asian–South China migration system

The Indian Ocean – Southeast Asian – South China migration system – earlier often termed a "coolie" system, though that word is now seen as a racial slur – in fact dated back two millennia, and began as coastal and trans-sea voyaging. When the British Empire, influenced by the white and black abolitionist movement, slaveholder calculations, and considerations on the part of the state ended slavery in the 1830s, consumer demand for tropical foods and other tropical products kept demand for labor high. To supply cheap and coerced labor, the British and, subsequently, the French Empire established labor regimes of "indentured servitude" in British India, French Indochina, and southern China. Indentured workers could be found in Burma, the Indonesian islands, Mauritius, Natal, and elsewhere, where British and other imperial governments did little to ameliorate their brutal working conditions. Such bound working men and women, however, accounted for only about 10 percent of over-the-seas migrations. More, especially Chinese people, were self-willed "credit-ticket" migrants working off the cost of passage in a year or less. Most were free "passenger" migrants. Some followed routes of long standing, others the new transshipment routes for plantation crops and indentured workers. With European and US moves to open Asian societies' markets, including the military–commercial opening of China (British "opium wars," 1840s), of Japan (US fleet, early 1850s), and replacement of the private East Indian Company's by Crown rule in India (1857–58), migration intensified. In India, British-appointed *zamindars*, a kind of tax farmers, impoverished peasant families; in China the British Empire's support for opium imports achieved the same effect; in Japan the Meiji Era's

4 José C. Curto and Renée Soulodre-La France, eds., *Africa and the Americas: Interconnections during the Slave Trade* (Trenton, NJ, and Asmara: Africa World Press, 2005); Katia M. de Queiros Mattoso, *To Be A Slave in Brazil, 1550–1880* (fourth edn.; New Brunswick: Rutgers, 1994).

industrial modernization, funded through heavy taxation of the peasantry, forced rural young people to migrate.

Wherever free, credit-ticket, or bound migrants arrived or were unloaded, demand for everyday necessities arose, and merchant family and trader migrations also increased. Mass production of rice for the indentured workers in British Burma, for example, required additional migrant labor. Migrants traveled as far away as Hawai'i and the Caribbean islands. In Caribbean societies, indentured workers and "passenger" migrants became part of ethno-culturally ("racially") mixed societies. Immigrant families and communities entered politics in societies from South and East Africa to Hawai'i. During World War I between one and two million Chinese, Indochinese, and Indian "colonial auxiliaries" were transported to Europe for war-related work – some settled, others joined anti-colonizer struggles, and India's nationalist elite negotiated the end of the indenture system. Self-willed migration continued unabated.[5]

North China–Manchuria migrations

From the 1880s, migrations from North China to Manchuria complemented the outbound migrations of southern Chinese and the vast internal long-distance migrations from coastal provinces to the inner provinces of Yunnan and Guizhou. Seasonally migrating single men but also whole families left the densely populated and extremely impoverished agricultural provinces of Shandong, Zhili, and Henan in northern China, crossed the Bohai Sea, and continued with the South Manchuria Railway, built beginning in 1896 with investments by newly imperial Japan. In rural regions of Manchuria immigrants became the majority. Others became industrial wage workers: Russia was developing its eastern cities and Japan had mining and industrial investments in Manchuria as well, which after 1932 became the Japanese-controlled province of Manchukuo. China's policy-makers and educated elites showed no regard for migrants in general and the Japanese colonizers exploited them, although the railroad company hired social scientists to study both the conditions that forced rural families to leave and the demand for labor in Manchuria. A rural pioneer as well as newly industrialized society emerged.[6]

5 David Northrup, *Indentured Labor in the Age of Imperialism, 1834–1922* (Cambridge University Press, 1995); Piet C. Emmer, ed., *Colonialism and Migration: Indentured Labour before and after Slavery* (Dordrecht: Martinus Nijhoff, 1986).

6 Adam McKeown, "Chinese Emigration in Global Context, 1850–1940," *Journal of Global History* 5 (2010), 1–30.

The Russian–Siberian system

Along the Amur River, Chinese in-migrants jostled with others traveling east via the Trans-Siberian Railway. The Russian–Siberian system began with fur traders and the deportation of criminals and political opponents, continued with large-scale peasant migrations to southern Siberia, and – in the context of competition with China – the dispatching of troops and administrators to develop Russia's Far East. Peasant families migrated "unofficially" to land, entrepreneurs to the fast growing cities. In European Russia, the communal character of village organization kept individual out-migrants to urban jobs tied to family and community, but after emancipation (1861) 13 million migrated within a decade, usually seasonally, to the "Central Industrial Region" of Moscow and St. Petersburg and to the mining and industrial centers of southern Donbass and the Urals. By 1900, more than 70 percent of the inhabitants of Moscow and St. Petersburg were in-migrants. While this migration system remained largely separate from the transatlantic one, small numbers of West and Central European experts, entrepreneurs, and skilled craftsmen migrated eastward to opportunities in Russia. From the 1880s, economic oppression of and pogroms against Jews, ethnic oppression of Ukrainians, and withdrawal of privileges once granted to Mennonite and other German-speaking agricultural immigrants forced large numbers to migrate westward to Europe and North America.[7]

In addition to these five large systems, a small Pacific migration system, from East Asia since the 1840s and from South Asia since the early 1900s, brought about one million people to the Pacific Coast of the Americas by the 1920s. The impact was sizeable because railroad projects and extractive industries as well as California and British Columbia agriculture depended on Chinese and, later Japanese, Philippine, and Sikh workers. Chinese merchants were irreplaceable mediators of the trade with Asia and visiting Chinese students were expected to spread US ideas and consumer practices after their return home. Like Germans and Irish before them, all faced racism.[8]

In all of these migrations, the search for minimum subsistence or better options was the motivating factor for individual and family decisions; from these large migration systems based on information flows and top-down investment strategies emerged. Several of Europe's dynastic states had had exit restrictions, but they dropped these in the mid nineteenth century, and

7 Donald W. Treadgold, *The Great Siberian Migration: Government and Peasant in Resettlement from Emancipation to the First World War* (Princeton University Press, 1957).
8 Hoerder, *Cultures in Contact*, pp. 393–400.

Russia somewhat later; and free exit had, to some degree, been forced on India, China, and Japan. Only from the end of the nineteenth century did nation-states begin to channel or exclude migrants, however.

Exclusion regulations

The exclusion of certain groups of migrants was motivated in part by mass departures from Europe's new nation-states, which led to a questioning of constructions of essentialized national identities, and by the development of ideas about racial and ethnic hierarchies. Exclusion regulations based on race are usually seen as originating with the US prohibition of entry of Chinese laborers in 1882, although Chinese women had been singled out already in the 1875 Page Act since – in the opinion of male lawmakers – they might engage in prostitution. Such ideas made entry difficult for any woman traveling alone, as single women arriving from Europe were to experience as well.[9] Racist and ethnocentric restrictions were everywhere, however: Prussia/ Germany attempted to exclude Polish laborers from the Partition zones of the Tsarist and Habsburg Empires (1885); France reacted negatively to migrants from Italy (1880s); Australia (1901) and South Africa (1911) excluded "Asians" from immigration. Since each state's economy required migrant labor, shipping companies and industries evaded the respective laws or had them changed. Step by step, however, such restrictions ended the so-called "open door"-period of immigration. To the early 1900s, US entry restrictions for Europeans remained few. However, fears of "the passing of the great – white Anglo-Saxon – race," as commentators put it at the time, through the arrival of (and even worse, marriage to) "olive" or "swarthy" southern Europeans, "dark" Slavic "stock," and Jews (no further label required), led to a mandatory literacy test in 1917. World War I largely halted migration, but when it resumed after the war, the quota laws of 1921 and 1924 rigorously restricted the entry of South and East Europeans. The land borders, however, remained almost uncontrolled – British Canadians were Anglo-Saxon, Mexicans were low-paid and needed workers, and French Canadians had become part of New England society in some areas. Canada, through the 1920s, continued to recruit farming families and labor migrants came on their own initiative.

The grid of regulations and complex new paperwork led to the invention or imposition of the passport system, and its circumvention by those who

9 The Act also excluded contract laborers but this provision was not regularly enforced.

claimed to be children of residents, known as "paper children."[10] From 1929, the Great Depression slowed migration and increased return migration, because in times of need family networks provided better support than did immigration states. Thus the social cost of unemployment was borne by the societies of origin. In the Plantation Belt, indenture, formally abolished in 1917, in practice ended in the 1930s.

Nationalism, assimilation, and population transfers, 1880s-1950s

The colonizer empires in Europe and, as new powers, the USA and – at first little noticed – Japan had achieved their largest extent and impact at the beginning of World War I. In the late nineteenth century, these states of numerous peoples ideologically reconstructed themselves as monocultural "nations." Under earlier dynastic systems, permanent immigrants and temporary in-migrants, if economically valued, had been admitted into many-cultured populations on the sole condition that they professed allegiance to the ruler. As "subjects" they could then continue their cultural practices, speak their language, and practice their religion if they did this discretely. Such incorporation of difference became impossible once ideology postulated peoples defined by one culture as a state's constituent element. In the Western World, the concept of one inclusive "nation" began to evolve into practices that scholars now term "othering": the regulation of in-migration, the complete exclusion of certain groups, and discrimination after arrival. None of the states had ethno-culturally homogeneous populations, but once the strongest group had appropriated to itself the status of nation, it labeled smaller resident groups of different cultural practices "minorities." Discrimination followed and, without equal access to societal resources, members of such groups felt pressured to emigrate, although their very lack of resources made this difficult. For in-migrants the space to negotiate their status or engage in diverse cultural practices contracted: Americanization, Germanization, Germanization in its Habsburg-Austrian variant, Russification, and the like demanded unconditional assimilation. A culture marked as somehow "ethnic" became a reason for segregation, as religion had been earlier and continued to be in colonizer–colonized hierarchies. Christian policies and personnel continued to view peoples of Hindu, Buddhist, or other faiths as inferior, and in colonial areas

10 John Torpey, *The Invention of the Passport: Surveillance, Citizenship and the State* (Cambridge University Press, 2000).

Christianity coincided, largely, with Whiteness. As Western polities developed republican or democratic forms of government, in which each and every person was to be equal before the law, the parallel adoption of the ideology of nationhood made "minorities" and immigrant "aliens" persons of lesser rights.[11]

To this discrimination against resident minorities and to enforced assimilation male state bureaucracies added a new type of forced migration motivated by nationalism. They decided who could belong and who was different, expelled or deported unwanted people, and imported others designated as co-nationals. Under the proto-typical if numerically small British Empire Settlement program, poor orphans, unwed women, and disabled veterans of colonial wars were to be sent to the White Dominions of South Africa, Australia, and New Zealand, where, it was assumed, they would find employment and not be a burden on public resources.[12] This targeting of nationals was supplemented by the targeting of "aliens." Many of these were Jews who had escaped pogroms in Tsarist Russia, and were increasingly defined as a race rather than a religion in this period. In the Habsburg Empire, self-defined as a state of many peoples, Austrian bureaucrats still marginalized non-German speakers. In the Ottoman Empire, the protected status of non-Muslim peoples eroded, and "Turkishness" became the badge of belonging, a nationalist idea picked up from other European nations. In the 1920s, with assent of the League of Nations, "Greeks" were deported from Turkey, "Turks" expelled from Greece and Bulgaria. In the USA fears of working-class radicalism also led to deportation of those identified as "anarchists" or "Reds." A nation had to be "clean," and thus "ethnic cleansing" was imposed on all those deemed of another culture or group.

From the Balkan wars of the 1880s through World Wars I and II to the late 1940s, Europe's political elites turned Europe into a region of refugees and migrants. The 1918/19 peace treaties drew new borders across culturally mixed regions and moved existing ones over people resident for generations. Those of different culture suddenly found themselves designated "foreigners" and the new (male) "national" bureaucracies pressured them to depart or flee "home" to "their" (equally new) nation-state. These borders fragmented the many-cultured Central Europe and cut through the German–Romance languages borderlands. In the new nations, one group occupied the

11 For a more detailed summary, see Hoerder, *Cultures in Contact*, Chapter 17.

12 At the same time poor and infirm Whites, not measuring up to ideologies of superiority, were removed from colonies or shunted into asylums as not to be visible to the colonized.

institutions of rule, while the others became minorities of lesser rights who lived on the margins. "The growth of the modern nation-state implied not only the naming of certain peoples as enemies of the nation, but also the expulsion of significant groups for whom the state would or could not assume responsibility . . . The war itself schooled the new masters of the state apparatus" how to eject unwanted groups.[13]

Economic readjustment after World War I and global depression from 1929 reduced labor migrations, but such deportations were repeated under fascism and Stalinism. Poles were shifted around by both German and Russian occupation forces, Ukrainians degraded by their Aryan masters to a subservient labor force. The most powerful of Europe's (nation-)states became refugee-generating apparatuses; their democratic neighbors refugee-refusing states. On the other side of the globe, Japan's elites (in some cases Western-educated) developed similar "nationalist imperialist" policies, conceptually a contradiction in terms, which also led to the generation of refugees in what Japan labeled the Greater Asia Co-Prosperity Sphere. Japanese aggression in China in 1937, for example, forced one hundred million Chinese to flee in a single year.

In this era of regimentation, military and government officials, themselves often migrants, imposed labor regimes in the globe's annexed segments; forced men, and sometimes women, into corvée labor or migration; labeled some cultural groups a reservoir of workers, and others "effeminate." Practices of forced labor, imposed on colonized peoples, were brought home: labor regimentation in the Netherlands; the import of Korean workers to Japan; internal passports and labor camps in the Soviet Union; involuntary labor from Jews or people identified as such, political opponents, "Gypsies," homosexuals, and whole subjected peoples in Fascist Germany and its occupied territories. "Cleansing" by deportation was pushed to a worse level, and became "cleansing" by annihilation in the Holocaust. At the war's end, "Displaced Persons" or DPs, survivors of the extermination and labor camps, were as stateless as many expellees had been after World War I.

Europe became the world's largest refugee-generating region, because its nation-state ideology led to forced migrations, and because it exported this nationalist ideology to other parts of the world, first to the Ottoman Empire and from the 1950s to the decolonizing world. When, after Europe's self-weakening 1914–18 and 1938–45, colonized peoples declared – or struggled

13 Michael R. Marrus, *The Unwanted: European Refugees in the Twentieth Century* (Oxford University Press, 1985), quote p. 51.

for – independence, indigenous elites adopted and implemented monoculturalist nation-state ideology, sometimes with the advice of Western political scientists and politicians. This led to the partition of British India in 1947 along religious lines with tens of millions of refugees, the establishment of states in West Africa that brought together the traditional spaces of residence of many peoples or divided such spaces into several states, and the establishment of Indonesia as a nation-state out of the remnants of the Dutch multi-ethnic empire. Under racial hierarchies, White-ruled South Africa imposed residential segregation and forced labor, imposing large forced migrations on the indigenous Black population.[14]

From the 1950s, refugee generation shifted to decolonizing states, later called the "Global South," and labor migrations to industrializing, job-providing regions diversified globally.

Decolonization, guestworkers, and global apartheid from the 1950s to the 1990s

At mid-century major new macro-regional migration systems emerged. From 1942, wartime demand induced the USA to negotiate with Mexico an inter-governmental "bracero" program. "Braceros" – that is "arms," or in British usage "hands"– implies a "body-parts" approach to labor migrants: Muscles count while emotions, spirituality, and everyday needs of reproduction do not.[15] Countries recruiting labor sequentialized in-migration: workers worked for a specified period, then were required to depart, and then a new cohort of rotatory labor migrants were brought in. Around 1900 Prussia regimented Polish labor in this way, bringing in 1.3 million workers annually around 1910, and around 2000 Arab oil-producing economies did so as well, bringing in about 9.6 million workers.[16] In Prussia, fear of "agitation" for an independent Poland among workers was a reason for this system, and in the oil-wealth countries fear of being overwhelmed by foreigners given the high ratio of migrants to residents – ranging from 70.4 percent of the total

14 For forced labor, see Hoerder, *Cultures in Contact*, Chapters 17.2 and 18.4.

15 The bodily aspects of labor migration have been intensively analyzed for the colonizer–colonized labor and sexual relations. Margaret Strobel, *Gender, Sex, and Empire* (Washington, DC: AHA, 1993); Ann L. Stoler, *Race and the Education of Desire: Foucault's History of Sexuality and the Colonial Order of Things* (Durham, NC: Duke, 1995).

16 Martin Baldwin-Edwards, *Migration in the Middle East and Mediterranean*. Paper prepared for the . . . Global Commission on International Migration (Athens, Dept. 2005) http://iom.ch/jahia/webdav/site/myjahiasite/shared/shared/mainsite/policy_and_research/gcim/rs/RS5.pdf (accessed Feb. 6, 2014).

populating in Qatar to 23.7 percent in Saudi Arabia. This imported labor force is essential to keeping the economy functioning in importing states, although both democratic and authoritarian states make them an underclass with lesser rights and limited access to the resources of the society to which they contribute labor and taxes. They become "denizens" rather than citizens, without political rights, equality before the law, and, sometimes, schooling for their children, which in democracies subverts the fundamental equality of citizens. In societies with social security provisions, opponents of "foreign labor" have posited that such workers deplete social resources. On the sending side, by the end of the twentieth century, states like the Philippines and Bangladesh had become export organizations for human labor. Such systems could also be internal. In the People's Republic of China, for example, the underserviced and undersupplied countryside delivered labor without rights and residence to the metropoles, a migration involving an estimated 200 million in 2010.

The wartime uprooting of the 1940s – which lasted longer in Africa, with France's war to prevent the independence of Algeria in 1962 and Portugal's to prevent the independence of Angola in 1974 – transformed millions of economically active people into displaced individuals, truncated families, and deportees. Such DPs – about 11 million in Germany alone in 1945 – needed to be resettled and (re-)integrated. Most desperately wanted (and want) to get on with lives disrupted by destructive states or intrastate rebel groups. After 1945 many helped rebuild housing and whole economies out of the rubble produced by military aggression. For some this meant settlement where the powers-that-were had deposited them; for others a further, self-decided migration to better options in a less destroyed country, if admission regimes permitted entry. Neither states nor international institutions have solved the contradiction between the human rights-principle of freedom to move and leave an oppressive state and the state sovereignty-principle of preventing people from in-migrating. This regulation was costly for individuals' and families' life projects, and the border guarding apparatus was costly for states' budgets. By the mid 1950s, however, the economic booms in Western Europe and, subsequently, in oil-producing regions and newly industrializing states, like South Korea or Singapore, provided chances for immigrants if they could gain entry. Entry controls of the 1920s, which had had limited impact during the 1930s Depression when there was little migration, showed their full force, but air transport also accelerated migrant travel.

In the Atlantic Migration System, most countries had refused entry to Jews fleeing Fascism, but a short early 1950s surge brought migrants, who saw little

Figure 1.3 Guatemalan illegal immigrants deported from the United States walk along the tarmac upon their arrival back to Guatemala
(EITAN ABRAMOVICH/AFP/Getty Images)

future in Europe's ruins, to the classic immigration states. No migrants from destroyed Japan were admitted. With economic recovery by the mid 1950s, the transatlantic connection ended and two separate south–north systems emerged. The first was in Europe, where "guest workers" – the new term for rotatory labor – moved from the Mediterranean to West and North Europe. The recruitment region expanded to socialist Yugoslavia and to Istanbul and (Muslim) Anatolia. While recruitment agreements with North African states were not operationalized after the crisis of rising oil prices in 1973, France became the destination for individual labor migrants and families from its former colonies and protectorates. The second system was in the Americas. While the inter-governmental bracero program was not renewed in 1964, workers from Mexico and refugees from Central America's right-wing dictatorships migrated, often temporarily, to the United States. Migration from the Caribbean, which – as in Mexico in the 1880s – had begun with US investments, had accelerated since the 1930s. Intellectual refugees from Latin America's – often US-supported – dictatorships sought asylum in Europe, and others left Cuba for the USA The continuity of flight from dictatorships, of remittance and information flows, as well as displacement through anti-drug campaigns and internal conflict, made northbound migration self-sustaining. While small numbers have gone to Canada, the ever tighter US control of its southern border has forced many transmigrants to remain in Mexico. Depending on economic development or decline and on conflict-related displacement, distinct intra-South American migration regions have emerged. They, too, achieve continuity through relay of information or quickly subside when economic conditions at the destination deteriorate.

In another post World War II system of state control of populations, the Socialist and Communist countries prohibited emigration and cut themselves off from other migration systems. Internal unequal regional and statewide development induced migrations within states and across borders. Large migrations from rural and peripheral regions expanded towns and cities. In Russia, investments in southern Siberia mobilized young people. In China, the Cultural Revolution involved deportation of "bourgeois" intellectuals to rural hinterlands, and the so-called Great Leap Forward resulted in mass flight from starvation. Since then, industrial and urban growth combined with a policy of underservicing of rural populations generated vast migrations to new industrial zones. These workers, labeled "floating population," were indispensable for the economy, but received neither equal rights nor permanent urban residence permits nor schooling for their children.

In Southeast Asia, the fight against re-imposed Dutch rule in Indonesia (to 1949) and against re-imposed French rule in Vietnam (to 1954, extended by US intervention to 1975) involved vast population displacement and, after warfare's end, resettlement and urbanization migrations. Indonesian Chinese, resident for generations, were expelled (or massacred) in 1965 under an allegation of communist allegiance. Singapore, totally dependent on an in-migrant labor force, made access to citizenship near impossible. Japan, globally a singularly nationalist case, rejected any in-migration and refused refugee admission. The state still discriminates against "foreigners" of long presence, especially Koreans who came or had been forced to come under Japan's occupation of Korea, 1910–1945. In South Asia, state and nation-formation, the separation of East from West Pakistan to form independent Bangladesh, and civil war in Sri Lanka between the Sinhalese majority's postcolonial self-assertion and South Indian Tamils resident for generations, involved large-scale displacement. Economic growth and fast urbanization, however, explain the vast majority of internal migrations in much of Asia.

In two further postcolonial regions, North and sub-Saharan Africa, colonizer-induced retarded development and inequalities as well as some post-independence governments' economic mismanagement and clique networking induced temporary and permanent out-migration. Migrants from the Mediterranean littoral's Maghreb, still partially French-speaking, select France, and Egypt's underemployed, the neighboring oil-economies. Given the regions' young population, some demographers and policymakers in the early 1970s projected the societies as a labor reservoir for Europe, but the 1973 crisis, racialization, and growing Islamophobia precluded even discussion of such plans. In sub-Saharan Africa, ecologically and culturally multiply divided, economically vibrant and warlord-destroyed regions attract and send migrants. Ghana and Kenya, post-apartheid South Africa, and metropoles in general attract large numbers of culturally heterogeneous migrants. Civil and factional wars, elite enrichment and warlordism (with migrant white mercenaries), often supported and funded by outside economic and political interests, have caused mass flight. Most refugees remain in camps rather than being resettled or admitted to states in safer and wealthier countries of the world. Some states with little development have become permanent suppliers of human beings / working men and women – mostly to other economically growing states in the region. Urban migrants, by keeping ties to their places of origin – as did Europe-to-North America migrants – fund developmental or prestige-yielding projects, thus contributing to economic development of regions of out-migration. Such investment may mobilize further migrants or reduce emigration through new infrastructures and jobs. The impact of development on staying or moving needs to be determined for each specific region.

Like Europe's post-imperial states, the postcolonial ones are not ethnoculturally homogeneous. In fact, around 1990 only one fifth of the world's states claimed that one ethno-national group amounted to more than 90 per cent of the population; in one third official statistics placed its share at 75–89 per cent, and in the rest it amounted to less than half.[17] Negotiated intercultural accommodation, a concept neglected for a century in political theory and the practices of nation-states, has reduced conflict and the resulting push to depart in some places, while imposed monoculturalism, along with de-facto ethno- or religio-cultural hierarchization, has been an important reason for emigration.

During the post-imperial and postcolonial reorganization of state structures, displacement involved the exchange of administrative personnel and the relocation of intellectuals and other elites; economic growth or

17 *The World Factbook, 1993–94* (Washington, DC: Brassey's, 1993).

collapse induced working- and middle-classes migrations. Wherever elites – schoolteachers for example – departed, in-migration of similarly qualified personnel (often of other ethnic or religious culture) was encouraged. Young migrants from any developing country are the population cohort "in the best years," who, at their destinations, are highly productive and require comparatively little health care and other services. They provide a free bonus to developed societies since their – often low-GDP – countries of birth have paid for their upbringing and education. Receiving states, France or Singapore for example, expect them to return before reaching a life-cycle stage in which demands on social security would become costly. Global inequalities are exacerbated by migration of cohorts in the most active life-cycle phase.

Two further socio-ecological macro-regions, a better unit of analysis than continents defined by physical geography, demand attention: the Eastern Mediterranean–Western Asian–Gulf of Hormuz region and the Pacific's two rims. In West Asia's north, since the 1960s Turkey experienced massive labor out-migration to Western Europe as well as the flight and exile of Kurds, who, like Armenians, rather than being granted a state of their own after 1918 had been parceled out into several states. In the 1990s Turkey's economic growth attracted migrants from post-1989 Eastern Europe as well as from unemployed second-generation Western European Turkish-background residents. Palestine as a region became the arena of (Jewish) refugee arrival which, in turn, generated (Palestinian) refugees. Even before Israel's statehood in 1948, European-cultured Holocaust survivors arrived, and subsequently – with ethnic hierarchization – Arab-cultured and Soviet Union-socialized refugees and emigrants came as well. In the process, resident Arab-Muslim Palestinians fled, were expelled, or discriminated against. These refugees were never resettled: many remained in camps, and by 2000, over three generations, many became migrant laborers in oil-producing economies, while others migrated to universities and became a cosmopolitan academic elite, just as people of Jewish faith had been in late nineteenth century and interwar Europe. Since the increase in the price of oil and in investment that began in the late 1970s, the oil states of the Gulf of Hormuz and West Asia have rigorously enforced a rotatory dual migrant labor regime, with Western technical personnel and Palestinian–Egyptian–Asian male workers and female domestics. Around 2000, with the training of local experts and in-migration of personnel from China, migration has culturally diversified. All migrants retain ties to their multiple, oil-consuming, states of origin.

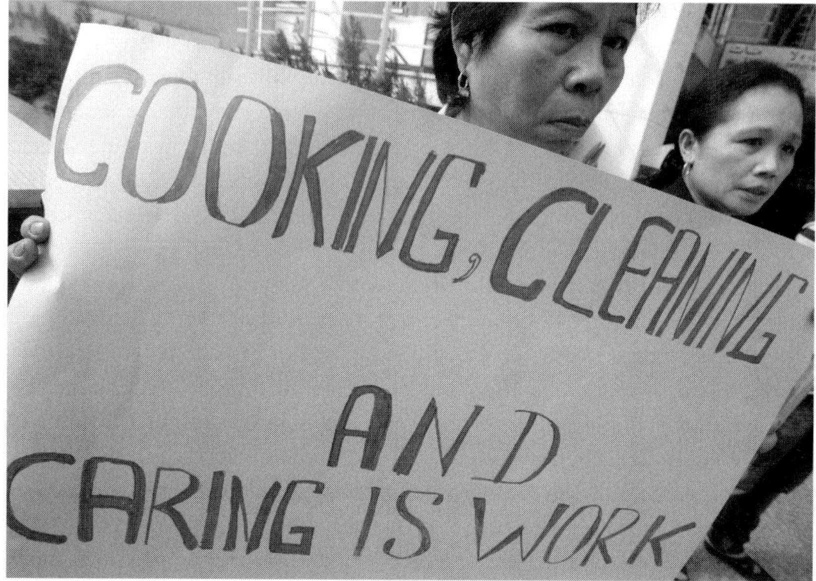

Figure 1.4 Migrant workers hold banners during a protest to support the rights of migrant domestic workers in Lebanon, on the occasion of International Women's Day in Beirut
(© Str/Reuters/Corbis)

Finally and paralleling the decline of Atlantic migrations, a new Pacific Migration System emerged. In the 1940s, when China was the major ally against Japan, exclusion of "Orientals" was cautiously questioned in the USA and Canada and, though legally abolished, was maintained by minuscule quotas. In the 1950s, Cold-War and racist dogmas kept the 1920s restrictions in place. In the 1960s, decolonization, new markets, intensifying economic relations, and new alignments led to major revisions of immigration policies first in Canada, then in the USA, and then in Australia. The Global North adjusted its color-coded entry barriers to professedly less racialized and intentionally economically more advantageous procedures. It was tacitly assumed that the "points system," privileging the highly qualified, would ensure that the ethnic composition of immigrants would remain unchanged. The assumption was not completely fulfilled, for not only did white societies have highly developed education systems, but so did several of Asia's societies. Within a decade transpacific migration was a major supplier of newcomers to the USA and Canada, joining the migrations of unskilled Mexicans and other Latinos/as.

All of these macro-regional and transpacific migrations are, on close analysis, as localized as all other self-decided migrations: People depart from some locales (but not from others), use the best-known and most reasonable routes, and target a locale with a personal anchor-point, such as kin, friends, acquaintances, a foreign student office, or a business partner. Policy consultants analyze macro-patterns and scholars focus on international migrants, but each and every migrant assesses local options at home and at the destination. Decisions are local-to-local within regional frames of options to earn one's living and exit and entry regulations of various states. Given the possibility of migrants' choice between multiple anchor-points, moves at the turn of the twenty-first century have been called "glocal," a far more precise empirical-analytical conceptualization than generalizations like "from China to America" or "from Bangladesh to Saudi Arabia." Migrants target societies with better chances and standards of living – and television makes standards of living in Buenos Aires or Shanghai visible to the shantytowns of the impoverished across the world. Given the selectivity of TV images, viewers may not be aware of the glittering metropoles' sprawling favelas, although information from earlier migrants can inform them of working conditions and entry barriers.[18]

Migration issues in the early twenty-first century

From the 1990s, the capital-induced macro-regional shift of production north–south and west–east to low-wage countries, as well as the demand for services in the north, changed migrant directions and gender composition. "Global apartheid," dividing South and North, extreme exploitation of many migrant workers, displacement by environmental deterioration and developmental projects, an assumed "feminization" and globalization of migration all characterize migration in the early twenty-first century, and form the major themes of research on the present.

In the decades after the White World ended official racial exclusion, "global apartheid" has divided a Global North from a Global South with the North's high living standards based on the South's low wages. "Globalization" – in its nth version since the integration of "old" world and "new" – links both through flows of capital and goods, but stymies the flow of people through the construction of barriers to human movement such as

18 Stephen Castles and Mark J. Miller, *The Age of Migration: International Population Movements in the Modern World* (New York: Guilford, 1993); Hoerder, *Cultures in Contact*, chapters 19, 20.

"fortress Europe" and a new Iron Curtain along the USA's southern border. Decolonization, a political-societal project, has been counteracted by re-colonization as an economic strategy of capital (and capitalists) and also, it needs to be emphasized, as a household-economy strategy of consumers. Present global inequalities, like the nineteenth-century Atlantic ones, push people to cross the borderlines etched by admission-exclusion regimes into human lives. In terms of life-chances and aspirations, the post-/re-colonial division of labor sets in motion vast local and regional migrations to quickly constructed (and as quickly abandoned) production complexes in many low-wage localities across the globe. Fenced in as free trade zones, they are free exploitation zones since within their perimeter laws regulating working hours and safety conditions do not apply.

Men and women migrate to such jobs pushed by the extreme constraints of their inhospitable "home" locales and regions. "Home," the place where accident of birth has placed people, may by unjust, unsupportable, and unsafe. At the other end, export of production facilities, called "delocalization," forces those workers whose jobs are exported to move. Since the establishment of the global plantation belt in the sixteenth century, any global transfer of investment capital forces or induces male, female, and child workers to move. Across fortified and heavily guarded borders, images of cosmopolitan centers from Dubai and Hong Kong to Moscow and Amsterdam are beamed, although these are countered by others of African migrants drowned in the Mediterranean, along with reports of inhuman conditions in Chinese factories and English sweatshops and of mass deportations of undocumented migrants. The global South's poorly remunerated working men and women, called "new helots" or "new untouchables" by some analysts, observe wage differentials from their front doors whether in the maquiladora along the Mexico–USA border or in Hong Kong's impoverished working-class neighborhoods. Women crossing without papers from Myanmar to Thailand to take jobs in one of the quick-to-move textile factories along the border know, from the stylish garments they sew, what consumers in wealthy countries can afford. Why not try to join them, even if the trip is fraught with dangers and requires funding by loan sharks? One risk involves the promise of (well-) paying jobs by facilitators-smugglers-entrepreneurs but, in fact being trafficked into sex work – another "body-parts" approach to migrant labor – or into slavery-like working conditions, which has been documented for oil- and western economies alike. While the cost of moving in relation to possible gains has dropped so that by the turn of the twenty-first century air travel has become affordable even to low-income migrants, and while it is now often possible to stay in touch with families in an instant – compared to the weeks or months that the millions of transatlantic letters of earlier migrants took – only some take the risks, because these have also massively increased because of the imposition of border regimes. Research, unfortunately, has not paid much attention to those who stay and to their motivations except for some psychologizing generalizations.[19]

Huge infrastructural development projects and environmental deterioration are additional migration-imposing factors. Inundation of peasant lands by dams to generate hydro-electricity and other "development displacement" displaces millions, which has been analyzed by the World Bank. Even if compensation is promised for such displacement, funds often do not reach those who are actually displaced because of their low social position. People have always fled natural disaster like volcano eruptions or famine-generating droughts but, increasingly, environmental displacement may be traced to human activity: toxic debris and emissions, global warming, urban sprawl, and rising sea-levels. Mass departure occurs from newly barren, stormy, or inundation-threatened regions, such as the Sahel's decennial drought, tropical storms as in New Orleans, or flooding rivers in Pakistan, Mississippi, or Thailand. The tsunami on the coast of Japan was a natural disaster, but the nuclear plant in the region's fissure zone was man-made.

Admission, exclusion, and discrimination regimes are gendered. Even environmental impact may be: men may depart more easily than women who, according to both ascription and self-perception, are responsible for home and children. Women have entered and are entering wage labor in large numbers. They migrate to factories, whether in China, the Philippines, or some other location where vagrant capital temporarily settles before moving on: textiles, electronics, toys, and other. Women from low-wage societies have also become sought-after domestic workers in high-income countries where resident women have gained access to labor markets and have entered better-paying echelons and most men do not share housework; domestic chores, childcare, support for the elder – all of the reproductive aspects of work – are delegated to them. In popular clichés and economic theory this is viewed as "unskilled work," but it often involves preparing high-standard meals, helping children learn, and providing "emotional labor." Since such service jobs, with no analytical but heavily ideological

19 Robin Cohen, *The New Helots: Migrants in the International Division of Labour* (Aldershot: Gower, 1987); Bridget Anderson, *Doing the Dirty Work? The Global Politics of Domestic Labour* (London: Zed Books, 2000).

grounding, are gendered female, wealthy states admit women from low-wage "colored" societies who thus may cross global apartheid's color-of-skin exclusion line in Italy or Singapore, Great Britain, or Japan. Labor in the unregulated sphere of private homes may be highly exploitative and, in some societies, also highly abusive, but it may also be rewarding.[20]

These processes have been labeled a "feminization" of migration, but women have always participated in global migrations. What is new is their visibility: they work and often live in middle-class residential neighborhoods rather than remaining "invisible" in ethnic quarters close to the factories employing them. What is also new is that women leave first, that (married) women leave their children in the care of female relatives, and that they become the main providers for families. Across time, single-gender migration, whether of men or women, results in skewed marriage markets. Whereas in the past men migrated first, and women established routes of their own, in the present, women from low-income societies are being recruited through international agencies as marriage partners for men, some of whom remain in the agricultural sector of high-income highly urbanized societies and others who do a variety of other types of work. Although such marriages are often described as exploitation for household and farm labor as well as for sex and emotional labor, they may be a valid strategy for women, who view them as the only possible way to escape poverty. Under prevailing exclusion regimes, women use marriage in their own or their family's interest, as a way to enter societies with more options, to gain a foothold in the labor market, and a trajectory to better occupations. Law and public opinion about such betterment strategies varies; in Canada and Sweden they are generally accepted, while in Muslim countries they are not. Analyses of such marriages combine labor/marriage market structures with discussion of migrant women's goals of supporting families, helping sustain marginal agriculture or crafts, and providing for their children's education.[21]

At the beginning of the twenty-first century patterns of migration are changing, but over the centuries men and women have always adapted life-course prospects to region-specific, continent-wide, transoceanic, and global inequalities and options. Entrepreneurs and financiers in demand of

20 Elsa Chaney, Mary Garcia Castro, and Margo L. Smith, eds., *Muchachas no More: Household Workers in Latin America and the Caribbean* (Philadelphia: Temple, 1989); Rhacel Salazar Parreñas, *Servants of Globalization: Women, Migration, and Domestic Work* (Stanford University Press, 2001).

21 Christiane Harzig, "Women migrants as global and local agents: new research strategies on gender and migration," in Pamela Sharpe (ed.), *Women, Gender and Labour Migration: Historical and Global Perspectives* (London: Routledge, 2001), pp. 15–28.

labor have always recruited working men and women or whole families from where a supply was available. Uneven economic, social, and political development results in migration – casual and skilled labor, student, entrepreneurial, elite – to increase individual or family options and to reduce labor shortages in societies of destination. Settlement and acculturation varied by culture and the economic structures at the destination. Reducing migration, if considered desirable, requires a relative equalization of chances across the globe. While the speed of information relay has increased, nineteenth-century telecommunication – letters via the mail – was sufficient to adjust migrant decisions to the availability of options at destination. Migrants, who carefully assess costs and rewards of their moves, are entrepreneurs in their own lives, trying to make the most of their human capital. Societies that provide for the easy entry of such individuals gained and gain the most.

Further reading

Anderson, Bridget. *Doing the Dirty Work? The Global Politics of Domestic Labour*. London: Zed Books, 2000.

Bilsborrow, Richard E. and Hania Zlotnik. "Preliminary report of the United Nations expert group on the feminization of internal migration," *International Migration Review* 26/1 (1992), 138–161.

Boyd, Monica and Elizabeth Grieco. "Women and migration: incorporating gender into international migration theory," *Migration Information Source* 1 March 2003, www.migrationinfromationsourse.org/Feature/display/cfm?ID=106 (accessed January 14, 2007).

Bryder, Linda. "Sex, race, and colonialism: an historiographic review," *International History Review* 20 (1998), 806–822.

Chaney, Elsa, Mary Garcia Castro, and Margo L. Smith, eds. *Muchachas no More: Household Workers in Latin America and the Caribbean*. Philadelphia: Temple, 1989.

Castles, Stephen and Mark J. Miller. *The Age of Migration: International Population Movements in the Modern World*. New York: Guilford Press, 1993.

Cohen, Robin. *The New Helots: Migrants in the International Division of Labour*. Aldershot: Gower, 1987.

Curto, José C. and Renée Soulodre-La France, eds. *Africa and the Americas: Interconnections during the Slave Trade*. Trenton, NJ, and Asmara: Africa World Press, 2005.

Gabaccia, Donna and Dirk Hoerder, eds. *Connecting Seas and Connected Ocean Rims: Indian, Atlantic, and Pacific Oceans and China Seas Migrations from the 1830s to the 1930s*. Leiden: Brill, 2011.

Harris, Nigel. *The New Untouchables: Immigration and the New World Worker*. London: Tauris, 1995.

Harzig, Christiane. "Women migrants as global and local agents: new research strategies on Gender and Migration," in Pamela Sharpe (ed.), *Women, Gender and Labour Migration: Historical and Global Perspectives*. London: Routledge, 2001, pp. 15–28.

Harzig, Christiane, Dirk Hoerder with Donna Gabaccia. *What is Migration History?* Cambridge: Polity, 2009.

Hoerder, Dirk. *Cultures in Contact: World Migrations in the Second Millennium*. Durham: Duke University Press, 2002.

Isajiw, Wsevolod W. *Understanding Diversity: Ethnicity and Race in the Canadian Context*. Toronto: Thompson, 1999.

Kaur, Amarjit. *Wage Labour in Southeast Asia since 1840: Globalisation, the International Division of Labour and Labour Transformations*. Basingstoke: Palgrave Macmillan, 2004.

Kuhn, Philip A. *Chinese among Others: Emigration in Modern Times*. Lanham, MD: Rowland and Littlefield, 2008.

Markovits, Claude, Jacques Pouchepadass, and Sanjay Subrahmanyam, eds. *Society and Circulation: Mobile People and Itinerant Cultures in South Asia 1750–1950*. Delhi: Permanent Black, 2003.

Marrus, Michael R. *The Unwanted: European Refugees in the Twentieth Century*. Oxford University Press, 1985.

McKeown, Adam M. "Global migration, 1846–1940," *Journal of World History* 15/2 (2005), 155–189.

Melancholy Order: Asian Migration and the Globalization of Borders. New York: Columbia University Press, 2008.

"Chinese emigration in global context, 1850–1940," *Journal of Global History* 5 (2010), 1–30.

Midgley, Clare, ed. *Gender and Imperialism*. Manchester University Press, 1998.

Morokvasic, Mirjana, ed. *Women in Migration, topical issue of International Migration Review* 18, no.68 (1984).

Moya, José C. "A continent of immigrants: postcolonial shifts in the western hemisphere," *Hispanic American Historical Review* 86/1 (2006), 1–28.

Moya, José and Adam McKeown. "World migration in the long twentieth century," in Michael Adas (ed.), *Essays on Twentieth-Century History*. Philadelphia: Temple University Press, 2010, pp. 9–52.

Nugent, Walter. *Crossings: The Great Transatlantic Migrations, 1870–1914*. Bloomington: Indiana University Press, 1992.

Parreñas, Rhacel Salazar. *Children of Global Migration: Transnational Families and Gendered Woes*. Stanford University Press, 2005.

Servants of Globalization: Women, Migration, and Domestic Work. Stanford University Press, 2001.

Phizacklea, Annie. "Migration and globalization: a feminist perspective," in Khalid Koser and Helma Lutz (eds.), *The New Migration in Europe: Social Constructions and Social Realities*. London: Macmillan, 1998.

Queiros Mattoso, Katia M. de. *To Be A Slave in Brazil, 1550–1880*. Fourth edn. New Brunswick: Rutgers, 1994.

Richmond, Anthony H. *Global Apartheid: Refugees, Racism, and the New World Order*. Oxford University Press, 1994.

Sassen, Saskia. *Guests and Aliens*. New York: New Press, 1999.

Simon, Rita James and Caroline Brettell. *International Migration: The Female Experience*. Totowa, NJ: Rowman & Allanheld, 1986.

Stoler, Ann L. *Race and the Education of Desire: Foucault's History of Sexuality and the Colonial Order of Things*. Durham, NC: Duke, 1995.

Strobel, Margaret. *Gender, Sex, and Empire*. Washington, DC: American Historical Association, 1993.

Torpey, John. *The Invention of the Passport: Surveillance, Citizenship and the State*. Cambridge University Press, 2000.

Treadgold, Donald W. *The Great Siberian Migration: Government and Peasant in Resettlement from Emancipation to the First World War*. Princeton University Press, 1957.

2

World urbanization, 1750 to the present

LYNN HOLLEN LEES

Today over half the total world population lives in cities, but in 1750, fewer than five percent did. The change from a predominantly rural society, dominated by villages, fields, and forests, to one of giant cities and urbanized regions is observable from the river valleys of East Asia to the plains of North America, from Scandinavia south through sub-Saharan Africa. During the past 250 years, New York City grew from a tiny port on the southern tip of Manhattan Island into the core of a metropolitan area with more than 16 million inhabitants. In a relatively brief period, urbanization has transformed the way that most of us work and live. We have become urban. This chapter examines city growth in the modern period, comparing patterns of change over time in different regions, to show how cities have come to dominate economic, social, and cultural life in every part of the world. It focuses on urbanization as a process, organized through city systems, not on the histories of individual cities.

Exploring the consequences of urbanization is a second focus. The shift into cities has changed the scale and types of typical human interactions and has altered natural environments as well. The green of fields and forests has given way to grey concrete, brown stone, and black asphalt. Endless strings of houses and businesses line roads that guide and multiply contacts among residents. Cities are necessarily social spaces, and their spatial organization and modes of transportation help to define social styles. Debates over the impact of city living raged during the nineteenth century and continue today. In 1870, Thomas Baines, former editor of *The Liverpool Times*, argued "Great cities and towns have always been nurseries of intelligence, from the time of Tyre, Athens, and Florence, which were seats of knowledge and the fine arts, as well as of trade and commerce." He claimed the same virtues for factory towns in Yorkshire. But where Baines saw progress, others found dirt, degradation, and moral as well as physical danger. Alexis de Tocqueville called Manchester, England, "this new Hades."[1] In the modern period, industrial cities triggered widespread fear, sharpened by moral disapproval.

What does urban living have to offer the millions of newcomers who move each year into cities? The answer, while heavily dependent upon public policies and the local economies, is also shaped by the normal constants and constraints of urban environments. While there are certainly differences between the cities of Algeria and those of Australia, there are also many similarities. One impact of contemporary globalization has been an increasing convergence worldwide of urban technologies, housing patterns, institutions, and consumer goods. The nature of this convergence and its limitations will shape urban societies in this century.

Definitions and proportions

Cities and towns are permanent settlements of substantial size and density, which have economic, cultural, and, sometimes, political functions that distinguish them from villages and hamlets. The essential basis of city creation is economic. Urban populations depend on imported resources, since their inhabitants do not grow enough food to support themselves. This requires the production of a food surplus elsewhere that can be gathered and brought into the towns. The resulting exchange of manufactures and services for food in markets serves both urban and the rural residents. The clarity of this distinction between urban and rural ought not to be exaggerated, however. Cities rarely have clear spatial boundaries. Even cities in the ancient world had suburbs – inhabited areas outside city walls, whose residents were part of regional economies and social systems. Moreover, there is no single size threshold for a city. In the ancient world, a settlement of several hundred people could qualify as urban, but today that limit is far too low. The United States and Mexico currently use a standard of 2,500 inhabitants, while India and Lebanon require a concentration of 5,000 people. Many countries – among them China, Brazil, and Belgium – define cities in legal or administrative terms.[2] Cities and towns are those places labeled as such by governments. Standards for what constitutes "urban," therefore, vary from country to country.

1 Thomas Baines, *Yorkshire Past and Present*, II, pt. 1 (London: Mackenzie, 1871), p. 218; Alexander de Tocqueville, *Journeys to England and Ireland*, J. P Mayer, ed. (Garden City: Doubleday, 1968), pp. 93–96.

2 Department of Economic and Social Affairs, Population Division, United Nations, *World Urbanization Prospects: The 1999 Revision* (New York: United Nations, 2001), pp. 112–127.

Table 2.1 World urbanization rates, 1700–2000

				1950		2000	
	1700	1800	1900	a	b	a	b
Africa	3.9%	4.0%	5.5%	12.0%	14.7%		37.9%
Americas North America	11.4%	12.3%	28.5%	47.9%	63.9%		77.2%
Latin American & Caribbean					41.4%		75.3%
Asia	10.9%	9.1%	9.3%	14.9%	17.4%		36.7%
Europe (excl. Russia)	12.3%	12.1%	37.9%	50.7%	52.4%		74.5%
Total	9.8%	9.0%	16.1%	25.6%	47%		51%

a= settlements of 5,000+
Source: Bairoch, pp. 284, 587, 634.
b= all urban settlements, national definitions
Source: United Nations, *World Urbanization Prospects*, 1999, p. 32.

The growth of urban populations depends on two processes: migration and natural increase, whose relationship sets the rate at which cities expand over time. Geographic mobility is normal, particularly among young adults, and industrialization and agricultural modernization increase pressures, as well as the opportunities, to move. Heavy immigration swells the size of a town and the ranks of those in their reproductive years, although many immigrants leave soon after arrival, and others die young, marry late, or not at all. Before 1850, cities were relatively unhealthy places with higher infant mortality and lower life expectancy than the countryside. Therefore most urban growth in Europe resulted from immigration, rather than natural increase.

Urbanization is most easily defined demographically. As a region urbanizes, a larger and larger proportion of its people live in cities and towns, rather than rural areas. As Table 2.1 indicates, only about nine percent of total world population lived in settlements larger than 5,000 in 1800, but that percentage swelled to about sixteen percent in 1900 and then to about twenty-six percent in 1950. Urbanization levels have varied from region to region, however, being much higher in the modern period in Europe and in the Americas than elsewhere. In these two areas, around half of the total population lived in cities and towns in 1950, while the proportion reached only about fifteen percent in Asia and twelve percent in Africa. In the second half of the twentieth century, levels of urbanization rose in Asia and Africa too, as their states gained independence from colonial rule and the world economy recovered from the impact of the world wars and the Depression.

Today the absolute number of urban dwellers in Asia is much higher than in Europe and North America, and Asian urbanization levels are climbing. Since 1950, the relationship between the rate of urbanization and the level of urbanization has been inverse: movement into cities has been fastest in areas with the fewest cities – Africa, Polynesia, Southeastern and East Asia. It has been much slower in regions with more advanced economies, such as Europe, North America, Australia, and New Zealand.[3] Higher fertility and declining mortality, combined with sustained movement out of rural areas, continue to fuel the intensified urbanization of poorer states.

Urbanization, however, is not just a matter of numbers. It must also be measured in structural terms: as activities located in space. Towns are centers where specialized services are offered and where those who deliver those services reside. For example, trade, large-scale manufacturing, governance, and education are most efficiently carried out or provided in central places, where there are markets, factories, and offices. Cities are multi-functional, diverse communities. If we look at a mid-nineteenth-century census of Paris, we can see the many different trades that constituted the economy of a capital city early in the industrial era. Its citizens administered, arrested, brewed, cleaned, carried, constructed, cooked, cured, danced, drove, and dug, trained in hundreds of different crafts and services. These activities not only produced goods for sale, but also helped to create and spread an urban way of life. Immigrants learned city habits in urban taverns, shops, theaters, and workplaces. Conversely, urban communities developed ways to integrate or segregate newcomers, who might speak another language or have a different religion. Formal organizations, such as police forces, schools, and neighborhood groups, communicated local standards and set limits on behavior. Today, given the ease of commuting and telecommunicating, urban models of behaving and consuming have spread far beyond city borders. Seeing urban and rural areas as separate, bounded entities is no longer possible.[4]

Cities as systems

Cities are not isolated units. They are tightly integrated into the territories surrounding them, importing food and other products and exporting services

3 Ibid, p. 50.

4 A. E. Smailes, "The definition and measurement of urbanization," in Ronald Jones (ed.), *Essays on World Urbanization*, The Commission on the Processes and Patterns of Urbanization of The International Geographical Union (London: George Philip, 1975), pp. 3–13.

and manufactures. In any given area, urbanization creates a hierarchy of central places, which house a range of political, economic, and cultural institutions, distributing them in space according to levels of demand. In such systems, diversity is positively correlated with size. Small market towns of a region are linked via roads to larger, more complex towns, which offer a wider range of products and services, ones that people are willing to travel longer distances to obtain. While even the smallest towns have primary schools and markets or food stores, they normally lack secondary schools, hospitals, and theaters, which are located in larger centers. To find a university, a government office, or an opera house, a rural person must travel farther, perhaps to the largest city in a county or a country. City systems also include specialized towns – ports, manufacturing centers, university towns, or holiday resorts, for example.

Local overland connections constitute, however, only part of the linkages that cities foster. Technologies of transport and communications have gone global, and cities are major relay stations in the journeys of people and information. Cities are the nodes from which long-distance travelers depart, from which television programs are transmitted, and in which cultural standards are set. Hollywood, Bollywood, and Nollywood movies flow from Los Angeles, Mumbai, and Lagos to global consumers. The music industries and audiences of Dakar, Paris, and the Caribbean are interlinked, as are those of Kingston, London, and New York. Cities operate within both Central Place and Network Systems, increasing their adaptability and their diversity through multiple linkages and exchanges. Cities are spaces of flows, in and out.[5]

Urban networks, reinforced by current technologies of transportation, also shape long-distance travel and emigration. The hub-and-spoke designs for trains and air travel point travelers to the larger towns and cities. In the early twentieth century, shipping lines based in Hamburg, London, New York, and Yokohama ran regular services to ports in the Americas, Africa, and East Asia, as well as the coastal cities of Europe. Map 2.1 shows the routes of the Hamburg America line in 1914. Thinking about urbanization requires examining cities in terms of their spatial and functional relationships to one another. Some of these relationships are economic, reflecting geographies of production and exchange. Others are cultural, deriving from the circulation of ideas, art, and ideologies. Political power also operates through

5 Paul M. Hohenberg and Lynn Hollen Lees, *The Making of Urban Europe, 1000–1994*, rev. edn. (Cambridge, MA: Harvard University Press, 1995), pp. 4–5; Manuel Castells, *The Informational City* (Oxford: Basil Blackwell, 1989), pp. 168–171.

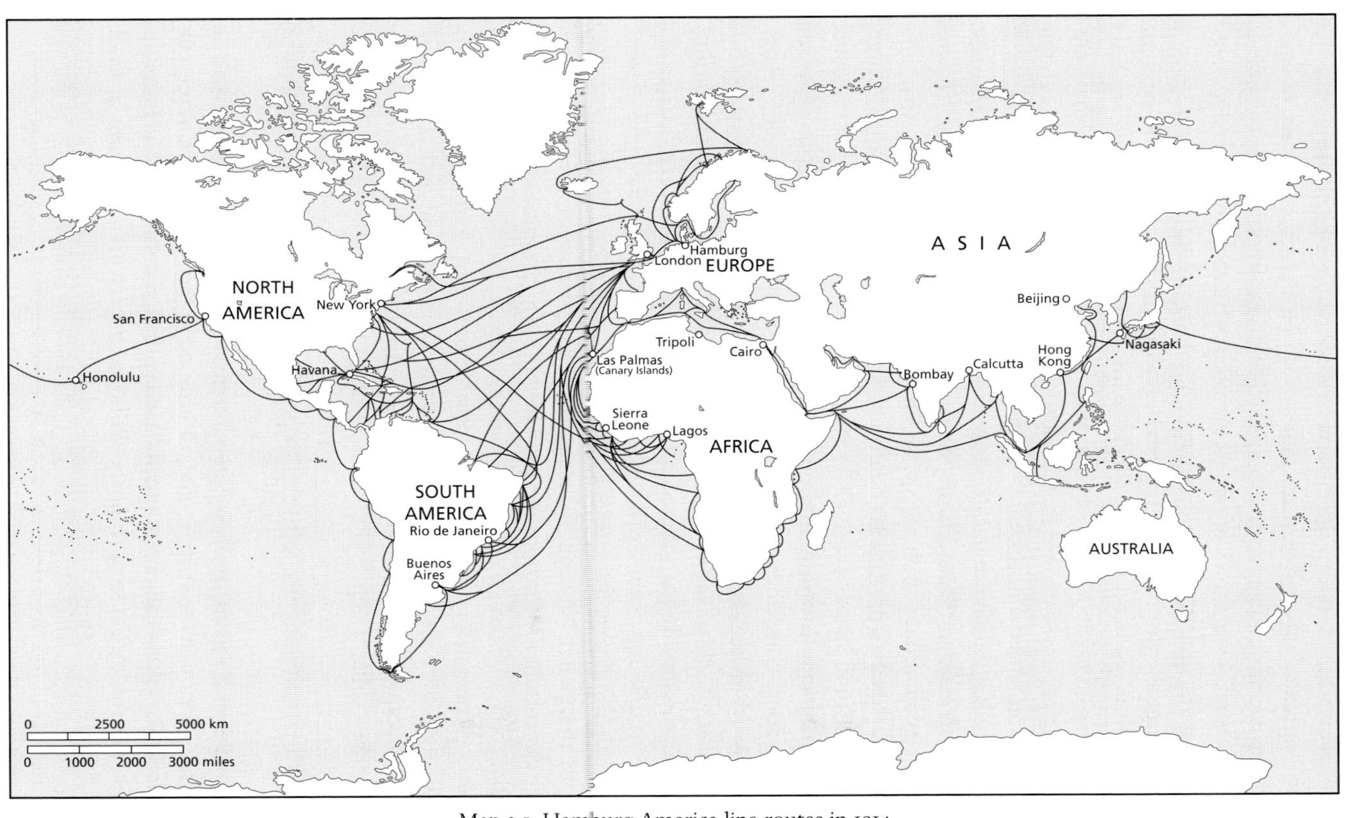

Map 2.1 Hamburg America line routes in 1914

systems of cities. Most states, for example France after the Revolution of 1789, have functioned through institutions located in a hierarchy of cities. Mayors of towns or communes have answered to prefects, who then have reported from their offices in the chief city of each department to the central government in Paris via letters, telegraph, telephone, or, now, the Internet.

The largest cities in many national systems have tended to be political capitals: Moscow, Jakarta, Cairo, and Buenos Aires, for example, each of which also serves as a national commercial and cultural center. Where the attractive power of a central city far outshines the appeal of regional capitals and it becomes disproportionately large, it is called a primate city because of its huge size and influence. Today almost 70 percent of the Lebanese population lives in Beirut, and Port-au-Prince houses 60 percent of the Haitian population. Small, highly urbanized countries have the most concentrated populations. Although London and Tokyo are also primate cities, both Britain and Japan have lively regional capitals and complex distributions of urban functions among a large array of towns. Their degree of urban concentration is comparatively less. Economic development fosters more balanced urban hierarchies within national boundaries.

Scholars of globalization have suggested that the growing interaction of national economies has created an international urban hierarchy. Saskia Sassen argues that New York, London, and Tokyo have become "global cities," because of their dominant role in providing financial services for the rest of the planet.[6] Although some types of manufacturing have become more decentralized, the opposite has taken place at the level of international finance, which benefits from a critical mass of firms, specialized services, and heavy investment in advanced telecommunications. London, Tokyo, New York, and, more recently, Hong Kong have acquired new centrality in the global economy because of their roles as receivers, processors, and dispensers of finance capital.

Regional differences

Urbanization is a global process, but it has not taken place evenly over time or in space. Although the earliest cities developed in the river valleys of present day Iraq, Egypt, Pakistan, and north China, urban systems could be found in many regions by the first century CE. These networks of towns proved

6 Saskia Sassen, *The Global City: New York, London, and Tokyo* (Princeton University Press, 1991).

fragile, declining along with the political powers that offered them protection. Extensive deurbanization of Western Europe followed the collapse of the Roman Empire in the fifth century CE. When population and agricultural productivity both increased after 800 CE, urban development accelerated again in much of Eurasia and northern Africa. This wave of urbanization slowed in the fourteenth and fifteen centuries when epidemics and the collapse of major empires hampered the flows of people and goods that sustained the towns. Where effective governments established themselves, urban growth continued, for example in the Aztec-dominated lands of central Mexico and the Yangzi delta towns in China under Yuan rule.[7]

Another spurt of urban growth took place between 1500 and 1700, pushed by rising agricultural productivity, trade, and political consolidation. Between 1580 and 1700, Japan became one of the most heavily urbanized territories in the world, when the new military ruler of the country Tokugawa Ieyasu founded Edo (the forerunner of Tokyo), and his samurai warrior allies administered their domains from fast-growing castle towns. In the Middle East, cities as diverse as Isfahan, Istanbul, Damascus, and Mecca thrived under Ottoman and Safavid control, linked by secure routes to other centers of Muslim power from the shores of the Mediterranean to Malacca. Urbanization expanded in the Americas, as the Spanish founded new towns through which they administered their vast empire. As states expanded their power, the larger administrative cities and ports grew rapidly. The largest and most dynamic cities in the world during the early modern period were, for the most part, located in Asia, although urban growth had slowed in the Mughal Empire and in China by the later eighteenth century.[8] In contrast, urbanization was limited in North America and sub-Saharan Africa.

In 1750, the most densely urbanized regions of the world (defined as proportion of total populations living in cities) could be found in the Netherlands, England, Brabant, Northern and Central Italy, and Japan, all heavily commercialized areas with integrated networks of multiple market towns and administrative centers.[9] These districts of high urbanization were located in economically advanced zones with prosperous agriculture, thriving merchant communities, and active ports and markets. London and Edo

7 Richard van Glahn, "Towns and temples: urban growth and decline in the Yangzi Delta, 1100–1400," in P. J. Smith and R. van Glahn (eds.), *The Song-Yuan-Ming Transition in Chinese History* (Cambridge, MA: Harvard University Press, 2003), pp. 176–211.

8 Peter Clark, ed., "Introduction," *The Oxford Handbook of Cities in World History* (Oxford University Press, 2013).

9 Jan de Vries, *European Urbanization, 1500–1800* (Cambridge, MA: Harvard University Press, 1984), p. 39.

(Tokyo) were huge, metropolitan districts, their populations spilling over formal boundaries. Even if its overall level of urbanization was comparatively low, China had well-developed urban hierarchies in regions organized around the drainage basins of major rivers. Growing commerce supported the rise of market towns. During the eighteenth century, the most advanced regions of Western Europe and China had similar levels of agrarian productivity, population growth, standards of living, and commercial development.

What Kenneth Pomeranz calls "the Great Divergence" in the economic organization and wealth of the most developed areas of Europe and China took place after 1800, and it had definite urban implications.[10] In England, the "Industrial Revolution" – the shift of textile manufacturing into factories and the use of steam engines and coal to provide cheap, continuous power – led to city creation, first in Britain, and somewhat later in Belgium, France, and New England. Rural sites of production attracted enough workers to transform villages into towns, and railways moved migrants and materials faster and farther to central places. Coal-burning steam engines freed textile manufacturing from its dependence on water power, permitting production sites in older cities. The combination of mining and metallurgy helped after 1870 to urbanize large areas near coal deposits in Poland, western Germany, and Pennsylvania. A second wave of industrialization based on the internal combustion engine, steel, oil, and chemicals reinvigorated economies in Western Europe in the late nineteenth century and stimulated both industrial and urban growth in Central Europe, North America, and Russia. Because technology is relatively "footloose," available for installation anywhere, entrepreneurs on several continents bought the new machinery, building factories in towns and refineries in ports. Not only industrial production, but also expanded transportation, trade, and services provided new jobs in many cities, thereby attracting migrants. During the nineteenth century, cities grew, albeit at different rates, throughout Europe, North America, Australia, New Zealand, and South Africa.

The early impact of industrialization in Europe and North America on Asia, Eastern Europe, and Latin America was uneven. Port towns that exported raw materials to the developed countries and imported manufactured goods could thrive whatever their setting. Witness the rapid growth of Manaus in Brazil during the rubber boom and Baku in the Russian Empire after the discovery of oil in its hinterland. Urban populations in Mexico,

10 Kenneth Pomeranz, *The Great Divergence: Europe, China, and the Making of the Modern World Economy* (Princeton University Press, 2000).

Brazil, and Argentina expanded along with their export and manufacturing sectors, while cities in the Andean regions stagnated. India experienced almost a century of deurbanization, as town artisans found their markets shrinking because of British competition, although ports such as Bombay and Calcutta thrived. In China, no single pattern dominated. Small market towns continued to grow during the later decades of the Qing empire, and after 1850, treaty ports expanded, but declining rates of population growth and political turmoil from the mid nineteenth century onward probably dampened urban expansion in the lower Yangzi region.

The absolute number of cities has also risen strikingly since 1800 in both industrialized and developing countries. In Europe, the number of towns with more than 10,000 inhabitants doubled between 1700 and 1800, and more than doubled again by 1870.[11] Planned towns multiplied in South Australia and New Zealand during the early years of European colonization. In 1883, surveyors laid out over 1200 new townships along the route of the Canadian Pacific Railway. After Latin America became independent, the number of centers with more than 20,000 inhabitants grew from 41 in 1800 to 207 in 1920.[12] Colonial governments and merchants founded new ports along coastlines. Singapore, Hong Kong, Rangoon, and Surabaya soon became important centers of export and transshipment. By the later nineteenth century, Durban, begun as a trading station by merchants from Cape Colony, developed into one of the world's largest sugar terminals. Expanding maritime empires generated international trade, which produced new cities and towns.

Urbanization during the early and mid twentieth century was uneven. World wars and economic depression hindered growth in much of the industrialized world. Not only did bombs and retreating armies level towns, but the list of urban casualties stretching from Coventry through Dresden, Warsaw, and Hiroshima was depressingly long. Meanwhile, Latin American cities, well outside the conflict zones, expanded rapidly, especially where protective tariffs encouraged industrial development. Then after 1945, rebuilding combined with the postwar economic boom fostered city growth in Europe, North America, and much of Asia. Expanding at twice the rate of towns in the industrialized regions, cities throughout the Third World exploded in size. The spatial distribution of that population within cities

11 Paolo Malanima, "Urbanization," in Stephen Broadberry and Kevin H. O'Rourke (eds.), *The Cambridge Economic History of Modern Europe*, Volume 1, 1700–1800 (Cambridge University Press, 2010), p. 246.

12 Paul Bairoch, *Cities and Economic Development*, trans. Christopher Braider (University of Chicago Press, 1988), p. 414.

changed too. Although central cities in many regions lost population, suburban settlements attracted immigrants.

Urbanization responds to political attitudes and policies as well as economic rhythms. Wars can destroy towns and force their populations to flee, at least temporarily. Where command economies replaced market systems, governments monitored urban residence and shaped urban design and growth. The Soviet state used passports and resident permits to block the rural population from moving into Russian cities. In 1958, the Chinese government instituted a system of household registration linked to place (hukou) that it used to limit migration from countryside into the towns. Then during the Cultural Revolution of the 1960s and early 1970s, the Maoist government exiled young people from the cities into the countryside for political reeducation. The determination of the Khmer Rouge to build an agrarian-based Communist society led them to virtually empty Cambodian towns during the later 1970s. Governments can also champion and finance urbanization. Governments have built new towns and revamped older ones according to prevailing views of a "good society." In Eastern Europe and the USSR, over 1000 new towns were built after World War II to ease housing shortages and jump-start the new socialist economies. Neighborhood units organized around large concrete apartment blocks and minimal sets of social services multiplied around industrial sites. After 1945, new towns, designed as garden cities, multiplied in the British Isles, the Netherlands, and Scandinavia, offering their residents artfully designed greenspace and modernist housing.

During the later twentieth century, the once-powerful link between manufacturing and urban growth broke in many areas, when much of Western Europe and North America deindustrialized. Formerly prosperous factory towns, such as Belfast, Liège, and Detroit, lost population and economic dynamism. Others turned with relative degrees of success to the production of culture or services. Today, the main drivers of the Philadelphia economy are education and health care. Lyon, once the leading producer of fine silks, now thrives on the combination of biotechnology, research, tourism, and transportation. While adaptation has served some major cities, others have not developed either a manufacturing sector or substitute trades able to employ their populations. The movement out of rural areas into towns has increased in Africa, Latin America, and the Middle East, far beyond the level at which migrants can be employed in manufacturing jobs. Yet the relative attraction of cities, where newcomers can find better schools, health care, entertainment, and perhaps a poorly paying job, remains strong. In cities such as Nairobi, Jakarta, and La Paz, thousands of men and women arrive yearly with many moving into shanty towns and decayed housing. While some find employment in established businesses or government offices, others can get work only in the informal economy, perhaps as street vendors or trash pickers. Demographic growth therefore continues, but on a relatively fragile economic base in the absence of industrialization. Low-level political conflict has resulted between newcomers and local governments over rights to land and city services.

In multiple countries today, over two-thirds of the total population lives in cities and towns. Levels are highest in North and South America, Australia, Japan, Western Europe, North Africa and the Gulf region. Map 2.2 allows easy comparison of urbanization levels in 1990 in large regions, although it gives a misleading impression of urban populations spread evenly throughout nation-states. Few countries today have less than a quarter of their population living in cities, and these tend to be small, relatively isolated states such as Rwanda, Cambodia, Nepal, and Papua New Guinea.

Coping with urban growth

New towns without adequate housing, sufficient clean water, and effective sanitation shocked contemporary observers. The stinks, the dirt, the noise were overwhelming, and the infrastructures were primitive. Local transportation was primarily on foot, and citizens could access few city services. Horses, which did much of the hauling and carrying, added to the cacophony of sounds with their clomping hooves and whinnies, while dropping manure on the streets. In the early nineteenth century, medical doctors and radical politicians compared cities to sewers, to "foul holes" that produced "poverty, plague, and disease."[13] Both conservatives who disliked change and progressives who demanded a better outcome became vocal critics of industrial cities, which they saw as death traps because of their physical conditions, and they were right. During the early and mid nineteenth centuries, not only did cities have higher death rates than rural areas, but those rates rose along with industrial urbanization.[14]

On the ecological level, cities change environments because of the pollution they create and the land that they use. John McNeill uses the term "urban

13 Andrew Lees, *Cities Perceived: Urban Society in European and American Thought, 1820–1940* (New York: Columbia University Press, 1985), pp. 71–73.

14 Michael R. Haines, "The Urban Mortality Transition in the United States, 1800–1940," National Bureau of Economic Research Historical Working Paper, #134 (July 2001).

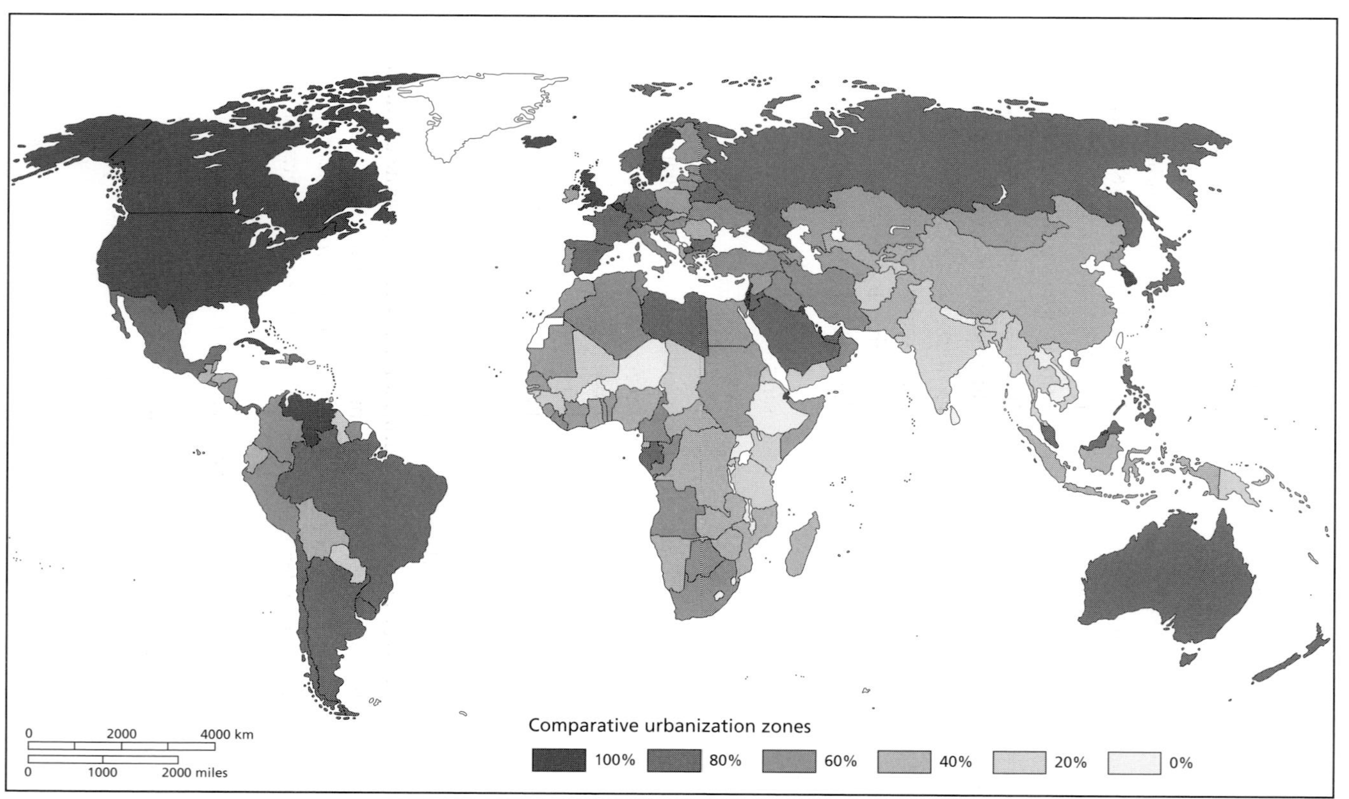

Map 2.2 World map of comparative urbanization rates, 2005

metabolism" to describe how cities every day take in enormous amounts of oxygen, water, food, fuel, building materials, and other products, and simultaneously send out carbon dioxide and monoxide, sulfur and nitrogen oxides, dirty water, sewage, and dust.[15] Concentrations of people produce concentrations of harmful waste products. The burning of coal by factories, home furnaces or hearths, and power plants sent skyward daily hundreds of tons of soot, gases, and toxic metals to darken skies and harm lungs. Supplying cities with sufficient, clean water became more difficult during the rapid urbanization of the nineteenth and twentieth centuries. Most cities drew their drinking water from local rivers, despite the fact that they also dumped untreated sewage into the same streams. In the mid nineteenth century, thousands of city dwellers died from cholera and other water-borne diseases.

Industrialization, which had initially worsened urban conditions, soon, however, produced the technologies and higher incomes that led to lower mortality. During the second half of the nineteenth century, urban death rates declined in most of Europe and in the United States, as inhabitants gained access to cleaner water, better sanitation, and improved housing. In 1849 a British doctor, John Snow, suggested that sewage-laden water carried cholera, and he later provided epidemiological evidence of the linkage between cholera deaths and polluted water. As his ideas gained support, the larger, richer cities in Western Europe built underground pipes and tunnels to divert sewage away from water sources, and they brought more clean water into the towns from distant springs and rivers via aqueducts. Engineers designed pumping stations, filtration plants, and piping systems to deliver the water to homes and businesses. By 1900, the larger cities in Britain, France, and Germany had waterworks and sewage treatment plants, and these technologies spread to other countries. Where these were introduced, cholera ceased to be an urban problem. Sanitizing cities became a central part of modernizing them, and urban administrators not only shared information on projects, but they competed with one another to introduce improvements. By 1900, urban death rates fell decisively in the larger cities of Western Europe and North America.

By the early twentieth century, infant mortality rates began to decline not only in Europe but also in colonial towns such as Cairo, Calcutta, and Singapore. Authorities funded increased water supplies, sewage systems, and public health services for at least part of the urban population. As

15 J. R. McNeill, *Something New Under the Sun: An Environmental History of the Twentieth-Century World* (New York: W.W. Norton & Co., 2000), pp. 289, 292.

antibiotics, DDT, and better urban sanitation spread widely after World War II, death rates both of infants and of adults declined sharply throughout developing regions. Natural increase now fuels urban growth, even where economic development lags. Nevertheless, this pattern has proved reversible, for example during wars, famines, or epidemics. The spread of HIV/AIDS has produced rising death rates in many cities throughout sub-Saharan Africa, and low-income urban populations remain at high risk from TB and malaria.

The sanitation and modernization of cities was neither automatic nor cheap. In Europe, governments commonly used tax money to make these investments, or they sold monopoly rights to a private company, requiring it to provide good service at reasonable prices. By 1900, the major cities of the German empire all had waterworks and gasworks, tramways and electricity plants.[16] Their inhabitants could use public baths, health clinics, and hospitals, with the result that they lived longer, healthier lives. These investments did not take place where towns lacked effective governance and a strong economic base.

Engineers, inventors, and entrepreneurs worked in tandem to redesign urban services, communications, and construction. Steam engines pumped water into elevated reservoirs to permit wide distribution. Gasworks and underground pipes permitted the lighting of town streets and homes. Cast iron could be turned into rails for horse-drawn trolleys and railway lines, while glass panels brought new light into railway terminals. Portland cement, patented in 1824, produced cheap sidewalks and sewer pipes. In the later nineteenth century, electricity powered trolleys and elevators. Cheap steel and reinforced concrete made possible skyscrapers and prefabricated housing. In the early twentieth century, the internal combustion engine revolutionized urban transport, permitting buses and, later, automobiles to swarm onto city streets, with the result that tailpipe emissions added waste gases and lead to the air. Cars have multiplied faster than roads, freeways, and garages can be constructed, slowing traffic and poisoning the air in cities around the world. Introducing new technologies in cities has not been a story of linear and uniform progress.[17] What has brought greater convenience to individuals can also bring high costs to communities and deepen inequalities.

16 Marjatta Hietalla, *Services and Urbanization at the Turn of the Century: The Diffusion of Innovations* (Helsinki: Finnish Historical Society, 1987), p. 195.

17 David Goodman and Colin Chant, eds., *European Cities and Technology: Industrial to Post-Industrial City* (London: Routledge, 1999).

Inequalities in the city

Debates about the consequences of urban life have continued throughout the twentieth century as analysts from many political and disciplinary camps have weighed in. Stressing the positive results of urbanization, Edward Glaeser, an American economist, argues that cities make us "richer, smarter, greener, healthier, and happier." Yet where Glaeser sees "human progress," Mike Davis, an urban theorist, finds "increasing inequality" and the "reproduction of poverty."[18] In his view, the negative results of contemporary urbanization for the many outweigh the positive implications for the few. Some of the debate arises from differences in values: should cities be measured against an index of prosperity or one of equality, against a yardstick of individual freedoms or one measuring communal well-being? Both of these men can be right. Market-driven economies work through inequality, which can be extreme, but they also concentrate wealth and other resources in the larger cities, where they encourage investment.

The evidence is clear that cities are engines of economic development and innovation. They offer inhabitants higher standards of living and higher wages than do rural areas. Moreover, people living in predominantly urbanized countries are richer and healthier on average than those living in states where more than 50 percent of the population lives in the countryside. However poor a developing country might be today, the share of its population living in poverty is significantly lower in its cities than in rural areas of those states.[19]

Nevertheless, inequality is built into the social and spatial organization of cities. Today the absolute numbers of the urban poor are growing because of migration of unemployed, disadvantaged people to major cities who settle in wherever they can find space and are tolerated by city governments. Mike Davis estimates on the basis of United Nations investigations that 78.2 percent of city populations in the "least-developed countries" (Nigeria, Nepal, Bangladesh, Sudan, for example) reside in slums.[20] He calculates that in India, slum dwellers constitute 55.5 percent of the urban population.

18 Edward Glaeser, *The Triumph of the City: How Our Greatest Invention Makes Us Richer, Smarter, Greener, Healthier, and Happier* (New York: The Penguin Press, 2011), p.1; Mike Davis, *Planet of Slums* (London: Verso, 2006), pp. 7, 16.

19 United Nations Department for Economic and Social Affairs, *Rethinking Poverty: Report on the World Social Situation 2010* (New York: United Nations, 2010). See also Alan Gilbert, "Poverty, inequality, and social segregation in the city," in Clark, *Handbook*, pp. 683–699.

20 Davis, *Planet*, p. 23.

The absolute amount of poverty to be found in many contemporary cities is striking because of its sheer magnitude, concentration, and contrast with nearby affluence. Skyscrapers and shopping malls look out over shanty towns, where inhabitants lack legal titles to their property and battle authorities for access to services and the right to remain. Low-level conflict between newcomers and officials contributes to the problems of crime and violence in slum communities.

Inequality has grown in tandem with the development of an informational economy, which has changed occupational structures in the cities of the industrialized world as well as those of developing areas. Growth of labor forces in the "global cities" at the top of the international hierarchy has resulted in high-paying jobs in finance and information technology and in low-paying service work, which is taken on disproportionately by minorities and foreign immigrants in the informal economy.[21] In combination with decreases in unionized manufacturing jobs, these changes have produced increased economic inequality and social segregation in London, New York, and Tokyo, the centers of the global economy.

Urban spaces and their allocations signal social values and shape everyday life for ordinary citizens. Cities are systems within their own boundaries, organizing their internal spaces around particular functions and settlement patterns that influence circuits of exchange and communication. City walls marked boundaries, separating insiders from outsiders. From ancient times, cities were split into areas of higher and lower status, in which residence was linked to religion, kinship, social class, and occupation. Governments and religious authorities usually pre-empted central spaces. The wealthy tended to live nearby, gaining status and visibility by being close to the loci of power, while the poorest citizens found housing in outer areas or in back streets. Rulers often forced foreign merchants to live in separate districts, and some European towns confined Jewish residents to enclosed ghettos. Segregation could also be vertical, as it was during the early nineteenth century in central Paris, where servants and other workers lived on upper floors, or it could be by occupation, as it was in Hanoi, where particular trades from specific villages settled on the same street. As long as most people moved around cities on foot, and the wealthy needed servants and supplies close at hand, different social classes lived in reasonably close proximity.

Industrialization and economic development then made possible extensive rearrangements of urban spaces. Homes and workplaces became separate

21 Sassen, *The Global City*, pp. 317–319.

places for more and more people. An expanding middle class who could afford newer housing and mass transit fares fostered suburban growth. Soon commuting became relatively easy as railroads, trolleys, and buses tied outer districts to central areas. Moving out let others move into what became Central Business Districts organized around banks, department stores, and office buildings. Manufacturing often located in, or was moved to, peripheral areas where land was cheaper and where noise, smoke, and stink would be less annoying. In the twentieth century, planners in many countries embraced functional zoning, which mandated housing separated from commerce and production. Segregation by social class increased as rapid transit and private automobiles made it even easier to move to newer quarters, where higher prices and rents kept out the poor. By the early twentieth century, large middle-class suburbs organized around single-family houses had appeared outside cities as diverse as Manchester, Munich, Chicago, Capetown, and Sydney. After World War II, similar housing estates could be seen all over the world, wherever rising incomes and improved transportation permitted the wealthier to isolate themselves from the less fortunate. In very recent decades, substantial numbers of the affluent have moved back into city centers, where luxury apartments and town houses provide relief from the inconveniences of commuting, while still offering sufficient distance from the poor.

Social segregation on the basis of ethnicity and culture became much more explicit in the modern period when the languages of color and race became intertwined with allocations of urban space. Carl Nightingale identifies empire building, land markets, and sanitary reform as the processes through which urban segregation deepened in the eighteenth and nineteenth centuries. The British organized the area of Madras into two walled settlements, White Town and Black Town, and Stamford Raffles' 1819 plan for Singapore centered on an administrative district and European quarters, flanked by separate sections reserved for Chinese, Malay, Arabs, South Asians, and Bugis. As town-building expanded throughout British India in the nineteenth century, British civilians lived in cantonments, self-contained, quasi suburban communities protected by the army and culturally insulated from local populations. In Morocco, the French added modern sections to Casablanca, Rabat, Meknes, and Marrakesh, which separated the rulers and their institutions from "traditional" neighborhoods. After the outbreak of the bubonic plague in 1894 in large Asian cities, doctors and public health officials redoubled efforts to segregate Europeans from "native" populations blamed for transmitting diseases. Several mechanisms – among them, relative land prices, zoning regulations, and restrictive covenants – reinforced racist assumptions about the need for segregation of populations. In the most extreme case, the Native Urban Areas Act of 1923 permitted South African towns to restrict districts to "whites only" and to remove others to separate locations.[22] Although anti-colonial and democratic governments dismantled the legal bases of urban racial segregation in the late twentieth century, differences in land and housing prices combined with income inequality permits de facto segregation to survive in many cities.

Although the political ideology of democracy promises equal rights to citizens, inequality of outcomes is built into free market economies, which is often justified in terms of religious and ethnic differences. Cities as economic and cultural centers exemplify the tensions between legal rights and social realities. Their diversity and multi-functionality hinders progress toward the broader social equality promised in the ideal of an urban "community."

The megalopolis

One of the most striking changes produced by the rapid urbanization of the planet during the past 250 years is the exploding size and diversity of the world's largest cities. Cities of more than a half million people were not unknown in the ancient world, but they were rare and generally lasted only as long as their political base remained strong. In modern times, the largest cities have not only remained large and retained their political importance, but they have continued to expand, in many cases faster than their national populations. In 1750, most of the ten largest cities in the world were located in China, Japan, or the Ottoman Empire, reflecting the long-term dominance of Asia in the world economy. Each had fewer than 900,000 people. The increasing sizes of London and Paris signaled, however, the growing strength of northwestern European states and the expanding Atlantic economy (see Table 2.2). By 1850 London had leaped to the top of the list with 3,320,000, and New York City had broken the half million mark. By 1950, four of the top ten cities – New York, Buenos Aires, Chicago, and Los Angeles – were in the Americas, but Moscow and Calcutta had also become urban giants. Each claimed more than 3,000,000 residents. Only half of the cities on the list were capitals. The others relied on industrial growth and trade to draw in immigrants by the tens of thousands.

22 Carl H. Nightingale, *Segregation: A Global History of Divided Cities* (University of Chicago Press, 2012).

Table 2.2 World's ten largest cities

1750		1850		1950	
Peking	900,000	London	2,320,000	New York	12,300,000
London	676,000	Peking	1,648,000	London	8,860,000
Constantinople	666,000	Paris	1,314,000	Tokyo	7,547,000
Paris	560,000	Canton	800,000	Paris	5,900,000
Edo (Tokyo)	509,000	Constantinople	785,000	Shanghai	5,406,000
Canton	500,000	Hangchow	700,000	Moscow	5,100,000
Osaka	375,000	New York	682,000	Buenos Aires	5,000,000
Kyoto	362,000	Bombay	575,000	Chicago	4,806,000
Hangchow	350,000	Edo (Tokyo)	567,000	Calcutta	4,800,000
Naples	324,000	Soochow	550,000	Los Angeles	3,900,000

Source: Tertius Chandler and Gerald Fox, *3000 Years of Urban Growth* (New York: Academic Press, 1974), pp. 322, 328, 337.

These sprawling, crowded places have proved hard to understand and easy to fear. Fritz Lang's 1927 film *Metropolis* identified the city of the future with looming skyscrapers, oppressive technology, deep economic inequality, and class conflict. Lewis Mumford, one of the twentieth century's most influential commentators on cities, thought that modern cities threatened social cohesion and the natural environment. He accused them of spreading conformism and mindless patriotism, while curbing individual liberty. Their size and mobility defeated attempts to maintain a sense of community or a coherent space.[23]

During the next fifty years, cities continued to multiply in size as well as in numbers. While only one city, metropolitan New York, had broken the 10,000,000 mark in 1950, nineteen had done so by 2000 (see Table 2.3). Of the world's largest cities in 1750, only three (Beijing, Edo now Tokyo, and Osaka) retained that rank in 2000, and they are all in Asia, as are a majority of the other mega-cities that have emerged. Neither "city" nor "metropolis" seems an adequate description of these urban giants. In 1961, Jean Gottmann coined the term "megalopolis" to describe the area from Boston to Washington, DC, which he argued had become one urbanized area, unified by transportation and communications.[24] City region seems an even better description of these gigantic, urbanized areas. The Greek city planner Constantinos Doxiadis predicted the creation of one worldwide city, "ecumenopolis," which would grow dynamically along transportation routes to link major settlements everywhere.[25] Planners, he hoped, would "build the frame" of this universal city, channeling urbanization into carefully designed, human-scale communities, while preserving greenspace and the natural environment. Some of Dioxiadis's predictions about runaway urban growth have come true. Today, the Japan Statistics Bureau recognizes a Tokyo metropolitan area of 13 million people, embedded in a National Capital Region of over 43 million inhabitants, which comprises not only Tokyo but three adjoining, urbanized prefectures – Chiba, Kanagawa, and Saitama – each of which includes multiple cities with their own boundaries, and the urban sprawl continues south along the coast to the Osaka conurbation. In extreme cases, urbanized regions have overleapt the boundaries of nation-states. French geographers identified as early as 1989 a European urban core

23 Lewis Mumford, *The Culture of Cities* (New York: Harcourt Brace, & Co., 1938), pp. 250–52, 273–74, 278.

24 Jean Gottmann, *Megalopolis: The Urbanized Northeastern Seaboard of the United States* (New York: The Twentieth Century Fund, 1961).

25 Constantinos A. Dioxiadis, "The coming world city: Ecumenopolis," in Arnold Toynbee (ed.), *Cities of Destiny* (New York: McGraw-Hill, 1967), pp. 336–358.

Table 2.3 Population of cities with 10 million inhabitants or more, 1950–2000 (* in millions)

City	1950	City	1975	City	2000
New York	12.3	Tokyo	26.6	Tokyo	35.0
Tokyo	11.3	New York	15.9	Mexico City	18.7
		Shanghai	11.4	New York	18.3
		Mexico City	11.4	São Paulo	17.9
		São Paulo	10.7	Mumbai	17.4
				Delhi	14.1
				Calcutta	13.8
				Buenos Aires	13.0
				Shanghai	12.8
				Jakarta	12.3
				Los Angeles	12.0
				Dhaka	11.6
				Osaka-Kobe	11.2
				Rio de Janeiro	11.2
				Karachi	11.1
				Beijing	10.8
				Cairo	10.8
				Moscow	10.5
				Manila	10.4
				Lagos	10.1

Source: United Nations, *World Urbanization Prospects: The 2003 Revision*, Table 1.7, p. 11.

extending from northwest England through Belgium, the Netherlands, and the Rhineland area into northern Italy. Nicknamed the "Blue Banana," for its curved shape and the color originally used for it by mapmakers, it depicts an area of dense settlement linked by high-speed rail, freeways, and airports, within which London functions as a financial capital and the Brussels bureaucracy exercises powers delegated to the European Union.[26] The different parts of these sprawling urban regions while unified by transport remain divided in many other respects.

The question of how to govern these urban giants has not been solved effectively anywhere. Solutions lie along a continuum ranging from extreme decentralization, such as that followed in much of the United States, where multiple independent local governments run their particular slices of the larger

26 Andreas Faludi, "The megalopolis, the Blue Banana, and global economic integration zones in European planning thought," in Catherine L. Ross, *Mega-regions: Planning for Global Competitiveness* (Island Press, 2009).

agglomeration, to centralized forms of regional governance, such as exist in Bangkok, Tokyo, and Shanghai.[27] But even where one authority has power over a designated metropolitan region, there are usually competing authorities who run particular services, and official boundaries rarely coincide with settlement patterns on the ground. Growing cities expand outward, faster than government can recognize and cope with changes. Even in the twenty-first century, urban sprawl outruns the capacity of city governments to provide needed infrastructures and services. Suburban shanty towns lacking electricity, sewers, and clean water have multiplied in parts of Latin America, Asia, and Africa, but metropolitan regions in Europe and North America also have neglected territory outside formal jurisdictions. Office buildings, shopping malls, and apartments, in clusters sometimes called "edge cities," have sprouted around the world near freeway exits or airports.[28] With no separate governing structures or clear identity, these neighborhoods sit uneasily among older town centers and overlapping administrative jurisdictions. Parasitic on the services and populations of other neighborhoods, they survive uneasily where transit systems intersect and commuting patterns converge.

The United Nations estimated that in 2003 the world urban population reached 3.04 billion people, a large majority of whom lived in the cities and towns of developing countries.[29] Urbanization has become the norm, rather than the exception. In the next two decades, virtually all of the the world's population growth will flow into the cities of less developed regions, many of which lack the resources to offer most newcomers decent housing, good education, and employment at a living wage. Although globalization has lessened differences among cities, which share technologies, cultural styles, and consumer goods, rising levels of social and economic inequality limit access to the benefits of urban modernity. Cities in the twenty-first century, as in earlier times, need to translate the benefits of higher incomes into improvements in the quality of life and widened opportunities for all of their citizens.

Further reading

Bairoch, Paul. *Cities and Economic Development*, trans. Christopher Braider. University of Chicago Press, 1988.

27 Aprodicio A. Laquian, *Beyond Metropolis: The Planning and Governance of Asia's Mega-Urban Regions* (Washington, DC: Woodrow Wilson Center Press, 2005).

28 Joel Garreau, *Edge City* (New York: Doubleday, 1991).

29 United Nations Department of Economic and Social Affairs, Population Division, *World Urbanization Prospects: The 2003 Revision* (New York: United Nations, 2004), p. 3.

Castells, Manuel. *The Informational City*. Oxford: Basil Blackwell, 1989.
Clark, David. *Urban World/Global City*. London: Routledge, 2003.
Clark, Peter, ed. *The Oxford Handbook of Cities in World History*. Oxford University Press, 2013.
Davis, Mike. *Planet of Slums*. London: Verso, 2006.
de Vries, Jan. *European Urbanization, 1500–1800*. Cambridge, MA: Harvard University Press, 1984.
Driver, Felix. *Imperial Cities: Landscape, Display, and Identity*. Manchester University Press, 2003.
Freund, Bill. *The African City: A History*. Cambridge University Press, 2007.
Garreau, Joel. *Edge City: Life on the New Frontier*. New York: Doubleday, 1991.
Glaeser, Edward. *The Triumph of the City: How Our Greatest Invention Makes Us Richer, Smarter, Greener, Healthier, and Happier*. New York: The Penguin Press, 2011.
Goodman, David and Colin Chant, eds. *European Cities and Technology: Industrial to Post-Industrial City*. London: Routledge, 1999.
Hall, Peter. *Cities of Tomorrow: An Intellectual History of Urban Planning and Design Since 1880*. 4th edn. Oxford:Wiley-Blackwell, 2014.
Hietalla, Marjatta. *Services and Urbanization at the Turn of the Century: The Diffusion of Innovations*. Helsinki: Finnish Historical Society, 1987.
Hohenberg, Paul M. and Lynn Hollen Lees. *The Making of Urban Europe, 1000–1994*, rev. edn. Cambridge, MA: Harvard University Press, 1995.
Jacobs, Jane. *The Economy of Cities*. New York: Vintage, 1970.
Laquian, Aprodicio A. *Beyond Metropolis: The Planning and Governance of Asia's Mega-Urban Regions*. Washington, DC: Woodrow Wilson Center Press, 2005.
Lees, Andrew. *Cities Perceived: Urban Society in European and American Thought, 1820–1940*. New York: Columbia University Press, 1985.
Lees, Andrew and Lynn Hollen Lees. *Cities and the Making of Europe, 1750–1914*. Cambridge University Press, 2008.
Nightingale, Carl H. *Segregation: A Global History of Divided Cities*. University of Chicago Press, 2012.
Ren, Xuefei. *Urban China*. London: Polity Press, 2013.
Sassen, Saskia. *The Global City: New York, London, and Tokyo*. Princeton University Press, 1991.
United Nations Department of Economic and Social Affairs, Population Division. *World Urbanization Prospects: The 1999 Revision* (New York: United Nations, 2001) and *World Urbanization Prospects: The 2003 Revision* (New York: United Nations, 2004).

3

The family in modern world history

PETER N. STEARNS

Changes and continuities in family structure and family life form an important element in world history over the past two and a half centuries. On the one hand, families have been subjected to intense pressures to shift and adapt, whether the focus is on gender roles within the family or the purpose of having children. Alterations in economic structure, including urbanization, provide one impetus for change, but so do other developments such as imperialism or, more recently, globalization. On the other hand, families remain intensely personal, and traditions can be closely guarded as part of cultural identity. Important tensions result, as well as considerable regional diversity along with some common trends.

Some broad patterns can be identified, ultimately affecting most societies though with important differences in timing. Whereas families in agricultural economies – the standard framework still in 1750 – emphasized the centrality of child labor to the family economy, increasingly attention shifted to the linkage between childhood and education. This in turn converted children from economic assets to the family, to economic liabilities, and was everywhere accompanied by a reduction in birth rates. This could in turn have still further implications for gender roles in families, by reducing some traditional demands on mothers. Still more broadly, though unevenly, the economic functions of families declined, as much production shifted to other units such as factories and as management structures moved beyond the capacity of family units. These processes could lead to some destabilization – divorce rates went up in many societies – but also to intense and often successful efforts to emphasize alternative functions for the family itself.

Another key development involved a tendency for nuclear family structures to gain precedence over the extended family, though this trend, too, needs careful handling. Urbanization and migration unquestionably placed great strain on extended families, as some members – disproportionately young – moved away. Of course networks with uncles and cousins could re-form, and extended families continued to provide not only emotional but economic service, helping relatives find jobs or loaning money for an individual unit to handle hard times. By the twentieth century, new technologies, such as the telephone, also helped relatives maintain contact even across distances. And in many cultures – the Middle East is one example – families continued to place great emphasis on solidarity as they socialized their children. But there was a common trend toward a focus on connections among parents and children alone. As life expectancy went up – another widespread global trend by the twentieth century – this could force some hard decisions about how to handle older family members. In the West, the rise of the welfare state substituted for family support for the elderly to some extent, but in other cases, such as Japan, a wider assumption that more traditional family responsibilities would prevail created real strain. Here was another complex mix of newer trends and older values.[1]

At some point in the past two centuries, then, families in many regions shifted away from some characteristics that had been standard in the long agricultural period of world history, to what might be called an industrial or modern family model. This shift has been complicated, however, by a number of factors. First, even ultimately standard changes have occurred at very different points in time. Families in Western Europe and the United States began altering the definition of childhood from work to schooling in the nineteenth century, with attendant impacts on birth rates, but Japan moved to a fuller emphasis on education only after 1872 and many African societies are just now experiencing the implications of schooling for average family size. At any given point, then, families have varied widely, from one region to the next or even within regions, in terms of the stage of their engagement with basic modern trends.

Specific sources of change have also varied. In the West, pressures on family traditions resulted particularly from economic shifts, beginning with the industrial revolution, supplemented by new directives from the state (through laws on child labor, for example, or school attendance). The pressures might be resented, but they were largely internal. In many other regions, change came in part from external sources, from imperialist regimes or, more recently, from global agencies, and this could generate different types of reaction and resistance.

1 On extended families and kinship, Maurice Godelier, et al., *The Metamorphoses of Kinship* (London and New York: Verso, 2011); on implications of greater longevity for the family, Katherine Lynch, *Individuals, Families and Communities in Europe, 1200–1800: The Urban Foundations of Western Society* (Cambridge University Press, 2003).

Finally, and obviously, common patterns of change have been strongly conditioned by prior differences in family structures and cultures. There was no single type of agricultural family in 1750, which meant that there would be no single reaction to pressures for change even aside from distinctions of timing and specific causation. While agricultural families generally promoted some respect for older family members, the emphasis was much stronger in Confucian cultures than in the Western tradition – and elements of this distinction still echo in the twenty-first century. Most agricultural families showed some preference for boys over girls – basic patriarchal assumptions were widespread. But the preference was stronger, or at least more resistant to change, in places like China and India – that is, in Confucian and Brahminical cultures – than in Western Europe or the United States, again with clear results in family practices today. Traditions of polygamy in Islam (for families with sufficient means) and in parts of sub-Saharan Africa, though hardly unaltered, continue to influence contemporary behaviors. Prior differences not only persist amid change. They can also be highlighted or even revived as part of a defense of cultural and family identity amid other, less governable, pressures.

Modern family history is, thus, complex. Separate regional treatments and comparisons remain essential. Yet common patterns must not be ignored. A case in point: in 1926 the song *Happy Birthday* was first composed; it began to be a standard part of family birthday celebrations by the 1930s in the United States. By the early twenty-first century the song had been translated into virtually every major language. Birthday celebrations for children gained ground not only in the West, where they tended to become steadily more elaborate, but also in urban cultures in the Middle East, China, and elsewhere where, traditionally, the whole phenomenon had been ignored. Amid important variety and, sometimes, resistance, some aspects of family life were gaining global characteristics.

The eighteenth century

The second half of the eighteenth century did not witness any systematic changes in family life, on a global basis. One historian has suggested that economic pressures during this period, thanks above all to higher rates of world trade, increased work requirements for various categories: slavery became more onerous and child labor more demanding, while older people had to labor more as well, with less possibility of partial, informal retirement as physical capacity began to wane.[2] These changes may have affected many societies, China for example as well as the Atlantic world, and they would certainly have conditioned family life. But the possibility is still somewhat speculative, and short of this a global proposition about family change would be misplaced.

There were, however, important regional developments, with a diverse set of directions involved. The spread of Confucianism in Tokugawa Japan began to encourage wider interest in schooling, by the later eighteenth and particularly early nineteenth centuries. This did not undo a primary commitment to work for most children, but it modified it to some extent. In southern Arabia the movement ultimately called Wahhabi, founded by Muhammed ibn Abd al-Wahhab (1703–92) and calling for a return to the original stipulations of Islam, had important implications for family life. Al-Wahhab was deeply concerned about loose morals, including what he saw as an increase in adultery; but he also wanted greater attention to the wellbeing of widows and orphans and stricter protection for the inheritance rights of women. Wahhabi Islam, which became the predominant version of Islam in what is now Saudi Arabia, was known for its strict enforcement of sexual morality and the subordination of women, but it had other features as well designed to shore up Islam's support for family life and family members, urging husbands, for example, to provide proper care for wives.

The Atlantic slave trade and European colonialism had important results for family life, not new in 1750 but continuing to gain momentum for another several decades. In West Africa and Angola the depredations of the slave trade, in emphasizing the seizure of young men, created gender disparities that significantly expanded reliance on polygamy as a means of integrating excess women into a functioning family structure. Even aside from this larger pattern, the capture of young people for slavery was profoundly wrenching to individual families.

The impact of colonialism in Latin America was even more profound, in terms of alterations of family life; and some of these changes applied as well to North America. In the first place, Europeans tended to disapprove strongly of some of the family patterns they encountered among Native Americans. Women often seemed to have too much power and independence, and as Europeans gained the opportunity during the sixteenth and seventeenth

2 Kenneth Pomeranz, *The World That Trade Created: Society, Culture and the World Economy, 1400 to the Present* (New York and London: M.E. Sharpe, 2006).

centuries, through laws and Christian missionary conversions, they tended to promote greater male authority in the family, sometimes even to the point of countenancing violence against wives and daughters in order to keep them in line. Imported slaves, for their part, often worked hard to reestablish African family patterns, for example the practice of naming children for other relatives and providing protection for all members of an extended family, including the elderly; but the practice of separating some families in subsequent slave sales was a deeply disruptive element.

In Latin America, the colonial experience also created unusually high rates of illegitimacy. Spanish and Portuguese colonists were disproportionately male, and for this reason as well as to take advantage of political superiority they often formed sexual liaisons with native women, rarely acknowledging any offspring that resulted. The result was a growing mestizo, or mixed-blood population that picked up some similar patterns, with high rates of illegitimacy and mother-headed households. Thus in the 1740s in the Sao Paulo parish in Brazil, 23 percent of all children born were illegitimate, and the figure was even higher in other areas.[3] To compensate, many Latin American communities shared responsibility for child care, to relieve individual mothers, and children were sometimes passed around among families, depending on where there were labor needs. Many children were also sent to orphanages, where again they were allocated to families for labor once they reached the age of five or six. The result could be unsettling, sometimes quite cruel, but it could also lead to caring de facto families, even when the children involved were in essence adopted. Upper classes in Latin America, of European origin, often criticized the family practices of the lower classes, and in the later nineteenth century various reform movements would seek to impose more "civilized" family patterns. Here too, the legacy of colonialism would have durable impact.

Probably the most significant changes in family life in the later eighteenth century occurred in Western Europe. It is important to be careful here: Europe was only one place among many in eighteenth-century world history, and its family patterns initially had no global resonance. In the long run, however, some of the family developments in Europe would spill over into other societies.

3 Tobias Hecht, *Minor Omissions: Children in Latin American History and Society* (Madison, WI: University of Wisconsin Press, 2002); Ernest Bartell and Alejandro O'Donnell, *The Child in Latin America: Health, Development and Rights* (Indiana: University of Notre Dame Press, 2001).

Two or three major changes began to modify European families in the eighteenth century, with some impact as well on the British colonies of North America. First was a cultural shift. Protestantism had already placed a new level of importance on the family: in countering Catholic belief in the importance of clerical celibacy, Protestants began to emphasize the centrality and validity of the family more fully. Then, in the eighteenth century itself, new beliefs began to emerge about the importance of love as the basis for appropriate family life. Many readers, in an increasingly literate society, began to read romantic novels. Individuals themselves began to expect more affection in family life, most obviously seeking to base courtship and marriage on romantic attraction rather than economic arrangements. In some cases, as in one part of Switzerland, even laws changed: courts began to rule that young people could turn down parental matches on grounds that there was no possibility that they could ever love the partner who had been selected. New cultural emphasis was also placed on the emotional value of motherhood. It is not clear how widely these new ideas were held, or how much impact they had against the more practical side of family formation; but they were in the air. Historians have also debated the results, particularly for women: the changes could give women a new voice, for example in courtship, but they could also confirm women's largely domestic role.[4] More companionate family ideals also emerged in China, though obviously within a different cultural framework.

Accompanying the greater valuation of romance, family life began to be associated with new forms of consumerism. While many Europeans remained desperately poor, a growing number began to have a bit of money to spare. In addition to some changes in diet, toward more consumption of products like sugar and coffee, growing consumerism focused on two categories, both family-linked. First, stylish clothing gained esteem, and this was directly connected to the desire to win love and affection. Second, household items won popularity: better furnishings, better table settings, specific utensils to serve products like coffee or tea. Arguably, these products both reflected and encouraged a greater richness in family life, including new insistence on practices like family mealtimes where the products could

4 Nancy Cott, *The Grounding of Modern Feminism* (New Haven, CT: Yale University Press, 1989). On the emergence of a more companionate family ideal in China, within an obviously different cultural framework, see William Rowe, *China's Last Empire: The Great Qing* (Cambridge, MA: Harvard University Press, 2009).

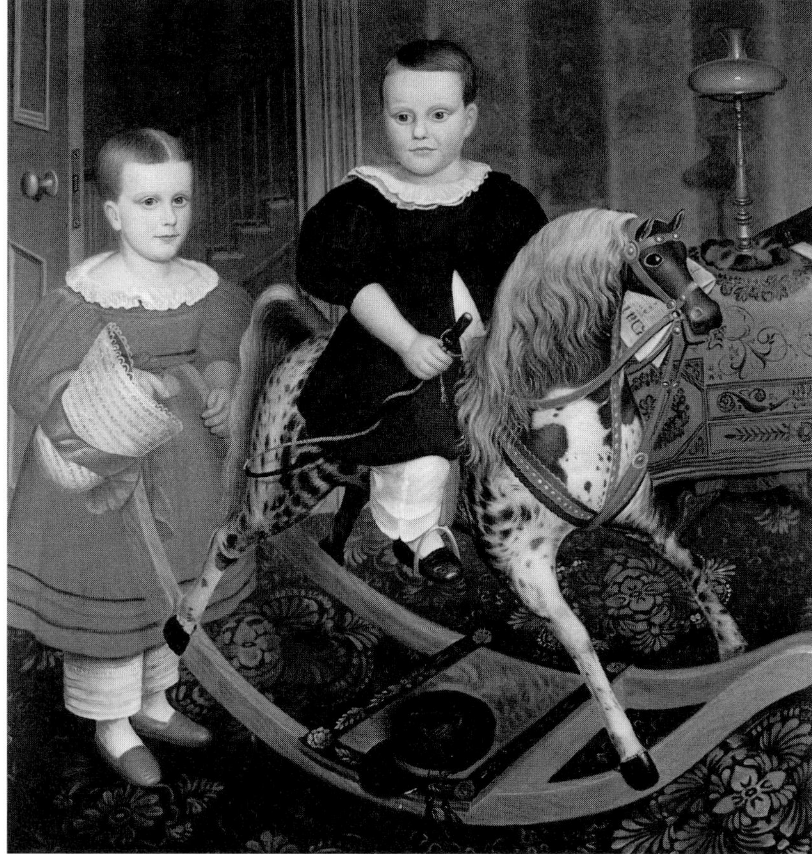

Figure 3.1 Children playing with hobby horse in American folk art painting from the 1840s (© Francis G. Mayer/Corbis)

be enjoyed but also greater family sociability developed. Almost certainly, many families were gaining a new significance in emotionality and social relationships, as the importance of wider communities and non-familial friendships began to recede.

At the same time, however, another pattern emerged that reflected a certain degree of destabilization, though it could be linked with the romantic theme to some extent. Rates of illegitimate births began to go up in Western society, particularly among the lower classes. More and more people were taking jobs partly outside the family economy, producing clothing or metal goods for sale on the market for example. This gave young people some earnings outside their parents' control, and it also generated wider social contacts, including urban contacts. The result was what some historians have termed the first modern sexual revolution.[5] Many young people began to have sex at a somewhat earlier age, and marriage did not always result. Historians continue to debate the gender implications of this shift: did women, as well as men, have new opportunities for sexual pleasure-seeking, or were they bullied or deceived into relationships that would often leave them burdened and stigmatized?

One point is clear, though it would not fully emerge until the early nineteenth century: respectable, propertied elements in Western society were deeply troubled by the new sexual behaviors and the unwanted children that could result. In response they constructed an elaborate extension of "traditional" sexual morality, in what became known as Victorian culture: sex became dangerous, capable not only of causing social and familial harm, but also generating ill health. In the extreme Victorian view, youthful sex, or too much sex at any age, could cause mental degeneration, sterility, stunted growth – this list was long. Proper parents had new responsibilities to supervise the sexual habits of their children, particularly working to prevent masturbation. Women had a special obligation – in the Victorian view, they were judged naturally more sexually reticent – to keep their virginity and, even in marriage, to discourage excess. In fact, many respectable Westerners took Victorianism with some grains of salt. Both husbands and wives might find pleasure in marital sex. Many men indulged in prostitutes or other opportunities to live up to standards within the family but enjoy pleasures without. But Victorianism undoubtedly influenced actual sexual standards, as well as rules about sexuality in culture and even legal codes. It would condition the way Europeans judged sexuality in other cultures, during the decades of imperialism. And while it did not in fact reverse the sexual revolution, it undoubtedly slowed it.

Overall, significant regional adjustments marked family history in the later eighteenth century, without much interconnection. Even within individual societies, like Latin America or Western Europe, trends were complex, to some degree contradictory. No full version of change had yet emerged.

5 One reason for illegitimacy was the fluctuation of earnings for young adults. Independent earnings, in other words, helped motivate new sexual behavior, but also new instability. See David Levine, *Is Behavioral Economics Doomed?: The Ordinary versus the Extraordinary* (Cambridge: Open Book Publishers, 2012).

The nineteenth and early twentieth centuries: the industrial revolution and imperialism

Two fundamental forces impacted family life in the nineteenth century. The industrial revolution generated a host of significant changes, some of them transient, some very durable. Initial industrialization centered in the West and was linked to some of the innovations that were emerging even before 1800. It was spreading beyond the West by 1900, most notably to Japan, with some similar results. But along with industrialization came an unprecedented surge of overseas imperialism, producing family disruption in its own right – particularly through the partial imposition of Western standards on regional family patterns. Many traditional family elements persisted: most of the world's population remained rural, often far removed from the major currents of change. And certainly there was no uniform pattern of change. There is no doubt, however, that the nineteenth century ushered in a number of new pressures and opportunities for the institution of the family.

Not all regions were deeply touched by either of the key developments, in terms of family life. The Ottoman Empire, for example, witnessed a variety of important changes, with the rise of nationalism, growing Russian and Western pressure, and the huge effort that went into the Tanzimat reforms until they were largely abandoned in the 1870s. The results did not, however, significantly alter family life, which continued to be affected more clearly by the religious traditions of the various communities within the multinational empire, the Islamic communities most important among them. Early factories drew in some women workers, which could affect family life, but these were still exceptions. Family issues did not define priorities in the Empire at this point. Western observers, to be sure, pointed to the Ottoman Empire as a hotbed of sexual excess, as they gossiped about, and greatly exaggerated, life in the Sultan's harem, with its many wives and concubines. This had little to do with the more standard conditions of family life in the region.[6]

The industrial revolution

The industrial revolution began to take shape in Britain in the later eighteenth century, and then spread to other parts of Western Europe and the United States from the 1820s onward. A powerful phenomenon, focused

6 Asli Çirakman, *From the "Terror of the World" to the "Sick Man of Europe,"* 2nd edn. (New York: Peter Lang Publishing, 2004). See also Beshara Doumani, ed., *Family History in the Middle East: Household, Property, and Gender* (Albany, NY: State University of New York Press, 2003).

on the growth of steam-powered factory industry and the more general growth of cities, it did not affect entire populations immediately, but intensified steadily over time. Its impacts on families were extensive. Results were not identical for all the groups involved: gender differentiations increased for a time, but there were also significant divergences between middle and working classes, for example on the extent to which women could be removed from the labor force. Finally, family impacts were further complicated by a distinction between short-term dislocations and longer-term patterns.

Especially in the initial decades of industrialization, sheer disruption bore heavily on many families. Intense, unfamiliar work and movement to the cities help explain increased rates of family abandonment and (depending on legal codes) rising rates of divorce. Drinking went up, another stress on some families. Early industrial consumerism now provided entertainment opportunities outside the family, with bars as early example, as the impact of this development became more complex.

More important in the long run was the growing separation of work and business from home and family, affecting middle- as well as working-class families. Several compensations resulted. Married women were increasingly withdrawn from the labor force, except for work in the home, in order to care for household and children. Male contact with families lessened, increasingly framed in terms of providing material support – the "breadwinner" role. Even in the many working-class families that in fact depended on supplementary earnings by wives and older children, the breadwinner ideal gained ground, giving adult male workers special standing in the family but some special pressures as well.

Fairly quickly, children's work function was also reconsidered, for the new production systems proved unsafe for young children while reducing parental control. Middle-class families led the way in seeking more schooling. Various reform pressures soon led governments to restrict child labor more generally, with initial laws emerging in the 1830s and 1840s in most Western nations. Wider school requirements were not far behind, though some families resented the resulting reduction of parental control over children and their work. More generally, growing government attention to features of family life was an important innovation in its own right.

Less child labor and the need to cover school costs prompted reconsideration of traditional birth rates, aided in some cases by new, factory-made contraceptive devices. Middle-class families led the way, followed by workers and then some rural families. By the early twentieth century average birth rates in the West were dropping below four per family. There is real debate over some of the results for families themselves: did fewer children increase parental attention and affection for the individual child, or did smaller sibling groups actually heighten tensions between the child and its parents?

One further result is less contested: lower birth rates prompted industrial societies and many parents to seek lower death rates.[7] Between 1880 and 1920, throughout the Western world, infant mortality began to drop rapidly, from 20–30 percent of all children born to 5 percent or below, with further reductions still to come. For the first time in human history, by the early 20th century, families no longer had to expect the death of at least one child. The *demographic transition*, to low birth and child death rates alike, reflected a quiet revolution in key aspects of family life.

The industrial revolution also affected the position of older people in the family during the nineteenth century. Industrial conditions in the West encouraged more elderly parents, especially widows, to live with younger kin, to gain some support but also to provide assistance with grandchildren. These patterns would change, from the 1920s onward, with growing residential separation but also the creation of new institutions to care for dependent elderly. Widespread unemployment of older workers, another result of industrialization, increased pressure on families to provide assistance, though gradually the emergence of retirement pensions reduced this pressure to a degree. Family responsibility for the elderly became, if not a new at least a clearer issue with industrialization, and then in the twentieth century rising rates of adult longevity added to the mix.

Finally, family imagery and some key functions changed. Faced with urban conditions and disruptive pressures, middle-class spokespeople began to create new family ideals, emphasizing love among family members and a sense that, guided by affectionate wives and mothers, the family could become something of a haven amid a harsh, competitive economic environment.[8] New beliefs in the innocence of children supplemented this picture, along with accelerating emphasis on love as the basis for marriage. More than symbolism was involved: urban conditions steadily promoted a

7 The birth rate/death rate relationship was complex. In the West, the birth rate drop did precede the largest decline in infant death rates, though there may have been more modest changes as the birth rate transition began. In most other societies however the relationship was clearly the other way around, as individuals and governments pushed for lower death rates first.

8 Christopher Lasch, *Haven in a Heartless World* (New York and London: W.W. Norton Books, 1977).

reduction in the use of dowries as part of contracting for marriage, in favor of less formal economic arrangements and, of course, more emphasis on emotion. Many families, of course, fell short of the new ideals, but they had wide currency and clearly shaped expectations to some degree. Some historians have indeed argued that higher emotional standards could actually produce new dissatisfaction, provoking divorce or parent-child dispute, when reality of family life fell short of the mark.

But the new imagery also promoted growing use of the family as a consumer unit, particularly when incomes rose above subsistence. In many middle-class homes, for example, the piano, a fairly expensive item, became a vital symbol of family solidarity. Other expenses for the home, many of them featured in the new consumer outlets called department stores, and purchases of a growing array of toys and books designed for children amplified this aspect of family life. Within marriage, though gradually, increasing interest in sexual pleasure – recreational rather than largely procreational sex – also gained ground. One study showed that American middle-class women born after 1870 reported markedly higher rates of orgasm, for example, than was true for the previous generation.[9] Overall, as production functions declined for the family, the emotional, consumer, and recreational roles expanded.

One other factor affected family life in the West during the industrialization period. Rising population rates, before birth rate control took full effect, prompted massive emigration. Germany and Ireland joined Britain in providing many migrants, and later other regions joined in. Mid-nineteenth-century migration affected gender balance, in both sending and receiving societies, with more young men leaving, and this obviously complicated family life again at both ends of the process. In receiving societies like the United States or Latin America, the presence of many single male immigrants was a source of great concern for family advocates for many decades.[10]

The emergence of the industrial family centered in Western Europe and North America through much of the nineteenth century. By the final quarter of the century, however, industrialization began to spread to other regions, especially to Russia and Japan. This expansion generated a number of parallel results in terms of family change, but also some key differences. The

9 Clelia Duel Mosher, *The Mosher Survey: Sexual Attitudes of Forty-Five Victorian Women* (New York: Arno Press, 1980).

10 Leslie Page Moch, *Moving Europeans, Second Edition: Migration in Western Europe since 1650* (Bloomington, IN: Indiana University Press, 2003).

Japanese moved quickly to limit child labor and require education through legislation, while new public health measures pushed down child mortality rates. Parents, particularly mothers, took on growing responsibilities for their children's school success. One historian has argued that a new appreciation for childhood as a separate phase of life took hold in Japan, and certainly the state showed growing interest not only in schooling but other aspects of child care; as in the West, for example, the government began to push educational programs to teach parents "modern" methods of hygiene and discipline.[11] But lower birth rates took hold more gradually in the Japanese case, and Japan would not complete this aspect of the demographic transition until after World War II. In Japan and even more in Russia, labor force needs also kept large numbers of married women in employment outside the home, juggling work and family responsibilities in ways that differed from Western patterns. Another distinction, in Japan, was the continued cultural emphasis on respect and family responsibility owed to older parents and grandparents.

Both Russia and Japan abundantly demonstrated the more general disruptive effects of the industrial revolution on family life. Divorce rates soared in Japan around 1900, though they would later stabilize. Rates of premarital sexual activity went up in Russia, recalling patterns in the Western "sexual revolution" a century before.

Nowhere did the industrial revolution destroy the family, though it obviously generated important challenges. Many families, however, faced dramatic redefinitions of roles and functions, creating new constraints and new opportunities alike.

Imperialism

Most of the world would not be involved in outright industrial revolutions until well into the twentieth century or beyond. As a result, more traditional family characteristics remained viable, from high birth rates to arranged marriage to continued use of the family as a production unit. Significant spillovers did occur however, as industrialization in some parts of the world affected economic and demographic patterns elsewhere.

New systems of immigration brought people from southern and eastern Europe and from Asia not only to the United States but also to regions such as Brazil or South Africa during the later nineteenth century, engaged in

11 Brian Platt, "Japanese childhood, modern childhood: the nation-state, the school, and 19th century globalization," *Journal of Social History* 38/4 (2005), 965–985.

growing export production for industrial markets. As before, immigration could disrupt extended families. It created novel opportunities for children, raised in a new region, to serve as brokers between their elders and the culture around them. Immigrants typically worked hard to maintain family cohesion – Italian Americans for example tried to prevent wives and daughters from working as domestics in other households, lest they be corrupted[12] – but some change and tension were inevitable. Correspondingly, studies of generational patterns among immigrants, such as Japanese Americans, become an important vehicle for grasping changes and continuities in family life. Some immigrant groups picked up new family habits, like lower birth rates, fairly quickly (Jewish Americans were a case in point), while others reacted more gradually.

New family ideals from the West did have some impact even aside from the immigrant experience. They certainly affected Western judgment of conditions in other societies – for example, the widespread use of child labor, now seen as a sign of backwardness – feeding a sense of superiority. Elites in some regions might also use elements of the new family ideals in their own judgments. Middle classes in Latin American cities, in countries such as Argentina, in the late nineteenth and early twentieth centuries, developed fierce critiques of lower-class family habits based in part on imported standards. In this view, radical reforms were essential to bring the lower classes up to a "civilized" approach to family life, in which less illegitimacy, less exploitation of child labor, more attention to domestic hygiene, more parental commitment to education for children would create more appropriate standards.

It was imperialism, however, that brought the clearest interaction between Western industrial nations and other world regions during the nineteenth century and often beyond. Imperialism generated some confrontations between Western family standards and conditions elsewhere, but also a wider set of economic and political changes that had somewhat different implications for family life.

Results were particularly dramatic in Africa, where imperialism gained ground from the 1860s onward. Several factors combined to impact many families, though by no means was every region or social group deeply affected. Religious conversions spread rapidly, as sub-Saharan Africans increasingly moved from polytheism to Christianity or Islam. Missionary

12 Donna R. Gabaccia, *Foreign Relations: American Immigration in Global Perspective* (Princeton University Press, 2012).

efforts often challenged traditional patterns of family authority at least for a time, when male elders, for example, tried to hold out for older beliefs against the conversion of wives and children. The same efforts could generate criticisms of some customary habits. Christians, of course, sought to challenge polygamy directly, though sometimes with mixed results, while conversion to Islam could affect gender relations within the family. Economic change was at least as significant. European countries and governments sought to develop mining and commercial agriculture. In the process, they frequently drew males' labor away from rural villages, obviously disrupting traditional family patterns. Female authority in village families increased, though often amid economic hardship, while male family contacts became more sporadic. On another front, some children gained access to formal schooling, in colonial or mission settings. Exposure to new education and urban jobs created new tensions between personal goals and the traditions of African extended families. A later African novel described a situation in Lagos, in the 1920s, when the mother of a young urbanite died back in the village. Family traditions insisted that the young man quit his job to go back for an elaborate funeral and a prolonged stay, to reintegrate with his rural kin. Attached to urban life and some consumer pleasures, the young man simply stayed put to the dismay of his relatives.[13] More widely, Western laws and standards cut into African practices, tending to reinforce the authority of husbands and reducing the vitality of older customs that had provided protections and voice for women in the extended family. Colonial regulations sometimes sought to limit women's activities as merchants, for example, because they were not subject to adequate family authority; the result could increase women's economic dependence on their husbands. Again, many features of African families persisted, including polygamy in several regions, and patterns of change and disruption were varied. Colonial authorities themselves were not eager to stir up opposition by too many reforms; Christian missionaries were often more active in pressing for changes in family habits. Overall there was change, and some family patterns were unsettled as a result.

British imperialism in India had less impact on family patterns, compared to Africa, partly because economic changes were more varied and complex, partly because so many family patterns were enshrined in well-established religions, Hinduism at their head. The British did venture one reform effort, from the 1830s onward, joined by some key Indian reformers: the

13 Chinua Achebe, *No Longer at Ease* (New York: Random House Anchor Books, 1994).

old practice of *sati*, in which widows had died on a husband's funeral pyre, was increasingly outlawed – but it had never been a universal practice in any event. Important resulting questions – how should widows be treated, and should they be allowed to remarry? – bedeviled Indian reformers for many decades. Later in the nineteenth century, Western missionaries and Indian reformers began to sponsor new educational opportunities, often particularly for girls, in ways that could affect the families involved. Reformers like Ishwar Chandra Vidyasogar worked to blend Western standards with a belief that older Hindu values, which had also protected women, could be revived, as he worked to promote marriage opportunities for widows and schooling for girls, while also opposing the widespread practice of committing girls to marriage at a young age (a stance that caused great controversy among nationalists). In the long run, new educational opportunities for women in India would encourage a reduction in traditional birth rates – the standard effect of such opportunities, in exposing women to new values and new knowledge of available alternatives – but larger changes of this sort developed very slowly.

Indeed, imperialist pressures could actually generate compensatory efforts to defend older patterns as part of traditional or nationalist identity, whether the subject was roles for children or conditions for women. A debate in Egypt, around 1900, over whether parents should allow girls to adopt more Western styles of dress, including abandoning the veil, generated great controversy, with many Egyptian women clearly opting for traditional styles against "foreign" standards and impositions. A generation later, nationalist leaders, such as Jomo Kenyatta in Kenya, might defend practices such as female circumcision on grounds that they were an integral part of distinctive traditions and should not be subjected to outside scrutiny – and in fact practices of this sort changed very slowly into the later twentieth century and beyond.

War and revolution: the twentieth century

Key world history developments in the middle decades of the twentieth century, headed by wars and the major communist revolutions, had important results for family life in many regions. World War I launched a century of recurrent violence that had huge impacts on family life. With industrial technology, war became increasingly deadly. Many families had death or injury to mourn in World War I, and the toll was great enough for some combatant nations, like Germany, that a "hollow generation" was created by the absence of a standard number of young men to launch families. The War's results also saw a wave of forced migrations, as Greeks and Turks realigned in the former Ottoman Empire, with additional family dislocation resulting. Further escalation and dislocation occurred in conflicts like the Spanish Civil War (1936–9) and Japanese attacks on China, and then World War II, where aerial bombardments on cities increasingly blurred the boundaries between civilian and military involvement. Nor did this pattern disappear after World War II, even though direct war between great powers has been very rare since 1945. It was estimated early in the twenty-first century that 15 million children had been killed in war and civil strife during the final three decades of the twentieth century alone, with many others orphaned or wounded.[14] The aftermath of World War II and then subsequent ethnic conflicts in many areas further magnified displacement of families, with refugee camps, often disproportionately filled with women and children, serving as surrogate centers for family life sometimes for several generations. Overall, as many as 4 percent of the global population has been forced to flee their homes because of violence at least once over the past century. During the 1990s ethnic conflict in Rwanda, 100,000 children were separated from their families, though some subsequent reunions did occur.

War as a disrupter of family was obviously not an invention of the twentieth century, but there seems little question that, thanks to new technology often combined with vicious hatreds, conflicts became unusually devastating.

The twentieth century also witnessed a spate of major revolutions, often with deliberate impacts on family life beyond temporary disruptions and violence. Communist revolutions in Russia, China, and elsewhere deliberately sought to redo key elements of family life, as part of exerting new state control and shaping new kinds of populations. The goals were both to undo elements of family tradition, including many that had been shaped by religion or (in China's case) Confucianism, but also to avoid aspects of the modern Western model, seen as inappropriately bourgeois as well as foreign.

Communist leaders worked to remove many traditional constraints on women in the family. Reformers in China had already made headway against the practice of foot binding, and twentieth-century revolutionaries

14 United Nations Children's Fund (UNICEF), "Children in war," State of the World's Children (1996).

(liberal as well as communist) completed the process. At the same time, Western patterns of withdrawing many women from the labor force were both impractical, in developing economies that needed a large workforce, and undesirable. Communist ideology saw no virtue in images of the family as a haven from the larger economy. As Russia industrialized further, most wives and mothers had to juggle family obligations with demanding work roles.

Communist states sought to enlist large numbers of young people in the revolutionary cause, not only through state-run schools but also through a variety of youth organizations. Families could not be fully trusted to indoctrinate the young appropriately, and indeed the new regimes often sought to use some young people to spy on their parents and report any secret political deviance. Allegiance to the state and the revolutionary cause should take precedence over family loyalty. In Russia and particularly China, efforts to organize collective farms sometimes included programs to share meals and other activities with the entire community, reducing family functions in this regard as well. Other family customs drew attention: the Russian regime for a time, for example, fought against Christmas trees as a wasteful, family-centered practice. Finally, while praising youth, the communist regimes struggled, though with mixed results, to prevent young people from gaining much contact with global youth consumer culture, seen by communists (as well as by conservatives in the West) as decadent and indulgent.

The new regimes also worked hard to change family life in some more familiar ways. Huge effort went into reducing child mortality. Despite economic constraints, the early revolutionary regime in Russia expanded clinical and pediatric services. China in the 1950s dispatched "barefoot doctors" to work on infant and maternal mortality. Strong results ensued: China's infant mortality rate, at 18 percent in the 1950s, had dropped to 3.7 percent by 2003. Medical services combined with government-sponsored advice to families, urging new measures of hygiene.

Communism also accelerated conversion of childhood from work to schooling. Some labor persisted: this was sometimes a function of the youth groups. But primary commitment to education emerged strongly, from nursery schools on up. Russia doubled the elementary school population between 1929 and 1939, while pushing secondary school attendance up eightfold. Correspondingly, within the family, both children and parents devoted increasing attention to school success, as a key feature of family life.

Figure 3.2 "Study hard follow Lei Feng," Chinese Cultural Revolution propaganda poster (© David Pollack/Corbis)

Schooling, along with more general urbanization and industrialization, prompted many families to begin to reduce birth rates. Officially, the Russian regime sought to promote population growth, but this aspect of policy was increasingly contradicted by the facts on the ground. Parents needed smaller families to adjust to urban housing limitations and the conversion of childhood from labor resource to school support, and they moved to adapt fairly rapidly. Chinese policy under Mao Zedong notoriously touted a high birth rate as a Chinese communist asset, but here too, quietly, as early as the 1960s urban families began to cut back. Then by the 1970s, the regime reversed course, deciding that population growth was an unacceptable economic drain: most families were now officially limited to a single child, and the government imposed this policy with great vigor, even requiring abortion or sterilization in some cases.

Clearly, communist revolutions forged an interesting combination of what might be seen as standard modern family change – notably in the area of childhood and family life – with some distinctive elements. The relaxation of communism, or its rejection outright in Eastern Europe at the end of the twentieth century, allowed a growing number of urban families to add shared consumerism to the list of family functions. Rapid industrialization in late-twentieth-century China had the familiar effect of disrupting extended families, as literally millions of migrants poured into the cities, returning however to villages once or twice a year to regain some contact. With smaller families and improvements in adult health, another familiar family theme began to emerge in China: the question of the family's role in caring for older members. Finally, distinctive policies had some ongoing distinctive results. China's population policy, combined with traditional preference for sons, led to a growing gender imbalance as many families used abortion or other means to avoid unwanted daughters. Several million more men than women began to reach the age of family formation by the early twentt-first century, a potentially destabilizing outcome.

Families in the age of globalization

A variety of forces affected families in many regions in the decades after World War II. More and more areas were drawn into some standard patterns of change: child labor declined now on a global basis, though with interesting regional variations, and schooling accelerated. In most areas, save in periods of war or severe economic hardship, child mortality declined. Many additional regions – for example, most parts of Latin America by the 1960s – began to experience a full demographic transition, as more and more families turned to lower birth rates as well. Often, women played a key role in these changes, seeking to avoid the burden of numerous children and informed as well by their growing access to some education. Yet common patterns were not the whole story. A number of regions and groups proudly asserted their commitment to particular versions of the family. The rise of religious fundamentalism in many areas in the 1970s was only one aspect of an ongoing effort to combine tradition with change in the definition of family life, or even to try to hold off change altogether.

The continuing spread of industrialization – to the Pacific Rim by the 1960s, to a wider swath of societies by the 1990s including India, China, and Brazil – obviously had impacts on family life, particularly in the growing cities. Not only smaller family size but also new stresses on links within extended families were key results. International migration patterns now featured movement, often over long distances and substantial cultural divides, between less industrial and industrial societies. Muslim immigrants poured into Europe, with substantial resulting tensions over family standards. Global communication devices, plus new opportunities to return "home" for visits, added some new complexity. Some immigrant groups maintained close contacts with kin in their societies of origin. This could help maintain family traditions – such as arranged marriage, in the case of South Asian immigrants – even in novel settings. But it also could bring examples of change, for example greater family consumerism, to the family members who stayed behind.

New international institutions contributed to change. The World Health Organization, for example, pressed for improvements in child and maternal mortality, throughout the less-developed world. Unprecedented global declarations of human rights had important implications, particularly for the position of women and children in the family, and they were supported not only by United Nations agencies but also the host of international Non-Governmental Organizations (NGOs) that began to proliferate from the foundation of Amnesty International, in 1961, onward.

Beginning with the Universal Declaration of Human Rights (1948), postwar definitions of human rights included strong assertions of women's equality, including their right to equal jobs and pay and to educational access. From 1965 onward, the United Nations pressed this point further through a recurrent series of "Year of the Woman" conferences, which often generated increasing human rights activity in particular regions, such as Latin America and Africa. Many national governments subscribed to relevant human rights commitments, which might then, when taken seriously, force alterations of traditional family law. In Africa, for example, many courts ruled in favor of property rights for wives and widows, against customary assumptions of male ownership, on the basis of the international engagements. Attention to women's access to education could, as we have seen, have implications for knowledge of birth control goals as well as other adjustments in family relationships. In the 1990s, against objections from several Muslim countries and the Catholic Church, a United Nations conference came out in favor of further efforts at birth control, mainly through the means of better education for women.

Discussion of rights for children was more complicated, but increasingly this category, also, was inserted into international human rights discussions. Children's rights to education, and to protection from exploitative work, loomed large in this connection, though a number of societies, including the United States and India, shied away from full renunciation of child labor. Finally a 1989 compromise targeted abusive labor, rather than work in general. In fact, however, regional efforts to promote education plus ongoing economic change led to fairly steady reductions of child labor on a

Figure 3.3 A bus which has been converted into a school called School on Wheels, is seen parked at a slum area in the southern Indian city of Hyderabad. The mobile school, run by CLAP Foundation, a non-governmental organisation, brings education to the doorstep of disadvantaged children every day, halting for several hours at a time in different parts of the sprawling city.
(© KRISHNENDU HALDER/Reuters/Corbis)

global basis. Children dropped from 6 percent of the global workforce in 1950, to 3 percent in 1990, or from 28 percent of all children under 14 to 15 percent.[15] There were some countercurrents. Global economic competition pressed some small businesses to rely more heavily on low-wage children, even as overall levels dropped. In South Asia, through similar mechanisms, use of child labor actually rose in the 1990s, only to begin to fall back in the twenty-first century. The overall pattern, including some global agreement on what families should be doing for and with children, was reasonably clear.

Global consumerism also had some bearing on family life in diverse regions. Many young people could define some independence from traditional family habits by patronizing Western or Japanese music and electronic games, or taking meals in Western-style restaurant chains. Families themselves often developed new routines. Urban Chinese families sometimes began to celebrate children's birthdays, often taking them to a

15 International Child Labour Programme, *Global Child Labour Developments* (London, 2010). See also Hugh Hindman, ed., *Child Labor: An American History* (Armonk, NY: M.E. Sharpe, 2002).

McDonalds as a special treat. Businesses catering to children's birthdays flourished in the United Arab Emirates and Egypt, drawing particularly on a wealthy middle class.

The currents of change did not, however, produce global uniformities. Economic conditions varied greatly, even as industrialization and urbanization spread. While Brazil participated strongly in economic growth, an urban lower class continued to struggle with continued high rates of illegitimacy and heavy dependence on children's efforts. Some African societies continued to reflect divisions between village men gaining jobs in cities, and women and children left behind in a limited rural economy.

More than economic variety was involved. Many families in India remained strongly attached to traditions such as arranged marriage, against foreign standards that seemed to urge love as a precondition. Some Indian spokeswomen explicitly argued that arranged marriages provided greater family stability and less pressure on women – pressure to remain constantly attractive, for example – than Western patterns generated. Many families in the Middle East, though aware of promptings to think of children in terms of individual rights, consciously worked to instill more collective, and traditional, family loyalties. Religious revivals, not only in Islam but among fundamentalist Christians, some Catholics, Hindus and Jews, reflected strong pressures to maintain more customary roles for women in the family including, often, higher-than-average contemporary birthrates. Some religious communities sought to reemphasize aspects of their family law, as with punishments against adulterers in some Islamic regions. Change was not excluded even here: in revolutionary Iran, educational gains for women continued, with 55 percent of university students female by the early twenty-first century,[16] despite overall emphasis on women's subordination within the family. Clearly, however, there was widespread reluctance around many aspects of change.

On occasion resistance could even take violent forms. Physical abuse of women may have increased in some settings, in protest against some of the wider currents promoting redefinitions of gender roles. A number of dowry murders – cases where husbands murdered their brides because they judged the dowry to be inadequate – occurred in the South Asian subcontinent early in the twenty-first century, arguably reflecting new levels of

16 The Business Year, "Review: access & quality," retrieved February 1, 2013, from www.thebusinessyear.com/publication/article/7/637/iran-2011/access-and-quality. In 2012, however, the government moved to exclude women from 77 majors, concerned about their growing educational role.

hostility to women as well as specific expectations about the economic arrangements accompanying marriage.

Still more widespread was a simple reluctance to change in the first place. An Indian reformer confronts a cobbler, who keeps his son at work rather than sending him to school. The response? "Young man, my father was a cobbler and my grandfather before him, and no one before you has ever asked me that question. We were born to work, and so was my son."[17] Many African mothers, confronted with sales pitches to buy strollers for their children, reject them outright: far more pleasant for all concerned to carry them in the customary fashion. Some modern family opportunities, in other words, make no sense for many still.

Other issues unquestionably complicated family patterns in many contemporary societies. Many African families still had to deal with tensions between extended family customs and the goals of urban, nuclear families. Assumptions that members of extended families could expect to visit for long periods, receiving hospitality as a matter of course, struggled against an interest in consumer standards and other issues in urban life. Treatment of the elderly was a growing concern, particularly in societies that had gone through the earlier demographic transition. Urban conditions continued to encourage older parents to live separately. But increasing longevity and, sometimes, health issues of later age placed new burdens on younger kin that were difficult to cope with. Retirement communities and assisted living provided some support, yet many families found themselves seriously burdened with decisions about older parents. Many older people, correspondingly, found their younger kin insufficiently attentive and respectful – an issue frequently voiced in countries like Japan. Here, as in so many respects, the most recent phase of world history produced complexities as well as a variety of differentiations in core features of family life.

Conclusion

Many traditional institutions have virtually disappeared amid the currents of change in modern world history. Guilds, monarchies, aristocracies, slave plantations – seemingly secure in 1750 – have declined or vanished, leaving only vestiges in the contemporary world. Families, in contrast, have fared surprisingly well. They survive as institutions and, according to most

17 Kailash Satyarthi, *The Wallenberg Medal and Lecture* (University of Michigan, October 30, 2002); retrieved from www.wallenberg.umich.edu, June 1, 2012.

international polls, they continue to be seen as a leading source of satisfaction as well. The core functions families serve have been amplified by a variety of newer roles and structural adjustments, an intriguing combination of change and continuity. At the same time, for many groups, families have also been supported through their linkage to other aspects of cultural identity – a common function which however maintains a variety of diverse regional family features. In all respects – in continuity, in flexibility, and in service to group identity – families help translate global trends and tensions into some of the most personal aspects of modern life.

Further reading

Chatterjee, Indrani. *Unfamiliar Relations: Family and History in South Asia*. New Brunswick, NJ: Rutgers University Press, 2004.

Cornell, V. J. *Voices of Islam: Voices of Life: Family, Home and Society*. Santa Barbara, CA: Praeger, 2007.

Dabhoiwala, Faramerz. *The Origins of Sex: A History of the First Sexual Revolution*. London: Pengion, 2012.

Doumani, Beshara, ed. *Family History in the Middle East: Household, Property, and Gender*. Albany, NY: State University of New York Press, 2003.

Ebrey, Patricia. *Women and the Family in Chinese History*. London: Routledge, 2003.

Fass, Paula S. *Children of a New World: Society, Culture, and Globalization*. New York University Press, 2006.

French, William E. and Katherine E. Bliss. *Gender, Sexuality and Power in Latin America since Independence*. Lanham, MD: Rowman and Littlefield, 2007.

Gillis, John R. *A World of Their Own Making: A History of Myth and Ritual in Family Life*. New York: HarperCollins, 1997.

Godelier, Maurice, et al. *The Metamorphoses of Kinship*. London and New York: Verso, 2011.

Goody, Jack. *The Oriental, the Ancient and the Primitive: Systems of Marriage and the Family in the Pre-Industrial Societies of Eurasia*. Cambridge University Press, 1990.

Hartman, Mary S. *The Household and the Making of History: A Subversive View of the Western Past*. Cambridge University Press, 2004.

Hecht, Tobias. *At Home in the Street: Street Children of Northeast Brazil*. Cambridge University Press, 1998.

Minor Omissions: Children in Latin American History and Society. Madison, WI: University of Wisconsin Press, 2002.

Jeppie, Shamil, Ebrahim Moosa, and Richard Roberts. *Muslim Family Law in Sub-Saharan Africa: Colonial Legacies and Post-colonial Challenges*. Amsterdam University Press, 2010.

Jolivet, Muirel. *Japan: The Childless Society? The Crisis of Motherhood*. London: Routledge, 1997.

Kirschenbawm, Lisa A. *Small Comrades: Revolutionizing Childhood in Soviet Russia, 1917 – 1932*. London: Routledge, 2000.

Lynch, Katherine. *Individuals, Families and Communities in Europe, 1200 – 1800: The Urban Foundations of Western Society*. Cambridge University Press, 2003.

Mintz, Steven and Susan Kellogg. *Domestic Revolutions: A Social History of American Family Life*. New York: The Free Press, 1989.

Stearns, Peter N. *Childhood in World History*. London: Routledge, 2006.

Therborn, Göran. *Between Sex and Power: Family in the World 1900 – 2000*. London: Routledge, 2004.

4

Continuities and change in sexual behaviour and attitudes since 1750

JULIE PEAKMAN

Global variations in sexual attitudes and practices depend to a large degree on elements such as religion, industrialisation, urbanisation, population growth and changes in technology; and on a more individual level, they depend on education, class, race, gender and age. The last two and a half centuries have witnessed dramatic changes in societies, which affected sexual behaviour around the world. However, only within the last sixty years or so would an effective separation between sex and procreation become possible; and only then would laws be enacted allowing a move towards greater sexual equality in Europe, the Americas, Asia and Oceania. Generally speaking, on both a national and international scale, unprecedented social mobility, opening economic opportunities, and expanding urban markets saw major shifts in relationships of men and women from the beginning of this period onwards, rapidly increasing during the twentieth century.

The study of the history of sexuality emerged around the 1970s and 1980s along with feminist and women's history and, with the development of gender history, began to incorporate the examination of male sexualities. Early studies concentrated disproportionately on heterosexuality and on Western civilization, with a few notable exceptions.[1] More recently, historians have tended to examine specific areas of sexuality, such as the history of the body, the family, homosexuality, prostitution, pornography or sexual perversions in particular times in the past.[2] Scholars of sexuality tend to fall

1 One of the great early pioneers was Vern Bullough; among other works, see his *Sexual Variance in Society and History* (New York: Wiley Interscience, 1976) and *Sex, Society and History* (New York: Neale Watson, 1976); also see Reay Tannahill, *Sex in History* (London: H. Hamilton, 1980).

2 For examples on the body, see Thomas Laqueur, *Making Sex: Body and Gender from the Greeks to Freud* (Harvard University Press, 1992); on pornography, see Julie Peakman,

into two camps, essentialists or social constructionists. Put simply, essentialists believe in an underlying truth of forms or essences; that these will be constant over time; and that certain phenomena are natural, inevitable, and biologically determined. Social constructionists believe that reality is constructed socially, and that language and 'discourse' play an important meaning in making and interpretation of history. The latter historians follow philosopher Michel Foucault, who focused on regulation, power and subjectivity in suggesting that the whole concept of sexuality is a creation of nineteenth-century bourgeois society.[3] Before then there were sexual acts, but not sexual identities understood as an intrinsic aspect of the self. Other historians have criticised his assertions – if sexuality and sexual identity are nineteenth-century social constructions, why can evidence of these be identified in medieval Europe or even earlier? The interplay between act and identity is therefore more complex than Foucault suggested.[4]

While it has been helpful to identify nuances in the past, it is essential to take a broader sweep if longer-term trends are to be identified.[5] One long-standing premise throughout the world was that vaginal penetrative sexual intercourse between a man and a woman, later termed 'heterosexuality', was 'normal' behaviour. The major belief systems, including Christianity, Judaism, Hinduism, Islam and Confucianism, reflected this understanding of sexuality as part of their code. Most deviant behaviours, including sodomy, bestiality and incest among others, were generally considered 'abnormal' or 'against nature' and thus were unacceptable – although there were exceptions to the rule. Marriage and reproduction were considered the natural path in an individual's life. Girls were expected to remain chaste until marriage, and young men were advised to control their sexual urges,

Mighty Lewd Books: The Development of Pornography in Eighteenth-Century England (Basingstoke: Palgrave, 2003); on perversions, see Julie Peakman, *The Pleasure's All Mine: A History of Perverse Sex* (London: Reaktion, 2013); James Penney, *The World of Perversion: Psychoanalysis and the Impossible Absolute of Desire* (Albany: State University of New York Press, 2006).

3 Michel Foucault (trans. Robert Hurley), *The History of Sexuality, Vol. 1. An Introduction* (Harmondsworth: Penguin, 1990); Domna C. Stanton, *Discourses of Sexuality: From Aristotle to AIDS* (University of Michigan Press, 1992).

4 See, for example, Lois McNay, *Foucault: A Critical Introduction* (Cambridge: Polity Press, 1994); Lin Foxall, 'Pandora unbound: a feminist critique of Foucault's *History of Sexuality*', in David H. Larmour, Paul Allen Miller and Charles Platter (eds.), *Rethinking Sexuality* (Princeton University Press, 1998), pp. 132–133.

5 See, for example, Julie Peakman (general ed.), *A Cultural History of Sexuality* (Oxford: Berg, 2011); Phillip Ariès and George Duby, *A History of Private Life* (Cambridge, MA: Harvard University Press, 1990); Peter N. Stearns, *Sexuality in World History* (London: Routledge, 2009).

although sexual activities among young men were generally tolerated. A premium was set on a girl's virginity and, without it, she could not expect to make a good marriage. Because the 'purity' of a woman reflected her honour and that of her family, the higher up the social scale, the more important this virginity became. Generally, women had fewer protective laws, work opportunities, and prospects of independence. This left them at a disadvantage when forging sexual relationships, either in or out of marriage.

Historians of sexuality generally agree that in the West at least, the control of the regulation of sex shifted from the church in the seventeenth century, to medicine in the eighteenth century, and to the state in the nineteenth century. Religious constructions of gender and sexuality were reinforced by science, politics and the law, all representing women as mentally and physically inferior to men, and homosexual men as inferior to heterosexual men.[6] However, I would argue that, on a global scale, religion has retained its influence on attitudes towards sexual matters in a large part of the world, including parts of the West, to today, and this influence can be seen in continued discrimination against women and homosexuals. However, discrimination has diminished over the last half century or so, and this shift I would argue, has been one of the most radical changes in history regarding sexuality.

Before examining this dramatic change, this chapter will discuss three topics that played a part in this. It will first examine sex and marriage during the eighteenth and nineteenth centuries in three areas – Europe, the European colonies, and East Asia – and then look at two more topics in greater detail, prostitution and homosexuality.

Sex and marriage in Europe

Although in post-Reformation Europe Catholics and Protestants had different ideas about the relative merits of celibacy and marriage and the possibility of divorce, all Christian churches taught that sex was to be within marriage,

6 Ludmilla Jordanova, *Sexual Visions: Images of Gender in Science and Medicine between the Eighteenth and Twentieth Centuries* (London: Harvester Wheatsheaf, 1989); Londa Schiebinger, *Nature's Body: Sexual Politics and the Making of Modern Science* (London: Pandora, 1993); Roy Porter and Mikuláš Teich, eds., *Sexual Knowledge, Sexual Science: The History of Attitudes to Sexuality* (Cambridge University Press, 1994); Margaret Somerville, *Sex and Subjection: Attitudes to Women in Early-Modern Society* (London: Arnold, 1995); Susan Mendus and Jane Rendal, eds., *Sexuality & Subordination* (London: Routledge, 1989); Vern Bullough, Brenda Shelton, Sarah Slavin, *The Subordinated Sex: A History of Attitudes towards Women* (Athens, GA: University of Georgia Press, 1998).

and then mainly for procreative purposes, not for pleasure. Sex outside marriage was 'fornication' and a sin. Despite this teaching, and despite the theoretical importance placed on female chastity in Europe, young men and women (at least those among the lower classes) could meet each other with relative ease. Premarital sex was evident in both Protestant and Catholic countries, and within certain boundaries was regarded an inescapable part of life. Young couples came together whenever they had the chance, at fairs, in church and at markets.[7] In some Protestant countries, they were sometimes allowed to sleep together in the same bed under their parents' roof. The young couple would remain semi- or fully clothed, with a bolster or plank placed between them, a custom known as 'bundling'. In Switzerland and Germany, couples followed a pattern of courting called *kiltgang* whereby young men would visit via the window of young single women. Sexual activities were not supposed to include full intercourse, although this sometimes occurred and pregnancy resulted. This might not be a catastrophe for the woman, however, if a promise of marriage had been extracted from the young man, preferably in front of witnesses.

Even in Spain, considered the exemplar of Catholic orthodoxy after the Catholic Reformation, local people often adapted church regulations and religion doctrine to suit their own needs. Although the majority of people abided by the church teachings, pre-marital sexual activity was sometimes tolerated by the immediate community.[8] Some couples who exchanged promises of betrothal had sex and cohabited, but did not always go on to marry, even if they had a child. Some took up with other partners when marriages failed, although divorce was forbidden by the Catholic Church. In Italy, premarital sexual activity seems to have been less common than in Spain, and more people followed the directives of the church.[9] Throughout Europe, pre-marital sex was rare for elite women. Daughters of these classes tended to marry younger, binding them early in a bid to protect their virginity and increase the length of their child-bearing years.

Since the 1970s, historians have debated how and when family structures changed in Europe to what is generally seen as the 'modern' family with

7 G. R. Quaife, *Wanton Wenches and Wayward Wives: Peasants and Illicit Sex in Early Seventeenth Century England* (London: Croom Helm, 1979); Julie Peakman, *Lascivious Bodies: A Sexual History of the Eighteenth Century* (London: Atlantic, 2004), pp. 32–35.

8 Allyson M. Poska, *Regulating the People: The Catholic Reformation in the Seventeenth-Century* (Leiden: Brill, 1998), pp. 1–2, 101–110.

9 Bruno P. F. Wanrooij, 'Italy: sexuality, morality and public authority', in Franz X. Eder, Lesley Hall and Gert Hekma (eds.), *Sexual Cultures in Europe*, Vol. 1: *National Histories* (Manchester University Press, 1999), pp. 114–137.

companionate marriage based on love and sexual passion. Lawrence Stone has argued that in most of Europe, marriage was a contract between two families before 1600, but by the eighteenth century companionate marriage became more common. Edward Shorter similarly made claims about the modern family, pointing to what he saw as a growth of maternal affection in the middle classes and sexual passion in the lower classes at the end of the eighteenth century. Other family historians have since nuanced these claims.[10] They have noted that although marriages were usually arranged by parents in Europe, young people generally agreed to them and were only rarely forced into marriages they did not want. Among the aristocracy, parental control over choice of partners was stronger, as these marriages were designed to tie two wealthy families together.

As cities developed in Europe, family ties became less strong and there was a loosening of control over sexual behaviour, especially in poorer families, although this happened at different times in different places for different reasons. Generally in Western Europe, by the eighteenth century greater commercialisation and increasing opportunities for wage labour led to young people having greater sexual freedom. However, in Russia, mobility was made possible by the abolition of serfdom in 1861, which weakened traditional social constraints.[11]

The Victorian period brought a reinforcement of the segregation of the sexes among certain classes in some countries. In much of Western Europe, middle-class women were increasingly viewed as 'angels in the house', that is, guardians of the household, although they were still in a secondary social, economic and political position relative to men, who were still firmly at the head of the household. Dramatic changes took place in sexual behaviour, however, with fertility rates dropping across Europe. Marital fertility in England and Wales fell by 32 per cent between 1871 and 1911, illegitimacy by 54 per cent. In France marital fertility fell steadily from 1831, with a rise in the age at marriage. Debates have arisen as to why this happened. According to Simon Szreter, in France this was achieved by a 'sophisticated and widely diffused positive and hedonistic culture of both marital and non-marital sexuality' with the encouragement of the use of prostitutes by both youths

10 Lawrence Stone, *The Family, Sex and Marriage in England, 1500–1800* (London: Peregrine Books, 1977); Edward Shorter, *The Making of the Modern Family* (New York: Basic Books, 1975); Helen Berry and Elizabeth Foster, *The Family in Early Modern England* (Cambridge University Press, 2007).

11 Alexandre Avdeev, Alain Blum and Irina Troitskia, 'Peasant marriage in nineteenth-century Russia', *Population-E 2004* 59/6, 721–764.

and married men, the use of *coitus interruptus* and a range of non-coital sexual activities. In Scotland and England, sexual abstinence was a more likely reason for falling fertility rates, as evangelical Christians campaigned for self-control over sexual urges from the 1860s onwards. Many women were involved, such as Josephine Butler who called for more sex education and moral restraint (mainly on the part of men). An increase in general education, too, may have led people to search for ways to prevent having too large a family.[12] In Italy, Spain, Portugal and Greece, the same shift in fertility was apparent, except it had different causes. Here, marriages in traditional agricultural settlements of older men to younger women were changing as a large part of the young population migrated to industrial cities for work; here they chose to marry later, pick their own partners, and limit their families.[13]

Sexual relations in European colonies and empires

Empire building played an important part in changing sexual attitudes and practices, and sex and gender helped shape the history of European colonies and empires.[14] Increased exploration, trade and travel led to sexual interactions between different groups, which ranged from violent rape to companionate marriage.[15] Christian missionaries preached self-control and monogamy, which affected local practices and attitudes. European settlers often criticised indigenous populations for their sexually loose morals; for example Native Americans were attacked for their 'impurity and immorality, even gross sensuality and unnatural vice'.[16] Yet along with new ideas about sexual restraint, European expansion also brought added promiscuity as well as an increase in venereal disease.

12 For an overall view of Victorian sexuality, see Michael Mason, *The Making of the Victorian Sexuality: Sexual Behaviour and Its Understanding* and his *The Making of the Victorian Sexual Attitudes* (both Oxford University Press, 1994).

13 Simon Szreter, 'Falling fertilities and changing sexualities since c. 1850: a comparative survey of national democratic patterns', in Eder, Hall and Hekma, *Sexual Cultures in Europe, Vol.* II, pp. 159–194; p. 163.

14 For examples, see Ronald Hyam, *Empire and Sexuality* (Manchester University Press, 1990); Anne McClintock, *Imperial Leather: Race, Gender, and Sexuality in the Colonial Contest* (London: Routledge, 1995); Philippa Levine (ed.), *Gender and Empire* (Oxford University Press, 2004); Ann Laura Stoler, *Carnal Knowledge and Imperial Power: Race and the Intimate in Colonial Rule* (Berkeley, CA: University of California Press, 2nd edn, 2010).

15 Richard C. Trexler, *Sex and Conquest: Gendered Violence, Political Order, and the European Conquest of the Americas* (Ithaca, NY: Cornell University Press, 1995); Carl J. Ekberg, *Stealing Indian Women: Native Slavery in the Illinois Country* (Urbana: University of Illinois Press, 2007).

16 John D'Emilio and Estelle Freedman, *Intimate Matters: A History of Sexuality in America* (University of Chicago Press, 1997), p. 7.

For Europeans abroad, 'home' domestic arrangements were clung to steadfastly and would to a large extent be transported to the colonies. For example, Australia and New Zealand both shared the English pattern of Victorian sexuality, although there was a lower average marriage age overseas than there was in Europe. John D'Emilio has argued that North American sexual history was reshaped by the changing economy and political situation from a family-centred reproductive sexual system in the colonial era to a romantic intimate nineteenth-century marriage, a picture similar to the one Stone depicted for Britain.[17] Just as in Britain, white middle-class authorities regulated sexual morality, and there was a search for more emotional intimacy and greater physical pleasure, although women's sexuality was also viewed as dangerous.[18] Such parallels with Britain tell only part of the story, however, because North America contained a diverse range of people from different areas of the world – and invariably this meant different attitudes to sex. As Helen Horowitz has pointed out, in the nineteenth-century United States of America an earthy acceptance of desire and sexual expression collided with the prohibitions broadcast from the pulpit, primarily by evangelical Protestant Christians.[19]

Slavery was an important part of the story of colonisation and had a dramatic impact on the sexual history of Africa and the European colonies. While Peter Stearns has argued that patterns of sexual behaviour did not alter in Africa, he also points to the fact that West Africa saw an altered gender ratio as men were taken as slaves more often than women (over 65 per cent of slaves were male). This brought an increase in polygamy and complaints by men that women were harder to control. In the Americas, with the importation of thousands of slaves, sexual interactions between male plantation owners and their female slaves often meant enforced sexual subservience and abuse. It was often considered acceptable by planters to use female slaves for sex, either in rape or taken as mistresses. Europeans tended to see non-white populations as 'bestial', and in reaction to their own highly imaginative sexualized images of African men, white authorities issued new laws in attempts to control them. As a result, in the United States hundreds of black men were put on trial for rape in separate public courts established

17 D'Emilio and Freedman, pp. xi–xii; Stone, p. 22.

18 Caroll Smith-Rosenburg, *Disorderly Conduct: Constructs of Gender in Victorian America* (New York: Alfred A. Knopf, 1985).

19 Helen Lefkowitz Horowitz, *Rereading Sex: Battles over Sexual Knowledge and Suppression in Nineteenth-Century America* (New York: Alfred A. Knopf, 2002).

for them at the beginning of the eighteenth century, with little hope of being acquitted.[20]

Sweeping changes due to imperialism also affected South Asia. At the beginning of the eighteenth century, women in well-to-do Hindu and Muslim households tended to be segregated in separate quarters, and spent their lives in the *andarmahal*, or inner sanctum of the house.[21] That continued, but the arrival of the British East Indian Company also had a further profound effect on sexual laws and practices. Initially, with an overwhelming amount of soldiers and so few white women, company authorities overlooked their employees taking Indian mistresses (*bibis*). Ronald Hyam has indicated that 'the keeping of a mistress in British India became a well-established practice'.[22] Company men often had children with these women, provided for their children when they left them behind on their return to England, and sometimes sent their mixed-race children to British boarding schools. However, from the second half of the eighteenth century in India (earlier in other colonies), voices of authority were increasingly raised against inter-racial relationships. Fear of company men 'going native' fed into already entrenched attitudes of white superiority. In order to discourage British men from consorting with Indian women, 'the fishing fleet' was introduced to bring in single British women as potential wives for employees of the East India Company. Soon more women came to India – older unmarried women and unwed governesses 'of the shrivelled and dry description', as one woman unkindly described them in 1779, as well as 'reformed' prostitutes.[23] Officers sometimes married back home and brought their wives with them, the couple setting up a mini-England within their Indian homes.

The pattern found in South Asia, of initial toleration for inter-racial and intercultural sexual relations followed by restrictions, can be found in many places in the colonial world. Laws against racial mixing were issued in North

20 Sharon Block, *Rape and Sexual Power in Early America* (Chapel Hill: University of North Carolina, 2006), pp. 243–244; also see Peter W. Bardaglio, 'Rape and law in the Old South: "Calculated to excite indignation in every heart"', *Journal of Southern History* 60 (November, 1994), 753–755; and Bardaglio, *Reconstructing the Household: Families, Sex and the Law in the Nineteenth-Century South* (Chapel Hill: University of North Carolina Press, 1995).

21 Sonia Nishat Amin, *World of Muslim Women in Colonial Bengal 1876–1939* (Leiden: E.J. Brill, 1996).

22 Hyam, *Empire and Sexuality*, p. 115.

23 Anne de Courcy, *The Fishing-Fleet: Husband-hunting in the Raj* (London: Weidenfeld & Nicolson, 2012); Margaret MacMillan, *Women of the Raj* (London: Thames and Hudson, 1988), p. 16.

and South America, India, Southeast Asia and Africa in an attempt to draw firm lines between the races, although these were only selectively enforced.

In some parts of the imperial world, along with men and women there were individuals understood to belong to a third gender. Though Europeans who encountered them focused on their sexuality, they were often distinguished from others by their work or religious roles, as well as their sexual activities. In South Asia, individuals known as hijras could (and still can) perform blessings at weddings and dance at celebrations, although they also worked as prostitutes to survive. In the twentieth century, hijras gained some civil rights, including the right to vote and run for local political office, although they must declare themselves male or female to do so. Among the Native Americans, third gender individuals, now generally termed 'two spirit people', acted as second wives, cooking and cleaning and playing domestic roles. Exactly how accepted they have been has been debated.[24]

Sex and marriage in East Asia

Just as sexual and marriage relations in Europe were influenced by Christianity, sexual relationships in East Asia during the Qing dynasty (1644 to 1912) were influenced to varying extents by Daoism, Buddhism and Confucianism, especially the latter. Marriages were arranged between families, usually with introductions made through a match-maker, even in poor rural villages.[25] The woman married 'out', taking up a role in her in-laws' home, and became subservient to her mother-in-law in a hierarchical system based on age and gender, in which filial piety and veneration of one's ancestors were central values. Married couples were not expected to be emotionally intimate, but were expected to produce children. Men were expected to find sexual fulfilment outside the home, with prostitutes or concubines, yet female virtue was central to morality.[26] Vivien Ng has argued that with the introduction of the new Qing Code of 1646 and a new rape law, a cult of chastity was promoted, which encouraged peasant women, and

24 Trexler, *Sex and Conquest*, p. 136; Gayatri Reddy, *With Respect to Sex: Negotiating Hijra Identity in South India* (University of Chicago Press, 2005); Sue-Ellen Jacobs, Wesley Thomas and Sabine Lang, eds., *Two Spirit People: Native American Gender Identity, Sexuality, and Spirituality* (Chicago: University of Illinois, 1997).

25 On betrothal and marriage customs, see Henry Doré, *Chinese Customs* (Singapore: Graham Brash, 1987), pp. 47–59; Dabing Ye (trans. Mark Bender and Shi Kun), *The Bridal Boat: Marriage Customs of China's Fifty-Five Ethnic Minorities* (Beijing: New World Press, 1993).

26 Alison Sau-Chu Yeung, 'Fornication in the late Qing legal reforms: moral teachings and legal principles', *Modern China* 29/3 (July 2003), 297–328.

especially widows, to remain chaste. Women who had died defending themselves from rape, or wives who had resisted pressure to act as prostitutes, were honoured as martyrs. Even virtuous ex-prostitutes (*cong liangi*) could be canonized as part of the cult of chastity.[27] Matthew Sommer has argued, however, that a cult of chastity had already been thriving earlier, in the Ming dynasty. By the 1820s, with economic change, this cult declined, and chaste widows were viewed as objects of charity rather than heroic figures.[28]

During the commercial expansion and rapid urbanisation of the eighteenth century, the volume of trade between Canton and Europe is reckoned to have doubled every eighteen years,[29] although foreign men were kept segregated in their own spaces. With the growth in population, people were shifting both physically and economically, migrating to work and moving up and down the social ladder. Female commoners might slide down the scale, and be sold into slavery; or move up it by becoming a concubine to a man of better status.[30] New regulations on sexuality emerged from growing concerns about social and demographic trends, which extended a more uniform standard of sexual morality, something akin to what would happen in Victorian society in Europe. Both men and women, higher and lower status, were now expected to conform to idealised marital roles. Elite men were in theory no longer exempt, but a general prohibition of extramarital intercourse was introduced, forbidding men the use of prostitutes or servant women for sex. In contrast to England, where 'mill girls' or women engaged in textile production were associated with promiscuity, in China, textile work was seen as a benefit to the family that would keep 'a check on female promiscuity'. Authorities showed particular concern over a surplus of young males at the bottom of the socio-economic scale, who threatened to disrupt family households. It was such young men who would suffer the brunt of the new laws; they were prosecuted for consensual sodomy, rape, pimping or selling their wives, and adultery with widows.

Until the middle of the nineteenth century, Japan remained relatively isolated from the rest of the trading world. Social relationships, based in part on Confucianism imported from China, were characterised in theory as

27 Vivien W. Ng, 'Ideology and sexuality: rape laws in Qing China', *Journal of Asian Studies* 46 (1987), 57–70.

28 Matthew H. Sommer, *Sex, Law and Society in Late Imperial China* (Stanford University Press, 2000); Susan Mann, 'Widows in the kinship, class and community structures of Qing Dynasty China', *Journal of Asian Studies* 46/1 (1987), 37–56.

29 Harry G. Gleber, *The Dragon and the Foreign Devils* (London: Bloomsbury, 2007), pp. 54–56.

30 Susan Mann, *Precious Records: Women in China in the Long Eighteenth-Century* (Stanford University Press, 1997), pp. 11, 35, 43.

several interlocking hierarchical systems: as 'five relations' (that of loyalty between ruler and minister; filiality between father and son; harmony between husband and wife; precedence between elder and younger siblings; and trust between friends) and, for women, 'three bonds' (that a woman was subject to her father, husband, and then son within her life cycle). Loyalty and obedience were at the core of the system, and the strength of the patriarchal family was understood to express itself in public morality. Within this structure, women were segregated in the home, most notably amongst elite families, but their model influencing the respectable middle classes. The lower classes had less opportunity to enforce strict rules regarding the etiquette and seclusion of women, as many women were obliged to work long hours in the fields or outside the home. As elsewhere in the world, women's status came primarily from being wives and daughters, not from their labor.[31] Polygamy was illegal, but second wives or concubines were taken, and their children were legally recognised.

Prostitution

The sale of sex has been an aspect of urban life since the world's earliest cities, but it has taken a variety of forms: unmarried women who had sex with their long-term partners, those who had casual sex with strangers, women 'kept' by richer men who were paid in gifts and rent, and professional sex workers who sold sex for money have all been labelled 'prostitutes'. In the cities of early modern Europe, classifications of those who sold sex were often dependent on the location of their work, from street-walking whores at the bottom through to women who worked in city brothels, to those who made arrangements for men to visit them in luxurious apartments. Often women drifted into prostitution on a seasonal basis affected by employment opportunities. With fewer safety nets in cities, away from wider family support networks that had been afforded to women in the past, they sometimes used prostitution as a way of supplementing their low wages.[32] Most people who sold sex were female, although Randolph Trumbach has argued that before about 1700, men in Europe had used both women and boys as prostitutes, with the primary

31 Gail Lee Bernstein, *Recreating Japanese Women, 1600–1945* (Berkeley, CA: University of California Press, 1991).

32 Judith R. Walkowitz and Daniel J. Walkowitz, '"We are not beasts of the field": prostitution and the poor in Plymouth and Southampton under the Contagious Diseases Acts', *Feminist Studies* 1 (Winter-Spring 1973), 73–106.

distinction that between the penetrator and the penetrated; after this, as the gender of one's partner became the primary marker of sexual identity, only men who identified as homosexual used male prostitutes.[33]

From the eighteenth century onwards, all over the world, prostitution was seen to be an ever-growing problem that needed regulating and containing.[34] Reactions towards prostitution were mixed, with some authorities bringing out new laws to prevent it, while others decided on a path of increased tolerance. In England, there was a notable shift in attitude towards the women who sold sex, with the image of the embittered whore gradually replaced in popular imagination by the penitent Magdalene.[35] Previously prostitutes had been seen as innately lustful women who had chosen a life of selling sex rather than entering the profession through a lack of any other viable choice. Increasingly women were seen as having 'fallen' into prostitution through no fault of their own, either seduced by employers or duped by their lovers through a promise of marriage. This image of the redeemable prostitute was evident in literature and art,[36] and was turned into practical action. Philanthropists and religious bodies established Magdalene houses in various European cities, including London, Vienna and Paris, in order to 'rescue' women from a life of prostitution. Although in theory they were protective institutions, in reality Magdalene houses were more of a punitive system established for women who had transgressed society's idea of sexual morality; harsh regimes in such houses saw women and young girls subjected to fines and punishments for misbehaviour. In France and Italy, fathers had their daughters incarcerated if they were considered to have behaved in a sexually immoral manner by applying to the courts to have them committed to asylums. These punitive patterns continued from the eighteenth into the twentieth century, with female offenders, especially juveniles, institutionalised for sexual transgressions in the USA, Canada and many European countries. As one historian points out, 'places like convents, conservatories, poorhouses, houses of patience, insane asylums, and prisons were used . . . to

33 Randolph Trumbach, 'Prostitution', in Peakman (ed.), *A Cultural History of Sexuality in the Enlightenment*, pp. 183–202.

34 For a comprehensive bibliography of prostitution up to 1999, see Timothy J. Gilfoyle, 'Prostitutes in history: from parables of pornography to metaphors of modernity', *American Historical Review* 104/1 (Feb., 1999), 117–141.

35 Tony Henderson, *Disorderly Women in Eighteenth-Century London: Prostitution and Control in the Metropolis, 1730–1830* (London: Longman, 1999), p. 2.

36 Julie Peakman, 'Introduction', *Whore Biographies* (London: Pickering and Chatto, 2007–8); Sophie Carter, *Purchasing Power: Representing Prostitution in Eighteenth-century English Popular Print* (Hants: Ashgate, 2004).

manage women's destinies that were deviant compared to the common destiny of normality'.[37]

Western imperialism brought with it a huge rise in prostitution in every part of the world, both colony and metropole, and invariably venereal disease flourished alongside it. In Britain, the Contagious Diseases Acts passed in the 1860s subjected women in military and naval towns to vigorous medical inspections. According to such laws, authorities could identify a woman as a common prostitute and subject her to fortnightly examinations. If she was found to be suffering from gonorrhoea or syphilis, she was forcibly interred in a Lock Hospital, a hospital specifically set up to treat women with venereal disease. Social purity movements emerged during the 1860s, with groups of middle-class women running campaigns to 'save' prostitutes from the streets, calling for the repeal of the Contagious Disease Acts, and urging chastity and fidelity for both men and women instead of a sexual double standard. Repeal organisations appealed to feminists and moralists, and gathered millions of signatures in petition campaigns, which were ultimately successful.[38]

Similar laws were passed elsewhere in Europe, and other major cities developed policies of regulation similar to those in Britain, all of which entailed the regular inspection of prostitutes. Because Italy was only unified in 1861, laws had previously varied from region to region; to rectify this, a new law, the Cavour Regulation, was issued in 1860. Prostitutes were required to be registered, if they wanted to work legally, and had to submit to bi-weekly medical examinations. By 1881, to prevent the spectacle of the procuring street whore, 10,422 prostitutes were licensed and permitted to work within enclosed premises only. Any woman wandering around alone at night might be arrested, even registered prostitutes.[39]

Authorities everywhere in Europe wanted to keep prostitution separate from family life, but in some places this led to spatial restrictions instead of prohibition. In France, state regulated brothels called *maisons de tolérance* opened up in burgeoning commercial areas, and there were reserved quarters where prostitutes were allowed to work, although again women had to

37 Sherrill Cohen, *Evolution of Women's Asylums Since 1500: From Refuges for Ex-Prostitutes to Shelters for Battered Women* (Oxford University Press, 1992), pp. 165–176, 168.

38 Lucy Bland, *Banishing the Beast: English Feminism and Sexual Morality, 1885–1914* (London: Penguin, 1995); Lesley Hall, 'Hauling down the double standard: feminism, social purity and sexual science in late nineteenth-century Britain', *Gender & History* 16/1 (2004), 36–56; Judith R. Walkowitz, *Prostitution and Victorian Society: Women, Class, and the State* (Cambridge University Press, 1980) and *City of Dreadful Delight: Narratives of Sexual Danger in Late-Victorian London* (University of Chicago Press, 1992).

39 Mary Gibson, *Prostitution and the State in Italy 1860–1915* (Columbus: Ohio State University Press, 1999).

submit to regular inspections for venereal disease.[40] As with many other countries, major towns had the highest concentration of prostitutes; in Paris, about 5440 prostitutes were registered between 1880 and 1886, 73 per cent of them over 21 years old. As Alain Corbin points out, brothels were related to industrialisation in several ways: they served an urban clientele, many of whom worked in factories, and, like factories, they provided an institution for the organized and profitable sale of goods and services with a regulated workforce. Changing patterns of urban consumption and burgeoning urban populations in the late nineteenth and early twentieth centuries spurred the expansion of unregulated prostitution, although the *maison de tolerance* would continue to serve those in search of more specified eroticisms. By the 1880s, unregistered itinerant Parisian prostitutes were found everywhere from vaudeville theatres and dance halls to parks and railway stations. Industrialisation was not the only cause of a burgeoning of prostitution, however. Laurie Bernstein argues that Russian prostitution followed a different and distinctive pattern: Russian regulation of prostitution was not directly linked to industrialisation, since regulation began in the mid nineteenth century before the massive economic transformation of the late nineteenth century.[41]

Meanwhile, in parts of the United States, prostitution flourished particularly in new towns emerging in the gold rushes of 1840s and 1890s, and the cattle industry boom, as women flocked to provide services for the influx of labourers and cowboys. As in many other areas in the world with new extractive industries, these boom towns acted as a magnet for prostitution. New settlements tended to be overpopulated by men, with few respectable single women making the journey, so the social position of prostitutes was sometimes less marginal than in older cities.[42]

In China, the first Opium War from 1839 to 1842 opened up China to foreigners and turned Shanghai into a major commercial centre. By the middle of the nineteenth century, the city was awash with all types of

40 Alain Corbin. *Women for Hire: Prostitution and Sexuality in France after 1850* (Cambridge, MA: Harvard University Press, 1990); Jill Harsin, *Policing Prostitution in Nineteenth-Century Paris* (Princeton University Press, 1985).

41 Laurie Bernstein, *Sonia's Daughters: Prostitutes and Their Regulation in Imperial Russia* (Berkeley, CA: University of California Press, 1995); Elizabeth Waters, 'Victim or villain: prostitution in post-revolutionary Russia', in Linda Edmondson (ed.), *Women and Society in Russia and the Soviet Union* (Cambridge University Press, 1992), pp. 160–177.

42 Anne M Butler, *Daughters of Joy, Sisters of Misery: Prostitutes in the American West 1865–90* (Urbana: University of Illinois Press, 1985); Marion S. Goldman, *Gold Diggers and Silver Miners: Prostitution and Social Life on the Comstock Lode* (Ann Arbor: University of Michigan Press, 1981).

prostitution.[43] From around 1860, lower-class brothels developed alongside elegant brothels in the Nanking Road, and prostitution spread from within the old walls of the city to the suburbs. After the Opium Wars, an International Settlement was established in Shanghai, which was divided into sections and administrated by different countries, including Britain and the United States. Here, foreign citizens enjoyed extraterritorial privileges and a multi-layered system of prostitution emerged to supply the area. In Shanghai and other cities, women were sometimes sold into prostitution, just as they were sold into domestic service.[44]

In Japan as in China, women who offered sexual services in the eighteenth and nineteenth centuries ranged from high-class geisha who offered entertainment to wealthy men and were important cultural figures to low-status streetwalkers.[45] Moves were made to place prostitution in separate areas.[46] In 1870, for example, the new emperor pronounced the Pontocho area in Kyoto a 'flower' district (a geisha community) and by 1906, more than 40,000 prostitutes were registered in Japan working in licensed brothels. However, by the turn of the century, a rivalry was emerging among prostitutes as new types of places arose and brought with them new sorts of sex workers; the café girl, similar to today's bar hostesses, began to compete with the geisha for wealthy clients. However, this period also saw a backlash; as in Europe some decades earlier, moves were made to restrict prostitution at the end of the nineteenth century in both Japan and in Japanese migrant communities in the western United States, as such measures were increasingly seen as a sign of being a 'civilized' country. However, although Japanese prostitution had visibly declined by 1920 in Pacific Coast cities, it continued to be a regular feature of public life in Japan.[47]

With the increase in travel, business and migration for work between continents in the nineteenth century, the structure of the sex trade changed.

43 Gail Hershatter, *Dangerous Pleasures: Prostitution and Modernity in Twentieth-Century Shanghai* (Berkeley, CA: University of California Press, 1999); Christian Henriot, *Prostitution and Sexuality in Shanghai: A Social History 1849–1949* (Cambridge University Press, 2000).

44 See Sue Gronewold, *Beautiful Merchandise: Prostitution in China, 1860–1936* (London: Routledge, 1982).

45 See Lesley Downer, *Geisha: The Secret History of the Vanishing World* (London: Headline, 2000).

46 The first regularisation of an area for prostitution was recorded in *The Great Mirror of the Way of Love* (1678); also see Teruoka Yasutaka, 'The pleasure quarters and Tokugawa culture', in C. Andrew Gerstle, *Eighteenth-Century Japan: Culture and Society* (Sydney: Allen and Unwin, 1989), pp. 3–29.

47 Kazuhiro Oharazeki, 'Anti-prostitution campaigns in Japan and the American West, 1890–1920', *Pacific Historical Review* 82/2 (May 2013), 175–214.

Millions of Indians, Africans, Chinese, Pacific Islanders, and others moved to provide labour for European colonial powers. Migrant communities were overwhelmingly male, and as a result, the demand for sexual service of women increased.[48]

Homosexuality

The debate between social constructionists and essentialists discussed above has been particularly extensive among historians of homosexuality. Mary McIntosh's crucial essay 'The Homosexual Role', published in 1968, was one of the first to identify the social construction of homosexuality from a sociologist's perspective, although it has often been overlooked. As Jeffrey Weeks has pointed out, 'There is a tendency to efface the theoretical origins of social constructionist approach to sexuality, with an accompanying tendency to privilege the contribution of Michel Foucault and his followers.'[49] Social constructionists tend to see a significant change in the late nineteenth century, at which point the idea of permanent sexual orientations developed. Essentialists saw same-sex attraction as innate, or in a person's character or biology, and thus were willing to identify people who engaged in same-sex relations or had same-sex desires as 'homosexuals' even before the invention of the word. The Hungarian journalist and human-rights advocate Karl-Maria Kertbeny is attributed to having first applied the term 'homosexual' to same sex desire in 1869. However, historians have identified homosexual sub-cultures and identities prior to the nineteenth century and arguments have ensued as to when the homosexual identity was actually constructed.[50] Studies of homosexual sub-cultures have shown 'mollies' congregating in London taverns together, Portuguese transvestites dancing together, male pickups in the Pont-Neuf in Paris who mimicked women and used female

48 Philippa Levine, *Prostitution, Race and Politics: Policing Venereal Disease in the British Empire* (London: Routledge, 2003); Raelene Frances, 'Prostitution: the age of empires', in Chiara Beccalossi and Ivan Crozier, *A Cultural History of Sexuality in the Age of Empire* (Oxford: Berg, 2011), pp. 145–170.

49 Jeffrey Weeks, 'The "homosexual role" after 30 years: an appreciation of the work of Mary McIntosh', *Sexualities* 1/2 (May 1998), 131–52; Mary McIntosh, 'The homosexual role', *Social Problems* 16 (1968), 182–92.

50 For a good introduction to the various debates, see D. Altman et al., *Which Homosexuality?* (London: GMP Publishers, 1989), and Edward Stein, ed., *Forms of Desire: Sexual Orientation and the Social Constructionist Controversy* (London: Routledge, 1990). Also see Jeffrey Weeks, *Sex, Politics & Society: The Regulation of Sexuality Since 1800* (London: Longmans, 3rd edn, 2012); Randolph Trumbach, *Sex and the Gender Revolution*, Vol. 1: *Heterosexuality and the Third Gender in Enlightenment London* (University of Chicago Press, 1998).

nicknames, and 'warm brothers' who gathered in boy bordellos in Germany. Many of these men were married. Some were male prostitutes.[51] These have come to light mainly through exploration of trial records.

Similar debates emerged around the lesbian, about her 'construction', what terminology to use for which periods, and whether she can be said to have existed prior to the eighteenth century. Again historians have found ample evidence of both lesbians and lesbians' self-identity as such at various times in history, as they have uncovered 'female husbands', 'female friendships' and 'lesbian-like' relationships.[52] Women who engaged in same-sex relationships were prosecuted more often for fraud – either because they married other women without revealing their true sex or for taking a male sexual role by using a dildo rather than for the sex alone. Many societies remained silent on sexual acts between women, no doubt because women rarely sought out sex in public places, and were considered less important and therefore less noticed. What they did sexually between themselves held little threat to society, especially when compared to homosexual men.

Along with debates about whether 'homosexual' should be used across time, more recently, queer theorists and trans activists have also questioned the polarisation between heterosexual and homosexual and introduced important questions about normative and non-normative sexualities. Historians of other parts of the world have also criticized the application of concepts and chronologies drawn from the West to other areas.

There has been less study of same-sex relations outside the West, but more is emerging. That on China, for example, has shown that although laws against consensual male homosexuality were already in existence, new regulations were introduced in 1740 against homosexual rape. This law was justified as a way to curb rampant homosexuality,[53] but it has also been seen

51 Norton, *Mother Clap's Molly House*; David Higgs, ed., *Queer Sites: Gay Urban Histories Since 1600* (London: Routledge, 1999); Michael Rey, 'Police and sodomy in eighteenth-century Paris: from sin to disorder', in K. Gerard and G. Hekma, *The Pursuit of Sodomy: Male Homosexuality in Renaissance and Enlightenment* (New York: Harrington Park Press, 1989), pp. 129–146; R. D. Tobin, *Warm Brothers: Queer Theory and the Age of Goethe* (Philadelphia: University of Pennsylvania Press, 2000); Robert Aldrich, ed., *Gay Life and Culture: A World History* (London: Thames & Hudson, 2006).

52 Lillian Faderman, *Surpassing the Love of Men: Romantic Friendships and Love Between Women from the Renaissance to the Present* (London: Junction Books, 1981); Alison Oram and Ann Marie Turnbull, *The Lesbian History Sourcebook: Love & Sex Between Women in Britain 1780–1970* (London: Routledge, 2002); Judith M. Bennett, '"Lesbian-like" and the social history of lesbianisms', *Journal of the History of Sexuality* 9/1–2 (January/April 2000), 1–24.

53 Vivien W. Ng, 'Homosexuality and the state in late imperial China', in Martin Duberman, Martha Vicinus, and George Chauncey (eds.), *Hidden from History: Reclaiming the Gay and Lesbian Past* (New York: Penguin, 1989), pp. 76–89.

as a reflection of an increasing concern about the rogue and 'rootless male', a result of a growing mobile population, with more men than women. This law aimed at punishing the consensual penetrated male, although desiring boys for sex was still considered understandable. Despite the laws, elite men would continue to patronize male prostitutes and cross-dressing actors.[54]

Meanwhile, although under sharia law same sex relations were condemned, France's colonies in North Africa, as well as other Islamic countries, conjured up images of an exotic availability of homosexuality in the minds of Europeans. ''Tis Common for Men there [Algiers] to fall in love with Boys, as 'tis here in England to be in Love with Women', commented one Joseph Pitts.[55] Tensions around homosexual desire and the exotic 'primitive' male also surfaced in other imperial territories, including Northern Australia in the late nineteenth century and early twentieth century.[56]

Religious strictures against homosexuality were transported across the Atlantic with European colonization. In North America, restrictions were placed on pre-marital sex, adultery and homosexuality. But urbanisation would bring a lessening of oversight by the nineteenth century. In New York, boarding houses were established where transient men who had come into town looking for work could find a bed for a month or two. These places provided opportunities for men to stay overnight together unnoticed. Poet Walt Whitman thus indulged his passion for working-class men in the 1860s, and brought back several working-class men he had picked up in the city. These relationships were not always just about sex, but friendships and affection sometimes developed between men.[57]

On the European continent, in countries under the Napoleonic Code of 1804, sex acts between men were tolerated, but local statutes and laws covering public indecency meant that after 1848 acts of sex between men were effectively criminalised. The threat of being perceived as a sodomite took on a more significant meaning in Britain during the nineteenth century, when a series of new laws came out which outlawed more acts of sexual

54 Sommer, *Sex, Law and Society*, pp. 305, 310–11; Matthew H. Sommer, 'The penetrated male in Late Imperial China: judicial constructions and social stigma', *Modern China* 23/2 (1997), 140–180.

55 Quoted in Khaled El-Rouayheb, *Before Homosexuality in the Arab-Islamic world, 1500–1800* (University of Chicago Press, 2005), p.1.

56 Stephen O. Murray and Will Roscoe, *Islamic Homosexualities: Culture, History and Literature* (New York University Press, 1997); Anne O'Brien, 'Missionary masculinities: the homosexual gaze and the politics of race: Gilbert White in northern Australia, 1885–1915', *Gender and History* 20/7 (2008), 68–86.

57 Jonathan Ned Katz, *Love Stories: Sex Between Men Before Homosexuality* (University of Chicago Press, 2001).

behaviour. With the introduction of the Offences Against the Person Act in 1861, capital punishment for sodomy was abolished, although the last execution had already taken place in 1835.[58] Instead, a new set of crimes were introduced relating to sexual activities between men – these included kissing, fondling, mutual masturbation and oral sex. The Criminal Amendment Act of 1885 with Clause 11, stretched the law to define *all* acts of sex between two men as criminal, whether in public or private.

The changing times of the twentieth century

The twentieth century brought some radical changes affecting sexual behaviour, particularly in terms of a move towards greater sexual equality. New, improved, and more widely available birth control, the legalisation of abortion in some places, and decriminalisation of homosexuality would all have a positive impact on the position of women and marginalised men. Although heterosexuality remained the 'norm' during the twentieth century, alternative lifestyles and sexual practices became more apparent.

A new 'science' of the study of sex called sexology emerged in the second half of the nineteenth century which provided a greater understanding of sexual behaviour. This system of study saw sociologists, psychologists and psychiatrists influence how people understood different types of sexuality, and would have an impact in the wider world during the twentieth century. Karl Heinrich Ulrichs, who was working as a legal advisor, was one of the first activists to call for toleration of homosexuals (whom he called urnings) in a series of his essays entitled *The Riddle of Male-Male Love* published between 1864 and 1879. He suggested that homosexuality was not a life choice but congenital. However, it was Richard von Krafft-Ebing who was the founding father of sexology. He categorised and explained sexual activities, as well as labelling 'perversions' such as fetishism, transvestism, flagellation, homosexuality and lesbianism in his book *Psychopathia Sexualis* (1886).

The study of sexual behaviour spread from Europe in the twentieth century. Part of this examination involved sexual surveys, which became highly influential in the understanding of sexual behaviour in America and Britain as popular newspapers printed up their findings to reach the wider population. Kinsey's study of male and female sexual behaviour in America in

58 A. D. Harvey, 'Prosecutions for sodomy in England at the beginning of the nineteenth century', *Historical Journal* 21 (1978), 939–948; Netta Murray Goldsmith, *The Worst of Crimes: Homosexuality and the Law in Eighteenth-Century London* (Aldershot: Ashgate, 1998).

1948–53 was one of the biggest sex surveys ever to take place. In 1949, the smaller British Mass Observation 'mini' sex survey (called 'Little Kinsey') recorded the attitudes and behaviour of thousands of volunteers. In China, Professor Liu Dalin undertook a nationwide study of Chinese sexual behaviour similar to the Kinsey Report in 1989–90 and published his findings in *Sexual Behaviour in Modern China* (1992). From 20,000 surveys, from all parts of China, the investigators found that people were becoming more enlightened in some areas. Early love relationships between young people were increasing, and 94.8 per cent of college students and 66.55 per cent of married couples believed that women should also take the initiative in sex. However, just over half of the college students questioned had never masturbated, which is possibly related to the fact that the view in traditional Chinese medicine is that masturbation is harmful to one's health, a view which changed only in the twentieth century in the West.[59]

Transsexuality was also studied, and with improvements in procedures became a real possibility for more people. Although partial transsexual operations had been experimented with in the 1930s, they were rare, and up until the 1960s, few people had an understanding of the phenomenon of transsexuality, including doctors. Sexologist Dr. Harry Benjamin began pioneering work publishing *The Transsexual Phenomenon* in 1966. He set up his own Gender Identity Foundation in 1972 to help people with sex and gender conflicts, receiving countless letters from transvestites and transsexuals asking for help. Since then, transsexuals have gone on to demand better treatment and legal recognition throughout the world.

Heterosexuality remained the norm for most people with marriages the usual pattern, but to some extent World War I led to an unravelling of Victorian restraints. In Britain, marriage rates leapt upwards during the first year of World War I, and divorce rates similarly rose at the end of it. Illegitimacy rates also rose. Both world wars were to create disruption of conventional relationships. At a time when no one knew whether they would return from the war, who would live and who would die, sex was a way of reaffirming life. Young couples raced to have sex or to marry before men were sent to the front, with single mothers and war-brides left behind to cope with pregnancy and newborns alone.

The wars not only saw the formation and breakdown of many marriages but also offered new sexual opportunities. As a result, venereal disease spread

59 Lui Dalin, Man Lun Ng, Li Ping Zhou and Erwin J. Haeberle, *Sexual Behaviour in Modern China* (New York: Continum, 1997).

despite public health officials' efforts to eradicate it through propaganda. A nationwide system in Britain and America offered free and confidential advice and treatment. Salvarsan was an effective treatment but the use of penicillin from the 1940s allowed easy and complete cure. In China, by 1923, venereal disease affected three times as many people as in the United States.[60] Few countries were left unaffected. In World War II, mass mobilisation of troops meant that there was greater sexual intermingling between different nationalities. American GIs in Britain and British soldiers in France had sex with local women, and illegitimacy rates shot up. Another detrimental effect was the shift in the sex ratio after the loss of so many men in the wars. Studies of the Soviet Union and Bavaria show how male population losses during World War II led to lower rates of marriage and fertility, and higher rates of out-of-wedlock births, abortions, and deaths from abortions than in regions less affected by war deaths.

Increasing control over fertility was crucial to the remaking of heterosexual behaviour and had a massive impact on women's lives.[61] Prior to World War I, Germany was one of the first countries to introduce sex education in schools. Limiting families became important throughout the world as the connection between large families and poverty was better understood. New groups sprang up to advocate birth control. In the United States, Margaret Sanger promoted pessaries, condoms, douches and various forms of birth control for the working classes in her book *Family Limitation* (1914). Two years later, she attempted to open a birth control clinic, but it was raided by the police and was closed down. Sanger went on to form the American Birth Control league in 1921 and continued to campaign for people's right to effective birth control. In her book *The Pivot of Civilisation* (1922), she argued that sex would make women freer and able to form more spiritual unions with their husbands, but the US Comstock Laws that prevented the sending of obscene material through the post, effectively banned the postal sale or distribution of birth control devices and information on family planning methods. In England, Marie Stopes took up where nineteenth-century family planning campaigners Charles Bradlaugh and Annie Besant had left off, publishing books such as *Married Love* and *Wise Parenthood* (both 1918) and later setting up birth control clinics to cater mainly for married women.

60 Frank Dikotter, 'Sexually transmitted diseases in modern China: a historical survey', *Genitourinary Medicine* 69 (October 1993), 341–345.

61 Hera Cook, *The Long Sexual Revolution: English Women, Sex and Contraception 1800–1975* (Oxford University Press, 2004).

In Latin America, demands for better birth control and more information grew stronger from around the 1920s. As a result, fertility rates have declined in the last 40 years, from over 6 children per woman to around 2. As expected, the most educated and wealthiest populations have the fewest children; the poorest of the population still have rates ranging from 4 to 6 children per woman and have more than 50 per cent of their fertility concentrated at very young ages. Some Catholic countries such as Chile and Guatemala lagged behind in use of new contraceptive methods and abortion remained illegal; 'maschismo' played a part in Latin American men's resistance to condoms and disease was more easily spread.

The baby boom in the United States from the end of the 1940s through to the early 1960s proved that reproduction was still important for postwar couples, but birth control was increasingly giving couples the right to choose the size of their families. In the USA and Britain, couples used birth control by choice to restrict families or prevent unwanted pregnancies, while in China and India state planners used it as a nationwide method of controlling population growth. Family size was limited by law or by levying penalties for large families. While China had been encouraging population growth as an asset to the state, by the 1970s, its policy was reversed when a one-child-only policy was introduced (two in the countryside). Abortion and condoms were the contraceptive choice, but infanticide was still practised to get rid of unwanted babies. In India, a sterilisation campaign in the 1970s introduced penalties for families with more than three children.

Although condoms and diaphragms had been used as protection in the West, it was the contraceptive pill which brought a greater freedom and most dramatically changed women's lives. Its easy access in Britain and the USA from the 1960s effectively allowed for the separation of sex and pregnancy. Planned Parenthood statistics reveal that by 1965, one out of every four married women in America under 45 had used the pill. By 1967, nearly 13 million women in the world were using it. By 1984 that number would reach 50–80 million. Today 100 million women use the pill.[62] Not all countries took up the pill easily. In Japan, women had to campaign for three decades before it was finally introduced in 1999. Prior to this, as in China, both Japan and Russia used abortion as the primary method of contraception.[63]

62 Planned Parenthood Federation, issue brief, 'The birth control pill: a history', March 2013: www.plannedparenthood.org/files/PPFA/pillhistory.pdf (accessed 23 July 2013).

63 On Russia, see Igor S. Kon, *The Sexual Revolution in Russia from the Age of the Czars to Today* (New York: The Free Press, 1995); Tiana Norgren, *Abortion Before Birth Control: The Political of Reproduction in Post-war Japan* (Princeton University Press, 2001); Warren

Overall, shifting social and economic roles, such as mass migration to cities and increasing dependency on wage labour, led to changes in relationships between men and women. In Western Europe and North America, the so-called 'sexual revolution' saw couples increasingly living together before marriage from the 1970s onwards, though they were still in a minority. People also had their first sexual encounters earlier. In India, urban Muslim women who gained education and embarked on careers increasingly questioned a social structure based on polygamy, concubinage, child marriage and subservience to men. All Indian women, including the Hindu majority, have had birth control issues thrust upon them, however, and elite assumptions have shaped fertility behaviour in the middle class.[64]

Changes in the law helped change sexual behaviour. Legalisation of abortion in many countries allowed women freedom from unwanted pregnancies for the first time. Initially, it was legalised in special cases only, such as rape or threat to the mother's health; this happened in Poland, Turkey, Denmark, Sweden, Iceland and Mexico in the 1930s. This was followed by abortion on demand. However, female foeticide in countries where limits were placed on family size, such as China and India, has led to unequal sex ratios and may create more problems in the future.[65]

Laws also changed on homosexuality, allowing people to choose their sexual partners and providing them with legal protection. The first homosexual rights movement, Wissenschaftlich-humanitäres Komittee, was formed in 1897 in Germany by Magnus Hirschfeld. Other countries followed over the coming decades with gay and lesbian societies formed to demand equal rights. In 1969 in New York, the Stonewall riots occurred after the police raided a gay bar, and hundreds gathered on the streets to demonstrate against the persecution. In 1978, the International Lesbian and Gay Association was founded and was joined by many different groups from different countries. The twentieth century saw a decriminalisation of homosexuality in Western countries. Norway in 1933, Sweden in 1944, England in 1967, the United States first with Illinois in 1962, then state by state, and nationwide in 2003.

C. Robinson and John A. Ross, eds., *The Global Family Planning Revolution: Three Decades of Population Policies and Programs* (Washington, DC: World Bank, 2007).

64 Sanjam Ahluwalia, 'Rethinking boundaries: feminism and (inter)nationalism in early-twentieth century India', *Journal of Women's History* 14/4 (Winter 2003), 188–195.

65 Tulsi Patel, ed., *Sex-Selective Abortion in India: Gender, Society and New Reproductive Technologies* (London: SAGE, 2006).

Freedoms gained were suddenly restricted with the emergence of HIV/AIDS in the early 1980s. HIV/AIDS is transmitted by the exchange of bodily fluids, and its initial victims in the West included many homosexuals and intravenous drug users. Bath houses, bars and other places for meeting were shut down, and there was a wave of anti-homosexual violence. Extensive medical research led to the development of antiretroviral drugs in the 1990s. For those who could afford these, AIDS became a chronic condition rather than a death sentence. In poorer parts of the world, AIDS spread first among prostitutes and their clients; drugs were far too expensive and many men objected to using condoms, which would have slowed its spread. Eventually huge numbers of people were infected, particularly in sub-Saharan Africa, where it is still a major killer.[66] AIDS is spreading fastest in countries where the government sometimes denies that it exists and, according to the World Health Organisation is now the leading cause of death for women aged 15–44 worldwide.[67]

Moves toward greater toleration of homosexuality in the West picked up again in the early twenty-first century, with same-sex marriage increasingly legalised in Europe and many states in the United States, and people in traditionally homophobic occupations, such as professional sports, coming out as gay. In Latin America as well, most countries have legalised same-sex relations, but there is still a struggle for the acceptance of gay marriage and equal rights worldwide.

Prohibition of homosexuality has continued into the twenty-first century in some places with criminal penalties, crackdowns and anti-gay violence increasing. Many Muslim countries retain their repressive laws against same-sex relationships and the death penalty still exists for homosexuality. In the majority of countries in Africa, same-sex relations are also illegal, and in some, including Uganda and Nigeria, harsher laws were enacted in 2013, in part because of the influence of American Christian fundamentalists. In 2009, the High Court in Delhi ruled that the law against homosexuality (a holdover from British imperial law which had never been rescinded) was unconstitutional, which in effect decriminalised homosexuality in India, although the Supreme Court of India reversed this in 2013, stating that decriminalisation would have to be done by legislative act, not court decision.[68] In the first couple of decades of the 2000s, Russia enacted a series of regulations

66 Jonathan Engel, *The Epidemic: A Global History of AIDS* (New York: Harper Collins, 2006).
67 www.who.int/mediacentre/factsheets/fs334/en (accessed 10/4/14).
68 Manoj Mitta, 'Will Delhi HC gay order apply across India?', *The Times of India*, 3 July 2009.

outlawing Gay Pride marches and other events the government termed 'propaganda of non-traditional sexual behaviour'.

Meanwhile, in other countries, homosexuality was not so much condemned as denied an existence. In China during the 1980s, homosexuality was closeted and, if detected by the authorities, was declared 'hooliganism' and the culprits imprisoned. Same-sex relations were made legal in the People's Republic of China in 1997, although there are no laws to prevent discrimination. Homosexuality has never been illegal in Japan except for a short time from 1872–1880, and although civil rights are not specifically protected, cases of discrimination are relatively rare.

Along with the decriminalisation of homosexuality, some countries in Western Europe, initiated by the Netherlands, legalised prostitution, thus making it safer for women to sell sex. Others countries, particularly Muslim-dominated ones, have severe punishment for prostitution; Sudan, for example, retains the death penalty for this 'crime'.

As with other aspects of the economy, sex work became increasingly globalised in the twentieth century as poor people, primarily women, migrated to cities or to different countries to find sex work or became involved in sex tourism. Around 200,000 Nepalese women, for example, were thought to be working in India in sex work in the early twentieth century.[69] With the fall of communism, Russia and Eastern Europe became a new source of prostitutes. Highways leading from Germany into the Czech Republic were lined with prostitutes. By 2008, an estimated 500,000 women from Eastern Europe and Asia were working in prostitution in the European Union. Governments have made some efforts to limit the sex trade and sex tourism, although these often parallel nineteenth-century campaigns against prostitution in that they focus on the providers, not the customers. This, however, is changing as new laws are targeting the customer rather than the prostitute in such countries as Sweden, Norway, Iceland and France. Here, it is now illegal to buy sexual services, although this too has led to accusations that such laws force prostitution underground leaving women yet more vulnerable.

Male prostitution, although by no means new, has become more evident; today services can be found online, on the streets, in bath-houses and in 'stables'. Western (and to a lesser degree Japanese) men and Asian, Eastern European, and Latin American women are primarily involved in sex tourism, a pattern resulting largely from the sharply unequal globalised economy, and

69 Stearns, *Sexuality in World History*, p. 149.

gendered and sexualised notions of cultural and racial differences. Sex tourism has also taken a new turn, as along with men from wealthy countries traveling to poorer ones for sex, older women are going abroad to seek willing young men in Brazil, Dominican Republic, the Caribbean and parts of Africa.[70] Most societies continue to have a two-sided attitude towards prostitution, with the authorities trying to prevent or control it, while public demand increases.

The twentieth century heralded a period of the development of a more highly sexualised public culture in nearly every society. Family planning, consumerism, new media – radio, televisions, films, videos and sex magazines – have had their impact on sexual culture. With the lifting of censorship in many countries, pornographic material has become more readily available than ever before, and new centres of porn emerged; in the 1990s, for example, Japan became the largest exporter of porn in the world. Meanwhile, the Internet has revolutionised access to pornography and sexual partners, but usage is increasingly surveyed by governments.[71]

Conclusions

In the eighteenth and nineteenth centuries, some marginalised people, including women, indigenous people in colonial areas, slaves and homosexuals managed to manoeuvre themselves into positions where they had some degree of control over their own sexuality, or at least attained some protection from those in more powerful positions. A few even managed to achieve a degree of independence in the burgeoning cities around the world, although this was rare. There were huge changes in terms of economic growth, migration, industrialisation and urbanisation in these centuries, but these often did little in terms of sexual or gender equality. Instead they brought increasing dangers, as many young women and men lost ties with family and communities with the move to the cities and became more vulnerable to sexual exploitation. Homosexual men continued to be persecuted for their activities and the majority of women remained in secondary economic and social positions.

In the twentieth and twenty-first centuries, gender and sexual equality increased, and now supposedly exists in much of the West, although even

70 Stephen Cliff and Simon Carter, eds., *Tourism and Sex: Culture, Commerce and Coercion* (London: Continuum, 2000).

71 See Katrien Jacobs, *People's Pornography: Sex and Surveillance on the Chinese Internet* (University of Chicago Press, 2013).

where there are laws prescribing equality, discrimination continues, against heterosexual women, gay men and lesbians. In other places, such as the Middle East, Africa and Russia, persecution of homosexuality continues, or has even increased. On other sexual issues there has also been both decline and advance. Economic disparities remain, access to abortion and birth control is opposed by religious leaders, and sexual violence continues, but better contraception, wider sex education, and changes in laws have at least contributed towards greater sexual and gender equality. In 2008, the United Nations stated that sexual violence as a weapon of war was a matter of national and international security. Mass rape and sexual enslavement in the time of war has been declared a crime against humanity by the World Court.

Further reading

Aldrich, Robert, ed. *Gay Life and Culture: A World History*. London: Thames & Hudson, 2006.

Bamber, Scott, Milton Lewis and Michael Waugh, eds. *Sex, Disease, and Society: A Comparative History of Sexually Transmitted Diseases and HIV/AIDS in Asia and the Pacific*. Westport, CT: Greenwood Press, 1997.

Beccalossi, Chiara and Ivan Crozier, eds. *A Cultural History of Sexuality in the Age of Empire*. Oxford: Berg, 2011.

Cliff, Stephen and Simon Carter, eds. *Tourism and Sex: Culture, Commerce and Coercion*. London: Continuum, 2000.

Cook, Hera. *The Long Sexual Revolution: English Women, Sex and Contraception 1800–1975*. Oxford University Press, 2004.

Corbin, Alain. *Women for Hire: Prostitution and Sexuality in France after 1850*. Cambridge, MA: Harvard University Press, 1990.

D'Emilio, John and Estelle Freedman. *Intimate Matters: A History of Sexuality in America*. University of Chicago Press, 1997.

Dikotter, Frank. *Sex, Culture and Modernity in China: Medical Science and the Construction of Sexual Identities in the Early Republican Period*. Honolulu: University of Hawaii Press, 1995.

Eder, Franz X., Lesley Hall and Gert Hekma, eds. *Sexual Cultures in Europe*. 2 vols. Manchester University Press, 1999.

Hyam, Ronald. *Empire and Sexuality*. Manchester University Press, 1990.

Jacobs, Katrien. *People's Pornography: Sex and Surveillance on the Chinese Internet*. University of Chicago Press, 2013.

Jordanova, Ludmilla. *Sexual Visions: Images of Gender in Science and Medicine between the Eighteenth and Twentieth Centuries*. London: Harvester Wheatsheaf, 1989.

Kon, Igor. *The Sexual Revolution in Russia from the Age of the Czars to Today*. New York: The Free Press, 1995.

Laqueur, Thomas. *Making Sex: Body and Gender from the Greeks to Freud*. Harvard University Press, 1992.

Levine, Philippa. *Prostitution, Race and Politics: Policing Venereal Disease in the British Empire*. London: Routledge, 2003.

Mann, Susan L. *Gender and Sexuality in Modern China*. Cambridge University Press, 2011.

Mason, Michael. *The Making of the Victorian Sexuality: Sexual Behaviour and Its Understanding*. Oxford University Press, 1994.

McClintock, Anne. *Imperial Leather: Race, Gender, and Sexuality in the Colonial Contest*. London: Routledge, 1995.

Murray, Stephen O. and Will Roscoe, eds. *Islamic Homosexualities: Culture, History and Literature*. New York University Press, 1997.

Boy Wives and Female Husbands: Studies of African Homosexualities. London: St. Martin's Press, 2001.

Norgren, Tiana. *Abortion Before Birth Control: The Political of Reproduction in Post-war Japan*. Princeton University Press, 2001.

Peakman, Julie. *The Pleasure's All Mine: A History of Perverse Sex*. London: Reaktion, 2013.

ed. *A Cultural History of Sexuality*. 6 vols. Oxford: Berg, 2011.

Porter, Roy and Mikuláš Teich, eds. *Sexual Knowledge, Sexual Science: The History of Attitudes to Sexuality*. Cambridge University Press, 1994.

Robinson, Warren C. and John A. Ross, eds. *The Global Family Planning Revolution: Three Decades of Population Policies and Programs*. Washington, DC: World Bank, 2007.

Schiebinger, Londa. *Nature's Body: Sexual Politics and the Making of Modern Science*. London: Pandora, 1993.

Sommer, Matthew H. *Sex, Law and Society in Late Imperial China*. Stanford University Press, 2000.

Stearns, Peter N. *Sexuality in World History*. London, Routledge, 2009.

Stoler, Ann Laura. *Carnal Knowledge and Imperial Power: Race and the Intimate in Colonial Rule*. Berkeley, CA: University of California Press, 2nd edn, 2010.

Weeks, Jeffrey. *Sex, Politics & Society: The Regulation of Sexuality Since 1800*. London: Longmans, 3rd edn, 2012.

5
Abolitions

ALESSANDRO STANZIANI

Debates about abolitions have essentially focused on two interrelated questions: (1) whether nineteenth- and early-twentieth-century abolitions were a major breakthrough compared to previous centuries (or even millennia) in the history of humankind during which bondage had been the dominant form of labour and human condition; (2) whether they express an action specific to Western bourgeoisie and liberal civilization.

It is true that the number of abolitionist acts and the people concerned throughout the extended nineteenth century (1780–1914) had no equivalent in history: 30 million Russian peasants, half a million slaves in Saint-Domingue in 1790, four million slaves in the US in 1860, another million in the Caribbean (at the moment of the abolition of 1832–40), a further million in Brazil in 1885 and 250,000 in the Spanish colonies were freed during this period. Abolitions in Africa at the turn of the nineteenth century have been estimated to involve approximately seven million people.[1]

Yet this argument has been criticized by those who have argued that the abolitionist legal acts take into consideration neither the important rate of manumission and purchase of freedom in Islamic societies, in areas such as Africa, South East Asia and the Ottoman empire[2], nor the important rate of manumission in Russia and Brazil prior to general abolition, nor the legal and social constraints on freed slaves and serfs.

1 Seymour Drescher, *Abolitions: A History of Slavery and Antislavery* (Cambridge University Press, 2009).

2 On this debate, see among others: Joseph Calder Miller, *Slavery and Slaving in World History: A Bibliography, 1900–1996* (Armonk, NY: M.E. Sharpe, 1999); Claude Meillassoux, *Anthropologie de l'esclavage* (Paris: PUF, 1986); Moses Finley, *Ancient Slavery and Modern Ideology* (New York: Viking Press, 1980); Orlando Patterson, *Slavery and Social Death: A Comparative Study* (Cambridge University Press, 1982); James Watson, ed., *Asian and African Systems of Slavery* (Berkeley and Los Angeles: University of California Press, 1980); William Gervase Clarence-Smith, ed., *The Economics of the Indian Ocean Slave Trade* (London: Frank Cass, 1989); Gwyn Campbell, ed., *The Structure of Slavery in the Indian Ocean, Africa and Asia* (London: Frank Cass, 2004).

This chapter seeks to provide answers which go beyond these standard oppositions between 'before' and 'after' the abolition, on the one hand, and between the 'West' and 'the rest', on the other hand. We will stress interrelations in terms of the circulation of ideas and the economic and social dynamics between various areas – Europe, Russia, Africa, the Indian Ocean and the Americas. Taking this as our starting point, we will attempt to identify continuities and changes in the long-term process of emancipation and the interaction between different notions and practices of 'freedom'. We will begin with Russian serfdom and its abolition, before analysing the transatlantic slave trade and the abolition of slavery in European colonies in connection with economic and social dynamics in Africa, India, Europe and Latin America. We will then show that abolition in the USA impacted different areas such as Brazil, Egypt, Russian Turkestan, India and, of course, Europe. We will conclude with the abolition of slavery in Africa and in the Ottoman Empire before World War I and a broader reminder of persistent forms of bondage and coercion through to the present day.

The abolition of serfdom

In continental Western Europe and Britain forms of serfdom and slavery were never officially abolished, they simply progressively disappeared between the eleventh and the fourteenth centuries. This was not the case in Russia and Eastern Europe where, on the contrary, new forms of bondage were introduced from the fourteenth century. Some have found close similarities between the so-called second serfdom in oriental Europe and American slavery.[3] This approach is misleading for several reasons: serfdom was not practised on foreigners on the basis of racial distinction, but on Russian themselves; unlike American slaves, serfs were not eradicated from their original community, but were fully integrated into the peasant village and the owner's estate; the introduction, evolution and abolition of serfdom followed completely different paths to that in the Americas. Yet before serfdom, Russia knew forms of slavery and bondage knows as *kholopostvo*. These were heterogeneous forms of bondage, varying from the indentured labour and debt slavery to domestic servants and chattel slavery. At its peak, i.e. at the turn of the sixteenth and seventeenth centuries, *kholopy* accounted for about 10 per cent of the Russian population. However, this category was

3 Peter Kolchin, *Unfree Labor: American Slavery and Russian Serfdom* (Cambridge, MA: Belknap, 1987).

abolished by Peter the Great in 1725 when he introduced the general capitation fiscal system. From that moment onwards, *kholopy* entered other legal categories – either that of peasants (serfs) or of lower urban groups.[4] This is where the identification of serfdom became crucial. Unlike interpretations which have remained dominant from the Enlightenment through to the modern day, serfdom as such was never institutionalized in Russia.[5] Limitations to peasants' mobility entered a wider game opposing Russian elites. These measures were dictated not only by the taxation and military requirements of the rising Russian state, which were linked to Russian territorial expansion[6] but overlapped with a significant redefinition of the relationships between social groups and that state.[7] The Russian elites welcomed requests from the provincial nobility to legitimize their properties, as these elites could thereby secure an important ally in their fight against the *boyari* (big estate owners). As such, constraints were above all a form of institutionalized extortion of peasants by landlords: the latter could forbid marriages, sideline activities and emigration and could also impose labour services.[8] In practice, all these rules could be negotiated and most landlords simply demanded a fee in order to give their permission. This explains why despite 'serfdom', and in accordance with its rules, peasants never stopped moving from one estate to another, from one region to another and the government even introduced measures to protect them, particularly if they accepted to move to the newly annexed southern and eastern provinces. As a result, between the mid sixteenth and the early seventeenth centuries, the colonization of the southern and eastern steppes was the most important event to occur in Russia. With the help of the State, half a million people moved to these new areas, despite the complaints of landowners in central Russia.[9]

From the last quarter of the eighteenth century, peasants and working people exploited conflicts between the elites in order to contest the latter's

4 Richard Hellie, *Slavery in Russia* (University of Chicago Press, 1982).

5 Tracy Dennison, *The Institutions of Russian Serfdom* (Cambridge University Press, 2011); Alessandro Stanziani, 'Serfs, slaves, or wage earners? The legal status of labour in Russia from a comparative perspective, from the 16th to the 19th century', *Journal of Global History* 3/2 (2008), 183–202.

6 David Moon, *The Russian Peasantry, 1600–1930: The World the Peasants Made* (London: Longman, 1996); Richard Hellie, *Enserfment and Military Change in Muscovy* (University of Chicago Press, 1971).

7 Pavel A. Zaionchkovskii, *Otmena krepostnogo prava v Rossii* [The Abolition of Serfdom in Russia] (3rd edn, Moscow, 1968).

8 Steven Hoch, *Serfdom and Social Control in Russia: Petrovskoe, a Village in Tambov* (University of Chicago Press, 1986).

9 Stanziani, 'Serfs, slaves, or wage earners?'.

rights over them. Through litigation or administrative decisions, between 1801 and 1861, when serfdom was officially abolished, half of the peasantry abandoned the status of 'private peasant' and became state peasants or urban inhabitants. Of the other fifty per cent – ten million males, plus their families (still private peasants at the moment of abolition) – barely half were still engaged in labour services, the others paying fees and rent to the landlord. Unlike world-capitalism theory,[10] detailed empirical analyses show that labour services went hand-in-hand with an increasing integration of the demesne in proto-industrial activity as well as in local and national markets for agriculture and commerce.[11] Both landlords and peasants took part in this process.[12] The output of both agricultural produce and proto-industrial products increased throughout the eighteenth and nineteenth centuries; in turn, this sustained the demand for manufactured goods which was mostly satisfied by local proto-industrial activity utilizing labour-intensive technology.[13] The well-being of peasants improved, as seen in decreasing mortality rates and the increasing height of conscripts.[14]

From this perspective, whilst the 'abolition of serfdom' in 1861 did not mark as big a break as has often been claimed, it was nevertheless a crucial step in the long-term process which had begun in the late eighteenth century and ended only on the eve of World War I. The major novelty of the reforms was not 'freedom' as such, nor the passage from 'feudalism' to 'capitalism', but the very fact that access to the ownership of inhabited estates was now extended to other social classes, namely urban residents and merchants. Peasants purchased lands and sold agricultural and proto-industrial products to the market. Peasants' standards of living strongly increased and recent estimates have shown that between 1861 and 1914 Russian's growth in agriculture, trade and industry kept pace with that of major Western countries.[15]

10 Immanuel Wallerstein, *The Modern World-System: Capitalist Agriculture and the Origins of the European World-Economy in the Sixteenth Century* (New York: Atheneum, 1976); Witold Kula, *An Economic Theory of the Feudal System* (London: New Left Book, 1976); Douglass North, *Structure and Change in Economic History* (New York: Norton, 1981).

11 Russian State Archives of Ancien Acts: fonds 1252, opis' 1, Abamelek-Lazarevy's estate, province of Tula ; fonds 1282, Tolstye-Kristi's estate, province of Riazan; fonds 1262, opis' 1, Prince Gagarin's estates in Saratov and Tambov provinces; fond 1287, Sheremetev's estate.

12 Russian Imperial State archives, fond 1088, opis' 10.

13 Alessandro Stanziani, 'Revisiting Russian serfdom: bonded peasants and market dynamics, 1600–1800', *International Labor and Working Class History* 78/1 (2010), 12–27.

14 Steven Hoch, 'Serfs in imperial Russia: demographic insights', *Journal of Interdisciplinary History* 13/2 (1982), 221–246.

15 Paul Gregory, *Russian National Income 1885–1913* (Cambridge University Press, 1982).

These outcomes confirm similar recent conclusions regarding east-European agriculture under serfdom.[16] Taken together, the experiences of Russia, Prussia, Lithuania and some parts of Poland lead to the conclusion that, as a whole, second serfdom was not so much a form of slavery as, above all, a set of legal constraints on labour mobility. These rules were dictated far less by scarcity of population in a context of absentee and backward landlords than by increasing demand for agricultural produce and proto-industrial products encouraging growth. Unlike Wallerstein's argument, Russia and Eastern Europe did not constitute the quasi-periphery of industrializing Europe. East-European cereals were not the feudal support of Western capitalism, but an important ingredient of its transformation.

Yet far from closing the file, these issues raise new questions: once one accepts that Russian serfdom was more flexible and market-oriented than is usually suggested and that its abolition was part of a long-term transformation, then analogies and differences with European colonial slavery also require new appraisals.

The abolition of the transatlantic slave trade

Russian emancipation was not so much due to pressure from urban groups as to a circumstantial event (the Crimean war) and the attitude of certain tsarist elites, a group of big estate owners and the peasants' resistance during previous decades. In a quite different manner, the first British abolitionist campaigns combined moral, political, religious and economic arguments. The latter were probably the weakest, not just because slavery was objectively profitable, but also because in England itself Adam Smith's arguments did not become widespread until the mid nineteenth century. Indeed, religious anti-slavery groups were opposed to both materialism and utilitarianism and used this argument to criticize slavery.[17]

The abolition of slave trade caused Britain to lose profits not only from this trade, but also from the reduced production of sugar in the West Indies in the years following the abolition. After that period, despite the slow recovery of

16 Hartmut Harnisch, 'Bäuerliche Ökonomie und Mentalität unter den Bedingungen der ostelbischen Gutsherrschaft in den letzen Jahrzehnten vor Beginn der Agrarreformen', *Jahrbuch für Wirtschaftsgeschichte* 24/3 (1989), 87–108.

17 Robert Fogel, *Without Consent or Contract: the Rise and Fall of American Slavery* (New York: Norton, 1994), Vol. 1, pp. 203–204.

production, on the European markets Britain constantly lost shares of sugar and coffee to the benefit of Spain and Brazil.[18]

The slave trade was nevertheless a global affair. In the Atlantic, between 1500 and 1850, 31 per cent of African slaves transported to the Americas went to Brazil; against 22 per cent to the French Caribbean, 23 per cent to the British Caribbean, 9.6 per cent to the Spanish colonies and 6 per cent to North America. In the Caribbean, slaves were mostly employed on sugar plantations. Unlike those in Brazil, these were huge plantations; they were also badly organized and essentially relied upon strong coercion. The history of slavery and sugar in the Caribbean is one of rampant profit-taking and strong slave resistance encouraged by the size of the plantations and by the high proportion of slaves compared to the population as a whole (about three-quarters, as against 44.8 per cent in the deep South USA in 1860). Resistance was also enhanced by the low rate of reproduction and the continuous flow of new slaves from Africa.

Indeed the abolition of the slave trade did not reduce the overall number of slaves carried across the Atlantic but enhanced it for a time. Encouraged by the demand for sugar and coffee in North America and Europe, increasing numbers of African slaves were carried to Brazil and Cuba.[19] Even worse, at least 90 per cent of the manufactured goods used in this slave trade to Brazil and Cuba came from Britain, while British credit financed half of the Cuban and Brazilian slave trade.[20]

In Africa itself, the export trade in African slaves northwards to Muslim countries continued to be significant, accounting for about 30 per cent of total slave exports from Africa in the seventeenth century, 20 per cent in the eighteenth century, and about 30 per cent between the seventeenth and the early nineteenth centuries. Overall, between 1500 and 1800, the Muslim trade probably accounted for about 40 per cent of African slave exports. During the first half of the nineteenth century, half a million African slaves were sent to the Indian Ocean and another 420,000 to the Red Sea.[21] As a consequence of British abolitionism, the initial decline in slave prices stimulated internal demand. The enslavement frontier was pushed further into the interior than ever before. The introduction of so called 'legitimate trade' (palm oil,

18 David Eltis, *Economic Growth and the Ending of the Transatlantic Slave Trade* (Oxford University Press, 1989).
19 David Eltis and David Richardson, eds., *Extending the Frontiers: Essays on the New Transatlantic Slave Trade Database* (New Haven: Yale University Press, 2008).
20 Eltis, *Economic Growth*, p. 59.
21 Paul Lovejoy, *Transformations in Slavery* (Cambridge University Press, 2002), p. 137.

coconuts) also contributed to the recrudescence of slavery in Africa and the Indian Ocean. In most cases, manumissions were extremely important, in particular in Islamic areas. On the other hand, there was no equivalent of the British notion and practice of abolitionism as they were progressively identified in the nineteenth century.

The abolition of slavery in practice: from slaves to apprentices

In England many had believed that the abolition of slave trade would lead to the progressive abolition of slavery. This was not the case, as France, Spain and Portugal continued to import slaves, while in the West Indies planters resisted any attempt to improve the conditions of slaves. A new antislavery society was founded; it shifted from gradual abolition to immediate abolition of slavery. A period (usually six to seven years, which typically reproduced the timeframe of individual emancipation as well as the apprenticeship contract) was imposed during which the quasi-former slaves were given an apprenticeship status.[22] Slaves did not enjoy full legal status inasmuch as they were not yet 'civilised'.[23] Apprentices worked 45 hours a week for their former owners in exchange for food, clothing, lodging and medical care. Absenteeism or bad performance (according to standards set by the planters themselves) led to severe penalties and increased the period and the amount of apprentices' obligations. Physical punishment, which had been supressed under slavery during the 1820s, was now re-introduced for apprentices. Abuse was thus extremely frequent.[24]

Thus, even though former slave-owners had received compensation of 20 million pounds, many planters used the apprenticeship programme as additional compensation and, to this end, they sought to extract as much unpaid labour as possible. The final social and economic outcome differed from one colony to another according to the availability of land, previous forms of bondage and types of culture, new forms of labour and their rules (different masters and servants acts enacted in each colony), and to systems of credit.[25]

22 Seymour Drescher, *Capitalism and Antislavery* (London: Palgrave, 1987); Robin Blackburn, *The Overthrow of Colonial Slavery, 1776–1848* (London: Verso, 1988).

23 House of Commons, 'Papers in explanation of the condition of the slave population, 5 Nov. 1831', *British Parliamentary Papers*, 1830–1 (230), 16.1, pp. 59–88.

24 J. R Ward, *British West India Slavery, 1750–1834: The Process of Amelioration* (Oxford University Press, 1988).

25 Mary Turner, 'The British Caribbean, 1823–1838: the transition from slave to free legal status', in Douglas Hay and Paul Craven (eds.), *Masters, Servants and Magistrates in*

In Barbados the planters kept almost all the land that they rented in part to former slaves, few of whom therefore left their original plantations. In Jamaica, Trinidad and English Guyana, many former slaves had formal access to land, but many of them ended up indebted to their former masters and found themselves back on the plantations.[26] This did not prevent former slaves (when they did not run away) from providing extremely irregular (in their masters' eyes) labour. A fall in sugar output in Jamaica was one of the major expressions of resistance.

In this context India was a special case within the British Empire; public opinion in Britain tended towards the adoption of a broader conception of slavery (from chattel slavery, to debt bondage, domestic and agricultural slaves, cast dependence, children dependence, etc.), a conception which would extend the range of reforms and the areas of the Empire concerned. However, in practice colonial officers supported a relatively restrictive interpretation of slavery, by arguing that many forms of 'dependence' were far milder than slavery and were part of local customs. In turn, the latter were to be preserved for social and political imperial equilibrium. Ever since, historians have fiercely debated whether the multiple forms of Indian bondage were or were not 'slavery' and, hence whether slavery decreased or increased over time. Indeed, the British administration openly supported masters' rights until 1843, when it adopted a comparatively neutral attitude up until the last quarter of the nineteenth century, when more aggressive anti-slavery policies were adopted.[27]

The French only abolished slavery in 1848; unlike the British they did not go through an intermediate period of 'apprenticeship' but rather practised disguised forms of enslavement. Recruitment in India, Madagascar, Mozambique and the eastern coast of Africa relied on networks that had been in place since the eighteenth century and it employed the same practices as the slave trade. It often involved violence, sometimes with the help of local tribal chiefs. Using the slave trade system already developed in the region with the rise of Islam, French traders, helped by local sultans, began importing libres *engagés* from Gabon, Zaire and West Africa – a name which fetished

Britain and the Empire, 1562–1955 (Chapel Hill and London: The University of North Carolina Press, 2004), p. 322.

26 Thomas, Holt, *The Problem of Freedom: Race, Labour and Politics in Jamaica and Britain, 1832–1938* (Baltimore and London: The Johns Hopkins University Press, 1992).

27 Dharma Kumar, *Land and Caste in South India* (New Delhi: Manohar, 1992); Gyan Prakash, *Bonded Histories: Genealogies of Labour Servitude in Colonial India* (Cambridge University Press, 1990).

freedom while practising enslavement.[28] There were also 'prior redemptions' (the term given to such purchases) in Madagascar, Zanzibar and Mozambique, causing conflicts with the Portuguese and the English. Ultimately, these disguised forms of slavery evolved only with the development of new massive worldwide forms of population displacements.

From apprentices to indentured immigrants

According to one approach, the indentured contract resembled forced labour and slavery and contracts were said to express a 'legal fiction'. This interpretation has an interesting history of its own: it was advanced by colonial elites in the nineteenth century and later renewed in 'subaltern studies'.[29] This approach deprives the abolition of slavery of any historical significance.[30]

Other scholars have opposed this view by demonstrating that the indenture contract was not considered an expression of forced labour until the second half of the nineteenth century, whereas until that date, it was viewed as an expression of free will in contract.[31] Indeed, indentured labour was not just disguised slavery, but an expression of what free labour was at that time, i.e. a contract based upon unequal rights between the master and the servant, the latter being subject to criminal prosecution. Masters in the colonies gradually obtained broader rights than in Great Britain. In Mauritius, 14,000 indentured and domestic servants were prosecuted every year in the 1860s; during the same period in Great Britain, proceedings were brought against 9,700 servants per year for breach of contract and almost always resulted in convictions. In contrast, masters were seldom indicted and even more rarely convicted for breach of contract, ill treatment or non-payment of wages. They could exercise corporal punishment, authorise the marriage of indentured servants, etc.[32]

28 Edmund Maestri, ed., *Esclavage et abolition dans l'Océan Indien, 1723–1869* (Paris: L'Harmattan, 2002).

29 Hugh Tinker, *A New System of Slavery: The Export of Indian Labour Overseas, 1830–1920* (London: Hansib, 1974).

30 David Northrup, *Indentured Labour in the Age of Imperialism, 1834–1922* (Cambridge University Press, 1995); Marina Carter, *Servants, Sirdars and Settlers: Indians in Mauritius, 1834–1874* (Oxford University Press, 1995).

31 Robert Steinfeld, *The Invention of Free Labour: The Employment Relation in English and American Law and Culture, 1350–1870* (Chapel Hill: University of North Carolina Press, 1991); Stanley Engerman, ed., *Terms of labor: Slavery, Serfdom and Free Labor* (Stanford University Press, 1999); Tom Brass and Marcel van der Linden, eds., *Free and Unfree Labour: The Debate Continues* (Bern: Peter Lang, 1997).

32 David Galenson, *White Servitude in Colonial America: An Economic Analysis* (Cambridge University Press, 1981).

In economic terms, it is not correct to interpret indentured labour as a simple and temporary substitute for slavery in the aftermath of its abolition. Indentured labour began far before slavery and persisted during and after it. The first phase, from the seventeenth century to the 1830s, concerned about 300,000 European indentured servants who were intended for tobacco plantations and to some extent for manufacturing. With the rapid development of plantations, African slaves gradually supplanted them. However, white indentured immigration retained all of its importance in North America and Canada until at least the 1830s and responded to both push factors in Europe (industrialisation, transformation of the countryside) and pull factors in North America.

The abolition of slavery gave new life to indentured immigration. The second phase (nineteenth and twentieth centuries) concerned 2.5 million indentured servants, mostly Chinese and Indian but also African, Japanese and immigrants from the Pacific Islands. They were employed in sugar plantations and in manufacturing. Unlike white settlers during the first phase of indentured immigration, during the 1850s and 1860s, many indentured immigrants returned home (mostly Indians). The proportion was one third in Mauritius, the Caribbean, Surinam and Jamaica but this was far from the 70 per cent repatriation recorded in Thailand, Malaya and Melanesia. Distance and the cost of transport were only two of the variables affecting repatriation; politics, concrete forms of integration and death from disease were also important factors.

The actual conditions endured by workers depended not only on their ethical origin and on the period during which they arrived, but also on the estates on which they worked. Small plantation owners were more concerned about fugitive, insubordinate and vagrant indentured servants.[33] On the other hand, owners of large plantations who complained of the excessive cost of slave surveillance often imposed a liberal ideology in the colonial systems; they found support for the indenture system in humanitarian and anti-slavery associations by stressing the benefits of free immigration (indenture) as opposed to slavery.[34]

Conditions for indentured immigrants improved over time. This was due to several factors, not least of which was the endurance of the immigrants themselves, who continued to report abuse despite the difficulties they

33 MNA (Mauritius National Archives), HA 66 (planters' petitions).

34 Alessandro Stanziani, 'Local bondage in global economies: servants, wage-earners, and indentured migrants in nineteenth-century France, Great Britain and the Mascarene Islands', *Modern Asian Studies* 1 (2013), 1–34.

faced in so doing, and their commitment to passive resistance as well as to absconding, forming groups and taking action through the courts. These approaches met with increasing 'benevolence' on the part of colonial elites, in some instances because they firmly believed in freedom and/or the virtues of the free market, while others were responding to political pressure from Paris and London. The India Office and officials in India were doubtless inclined to protect Indian immigrants on Reunion Island not only for humanitarian reasons but also to guarantee a labour force for British employers in India.

Market trends strongly affected conditions for immigrants. The steady fall in the price of sugar on international markets (from 39 pounds a ton in the early 1840s to 22 pounds in the early 1870s and down to a low of 9.60 pounds in 1896)[35] pushed small producers to impose harsh labour conditions, which led to massive worker absconding and resistance. As a result, in Reunion Island and Mauritius, many *petits blancs* sold their properties and moved to the highlands,[36] where they were joined by immigrants and former slaves who began buying land or, more often, cultivating it under new forms of renting.

Together with the declining price of sugar, the generally increasing supply of migrants influenced conditions on local and global labour markets. Between 1840 and 1940, 55–58 million Europeans, 2.5 million Africans and Asiatic reached the Americas; during this same period, other 29 million Indian, 19 million Chinese and 4 million Africans and Europeans moved to southeast Asia, the Pacific Islands and the Indian Ocean Rim. Finally, 46–51 million people from north-eastern Asia and Russia moved (or were compelled to move) to Siberia, Manchuria and Central Asia.[37] Many of these movements were coerced – especially those working for European enterprises – but many others also moved without physical coercion.[38] 'Free' migration expanded with the increasing restriction of indentured contracts, imperial dislocations, global economic dynamics and, in particular, the abolition of slavery in the USA.

35 Richard Allen, *Slaves, Freedmen and Indentured Laborers in Colonial Mauritius* (Cambridge University Press, 1999), p. 23.

36 CAOM (*Centre des archives d'outre-mer*, Aix-en-Provence) FM SG/Reu c 400 d 3688 and c 515 d 6005.

37 Adam Mckeown, *Melancholy Order: Asian Migration and the Globalization of Borders* (New York: Columbia University Press, 2008).

38 Frederick Cooper, *From Slaves to Squatters: Plantation Labor and Agriculture in Zanzibar and Coastal Kenya, 1890–1925* (New Haven and London: Yale University Press, 1980).

Abolition in the United States

As in England, US Quakers engaged in antislavery mainly because they were concerned by domestic problems of labour discipline. Yet, unlike England or France, in the USA a civil war was needed for the abolitionist movement to succeed. The origins of this war were far more political than purely economic. Whilst it is true that international tariff policies (protectionism versus free trade), the structure of the economy (agriculture vs. manufacture), monetary and fiscal policies (stability versus. inflation) and the availability of labour (needed by both the North and the South) were real points of disagreement between northern and southern states, the ultimate source of conflict was the equilibrium in the Congress between slave and free states.[39]

However, this conclusion does not explain, why, in the end, former slaves were granted so few rights. The strong heritage of slavery in post-abolition American society – often evoked in historiography – reflects only part of the story. Former slaves were not granted 'false freedom' but freedom as it was generally understood at that time for people such as servants, apprentices and children. In the USA a fundamental difference separated wage labour from indentured contracts. By 1800 wage work was different from its equivalent in England, at least for adult white native-born workers, in that penal sanctions had already been abolished; wage forfeiture was the most widespread remedy to enforce contracts. By contrast, criminal penalties were extremely important in the enforcement of indentured and seamen's contracts. With the abolition of slavery, criminal punishments were generalized to all former slaves. In agriculture, in particular in cotton fields, employers found it increasingly difficult to retain freedmen over an entire year.[40] The fixed-wage system with a year-long contract prevented a midseason reservoir of unemployed workers and contributed towards reducing the number of dismissals for neglect of work. On the contrary, it did not offer the planter enough control over seasonal variations of labour supply. Sharecropping was seen as the best solution to this problem. Under this system, supervision costs would be reduced and the supply of labour over the entire year could be ensured.

The issue was different in sugar areas. In Louisiana, planters sought to face limited credit and financial resources with long-term contracts for gangs of

39 David Brion Davis, *Challenging the Boundaries: Migration in African History* (Markham Press Fund, Baylor University Press, n.d.).

40 Ralph Shlomovitz, 'Bound or free? Black labor in cotton and sugar cane farming, 1865–1880', *Journal of Southern History* 50 (1984), 569–96.

workers and later, with the collapse of the sugar price in the 1870s, with increasing pressure on labour. Workers initially reacted with increasing mobility, which gave rise to an attempt to more strictly enforce the rules on criminal punishments. Another consequence was that small planters stopped processing the sugar themselves, with 'central stations' receiving the sugar from several units. Faced with this increasing pressure, workers reacted with collective action and strikes. Repression was severe, leading to concentration and mechanization.[41]

The global impact of American abolition

The international impact of American abolition was recently very firmly asserted.[42] The lack of cotton on the international markets led to increased production in various other areas such as Egypt, Russian Turkestan, India and Brazil. Yet the long-term impact on local forms of labour and economic growth depended on the one hand on the recovery of US production and on the other hand on local dynamics. By the end of Reconstruction in 1877, US production was approximately 25 per cent above 1860 levels, and exports were almost at the level of the total crop for 1860. Between 1877 and 1900, exports had more than doubled. At the same time, Russian imperialism in central Asia and the development of cotton fields in the Fergana valley were not only a reaction to the American Civil War, but a response to long-term (since the seventeenth century) Russian efforts to stabilize their south-eastern frontier while threatening British India.[43] Attention to cotton certainly increased in the 1860s, but it only really began to develop twenty years later as a combined result of Russian customs policy and railroad construction.[44]

Egypt was the second major area influenced by the collapse of American cotton production. Higher production levels were essentially achieved through increasing imports of slaves – in part Circassians from Russia and central Eurasia, in part from Africa. Imports from Africa jumped from about

41 Rebecca Scott, 'Defining the boundaries of freedom in the world of cane: Cuba, Brazil, and Louisiana after emancipation', *American Historical Review* 99/1 (1994), 70–102.

42 Sven Beckert, 'Emancipation and empire: reconstructing the worldwide web of cotton production in the age of the American Civil War', *American Historical Review* 109/5 (2004), 1405–1438; Sven Beckert, *Empire of Cotton: A Global History* (New York: Knopf, 2014).

43 Seymour Becker, *Russia's Protectorate in Central Asia, Bukhara and Khiva, 1865–1924* (London: Routledge, 2004).

44 Maria Rozhkova, *Ekonomicheskie sviazi Rossii so Srednei Aziei: 40–60gg XIX veka* [The economic links between Russia and Central Asia in the 40s-60s of the 19th century], (Moscow: Nauka, 1963).

5000 per year during the 1840s and the 1850s to about 30,000 per year in the 1870s, at which point they fell once again due to the recovery in the USA.[45]

India was the third area where abolition in the USA exerted a major impact. Immediately after the outbreak of the American Civil War, British producers increased their pressure in Indian cotton-producing areas where masters' and servants' rules were far more strongly enforced. At the same time, the rising price of cotton pushed Indian producers to increase their own production. The British were thus competing with the French to obtain the most cotton while at the same time trying to divert it from the Indian internal market. In millions of pounds, Indian exports of cotton grew from approximately 346 in 1860 to 806 in 1866. This was not a temporary boom, as unlike the conventional history of Indian deindustrialization, recent works show that Indian demand supported local production throughout the nineteenth century and in particular from the 1870s onwards.[46]

In Brazil, imports of slaves had increased during the nineteenth century, in particular after the British and US abolition of the slave trade. The peak was reached in the 1830s when the number of slaves in Brazil was about 2.5 million. More active policies were only adopted in 1850, with the major decline in imports of slaves. With high mortality, the lack of women and the high rate of manumission, the number of slaves decreased to 1.5 million in the 1850s to 750,000 at the eve of abolition in 1886. The slave society of Brazil was also particular in that although they were of African descent, numerous men and women shed their slave status. In the early nineteenth century this accounted for 12.5 per cent of the Brazilian population, similar to Spanish America at that time but very different from southern USA where it barely reached 4.5 per cent. In Brazil, the sugar industry was not based as much on huge plantations as was the case in the Caribbean, and mining and urban slavery also played a prominent role (unlike in the USA). Slave ownership thus rested on a very broad social base and the abolition of trade did not halt the internal market: between 1850 and 1880, a buoyant internal market persisted for slaves.[47] An abolitionist movement won attention in the 1860s, by echoing the politics of the USA. Yet as in the other cases mentioned above, continuities in social conditions were as important as official abolition. Since the 1870s, many slaves had already signed official contracts of labour, selling,

45 Lovejoy, *Transformations*, p. 149.

46 Thirtankar Roy, *Traditional Industry in the Economy of Colonial India* (Cambridge University Press, 1999).

47 Robert Conrad, *The Destruction of Brazilian Slavery, 1850–1888* (Berkeley, CA: University of California Press, 1972).

etc. while after 1888, the criminal punishment and harsh treatment of now free slaves were common practice.[48]

To sum up, the second half of the nineteenth century was not solely a 'global march towards freedom'. Not only in Brazil, Egypt and India, but also in Russia, expansion was supported by various forms of legal constraint on working people. This analysis is all the more problematic because, on a wider scale, these transformations interacted with the collapse of the Ottoman Empire and the scramble for Africa.

Last stages? The abolition of slavery in Africa and the Ottoman Empire

In the Ottoman Empire, military, domestic and sexual slaves were added to rural and urban slaves, who were in turn hard to distinguish from other forms of coercion, such as that practised on serfs or convicts. There was a continuum of various degrees of servitude rather than a dichotomy between 'slave' and 'free'. Slaves could be public or private and they were imported from Africa, central and southern Asia and the near east, not to mention Christian captives in the Mediterranean. Imports were important not so much because of the high rate of mortality but because of the high rate of manumission.

Abolitionism started when British public opinion and the British government took interest in the abolition of slavery in the Ottoman Empire. This was in the 1840s; geopolitical considerations linked to the decadence and fragmentation of the Ottoman Empire intervened with the usual humanitarian consideration to pump up British pressure. Pressure started with the prohibition of the slave trade in the Persian Gulf and in Africa in 1857. It increased with the emigration of Circassians from Russia to the Ottoman Empire, notably Egypt and Turkey as a consequence of the Crimean war. Britain seized this occasion to warn Ottoman authorities to stop this trade. From this perspective, the Crimean war marked a huge break in both diplomatic equilibria and the global labour market. The war incited the abolition of serfdom in Russia whilst encouraging European powers to exert pressure on Istanbul to abolish slavery. However, despite the Conventions signed with Egypt in 1877 and the Porte in 1880, British pressures significantly reduced the slave trade but had little effect on domestic

48 Katia de Queirós Mattoso, *To be a Slave in Brazil, 1550–1888* (New Brunswick, NJ: Rutgers University Press, 1987).

practices.[49] There was also considerable abolition impetus within the Ottoman Empire; yet despite their interest in 'modernization', they opposed any external Western influence. As a consequence, Britain ultimately adopted a cautious attitude towards slavery in Turkey. British pressure was much more effective in Egypt, where anti-slavery movements against Islam converged with the overall movement for the 'abolition of slavery' in Africa.

Between the 1890s and World War I, European powers decreed the abolition of slavery in Africa. Indeed, Europeans justified their occupation of Africa by the argument that it was necessary to abolish the slavery which still existed in these regions. Public opinion and administrative rulers in Europe stressed the 'barbarian' and backward attitude of African elites willing to enslave other Africans and called for a 'civilizing mission' by the West.[50] This action was intended to have two principal phases: firstly, 'slaves' had to be freed and the slave trade stopped; secondly, an appropriate labour market had to be established. However, on the ground, these ambitions encountered more pragmatic attitudes. British officials sought to avoid confrontation with Islamic authorities; concubinage was left intact and Islamic customary law was evoked to justify this attitude. Indeed, colonial policy was to refuse to implement immediate abolition for fear of a quick collapse of local societies and maybe even of European control.[51] The colonial state was therefore supposed to intervene to ease the transition to free labour and to maintain discipline. Officials believed that Africa's development required Africans not being allowed to work when, where and how they chose. In both French and British Africa, there was a campaign against vagrancy, theft, drinking and personal violence. Colonial intentions must not however be taken to be achievements. African slave owners and slaves practised emancipation in a manner which the British (or French) did not necessarily approve. Instead of becoming 'capitalists', 'landowners', 'proletarians' (as the British hoped in Kenya and Tanzania) or 'peasants' (as the French wished), most Africans worked as 'peasant-workers' moving back and forth between their own plots and plantations or urban activities.[52]

These policies took different shapes in different parts of Africa. Important differences existed between colonial policies in the British

49 Toledano, *Slavery and Abolition*.

50 Frederick Cooper, 'From free labour to family allowances: labour and African society in colonial discourse', *American Ethnologist* 16/4 (1989), 745–765.

51 Paul Lovejoy and Jan Hogendown, *Slow Death of Slavery: The Course of Abolition in Northern Nigeria, 1897–1936* (Cambridge University Press, 1993).

52 Cooper, *From Slaves*.

territories of Kenya and Zanzibar, which were in turn different from the legislation in the Cape, mostly influenced by labour in the mines. Gold Coast legislation, on the other hand, attempted to closely follow the evolution of labour law in Britain and therefore sought to make breach of contract a civil rather than criminal offence. None of these policies was implemented in Nigeria and Sierra Leone. There were prosecutions under these laws but there was little uniformity across British Africa. For example, employers and employees in Nigeria and Sierra Leone appear to have made very little use of the legislation.[53] Indeed, the rate of prosecution was much higher in the mines, not only in South Africa and Rhodesia, but also in the Gold Coast.[54]

Analogous differences existed in French Africa.[55] In 1887, the code of 'indigenous people' provided criminal sanctions and repressed vagrancy. Obligatory labour was the rule in both private and public companies and plantations.[56] At the same time, 'obligatory labour' was carefully distinguished from slavery; to some extent it was even presented as a way of escaping it. Limitation of freedom in the name of freedom was a constant refrain which was not considered to be a contradiction in terms. So-called *prestations* were legalized in 1912 but they had been in use since the end of the nineteenth century. Local inhabitants were compelled to work to pay their taxes, to work off their sentences or as a form of military conscription. Governors pressured Africans to produce certain crops for export and to work for concessionary companies especially in AEF. In turn, local concessionaires and planters could apply to receive part of this workforce. French attitudes were much more brutal in central Africa (AEF) than in western Africa (AOF). The reasons for this were complex: lack of control, thin population and greater reliance on concession companies. There were also huge differences within regions. In Senegal numerous slaves were found and redeemed by kin; people often moved far away.

As result of this, the three main options open to former slaves (emigrate, stay nearby under new ties with local communities, or stay with their former

53 *Blue Book of Sierra Leone: Years 1905–1914* (London: Government Printing Office, 1915).

54 Giles Hunt to Colonial Secretary, 30 May 1909, Enc. 5 in Governor Rodger to Lord Crewe, 30 Oct. 1909, TNA (The National Archives, Kew), CO 96/486.

55 Alice Conklin, *A Mission to Civilize: the Republican Idea of Empire in France and West Africa, 1895–1930* (Stanford University Press, 1997); Ann Laura and Frederick Cooper, eds., *Tensions of Empire: Colonial Cultures in a Bourgeois World* (Berkeley, CA: University of California Press, 1997).

56 Babacar Fall, *Le travail forcé en Afrique Occidentale Française 1900–1946* (Paris: Karthala, 1993); Suzanne Miers and Richard Roberts, eds., *The End of Slavery in Africa* (Madison, WI: University of Wisconsin Press, 1988).

masters) took on varying proportions and forms in different areas. Spontaneous long-distance movement was always discouraged by colonial authorities for political stability in both Africa and Europe, but they were important in British Nigeria and French Sudan not to forget immigration to South African mines. New settlements were widespread in Senegal (coconut farmers) and in some areas of Guinea.

Resurgence and persistence of slavery in the twentieth century

The 'march towards freedom' which seemed to be an irreversible achievement at the turn of the twentieth century would not be confirmed. On the contrary, during World War I, requisition, militarization of labour and obligatory labour were practised on a massive scale in Europe and even more so in its colonies.[57] The heritage of World War I was important: in Europe, German and Soviet leaders took inspiration from their experiences during World War I (and in the Russian Civil War), to develop new forms of coercion. At the end of World War II, the two powers employed about 30 million forced labourers: over 23.5 million by Soviet Russia and about 7.7 million by Nazi Germany. Of this number, over 2 million were in concentration camps. Furthermore, over 5 million were Russians, with 2.8 million put to work by the Nazis as prisoners of war and conscripted labourers.[58] The Soviet Gulag main aim was political: every real or presumed opponent to the Soviet regime was imprisoned in the camps: peasants hostile to collectivization, small entrepreneurs and traders, specialists, political activists and, ultimately, gypsies and Jewish and 'ethnical minorities'.[59] The profitability of the gulag is more difficult to evaluate: like many Western scholars, some Soviet leaders seemed to justify the use of forced labour in remote semi-deserted areas where any other kind of 'voluntary' labour would have been more expensive. Yet the camps proved to be extremely inefficient; they caused huge destruction of resources and human capital. It was not by chance

57 Peter Gatrell, *Russia's First World War: A Social and Economic History* (London: Pearson Education, 2005); Christopher Fischer, *Civilians in a World at War* (New York University Press, 2010).

58 Ulrich Herbert, *Hitler's Foreign Workers* (Cambridge University Press, 1997); Edwin Bacon, *The Gulag at War: Stalin's Forced Labor System in the Light of the Archives* (New York University Press, 1994); Paul Gregory and Valery Lazarev, eds., *The Economics of Forced Labor: The Soviet Gulag* (Stanford: Hoover Institution Press, 2003).

59 Oleg Khlevniuk, *History of the Gulag: From Collectivization to the Great Terror* (New Haven: Yale University Press, 2004).

that the best economic performances related to the practice of leasing workers to outside employers.[60]

During the same period, international organizations made their first attempts to fight slavery outside of Europe (1926: League of Nations' Convention) and, more generally, forced labour (1930: Convention of the International Labour Organization (ILO)). The 1926 Convention widened the definition of slavery and marked the beginning of the attack on a wide range of exploitative practices. Yet it was difficult to enforce, partly because of the ambiguity of some formulations, partly because many states, such as France, opposed practices of monitoring as infringements of national sovereignty.[61]

After World War II, while forced labour was banned in Europe, it was also abolished in the declining French Empire, due to the presence of African members of parliament in the *Assemblee Nationale Constituante* in 1946. A strong international consensus was reached that forced labour was both identifiable and unacceptable. The ILO tried to argue that social legislation for Europe should apply to colonies – i.e. that labour was a universal social issue. However, this motion was strongly denied in both Britain and France. Liberation in one sense – sovereignty – provided a screen behind which practices agreed in international circles to be unacceptable reappeared, with the connivance of European and American corporations.

Quarrels over slavery were embedded in the broader tensions and framework of the Cold War. Thus in Saudi Arabia, the British complained that because of the increasing involvement of the USA with regard to oil, slavery persisted to a large extent. The French confirmed the importance of the trans-Saharan slave trade to Saudi Arabia. By 1962, slavery had become a political issue in Saudi Arabia itself; twenty Saudi princes involved in an abortive coup fled to Egypt, where they denounced slavery, thus fuelling Nasser's campaign against the Saudi royal family. After the new coup in 1963, the new Saudi regime declared the official abolition of slavery. Yet charges that slavery still existed in Saudi Arabia continued into the 1980s.

Forms of welfare were introduced in Africa, but the discrepancy between European legal and economic categories and labour practices in Africa made it difficult to implement these rules.[62] Even worse, most of these rules were preserved in postcolonial Africa and have contributed to legitimizing abuse. Multinational firms and new states such as Ivory Coast evoked formal labour

60 Anne Applebaum, *Gulag: A History* (New York: Random House, 2003).

61 Suzanne Miers, *Slavery in the Twentieth Century* (Walnut Creek and Oxford: Altamira Press, 2003).

62 Frederick Cooper, *Decolonization and African Society* (Cambridge University Press, 1996).

rules to deny any accusation of practising slavery. Quite ironically, these arguments were the same as those used by people who, at the opposite end of the political and intellectual spectrum, criticized the categories and rules derived from the West as a form of neo-colonialism. These orientations ignored the fact that European colonial powers had supported this argument as early as the nineteenth century.

Further reading

Allen, Richard. *Slaves, Freedmen and Indentured Laborers in Colonial Mauritius*. Cambridge University Press, 1999.

Bacon, Edwin. *The Gulag at War: Stalin's Forced Labor System in the Light of the Archives*. New York: New York University Press, 1994.

Beckert, Sven. *Empire of Cotton: A Global History*. New York: Knopf, 2014.

Blackburn, Robin. *The Overthrow of Colonial Slavery, 1776–1848*. London: Verso, 1988.

Brass, Tom and Marcel van der Linden, eds. *Free and Unfree Labour: The Debate Continues*. Bern: Peter Lang, 1997.

Campbell Gwyn, ed. *The Structure of Slavery in the Indian Ocean, Africa and Asia*. London: Frank Cass, 2004.

Campbell, Cameron and James Lee. 'Free and unfree labour in Qing China: emigration and escape among the bannermen of northeast China, 1789–1909', *History of the Family* 6 (2001), 455–476

Carter, Marina. *Servants, Sirdars and Settlers: Indians in Mauritius, 1834–1874*. Oxford University Press, 1995.

Clarence-Smith, William Gervase, ed. *The Economics of the Indian Ocean Slave Trade*. London: Frank Cass, 1989.

Conrad, Robert. *The Destruction of Brazilian Slavery, 1850–1888*. Berkeley, CA: University of California Press, 1972.

Cooper, Frederick. *From Slaves to Squatters: Plantation Labor and Agriculture in Zanzibar and Coastal Kenya, 1890–1925*. New Haven and London: Yale University Press, 1980.

Davis, David Brion. *Challenging the Boundaries of Slavery*. Cambridge, MA: Harvard University Press, 2003.

The Problem of Slavery in the Age of Revolution. Oxford University Press, 1999.

de Queirós Mattoso, Kátia. *To Be a Slave in Brazil, 1550–1888*. New Brunswick, NJ: Rutgers University Press, 1987.

Dennison, Tracy. *The Institutions of Russian Serfdom*. Cambridge University Press, 2011.

Drescher, Seymour. *Abolitions: A History of Slavery and Antislavery*. Cambridge University Press, 2009.

Drescher, Seymour and Stanley Engerman, eds. *A Historical Guide to World Slavery*. Oxford University Press, 1998.

Eltis, David. *Economic Growth and the Ending of Transatlantic Slave Trade*. Oxford University Press, 1989.

Coerced and Free Migration: Global Perspectives. Stanford University Press, 2002.

Engerman, Stanley, ed. *Terms of Labour: Slavery, Serfdom and Free Labour*. Stanford University Press, 1999.

Espada Lima, Enrique. 'Freedom, precariousness, and the law: freed persons contracting out their labour in nineteenth-century Brazil', *International Review of Social History* 54/3 (2009), 391–416.

Fall, Babacar. *Le travail forcé en Afrique Occidentale Française 1900–1946*. Paris: Karthala, 1993.

Fogel, Robert. *Without Consent or Contract: the Rise and Fall of American Slavery*. New York: Norton, 1994.

Gregory, Paul and Valery Lazarev, eds. *The Economics of Forced Labor: The Soviet Gulag*. Stanford: Hoover Institution Press, 2003.

Hansson, Anders. *Chinese Outcast: Discrimination and Emancipation in Late Imperial China*. Leiden: Brill, 1996.

Herbert, Ulrich. *Hitler's Foreign Workers*. Cambridge University Press, 1997.

Hoch, Steven. *Serfdom and Social Control in Russia: Petrovskoe, a Village in Tambov*. University of Chicago Press, 1986.

Holt, Thomas. *The Problem of Freedom: Race, Labour and Politics in Jamaica and Britain, 1832–1938*. Baltimore and London: The Johns Hopkins University Press, 1992.

Kolchin, Peter. *Unfree Labor: American Slavery and Russian Serfdom*. Cambridge, MA: Belknap, 1987.

Kumar, Dharma. *Land and Caste in South India*. New Delhi: Manohar, 1992.

Lovejoy, Paul. *Transformations in Slavery*. Cambridge University Press, 2002.

Lovejoy, Paul and Jan Hogendown. *Slow Death of Slavery: The Course of Abolition in Northern Nigeria, 1897–1936*. Cambridge University Press, 1993.

Maestri, Edmund, ed. *Esclavage et abolition dans l' Océan Indien, 1723–1869*. Paris: L'Harmattan, 2002.

Meillassoux, Claude. *Anthropologie de l'esclavage*. Paris: PUF, 1986.

Miers, Suzanne. *Slavery in the Twentieth Century*. Walnut Creek and Oxford: Altamira Press, 2003.

Miers, Suzanne and Richard Roberts, eds. *The End of Slavery in Africa*. Madison: University of Wisconsin Press, 1988.

Miller, Joseph Calder. *Slavery and Slaving in World History: A Bibliography, 1900–1996*. Armonk, New York: M.E. Sharpe, 1999.

Northrup, David. *Indentured Labour in the Age of Imperialism, 1834–1922*. Cambridge University Press, 1995.

Patterson, Orlando. *Slavery and Social Death: A Comparative Study*. Cambridge University Press, 1982.

Prakash, Gyan. *Bonded Histories: Genealogies of Labour Servitude in Colonial India*. Cambridge University Press, 1990.

Reid, Anthony. *Slavery, Bondage, and Dependency in South-East Asia*. London: MacMillan, 1984.

Renault, François. *Libération d'esclaves et nouvelle servitude: les rachats de captifs africains pour le compte des colonies françaises après l'abolition de l'esclavage*. Abidjan, 1976.

Roy, Thirtankar. *Traditional Industry in the Economy of Colonial India*. Cambridge University Press, 1999.

Scarr, Derrick. *Slaving and Slavery in the Indian Ocean*. London and New York: Macmillan, 1998.

Scott, Rebecca. 'Defining the boundaries of freedom in the world of cane: Cuba, Brazil, and Louisiana after emancipation', *American Historical Review* 99/1 (Feb., 1994), 70–102.

Scott, Rebecca, Thomas Holt, Frederick Cooper and Aims McGuinness. *Societies After Slavery: A Selected Annotated Bibliography of Printed Sources on Cuba, Brazil, British Colonial Africa, South Africa and the British West India*. University of Pittsburgh Press, 2004.

Shlomovitz, Ralph. 'Bound or free? Black labor in cotton and sugar cane farming, 1865–1880', *Journal of Southern History* 50 (1984), 569–96.

Stanziani, Alessandro. 'Free labour-forced labour: an uncertain boundary? The circulation of economic ideas between Russia and Europe from the 18th to the mid-19th century', *Kritikaa: Explorations in Russian and Eurasian History* 9/1 (2008), 1–27.

'Local bondage in global economies: servants, wage-earners, and indentured migrants in nineteenth-century France, Great Britain and the Mascarene Islands', *Modern Asian Studies* 1 (2013), 1–34.

'Serfs, slaves, or wage earners? The legal status of labour in Russia from a comparative perspective, from the 16th to the 19th century,' *Journal of Global History* 3/2 (2008), 183–202.

'The traveling panopticon: labor institutions and labor practices in Russia and Britain in eighteenth and nineteenth centuries', *Comparative Studies in Society and History* 51/4 (2009), 715–741.

ed. *Labour, Coercion and Growth in Eurasia, 17th-20th Centuries*. Leiden: Brill, 2012.

Steinfeld, Robert. *The Invention of Free Labour: The Employment Relation in English and American Law and Culture, 1350–1870*. Chapel Hill: University of North Carolina Press, 1991.

Tinker, Hugh. *A New System of Slavery: The Export of Indian Labour Overseas, 1830–1920*. London: Hansib, 1974.

Toledano, Ehud. *Slavery and Abolition in the Ottoman Middle East*. University of Washington Press, 1997.

Turner, Mary. 'The British Caribbean, 1823–1838: the transition from slave to free legal status', in Douglas Hay and Paul Craven (eds.), *Masters, Servants and Magistrates in Britain and the Empire, 1562–1955*. Chapel Hill and London: The University of North Carolina Press, 2004, pp. 303–322.

Ward, J. R. *British West India Slavery, 1750–1834: The Process of Amelioration*. Oxford University Press, 1988.

PART II

★

CULTURE AND CONNECTIONS

6

Department stores and the commodification of culture: artful marketing in a globalizing world

ANTONIA FINNANE

Around the middle of the eighteenth century, a time that in China was marked by a general social conservatism, the scholar–painter Zheng Banqiao (1693–1765) caused a stir in the lower Yangtze city of Yangzhou by attaching a price list for his paintings on the door of his residence. Zheng, a retired official, belonged to a stratum of Chinese society where painting was a polite activity, not a commercial one. In presenting a social peer with a painted scroll, a scholar should do so as if it were a gift; and if he accepted remuneration for his brushwork, it should be after the fashion that Anthony Trollope prescribed for a physician in English society: "without letting his left hand know what his right hand was doing." A well-placed client did not wish to know very clearly that the painting of bamboo had just been handed cost two taels of silver.[1]

Except perhaps for the names, this scenario will be familiar to students of art history in the West. The seventeenth-century printmaker Abraham Bosse (1604–1676) captured the juxtaposition of the scholar–painter and the artisan painter in China almost perfectly when he depicted the "vulgar artist" forced by circumstance to work for his living alongside the dignified painter of the French court.[2] Social status was plainly at issue in both cases, but so was the status of art itself. The commercialization of painting was by then already well advanced: in the Dutch Republic, even a shoemaker was likely to have paintings hanging on his walls.[3] That fact hardly softened the jarring effect of conjoining art and commerce.

1 Ginger Cheng-chi Hsü, *A Bushel of Pearls: Painting for Sale in Eighteenth-Century Yangchow* (Stanford University Press, 2001), pp. 146–147.

2 Svetlana Alpers, *Rembrandt's Enterprise* (University of Chicago Press, 1988), p. 91.

3 Jan De Vries, *The Industrious Revolution: Consumer Behavior and the Household Economy, 1650 to the Present* (Cambridge University Press, 2008), p. 54.

Underway in both East and West was a process that has become known as the commodification of culture, a term that is used descriptively and often also critically to denote the shift of cultural products from the realms of ritual and relationships to the market place. Evident in the small-scale commercial practices of artists, shopkeepers and customers active in the markets of early modern towns, this process became a phenomenon of some scale during the nineteenth century.

Central to the process were department stores, unknown in the lifetimes of Bosse and Zheng. Like microcosms of the overseas empires that proliferated in this same century, these mega-stores, with their many separate yet linked component sectors, made available to their customers paintings and music along with apparel, furnishings, and the more obvious material requirements of middle-class daily life. In the USA, writes Neil Harris, they "challenged the monopoly of the new museums in the display of art and costly manufactured arts and objects."[4] As the most obvious site of commodity accumulation in this period, with manifestations in numerous parts of the world, they were characteristic institutions of that in-between century, 1850–1950. They provide a good vantage point from which to view the merging of market and culture. How general was the process? How uniform? How complete?

Department stores

Shops, and particularly department stores, have been much studied by historians in recent years, usually in national contexts and often with a focus on individual stores. Over time, they have provided the foundations for debates in a variety of historical areas, including comparative economics, gender, and architecture. In Paris between the wars, Walter Benjamin spent hundreds of hours taking notes about them. From the boutique came the magasin, he observed, and from the arcade came the department store, where (in the course of the nineteenth century) art and literature "entered the market as commodities."[5]

As with many other aspects of modern consumer culture, precedents can be found in the early modern era. In the Netherlands, England, and France, retail outlets for handicrafts proliferated in the century leading up to 1750.[6]

4 Neil Harris, *Cultural Excursions: Marketing Appetites and Cultural Tastes in Modern America* (The University of Chicago Press, 1990), p. 65.

5 Walter Benjamin, *The Arcades Project* (Cambridge, MA: Harvard University Press, 1999), Exposé of 1935, p. 13.

6 De Vries, *The Industrious Revolution*, p. 69.

Thread, cloth, notions, and ready-to-wear items were major items in the burgeoning retail trade, but bookshops also abounded, and so did shops dealing in artworks. Ann Bermingham captured the temper of that age when she depicted Antoine Watteau as a young man, churning out religious images for merchants from the provinces.[7]

From the wealth of studies on consumer society in early modern Europe it would be easy to imagine that the flourishing material and commercial culture that gave rise to the Industrial Revolution was unparalleled in the world, and of course it had its distinctive aspects. But it is worth taking a brief look at the other side of the world, for in East Asia we find counterparts to the shops of Europe in this period. In a rare attempt at a comparative treatment of shops in early modern Europe and China, Robert Batchelor has suggested that Chinese shops were rather temporary structures compared to those emerging in, say, London in the seventeenth century.[8] That comparison probably holds true only for the lower end of Chinese retail. Shops in the prosperous cities of seventeenth to eighteenth-century China were well integrated into the material fabric of the city, probably approximating at least something like shops in Antwerp.[9] In the early 1800s, Henry Ellis was impressed by the shops of Wuhu, in Jiangsu, which he thought "would not disgrace the Strand or Oxford."[10]

In shopping, as in some other respects, there was a "great divergence" between China and Europe in the nineteenth century.[11] That shop styles were changing rapidly in London and Paris at this time can be deduced from John Thomson's (1837–1921) description of shops in China around 1870: "A granite base . . . supports the upright sign-board, which, *as with us in former days*, is the indispensable characteristic of every shop in China"[12] (emphasis added).

7 Ann Bermingham, 'Introduction – the consumption of culture: image, object, text," in Ann Bermingham and John Brewer (eds.), *The Consumption of Culture, 1600–1800: Image, Object, Text* (London: Routledge, 1997), p. 2.

8 Robert Batchelor, "On the birth of consumer society as interactions of exchange networks, 1600–1750," in John Brewer and Frank Trentmann (eds.), *Consuming Cultures, Global Perspectives, Historical Trajectories* (London: Berg, 2006), pp. 95–122.

9 Xu Min, "Wan Ming chengzhen shangye de kongqian fazhan – yi dianpuye wei zhishi" (The unprecedented growth of urban commerce in the late Ming: shops as an indicator), *Zhongguo jinggjishi luntan saojiao* (Selections from the China economic history forum) (May 2006). http://economy.guoxue.com/article.php/8569 (accessed 11 February 2008); Wallace Chang Ping Hung, "The city so prosperous: episodes of urban life in Suzhou," *Journal of Architecture* 5 (Autumn 2000), 267–291.

10 Henry Ellis, *Journal of the Proceedings of the Late Embassy to China* (London: Edward Moxon, 1840), pp. 44, 78.

11 Phrase adapted from Kenneth Pomeranz, *The Great Divergence: China, Europe, and the Making of the Modern World Economy* (Princeton University Press, 2001).

12 John Thomson, *Through China with A Camera* (London: Harper & Bros, 1899), p. 68.

In fact, while Thomson was in China, developments in retail back in Europe were taking shopping in new directions that via a circuitous route would soon be evident in China as well. In the second half of the nineteenth century and the first half of the twentieth, great department stores were built in one major city after another around the world. Macy's in New York, Whiteley's in London and Bon Marché in Paris were among the earliest examples, but these are only the most famous. Between the 1840s, when departmentalized prototypes were developing on both sides of the Atlantic, and the 1880s, when the first department stores began to appear in the British colonies, a large number of these emporia were created. The stages of development through which they typically passed render precise dates of opening difficult to determine, and a clear historical sequence of stores almost impossible to establish.[13]

Department stores retain great appeal as icons of consumer culture, especially historically. They stimulated and satisfied the appetites of people in industrial societies – those people, at least, who profited most from the changes being wrought by the Industrial Revolution. Quintessentially bourgeois institutions in the nineteenth century, they expanded to accommodate a post-bourgeois urban mass in the twentieth. In this way they prefigured the premier sites of mass consumption of a later period, the shopping malls, those later "cathedrals of consumption" into which they were either transformed or incorporated.

Their origins lay in dry-goods stores – draperies and haberdasheries – although in the USA the relationship with the warehouse was also close, a fact reflected in architectural features.[14] These origins remained evident in the clothing departments that dominated the fully fledged department stores of later times. In places such as Cairo or Shanghai, the stock of ready-to-wear apparel in a department store was much smaller, but the fabrics department likely to be extensive.[15] In all cases, these stores catered specifically, although not exclusively, for female customers, recognizing women's spending capacity and offering them a relatively sheltered environment for shopping. Propriety was

13 Michael B. Miller, *The Bon Marché: Bourgeois Culture and the Department Store, 1869–1920* (Princeton University Press, 1981); Harry E. Resseguie, "Alexander Turney Stewart and the development of the department store, 1823–1876," *Business History Review* 39/3 (Autumn, 1965), 30; For a table of early stores and dates of founding, see Douglas J. Goodman and Mirelle Cohen, *Consumer Culture: A Reference Handbook* (Santa Barbara: ABC-CLIO, 2004), p. 14, Table 1.3.

14 Sigfried Giedion, *Time, Space, and Architecture* (Cambridge, MA: Harvard University Press, 1967), p. 238.

15 Nancy Reynolds, *A City Consumed: Urban Commerce, the Cairo Fire, and the Politics of Decolonization in Egypt* (Stanford University Press, 2012), p. 59.

important to retaining the custom of women from the moneyed classes. For Bon Marché, "virtue was a trademark."[16]

The term "department store" itself, general in the Anglophone world and evident in phonetic appropriations in some other languages, is of US origin, as were many generic features of these stores internationally. Germany's early department stores, opened around the turn of the century by the Teitz brothers, were created "in conscious imitation of the American model."[17] So too were the railway *depāto* that sprang up in Japan in the late twenties and thirties.[18] The founders of Almacenes El Siglo ("Century Stores") in Barcelona were introduced to American retailing methods in Cuba then traveled to New York and Chicago to learn more.[19] In New Zealand, where British and Australian models were paramount up until World War II, there was a decided shift towards the American model thereafter.[20]

Yet in the early history of department stores, as the New Zealand example suggests, North American models were not always the most obvious. In fact, the term "department store" lacks general applicability for the nineteenth century. It was introduced to Britain only in 1909, when the American Harry Gordon Selfridge, after a quarter of a century's employment with Marshall Field and Co. in Chicago, set up Selfridge's Department Store in London.[21] (Figure 6.1) In Britain a more familiar expression was "universal providers," a term with religious connotations ("He Who provides all") that was applied first and most famously to William Whiteley's store in West London, developed from a haberdashery opened by Whiteley in 1863.[22] From London, the term spread through the British world, turning up in Cape Town in application to Mr. J. Oarlick's emporium[23] and in Sydney, where Anthony Hordern's was the self-proclaimed "largest and most popular Universal Providers in the Southern Hemisphere."[24] In 1885 the Scottish firm Muir and Mirrielees

16 Miller, *Bon Marché*, p. 220.

17 Donal L. Niewyk, *The Jews in Weimar Germany* (New Brunswick: Transaction Publishers, 2001), p.13.

18 Brian Moeran, "The birth of the Japanese department store," in Kerrie McPherson (ed.), *Asian Department Stores* (Richmond: Curzon Press, 1998), p. 163.

19 Jesus Cruz, *The Rise of Middle-Class Culture in Nineteenth-Century Spain* (Baton Rouge: Louisiana State University Press, 2011), p. 127.

20 Evian Roberts, "'Don't sell things: sell effects': overseas influences in New Zealand department stores, 1909–1956," *Business History Review* 77/2 (Summer 2003), 266–267.

21 Lindy Woodhead, *Shopping, Seduction, and Mr Selfridge* (London: Profile Books, 2007), p. 2.

22 Erika Rappaport, *Shopping for Pleasure: Women in the Making of London's West End* (Princeton University Press, 2001), p. 27.

23 James Salter-Whiter, *A Trip to South Africa* (London: W. Pile, 1892), p. 63.

24 *Sydney Morning Herald*, March 7, 1885, p. 17.

Figure 6.1 Confectionery section in Selfridges department store, early twentieth century
(Private Collection / © Look and Learn / Peter Jackson Collection / Bridgeman Images)

opened a "Universal'nyi magazin" in Moscow.[25] Otherwise the term basically followed the routes of the British empire. From Sydney it traveled to Hong Kong, Canton, and Shanghai, where, beginning in 1901, Chinese Australian entrepreneurs one after the other set up "universal providers" – the famous Sincere, Wing On, Sun Sun, and Dah Sun companies, inspired by Anthony Hordern's.[26] These stores were in British-dominated parts of the empire-turned-republic: the colony of Hong Kong; Shamien in Guangzhou, and the International (non-French, non-Japanese) Settlement in Shanghai.

Another great imperial route was carved out by France, using a combination of hard and soft power. In the Middle East, French and British spheres of influence overlapped, so that in Alexandria and Cairo, stores with names such as Davies Bryan and Roberts, Hughes & Co. sat virtually alongside *grands magasins* such as Cicurel and Orosdi-Back. But French cultural influence was paramount. Not only were many of the local department stores owned by Francophone families; branches of French department Stores – Bon Marché,

25 Marjorie L. Hilton, *Selling to the Masses: Retailing in Russia, 1880–1930* (University of Pittsburgh Press, 2012), p. 22.

26 Wellington K. Chan, "Personal styles, cultural values, and management: the Sincere and Wing On Companies in Shanghai and Hong Kong, 1900 –1941," in McPherson (ed.), *Asian Department Stores*, pp. 66–89; John Fitzgerald, *Big White Lie: Chinese Australians in White Australia* (Sydney: UNSW Press, 2007), pp. 190–199.

Printemps, Galeries Lafayettes, Louvre – were also established there.[27] Likewise in Turkey, elite culture was to all intents and purposes French culture, and the grandest of the many Western department stores in Istanbul was the EOB (Etablissements Orosdi-Back).[28] On the other side of the world, in Brazil, French merchants had dominated high-end commerce from the 1820s. Rio fashions followed "the Parisian timetable," and the burgeoning department stores of the 1870s, bearing names such as Notre Dame de Paris, carried only imports.[29] In Argentina, the British presence was strong enough for Harrod's to establish a branch of its famous store in Buenos Aires in 1910, but Italian and French cultural influence predominated.[30]

Lesser empires, too, can be tracked through international commercial routes in which department stores stand like milestones. In Berlin in 1903, Bruno Antelmann constructed the orientalist-inspired German Colonial House, described by Jeff Bowersox as "a sort of department store for goods from Germany's colonies."[31] The very first German department store had been built eighteen years earlier, in Vladivostok, one of a chain created by the firm Kunst and Albers, merchants of Hamburg active in the Far East. By 1903, this firm had expanded into China and was busy developing a store in Dalian (Port Arthur), within easy reach by sea of Germany's Chinese colony, Qingdao. Their efforts here were stymied by imperial expansion on the part of the Japanese, who defeated Russia in a short, sharp war in 1905 and began their inexorable move into north China.[32] Where the Japanese army went, department stores followed, springing up across the face of the Japanese empire and becoming established features of life in Korea, Taiwan, and Manchukuo, as also in Japan itself (Figure 6.2). Mitsukoshi, Japan's premier department store, had branches in the colonies.[33]

27 Reynolds, *City Consumed*, p. 56.

28 Yavuz Köse, "Vertical bazaars of modernity: western department stores and their staff in Istanbul (1889–1921)," in Touraj Atabaki and Gavin Brockett (eds.), *Ottoman and Republican Turkish Labour History. International Review of Social History*, Vol. 17, Supplement. (Cambridge University Press, 2009), p. 97.

29 Jeffrey D. Needell, *A Tropical Belle Epoque: Elite Culture and Society in Turn-of-the-century Rio de Janeiro* (Cambridge University Press, 1987), p. 288, n.20.

30 Matthew Brown, "Introduction," in Mathew Brown (ed.), *Informal Empire in Latin America: Culture, Commerce and Capital* (New York: John Wiley and Sons, 2009), p.12.

31 Jeff Bowersox, *Raising Germans in the Age of Empire: Youth and Colonial Culture, 1871–1914* (Oxford University Press, 2013), p. 90.

32 Lothar Deeg, *Kunst and Albers Vladivostok: The History of a German Trading Company in the Russian Far East, 1864–1924*, Sarah Bohnet trans. (Berlin: epubli, 2013).

33 Sang Chul Choi, "Moves into the Korean market by global retailers and the response of local retailers: lessons for the Japanese retail sector?"' in Sang Chul Choi, John Dawson, Roy Larke and Masao Mukoyama (eds.), *The Internationalisation of Retailing in Asia* (London: Routledge Curzon, 2003), pp. 49–66, here p. 51.

Figure 6.2 Interior of a modern department store in Tokyo, Japan, *c.*1895–1900 (Private Collection / The Stapleton Collection / Bridgeman Images)

To draw attention to these imperial formations as the context for department stores is not to exclude the USA from the early chapter in the story, because American entrepreneurial might and influence, too, was exercised in a world of empire-building.[34] Nonetheless, it was after the zenith of European maritime empires that the USA came into its own in this domain, emerging as the obvious model of business practice in respect of department stores among other institutions. From this perspective, it seems entirely appropriate that the "universal providers" of the English-speaking world should one by one have ceased to be known as such, becoming instead "department stores" in name as well as in internal organization. Between the wars, the universal embrace of empire was after all gradually relaxing. The empires would break up. In the compartmentalized world of nation-states, the idea of a "department store," whatever the route by which it attained hegemony, was perhaps more meaningful than "universal providers."

As products of empire, department stores of the nineteenth and early twentieth centuries positioned themselves, in Nancy Reynolds' words, as

34 Mona Domosh, *American Commodities in an Age of Empire* (New York: Taylor and Francis, 2006), pp. 11–12.

"cultural primers for a certain cosmopolitan modernity."[35] Reynolds was writing of Cairo, but the statement holds true for most places. The department store was a place where the customer met the world. While a store such as Whiteaway Laidlaw was designed to bring British products to the colonies, back in London the Liberty emporium owed its great commercial success to Indian and Chinese arts and crafts.[36] It was desirable that within the confines of a department store, the customer should encounter a world of goods, not merely a selection of local products. In Korea, it was the Japanese store, with its metropolitan sophistication, that was heavily patronized by its colonial subjects, not the provincial Korean stores.[37]

The obverse of empire and cosmopolitanism was colony and nationalism. Overall, little is known about stores in the colonial world, but in India and sub-Saharan Africa they were largely non-indigenous. In Ghana, or the Gold Coast as it was then known, the Kingsway Department Store was set up in 1920 to help Europeans live in the style to which they were accustomed back home.[38] The same was presumably true of S. Jacobs Co. in Nairobi, the largest store in East Africa, established by Sammy and Gertie Jacobs in 1906.[39] In Kitwe, Northern Rhodesia, Sid Diamond ran "the finest department store in central Africa," an entity with the prosaic name of Standard Trading.[40] In India, prominent department stores included Whiteaway Laidlaw (which had branches also in East Africa and China), Evans Fraser, and Hall & Anderson.[41] It is possible that such stores were patronized mainly by the colonial elites, but the assumption would need testing case by case. In Shanghai in the 1910s, Whiteaway Laidlaw was regularly advertising in the main Chinese-language daily, *Shenbao*, from which it can be assumed that it was dependent on Chinese customers for its profit margin. In Accra on the eve of independence, Kingsway's customer base was at least half local.[42]

35 Reynolds, *A City Consumed*, p. 76.
36 Saloni Mathur, *India by Design: Colonial India and Cultural Display* (Berkeley, CA: University of California Press, 2007), p. 42.
37 Kataryna J. Cwiertka, "Dining out in the land of desire: colonial Seoul and the Korean culture of consumption," in Laura Kendall (ed.), *Consuming Korean Tradition in Early and Late Modernity: Commodification, Tourism, Performance* (Honolulu: University of Hawai'i Press, 2011), pp. 29–31.
38 Bianca Murillo, "'The modern shopping experience': Kingsway Department Stores and consumer politics in Ghana," *Africa* 82/3 (August 2012), 372.
39 John Spencer, *KAU* (London: Taylor and Francis, 1985), p. 296.
40 Hugh Macmillan, *An African Trading Empire: The Story of the Susman Brothers and Wulfsuhn, 1901–2005* (London: I.B.Tauris, 2005), p. 304.
41 Ranjani Mazumdar, *Bombay Cinema: An Archive of the City* (University of Minnesota Press, 2007), p. 223.
42 Murillo, "'The modern shopping experience,'" p. 372.

In the early decades of the twentieth century, the cultural character of commodities traded by stores in the colonial world came under scrutiny and national products campaigns broke out like spot fires. The "Grand Emporium of Swadeshi Goods" in Grey Street, Calcutta, trumpeting its vast range of locally made goods to patriotic customers in 1905 set the tone for probably the most famous of campaigns, a hallmark of the Indian independence movement.[43] The big British department stores all fell prey to campaigns of opposition to foreign-made goods during the Quit India movement, and none survived Indian independence.[44] In Cairo in the 1930s, the French department stores closed down, one after the other, in the face of an energetic national products campaign.[45] In China there were boycotts of foreign goods sporadically from 1905 and with growing intensity in the twenties and thirties, especially in the context of the Japanese advance in the years leading up to the Pacific War.[46] More clearly than the actual inventories of stores, such campaigns expose the meanings invested in material goods within the framework of modern world retail practices.

The commodification of art

National sensitivities concerning the origins of commodities indicate one important sense in which culture became caught up in the process of exchange in department stores. What constituted this "culture"? Pondering the question in the middle of the twentieth century, Raymond Williams concluded that culture was a work in progress that took shape and became a named phenomenon during, and as a reaction to, the Industrial Revolution. He traced it etymologically, from its origins as meaning "tending natural growth" through different stages of development leading up to its application to "the general body of the arts" (a still familiar definition). The end of his journey brought him to broad and encompassing domain: culture as "a whole way of life, material, intellectual, and spiritual."[47] Had he looked across space as well as through time, he would have observed culture's

43 Arun Chaudhuri, *Indian Advertising, 1780–1950 A.D.* (New Delhi: Tata McGraw Hill Publishing Company, 2007), p. 157.

44 Ranjani Mazumdar, *Bombay Cinema: An Archive of the City* (University of Minnesota Press, 2007), p. 223.

45 Reynolds, *A City Consumed*, pp. 92–93.

46 Karl Gerth, *China Made: Consumer Culture and the Creation of the Nation* (Cambridge, MA: Harvard University Asia Centre, 2003).

47 Raymond Williams, *Culture and Society, 1780–1950* (Harmondsworth: Penguin Books, 1958), p. 16.

dissemination in different linguistic forms (*Kultur, cultura, kültür*, and so on) across Europe and into Asia. In East Asia, the late nineteenth-century Japanese neologism *bunka* (culture) made its way into Chinese, Korean, and Vietnamese (*wenhua, munhwa, văn hóa*). These etymological networks were linked to the rise of nationalism and the plethora of nation-state projects in the nineteenth and twentieth centuries, and indeed nationalism affected the idea of culture more closely than Williams allowed.

For critics of the commodification of culture, however, culture meant the creative arts, or "high" culture. It is by no means easy to disentangle literature, painting, and music from a "whole way of life," especially if these art forms are used to express and defend that way of life. Yet a view of the arts as constituting culture was general in the nineteenth century and through much of the twentieth. The arts had an unrivalled place in the value system of educated elites, for whom they were gradually coming to replace religion as a way of understanding the world. To see them reduced to the status of commodities could be as painful to the beholder as seeing money-changers in the temple of God.

As the opening paragraphs of this chapter indicate, the process of commodification of the arts has a long history. Theodore Adorno traced the "system of 'merchandising' culture" to around 1700, in England, and the beginning there "of an approach to literary production that consciously created, conserved and finally controlled a 'market.'"[48] From this market emerged what he called the culture industry, a blighted thing characterized by repetitiveness, self-sameness, and ubiquity. In this bleak indictment of the culture of his times, Adorno was not alone. Writing on the eve of World War II, Clement Greenberg described mass culture as a sort of virulent disease that was rampaging through the world "wiping out folk culture," and "defacing native cultures," to a point where (he prophetically remarked) it was fast becoming "the first universal culture ever beheld."[49]

Department stores (for Adorno "cemeteries of culture"[50]) became caught up in this process most obviously by including artworks for display and sale alongside household goods. Bon Marché's second floor, with its reading

48 Theodor Adorno, "How to look at television," in Adorno, *The Culture Industry* (London: Routledge, 2001), p. 160.

49 Clement Greenberg, "Avant-garde and kitsch (1939)," in Sally Everett (ed.), *Art Theory and Criticism: An Anthology of Formalist, Avant-Garde, Contextualist and Post-Modernist Thought* (Jefferson: McFarland, 1995), p. 33.

50 Andreas Huyssen, "Adorno in reverse: from Hollywood to Richard Wagner," in J. M. Bernstein (ed.), *The Frankfurt School: Critical Assessments* (London: Routledge, 1994), p. 94.

room and picture gallery, set the tone, providing a space for customers to take respite from the ardors of shopping. The two rooms were eventually merged, writes Michael Miller, to form a salon "conceived in the grand style of a Louvre Museum gallery."[51] Such an environment was felt to be "improving," as economist M. N. Sobolev later remarked. Sobolev listed art exhibitions, concerts, and reading rooms as among the benefits middle-class Muscovians could derive from visiting Muir & Mirrielees.[52] In Japan, department stores typically included an art department, used both for the exhibition and for sale of paintings and other national artworks.[53] This was undertaken in fulfillment of what now would be called corporate social responsibility: it was part of a store's duty to educate the public.[54] A comparable spirit of social responsibility can be detected in the undertakings of American retailers. In Chicago, for example, Marshall Fields sponsored local art through holding a yearly exhibition of Hoosier paintings (paintings made in the nearby state of Indiana), beginning in 1925.[55]

These new spaces for the exhibition and sale of art became available during a general shift in the structure of the art market. In France in the second half of the nineteenth century, the once all-powerful Salon was losing ground to private galleries and dealers; in Germany, art associations proliferated in a move towards professionalization; in China, particularly Shanghai, overt commercialization of painting followed by the first public exhibitions pointed to the same end. In the USA, paintings were being put to auction, creating a new benchmark in the commercialization of fine art.[56] The department stores were entering into a market that might not have been wide open, but was open enough for their purposes.

The agency of department stores in the commodification of the creative arts was to some degree shaped by the same national, and occasionally nationalist, circumstances that gave rise to national products campaigns. Thus the Cairo branch of Bon Marché advertised its local loyalties by

51 Miller, Bon Marché, p. 168.

52 Marjorie L. Hilton, *Selling to the Masses: Retailing in Russia, 1880–1930* (University of Pittsburgh Press, 2012), p. 123.

53 Ellen P. Conant, *Challenging the Past and the Present: The Metamorphosis of Nineteenth-Century Japanese Art* (Honolulu: University of Hawai'i Press, 2006), p. 13.

54 Millie Creighton, "Something more: Japanese department stores' marketing of a meaningful life," in McPherson (ed.), *Asian Department Stores* (Richmond: Curzon Press, 1998), p. 210.

55 Jan Whitaker, *Service and Style: How the American Department Store Fashioned the Middle Class* (New York: St. Martin's Press, 2006), p. 147.

56 Walter Adamson, *Embattled Avant-Gardes: Modernism's Resistance to Commodity Culture in Europe* (Berkeley, CA: University of California Press, 2007), p. 55; Kirsten Swinth, *Painting Professionals: Women Artists and the Development of Modern American Art, 1870–1930* (Durham: University of North Carolina Press, 2001), p. 99.

exhibiting the pottery made by the female students in a nationalist vocational school.[57] In Sydney, the art departments of Hordern's and Farmers department stores promoted Australian painting in particular, this in an era when recognition of a distinctive local painting tradition was growing.[58] With nationalism intensifying worldwide from the 1890s onward, apart from a brief respite in the 1920s, this evidence of patriotic partisanship in the arts is to be expected.[59] Through the display and sale of local art, the department stores achieved commercial exposure for national art products, and simultaneously underscored their own national character.

Although department stores are often compared to museums in scholarly literature, the standing of their art departments is generally not high. Jan Whitaker draws attention to some progressive undertakings in the USA, including Gimbels' travelling exhibition of cubists in 1913 and Hearn's "Art Created by Women" in the 1930s.[60] In Chicago, beginning in 1925, Marshal Field promoted local art through an annual exhibition of Hoosier paintings.[61] But these were unusual undertakings. The art collection of Alexander Turney Stewart, owner of the famous Marble Palace and Great Iron Store in Manhattan, consisted of sentimental middle-brow works with names such as *An Eastern Princess, The Little Lamb*, and *The First Smoke*.[62] The collection was auctioned after Stewart's death and failed by a considerable margin to realize expectations. The paintings hung in Bon Marché were probably very similar, to judge from a comment by Emile Zola.[63] In Sydney, Charles Lloyd Jones, who had studied painting in London, used his position as heir to David Jones department store to support a journal called *Art in Australia*. His own tastes in art were conservative, and so was the journal.[64]

In fact, it was not simply or even primarily by playing the role of art gallery that the department store became engaged with the arts. Rather, bearing out Adorno's insistence on the thorough interpenetration of commerce and the arts in the twentieth century, stores became structurally integrated into the arts world in multiple aspects of their institutional existence, including

57 Reynolds, *A City Consumed*, p. 56.
58 Heather Johnson, *The Sydney Art Patronage System 1890–1940* (Marrickville: Bungoona Technologies, 1997), pp. 86–95.
59 Mathur, *India by Design*, p. 42.
60 Jan Whitaker, *Service and Style: How the American Department Store Fashioned the Middle Class* (New York: St. Martins Press, 2006), p. 147.
61 Whitaker, *Service and Style*, p. 147.
62 *Catalogue of the A. T. Stewart Collection Of Paintings, Sculptures, and Other Objects of Art to be Sold by Auction* (New York: American Art Association, 1887), pp. vii–ix.
63 Miller, *Bon Marché*, p.168. 64 Johnson, *The Sydney Art Patronage System*, pp. 97–9, 117.

architecture, window-dressing, personnel (including management), the actual stock in a store, and of course their customers, their critical audience. Taken one by one, these features are not peculiar to the times. Advertising, the display of goods, the social ambitions of merchants expressed through patronage of the arts, grandiose shop-fronts, the wedding of aesthetics and function in everyday objects – these features can all be identified in prosperous urban societies of earlier centuries. Present in regular combination in buildings of scale at numerous sites across the world, however, they present as a specific historical phenomenon produced by economic growth and technological change during the "in-between" century.

Technological advances in the second half of the nineteenth century, especially the harnessing of electricity, underpinned the department store in its material aspects. They also affected art forms. Photography in particular marked a striking expansion of the domain of the conventional, flat, framed image. In a now widely read essay, Walter Benjamin commented on the effects of reproducibility on the "aura" of a work of art, which he saw as a process of decay caused by the desire of the masses to assimilate the work as reproduction, but inevitably leading to a democratization of art ownership.[65] Although this prediction was not quite borne out, technological changes in printing and image making had other effects. Specifically, they served to transform large areas of work and production in industrializing societies. There was resistance to its effects.[66] The same William Morris whose designs and creations were being sold at Marshall Field's denounced the uses to which the "wonderful machines" of the present age had been put, creating a system "that has trampled down Art, and exalted Commerce into a sacred system."[67] But on Morris's own premises of art "by and for the people," a meaningful art, others embraced the machine age and worked to reconcile art and industry. The machines and the reaction to them combined to effect the rise and recognition of the decorative arts in precisely the decades in which department stores were emerging as a noted feature of cityscapes. The decorative arts, in which art and function were fused, found in the department store a natural home.

65 Walter Benjamin, "The work of art in the age of its technological reproducibility," in Walter Benjamin, *The Work of Art in The Age of Its Technological Reproducibility, and Other Writings on the Media*, Edmund Jephcott, trans. (Cambridge, MA: Belknap Press, 2008), pp. 19–55.

66 Angela Davis, *Art and Work: A Social History of Labour in the Canadian Graphic Arts* (Montreal: McGill-Queen's University Press, 1995), p. 21.

67 William Morris, *Art and Socialism* (Whitefish: Kessinger Publications, 2004), p. 3.

Architectural innovation in the construction and internal organization of stores was among the more obvious ways in which art met function. By and large the architecture of department store buildings was conservative. The multi-story Renaissance-style buildings built to house the department stores in Japan were not untypical of global styles, "monumental expression[s] of commercial prestige" in the word of Henry-Russell Hitchcock.[68] In Japan, and also in China, these examples of European classical architecture were seen as emblematic of civilization and progress. In the West, they were "vaguely historicizing" rather than modern, and imposing without being challenging.[69] They might be compared to the paintings exhibited in the galleries of the various museums, designed to maximize the customer's feelings of comfort. Yet a combination of advances in engineering and design vision did produce some strikingly innovative buildings. Among these were Alexander Turney Stewart's "Great Iron Store," with its internal iron framework and cast-iron facades, Marshall Field's building of 1907 (a "superb example of the new Chicago School"), and Frantz Jourdain's innovative if controversial design for the Samaritaine department store on the River Seine.[70]

The impact of such buildings on streetscapes and urban development can hardly be overstated. Writing in 1908, Leo Colz remarked on their effect in Berlin, which was to transform the city into "a major metropolis, a world class city."[71] In New York, Stewart's Great Iron Store, demolished in 1956, occupied an entire block along Broadway between 9th and 10th Streets. Its construction in 1862 spurred the commercial development of the quarter, with other retailers following in Stewart's wake. The largely residential area north of 10th Street was gradually turned over into a retail and entertainment.[72] The same phenomenon was evident elsewhere. In Shanghai, the Sincere and Wing On

68 Quoted in Helle B. Bertramsen, "Remoulding commercial space: municipal improvements and the department store in Manchester," in John Benson and Laura Ugolini (eds.), *A Nation of Shopkeepers: Five Centuries of British Retailing* (London: I.B. Tauris, 2003), p. 218.

69 Richard Longstreth, *The American Store Transformed, 1920–1960* (New Haven: Yale University Press, 2010), p. 38.

70 Joan Marten, ed., *The Grove Encyclopedia of American Art* (Oxford University Press, 2007), p. 566; William Lancaster, *The Department Store: A Social History* (Leicester University Press, 1995), p. 66; Anthony Sutcliffe, "Architecture, planning and design," in Nicholas Hewitt (ed.), *Cambridge Companion to Modern French Culture* (Cambridge University Press, 2003), p. 62.

71 Lauren Kogod, "The display window as educator: the German Werkbund and cultural economy," in Peggy Deamer (ed.), *Architecture and Capitalism, 1845 to the Present* (New York: Routledge, 2013), p. 52.

72 Mona Domosh, "Creating New York's nineteenth-century retail district," in Keith Eggener (ed.), *American Architectural History: A Contemporary Reader* (New York: Routledge, 2004), p. 213.

Figure 6.3 Nanjing Road in Shanghai, 1934
(© Bettmann/CORBIS)

buildings were built in 1917 and 1918 amidst a host of inconsiderable small shops and eating places. After this, writes Wellington Chan, "Nanjing Road took off"[73] (Figure 6.3).

A significant site of artistic work in the department store was the display window, which the spread of department stores through cities made a major feature of urban design everywhere. In the 1920s, Ye Qianyu captured its visual impact in a cartoon depicting a scene in Nanjing Road: a modern miss and a migrant worker stand juxtaposed against the brilliantly lit window of Sincere department store, Western mannequin looming behind the plate glass. Ye may not himself have been a window dresser, but he had started his working life in a shop in Nanjing Road in 1921 and within a few years was busy organizing what he claimed was Shanghai's first fashion parade, held in

73 Wellington K. Chan, "Selling goods and promoting a new commercial culture: the four premier department stores on Nanjing Road, 1917–1937," in Sherman Cochran (ed.), *Inventing Nanjing Road: Commercial Culture in Shanghai, 1900–1945* (Ithaca: East Asia Program, Cornell University, 1999), p. 30.

Whiteaway Laidlaw, where he was employed.[74] Destined to become one of most famous graphic designers and cartoonists in China, he was not untypical of twentieth-century artists internationally in respect of his close association with the retail sector. James Narramore identifies a long list of notable arts figures in the USA who had at some time dressed a shop window: Vincent Minnelli, Man Ray, Salvador Dali, and Andy Warhol among others.[75] In Japan, Yu Ryūtanji must have been drawing on a similar occupational history when he made an artist turned window dresser the protagonist in his prize-winning novel, *A Vagabond Era*.[76]

The art of window dressing is often described as originating in North America in the late nineteenth century, and specifically with L. Frank Baum's spectacular efforts in Chicago in the 1890s.[77] The fact that an American visitor to Europe could be struck by the wonderful window displays before this date points to a distinction between the artful display and the merely sumptuous one.[78] In great European cities such as London, Paris, and Brussels the use of plate glass windows for seductive displays of goods was already well known in the eighteenth century, and increasingly obvious in the nineteenth. Attention to display even in the absence of plate glass must have been more widespread again. Melchior Yvan was struck by display of goods by Chinese retailers in the early nineteenth century. "In no country, not even Paris," he wrote, "have people ever invented such ingenious means of puffing goods by exhibiting them, and of *speaking to the eyes*."[79] L. Frank Baum served notice, then, of the arrival of a phenomenon not utterly novel in its material components but rather one that was historically distinctive in its assemblage. Stewart Culver describes the window display in Baum's hands as "a distinctly new medium of artistic expression, one characterized by a unique tension between commercial and aesthetic interests" and one capable, moreover, of transforming pedestrians on the city streets into "an audience of absorbed spectators."[80]

74 Antonia Finnane, *Changing Clothes in China: Fashion, History, Nation* (New York: Columbia University Press, 2008), p. 131.

75 James Naremore, *The Films of Vincente Minnelli* (Cambridge University Press, 1993), p. 14.

76 Joan E. Ericson, *Hayashi Fumiko and Modern Japanese Women's Literature* (Honolulu: University of Hawai'i Press), p. 66.

77 Lancaster, *The Department Store*, p. 64.

78 Elizabeth Biddell Yarnall, *Addison Hutton: Quaker Architect, 1834–1916* (Associated University Press, 1974), p. 56.

79 Melchior Yvan, 1858. *Inside Canton* (London: Henry Vizetelly, 1958), p. 55.

80 Stewart Culver, "What manikins want: the wonderful Wizard of Oz and the art of decorating dry goods," *Representations* 21 (Winter, 1988), p. 106.

Baum's influence in Chicago in the 1890s has been described as a factor in the disintegration of the distinction between art and commerce.[81] That distinction did indeed seem to be dissolving through the early decades of the twentieth century. In Wilhelmine Berlin, department store display windows became the site of struggles between commerce and religion, between art as individual expression and art for society, between Romanticism and modern style.[82] In Amsterdam, Joseph de Leeuw made the Metz and Co. store central to the establishment of an industrial arts ("Art Deco") aesthetic in the Netherlands through the employment of artists and designers for the production of store wares and household goods.[83] Personnel in this store were key contributors to *de Stijl* (Style), the arts journal that constituted the Netherlands' most influential contribution to Modernism.[84] In Paris, Art Deco was spectacularly displayed in a great exhibition in 1925, when leading department stores competed with architectural firms for the public's attention in an international show meant to show consumption in a contemporary context.[85] In New York in 1928, Macy's followed suit with an international exhibition of modern furnishings. Significantly, Robert W. De Forest, President of the Metropolitan Museum of Art in New York, was invited to write the foreword to the exhibition.[86]

Macy's exhibition was among the more obvious signs of how the globalization of art deco and modernist aesthetics was effected in the 1920s. The visual effects internationally were not overwhelming but nearly everywhere apparent. A certain "look" was evident in print media, furniture designs, fashion, and fine arts in urban societies worldwide. In Japan in the 1920s, followers of Muroyama Takahashi's Mavo movement, strongly influenced by the Bauhaus School, engaged intensively in commercial art, working in advertising, department stores, and the popular press and striving to

81 Bill Lancaster, *The Department Store: A Social History* (London: Leicester University Press, 1995), p. 64.

82 Kogod, "The display window as educator."

83 Tim Benton, Charlotte Beaton, and Ghislaine Wood, eds., *Art Deco, 1910–1939*, Ex. Cat (London: V&A, 2003), p. 187; Jan Middendorp, *Dutch Type* (Rotterdam: OIO Publishers, 2004), pp. 79–80; Michael White, *De Stijl and Dutch Modernism* (Manchester University Press, 2003), p. 99.

84 Marijke Kuper, ed., *Gerritt Th. Rietveld: The Complete Works* (Utrecht: Centraal Museum, 1992), p. 145.

85 N. J. Troy, *Modernism and the Decorative Arts in France: Art Nouveau to Le Corbusier* (New Haven and London: Yale University Press, 1991), chapter four, "Reconstructing Art Deco: purism, the department store, and the Exposition of 1925," pp. 159–266.

86 Robert De Forest, "Foreword," in *An International Exposition of Art in Industry From May 14 to May 26, 1928, At Macy's, Fourth Floor West Building, 34th Street and Broadway, N.Y.* (Exhibition Catalogue, New York Public Library), p. 5.

overcome the distance between art and everyday life.[87] Likewise in Brazil, art deco and Bauhaus influence was everywhere evident in the industrial fine arts.[88] With Paris and Berlin magnets for aspiring artists and writers from around the world, and London and New York exerting their own forms of cultural hegemony, it should be no surprise to find these commonalities in place.

The flows were by no means one-directional. The Netherlands Pavilion at the Paris Exhibition in 1925 showed the influence of an Indonesian (Dutch East Indies) aesthetic.[89] At the same exhibition, locally manufactured batik, again inspired by Indonesian arts, was on show in no fewer that twelve different pavilions.[90] French department stores were around this time selling turbans and Turkish-inspired harem pants that were worn by fashionable Chinese women on their world travels.[91] "Art deco," as Rosie Thomas writes, "was coming to connote modernity around the world. "[92] The part played by department stores in communicating this aesthetic was considerable: in their showrooms and behind the counters of stores everywhere were industrial products that combined function, line, and surface in a distinctive style that everyone came to recognize as belonging to that time.

Critiques and conclusions

The role of department stores in the world of the arts was not constant across time and space, but nearly everywhere they had the capacity of "*speaking to the eyes*." Looking at Accra with the eyes of a future President, Kwame Nkrumah sensed this: he wanted a department store in the main street of capital that would speak "modernity."[93] The leadership of the newly established People's Republic of China felt the same.[94] That these revolutionary leaders with their

87 See Gennifer Weisenfeld, *Mavo: Japanese Artists and the Avant-garde, 1905–1931* (Berkeley, CA: University of California Press, 1931), p. 70.

88 Daryle Williams, *Culture Wars in Brazil: The First Vargas Regime, 1930–1945* (Durham: Duke University Press, 2001), p. 48.

89 Dennis Sharp, ed., *Twentieth Century Architecture: A Visual History* (Mulgrave: Images Publishing, 2002), p. 79.

90 P.B., "Review of *Paris International Exhibition 1925: Report on the Industrial Arts* (Department of Overseas Trade)," *Journal of the Royal Society of Arts*, 75, 3894 (July 8, 1927), p. 835.

91 Hui-lan Oei Koo with Mary Van Rensselaer Thayer, *Hui-lan Koo: An Autobiography* (New York: Dial Press, 1943), p. 104.

92 Rosie Thomas, "Thieves of the Orient: the Arabian Nights in early Indian cinema," in Philip F. Kennedy and Marina Warner (eds.), *Scheherazade's Children: Global Encounters with the Arabian Nights* (New York: New York University Press, 2013), p. 376.

93 Murillo, "'The modern shopping experience,'" p. 372.

94 Guo Hongchi and Liu Fei, "New China's flagship emporium: the Beijing Wangfujing Department Store," in McPherson (ed.), *Asian Department Stores*, p. 116.

critical attitudes towards capitalism and imperialism should deem a department store necessary to the contemporary, international look of the capital was powerful testimony to its paradigmatic status in modern retail.

In the course of the second half of the twentieth century, however, the department store suffered a diminution in status. In the world's advanced economies, suburban sprawl sent the major retailers in pursuit of populations located far from city centers. New stores built to serve these populations were effectively lost to sight within vast shopping malls. Display windows, if evident at all, lost their discrete character and ceased to be artful. Art departments gradually disappeared from stores, and department stores from towns. The palatial buildings were sub-divided for lease to multiple tenants, or else demolished. This was not the fate of every one, of course, but it signified a major shift in the visibility and social roles of department stores. The prominent place they had occupied in the domain of the arts in the opening decades of the twentieth century was theirs no longer.

At the same time the art market was being reconfigured in ways that diversified and transformed the process of commodification with far-reaching effects. In 1981, when canvas painting was introduced to the Aboriginal community Balgo Hills, Western Australia, it was as an activity with religious meaning in a church community context. The initiative coincided with the emergence of a viable market for Aboriginal artworks at home and abroad. When the Warlayirti Art Centre was established in 1987, it was nicely positioned to reap the benefits of the international exposure of Aboriginal art at the Asia Society exhibition "Dreaming," held in New York in 1988 (Figure 6.4).[95] The creation of the World Wide Web subsequently allowed it to emerge as a tourist site with multiple connections to the outside world. Its website advertises a wide range of products for sale, ranging from paintings to objets d'art and souvenirs. The mail plane comes only once a week, but the Internet links the community to the world, and provides the means for money earned in post-industrial economies to be exchanged for works done by hand that are substantially about the relationship of the painters to the land.

Is this a relationship to which everyone has finally become accustomed? One of the earliest art journals to emerge in China after the Mao era was called *Art Market*. It was established by a group of art critics who wanted to put painting in China on an economic footing. Chinese art was "heading

95 Zohl Dé Ishtar, *Holding Yalwulyu: White Culture and Black Women's Law* (North Melbourne: Spinifex Press, 2006), pp. 213–214; Howard Morphy, "Aboriginal art in a global context," in Daniel Miller (ed.), *Worlds Apart: Modernity Through the Prism of the Local* (London: Routledge, 1995), pp. 215–218.

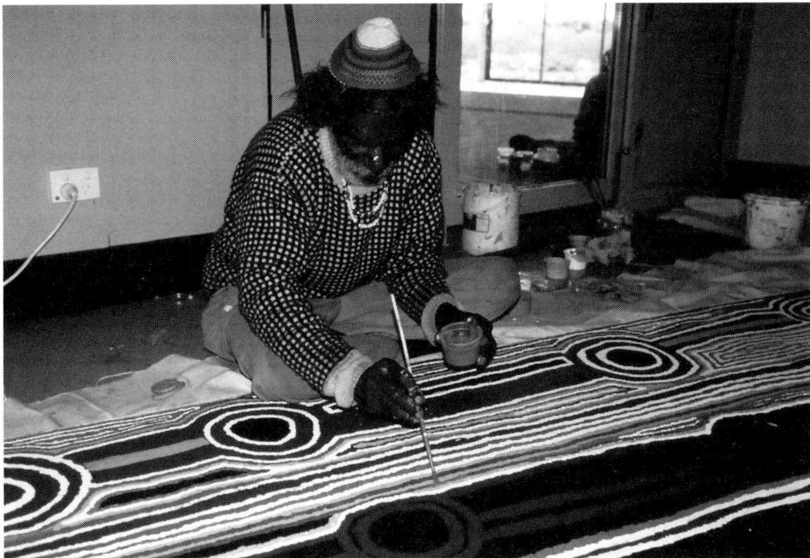

Figure 6.4 Balgo Community desert artist, the late Tjumpo Tjapanangka, working on a dot painting at the Warlayirti Culture Centre in the north-west desert region of Western Australia south of Halls Creek
(Werner Forman Archive / Bridgeman Images)

full-force toward the market," wrote painter Lü Peng in its pages. He defined "heading towards the market" very simply: "art ought to be produced for the purpose of sale."[96] This was a radical break indeed from the ideals of a revolutionary art for "the workers and peasants, soldiers, and petty urban bourgeoisie," enunciated by Mao in 1942,[97] and suggests a commonsensical approach to material life that Max Weber would have recognized. But it was not long before creating for the market revealed some problems. For Wang Nangming, Chinese artists abroad, "seeking to carve out a niche in order to survive within the order of the dominant culture," had been reduced to creating art projects that "are at best only on par with mass recreational activities in China's tourist industry . . . "[98]

96 Lü Peng, "Heading towards the market," in Wu Hung with Peggy Wang (eds.), *Contemporary Chinese Art: Primary Documents* (New York: MOMA, 2010), p. 290.
97 Mao Zedong, "Talks at the Yan'an Forum on literature and art," in Mao Zedong, *Selected Works* (Peking: Foreign Languages Press, 1965), pp. 250–286.
98 Wang Nanming, "The Shanghai Art Museum should not become a market stall in China for Western hegemony – a paper delivered at the 2000 Shanghai Biennale (2000)," in Wu Hung with Peggy Wang (eds.), *Contemporary Chinese Art: Primary Documents* (New York: MOMA, 2010), p. 353.

Here is a critique of the commodification of culture that would have been familiar to the ears of department store owners a century earlier, and even perhaps to Zheng Banqiao in an earlier time again. In these pages I have focused on a period of history during which the position of the fine and decorative arts in the market was profoundly affected by department stores, but it is mainly as an institutional history that the period can be said to be discrete. It is possible that a historian of the emotions, investigating attitudes to the relationship between art and commerce, would find continuities over a much longer period.

Further reading

Adamson, Walter. *Embattled Avant-Gardes: Modernism's Resistance to Commodity Culture in Europe*. Berkeley, CA: University of California Press, 2007.

Benjamin, Walter. *The Arcades Project*. Cambridge, MA: Harvard University Press, 1999.

"The work of art in the age of its technological reproducibility," in Walter Benjamin, *The Work of Art in The Age of Its Technological Reproducibility, and Other Writings on the Media*, Edmund Jephcott, trans. Cambridge, MA: Belknap Press, 2008, pp. 19–55.

Bermingham, Ann and John Brewer, eds. *The Consumption of Culture, 1600–1800: Image, Object, Text*. London: Routledge, 1997.

Benson, John and Laura Ugolini, eds. *A Nation of Shopkeepers: Five Centuries of British Retailing*. London: I.B. Tauris, 2003.

Brewer, John and Frank Trentmann, eds. *Consuming Cultures, Global Perspectives, Historical Trajectories*. London: Berg, 2006.

Chaudhuri, Arun. *Indian Advertising, 1780–1950 A.D.* New Delhi: Tata McGraw Hill Publishing Company, 2007.

Choi, Sang Chul, John Dawson, Roy Larke, and Masao Mukoyama, eds. *The Internationalisation of Retailing in Asia*, London: Routledge Curzon, 2003.

Cochran, Sherman, ed. *Inventing Nanjing Road: Commercial Culture in Shanghai, 1900–1945*. Ithaca: East Asia Program, Cornell University, 1999.

Culver, Stewart. "What manikins want: The Wonderful Wizard of Oz and the art of decorating dry goods," *Representations* 21 (Winter 1988), 97–116.

Deeg, Lothar. *Kunst and Albers Vladivostok: The History of a German Trading Company in the Russian Far East, 1864–1924*, Sarah Bohnet trans. Berlin: epubli, 2013.

Domosh, Mona. *American Commodities in an Age of Empire*. New York: Taylor and Francis, 2006.

Finnane, Antonia. *Changing Clothes in China: Fashion, History, Nation*. New York: Columbia University Press, 2008.

Gerth, Karl. *China Made: Consumer Culture and the Creation of the Nation*. Cambridge, MA: Harvard University Asia Centre, 2003.

Goodman, Dougles J. and Mirelle Cohen. *Consumer Culture: A Reference Handbook*. Santa Barbara: ABC-CLIO, 2004.

Harris, Neil. *Cultural Excursions: Marketing Appetites and Cultural Tastes in Modern America.* Chicago: The University of Chicago Press, 1990.
Hilton, Marjorie L. *Selling to the Masses: Retailing in Russia, 1880 – 1930.* University of Pittsburgh Press, 2012.
Kogod, Lauren. "The display window as educator: the German Werkbund and cultural economy," in Peggy Deamer (ed.), *Architecture and Capitalism, 1845 to the Present.* New York: Routledge, 2013, pp. 50–70
Köse, Yavuz. "Vertical bazaars of modernity: western department stores and their staff in Istanbul (1889–1921)," in Touraj Atabaki and Gavin Brockett (eds.), *Ottoman and Republican Turkish Labour History. International Review of Social History,* Vol. 17, Supplement. Cambridge University Press, 2009, pp. 91–114.
Lancaster, William. *The Department Store: A Social History.* Leicester University Press, 1995.
Longstreth, Richard. *The American Store Transformed,* 1920–1960. New Haven: Yale University Press, 2010.
Mathur, Saloni. *India by Design: Colonial India and Cultural Display.* Berkeley, CA: University of California Press, 2007.
MacPherson, Kerrie L., ed. *Asian Department Stores.* Honolulu: University of Hawaii Press, 1998.
Miller, Michael B. *The Bon Marché: Bourgeois Culture and the Department Store, 1869–1920.* Princeton University Press, 1981.
Murillo, Bianca. "'The modern shopping experience': Kingsway department stores and consumer politics in Ghana," *Africa* 82/3 (August 2012), 368–392.
Rappaport, Erika. *Shopping for Pleasure: Women in the Making of London's West End.* Princeton University Press, 2001.
Whitaker, Jan. *Service and Style: How the American Department Store Fashioned the Middle Class.* New York: St. Martin's Press, 2006.
The World of Department Stores. New York: Vendome Press, 2011.
Woodhead, Linda *Shopping, Seduction, and Mr Selfridge.* London: Profile Books, 2007.

7

Religion after 1750

PETER VAN DER VEER

The sacrality of the traditional state

In 1715 Pope Clement XI declared that Chinese Catholics were not allowed to conduct Confucian ritual or ancestral ritual.[1] Moreover, they should not use the Chinese term for Lord of Heaven to designate the Christian God. In 1721 the Chinese Emperor Kangxi banned Christian missions to China in response.[2] This ended a period during which in the sixteenth and seventeenth century the Jesuits had tried to accommodate their doctrine of God, the Lord of Heaven, with the Confucian worldview, for which (among other texts) we have Matteo Ricci's Tianzhu Shiyi (天主實義), "the substantial meaning of the Lord of Heaven," published in 1603.[3] The Confucian cosmology emphasizes Heaven (tian) as a metaphysical force that is impersonal and directs the universe and human society through its Mandate (tianming, 天命). This conception of a morally positive universe directed by the Mandate of Heaven had important ritual and political consequences: the emperor was the chief executor of the heavenly mandate in his ritual role as Son of Heaven. He was the performer of the great sacrifices to Heaven and Earth, the apex of a ritual-political system that integrated the Empire. This system was zheng 正, which one may translate as orthodoxy, but which is perhaps better translated with legitimate rule. Everything that was not in accordance with this political cosmology risked being xie 邪 (heterodox or illegitimate).

1 I want to thank Hartmut Lehmann for helpful comments on an earlier draft of this chapter.

2 David E. Mungello, ed., *The Chinese Rites Controversy: Its History and Meaning* (Nettetal: Steyler Verlag, 1994).

3 Matteo Ricci, *Tianzhu Shiyi* (Beijing 1603), translated, with introduction and notes, by Douglas Lancashire and Peter Hu Guozhen; edited by Edward J. Malatesta (Taipei: Institut Ricci, 1985).

At the level of the state Confucianism can be understood as a political cosmology. If one accepted this cosmology one could fill in personal spiritual needs with Buddhist devotion or Taoist magic or indeed by the Jesuit doctrine of the Lord of Heaven. This looks syncretistic and tolerant, but it is under the condition that one accepts the political cosmology. All this points at the important fact that if we compare Confucian China with Christian Europe in the eighteenth century we need to look at political formations, the politics of religion and certainly from the sixteenth century onwards at global interactions. It is the Catholic Counter-Reformation that is significant in China–Europe interactions, because of the presence of the Jesuits in China.

The Jesuits brought the latest products of Western science to China.[4] Certainly, they did think that the belief in Christ as the Savior was the true faith, but one of the most important issues was to introduce the Christian doctrine without emphasizing its difference, rather by emphasizing the extent to which it could be adopted within already existing cultural schemata. This Jesuit policy of accepting the imperial order in which they could give Christianity a place came under increasing pressure from other Catholic missionary orders, such as the Franciscans and Dominicans, in the early eighteenth century, which led to the Pope's condemnation of the Jesuit strategy. On the Chinese side one needs to remember here that the Qing rulers were Manchu "barbarians" and had adopted the Confucian cosmology in order to establish the legitimacy of their rule. Being outsiders they had to constantly show their orthodoxy in defending the Confucian political cosmology, while keeping their ethnic identity alive. In passing one might compare India and China and see how different the Qing strategy of adoption of Confucian political cosmology was from the Mughal strategy of keeping Islam as their faith while creating political alliances with Hindu rulers.

The confrontation between the Pope and the Emperor (both central in their respective cosmologies) led in 1721 to the banning of Christianity in China which lasted for a century. Civilizational superiority was not the issue in this dispute but power and the authority to determine ritual matters, as indeed it had been in Medieval Europe. Chinese intellectuals embraced the empirical science that the Jesuits informed them about, while Leibniz was inspired by Chinese ideas that were brought to Europe by the Jesuits.[5] The

4 Jonathan D. Spence, *The Memory Palace of Matteo Ricci* (New York: Viking, 1984).
5 David E. Mungello, *Leibniz and Confucianism: The Search for Accord* (Honolulu: The University Press of Hawaii, 1977).

issue was ritual power and thus a clash between the claim that the Emperor had the Mandate of Heaven as Son of Heaven and the claim that the Pope had the Mandate of Heaven as Primus Apostolus (the successor of Peter) and Vicarius Christi. The claims of the Pope were deeply politico-theological and disputed in the Reformation, which led to the wars of religion in early modern Europe. One of the ways to solve these conflicts was the emergence of a kind of territorial sovereignty that determined the state religion (cuius regio, eius religio). In China also any mobilization around heterodoxy (xiejiao, 邪教) could lead to rebellion against imperial authority and had thus to be repressed violently. In China these heterodoxies often took the form of millenarianism with a promise of an end to injustice, and the coming of a just polity, a Paradise on Earth with some Buddhist overtones, gesturing to the Maitreya, the Buddha who is to come to Earth at the end of time (at the end of the age of lawlessness).

In India there had been a similar confrontation between the Jesuits and the Pope, called the Malabar Rites Controversy. Here the so-called adaptationist method (accommodatio) of missionization was developed by the Jesuit Roberto de Nobili (1577–1656), the founder of the Madurai Mission. De Nobili adopted a Brahmanical way of life and attitude, thereby dissociating himself from the lower castes. While the Jesuits in China adapted to the ritual hierarchies of the Emperor, they adapted in India to Brahman priesthood and caste. These social discriminations were the subject of a conflict among Jesuits which ultimately led to a change in missionary policy.[6] Since this dispute did not involve a direct conflict with political authority it did not have the consequences that it had in China. Again, it was not so much civilizational superiority that was at issue here, but rather a strategic difference about how to approach a deeply hierarchical society with an egalitarian Christian message. India and China were not the only societies in which the Jesuits ran into difficulties, though. By the mid eighteenth century the Jesuit order was banned in most of the world, even in Latin America, where it had become a considerable economic and political power. Both in India and in China Christianity has remained marginal in proportion to the population. Political authority in China and caste authority in India have continued to be a challenge for Christian expansion. It was tribal Africa (as well as Melanesia and Oceania) from the end of the nineteenth century that was going to prove the most fertile ground for Christian

6 Ines Zupanov, *Disputed Mission: Jesuit Experiments and Brahmanical Knowledge in Seventeenth-Century India* (Oxford University Press, 1999).

(both Protestant and Catholic) conversion after the sixteenth- and seventeenth-century Christianization of Latin America.[7]

Eighteenth-century Hinduism was not connected to imperial authority as Confucianism was in China. Large parts of India were ruled by Muslim dynasties, foremost among which were the Mughals. The Mughals were challenged by Muslim Sultans in the South and East of India and by Hindu Maratha rulers in the West, while they had created alliances with Hindu rulers, primarily in the desert region of Rajasthan. Islamic (both Sunni and Shi'a) and Hindu rituals were part of the legitimation of these dynasties, but it would be anachronistic to speak of religion as the organizing principle of political power. Sanskrit and Persian were the languages of civilization, while Arabic was the language of the Quran, but those involved in administration would use several languages, including vernacular ones, such as Hindi (with Sanskrit script and vocabulary) and Urdu (with Persian script and vocabulary). Caste hierarchy was an important principle of societal organization, but it had a quite open and flexible relation to Hindu traditions of purity and purification. The Brahman caste had spread all over the subcontinent and was the guardian of traditions of law, ritual, and philosophy. Equally important were the devotional non-Brahmanical movements that swept large parts of the continent from the fifteenth century onwards. One of these movements, founded by Guru Nanak, in North India, called the Sikhs, became the basis of a politico-religious formation that challenged the Mughal empire in the eighteenth century and is still of political importance today.[8]

Muslim rulers in India and in the Ottoman Empire were under regular pressure from clergy to confirm to the fundamental tenets of Islam. The eighteenth-century Delhi-based preacher Shah Waliullah was probably the most important of those who called for a purist Islam.[9] In the same period Muhammad ibn Abd al-Wahhab (1703–1792), founder of the Salafi movement that has influenced Islamicists till today, argued along similar lines, but was able to consolidate his influence and that of his descendants by connecting to the emerging house of Saud, the dynasty that was going to rule Saudi Arabia (then still part of the Ottoman empire) and to be the

7 Jean and John Comaroff, *Of Revelation and Revolution*, Vol. I: *Christianity, Colonialism, and Consciousness in South Africa* (University of Chicago Press, 1991).

8 W. H. McLeod, *The Sikhs: History, Religion, and Society* (New York: Columbia University Press, 1989).

9 B. J. S. Baljon, *Religion and Thought of Shāh Walī Allāh Dihlawī, 1703–1762* (Leiden: Brill, 1986).

guardian of Mecca, the premier holy site of Islam. The criticism of these purists remained marginal till the twentieth century, however. Worship of Saints at Sufi shrines was universal in the eighteenth-century Islamic world (from Bosnia to Java) and that worship was open to participation for all and not restricted to Muslims.

Buddhism in the eighteenth century had hardly any remaining importance in the Indian subcontinent where it originated, but had been successfully exported to Tibet, Mongolia, China, Korea, and Japan as well as to Sri Lanka, Burma, Thailand, Cambodia, Laos, and Vietnam. In these societies it was always an important social and political force by way of its strong monastic organization, but variably connected to royal power. After having been a state religion in Korea, for instance, it was largely suppressed for many centuries till the twentieth century. In Beijing the Qing rulers gave patronage to Tibetan Buddhism, but in general kept Buddhist and Daoist orders under strict control.

Before the nineteenth century religion everywhere in the world was an integral part of statecraft. Surely, religion dealt with rites of passage, with agriculture, with health, with evil, and a range of other human concerns, but in all these cases it marshaled powers that had political salience. The legitimation of rulers came from heaven and was mediated by priestly and monastic classes. This is true in Christendom, but also in Islam, Hinduism, Buddhism, Confucianism, Shintoism, as well as for the tribal powers in Africa. The relation between worldly powers and religious authorities could range from forms of divine kingship as in China or Japan to the uneasy power struggles between state and church in Europe, but religion was central to state and society. It is the French (and American and Dutch) revolution at the end of the eighteenth century that signifies the change of the location of religion in Europe and North America. Similar changes happened in the rest of the world in the era of imperialism. Instead of kingship it is the sovereignty of the people that becomes the basis of the state. Nationalism is the ideology that enables the production of the people as a nation.

Religion in the modern nation-state

While nationalism is seen as modern, religion is commonly seen as either ancient or transcending history. In the common view of historians of ideas it is the European Enlightenment in its critique of religion that is the harbinger of modernity. The political expression of that critique was anti-clericalism in the French Revolution and laicite (secularism) in the French Republic. Anti-clericalism was also an important feature of nineteenth-century liberal politics in Latin America, where the Catholic Church wielded considerable power. Leading students of nationalism have argued that modern, national society is by definition secular and depends on the disappearance or marginalization of religious worldviews and communities.[10] Similarly, an important distinction is made between civic identity, based on citizenship in a territorially defined nation-state, and primordial identity, based on kinship or language or religion or a combination of these elements.[11] According to this view civic identity should replace primordial identity in modern nation-building. The historical process producing modernity by replacing religious identity with civic identity is called secularization.

Much sociological attention and imagination has gone into first the development of the secularization thesis and more recently in its dismantling.[12] The secularization thesis has three propositions, namely the decline of religious beliefs, the privatization of religion, and the differentiation of secular spheres and their emancipation from religion. The causality of these connected processes is to be found in modernization. In Europe one can certainly find ample evidence for one or the other of these propositions, but it is hardly possible to combine them in one convincing narrative of secularization let alone connect them to stages of political or economic modernization. While generally there is an unchurching in Europe that process is highly uneven, both geographically and historically. At the same time, Christian Democratic parties are still important in the politics of a number of European nation-states and, especially, the highly advanced political economies of Western Europe, as in Germany, the Netherlands, and Belgium. The process of unchurching that can be found in Europe in various stages, moreover, cannot be found in the USA, another highly advanced modern society. While the USA has had secular arrangements of the relation between church and state from the late eighteenth century, it does not show evidence of unchurching. Interestingly enough, it seems that the uncoupling of state and church in the USA has had a positive effect on the growth of churches. The narrative of decline of religion in the face of modernization does not fit the American case, while in Europe it is a much

10 Ernest Gellner, *Nations and Nationalism* (Ithaca: Cornell University Press, 1983).
11 Clifford Geertz, *The Interpretation of Cultures* (New York: Basic Books, 1973).
12 Jose Casanova, *Public Religions in the Modern World* (University of Chicago Press, 1994).

more diverse narrative that cannot be connected to modernization per se. In the rest of the world the secularization thesis makes even less sense.

Nationalizing religion

While one cannot today accept many of the assumptions implicit in modernization theory one can still argue that both nationalism and religion are modern transformations of pre-modern traditions and identities. Indeed, there are continuities and sometimes really deep histories. First of all, proto-nationalist formations in ethnicity, language, or religion provide the material of nationalism. National traditions can be "invented" and nations are "imagined," but this is not done from scratch. Moreover, they do not form a seamless whole, a monolithic culture, but rather a discourse in which different versions compete with each other in social debate and conflict. But, deeper than proto-nationalism that precedes nationalism, there are ancient understandings of linguistic, religious, and ethnic unity, coupled with notions of territorial sovereignty that can be found among the ancient Hebrews, Greeks, Indians, and Chinese, for instance. These ancient understandings of sacred geographies together with sacred histories of particular peoples provide much of the material used in nationalist imagination. All of this material has to be transformed to serve for the nationalist cause. Religion thus has to be nationalized in the modern period.

In societies where religions were pitted against each other (like Catholicism against Protestantism or Sunni Islam against Shi'a Islam) they have to be (at least partially) cleansed of their divisive potential by being encapsulated in nationalism. They have to be made part and parcel of national identity and histories of religious conflict have to be tailored to fit a tale of national unity. Religious worship comes to be connected to moments of national glory and national remembrance. This process of homogenization is never entirely successful, because nationalism not only unifies but also diversifies by sprouting alternative nationalisms or regional identities. Well-known examples are modern Ireland and the Partition of India and Pakistan (as well as the further splitting of Pakistan and Bangladesh). Since in modern nation-states a politics of numbers, producing majorities and minorities, is important, religion can be used as the foundation of majority nationalism as well as the foundation of minority identities. Hindu nationalists in India had to constantly attempt to transcend caste boundaries as well as linguistic differences. Their efforts, however, also created deeper divisions between Hindus and Muslims. In Britain and the Netherlands, which were seen as Protestant nations till deep in the nineteenth century, Catholics were included in the nation.[13]

In Germany unification under Bismarck resulted in the conflictual incorporation of the Catholic minority in the state. Whatever the successful incorporation of Catholics in Protestant nations may have been, the exclusion of Jews from the German nation a few decades later and the resulting Holocaust provides overwhelming historical evidence of the terrible consequences of connecting race and religion in the twentieth century. While the Holocaust is unique in its specificities dangerous combinations of race or ethnicity and religion have been made from the late nineteenth century till today. In the nineteenth century the British, French, and Dutch colonizers acquired a sense of religious and racial superiority towards the colonized people in the empire. In the postcolonial era the immigration of Muslims in Europe reminds us that these struggles are never completed and by their very instability important in the production of nationalism.

Secular nationalism and religion

Besides nationalized religion we find secular nationalism in the nineteenth century. At a theoretical level secular nationalism has sometimes been seen as the replacement of religion and as the religion of the nation-state, while modern statecraft can be seen as a secularized, political theology. Even in this view, however, religious communities are never entirely absorbed by nationalism and continue to be the object of secular regulation, such as in the separation of state and church. Secular nationalism as an ideology is important in creating and defining the spheres in which religions are allowed to operate. Forms of separation of church and state are defined in ways that are different in France, Britain, and the USA and Turkey and India, to mention just a few cases. The extent to which science is separated from religion differs greatly, although the power of science is such that it defines the spaces in which religious arguments can be allowed. In the political sphere democracy is often argued to be secular or that it ought to be secular, but it is not. There are several possible connections between democracy and secularity, but there is no necessary one. Secularity can be

13 Peter van der Veer and Hartmut Lehmann, eds., *Nation and Religion: Perspectives on Europe and Asia* (Princeton University Press, 1999).

promoted in a society by democratic means, but also, as in communist or fascist regimes, by dictatorial means.

Communism provides an important historical case of a radical atheist project to eradicate religion. This project has had major consequences in societies that came under communist rule (Soviet Union in 1922, most of the others after the Second World War), but it has nowhere succeeded in getting rid of religion with perhaps the exception of the former DDR which is one of the most secular societies in the world. In most cases the state kept a tight control over religious institutions and its resources (especially targeted by land reforms) and clamped down quickly on religious movements that seemed to constitute a challenge to its rule, as in the case of the Falun Gong in China in the 1990s. Under post-socialist conditions we see a resurgence of public manifestations of religiosity in many of these societies.[14]

Democracy, however, by no means depends on secularization. In fact, there are hardly any secular democracies in the world, because there are hardly any secular societies. As a form of political participation and representation democracy is typical for the modern nation-state. Liberal secularists may demand that the state is secular and that it treats religions equally and neutrally, but they have to acknowledge that if one allows freedom of religious expression religion more often than not will play an important role in the democratic process. One therefore needs to distinguish between the relative secularity of the state and the relative secularity of society and make clear how one defines that secularity. Modern states like England, Holland, and the USA all have had their own specific arrangements for guaranteeing a certain secularity of the state, but these states have found their legitimation in societies in which religion plays an important public role. To give one clear example: It can be safely said that the wall of separation in the USA is a demand that has emerged not from secularists, but from religious minorities that were persecuted in England and therefore that, at least in this case, the secularity of the state is in fact a religious demand. Such a religious demand for the separation of State and Church can in fact also be found in the Netherlands among Protestant dissenters in the second half of the nineteenth century who wanted to have an education system that was not controlled by the established state church.

14 Tam Ngo and Justine Quijada, eds., *Atheist Secularism and Its Discontents: A Comparative Study of Religion and Communism in Eastern Europe and Asia* (forthcoming).

The role of the secular in relation to the religious is not only limiting, since religious traditions that are interpreted in a nationalist way are crucial in the formation of state–society and society–individual relations in the modern nation. These traditions become fields of disciplinary practice in which the modern civil subject is formed. They are also important in creating the modern public. In Britain Evangelicals have been instrumental in mobilizing a large public in anti-slavery societies as well as global mission societies. During the industrial revolution an entire spectrum of societies of "moral uplift" have targeted the working class. On the one hand religious institutions enable notions of individual conscience and civilized conduct; on the other hand notions of publicity, the public, and public opinion are produced by religious movements.

Religious nationalism

Nationalism does not have to be secular. It can also be explicitly religious in nature.[15] Religious nationalism may amount to not more than a civil religion in the sense that national leaders, for instance in the USA, express their belief that the nation is "a nation under God." Themes of death, sacrifice, and rebirth as well as that of a mission in the world are celebrated in a religious fashion in national holidays and with national monuments. This is especially the case when war and death are involved in relation to which the nation has to acquire a metaphysical existence beyond individual life. Important theological notions like that of the chosenness by God can be used to fuel nationalist projects abroad and at home. As important is the notion of rebirth or revival of the nation that is connected to the Protestant metaphor of Awakening. Finally, there is the notion of the coming of a messiah, a leader who is leading his people to the Promised Land. This important notion is shared by Judaism, Christianity, and Islam, but variations of it are found in Hinduism, Buddhism, and forms of Chinese religion. A religious symbolic repertoire of divine election, of ordeals to test one's convictions, conversion to higher truth, and martyrdom is routinely applied to the biographies of great, nationalist leaders.

Examples of radical religious nationalism can be found in India, Pakistan, Ireland, and Israel, but in all these cases they are contained within secular constitutions and state institutions. A case of radical religious nationalism that was able to capture the state is that of the Iranian revolution of 1979,

15 Peter van der Veer, *Religious Nationalism: Hindus and Muslims in India* (Berkeley, CA: University of California Press, 1994).

leading to an Islamic state under Shi'ite clerical leadership. Islam (like Christianity, Confucianism, and Buddhism) contains ideas about just rule and divinely sanctioned law that were important in the ritual legitimacy of traditional states. To make them important in modern states is something quite different and requires a complicated relationship between clerical authority and democratic elections. While Iran may have wanted to export its Islamic revolution to other societies it has not been able to do so.

Imperialism and religion

The nineteenth century is not only the period of nationalism, but also of imperialism. Nationalism and the nation-state are not singular phenomena, but emerge during a process of European expansion and the creation of a world-system of economies and states.[16] Although sovereignty and self-determination are important elements of nationalism they are conceptualized in a larger framework of international relations on a global scale. Similarly, so-called "world religions" like Christianity can never be entirely captured by individual nationalisms, since they have a global mission. Europe has been globalizing and has been globalized over many centuries, depending on which starting point one wants to take for which kind of globalization. Religions like Christianity and Islam are globalizing formations. They have spread through expansion and conversion along trading routes and military campaigns within Europe and outside of Europe. This larger history of both competition and contact between Muslim and Christian expansionists is of importance for the way Muslims are perceived in Europe today. However long and important the history of religious encounters in Asia may have been, the modern period of imperialism and nationalism provides a specific rupture with the past, because of the externality of imperial power and the ideological emphasis on the difference of modern society from both its own past and from other, so-called backward societies. Comparison and an evolutionary perspective on difference became crucial in the high days of the empire. As Edward Said has argued, the new scientific knowledge of Orientalism also provided the colonized with a new understanding of their traditions.[17] Hinduism, Buddhism, Confucianism, Daoism (all western terms translating such terms as dharma and jiao (teachings)) were discovered and evaluated by

16 Peter van der Veer, *Imperial Encounters: Religion and Nationalism in Britain and India* (Princeton University Press, 2001).

17 Edward Said, *Orientalism* (New York: Vintage, 1978).

philologists, archeologists, and other historians while traders, missionaries, and colonial officers tried to deal with the contemporary forms of these traditions. This apparatus of imperial knowledge has created an archive that is still crucial for any understanding of Asian traditions that have been transformed into "world religions."

Much has been written about the "British Discovery of Hinduism" in the eighteenth century and the question what "Hinduism" stands for has been repeatedly asked. The common view is that "Hindu" is a term applied by people coming from outside to the inhabitants of the Indus region and their culture. These Hindus had a great variety of traditions that were systematized and unified under the name "Hinduism" by orientalist scholars in the eighteenth and nineteenth century as part of the colonization of India. It is an argument that has elicited the counter-argument that these various traditions were in fact already in constant conversation and, to an extent, unified and carried by a priestly caste of Brahmans that had spread all over the subcontinent. Both arguments contain elements of truth. It depends on which period is being examined. In the nineteenth century one has to account for the enormous impact of "European modernity" on the conceptualization of Asian traditions. The translation of Hindu traditions into the English-language category of Hinduism, being the religion of Hindus, has been of immense significance for Hindu understanding of their own traditions.

Rather than speaking of "the invention of Hinduism" in the eighteenth and nineteenth centuries, it is preferable to note that Hindu traditions had already existed for a long time and were only reconceived and reformulated in debates in that period. Protestant missionaries were important interlocutors in those debates. Protestantism has, of course, always been seen as an important historical site of thinking about the reflexive subject, about unmediated access, and about agency. In Protestant conversion missionaries are concerned with the purification of improper forms of agency, a purification that is seen as liberation from false understandings of nature. These Protestant notions are paradigmatic of a wider Western and ultimately global discourse of the modern self.[18] These are issues that are crucial in missionary projects everywhere. They raise questions about materiality and transcendence that feed into nineteenth-century constructions of spirituality as opposed to materialism, as we will examine later.

18 Webb Keane, *Christian Moderns: Freedom and Fetish in the Mission Encounter* (Berkeley, CA: University of California Press, 2007).

Directly related is another important issue, namely the tendency to define Christian religion not only as universalistic, but also as rational. The idea that Christianity is not backward, but in harmony with scientific progress becomes central in later Victorian evolutionism. It is the nature of modern rationality that needs to be explored further in its Protestant antecedents and secular consequences. It is not only the nature of religion that is under construction but also the nature of secularity and secularism.

Protestant missionary societies had become the most important cultural modernizing force in Asia and Africa in the late nineteenth century. Large parts of the population in sub-Saharan Africa were converted to Christianity. Education, healthcare, and in some cases part of the agrarian economy were managed by missionary societies. Also in Asia (India, China, Indo-China) these societies were important modernizing forces, but there they were soon imitated by Hindu, Muslim, Buddhist, and other religious groups who also started occupying civil society. After decolonization Christian churches were made indigenous by having native clergy. In sub-Saharan Africa a proliferation of independent churches has created a very diverse religious landscape despite the fact that it is majority Christian. The greatest competition in some African societies such as Nigeria comes from Islam, which is also expanding its reach.

In the later part of the nineteenth century the encounter between missionaries and heathens continues, but an important voice is added as a result of the secularization of the European mind, namely a new discipline, called "science of religion." One element of the modern transformation of religion is "the invention of world religions," as Tomoko Masuzawa calls it.[19] "World Religions" as a category is a product of comparative theology and the science of religion. Comparative theology begins and ends with the singularity of Christianity in comparison to other religions, while science of religion attempts to be a science that deals with all religions evenhandedly. In addition, science of religion derives part of its scientific status from being closely connected to historical linguistics and philology.

Of special importance is the "discovery" of Buddhism as another world religion besides Christianity. Buddhism came to be recognized in the nineteenth century as existing in various parts of Asia and thus as transnational. In contrast to the old enemy Islam it was also regarded as an ethically high religion with universal pretensions like Christianity. Scholars like Monier

19 Tomoko Masuzawa, *The Invention of World Religions* (The University of Chicago Press, 2005).

Monier-Willams (1819–1899), the Sanskritist at Oxford, declared that Buddhism was a philosophy or system of morality, but not a religion. This is certainly an important issue that is debated over and over again till the present day, but besides such Western discussions on the essence of religion, whatever their importance, there were also crucial developments in colonized Asia. Above all, there were archeological attempts to find ancient Buddhism under layers of Hinduism in India in the same period. Major General Alexander Cunningham (1814–1893), the founder of the Indian Archeological Survey, found and explored long forgotten Buddhist sites in India, such as the famous Sarnath. These findings were an important element in establishing ancient Indian history in which Buddhism was portrayed as the enemy of Brahmanism, and came to be destroyed by Islam and ultimately supplanted by Hinduism. This was essential to the grand narrative of Indian history in which Buddhism was also seen as an alternative to caste-ridden Hinduism and taken up as such, half a century later, by egalitarian reformists like the leader of the Untouchables and leading politician Ambedkar. It is this simultaneous production of Buddhism as native to India and as a world religion that could be universally respected for its modern, egalitarian message that becomes important in the Indian location from where it had almost entirely disappeared as a living tradition.

In Sri Lanka something else happened. Here Buddhism comes to be reframed first by the publication of 26,000 pages of Buddhist texts (in Roman transliteration!) by the Pali Text Society, founded in 1881 by Rhys Davids (1843–1922) who had been a British civil servant in Sri Lanka and, as such, involved in the excavation of a famous site, the ancient city of Anuradhapura. Subsequently it is the Theosophist Colonel Olcott (1832–1907) who designs the Sri Lankan flag and creates a Buddhist catechism which transforms Sri Lankan Buddhist traditions into a recognizable religion. And finally, and most importantly, it is the efforts of the reformist monk Anagarika Dhammapala (1864–1933), who has been deeply influenced by Theosophy that result in the formulation of Sinhala Buddhist nationalism, which is of central importance in contemporary conflicts between Tamil Hindus and Sinhala Buddhists in Sri Lanka. It is precisely the reconfiguration of Buddhism in Western scholarship as a world religion within the imperial framework that enables it to become such an important element of religious nationalism among the Sinhalese in Sri Lanka. On the side of the metropolis Buddhism is seen as a prime example of universal spirituality, a non-religious philosophy that fits with the unease about institutional religion that many intellectuals feel at the end of the nineteenth century. The dialectics of orientalism and nationalism is of great importance on both sides of the imperial imagination.

The way in which colonial knowledge about religion was gathered to control populations can be well illustrated by two examples of first-class Dutch scholarship. The Dutch Ministry of Colonies supported research by Christiaan Snouck Hurgronje (1857–1936) on Islam in Arabia with a clear focus on gathering information on Muslims from Aceh who were living in Mecca. The colonial fear of Pan-Islamism (a suspected anti-imperialist plot to unify all Muslims) was operative then, as it is today. Christiaan Snouck Hurgronje began as a student of Theology at Leiden University in 1874 and went on to become one of the most prominent scholars of Islam of his time. He stayed in Mecca in 1884–1885 and came in close touch with pilgrims from the Netherlands Indies. In 1891–1892 Snouck stayed in Aceh as an advisor of the colonial government. His analysis of local forms of insurgency led in 1898 to the bloodiest military expedition of the Dutch in the Indies, the war in Aceh that left 60,000 to 70,000 dead in a population of about 500,000. While Snouck's work is a good illustration of Said's arguments in *Orientalism*, it is also fundamental for imperial understandings of Islam as a rather recent layer of religion that has grown on top of earlier, more harmless layers of Hindu–Buddhism. Islam is seen as an aggressive, dangerous religion while Javanese and Balinese culture are seen as suffused by a more quietist and mystical Hindu–Buddhism. There is an uncanny relation between the Dutch colonial need for a de-politicized law and order (or Suharto's New Order) and the interpretation of Hindu–Buddhist culture as a deep structure of quietistic civilization in the Netherlands-Indies. The archeological recovery of the Borobudur as a world monument of Indonesian Buddhism from under the veil of a superficial Islam signifies this colonial theory. It is within the imperial context of Dutch control of the Dutch Indies and British control of British India that knowledge, archeological, philological, ethnographic, was acquired about religions that became the subject of the science of religion.

This is not only true in relation to the study of Islam, but of religions in general. An important contribution to our understanding of Chinese religion, including Chinese Buddhism, was made by the Dutch sinologist J. J. M. de Groot (1854–1921) who studied Chinese rituals in Amoy (Xiamen) in Southern China and then went on as colonial officer for "Chinese Affairs" in Borneo to advise the government on how to deal with the Chinese communities that were known in Borneo as "kongsis." When the Dutch established control over the Malay principalities in Borneo in 1854 they destroyed most kongsis except for the Langong kongsi that was only dismantled in 1884 when de Groot was in Borneo. When de Groot returned to the Netherlands he was internationally recognized as one of the greatest experts on Chinese religion. It is the productive relation between these disciplines, based on fieldwork and textual study, and the colonial challenges of rule that should be central in our understanding of the Western approach to religion in the nineteenth century.

Modern spirituality

Besides the emergence of the twin concepts of religion and secular one can find the rise of the spiritual as a modern category in the second half of the nineteenth century.[20] As such it is part of nineteenth-century globalization, a thorough-going political, economic, and cultural integration of the world. The emergence of spirituality is tied to the better-known ascendancy of the secular. As many scholars have been arguing, religion as a universal category is a modern construction with a genealogy in universalist Deism and in sixteenth- and seventeenth-century European expansion.[21] One needs therefore to analyze how the categories of "religion," "secularism," and "spirituality" are universalized. This is also true for the category of the secular that has a genealogy in Church–World relations in European history but is transformed in modernity both in Europe and elsewhere. The modern origins of "the secular" are already clear when we look at the first use of the term secularism in England by George Holyoake in 1846. Holyoake attacked Christianity as an "irrelevant speculation" and his attack was carried forward by Secular Societies that were formed in the early 1850s. One of the interesting aspects of these societies is that they combined radical anti-Church attitudes, anti-establishment socialism and freethinking with spiritual experimentation. Secular Societies had a membership that was hugely interested in connecting to the other world by do-it-yourself science. These practices were not considered to be anti-rational, but rather to constitute experiments that were scientific though different from what was going on in the universities. They did not need (or want) to be legitimated by a scientific establishment that was considered to be intimately intertwined with high society and the established church, as indeed Oxford and Cambridge were in this period.

20 Peter van der Veer, *The Modern Spirit of Asia: The Secular and the Spiritual in India and China* (Princeton University Press, 2013).

21 Talal Asad, *Genealogies of Religion* (Baltimore: Johns Hopkins University Press, 1993).

A good example of the combination of socialist radicalism, secularism, and spirituality is the prominent feminist Annie Besant. In the 1870s Annie Besant became a member of the Secular Society of London and began to collaborate with Charles Bradlaugh, a prominent socialist and President of the National Secular Society, in promoting birth-control and other feminist issues. She combined her radical socialist views and her scientific training as the first woman graduating in science at University College in London with a great interest in spiritual matters. After meeting Madame Blavatsky she became a leading Theosophist and after going to India she even became for a short moment President of the Indian National Congress.[22]

The idea of a spirituality that transcended the division of nations and religions gained in influence in response to imperialism and to the massacre of the First World War. Thinkers like the Indian poet Tagore rejected the aggressive materialism of the West and saw in Asian traditions a viable alternative. This optimism was more or less dashed with the emergence of Japan as an imperialist power. Nevertheless, in many religions forms of ecumenical peace-seeking emerged in this period and are still influential today.[23]

Science and scientific rationality are fundamental to the secular age and scientific progress is often seen to depend on the secularization of the mind. From our contemporary viewpoint it seems strange that spirituality and secular science were not seen as at odds with each other in the nineteenth century. A common view of the history of science is that science purifies itself from unwarranted speculation. So, for instance, while the contribution of Alfred Russell Wallace in developing evolutionary theory concurrently with that of Darwin is generally acknowledged, Wallace's spiritual experiments are generally seen as an aberration from which science has purified itself.[24] What falls outside of this teleological perspective on science as a process of progressive purification is the socially and politically embedded nature of both the elements from which science is purified and of purified science itself. Spiritualism was seen as a secular truth-seeking, experimental in nature and opposed to religious obscurantism and hierarchy. This was a truth-seeking that was hindered by both the State and the

22 Arthur Nethercott, *The First Five Lives of Annie* Besant (University of Chicago Press, 1960), and *The Last Four Lives of Annie Besant* (University of Chicago Press, 1963).

23 E.g. Hans Küng, *Theology for the Third Millennium: An Ecumenical View* (New York: Doubleday, 1988).

24 Peter Pels, "Spirits of modernity: Alfred Wallace, Edward Tylor, and the visual politics of fact," in Birgit Meyer and Peter Pels (eds.), *Magic and Modernity: Interfaces of Revelation and Concealment* (Stanford University Press, 2003), pp. 241–271.

Church, in England two intertwined institutions. It is within the context of spiritualism, spirituality, and the antinomian traditions of Britain that an anti-colonial universalism was born.

An important element in the emergence of spirituality was that it offered an alternative to religion. This was first and foremost institutionalized religion. In the West spirituality formed an alternative to Church Christianity. Together with the so-called secularization of the mind in nineteenth-century liberalism, socialism, as well as in science (especially Darwin's evolution theory) one can find widespread movements in different parts of the world that search for a universal spirituality that is not bound to any specific tradition. Good examples in the United States are the transcendentalists from Emerson to Whitman as well as Mary Baker's Christian Science. Theosophy is another product of spirit-searching America. In fact not only America is full of spirituality, as Catherine Albanese has shown, but there is a huge proliferation of this kind of movement that parallels the spread of secularist ideologies around the world.[25]

Simultaneously there is a search for a universal spirituality that transcends specific religions and for which the religions of the East are privileged sources. In Christianity, the religion of the colonial powers, we find in the second half of the nineteenth century attempts not so much to convert people to Christianity but to find a universal morality or spirituality in other religious traditions and thus a kind of Hegelian *Aufhebung* of all traditions. This is exemplified in the Unitarian organization of the World Parliament of Religions in 1893 at Chicago, where representatives of World religions were invited to speak on a common platform, as well as in the newly developed discipline of Science of Religion that went beyond Christian theology. The term "world religions" was coined in this period to designate religious traditions of a high morality that could be treated as relatively equal. Buddhism was a perfect candidate to be included in this category, while Islam, despite its clear global presence and similarity to Christianity, was excluded at first.

Global religions today

After the Iranian Revolution of 1979 there has been an increasing awareness of the continuing significance of religion in most parts of the world. Islam has

25 Catherine Albanese, *A Republic of Mind and Spirit: A Cultural History of American Metaphysical Religion* (New Haven: Yale University Press, 2007).

received the bulk of the attention partly because of the geopolitical importance of the Middle East, where much of the world's oil supply is today, political structures of the nation-state are fragile, and the Palestinian conflict pits Jews and Muslims against each other. Islam under these conditions has a strong political significance that goes far beyond this region. In 2001 the United States were attacked by a radical islamicist group, Al-Qaeda, in response to what the Islamicists considered to be the nefarious geopolitical hegemony of the United States. This "holy war" against America was interpreted by the American political scientist Samuel Huntington as the new battleground of the twenty-first century, between civilizations (mostly defined by religion), replacing the older battle between capitalism and communism.[26] Such an emphasis on unclearly defined civilizations obscures the fact that most warfare continues to be between nation-states or inspired by nationalism, including the struggle of the Palestinians. Nevertheless, globalization does produce a larger playing field for transnational religious movements.

Christianity, Islam, and Buddhism have always been potentially global religions, depending on expansion of trade networks or political formations, but in the current phase of globalization, enhanced by new forms of communication such as the Internet, they have followed patterns of labor migration and have become truly global. In this they are joined by a variety of new movements, such as the Bahai, the Hare Krishnas, the Falun Gong, etc.

Most of these transnational movements are not of a radical political nature, although, as usual, they do have political significance. The most important Christian movement today is that of the Protestant Pentecostals and Evangelicals. They have a significant influence on American politics, but also on the politics (for or against them) in large parts of Latin America, Africa, and Asia. The most important Islamic movement today is a pietistic movement, called Tablighi Jama'at, which originated in South Asia but has now spread to wherever Muslims live. A very significant Buddhist movement is that of Tzu Chi, originating in Taiwan, but spreading its humanitarian message globally. Such movements fit the emergence of the network society that does not replace the nation-state but is an important transformation of it.[27] Important in the network society is the development of the Internet

26 Samuel Huntington, *The Clash of Civilizations and the Remaking of World Order* (New York: Simon & Schuster, 1996).

27 Manuel Castells, *The Information Age: Economy, Society and Culture,* Vol. I: *The Rise of the Network Society*; Vol. II: *The Power of Identity*; Vol. III: *End of Millennium* (Oxford: Blackwell, 1996–1998).

which may turn out as significant for religious change as the invention of the printing press. The Internet provides new possibilities to engage theological questions and discuss religious matters in a virtual online community.[28] To an extent the Internet gives a new twist to an old problematic in religion, namely the virtuality of communicating with the supernatural, but also the social character of religious communication. The movement through space in international migration which is an important aspect of today's global society is accompanied by transnational communication that produces new forms of religious sensibility and community.

Further reading

Albanese, Catherine. *A Republic of Mind and Spirit: A Cultural History of American Metaphysical Religion*. New Haven: Yale University Press, 2007.

Asad, Talal. *Genealogies of Religion*. Baltimore: Johns Hopkins University Press, 1993.

Baljon, B. J. S. *Religion and Thought of Shāh Walī Allāh Dihlawī, 1703–1762*. Leiden: Brill, 1986.

Bunt, Gary R. *Islam in the Digital Age: E-Jihad, Online Fatwas and Cyber Islamic Environments*. London: Pluto Press, 2003.

Casanova, Jose. *Public Religions in the Modern World*. University of Chicago Press, 1994.

Castells, Manuel. *The Information Age: Economy, Society and Culture*, Vol. I: *The Rise of the Network Society*; Vol. II: *The Power of Identity*; Vol. III: *End of Millennium*. Oxford: Blackwell, 1996–1998.

Comaroff, Jean and John. *Of Revelation and Revolution*, Vol. I: *Christianity, Colonialism, and Consciousness in South Africa*. University of Chicago Press, 1991.

Geertz, Clifford. *The Interpretation of Cultures*. New York: Basic Books, 1973.

Gellner, Ernest. *Nations and Nationalism*. Ithaca: Cornell University Press, 1983.

Huntington, Samuel. *The Clash of Civilizations and the Remaking of World Order*. New York: Simon & Schuster, 1996.

Küng, Hans. *Theology for the Third Millennium: An Ecumenical View*. New York: Doubleday, 1988.

Masuzawa, Tomoko. *The Invention of World Religions*. The University of Chicago Press, 2005.

McLeod, W. H. *The Sikhs: History, Religion, and Society*. New York: Columbia University Press, 1989.

Mungello, David E. *Leibniz and Confucianism: The Search for Accord*. Honolulu: The University Press of Hawaii, 1977.

Mungello, David E., ed. *The Chinese Rites Controversy: Its History and Meaning*. Nettetal: Steyler Verlag, 1994.

Nethercott, Arthur. *The First Five Lives of Annie Besant*. University of Chicago Press, 1960.

The Last Four Lives of Annie Besant. Chicago: University of Chicago Press, 1963.

28 Gary R. Bunt, *Islam in the Digital Age: E-Jihad, Online Fatwas and Cyber Islamic Environments* (London: Pluto Press, 2003).

Ngo, Tam and Quijada Justine, eds. *Atheist Secularism and Its Discontents: A Comparative Study of Religion and Communism in Eastern Europe and Asia*. New York: Palgrave, forthcoming.

Pels, Peter. "Spirits of modernity: Alfred Wallace, Edward Tylor, and the visual politics of fact," in Birgit Meyer and Peter Pels (eds.), *Magic and Modernity: Interfaces of Revelation and Concealment*. Stanford University Press, 2003, pp. 241–271.

Ricci, Matteo. *Tianzhu Shiyi*. Beijing 1603, translated, with introduction and notes, by Douglas Lancashire and Peter Hu Guozhen; edited by Edward J. Malatesta. Taipei: Institut Ricci, 1985.

Said, Edward. *Orientalism*. New York: Vintage, 1978.

Spence, Jonathan D. *The Memory Palace of Matteo Ricci*. New York: Viking, 1984.

van der Veer, Peter. *Imperial Encounters: Religion and Nationalism in Britain and India*. Princeton University Press, 2001.

Religious Nationalism: Hindus and Muslims in India. Berkeley, CA: University of California Press, 1994.

The Modern Spirit of Asia: The Secular and the Spiritual in India and China. Princeton University Press, 2014.

van der Veer, Peter and Lehmann Hartmut, eds. *Nation and Religion: Perspectives on Europe and Asia*. Princeton University Press, 1999.

Webb, Keane. *Christian Moderns: Freedom and Fetish in the Mission Encounter*. Berkeley, CA: University of California Press, 2007.

Zupanov, Ines. *Disputed Mission: Jesuit Experiments and Brahmanical Knowledge in Seventeenth-Century India*. Oxford University Press, 1999.

8

Science since 1750

JAMES E. MCCLELLAN III

This article treats the history of science since 1750 from a history of the world perspective. The world and humankind entered a new era over the last three hundred years, and what we know as science has come to play a formidable role in the making of modern history. But traps await if we do not first examine the analytical categories and conceptual parameters that necessarily underpin any consideration of the topic of science and world history since 1750.[1]

Framing the topic: science and world history

We need to problematize several aspects of our topic. What do we mean by "science," for example? What *can* we mean in today's world of postmodern critical thought? Science as natural philosophy and a body of knowledge? Science as a social institution? Science as a research enterprise? The sociology of science as a profession, say? Science and the scientific enterprise as institutions in society ... ones supported by governments and states, for example? What about science as a force of production tied to technology? It is a tall order to combine these diverse elements of what we commonly understand as science, much less to sketch the broad outlines of change over the last two to three hundred years.

These considerations regarding how to think and write about science are only compounded when we ask about world history. An elaborate historiographical introduction is not germane here either, especially with the

1 In presenting the historiography and problematizing the subject, the 2010 special Focus section of *ISIS*, "Global histories of science," organized by Sujit Sivasundaram [*ISIS* 101 (2010), pp. 95–158], is the starting point today for thinking about the history of science on a global scale; see Sivasundaram, "Introduction," and Forum papers by other contributors. Sivasundaram et al. support the necessity of reflexivity and historiographical self-consciousness in taking up the subject.

serious historiographical consideration in other chapters and other volumes in *The Cambridge World History* that more than adequately address the issues involved.[2] Here, it suffices to point out that there are distinctions to be made between and among possibilities for world history. Is it universal history as in a history of the universe that includes the Earth and humans? Is it a *unitary* global history of humankind with one perspective on the global past and considered on a world scale, a single history of the world, governed by factors, like population growth or migration, playing themselves out over the *longue durée*? Is there such a thing as international history? Or, is our world history simply the sum of many histories, the addition of the multifaceted stories of individual peoples, societies, and cultures and all the multicultural diversity of the human experience so far? Or yet, are we still saddled with teleology, the end of history, or crossing some new threshold. All of these approaches have implications for how we think about *science* in world history.

One point becomes immediately apparent when we juxtapose "science" and "world history" in this way: ours cannot be simply the story of Western science and the Western scientific tradition.[3] Multicultural perspectives are essential. More than one culture and scientific tradition is at play even in the period from 1750 down to today. One has only to think of science and civilization in China and India in order to realize we have to deal with scientific traditions and knowledge systems in a variety of cultural contexts.[4] To be sure, the story involves the globalization of "Western science" emerging out of Europe, particularly after the Scientific Revolution of the sixteenth and seventeenth centuries and then continuing with the union of modern science and technology in the nineteenth century. Any history of science on a global scale since 1750 therefore must account for the success of the West and the maturation of what today can only be called world

2 See especially the introduction to this volume, and the essays on historiography in Volume One of this series. Benedikt Stuchtey and Eckhardt Fuchs, eds., *Writing World History, 1800–2000* (Oxford: Oxford University Press / German Historical Institute London, 2003), is also an important volume of historiographical studies on world histories. Textbooks, teaching films and videos, and world history encyclopedias are other manifestations of how world history is constituted, presented, and discussed. This variety suggests other contexts in which we need to integrate consideration of science.

3 Marwa Elshakry, "When science became Western: historiographical reflections," *ISIS* 101 (2010), pp. 98–109, elaborates the historiography that has shaped notions of Western science.

4 Sujit Sivasundaram, "Sciences and the global: on methods, questions, and theory," ISIS 101 (2010), pp. 146–158, discusses the current state of writing global histories of science. Joseph Needham's *Science and Civilization in China* remains canonical in this regard.

science. Yet at the same time, historians have now "provincialized" and decentralized Europe in framing accounts from a global perspective.[5]

By and large, science and its history seem little taken up in the historiography of global or world history studies. The subject does not figure in Stuchtey and Fuchs's 2003 volume on writing world history, and Anthony Giddens does not speak about science at all in his authoritative volumes on Europe and modernity.[6] Science does not appear in the special number of *Storia della Storiografia* in 1999 devoted to world history. In textbooks on world history, the Scientific Revolution gets mentioned in a rote way, particularly as tied to the Enlightenment, sometimes accompanied by "documents" of one sort or another, but science otherwise receives largely token treatment, sometimes, as in the present volumes, mixed up as an element of "culture."

In a highly productive realm of historiography, over the last half-century historians of science have intensely studied science and European colonial expansion, and they have developed a thriving academic field called Science & Empire Studies, but they, too, have only relatively recently turned to more explicitly global and world histories of science.[7]

Our story also connects historiographically with an elaborate literature in the social sciences pertaining to modernity and globalization. Here one has in mind the works of Francis Fukuyama, Samuel Huntington, and Thomas

5 Benedikt Stuchtey, "Introduction," in Benedikt Stuchtey (ed.), *Science across the European Empires, 1800–1950* (New York: German Historical Institute/Oxford University Press, 2005), p. 29, citing the work of Dipesh Chakrabarty; on these topics, see further James E. McClellan III, "Science and empire studies and postcolonial studies: a report from the contact zone," in Gesa Mackenthun and Klaus Hock (eds.), *Cultural Encounters and the Discourses of Scholarship*, Vol. 4 (Münster: Waxmann, 2012). Patrick Karl O'Brien, "The deconstruction of myths and reconstruction of metanarratives in global histories of material progress," in Stuchtey and Fuchs (eds.), *Writing World History*, pp. 67–90, sees the technological as an important and active area of work in "the growing field of global history" (p. 69).

6 Stuchtey and Fuchs, *Writing World History*; Anthony Giddens, *The Consequences of Modernity* (Stanford University Press, 1990) and *Europe in the Global Age* (Cambridge: Polity Press, 2007).

7 See the 2010 *ISIS* Forum section devoted to world histories of science mentioned in note 1; see also McClellan, "Science and empire studies" and " Colonialism and science," in Arne Hessenbruch (ed.), *Reader's Guide to the History of Science* (London and Chicago: Fitzroy Dearborn, 2000), pp. 143–144. James E. McClellan III and Harold Dorn, *Science and Technology in World History: An Introduction*, 2nd edition (Baltimore: The Johns Hopkins University Press, 2006), illustrates this trend. The internationalism and cosmopolitanism of René Taton's earlier multivolume history of the sciences is not to be forgotten, nor, again, the issues and questions that Needham's volumes have forced us to consider since they began appearing in the 1950s.

L. Friedman, if not going back to Schumpeter, Marx, or Hegel.[8] But in particular we need to signal Immanuel Wallerstein and world systems theory. Wallerstein's and Samir Amin's updated vision is of capitalist imperialism as the globalizing force in modern world history.[9] Although science has always been vaguely part of discussions about modernity, it seems that the social science literature has not paid too much attention to science per se. Wallerstein himself, for example, does consider *technology* as key (shipbuilding, iron, textile industries), but science hardly at all, except to remark very parenthetically on "the triumph of scientific rationalism as the reigning *ideology* of the modern world-system."[10] This blind spot in world systems theory not only largely omits science as an *explanandum*, but misses the key point, ironic for Wallerstein, that in the period under consideration here what's at least partly involved is a transformation of science from disinterested natural philosophy into a force of production, with in essence science moving from Marx's superstructure to the economic base.

World systems theory has come in for criticism for its Marxist orientation and reducing everything to economics.[11] It has now been refined by Anthony Giddens to encompass several different domains: (1) the world capitalist economy (per Wallerstein), (2) the nation-state system, (3) world military order, (4) international division of labor.[12] Obviously modern science is involved in all of these ways. Increasingly, globalization, too, is attracting wide critical attention, and thinkers likewise see it as a multifaceted subject.[13]

8 Francis Fukuyama, *The End of History and the Last Man, with a New Afterword* (New York: Free Press, 2006 [original edn. 1992]); Samuel P. Huntington, *The Clash of Civilizations and the Remaking of World Order* (New York: Simon Schuster, 1996); Thomas Friedman, *The Lexus and the Olive Tree* (New York: Anchor, 2000) and *The World is Flat* (New York: Farrar, Straus and Giroux, 2005).

9 Immanuel Wallerstein, *The Modern World System II: Mercantilism and the Consolidation of the European World-Economy, 1600–1750* (New York, London: Academic Press, 1980) and *The Modern World System III: The Second Era of Great Expansion of the Capitalism World-Economy, 1730–1840s* (San Diego, New York: Academic Press, 1989); see also Samir Amin, *L'Empire du chaos: la nouvelle mondialisation capitaliste* (Paris: L'Harmattan, 1991), and earlier works by this thinker.

10 Wallerstein, *Modern World System III*, frontispiece (sic) (my emphasis). Jerry H. Bentley, "World history and grand narrative," in Stuchtey and Fuchs (eds.), *Writing World History*, pp. 53–58, likewise makes technology determinative, but does not see science playing much of a role, even in post-Industrial Revolution technologies.

11 Roxann Prazniak, "Is world history possible? An inquiry," in Arif Dirlik, Vinay Hahl, and Peter Gran (eds.), *History after the Three Worlds: Post-Eurocentric Historiographies* (Lantham, MD: Rowman & Littlefield, 2000), pp. 221–239.

12 Giddens, *The Consequences of Modernity*, pp. 70–78; also Prazniak, "Is world history possible?," p. 214.

13 On globalization, see Gidden's definition and discussion, *Europe in the Global Age*, pp. xii, 8; *The Consequences of Modernity*, p. 64.

For Timothy Brennan in 2004, for example, globalization can variously mean: (1) political unification, (2) trade, commerce and finance, (3) geopolitical and American power, (4) new forms of colonization and imperialism, or even (5) that globalization doesn't exist, that the nation-state and the local are still the norm.[14] Once again, how we want to factor science into these equations complicates any account.

The field of Postcolonial Studies developed in the wake of Edward Said's *Orientalism* (1978), and how science is treated or ignored in this literature should be remarked upon.[15] Because of its roots in literary studies and the humanities, Postcolonial Studies, too, has tended not to treat science. Insofar as it has, the field has offered critiques of Western science as arrogant and an instrument of colonial and imperial rule, as we will detail further. More than that, the field of Postcolonial Studies embodies serious postmodern critiques of language and a rejection of master narratives, which has implications not only where science and world history are concerned, but reflexively in framing this account as well.

Another feature of our story has to do with the universalist claims of science. It concerns a contrast to be drawn between universalist knowledge claims on the one hand and the universality of the social penetration and practice of science on the other. That is, since the Pre-Socratics, the claims of science have been universal in scope and applied to all natural phenomena. Yet, the social reality has been that knowledge of such claims has been limited to restricted circles and far from universally accepted. In other words, we can differentiate the universalist claims of science from the historical reality of how deeply they have penetrated intellectually and culturally. To illustrate this key point, consider that at the time of the first edition of Newton's *Principia* in 1687, only two people – Isaac Newton and Edmund Halley – knew of or subscribed to any universal law of gravity wherein every particle in the universe attracts every other particle in mathematical proportion. In 1750 the number of subscribers was

14 Timothy Brennan, "From development to globalization: postcolonial studies and globalization theory," in Neil Lazarus (ed.), *The Cambridge Companion to Postcolonial Literary Studies* (Cambridge University Press, 2004), pp. 120–138.

15 Edward Said, *Orientalism* (New York: Pantheon Books, 1978) and *Culture and Imperialism* (London: Chatto & Windus, 1993); see further McClellan, "Science and empire studies and postcolonial studies"; Sünne Juterczenka and Gesa Mackenthum, eds., *The Fuzzy Logic of Encounter: New Perspectives on Cultural Contact* (Münster: Waxmann, 2009), and related symposia volumes issuing out of the University of Rostock and the program "Cultural Encounters and the Discourses of Scholarship."

already much greater, but not universal by any means when considered from a global point of view. And one can reasonably ask about the extent to which these universal claims of science are recognized or implanted universally today, which adds another dimension to the topic.

The Enlightenment movement of the eighteenth century comes to mind in this same connection. The place of science in the Enlightenment and in the making of modern identities is well known. Even if contested, the story of the Enlightenment and how "reason" became reasonable is an important one to tell. This science-and-Enlightenment perspective begs the question about the fate of the Enlightenment program and the state of science in culture today. What of the continuing cultural wars involving science, not to mention "vernacular" sciences, aboriginal "native" knowledge, or the persistence of odd-ball beliefs?[16]

Finally, we have to keep in mind the formal international organization of science on a world level. Such was already a feature of European science in the eighteenth century.

With these requirements, pitfalls, and perspectives before us, and to simplify embracing all these topics simultaneously within this small compass, let us begin by taking a snapshot of science on a world scale in 1750.

A snapshot circa 1750

The Western scientific tradition that stretched back to an earlier medieval age in Europe, the Islamic world, and the Greeks was alive and well implanted in Europe in 1750. Science was solidly institutionalized in European universities, in a transnational network of academies and societies of science, astronomical observatories, botanical gardens, hospitals, and in a variety of other niches, many state supported.[17] The earlier Scientific Revolution transformed

16 Helen Tilley, "Global histories, vernacular science, and African genealogies; or, is the history of science ready for the world," [Forum: Global Histories of Science] *ISIS* 101(2010), pp. 110–119, examines non-Western knowledge systems and epistemological conflict particularly as it applies the globalization of science and the universalist claims of science; Neil Safier also takes up non-normative epistemologies and knowledge production on a global scale in "Global knowledge on the move: itineraries, Amerindian narratives, and deep histories of science," [Focus: Global Histories of Science] *ISIS* 101 (2010), pp. 133–145, and *Measuring the New World: Enlightenment Science and South America* (University of Chicago Press, 2008).

17 See James E. McClellan III, "Scientific institutions and the organization of science," in Roy Porter (ed.), *The Cambridge History of Science*, Vol. 4: *Science in the Eighteenth Century*, (Cambridge University Press, 2003), pp. 99–120; *Science Reorganized: Scientific Societies in the Eighteenth Century* (New York: Columbia University Press, 1985); "Europe des Académies: Forces centripètes, forces centrifuges," *Dix-Huitième Siècle* 23 (1993),

the understanding of nature and bequeathed to contemporary science and its practitioners new heroes in Bacon, Descartes, and Newton, a new cosmology, a new physics, and new ideas about the practice of natural philosophical inquiry. Sophisticated communities of academicians, physicians, savants, and amateurs actively pursued research along various lines and on various fronts and contributed to scientific inquiry and a burgeoning enterprise of science in Europe at the time.

Looking at Europe and Western science on the world stage in 1750, European power along with European science extended outward considerably, notably to North and South America, the Caribbean, India, and China. The empires and science of Spain and Portugal were stagnant, but not to be overlooked, and the Dutch with their outposts in Batavia, including the scientific society, the *Bataviaasch Genootschapt van Kunsten en Wetenschappen* (1778), were more important players than usually credited. The British and the French were the major colonial powers, and science and medicine were both instrumentalities of overseas expansion and also beneficiaries of the global spread of European power and influence. With the scientific expeditions of Bougainville, Cook, and La Pérouse in the second half of the eighteenth century, Western science clearly demonstrated a global reach. The European outpost at Botany Bay in Australia speaks volumes in this regard. Yet, that grasp was more tentative than it would become in the nineteenth century and today. The Jesuits did run the Astronomical Bureau for the emperor in China, and there were European traders in Canton, but much else of the mandarinate in China in 1750 had its own institutions and cadres of experts with their special knowledge and remained far from touched or assimilated by Europeans. The same can be said of contemporary high civilization in India. Europeans displayed a probing interest in various aspects of Chinese and Indian science and medicine,

pp. 153–165; James E. McClellan III and François Regourd, *The Colonial Machine: French Science and Overseas Expansion in the Old Regime* (Turnhout: Brepols Publishers, 2011). See also earlier foundational works, including René Taton, ed., *Enseignement et diffusion des sciences en France au dix-huitième siècle* (Paris: Hermann, 1964; reprint, 1986), and Charles C. Gillispie, *Science and Polity in France at the End of the Old Regime* (Princeton University Press, 1980). E. C. Spary, *Utopia's Garden: French Natural History from Old Regime to Revolution* (The University of Chicago Press, 2000), throws further light on the organization of contemporary science and its institutionalization and pursuit across Europe and around the world. Bertrand Daugeron, *Collections naturalistes entre science et empires, 1763–1804* (Paris: Muséum national d'histoire naturelle, 2009), offers the same for the period stretching into the nineteenth century.

in addition to a respectful stance towards medical and botanical knowledge held by aboriginal peoples everywhere.[18]

For its adepts in Europe, America, and to a small extent elsewhere around the world in 1750 the enterprise of science and its goal remained largely natural philosophy, the disinterested pursuit of knowledge for knowledge's sake, a noble quest to decode the secrets of nature. Nevertheless, the support of science and useful knowledge by contemporary governments needs to be pointed out. The link between science and government goes back to the first civilizations, of course, and polities of all sorts have always needed and deployed experts in the service of governance.[19] This was no less true for the nation-states of Europe in the eighteenth century. Some institutions have been mentioned, and it is not for nothing that Isaac Newton left the university to become Master of the Mint in London, as well as President of the Royal Society of London. Many institutional and individual examples could be cited to show the contemporary science and government link. As it turns out, then, government-sponsored science and expertise facilitated the outward expansion of Europe and the maintenance of overseas colonies and trade. With state support, work in astronomy, botany, cartography, medicine, and a host of related areas was bent to colonial and later imperialist ends. In turn, the enterprise and practical bounds of science in Europe became enlarged by the overseas experience and expanded contact with the rest of the world. Contemporary European science thereby became complicit in bolstering

18 McClellan and Dorn, *Science and Technnology in World History*; McClellan and Regourd, *The Colonial Machine, passim* and pp. 14–16; McClellan, *Colonialism & Science*, esp. general remarks, pp. 2–14; "Science and Empire Studies and Postcolonial Studies," *Science Reorganized*, pp. 125, 263. On the contact zone, see canonically Mary Louise Pratt, *Imperial Eyes: Travel Writing and Transculturation* (London and New York: Routledge, 1992), and also Francis Barker, Peter Hulme, and Margaret Iversen, "Introduction," in *Colonial Discourse/Postcolonial Theory* (Manchester University Press, 1994), pp. 1–23; Bernhard Klein and Gesa Mackenthun, eds., *Sea Changes: Historicizing the Ocean* (New York: Routledge, 2004); Kapil Raj, *Relocating Modern Science: Circulation and the Construction of Knowledge in South Asia and Europe, 1650–1900* (Delhi: Permanent Black; New York: Palgrave Macmillan, 2007); Juterczenka and Mackenthun, eds., *The Fuzzy Logic of Encounter*. For the latest on postcolonialism and travel literature, see Siegfried Huigen, *Knowledge and Colonialism: Eighteenth-Century Travellers in South Africa* (Leiden and Boston: Brill, 2009). Carol Lynn Moder, "Discourse across cultures, across disciplines: an overview," in Carol Lynn Moder and Aida Martinovic-Zic (eds.), *Discourses Across Languages and Cultures* (Amsterdam/Philadelphia: John Benjamins Publishing Company, 2004), pp. 1–11, adds a key perspective from the world of linguistics.

19 This theme runs throughout and is developed by Harold Dorn, *The Geography of Science* (Baltimore and London: The Johns Hopkins University Press, 1991), and by McClellan and Dorn, *Science and Technology*.

the institution of slavery and retrogressive state economic policies of mercantilism.

In eighteenth-century Europe, as elsewhere, science and technology were still largely separate enterprises. Sociologically and intellectually, the world of everyday technologies took place at considerable remove from the contemporary world of science and natural philosophy. We can speak of applied science in the context of government patronage mentioned above, wherein mapmaking and using astronomical methods to determine longitude can serve as examples. Contemporaries didn't spurn opportunities to turn science into practical application, for which Franklin's electrical science and the lightning rod provide a nice example.[20] Science, rationality, and experiment had a large cultural impact at the time, but science and contemporary industry had little to do with one another, again sociologically or intellectually.[21] The connection was between science and government, not science and industry. The Industrial Revolution that took off in England in the second half of the century arose out of the world of technology, not science. Effected for the most part by unlettered mechanics in the countryside in England, the Industrial Revolution with its steam engines, coal and iron mining industries, mechanization of the textile industry, and the rest had nothing to do with science in the city or any effort to apply science in industry.[22] The ideology of Francis Bacon that science could or should be tapped for its useful application was without direct effect. The Industrial Revolution only coincidentally followed the Scientific Revolution.

In the eighteenth century the natural sciences anchored a broad and consequential intellectual and social movement, the Enlightenment. As is well known, science and the Scientific Revolution sparked the Enlightenment movement and inspired rational inquiry across a broad range of subjects in the social and political sciences, psychology, theology, and jurisprudence.[23] Jefferson and the Declaration of Independence are unthinkable without Newton and a universal gravity of political atoms; Condorcet's *Sketch of the Progress of the Human Mind* of 1793 and the French Revolution likewise make

20 James E. McClellan III, "Benjamin Franklin and the lightning rod," in James E. McClellan III (ed.), *The Applied Science Problem* (Jersey City, NJ: Jensen/Daniels Publishers, 2008), pp. 92–111, provides an authoritative account.

21 See Margaret C. Jacob, *Scientific Culture and the Making of the Industrial West* (Oxford University Press, 1997).

22 McClellan and Dorn, *Science and Technology*, pp. 279–94.

23 Peter Gay, *The Enlightenment: An Interpretation*, 2 vols. (New York and London: W. W. Norton, 1995) [Original edition, New York: Knopf, 1966–1969] remains a touchstone here, not least in framing his presentation around science and the history of science.

this clear. The renowned Republic of Letters was characteristic of the period of the Enlightenment, organized internationally across Europe and abroad with the academies serving as its capitals, and this Republic is not to be overlooked as indicative of the cultural impact and penetration of science in contemporary Western civilization.[24]

As far as concerns the intellectual history of science, in the useful model put forward by Thomas S. Kuhn, scientific research in the eighteenth century generally speaking unfolded along two large and largely separate arcs: research in the more theoretical, mathematical and demanding sciences like astronomy and mechanics with their roots in antiquity – the so-called Classical sciences – and the so-called Baconian sciences, more experimental, empirical and easily accessible domains of scientific inquiry such as electricity, magnetism, or meteorology that largely originated in the seventeenth century.[25] Considerable empirical work expanded domains in botany, natural history, geology, and geography across the century, not least because of the overseas expansion of Europeans. The multinational observations of the Transits of Venus in 1761 and 1769 that included Captain Cook observing from Tahiti are exemplary in this regard. In this context, too, Lavoisier and the Chemical Revolution of the eighteenth century stand out: Historiographically always something of a revolutionary outlier, with important developments in pneumatic chemistry, the chemistry of combustion, chemical nomenclature, and ultimately chemical atoms, the Chemical Revolution makes sense in Kuhn's model in terms of rationalizing chemistry within the Baconian sciences and under the theoretical aegis of Newton of the *Opticks* (1704). As vibrant, manifold, and growing as were these research endeavors, overall the natural sciences collectively lacked conceptual unity in 1750.

The wedding of science and industry

The important story behind science in the nineteenth century concerns the union of science and industry. The connection between science and government did not go away and, in fact, expanded as industrialization proceeded.

24 On the contemporary Republic of Letters, see McClellan, "Europe des Académies," and McClellan and Regourd, *The Colonial Machine*, pp. 429–445.

25 Thomas S. Kuhn, "Mathematical versus experimental traditions in the development of physical science," *Journal of Interdisciplinary History* 7 (1976), pp. 1–31. [reprinted in Kuhn, *The Essential Tension* (University of Chicago Press, 1977), pp. 31–65]; McClellan and Dorn, *Science and Technology*, pp. 295–302.

But a potent novelty in this new era was what we can more readily identify as the union of science and industry and the emergence of modern applied science.[26] The ideology goes back to Bacon, but this kind of applied science began in earnest in the nineteenth century as part of ongoing industrialization and the development of capitalism. Posed this way, we have to specify what was the science involved, what were the industries, and precisely how science conjoined with technology to become a powerful motor in the making of industrial civilization today.

The Industrial Revolution that began in England in the eighteenth century unleashed a momentous social and economic transformation, comparable in its effects to the Neolithic and Urban Bronze Age revolutions of so many millennia earlier. The result – still ongoing – was the rise of industrial civilization and a new mode of human existence. To repeat, the Industrial Revolution got off the ground without the aid or application of science in any notable way, but that changed as the nineteenth century unfolded and as applied science in industry developed. Historians of technology debate whether there have been multiple "industrial revolutions" that have given rise to the world order we have today, and distinctions need to be drawn. But from the big picture perspective, one overarching, snowballing process seems to have been at play, transforming and continuing to transform life and the world as we know it. Science and science-based technologies have self-evidently contributed to the making of industrial civilization today.

Over the course of the nineteenth century the intellectual accomplishments of science, particularly the physical sciences, were tremendous, and it was this body of knowledge that leaked into practical and world-transforming new technologies. The details are fairly straightforward.[27] One account starts with Newtonian ethers, Galvani's frog legs, and the invention of the battery by Alessandro Volta in 1800. Current electricity was virtually a new phenomenon of nature created by science, and it had wide scientific and technological impact. For science, the ramifications passed through Humphry Davy (1778–1829) and electrochemistry, John Dalton (1766–1844) and chemical atomism, and the mathematization of electricity and magnetism by way of André-Marie Ampère and the calculus.

26 McClellan and Dorn, *Science and Technology*, pp. 318–22, 412–14; McClellan, "What's problematic about 'applied science'?," in James E. McClellan III (ed.), *The Applied Science Problem* (Jersey City, NJ: Jensen/Daniels Publishers, 2008), pp. 1–36.

27 See again, Kuhn, "Mathematical versus Experimental Traditions"; McClellan and Dorn, *Science and Technology*, pp. 302–311.

Compliments of Hans Christian Oersted and Michael Faraday, by 1831 scientific understanding had led to the technological development of motors, generators, and electromagnets. The telegraph was a new and consequential technology that emerged in 1837. Thomas Alva Edison inaugurated the first electric lighting system in New York City in 1882. The telephone, invented by Alexander Graham Bell in 1876, is a related and likewise consequential technological outcome stemming from nineteenth-century physical science. Another stream in this same flow emerges out of James Clerk Maxwell's work and the mathematization of Faraday's electromagnetic field, notably in Heinrich Hertz's discovery of radio waves in 1887 and their almost immediate application by Guglielmo Marconi, as "wireless telegraphy," which ultimately turned into radio and then television.

The dye industry in Germany proved another influential locus of applied science in the nineteenth century. This confluence depended on the formidable maturation of analytical and organic chemistry in the context of German universities revived after Napoleon as research institutions, as well as peculiarities of German patent law and the state of German unification. Beginning with the first synthetic aniline dye by William Perkin in 1856 and moving on to the whole spectrum of coal tar dyes and their widespread application in dying, cosmetics, pharmaceuticals, and explosives, companies like Bayer embraced science and forged tight links with responsive chemistry departments in universities. The novelty in this case was the creation of the first industrial research lab by the Bayer Company in 1874. The model was taken up by other industries in the nineteenth and twentieth centuries. A new model of invention and technology as applied science had finally arrived.[28]

As much as we need to highlight new connections between science and industry in the nineteenth century, we cannot overlook continuing connections between science and governments and the industrialization of war that took place on a vast scale in this period.[29] Chemical warfare used in World War I is a telling example, and a host of war-related examples come to mind (the gunboat, rifled artillery, the machine gun, the dreadnought, chemical weapons, tanks, and airplanes, not to mention the trusty telegraph) showing the potency of applied science in the military. Governments thereby supported and added to the momentum of industrialization and the integration

28 McClellan and Dorn, *Science and Technology*, pp. 318–322.
29 McClellan and Dorn, *Science and Technology*, pp. 311–318.

of science into government as well as industry. It is not too crude to say that the place and role of science in society moved from the superstructure of natural philosophy to become part of the base and the means of production of contemporary industrial civilization.

Applied science in the military increased the ability of the West to impose itself on the rest of the world, and in this way science became a tool of empire. All Western colonial and imperial powers deployed scientists, physicians, engineers, and like experts in support of their burgeoning colonial and imperial endeavors.[30] The various Pasteur Institutes spread around the French empire, for example, illustrate the reach and role of science in the colonial context of the nineteenth and first half of the twentieth centuries.

As a concommitant feature of these developments, science in the West became professionalized in the nineteenth century in recognizably modern ways.[31] That William Whewell coined the English word "scientist" in 1840 is emblematic of what was involved. The above-mentioned reform of German universities after 1815 as research institutions with laboratories and graduate programs, the explosion of specialized institutions such as the Geological Society of London (1807), and professional associations like the British Society for the Advancement of Science (1831) or its American counterpart, the AAAS (1847) bespeak these changed circumstances as science became a full-time occupation pursued by Ph.D. researchers in social roles that had become plainly demarked and acknowledged. While French had been the international language of science in the eighteenth and first decades of the nineteenth century, it was German for the rest of the nineteenth and first part of the twentieth centuries.

Although not without antecedents in the previous Republic of Letters, new forms for the organization and pursuit of science emerged on the international level in the nineteenth century. Formal relations between

30 The works of Lewis Pyenson demand citation here; see his masterful trilogy: *Cultural Imperialism and Exact Sciences: German Expansion Overseas 1900–1930* (New York: Peter Lang, 1985); *Civilizing Mission: Exact Sciences and French Overseas Expansion, 1830–1940* (Baltimore and London: The Johns Hopkins University Press, 1993); *Empire of Reason: Exact Sciences in Indonesia, 1840–1940* (Leiden; New York: E. J. Brill, 1989). See also Michael A. Osborne, *Nature, the Exotic, and the Science of French Colonialism* (Bloomington: Indiana University Press, 1994) and "Science and the French Empire," *ISIS* 96 (2005): pp. 80–87. Regourd, "Science in the French colonies," provides additional background and context. The "civilizing mission" is particularly characteristic of France in the nineteenth and twentieth centuries, but is evident in other European colonial and imperial endeavors also.

31 McClellan and Dorn, *Science and Technology*, pp. 309–311; McClellan, *Science Reorganized*, pp. 256–259; "Scientific institutions and the organization of science," pp. 105–106.

and among European and American scientific institutions continued, as did common research projects, such as the international geomagnetic survey of 1827–1848. But international scientific congresses were the novelty in the international organization of science beginning in the nineteenth century.[32] They set the pattern for the exchange of the latest research findings and organizing international projects. Such specialized disciplinary meetings forged scientific contacts across borders and new forms of international scientific relations. They created international communities of scientists and spurred an identity of scientific internationalism, although still almost wholly within the Western imperium. But nationalistic sentiments formed the backdrop to such conferences and continued to shape international congresses and the international organization of science down to today.

As far as the intellectual history of science in the nineteenth century is concerned, to reprise Kuhn's model, we can simplify by pointing to what has been labeled the Second Scientific Revolution. This overlooked conceptual transformation involved the mathematization of the Baconian sciences (notably electricity and magnetism) and the unification of the previously separate Classical and Baconian sciences. The result is modern physics, something as we know it today. By the end of the nineteenth century, a grand intellectual synthesis and picture of the world – the Classical World View – emerged. For a brief period before 1905 and Einstein, physicists and chemists achieved a powerful if fragile and not uncontested scientific vision of the cosmos. Starting with Newton's absolute space and time (and therefore the flow of history), this vision held the universe to consist of three components: immutable chemical atoms endowed with the power of universal gravity, combining chemically, and bouncing around according to the laws of mechanics; the force of energy that changed from one form to another, but conserved itself in its protean guises; and a universal ether, the physical substrate of light and electromagnetic radiation. Thermodynamics and the discovery and mathematical mastery of energy and its behavior, incidentally, was one of the great achievements of nineteenth-century physics brought about by Joule, Kelvin, Maxwell, Clausius, and others. These discoveries and accomplishments cemented the moral authority of science, particularly the physical

32 Eckhardt Fuchs, "The politics of the Republic of Learning: international scientific congresses in Europe, the Pacific Rim, and Latin America," in Eckhardt Fuchs and Benedikt Stuchtey (eds.), *Across Cultural Borders: Historiography in Global Perspective* (Lanham, MD: Rowman & Littlefield, 2002), pp. 205–207, 226–228.

sciences, as a body of knowledge and a means of knowing, as well as a font of utility. Ironically, another of those pillars of modern scientific understanding – Darwinian evolution – was likewise the product of nineteenth-century science, but remained on the margins at the turn of the twentieth century, in good measure because the physicists denied Darwin the time needed to permit evolution. Much would change in science after Einstein and 1905.

World science and industrial civilization today

By 1900 the world had become a very different place than it was in 1800, as industrialization worked its transforming effects. We need to distinguish between and among the industrial revolution as something that unfolded in England, the larger process of industrialization that spread around the world, and industrial civilization as the practical and social/cultural result. Industrialization and industrial civilization have expanded and spread over the last two hundred years to the point where the Earth is entangled in one interconnected, intertwined, and interdependent global ecology of humans and the natural world. The most remote human outposts and regions of the globe today are not untouched by industrial civilization, but are now connected by the tentacles of progress. That the world population has grown from one billion in 1800 past the threshold of seven billion today is only one measure of the dramatic global changes that have developed in the period under review here. The exponential growth of science beyond even these indicators underscores the importance of science and industrial civilization on a world scale today.[33] With increasing momentum in the twentieth and now twenty-first centuries, science and science-based technologies have been and remain non-trivial factors driving world-historic change.

A simple laundry list shows the place and role of science and science-based technologies in industrial civilization on a world scale today. Almost randomly consider airplanes, automobiles, . . . transportation systems, . . . instantaneous global communication facilitated by orbiting satellites. Let's not forget about computers and the Internet and all that has come with, compliments of materials science and the silicon chip. Think how these technologies have restructured the world and everyday life in only the last

33 Derek J. de Solla Price, *Little Science, Big Science . . . and Beyond* (New York: Columbia University Press, 1986), esp. pp. 8, 135–154, documents this critical point.

half century. Any number of examples of continuing connections between science and the military tell the same tale, from stealth bombers to remotely operated drones to God knows what else. And, we should not overlook scientific medicine and what has resulted from medical applications of scientific research in biology, chemistry, and a host of related fields. At least in part, today's hyper-connected and global world owes itself to science and in some sense is the product of science. This begs the question of how exactly science has been tapped and applied in the technologies of contemporary civilization.

The atomic bombs dropped on Japan in 1945 represent an iconic case of applied science in the modern age, not least because they ended one war and started another, the Cold War, wherein physicists and nuclear weapons held the balance. The Bomb is a bad example to the extent that it uncritically inspires the cliché of technology as applied science.[34] The Bomb *was* a clear-cut and direct application of scientific *theory* to a practical application, knowledge from the cutting edge of the research front being turned directly to practical application, in this case from Lise Meitner and Otto Hahn and the conceptualization of nuclear fission in 1938/1939 to the Americans obliterating Japanese cities in 1945.

The reality of applied science in industrial and increasingly world civilization, however, is somewhat different from this sexy sense of science in society. More often, it involves what the historian Derek Price labeled "boiled down science" or the mundane (but hardly trivial) exploitation of knowledge by engineers or R&D specialists using what's available in textbooks, say, or online.[35] The invention of xerography and photocopying is exemplary here. Chester Carlson, a chemist and lawyer, developed the process by himself in his kitchen in 1938 using what he knew of optics and photochemistry. That for decades Carlson had to peddle his invention (with a wall of patent protection around it) or that photocopying machines did not come into general use until the 1960s says that much else is always involved when "science" gets transmuted into "technology." In this case considerable R&D, financing and business arrangements, and key marketing decisions had to be made before the technology migrated into copiers and printers and became a technological commonplace everywhere in the world. This instance turns another cliché on its head, with invention becoming the mother of necessity.

34 On these points, see McClellan and Dorn, *Science and Technology*, pp. 391–414, and papers in McClellan (ed.), *The Applied Science Problem*, including his own "What's problematic about 'applied science'?," pp. 1–36.

35 de Solla Price, *Little Science, Big Science*.

In the 1980s historians of technology, among others, introduced the concept of a technological system, or the idea of an entire set of things and ways of doing things required for any working technology, distinguishing, for example, between the artifact of a light bulb from all that's required to make it glow. Science and applied science are probably better thought of as part of the coming into being of technological systems, rather than as science somehow, almost mechanically, turned into technology. The concept of technological systems has proved most useful in conceptualizing today's incredible technologies and the place and role of science in innovation and new product development. The work of Thomas Parke Hughes stands out in this regard, and for Hughes and like-minded colleagues, rightly, science is only a piece of the whole puzzle that has to fall into place for a new science-based technology to emerge.[36] The electric car or wind or solar power technologies come to mind as examples. These days, systems thinking transcends privileging science or its application, as we somehow used to think.

Industrial civilization brought the industrialization of scientific research itself or what is known as Big Science. In Big Science today industrial-scale teams pursue scientific and applied science research in huge facilities on a large scale. The Manhattan Project and building the atomic bomb is a paradigmatic example; the best example currently is the Large Hadron Collider (LHC), the world's largest and highest-energy particle accelerator operated by CERN (European Center for Nuclear Research) on the Franco-Swiss border outside of Geneva. The LHC is a 26-kilometer ring built 100 meters underground and outfitted with particle detectors the size of six-story buildings; CERN itself employs 4,400 people. A list of such Big Science projects would go on to include other particle accelerators, national space programs, or the race to build the world's fastest computer. Any deep-space project and many ground-based astronomical observatories fit this category. All of these projects and more like them in the physical and biological sciences (such as the Human Genome Project) involve bringing together large, complex teams of researchers developing and using complex technological instruments for sophisticated research and application. Teams and individuals are inevitably specialized scientific workers, numbering in the

36 See Thomas P. Hughes, *American Genesis: A Century of Invention and Technological Enthusiasm, 1870–1970* (New York: Viking, 1989) and "The evolution of large technological systems," in Wiebe E. Bijker, Thomas P. Hughes, and Trevor Pinch (eds.), *The Social Construction of Technological Systems: New Directions in the Sociology and History of Technology* (Cambridge: MIT Press, 1989), pp. 51–82. See also Bruno Latour and Steve Woolgar, *Laboratory Life: The Construction of Scientific Facts* (Princeton University Press, 1986).

hundreds and even thousands in multinational collaborative networks, connected by computer and massive data processing. The expenses involved in this kind of research and development are enormous, funding at this scale mostly coming from governments, but also from regional, multinational, and industry sources. Thirty countries funded the LHC at a total cost of nearly two billion dollars. The Hubble Space Telescope cost approximately three billion dollars to build, service, and operate over the course of the period 1990–2007; the 2003–2005 Mars Exploration Rover Mission project cost $820 million. Nationalistic and military research may be less multinational, but no less industrial and managerial in this regard, and the phenomenon is worldwide. Small-scale science done by individuals or small teams, characteristic of the enterprise of science before the twentieth century, has not gone away and often, as in botany, paleontology, or mathematics, for example, produces important results. The industrialization of scientific research in the twentieth century is so new and such a marker of the blending of science and technology and of modernity on a global scale that it has been given the name Technoscience.[37] The term is a loose one with shades of meaning suggesting a seamless merger of what might be thought of separately as science and technology.

An argument can be made that science today is no longer "Western" per se, but has now gone global and become a world phenomenon, not in the sense of science studying the world as a whole, but institutionalized and implanted worldwide.[38] That is, what we think of as science or human understanding of nature may have (but only for the most part) come out of Europe and the West, but science today has vaulted to and implanted itself on the global level. To the extent that this claim is true, the globalization of Western science is a remarkable phenomenon in the history of science and world history since 1750. For current circumstances concerning science in society the suggestion is to drop the strawman label of "Western" science and substitute "modern science" or "science today" instead.[39] Plenty of evidence

37 Peter Galison and Bruce Hevly, eds., *Big Science: The Growth of Large-Scale Research* (Stanford University Press, 1992); McClellan and Dorn, *Science and Technology*, pp. 429–33. Giddens, *Europe in the Global Age*, pp. xii, 186, points to the development of a "knowledge economy," signaling a changing role of universities as "factories of the knowledge economy." Gidden's perspectives help further situate the enterprise of science, however fuzzy the concept be around the edges, in society and the economy today.

38 Tilley, "Global Histories," encourages this perspective, pp. 112–114.

39 McClellan, "Science and empire studies and postcolonial studies," makes this plea; on the historiographical background and context, see again Elshakry, "When science became Western."

supports this approach. Consider what is taught in university-level science courses, say physics or even biology 101, in China or India or Malaysia or Korea, Taiwan, or anywhere around the globe. Consider the rankings of nations in science and technology. And, world science is also the implantation of industries and R&D culture internationally. The spread of nuclear power and nuclear weapons to places like Pakistan in its way testifies to the global frame of reference that we now need to deploy in thinking about science and science-based technologies far and wide. The globalization of Western medicine and scientific medicine is only more true, with organized and institutionalized medicine of this sort found in hospitals and medical centers around the world today. The return of overseas Chinese scientists to their homeland is a recognized phenomenon, and China and India are already building cadres of scientific and technical experts and attractive facilities to support them at home. Places like Saudia Arabia and Qatar are not to be overlooked as developing centers of scientific research and application.[40] R&D is no longer strictly nationally based; what is important is innovation and application via global communication networks, not national or industry-based traditional R&D. Here, the multinational corporation versus the nation-state needs to be brought into focus in discussing the globalization of science. Europe and the USA account for slightly less than two-thirds of world R&D spending, but that share is decreasing, and other parts of the world spend proportionately much more on science R&D than does the USA[41] The rest of the world is producing an increasing share of research spending, patents, and scientists and engineers outside of traditional areas in Europe and the USA.

Such a change in terminology and perspective shifts the emphasis to where it belongs, away from the loaded term "Western science" and postcolonial conflict with the West (and its science) toward a more encompassing perspective and a range of other issues: the distribution of wealth within societies and across the globe; the state of the nation-state and the global organization of nations; the state of the world economy and world capitalism today; the success or inexorability of global and other globalizing institutions; centrifugal forces be they regional, local, or cultural; population, production, consumption, and the huge ecological effects of how we are living today, . . . in short, to straight thinking about industrial civilization and the state of the planet today. Science today is both part of these concerns and affected by

40 Tom Price, "Globalizing science," *CQ Global Researcher* 5 (2011), pp. 53–78; McClellan and Dorn, *Science and Technology*, pp. 311–318.

41 McClellan and Dorn, *Science and Technology*, pp. 418–419.

them. In this connection, Postcolonial Studies scholars Gesa Mackenthun and Sünne Juterczenka have suggested that the epistemological "fuzziness" we must bring to thinking about science is partly the result of its internationalization and globalization.[42]

In the meantime, what can we say of the remarkable development of science as natural philosophy in the twentieth and now twenty-first century? That is, science as a body of knowledge not only to be put to use in industrial civilization, but to explain the natural world around us. That story involved the collapse of the Classical World View of the nineteenth century and can only be suggested here by waving at Einstein and general and special relativity, the discovery of radioactivity and particle physics as these fields developed, the quantum theory of light and then the quantum mechanics and uncertainty as understood and articulated by Werner Heisenburg and Erwin Schrödinger and later Niels Bohr; Edwin Hubble and an expanding universe, Big Bang cosmology, and the Robert Wilson and Arno Penzias discovery of the 3° Kelvin background radiation in 1965. A notable theoretical and practical development in twentieth-century science was the revival and success of Darwinian evolution along with Mendel's genes and their confirmation in the discovery of the double helical nature of DNA by James Watson and Francis Crick in 1953. Subsequent developments in genetics, consequential for natural philosophy and for practical application (think of DNA forensics, for example), have been spectacular over the last half century, and evolutionary thinking has refracted into huge areas of scientific thought, not least concerning sociobiology and evolutionary psychology. Add to this psychology, paleontology, plate tectonics, and the full panoply of scientific knowledge today, and we are well equipped to tell unprecedentedly sophisticated stories about ourselves and the natural world around us. With every epistemological and postmodern caveat in mind, these incredible stories make science a great human intellectual and cultural achievement. It is a human-based explanatory enterprise that remains open-ended. Scientific questions over dark matter and dark energy, for example, and related speculations at the research front of so many fields today are both fascinating and make us ultimately tentative about an "end of science." But science's claims are the best we've got presently and in this author's opinion the best we can get in principle.

More than one international association and commission now binds scientific research and researchers together on a global level, including

42 Juterczenka and Mackenthun, "Introduction," p. 11.

UNESCO (the United Nations Educational, Scientific and Cultural Organization) and the umbrella organization, the International Council for Science, founded in 1931 as the International Council of Scientific Unions (ICSU), with well over one hundred affiliated organizations, including that for the history and philosophy of science. The ICSU and its subordinate unions sponsor many congresses, conferences, symposia, and meetings around the world annually. There are hundreds and thousands of international scientific and specialist conferences with as many specialist societies and organizations sponsoring these events. If the international language of science was German in the nineteenth and first part of the twentieth centuries, then after a detour through Russian, it is now almost universally English.

Science and industrial civilization have been the subject of criticism, especially in the postcolonial period following the Second World War. Decolonization has not entailed a democratization of science, although it has a bit with science-based technologies, such as cell phones, that have significantly impacted economically disadvantaged countries and peoples. But nevertheless, rich and poor countries and peoples separate themselves out today not just economically, but also scientifically and technologically.[43] A divide exists, an imbalance between haves and have-nots that offers further perspectives on the enterprise of science on a world scale today. Many topics involving science and global issues have not been sufficiently broached. These include the existence and character of whatever "colonial science" remains in former colonies, the Third World Academy of Science, brain drain, the skewed investments of multinational corporations in R&D overseas, biopiracy, biopatents, "ethno botany," native patrimony and rights, and intellectual property.[44]

The Postcolonial Studies critique mentioned above sees science too often as part of a grand narrative about the Enlightenment, reason, progress, freedom, democracy, equality, justice, and a universalizing rationality of European origin.[45] The field proposes a counter narrative about science from a global vantage point that involves imperialism, colonialism, racism, sexism, slavery, subjugation, domination, appropriation, exploitation, profit, and self-interest.[46] Other critics have bemoaned cultural homogenization and the decline of and threats to local cultures brought on by science and

43 Vertus Saint-Louis, "Foreword," in McClellan, *Colonialism and Science*, esp. p. xi.

44 Safier, "Global knowledge on the move," pp. 139–143.

45 Jörn Rüsen, "Comparing cultures in intercultural communication," in Fuchs and Stutchey (eds.), *Across Cultural Borders*, pp. 335–347; here pp. 337–338.

46 Paraphrased from Bentley, "World history and grand narrative," p. 49.

industrialization, especially with world science now closely tied to technological progress, the market economy, and doctrines of rationality. Science and scientists are part of the "technical-managerial elite" in cahoots with universities, industry, and government to rule the world. Regionalism, ethnocentrism, superstitions, and fundamentalisms of various sorts continue to challenge the hegemony of world science and industrial civilization. The ecological effects of industrial civilization hardly need to be remarked upon, including science and industries as contributing factors to climate change and environmental issues affecting world history. How humanity lives today is astounding and begs the question about the future of industrial civilization. In this sense science today is part of the problem, but potentially part of the solution.

The distinction is made in French between "mondalisation" and "globalisation." The former is taken to mean something local, raised informally from the bottom up, almost by diffusion, to the world level, as in your local Chinese, Thai or Mexican take-out, versus "globalisation" which implies the homogenization of global culture, more like the McDonalds or Starbucks on your corner. From this perspective the enterprise of science is indicative of something in between. It is surely global, as experts can migrate from one lab or project to another. But there is no single mark or brand. The enterprise of science is still very nation-based and supported by local interests, yet to an extent free from them and corporate interests, too. Not just anyone can do science, either, as we might open an ethnic restaurant. Then, if there is such a thing as "démondialisation," will science, too, retreat into regional or local identities?

The cultural impact of science in the modern world has been great, certainly in secular democratic societies, but sadly, it is not uncontested even there. Around the globe one can ask about the reality of science as simply an instrument providing powers versus science linked to values and the Enlightenment program of reason, human understanding, and human progress

Further reading

Bijker, Wiebe E., Thomas P. Hughes, and Trevor Pinch, eds. *The Social Construction of Technological Systems: New Directions on the Sociology and History of Technology*. Cambridge: MIT Press, 1989.

Daugeron, Bertrand. *Collections naturalistes entre science et empires, 1763–1804*. Paris: Muséum national d'histoire naturelle, 2009.

de Solla Price, Derek J. *Little Science, Big Science ... and Beyond*. New York: Columbia University Press, 1986.

Dorn, Harold. *The Geography of Science*. Baltimore and London: The Johns Hopkins University Press, 1991.

Fuchs, Eckhardt. "The politics of the Republic of Learning: international scientific congresses in Europe, the Pacific Rim, and Latin America," in Eckhardt Fuchs and Benedikt Stuchtey (eds.), *Across Cultural Borders: Historiography in Global Perspective*. Lanham, MD: Rowman & Littlefield, 2002, pp. 205–244.

Galison, Peter and Bruce Hevly, eds. *Big Science: The Growth of Large-Scale Research*. Stanford University Press, 1992.

Elshakry, Marwa. "When science became Western: historiographical reflections." *ISIS* 101 (2010), 98–109.

Gillispie, Charles C. *Science and Polity in France at the End of the Old Regime*. Princeton University Press, 1980.

Hughes, Thomas P. *American Genesis: A Century of Invention and Technological Enthusiasm, 1870–1970*. New York: Viking, 1989.

Huigen, Siegfried. *Knowledge and Colonialism: Eighteenth-Century Travellers in South Africa*. Leiden and Boston: Brill, 2009.

Jacob, Margaret C. *Scientific Culture and the Making of the Industrial West*. Oxford University Press, 1997.

Juterczenka, Sünne and Gesa Mackenthum, eds. *The Fuzzy Logic of Encounter: New Perspectives on Cultural Contact*. Münster, New York, München, Berlin: Waxmann, 2009.

Kuhn, Thomas S. "Mathematical versus experimental traditions in the development of physical science," *Journal of Interdisciplinary History* 7 (1976), pp. 1–31. [Reprinted in Kuhn, *The Essential Tension*. University of Chicago Press, 1977, pp. 31–65.]

Latour, Bruno and Steve Woolgar. *Laboratory Life: The Construction of Scientific Facts*. Princeton University Press, 1986.

McClellan, James E. III. *Colonialism and Science: Saint Domingue in the Old Regime*. Baltimore and London: Johns Hopkins University Press, 1992; reprint with a new preface by Vertus Saint-Louis, Chicago: University of Chicago Press, 2010.

"Science and empire studies and postcolonial studies: a report from the contact zone," in Gesa Mackenthun and Klaus Hock (eds.), *Cultural Encounters and the Discourses of Scholarship*, vol. 4. Münster: Waxmann, 2012, pp. 51–74.

Science Reorganized: Scientific Societies in the Eighteenth Century. New York: Columbia University Press, 1985.

"Scientific institutions and the organization of science," in Roy Porter (ed.), *The Cambridge History of Science*, Vol. 4: *Science in the Eighteenth Century*. Cambridge University Press, 2003, pp. 99–120.

McClellan, James E. III, ed. *The Applied Science Problem*. Jersey City, NJ: Jensen/Daniels Publishers, 2008.

McClellan, James E. III and Harold Dorn. *Science and Technology in World History: An Introduction: Second Edition*. Baltimore and London: The Johns Hopkins University Press, 2006; 3rd edn. 2015.

McClellan, James E. III and François Regourd. *The Colonial Machine: French Science and Overseas Expansion in the Old Regime*. Turnhout: Brepols Publishers, 2011.

Osborne, Michael A. *Nature, the Exotic, and the Science of French Colonialism.* Bloomington: Indiana University Press, 1994.

"Science and the French Empire," *ISIS* 96 (2005), pp. 80–87.

Price, Tom. "Globalizing Science," *CQ Global Researcher* 5 (2011), pp. 53–78.

Pyenson, Lewis. *Civilizing Mission: Exact Sciences and French Overseas Expansion, 1830–1940.* Baltimore and London: The Johns Hopkins University Press, 1993.

Cultural Imperialism and Exact Sciences: German Expansion Overseas 1900–1930. New York: Peter Lang, 1985.

Empire of Reason: Exact Sciences in Indonesia, 1840–1940. Leiden; New York: E. J. Brill, 1989.

Raj, Kapil. *Relocating Modern Science: Circulation and the Construction of Knowledge in South Asia and Europe, 1650–1900.* Delhi: Permanent Black; New York: Palgrave Macmillan, 2007.

Regourd, François. "Science in the French colonies," in George N. Vlahakis, Isabel Maria Malaquias, Nathan M. Brooks, François Regourd, Feza Gunergun, and David Wright (eds.), *Imperialism and Science: Social Impact and Interaction.* Santa Barbara, Denver, Oxford: A.B.C. Clio, 2006, chapter 3.

Safier, Neil. "Global knowledge on the move: itineraries, Amerindian narratives, and deep histories of science," [Focus: Global Histories of Science] *ISIS* 101 (2010), pp. 133–45.

Measuring the New World: Enlightenment Science and South America. University of Chicago Press, 2008.

Sivasundaram, Sujit. "Introduction" and "Sciences and the global: on methods, questions, and theory," *ISIS* 101 (2010), pp. 95–97 and 146–58. [Focus: Global Histories of Science, *ISIS* 101 (2010), pp. 95–158.]

Spary, E. C. *Utopia's Garden: French Natural History from Old Regime to Revolution.* The University of Chicago Press, 2000.

Stuchtey, Benedikt, ed. *Science across the European Empires, 1800–1950.* Oxford: German Historical Institute/Oxford University Press, 2005.

Stuchtey, Benedikt and Eckhardt Fuchs, eds. *Writing World History, 1800–2000.* Oxford: Oxford University Press/German Historical Institute London, 2003.

Taton, René, ed. *Enseignement et diffusion des sciences en France au dix-huitième siècle.* Paris: Hermann, 1964; reprint, 1986.

Tilley, Helen. "Global histories, vernacular science, and African genealogies; or, is the history of science ready for the world." [Forum: Global Histories of Science] *ISIS* 101 (2010), pp. 110–119.

9

Music on the move, as object, as commodity

TIMOTHY D. TAYLOR

This chapter treats the production, distribution, and consumption of musics around the world. As a result of the rise of digital and other technologies in the last few decades, the distribution and consumption of music has become ubiquitous, leading to a condition that composer R. Murray Schafer and anthropologist Steven Feld have termed "schizophonia," the separation of sounds from their makers.[1] The discussion begins, however, with a capsule history of the various modes of the objectification and later commodification of music that preceded today's schizophonia and the ideologies surrounding the production and consumption of music, particularly musics places far from western metropoles.

Music for most of human history was not recorded in any fashion. Even today, recordings of music as sound or in notation are more the exception than the norm. The history of the objectification and later commodification of music that has led to ideologies of the exchangeability and appropriability of music in the West must begin with its earliest form of objectification in the form of notation. In the European Middle Ages, the same texts were being sung differently in different churches in different locations since their music was transmitted orally, stored in people's memories. Notation was introduced at the behest of Charlemagne in the eighth century as a means of standardizing musical treatments of the liturgy from one church to the next, and from one generation to the next. Notation began as a simple *aide mémoire*. Music would be copied by hand, as were religious texts, though composers came to learn that notation afforded them the opportunity to test its limits, and their

1 R. Murray Schafer, *The Soundscape: Our Sonic Environment and the Tuning of the World* (1977; reprint, Rochester, Vermont: Destiny, 1994); Steven Feld, "From schizophonia to schismogenesis: on the discourses and commodification practices of 'world music' and 'world beat,'" in Charles Keil and Steven Feld, *Music Grooves: Essays and Dialogues* (University of Chicago Press, 1994).

creativity, so that by the fourteenth century, musical works by Guillaume de Machaut (*c.* 1300–77) and others had become ingeniously constructed and quite intricate. Notation had ceased to be simply a mode of standardization or even a memory aid, but began to be considered to be an end in itself, though, of course, most written compositions were still made for the glory of God.

The next major shift in the objectification of music emerged with the rise of music printing at the end of the fifteenth century. Printing with moveable type was as much a revolution in music publishing as in the printing of texts and drawings, facilitating the further movement of music around the European continent, permitting composers a broader audience outside of the church, and objectifying music in a new way.

Capitalism

While these developments in the history of music were crucial, in some ways they were less important than those that followed in the eighteenth and nineteenth centuries, when musicians' livelihoods changed dramatically. There were several intertwined developments that bear directly on the conceptions of music that are still common today, and I will consider them separately here.

Copyright

First, while composers and performers had long worked for the church or for a member of the nobility in what is known as the patronage system, with the decline of the aristocracy and the rise of a capitalist middle class in the late eighteenth century, composers increasingly were subject to the whims of the market, and had to think increasingly in entrepreneurial terms. They were aided in this by a number of cultural and legal shifts, the first of which was the introduction of copyright in the late eighteenth century, which allowed composers or their publishers ownership of their works, which was a right that had previously been the monarch's to give. With the entry of musical works into the capitalist marketplace, composers increasingly saw themselves as artists, even geniuses (a concept that would arise later, in the nineteenth century). These were – and remain – powerful ideologies by which composers attempt to differentiate themselves from others in a capitalist market of works.

Aesthetics

Another important shift was the rise of aesthetics, or the notion of "art for art's sake," an idea that has a rather curious history. I have written at greater length elsewhere of the crisis of use-value of artworks with the decline of the patronage system.[2] In the work of almost every important classical philosopher, music – in particular, instrumental music – poses a unique problem. Opera and other musical genres with words, or accompanied by dance, represent something – such music tells a story, paints a picture with sound. Instrumental music, however, does not. Jean-Jacques Rousseau wrote in his *Dictionnaire de Musique* (1767) under the entry for "sonata" that

> in order to know what all these jumbles of *sonatas* mean, one would have to be like a crude painter who must write above his figures; *this is a tree, this is a man, this is a horse*. I shall never forget the flash of wit of the famous Fontenelle, who, finding himself overburdened with these interminable Symphonies, cried out in fit of impatience: *sonata, what do you want of me?*[3]

Something as apparently useless – devoid of use-value – as instrumental music had to be dealt with in this new market of music, and it was Adam Smith who first proposed the idea that instrumental music does not need to signify anything at all – it can simply signify itself. In an essay published in 1795, Smith writes,

> That music seldom means to tell any particular story, or to imitate any particular event, or in general to suggest any particular object, distinct from that combination of sounds of which itself is composed. Its meaning, therefore, may be said to be complete in itself, and to require no interpreters to explain it. What is called the subject of such Music is merely . . . a certain leading combination of notes, to which it frequently returns, and to which all its digressions and variations bear a certain affinity.[4]

He continues, after comparing music to painting, by writing that the melody and harmony of music do not "suggest" anything other than themselves, and, "in fact [they] signify and suggest nothing."[5] I would be remiss not to mention Alexander Baumgarten's monumental eight-volume *Aesthetica*, published from 1750–8, which marks the first use of the term "aesthetics."

The overall point is that with the entry of music into the capitalist marketplace in the late eighteenth century, there was not only a crisis of use-value,

2 Timothy D. Taylor, *Beyond Exoticism: Western Music and the World* (Durham, NC: Duke University Press, 2007).

3 Jean Jacques Rousseau, *Dictionnaire de Musique* (Hildesheim: Georg Olms Verlagsbuchhandlung; New York: Johnson Reprint Corporation, 1969), p. 452; emphases in original). Fontenelle was Bernard le Bovier de Fontenelle (1657–1757), scientist and man of letters, highly regarded by Voltaire.

4 Adam Smith, *Essays on Philosophical Subjects*, ed. W. P. D. Wightman and J. C. Bryce (Oxford: Clarendon Press, 1980), p. 205.

5 Smith, *Essays*, pp. 205–206.

particularly with respect to instrumental music, but also, the establishment of exchange-value, coupled with the rise of aesthetics. And this development was important for composers, who began to justify all manner of appropriation and representation by appealing to the new concepts of art, genius, and masterpiece. Copyright and aesthetics objectified music in new ways, particularly as a commodity in a capitalist market of musical goods.

Nationalisms/Colonialisms

European composers who actively appropriated or represented folk musics from their own regions in their music were common in the nineteenth century, whether Bedřich Smetana (1824–1884) or Antonín Dvořák (1841–1904) in Czechoslovakia, or representations of "gypsy" music by Franz Liszt (1811–1886), Johannes Brahms (1833–1897), and many others.

But, despite the liberation achieved by the rise of aesthetics, as well as the concepts of, genius, and masterpiece, Western musicians – and audiences – did not show much interest in musics from other places until the beginning of the late nineteenth / early twentieth centuries. In part this newfound interest was a result of both nationalist tendencies, as well as the experience of some European states, particularly France, slowly coming to grips with their colonialized Others voyaging to Paris and other European metropoles. Some of this interest in sounds from other places was a result of the widespread belief among composers that tonality, the do-re-mi musical language that had been dominant since the beginning of the seventeenth century, had been worn out, that innovation through the manipulation of pitches was no longer possible after the works of Richard Wagner (1813–83) and others, who were thought to have stretched tonality to the breaking point. New musical resources were needed, and they were found, by some composers at least, in non-Western musics, or in the musics of rural folk musicians.

By the end of the nineteenth century in France, musicians, and the French public in general, first came into contact with sounds from other places through attendance at international exhibitions beginning in the late nineteenth century. There was plenty of music at these exhibitions, from France's colonized peoples and others. The sights and sounds from these exhibitions exerted a profound effect on artists in France in this period, helping them make new forms of modernist art.

Claude Debussy (1862–1918), the first of the modernist French composers, visited the 1889 exposition, and wrote in 1913, using the romanticizing language of this era:

> There were, and still are, despite the evils of civilization, some delightful native peoples for whom music is as natural as breathing. Their conservatoire is the eternal rhythm of the sea, the wind among the leaves and the thousand sounds of nature which they understand without consulting an arbitrary treatise. Their traditions reside in old songs, combined with dances, built up throughout the centuries. Yet Javanese music is based on a type of counterpoint by comparison with which that of Palestrina is child's play. And if we listen without European prejudice to the charm of their percussion we must confess that our percussion is like primitive noises at a country fair.[6]

Debussy employed or referred to Javanese music in several compositions.[7]

Other composers in this period turned inward to their own cultures as a means of devising new musical languages, whether Igor Stravinsky (1882–1971) cultivating a relationship to Russian folk music in such celebrated works as *Le Sacre du printemps* (1913), which makes use of many Russian folk songs[8]; or the Hungarian composer Béla Bartók (1881–1945), who collected folk music from all over Eastern Europe, some of which found its way into many of his works. Bartók, like many composers of his time, believed that music needed to be renewed. For him, the solution was to seek inspiration from folk music of his region.[9]

The interests of Stravinsky, Bartók, and others in non-Western musics, or musics "other" to their own music, were driven in part by the rising hegemony of finance capital in the late nineteenth/early twentieth centuries, which slowly helped to promote an ideology of the importance of

6 Quoted by Edward Lockspeiser, *Debussy: His Life and Mind*, vol. 2 (Cambridge University Press, 1978), p. 115. For more on music at this particular exhibition, see Annegret Fauser, *Musical Encounters at the 1889 Paris World's Fair* (University of Rochester Press, 2005).

7 See Roy Howat, "Debussy and the Orient," in Andrew Gerstle and Anthony Milner (eds.), *Recovering the Orient: Artists, Scholars, Appropriations* (London: Harwood, 1995).

8 See Richard Taruskin, "Russian folk melodies in *The Rite of Spring*," *Journal of the American Musicological Society* 33 (Fall 1980), 501–543.

9 See Béla Bartók, "The influence of peasant music on modern music," in Benjamin Suchoff (ed.), *Béla Bartók Esssays* (London: Faber & Faber, 1976), and "The relation of folk song to the development of the art music of our time," in *Béla Bartók Essays*. For more on Western treatments of non-Western musics, see Georgina Born and David Hesmondhalgh, eds., *Western Music and Its Others: Difference, Representation, and Appropriation in Music* (Berkeley, CA: University of California Press, 2000); Yayoi Uno Everett and Frederick Lau, eds., *Locating East Asia in Western Art Music* (Middletown, CT: Wesleyan University Press, 2004); Ralph Locke, *Musical Exoticism: Images and Reflections* (Cambridge University Press, 2009); and Michael Tenzer, "Western music in the context of world music," in Robert P. Morgan (ed.), *Modern Times: From World War I to the Present* (Englewood Cliffs, NJ: Prentice Hall, 1994).

exchange-value over use-value and, indeed, everything else.[10] Other musics were slowly reconceptualized not as "other," but as sounds that could be incorporated into one's own music, just as, in the visual arts, Picasso and Georges Bracque began to appropriate everyday objects into their artworks.[11]

New technologies of recording and reproduction

Bartók and others were aided in the collecting of folk songs by new technologies such as the phonograph. This device, invented in the USA and Europe about the same time, the late 1870s, made possible recording and playback of sounds. While Thomas Edison, the inventor in the USA, famously did not conceive of recording music as an important use for the phonograph, instead viewing it as a more homely device that could record the last words of a dying family member, or a song that one could bring to a friend later to play for her amusement.[12]

Nonetheless, the player piano, phonograph, and, later, radio, and sound film all had a profound effect on people's relationships to music, for all of these devices not only continued the objectification and commodification of music that had begun with music printing – they objectified and commodified music as sound.

To be sure, consumers in both Europe and the USA were slow to adopt these new technologies. Learning to conceive of musical sound as something that someone purchased instead of making it oneself was a slow and lengthy process that took decades, aided in part by the rise of a modern consumer culture that was buttressed by the new advertising industry in the late nineteenth century, which helped promote new sound reproduction technologies such as the player piano, phonograph, and radio.[13]

10 Rudolf Hilferding, *Finance Capital: A Study of the Latest Phase of Capitalist Development*, ed. Tom Bottomore, trans. Morris Watnick and Sam Gordon (London: Routledge, 1981). See also Giovanni Arrighi, *The Long Twentieth Century: Money, Power, and the Origins of Our Times* (New York: Verso, 1994).

11 See Fredric Jameson, "Culture and finance capital," *Critical Inquiry* 24 (1997), 246–265; and Timothy D. Taylor, "Stravinsky and others," *AVANT: The Journal of the Philosophical-Interdisciplinary Vanguard* 4 (2013), http://avant.edu.pl/wp-content/uploads/Timothy-D-Taylor-Stravinsky-and-Others1.pdf.

12 For Edison's first writing on the uses of the phonograph, see Timothy D. Taylor, Mark Katz, and Tony Grajeda, eds., *Music, Sound, and Technology in America: A Documentary History of Early Phonograph, Cinema, and Radio* (Durham: Duke University Press, 2012).

13 See David Suisman, *Selling Sounds: The Commercial Revolution in American Music* (Cambridge, MA: Harvard University Press, 2009). The player piano was a device invented in the late nineteenth century that attached to a piano and could, through the use of a paper roll punched with holes that allowed air to pass through that moved a

Even though many musicians and intellectuals initially opposed what they decried as "mechanical music," these new technologies caught on.[14] Recordings, and even player piano rolls, made available musics from other places that allowed composers to hear different sounds and employ them in their own music. With the advent of magnetic tape immediately after World War II, recorded music could be manipulated electronically, as it was in several well-known composers' works, such as Pierre Boulez (1925–) and Karlheinz Stockhausen's (1928–2007), whose *Hymnen* (1966–7) conglomerates national anthems from all over the world, and whose *Telemusik* (1966), he says, is an attempt to realize an "old and ever-recurrent dream: to go a step further towards writing, not 'my' music, but a music of the whole world, of all lands and races."[15] Music was thus ever more divorced from its original makers, ever more an object, a commodity.

Production, distribution, and consumption of music in globalized neoliberal capitalism

With this section I arrive at the main focus of this chapter, a consideration of recent forms of the objectification and commodification of music facilitated in part by new digital technologies, which also enable the increasing consumption of musics from around the world. Capitalism has changed as well – also made possible in part by new digital technologies – so it is necessary to lay the groundwork for what follows.

Generally I am in agreement with those who have posited a new form of capitalism that emerged a few decades ago, though commentators do not always agree on what to call it, whether late capitalism, disorganized capitalism, neoliberal capitalism, or something else altogether, such as "globalization" or "information age" or "network society." I have come somewhat reluctantly to prefer the term neoliberal capitalism, a form of capitalism that is being shaped by policies that have sought to enrich elite groups by aggressively utilizing the powers of the state, new technologies, and seeking global markets and labor. Thus, while I agree with those who describe today's capitalism as neoliberal, I find much of this work to be

mechanical "finger," "play" the piano. Later player pianos incorporated the playing mechanism inside the piano itself.

14 Taylor, Katz, and Grajeda, *Music, Sound, and Technology in America*, collects some writings by these detractors.

15 Karl H. Wörner, *Stockhausen: Life and Work*, ed. and trans. Bill Hopkins (Berkeley, CA: University of California Press, 1973), p. 58. See also Karlheinz Stockhausen, "World Music," trans. Bernard Radloff, *Dalhousie Review* 69 (1989), 318–326.

economistic, failing to pay sufficient attention to the culture that neoliberalism is shaping, one that is increasingly globally interconnected.

While the international record industry distributed European and American music abroad almost from its inception at the beginning of the twentieth century, mainly along colonial pathways, musics from non-Western Elsewheres were not easily available in Western metropoles until fairly recently. There were, of course, ethnographic and other kinds of field recordings that one could hear, but commercial recordings from, say, India or Africa were not common until the last few decades. In part this was simply because many small, or even large, countries did not have recording industries.[16] But once these countries increasingly became capitalist and increasingly developed a music industry, exports became more common.

Important precursors to what became known as world music was the rise of, first, ska, and later reggae in Jamaica, musics that gained worldwide popularity. Ska originated in the 1950s and developed both from other Caribbean musics such as calypso, but also African American popular musics. Reggae, which grew out of ska and rocksteady a decade or so later, produced the first non-US and non-European international music superstar, Bob Marley (1945–1981), whose belief that all black and brown people are brothers and sisters had an incalculable influence around the world. As an Australian radio DJ recalled, "Bob Marley played Adelaide in early 1979. The dust raised by that tour never really settled."[17] Australian aboriginal musicians, as did musicians around the world, began to make reggae and other popular musics themselves.

But Marley sang in English, and his music, owing as it did to African American sounds and styles, was not so different to listeners accustomed to American and European popular music that it couldn't find an international market. What was different in the 1980s and after was that more and more music from the West's Elsewheres was entering record shops. Retailers didn't know where to shelve it. The old "International" section that included German polkas and Irish drinking songs didn't seem to be the right place to shelve music from South Africa that sounded like Western popular music, though sung in languages nobody in the shops knew. So, a group of retailers and journalists and radio DJs gathered in London in 1987 and selected the term "world music" to describe these new sounds, which were mostly music

16 See Roger Wallis and Krister Malm, *Big Sounds from Small Peoples: the Music Industry in Small Countries* (London: Constable, 1984).

17 Quoted by Marcus Breen, ed., *Our Place, Our Music, Australian Popular Music in Perspective*, Vol. 2 (Canberra: Aboriginal Studies Press, 1989), p. 121.

influenced by British and American popular music but which were at the same time, new.[18] As the influential British DJ and author Charlie Gillett recounted,

> We had a very simple, small ambition. It was all geared to record shops, that was the only thing we were thinking about. In America, King Sunny Ade (from Nigeria) was being filed under reggae. That was the only place shops could think of to put him. In Britain they didn't know where to put this music – I think Ade was just lost in the alphabet, next to Abba. In 1985 [*sic*] Paul Simon did Graceland and that burst everything wide open, because he created an interest in South African music. People were going into shops saying: "I want some of that stuff" and there wasn't anywhere for them to look.[19]

"World music" gave many musicians from around the world a platform, even as the international music industry attempted to turn this vast collection of different musics into a "genre." But the term also advertised the presence of new music from everywhere, and many composers and musicians saw them, as did musicians early in the twentieth century, as a way of revitalizing their music, whether their field was composition or songwriting.

Thanks to centuries of the objectification and commodification of music and the liberatory effects of the ideology of aesthetics, which had been extended to rock musicians in the realm of popular music (who are akin to composers in the classical world in the license they are permitted to realize their creativity), world music of all kinds was viewed as ripe for the picking. Or, rather, it was frequently viewed as a natural resource that was ready to be mined. Discourses about world music from the 1980s and 1990s are replete with Western musicians characterizing non-Western popular musics as natural resources that were waiting to be discovered by the right explorer or curator.

Stewart Copeland, former drummer of the 1980s megaband The Police, issued a recording 1985 called *The Rhythmatist* that employed sounds from around Africa. The liner notes showed a photograph of Copeland all dressed in black, holding a huge, phallic, microphone, a new explorer in a neoliberal world. Copeland characterized the album, and its title, thus:

18 See Timothy D. Taylor, *Global Pop: World Music, World Markets* (New York: Routledge, 1997).

19 Robin Denselow, "We Created World Music," *Guardian*, June 29, 2004, 10. For more on the rise of world music, see Steven Feld, "Notes on 'World Beat,'" in Charles Keil and Steven Feld, *Music Grooves: Essays and Dialogues* (University of Chicago Press, 1994); George Lipsitz, *Dangerous Crossroads: Popular Music, Postmodernism and the Poetics of Place* (New York: Verso, 1994); Martin Stokes, "Music and the global order," *Annual Review of Anthropology* (2004), 47–72; and Taylor, *Global Pop*.

> "Rhythmatism" is the study of patterns that weave the fabric of life; with this speculation in mind a black clad figure is on his way across the so-called dark continent. He meets lions, warriors, pygmies and jungles before stumbling across the **rock**.[20]

When confronted with the idea that perhaps he was simply appropriating other peoples' music, Copeland responded by ridiculing the idea that he was "mining" other people's music, and insisted that musicians around the world derived pleasure from knowing that faraway people enjoyed their music.[21]

Paul Simon, for another example of the assumption of the naturalness of cultural production outside of Western metropoles, said, "Culture flows like water. It isn't something that can just be cut off."[22] Elsewhere, in response to a charges that he had appropriated black music as early rock 'n' roll musicians had done, Simon retorted, "You think it's easy to make a hit out of [that]?," as though Ladysmith Black Mambazo's and other South African musicians' music was raw material in need of refinement by a westerner with superior knowledge and technologies.[23]

These kinds of attitudes remain quite common, as rock musicians, as well as composers of contemporary classical music, believe that anything goes in the feeding of their muse.

Paul Simon and Graceland (1986)

Indeed, it was Simon's *Graceland* album from 1986 that awakened many, even most, listeners to world music, and in particular, African popular musics. Simon, like many Western stars who work with musicians from other cultures, says that he had been listening to South African popular musics for some time before he began to learn about them and began to desire making an album with local musicians. This kind of claim of a longstanding relationship is common among Western stars, who presumably don't want to be seen as carpetbaggers; establishing a kind of long-term connoisseurship is part of this strategy, before these musicians can be seen as curators of non-Western musics, or even, collaborators.[24]

Simon violated a United Nations boycott of trade with South Africa to make his recording, though he paid his musicians well. The album, while

20 Stewart Copeland, liner notes to *The Rhythmatist*, A&M CD 5084, 1985.

21 David N. Blank-Edelman, "Stewart Copeland: the rhythmatist returns," *RMM*, February 1994, 38.

22 Denis Herbstein, "The hazards of cultural deprivation," *Africa Report*, July-August 1987, 35.

23 *Paul Simon: Born at the Right Time*, directed by Susan Lacy and Susan Steinberg, 1991.

24 Louise Meintjes, "Paul Simon's Graceland, South Africa, and the mediation of musical meaning," *Ethnomusicology* 34 (Winter 1990): 37–73.

popular for its music, nonetheless was criticized by many for violated this boycott and Simon's perceived appropriation of South African popular musics.[25] At the same time, the musicians with whom Simon worked defended him, and their work on the album. They, like so many musicians around the world, had been seeking international recognition and working with an American superstar like Paul Simon was a way to achieve this. As Ray Phiri, a guitarist from the album, said,

> *We* as South African musicians, we were using him more than he was using *us*, if ever there was any [appropriate] word like "using." Because here we were, isolated from the world, and trying really hard to get involved in the international community. And it wasn't happening. And suddenly here was this guy who was known, and was writing beautiful words. And I thought maybe if we mix our rhythms with his thoughts we might get some kind of musical osmosis that would simply... say, "this is the direction of the music."[26]

Clearly, the *Graceland* case raised complicated questions about stars' and local musicians' desires, and began what has been a fairly common string of recordings in which a famous western musician, such as David Byrne, Peter Gabriel, or Ry Cooder, collaborates, or curates, or brokers, local musicians, often accompanied by some controversy, or at least critical disapprobation.

Non-Western, or, more precisely, non-European and non-American musicians, have benefited from their work with Western stars and some have slowly become better known in the Western metropoles, though superstardom has proved elusive for all of them, hampered as they are by not singing in English to audiences who are accustomed to popular music in that language. But they well ensconced in university concert series, college radio, public radio in the USA, which has hosted a program called *Afropop Worldwide* since 1988.

These musicians, especially those from the African continent, continue to fight stereotypes that they are premodern people from the bush who are ignorant of the ways of the West, including its musics and technologies. The great Beninoise singer, Angélique Kidjo, said, "There is a kind of cultural racism going on where people think that African musicians have to make a certain kind of music."[27] Elsewhere, she said,

25 For just one critique, see Charles Hamm, "*Graceland* revisited," in *Putting Popular Music in its Place* (Cambridge University Press, 1995).

26 *Born at the Right Time.*

27 Ty Burr, "From Africa, three female rebels with a cause," *New York Times*, July 10, 1994, §H, 28.

> I won't do my music different to please some people who want to see something very traditional. The music I write is me. It's how I feel. If you want to see traditional music and exoticism, take a plane to Africa. They play that music on the streets. I'm not going to play traditional drums and dress like bush people. I'm not going to show my ass for any fucking white man. If they want to see it, they can go outside. I'm not here for that. I don't ask Americans to play country music.[28]

Le Mystère des voix bulgares *(1975)*

In addition to *Graceland*, another extremely influential recording that helped to establish world music in retail establishments and in the musical culture of the west, *Le Mystère des voix bulgares* ("The Mystery of Bulgarian Voices"), was released in 1975 on a small label but received little attention until it was re-released in 1986 in the UK and the following year in the USA. The album was the result of many years of research by an ethnomusicologist and featured the sound of a Bulgarian women's chorus, a kind of music that frequently employ diaphanous harmonies, that is, harmonies based on seconds rather than thirds as in the western European tonal system mentioned earlier. This sound, unfamiliar to western ears as music and language, captivated many listeners. Jon Pareles observed in the *New York Times* that this music "suddenly became as hip as hip-hop," and noted that the lack of information on the recording, including the absence of translations of song texts, "encouraged listeners to enjoy the music as a pure, alien emanation, immaculate and miraculous."[29] This album became an early world music best seller, and was even used in television advertisements. The "exotic" sound of a women's chorus singing in a language unknown to most listeners became such a "feature" of world music generally that women soloists or choruses singing in nonsense syllables are frequently used to simulate world music in film and broadcasting.[30]

Other influential recordings

Other recordings were also influential in promoting the recognition of world music. One was rock musician Peter Gabriel's score to Martin Scorsese's film *The Last Temptation of Christ* (1988), released as an album in 1989 as *Passion:*

28 Brooke Wentz, "No kid stuff," *Beat*, 1993, 43.

29 Jon Pareles, "Pop from the Black Sea, cloaked in mystery," *New York Times*, October 30, 1988, §H, 27.

30 See Taylor, *Beyond Exoticism*, and "World music today," in Bob W. White (ed.), *Music and Globalization: Critical Encounters* (Bloomington: Indiana University Press, 2012).

Music for The Last Temptation of Christ. Gabriel employed musics and musicians from the Middle East, Africa, and South Asia, though perhaps the most remarked-upon track was "Lazarus Raised," featuring the *duduk*, a wind instrument from Central Asia. Its haunting sound has become familiar in soundtracks and recordings that sample world music. (A sample is a digital snippet of music or other sound that can be copied from one source and pasted into another.)

Another influential recording that helped to popularize world music was a recording entitled *Deep Forest*, which was released in 1992, and nominated for a Grammy award. The track "Sweet Lullaby" was a top 10 hit in the UK. This album, produced by two French musicians, featured infectious, danceable beats, electronic music, and samples of "pygmy" music – music by the Baka people of central Africa, and proved to be an unexpected hit, in part, I would venture, because of its romanticization and exoticization of "pygmies" as happy, premodern children.[31] This album helped launch a new genre of techno music that made liberal use of samples of musics from around the world, though it had an important precursor in an album by Brian Eno and David Byrne from 1981, *My Life in the Bush of Ghosts*.[32]

Sampling and consumption

One of the contributing factors to conceptions of world music as something that could be appropriated with impunity was the rise of digital sampling. Sampling is a technique made possible by new digital technologies that permit users to copy exactly prerecorded music and incorporate it into their own music. Sampling was first common in hip hop but quickly spread to other kinds of popular musics. In the realm of electronic dance music, sampling of world music became quite common in certain subgenres. Electronic dance musicians came to think in terms of the "samplability" of recordings, recordings that featured snippets of music that were striking enough to be sampled and used in new music. One such musician was asked about whether he has musical ideas first, or if he works from samples. He responded,

31 For a discussion of representations of "pygmies" and this recording, see Steven Feld, "Pygmy pop: a genealogy of schizophonic mimesis," *Yearbook for Traditional Music* 28 (1996), 1–35, and Feld, "A sweet lullaby for world music," *Public Culture* 12 (2002), 145–171.

32 For more on this album, see Steven Feld Feld and Annemette Kirkegaard, "Entangled complicities in the prehistory of 'World Music': Poul Rovsing Olsen and Jean Jenkins encounter Brian Eno and David Byrne in the Bush of Ghosts," *Popular Musicology Online* 4, www.popular-musicology-online.com/issues/04/feld.html.

> It various [*sic*]. Sometimes I'll just come across something I think is amazing and I might be able to imagine a tune built around it. Other times I stockpile stuff and when I'm working on a tune if I need a male Arabic vocal to fit a section I'll see if I have anything which would be suitable. But it tends to vary. Sometimes a sample will suggest the whole tune to me, but not very often unfortunately. It would be far too easy if that happened all the time![33]

It is difficult to imagine an earlier musician conceptualizing music in this kind of digitized, atomized way. When Beethoven famously used the sound of a Turkish march in his ninth symphony, it was for a whole host of complex reasons – part fashionableness (for things Turkish were all the rage in Vienna at the time), part straightforward celebration, and part of a more complex form of celebration, since the Turks had very nearly taken his adopted city of Vienna in 1683.[34]

The kind of extremely specific listening – or, to be more culturally and historically precise – consumption of music is not unique to musicians but is part of a culture in which consumption has come to play an ever-increasing role in people's leisure time and constructions of self. Sampling, as I have written elsewhere, emerged in a new moment of heightened consumption in the USA and the UK, when both Ronald Reagan and Margaret Thatcher were promoting it as a way to boost the economy, in line with neoliberal ideologies.[35] The sampler was invented as a machine to sample complex instrumental sounds as a short cut around attempting to synthesize them, but musicians soon began to use these new machines to sample pre-recorded music, launching a new relationship to music as we have seen.

The kind of relationship to music evident in sampling was not confined to hip hop or musicians who sampled, but has become increasingly common as listening habits, at least those of economic and social elites, have become increasingly eclectic. Sociological studies in the USA and several European countries have revealed classical music is no longer the primary music listened to by these groups, and that their members listen increasingly to a variety of musics, including world music, which has an audience mostly among educated middle-class people. This was perhaps first apparent with *Le Mystère des voix bulgares*, which one could find in many yuppie homes in the late 1980s and early 1990s. Increasingly eclectic modes of listening have thus

33 Toby Marks, "Banco de Gaia" interview, www.chaoscontrol.com/archive2/banco/bancosamples.html. This URL is no longer active.

34 See Taylor, *Beyond Exoticism*.

35 Timothy D. Taylor, *Commercializing Culture: Capitalism, Music, and Social Theory after Adorno* (University of Chicago Press, forthcoming).

become the norm, at least among the upper classes in the USA.[36] This, I have argued elsewhere, is a result of the growing importance of the ideology of the hip and the cool, which for decades has driven the advertising industry, which itself increasingly drives the production of culture generally.[37]

But whatever social group is listening, musicians around the world now make and consume a dizzying variety of music, in large part because of digital technologies that make it instantly available, whether on YouTube, iTunes, or a streaming service such as Spotify or RDIO. Young Hopi musicians make reggae music, Japanese musicians make salsa music indistinguishable from their American and Caribbean counterparts as Orquesta de la Luz, Irish music grows in popularity around the world.[38] Music, at least for those in wealthy countries, has become a just another commodity available to be consumed, or produced, the result of the long historical processes of objectification and commodification under consideration here.

World music today

World music in the West continues to enjoy the position of prestige it has slowly wrested from classical music as the music associated with elites, even though, like classical music, its sales remain small. Nonetheless, the presence of world music on BBC Radio 4, which once played classical music only but has added jazz and world music, is but one demonstration of the cultural prestige it enjoys today.

Music industries have sprung up around the world, particularly with the demise of the long-playing record and the rise of the cassette tape in the 1970s, which was much cheaper to produce. Today, populous countries such as

36 For studies of changing tastes in the USA, see Richard A. Peterson, "The rise and fall of highbrow snobbery as a status marker," *Poetics* 25 (November 1997), 75–92; and Richard A. Peterson and Roger M. Kern, "Changing highbrow taste: from snob to omnivore," *American Sociological Review* 61 (October 1996), 900–907. For European cases, see Philippe Coulangeon, *Sociologie des pratiques culturelles*, 2nd edn. (Paris: La Découverte, 2010); and Koen van Eijck, "Social differentiation in musical taste patterns," *Social Forces* 79 (March 2001), 1163–1184. See also Timothy D. Taylor, "Advertising and the conquest of culture," *Social Semiotics* 4 (December 2009), 405–425.

37 Taylor, "Advertising and the conquest of culture." See also Timothy D. Taylor, *The Sounds of Capitalism: Advertising, Music, and the Conquest of Culture* (University of Chicago Press, 2012). Workers in the advertising industry never define "hip" or "cool" (or another frequently used term that is employed interchangeably, "edgy") but all speak to forms of cultural production that are associated with youth culture (especially the cool), ironic (especially the hip), and that go against the mainstream (especially the edgy).

38 See Shuhei Hosokawa, "'Salsa no Tiene Frontera': Orquesta de la Luz and the globalization of popular music," *Cultural Studies* 13 (July 1999), 509–534; and Neal Ullestad, "American Indian rap and reggae: dancing 'to the beat of a different drummer,'" *Popular Music and Society* 23 (Summer 1999), 62–81.

India and China are home to prodigious and sophisticated music industries. Chinese and Indian pop stars can sell millions of recordings. The center of Indian film production, Bollywood, releases around 1,000 films annually, most of which are musicals. The global flow of musics is omnidirectional, as it has been for many decades, though the most influential centers of production continue to be in the west. And some of these flows are not global but regional or transregional, as is the case with the movement of music across diasporas. In some cases, such as the Persian and Vietnamese communities in southern California, music and films are produced locally and sent back to audiences in Iran and Vietnam.[39]

As musicians from outside of the West become increasingly connected to the west with digital technologies but, most especially, cellular phones that can exchange data, they increasingly position themselves in complex fashions as local, indigenous musicians rooted in ancient pasts, but at the same time part of a diaspora. Hip hop musicians in Dakar, Senegal, for example, appeal to the history of the griot, the bardic poets of parts of Africa, while fashioning hip hop musics that combine local sounds with transnational ones, viewing themselves as participating musically in a global black musical diaspora.[40] Non-Western musicians who once wanted to become their country's version of Michael Jackson or Madonna now just as frequently seek connections with diasporic ethnic or racial groups. As a Malian hip hop musician, Amkoullel, said in a visit to Los Angeles, "We don't have an American dream. We have an African dream."

Conclusions: schizophonia today

Today, it is not just sounds that have been separated from their makers, but listeners who have been separated from one another as well. The rise of the Sony Walkman, introduced in 1979, ushered in a new mode of listening privately to music in public. Technologically, this was possible long before the advent of the Walkman (even some very early radios were portable, and listening with headphones preceded listening with loudspeakers), but it wasn't until the rise of neoliberal ideologies of personalized consumption

39 See Farzaneh Hemmasi, "Iranian Popular Music in Los Angeles: Mobilizing Media, Nation, and Politics," Ph.D. diss., Columbia University, 2010; and Kieu Linh Caroline Valverde, "Making Vietnamese music transnational: sounds of home, resistance and change," *Amerasia Journal* 29 (2003), 29–49.

40 Catherine Appert, "Rappin' griots: producing the local in Senegalese hip hop", in P. Khalil Saucier (ed.), *Native Tongues: An African Hip-Hop Reader* (Trenton, NJ: Africa World Press, 2011).

that such a mode of listening to music really became widespread.[41] Later, with the development of the mp3 audio format system and mp3 players, and now, cellphones that play digital audio, personalized, individualized, atomized listening is quite common.

The experience of listening to music with friends, sharing music with friends with mix tapes or CDs is giving way to sharing music recommendations online, through such services as Spotify, which offers streaming audio selections and is linked to Facebook, so one can share what one is listening to with one's friends. It is also possible to share playlists. This replacement of social listening with individualized listening which is then made social through software and services for which one pays is another marker of today's neoliberal world, in which, as Duménil and Lévy have observed, social relationships are commercialized.[42]

The sociologist Alfred Schütz wrote famously in the 1950s that wherever there is music, there is something social, a "mutual tuning-in relationship," even when music is mechanically reproduced.[43] But with social relationships increasingly mediated by commercial interests, I wonder if this mutual relationship is waning. The atomized, disjunct nature of the production of music today is mirrored in its consumption.

Further reading and listening

Primary materials

Bartók, Béla. "The influence of peasant music on modern music," in Benjamin Suchoff (ed.), *Béla Bartók Essays*. London: Faber & Faber, 1976.

"The relation of folk song to the development of the art music of our time," in Benjamin Suchoff (ed.), *Béla Bartók Essays*. London: Faber & Faber, 1976.

Copeland, Stewart. Liner notes to *The Rhythmatist*. A&M CD 5084, 1985.

Denselow, Robin. "We created world music." *Guardian*, June 29, 2004, 10.

Lockspeiser, Edward. *Debussy: His Life and Mind*, vol. 2. Cambridge University Press, 1978.

Marks, Toby. n.d. "Banco de Gaia" interview. www.chaoscontrol.com/archive2/banco/bancosamples.html. This URL is no longer active.

Stockhausen, Karlheinz. "World Music." Translated by Bernard Radloff. *Dalhousie Review* 69 (1989), 318–326.

41 See Shuhei Hosokawa, "The Walkman effect," *Popular Music* 4 (1984), 165–180, and Michael Bull, "No dead air! The iPod and the culture of mobile listening," *Leisure Studies* 24 (2005), 343–355.

42 Gérard Duménil and Dominique Lévy, *Capital Resurgent: Roots of the Neoliberal Revolution*, trans. Derek Jeffers (Cambridge, MA: Harvard University Press, 2004), p. 2.

43 Alfred Schütz, "Making music together: a study in social relationships," *Social Research* 18 (1951), 76–97.

Discography

Deep Forest. 550 Music/Epic BK-57840, 1992.

Eno, Brian and David Byrne. *My Life in the Bush of Ghosts. Sire/Warner Bros.* 9 45374–2, 1981.

Copeland, Stewart. *The Rhythmatist*. A&M CD 5084, 1985.

Gabriel, Peter. *Passion: Music for* The Last Temptation of Christ. Geffen Records M5 G 24206, 1989.

Simon, Paul. *Graceland*. Warner Bros. W2–25447, 1986.

Filmography

Paul Simon: Born at the Right Time. Directed by Susan Lacy and Susan Steinberg, 1991.

Secondary materials

Appert, Catherine. "Rappin' griots: producing the local in Senegalese hip hop," in P. Khalil Saucier (ed.), *Native Tongues: An African Hip-Hop Reader*. Trenton, NJ: Africa World Press, 2011.

Arrighi, Giovanni. *The Long Twentieth Century: Money, Power, and the Origins of Our Times*. New York: Verso, 1994.

Bellman, Jonathan, ed. *The Exotic in Western Music*. Boston: Northeastern University Press, 1998.

Blank-Edelman, David N. 1994. "Stewart Copeland: the rhythmatist returns," *RMM*, February, 38–9.

Born, Georgina and David Hesmondhalgh, eds. *Western Music and Its Others: Difference, Representation, and Appropriation in Music*. Berkeley, CA: University of California Press, 2000.

Breen, Marcus, ed. *Our Place, Our Music: Australian Popular Music in Perspective*, vol. 2. Canberra: Aboriginal Studies Press, 1989.

Bull, Michael. "No dead air! The iPod and the culture of mobile listening," *Leisure Studies* 24 (2005), 343–355.

Burr, Ty. "'From Africa, three female rebels with a cause." *New York Times*, July 10, 1994, §H, 26.

Coulangeon, Philippe. *Sociologie des pratiques culturelles*, 2nd edn. Paris: La Découverte, 2010.

Duménil, Gérard and Dominique Lévy. *Capital Resurgent: Roots of the Neoliberal Revolution*. Translated by Derek Jeffers. Cambridge, MA: Harvard University Press, 2004.

van Eijck, Koen. "Social differentiation in musical taste patterns," *Social Forces* 79 (March 2001), 1163–1184.

Everett, Yayoi Uno and Frederick Lau, eds. *Locating East Asia in Western Art Music*. Middletown, CT: Wesleyan University Press, 2004.

Fauser, Annegret. *Musical Encounters at the 1889 Paris World's Fair*. University of Rochester Press, 2005.

Feld, Steven. "A sweet lullaby for World Music," *Public Culture* 12 (2002): 145–171.

"From schizophonia to schismogenesis: on the discourses and commodification practices of 'World Music' and 'World Beat,'" in Charles Keil and Steven Feld, *Music Grooves: Essays and Dialogues*. University of Chicago Press, 1994.

"Notes on 'World Beat,'" in Charles Keil and Steven Feld, *Music Grooves: Essays and Dialogues*. University of Chicago Press, 1994.

"Pygmy pop: a genealogy of schizophonic mimesis," *Yearbook for Traditional Music* 28 (1996): 1–35.

Feld, Steven and Annemette Kirkegaard. "Entangled complicities in the prehistory of 'World Music': Poul Rovsing Olsen and Jean Jenkins encounter Brian Eno and David Byrne in the Bush of Ghosts," *Popular Musicology Online* 4. www.popular-musicology-online.com/issues/04/feld.html.

Hamm, Charles. "*Graceland* revisited," in *Putting Popular Music in its Place*. Cambridge University Press, 1995.

Herbstein, Denis. "The hazards of cultural deprivation," *Africa Report*, July-August 1987, 33–35.

Hemmasi, Farzaneh. "Iranian popular music in Los Angeles: mobilizing media, nation, and politics." Ph.D. diss., Columbia University, 2010.

Shuhei Hosokawa. "'Salsa no Tiene Frontera': Orquesta de la Luz and the globalization of popular music," *Cultural Studies* 13 (July 1999), 509–534.

"The Walkman effect," *Popular Music* 4 (1984), 165–180.

Howat, Roy. "Debussy and the Orient," in Andrew Gerstle and Anthony Milner (eds.), *Recovering the Orient: Artists, Scholars, Appropriations*. London: Harwood, 1995.

Jameson, Fredric. "Culture and finance capital," *Critical Inquiry* 24 (1997), 246–265.

Lipsitz, George. *Dangerous Crossroads: Popular Music, Postmodernism and the Poetics of Place*. New York: Verso, 1994.

Locke, Ralph. *Musical Exoticism: Images and Reflections*. Cambridge University Press, 2009.

Meintjes, Louise. "Paul Simon's Graceland, South Africa, and the mediation of musical meaning," *Ethnomusicology* 34 (Winter 1990), 37–73.

Pareles, Jon. "Pop from the Black Sea, Cloaked in Mystery," *New York Times*, October 30, 1988, §H, 27.

Peterson, Richard A. "The rise and fall of highbrow snobbery as a status marker," *Poetics* 25 (November 1997), 75–92.

Peterson, Richard A. and Roger M. Kern. "Changing highbrow taste: from snob to omnivore," *American Sociological Review* 61 (October 1996), 900–907.

Rousseau, Jean Jacques. *Dictionnaire de Musique*. Hildesheim: Georg Olms Verlagsbuchhandlung; New York: Johnson Reprint Corporation, 1969.

Schafer, R. Murray. *The Soundscape: Our Sonic Environment and the Tuning of the World*. 1977. Reprint, Rochester, Vermont: Destiny, 1994.

Schütz, Alfred. "Making music together: a study in social relationships," *Social Research* 18 (1951), 76–97.

Stokes, Martin. "Music and the global order," *Annual Review of Anthropology* (2004), 47–72.

Suisman, David. *Selling Sounds: The Commercial Revolution in American Music*. Cambridge, MA: Harvard University Press, 2009.

Taruskin, Richard. "Russian folk melodies in *The Rite of Spring*." *Journal of the American Musicological Society* 33 (Fall 1980), 501–543.

Taylor, Timothy D. "Advertising and the conquest of culture," *Social Semiotics* 4 (December 2009), 405–425.

Beyond Exoticism: Western Music and the World. Durham, NC: Duke University Press, 2007.

Commercializing Culture: Capitalism, Music, and Social Theory after Adorno. University of Chicago Press. In preparation.

Global Pop: World Music, World Markets. New York: Routledge, 1997.

"Stravinsky and others," *AVANT: The Journal of the Philosophical-Interdisciplinary Vanguard* 4 (2013). http://avant.edu.pl/wp-content/uploads/Timothy-D-Taylor-Stravinsky-and-Others1.pdf.

The Sounds of Capitalism: Advertising, Music, and the Conquest of Culture. University of Chicago Press, 2012.

"World music today," in Bob W. White (ed.), *Music and Globalization: Critical Encounters*. Bloomington: Indiana University Press, 2012.

Taylor, Timothy D., Mark Katz, and Tony Grajeda, eds. *Music, Sound, and Technology in America: A Documentary History of Early Phonograph, Cinema, and Radio*. Durham: Duke University Press, 2012.

Tenzer, Michael. "Western music in the context of world music," in Robert P. Morgan (ed.), *Modern Times: From World War I to the Present*. Englewood Cliffs, NJ: Prentice Hall, 1994.

Ullestad, Neal. "'American Indian rap and reggae: dancing 'to the beat of a different drummer,'" *Popular Music and Society* 23 (Summer 1999), 62–81.

Valverde, Kieu Linh Caroline. "Making Vietnamese music transnational: sounds of home, resistance and change," *Amerasia Journal* 29 (2003), 29–49.

Wallis Roger and Krister Malm. *Big Sounds from Small Peoples: The Music Industry in Small Countries*. London: Constable, 1984.

Wentz, Brooke. "No kid stuff," *Beat*, 1993, 42–45.

Wörner, Karl H. *Stockhausen: Life and Work*. Edited and translated by Bill Hopkins. Berkeley, CA: University of California Press, 1973.

10

Sport since 1750

SUSAN BROWNELL

A history of world sport since 1750 is a history of the peaceful connection of the world's peoples. Why and how amicable sports competitions flourished during the century of history's most brutal wars is the central riddle of sport's place in the history of the modern world. The institutional backbone of today's international sport system consists of a structure of voluntary associations segmented into local, national, and international levels, with the International Olympic Committee (IOC) at its pinnacle. This system took shape in only two decades, between the founding of the IOC in 1894 and the start of World War I. The new sport organizations were part of a much larger phenomenon: in the second half of the nineteenth century, voluntary associations moved like wildfire around the planet, jumping from continent to continent within only a few years even when travel could take weeks or even months. They facilitated the new kinds of social networks that rapidly traversed the globe along with Western capitalism, colonialism, and Christian missionizing. Observers of the times were aware of the new phenomenon – nineteenth-century Greeks labeled it *syllogomania* ("association mania").

The world history of sport

Previously, world histories of sport typically focused on the discrete segments of the global system – particular sportspersons, sports, Olympic Games, nations, and world regions – rather than on the ties that knitted the segments together.[1] The groundwork for the present chapter began to be laid in the

1 Recent world histories of sport are Allen Guttmann, *Sports: The First Five Millennia* (Amherst: University of Massachusetts Press, 2004); Richard D. Mandell, *Sport: A Cultural History* (New York: Columbia University Press, 1984); S. W. Pope and John Nauright, *Routledge Companion to Sports History* (New York: Routlege, 2009); Horst Ueberhorst, *Geschichte der Leibesübungen*, 6 vols. (Berlin: Bartels and Wernitz, 1971–1989).

1980s by social histories that viewed sports in the context of bourgeois sociability, urbanization, and citizenship.[2] A second development was recognition of the central role of international organizations in the "making of the contemporary world."[3] What still remains is for local athletic clubs and international organizations to be fully explored as a single isomorphic form of sociability – after all, international organizations share the same internal structure as local clubs, the difference being the scope of the territory over which they claim jurisdiction. Both manifest a modern mode of sociability that still today is largely – but not exclusively – dominated by white, middle-class men, and by Western culture.

From classicism to athleticism

The process of linking thousands of local games and contests into a global system started in Western Europe at the end of the eighteenth century. As modern transportation and communications linked people across long distances, they did so on the foundation of a sense of "imagined community" that already existed among educated men who had never met face-to-face, but who had received a classical education and believed themselves to share membership in "Western civilization." The classics also provided a reservoir of ideas upon which educated men drew for their design of novel social forms in an era when the old society was collapsing. The parallel between warring ancient Greek city-states and warring modern nation-states was not lost on these men; they knew that in antiquity athletic games had been important forums for inter-state diplomacy, and they sought to replicate this function in their times.

The first book on the history of the ancient Olympic Games was published in the Netherlands in 1732. A call to revive the Olympics appeared

2 Pierre Arnaud and Jean Camy eds., *La naissance du mouvement sportif associatif en France; Sociabilités et formes de pratiques sportives* (Lyon: Presses universitaires de Lyon, 1986); Richard Holt, *Sport and Society in Modern France* (London: Palgrave, 1981) Richard Holt ed., *Sport and the Working Class in Modern Britain* (Manchester University Press, 1991); Steven A. Riess, *City Games: The Evolution of American Urban Society and the Rise of Sports* (Champaign: University of Illinois Press, 1991); Christina Koulouri, *Sport et Société Bourgeoise: Les Associations Sportives en Grèce 1870–1922* [*Sport and Bourgeois Society: Sport Associations in Greece, 1870–1922*] (Paris: L'Harmattan, 2000); Christiane Eisenberg, *"English Sports" und Deutsche Bürger. Eine Gesellschaftsgeschichte 1800–1939* [*English Sports and German Citizens: A Social History, 1800–1939*] (Paderborn: Schöningh, 1999).

3 Akira Iriye, *Global Community: The Role of International Organizations in the Making of the Contemporary World* (Berkeley, CA: University of California Press, 2002); John Hoberman, "Toward a theory of Olympic internationalism," *Journal of Sport History* 22/1 (1995); Barbara Keys, *Globalizing Sport: National Rivalry and International Community in the 1930s* (Cambridge, MA: Harvard University Press, 2006).

in 1790 in France, where the foundational thinkers of the French Revolution had linked sports with notions of ancient Greek democracy. By the mid nineteenth century, the transformation of the class structure under the growth of capitalism and imperialism had provoked calls across Europe for reform of the traditional classical education, including a greater emphasis on the physical health of students. Physical education emerged as a professional field in the 1880s, and its practitioners used classicism to legitimize their craft, claiming that *mens sana in corpore sano* (a sound mind in a sound body) was an ancient Greek ideal (albeit expressed in a Latin phrase). Pierre de Coubertin was a French aristocrat and an educational reformer. He convened the first International Olympic Committee in 1894, and many of the members whom he invited to join were educationalists and classically educated intellectuals.

German universities were the world centers for classical studies, and with their scholarship on the Olympic Games they created a new image of an ancient Greek lifestyle that exalted sports for male, amateur athletes. This erroneous, romantic construction then became the model for Germans as the "New Greeks," the heirs of Aryan civilization. It was not until the mid 1980s that scholars would seriously attack the popular wisdom by documenting that ancient Greek athletes were professionals, and contests for women in honor of Hera were also held regularly at the ancient Olympic complex.[4]

Around the world, physical education was included in the curricula of the schools and universities established by colonial administrators, Christian missionaries, and governments emulating the Western model of national education. Young people who had learned sports in schools went out into the world and formed sports clubs, so that the global educational network became the foundation upon which the international sport system was built. School sports were never integrated into a global structure; rather, they serve as the training ground and the feeder system for the global sport system, which is functionally independent from them.

Greece turned the Western fascination with ancient Greece to its advantage as it sought to claim membership in the West and expunge the remnants of the Ottoman occupation. The inaugural 1896 Olympic Games, as well as the 1906 Intercalary Olympic Games (planned for each Olympiad, but held only once due to Greece's subsequent instability) were both held in Athens. Unlike the 1900, 1904, and 1908 Olympic Games, they were stand-alone events

4 David C. Young, *The Olympic Myth of Greek Amateur Athletics* (Chicago: Ares, 1984); Angeli Bernardini, "Aspects ludiques, rituels et sportifs de la course féminine dans la Grèce antique," *Stadion* 12–13 (1986–87), 17–26.

not attached to the premier mass spectacle of the time – world's fairs. The Greek Olympic Games attracted substantial government and private support – particularly from diasporic Greeks, whose donations totaled one-sixth of the total revenues – because of their importance to modern Greek national identity, an importance that they retained when, in 2004, the Olympics "went home" to Athens (as one official slogan put it).

Neoclassicism was integral to the nationalism that was to dominate in Western Europe until World War II. It reached the height of its extravagance in the 1936 "Hitler" Olympics in Berlin, as documented in Leni Riefenstahl's classic documentary, *Olympia*.

German gymnastics vs. British sports

In the last half of the nineteenth century, two sporting traditions radiated out from two centers in Germany and Britain. The German model, the Turner (gymnastics) movement, included gymnastics, dancing, and calisthenics, and favored mass festivals of solidarity over individual competitions. Swedish gymnastics and the Czech Sokol movement were related systems. Additionally, figure skating, equestrian dressage, and fencing were popular in Europe. The hallmark sports of the British model were horseracing, boxing, cricket, soccer, and rugby. Basketball, baseball, volleyball, and American football were American inventions based on the British model. Both models included track and field. Both linked masculinity with Christianity and service to nation and empire – an ideology labeled "Muscular Christianity" by British writers in the 1850s. In both Britain and Europe, the inclusion of sport in the education of adult males made sport into a "male preserve" that reinforced gender differences among the middle and upper classes.[5]

German gymnastics were preferred in military schools worldwide, modeled after the admired Prussian military. British sports were preferred in schools modeled after the British "public" schools (Harrow, Eton, Rugby, etc.) that prepared young men for capitalism and colonial service. Soccer was the British sport that spread most widely throughout the European continent because it traced the path of capital as it was carried by men from wealthy families who had attended schools in England or Switzerland. Cosmopolitan private schools and polytechnics in Switzerland were the launching point on

5 Eric Dunning, "Sport as a male preserve: notes on the social sources of masculine identity and its transformations," in Norbert Elias and Eric Dunning, *Quest for Excitement: Sport and Leisure in the Civilizing Process* (Oxford: Basil Blackwell, 1986), pp. 267–83.

the continent because British sports – soccer in particular – helped to attract the sons of the British capitalists who dominated the international economy. The Anglophilia that accompanied British sport provoked nationalistic anti-British responses throughout Europe, particularly Germany. By contrast, state schools in Europe were associated with nationalist movements and emphasized gymnastics.

From ritual to record

Association mania and modern sport were both linked with the bourgeois "record-breaking mania" (as Communist Soviet critics were later to call it; Chinese Communists called it "medals-and-trophyism"). The original 1888 version of the Oxford English Dictionary could not find a usage of the word "sport" in its current sense prior to 1863.[6] The modern concept of sport appeared at the same time as the concept of the sport record. One of the earliest usages of the word "record" as a best-ever, measured performance occurred in an 1868 training manual for track and field.[7]

Allen Guttmann proposed that the simultaneous emergence of modern sports and industrial capitalism manifested the development of an empirical, experimental, mathematical worldview that underlay both. He maintained that a key feature distinguishing modern from pre-modern sports was a process of secularization and bureaucratization in which measured achievements replaced religious beliefs.[8] The "from ritual to record" theory has inspired heated debate, and both sides still have their adherents. Research has revealed sports record-keeping in other cultures and epochs, leading some scholars to argue that the sports record is not distinctly modern.[9] Nevertheless, even if an obsession with record-keeping and quantification per se is not modern, what *is* decidedly modern is a bureaucratic system in which associations keep records classified into local, national, and world levels.

6 Oswyn Murray, "The Olympic Games and the cult of sport in ancient Greece," in Susan Brownell (ed.), *From Athens to Beijing: West Meets East in the Olympic Games*, Vol.1: *Sport, the Body, and Humanism in Ancient Greece and China* (New York: Greekworks, 2013), p. 25.

7 Richard Mandell, "The invention of the sports record," *Stadion* 2/2 (1976), 250.

8 Allen Guttmann, *From Ritual to Record: The Nature of Modern Sports* (New York: Columbia University Press, 1978); Guttmann, "The development of modern sports," in Jay Coakley and Eric Dunning (eds.), *Handbook of Sports Studies* (London: Sage, 2000), p. 256.

9 Wolfgang Behringer, "Arena and Pall Mall: sport in the early modern period," *German History* 27/3 (2009), 331–357; John Marshall Carter and Arnd Kruger, eds., *Ritual and Record: Sports Records and Quantification in Pre-Modern Societies* (Westport, CT: Greenwood, 1990).

Sport records resulted from the modern capacity to imagine a runner in North America and one in England as members of a single sporting community, even if they never actually met in face-to-face competition. Records set by athletes excluded from the community were disregarded, such as the American pole-climbing records set by the natives in the 1904 Anthropology Days at the St. Louis World's Fair (personally observed by James Sullivan, the editor of Spalding's Almanac, which published American records); or the women's high jump world record of 1.77 m set by Zhang Fengrong in 1957, when China was not a member of the International Amateur Athletic Federation (IAAF) due to its exclusion from world organizations after the communist revolution.

The growth of associational life

Before 1800, horse racing, golf, cricket, boxing, rowing, and fencing became the first sports in which written rules were codified, clubs established, and regulated competitions held. In England boxing was codified in 1743, cricket in 1744. Between 1800 and 1840, shooting and yachting were codified and regulated. Between 1840 and 1880, baseball, soccer, rugby, swimming, track and field, skiing, cycling, canoeing, football, tennis, badminton, and field hockey were codified and regulated. By 1900, twenty-two of the approximately thirty sports that have been or will be summer Olympic sports were systematized.[10]

Early modern sport had been organized by courts, municipal governments, academies, and universities. Now, volunteer associations popped up everywhere. At first they were local, single-sport clubs. In England, the Jockey Club was formed in 1752, the Marylebone Cricket Club in 1787. In Germany, the Hamburg Turner Society was formed in 1816.

The social life of sport clubs was similar across space and time. A description of two sport clubs in Athens at the turn of the last century would still characterize countless sports clubs today. Selective recruitment of club members ensured that they came from similar backgrounds. Leading citizens of the community served as the governing board. A high level of discipline was enforced through sanctions and expulsion. Members met to play or watch sports, accompanied by dances, dinners, or other social activities in which women played a greater role than they did in the sports. The biggest event of the year was often not a competition, but a social dance. The mix of

10 Maarten van Bottenburg, *Global Games* (Urbana: University of Illinois Press, 2001), p. 4.

cooperation and rivalry with other clubs motivated the hosting of national games, through which clubs gained prestige.[11]

For-profit clubs in revenue-generating sports might look different on the outside, but the internal leadership structure was similar. The soccer club West Ham United, renowned for the loyalty of its East London followers, was started when Arnold F. Hills, president of the Thames Ironworks, sought to dissipate worker discontent. In 1900 it was registered as a company. Among the original shareholders, Hill was the only "gentleman," but within two years, only 41 of the 211 shareholders were laborers. Succeeding generations of two prominent local families have served on the board from its inception to the present.[12]

As the "imperial sport," cricket clubs in the British colonies provided the ritualized social meetings where British imperial ideology was reinforced and the social ties that knit together the empire were negotiated. Membership in cricket clubs was limited to the British and to local elites who had been properly inculcated in British ideals; people of color were largely excluded until the 1930s due to the concern with maintaining proper social distance. In sub-Saharan Africa, the formation of sports clubs by and for the locals was particularly strongly suppressed. The Football Association of Kenya, founded in 1922, may have been the first association for black players in Africa. Sport clubs for Africans finally began appearing in the 1920s and 1930s.[13]

The colonizer's romantic ideal of civilizing the colonized through sport was underpinned by a darker reality. Contests between people of color and white Europeans or North Americans were seen as demonstrations of racial and civilizational superiority, and sports clubs were powerful symbols of colonial subordination. In 1896, a team of Tokyo schoolboys resoundingly defeated the Yokohama Athletic Club, a team of foreigners that had disdained to compete with Japanese five years earlier. The defeat of the imperialists at their own game sent baseball on its way to becoming Japan's national sport.

After the Anglo-Egyptian War in 1882, the Gezira Sporting Club was founded in Cairo at the request of the British Army of Occupation that had been sent to quell the uprising against the ruling pasha of Egypt and Sudan. Its members were mostly British (but sometimes French or German) aristocrats,

11 Christina Koulouri, "Voluntary associations and new forms of sociability: Greek sports clubs at the turn of the nineteenth century," in Philip Carabott (ed.), *Greek Society in the Making, 1863–1913: Realities, Symbols and Visions* (Aldershot: Ashgate, 1997), pp. 146–157.

12 Charles Korr, *West Ham United: The Making of a Football Club* (London: Duckworth, 1986), pp. 1–9, 20, 28, 205–207.

13 Allen Guttmann, *Games and Empires: Modern Sports and Cultural Imperialism* (New York: Columbia University Press, 1994), pp. 67–69.

army officers, and high government officials; only one out of every fifty members was Egyptian, and almost all of them were pashas or beys. The only female members were governesses, commoner nurses, and teachers – the last two admitted in order to supply female companionship to junior military officers. During the July revolution of 1952 against the British occupation, the government took control of the club and replaced its leadership with Egyptians. After the Suez crisis of 1956 the old elite was replaced with the new, but this was new wine in an old bottle: it has been the most prominent sporting club in the Middle East from its inception to the present.[14]

Association mania moved from the local to the national level in the mid nineteenth century. In the USA, the National Association of Base Ball Players was formed in 1859. The German Turner Society was founded in 1860. England's Football Association was founded in 1863, the Rugby Football Union in 1871.

National associations for single sports were followed by associations for multiple sports. The British National Olympian Association was founded in 1865 to promote "Olympian" contests throughout Britain; the British Olympic Association (est. 1905) was a continuation of it. The American Amateur Athletic Union (AAU) was founded in 1888, the French *Union des Sociétés Françaises de Sports Athlétiques* (USFSA) in 1890.

The IOC was one of the several hundred international organizations founded between 1860 and 1910.[15] It was one of the earliest international sport organizations, and perhaps the first to claim jurisdiction over multiple sports. Internationalism was not simply a cumulative total of nationalisms, but rather the two developed simultaneously: often the formation of an international organization stimulated the formation of lower-level organizations by people wishing to be represented in it. The first three Olympic Games faced the daunting challenge of identifying a person and address to which an invitation could be sent; national Olympic Committees were formed in response, and the Athens 1906 Intercalary Games were the first at which national team members were selected by the national Olympic Committees, and clubs and individuals could not submit entries. A second challenge was establishing common rules of play; international sport federations were formed in response. By 1914, fourteen of them had been established and they organized increasing numbers of world championships.

14 Jean-Marc Ran Oppenheim, "The Gezira Sporting Club of Cairo," *Peace Review: A Journal of Social Justice* 11/4 (1999), 551–556.

15 John Boli, "Contemporary developments in world culture," *International Journal of Comparative Sociology* 46/5–6 (2005), 387.

The growth of mass culture along with global capitalism

The legacy of this historical process is that many, if not most, of the associations that administer profitable sporting empires are actually incorporated as non-profit organizations, including the International Olympic Committee; international sport federations such as FIFA; and the associations that oversee US professional sport, such as the NFL, NHL, NBA, and so on (Major League Baseball gave up its tax-exempt status in 2007). Sport grew as one component in the mass culture that emerged in the mid-nineteenth century along with the concentration of populations in cities. These organizations invented the mechanisms that made mass spectatorship possible, such as advertising, crowd control, close collaboration with the mass media, corporate sponsorship, and a reconfigured relationship between elite club owners and the commoner fans whose loyalty they needed.

Corporate sponsorship was an inherent part of modern sport from the beginning; sponsorships of cricket matches have been identified as early as the 1860s. Baseball was perhaps the first commercialized team sport: the National Association of Base Ball Players, established in 1859, was one of the world's earliest national sport associations; it was replaced by the National League in 1876, the world's oldest extant professional sports league. In that same year, the world's first major sporting goods company was formed, Spalding Athletic Goods, and it prospered together with the sport of baseball. In its advertisements, Spalding thoroughly utilized the first American Olympics in St. Louis in 1904 to promote its products. Coubertin complained about the deviation of "utilitarian America" from his neoclassical ideals, and did not attend the games. In 1899, Coca Cola developed the first bottled drinks in order to sell their product at baseball games. In 1928 it shipped crates of bottles to the Antwerp Olympic Games and became the first Olympic corporate sponsor; it has remained an Olympic sponsor ever since. While the influx of corporate capital fit rather comfortably into the owner–player hierarchy of professional sports, it exacerbated class conflict in sports organized by voluntary associations. Sport clubs with corporate sponsors could afford to pay athletes to train, which broke down the barriers to participation for proletarians lacking the leisure time and financial wherewithal. As the twentieth century proceeded, the "amateur ideal" was invoked in increasingly rigid ways against the incursion of working-class athletes into bourgeois sports, and the IOC became its most prominent defender.

Soccer has been contested in every Olympic Games except 1896 and 1932, and the Olympics served as the soccer world championship for more than two decades. However, its mass spectator appeal inevitably led to commercialization. By the 1920s, soccer had become the most popular spectator sport in the Olympics, and professional leagues were becoming more numerous. The IOC threatened to exclude soccer from the Olympics for violating the ban on professionals. FIFA's response was to organize the first soccer world championships in Uruguay in 1930 and open it to professionals; Uruguay was selected because it had won the title in the two most recent Olympics. The commercialization of soccer and the huge global audience ultimately made FIFA the only sport organization with enough wealth and power to rival the IOC.

The leadership of the IOC continued to perceive professionalism as the major threat to the Olympic system up until the Cold War, when the threat of national boycotts came to overshadow it. Until the 1980s the "amateur ideal" prohibited athletes in the Olympic sport system from receiving compensation, under penalty of expulsion.

The growth of radio and television dramatically increased the flow of money from corporations into sport. Ford Motor Company paid $100,000 for the radio broadcast rights of the 1935 Baseball World Series. The Rome 1960 Olympic Games were the first Olympics broadcast to televisions in multiple countries, and the first satellite broadcast took place during the Tokyo 1964 Olympics.

Despite the high levels of commercialization of many sports inside individual countries, the global sports system was surprisingly impervious to market forces until the end of the Cold War. The primary function of the Olympic Games was as a vehicle in international relations, and the hosting of games was spearheaded by national governments for political, not economic, purposes. As the global economy evolved, Olympic sport became a valuable commercial property, but the legal framework that enabled the IOC to claim ownership of it did not exist until the Nairobi Treaty on the Protection of the Olympic Symbol was adopted in 1981 under the auspices of the World Intellectual Property Organization. National trademark law in Switzerland – as was common worldwide – limited registration of trademarks to commercial companies until it was amended in 1993, enabling the IOC (headquartered in Lausanne) to register the Olympic rings and the word "Olympic" as trademarks. In 1988 the IOC finally opened up the Olympics to professional athletes. It also created a global corporate sponsorship program and asserted control over the revenues from television broadcasting rights. It used these revenues, which have increased continuously ever since, to bind the components of the Olympic system more tightly to it by distributing them to the national Olympic committees, international sport federations, and Olympic organizing committees, as well as to individual athletes in developing countries. In the 1990s, the amalgam of corporate sponsorship, mass media coverage, and sports events – which had been perfected in the USA – permeated sport at the global level, and in the first decade of the new millennium began to seep down into greater numbers of national sport systems.

In all of this, sport reflected the changing nature of global capitalism.

Why some sports globalized, and others did not

A comparison of the two sports with the widest worldwide participation – soccer and track and field – with three major sports that did not globalize – cricket, baseball, and Turner gymnastics – provides insight into why some sports attained global reach while others did not.

Cricket

Because of its importance to British power, the administration of the rules and behavior codes of cricket was tightly controlled from London, first by the Marylebone Cricket Club and then by the Imperial Cricket Conference (est. 1909). The first Commonwealth Games in 1930 presented an image of the unity of the British Empire just as it was starting to disintegrate. Allowing the colonial subjects onto the same playing fields counteracted the increasing "glocalization" of cricket that had been occurring since the 1920s as the locals altered the sport in conformity with their own cultures; the amalgamation of cricket and traditional dances and feasts in the Trobriand Islands is the best-known example.[16] It was not until the dissolution of the empire was well under way in 1965 that the Imperial Cricket Conference admitted members outside of the Commonwealth and replaced "Imperial" with "International" in its name. To this day, the popularity of cricket is limited to the former members of the British Empire.

Baseball

While baseball had spread throughout the American sphere of influence starting in the 1860s (Cuba, the Caribbean, Central America, Japan, and

16 Brian Stoddard, "Sport, Cultural Imperialism and Colonial Response in the British Empire," *Comparative Studies in Society and History* 30/4(1988).

Korea), the center of power never wavered from the USA, and Major League Baseball succeeded in subordinating leagues in other countries in an unequal system that expropriated talented athletes for US teams. MLB resisted the creation of a genuine world championship, and when the first World Baseball Classic was finally held in 2006, it was overseen not by an international organization as was typical of other sports, but by MLB, which kept a large share of the proceeds. Baseball was contested in the Olympic Games in 1912, 1936, and from 1992 to 2008, but it was removed starting in 2012.[17]

Soccer

The British establishment attempted to maintain control over soccer just as the American establishment did with baseball. While control over the organization of the sport escaped Britain's grasp, it maintained control over rule-making. The International Football Association Board (IFAB) was formed in 1886 to standardize rules of play and coordinate relations between the national football associations in England, Scotland, Ireland, and Wales. The *Fédération Internationale de Football* (FIFA) was founded in 1904 as a continental initiative, and the (British) Football Association was not a founding member. It joined FIFA shortly thereafter, but the relationship was unstable, and after World War I Britain withdrew from international competition and from FIFA. It did not become a full participant in FIFA until 1946. However, the FIFA statutes recognized the IFAB as the sport's rule-making body; FIFA did not gain representation on IFAB until 1913 and gained equal representation only in 1928.

At first, soccer clubs in Europe had a smaller membership than Turner gymnastics clubs, but Turner clubs were characterized by xenophobia and nationalism. Almost every Turner club had a nationality clause, but soccer clubs rarely discriminated on the basis of citizenship. This made soccer the sport of choice of the transnational elite, while gymnastics only went where Germans did.[18] Still, Germans and German diasporas constituted a huge participation base worldwide, augmented by the Turner influence in the worker's sport movement. Ultimately, the Turner movement went into decline for two reasons. One was that the downplaying of competition meant that Turner activities had less popular appeal than competition-oriented

17 William W. Kelly, "Is baseball a global sport? America's 'national pastime' as global field and international sport," *Global Networks* 7/2 (2007), 187–201.

18 Udo Merkel, "The politics of physical culture and German nationalism: Turnen versus English sports and French Olympism, 1871–1914," *German Politics and Society* 21/2 (2003), 69–96.

British sports. The second was Germany's defeat in two world wars. The conflict between German gymnastics and British sport worldwide was not finally resolved in favor of the latter until Germany's defeat in World War II.

Tight control exercised by an organization based in a single powerful nation limited the spread of cricket and baseball to the British and American spheres of influence. The defeat of Germany in two wars and its political isolation led to demise of Turner gymnastics as a sport, although Turner clubs are still the backbone of the German sport system. The emergence of several centers of control in soccer – Britain, the Continent, and Latin America – was a major factor in its global spread. Popular interest in soccer before 1930 was also facilitated by its inclusion in the Olympic Games, while cricket has never been contested in the Olympics, and baseball was contested only twice before 1992.

Track and field

By contrast with soccer, the world's other global sport – track and field – was always heavily dependent on the Olympic Games. The IAAF was only formed in 1912 after providing assurances to the IOC that it would not organize its own world championships – and it did not, until 1983. As an individual sport with many events that only require rudimentary equipment, athletics did not require the high level of organization that soccer did. The sport was not openly professionalized until the Olympic Games were opened to professionals, and the Olympics remain the only track and field championship that attracts a global audience. Being so closely intertwined with the Olympic Games may have facilitated its early globalization, but hindered its later ability to compete in the increasingly commercialized sports world.

Marginalized groups and the replication of sport associations

Because elite European men utilized sport associations to strengthen their networks and reinforce their social privileges, marginalized groups saw the necessity of doing the same. The result was that (with the exception of worker sport), marginalized groups never mounted serious challenges to the system itself, but merely replicated it. When their numbers and strength reached the stage that they were a threat to the core system, their organizations were neutralized by being incorporated into it.

Jewish sports

The wave of anti-Semitism that began in the late 1880s resulted in the exclusion of Jews from most sport and country clubs in Europe and America by the turn of the century. Jews responded by excelling in sports when they were allowed to, and establishing parallel institutions when they were not. Excluded from the German Turner Society, Jews formed the Jewish Turner Society. Excluded from the YMCA, they formed the Young Men's Hebrew Association, which became the Jewish Community Center movement in America. Being stateless, they were not represented inside the IOC and FIFA, and so proposed to host a "Jewish Olympic Games" in Palestine. This plan was finally realized after the creation of the first Jewish state: the first Maccabiah Games were held in Tel Aviv in 1932 and, except for a break during World War II, they have been held ever since.

As a diaspora, Jewish people needed a means of sociability in their host countries just as much as the Protestant industrialists did. The "most prolific" soccer club founder in Europe was Walter Bensemann, the son of a Jewish medical doctor. Educated at a Swiss private school, he founded Club Karlsruhe at the age of sixteen, followed by other clubs in German towns before moving to Britain in 1901; after the war he founded the weekly soccer magazine *Kicker*.[19]

By adding to the proliferation of sporting institutions, Jews played an integral role in building up the global sport system. As they were integrated into the middle classes, their prominence in sports waned.

Women's sports

The German Turner movement might have been more closed to foreigners and Jews, but it was more open to women than British sports were. Turner clubs for girls and women were established as early as the 1840s. In the USA and Great Britain, faced with exclusion by men's sports clubs, women who had learned sports in schools began forming their own clubs in the 1870s. The traditionally elite sports of archery, croquet, golf, and tennis were more open to women than other sports: the first national championship in tennis for women was played on the courts of Wimbledon in 1884; and in Scotland, the Ladies Golf Union was established in 1893.

Coubertin was opposed to the participation of women in the Olympic Games, but against his will the second games included women's golf and tennis, the third included archery, and the fourth included tennis, archery, and figure skating. The growing women's sports movement led to the

19 Pierre Lafranchini and Matthew Taylor, *Moving the Ball: The Migration of Professional Footballers* (Oxford and New York: Berg, 2001), p. 29.

organization of the first "Women's Olympics" in Monaco in 1921 and 1923. Alice Milliat founded the *Féderation Sportive Féminine Internationale* (FSFI) in 1921 and organized the International Women's Games in Paris in 1922. She began lobbying the IOC to include women's track and field events on the Olympic program, but neither the IOC nor the IAAF was receptive until she organized a second successful Women's Olympics in Paris in 1926. Then the IAAF requested her to delete *Olympiques* from the name of her events in return for membership in the IAAF and the inclusion of five track and field events on the 1928 Olympic program. When, at those games, several women displayed fatigue at the end of the 800 meters, the IOC decided to eliminate track from the program, but it was forced to reconsider. The IOC and IAAF demonstrated little interest in expanding women's track and field. The 800 meters would not be reinstated until 1960, and it would remain the longest event for women until the 1500 m was added in 1972; the marathon held at the Los Angeles 1984 Olympics was a quantum leap forward.

The IOC presided over a steady increase in the proportion of female Olympians over the years. Women constituted 42 percent of the athletes taking part in the London 2012 Olympics. However, the percentage of women in sport leadership positions did not increase accordingly. The first woman was not admitted as an IOC member until 1981, and three decades later there were only 19 women among the 115 IOC members, no female department head on the IOC headquarters staff, and few or no female officers in numerous national and international sport organizations. Participating in sports does not imply the same degree of power as does organizing them, and the dearth of women in leadership positions demonstrates that the essentially male, middle- and upper-class character of the global sport network has changed little in more than one hundred years.

Worker sports

Since the German Turner Society excluded workers, the Worker's Turner Federation of Germany was founded in 1893. It became the center of the worldwide worker sports movement. By 1928 there were two million members of various worker sport organizations in Germany, and in most Western countries, including Eastern Europe, the total membership ranged from tens of thousands to several hundreds of thousands.[20]

20 James Riordan, *Sport, Politics and Communism* (Manchester University Press, 1991), pp. 35–36.

The Olympic amateur rule effectively excluded workers from sport if they did not have the financial resources to support training. Four "Workers' Olympics" took place between 1921 and 1937. The second and third were organized by the Socialist Workers' Sports International, which claimed two million members at the time of the third Workers' Olympics in 1931. At the final installment, it negotiated a truce with its rival, the communist Red Sports International, and the two organized an event in opposition to the Berlin 1936 Olympics. In contrast to the campaigns by Jews and women, the worker sports movement sought to develop an alternative model not characterized by the bourgeois "record-breaking mania." Athletes did not represent nations, and the games symbolized the unity of workers of the world by being open to all regardless of sex, race, or performance level. They included poetry, song, political lectures, artistic displays, and pageantry. After World War II the worker sports movement began to shift toward competitive team sports in response to their greater popular appeal. This ended the rivalry with the Olympic system, but many worker sport organizations still exist.

The socialist sport model

Inside the Soviet Union, a grand experiment after the 1917 Revolution attempted to create an alternative model to the bourgeois sport system. To block the resurgence of "bourgeois" sport associations, in 1923 the USSR's Supreme Council of Physical Culture became the world's first permanent government body in charge of sport. Sport clubs housed within branches of the military, security forces, and trade unions became the pillars of the Soviet sport system. This model was adopted by other socialist countries after the war; in the East German and Chinese systems sports were directly under the control of units of the government, rather than indirectly through trade unions.

Expressing their opposition to colonialist uses of sport, the Soviet Union and China convened large-scale games for ethnic minorities intended to showcase their inclusive policies, beginning with the Central Asian Olympics in Tashkent in 1920. Soon after the Communist Party came to power in 1949, China held its first National Minority Games in 1953, and since 1982 they have been held every four years. These games allowed ethnic groups to showcase their traditional sports, rather than forcing them to engage in the sports of the dominant culture.

The Soviet Union emerged from World War II with newfound confidence, and almost immediately began to rejoin international sport organizations.

The first Soviet Union participation in the Olympics was in Helsinki in 1952. Hoping to strengthen the socialist presence in Olympic Games, the USSR persuaded China to attend. Chinese foreign policy did not allow participation in any event or organization that recognized the "Republic of China," the name of the defeated regime that had fled to Taiwan and still claimed to be the legitimate government of mainland China. Taiwan withdrew from the Helsinki games, but afterwards the IOC refused to expel Taiwan, so Helsinki was China's last Olympic participation for twenty-eight years.

Sports outside the West

East Asia is the only world region outside the West and its former colonies to have hosted Olympic Games. Tokyo 1964 was the first summer Olympics in East Asia; Seoul 1988 was the second, and Beijing 2008 was the third (Figure 10.1). In addition, Japan hosted two Winter Games, and Korea will host its first Winter Games in 2018. Japan and Korea jointly hosted the 2002 FIFA World Cup. In 1968, Mexico became the first developing country to host an Olympic Games. In 2014, Brazil hosted the FIFA World Cup, and in

Figure 10.1 Man takes a picture of the Beijing National Stadium shortly before the official opening of the 2008 Summer Olympic Games (© ITAR-TASS Photo Agency / Alamy)

2016 it will become the first South American nation to host the Olympic Games. The African continent hosted its first FIFA World Cup in South Africa in 2010, and has never hosted an Olympics.

East Asia

Because the institutional basis for sports in East Asia was strongly shaped by the YMCA and the USA, the early emphasis was on Olympic sports and baseball, rather than on soccer or cricket. The Far Eastern Games, launched by the YMCA from the Philippines in 1913, were the world's first regional games. Ten installments were held in Japan, China, and the Philippines up until 1934, when Japan's occupation of northeast China ended cooperation. The strong YMCA presence explains the early incorporation of East Asia into the Olympic system. The YMCA organizer Elwood Brown envisioned that regional games would be a feeder system for the Olympic Games, a concept that secured the IOC's support. This idea galvanized the patriotism of East Asians who wanted to see their countries take their place among the strong nations of the world, symbolized by hosting Olympics and winning medals.

Kanō Jigoro became the IOC member in Japan in 1909, making him the first Asian and first non-European member. Kanō was the creator of the sport of judo, which in 1964 became the first sport based outside the West to enter the Olympic Games (taekwondo was the second and last). Kanō apparently anticipated that a sport perceived as too non-Western would not be accepted in the West, because when speaking about judo before international audiences he was careful to use scientific language and avoid Confucian philosophy or religion, which he used when speaking in Japanese.[21] This had been forgotten by the time that China began promoting its martial arts form, wushu, with the expectation of seeing it included on the program for the Beijing 2008 Olympics. When the IOC failed to vote it onto the program, it initiated a debate inside China about whether the West was capable of accepting Chinese culture. A century after Kanō became the first non-Western IOC member, the presence of "Eastern culture" in the Olympic system was still a problem.

Latin America

Based on the success of the Far Eastern Games, the IOC entered into a partnership with Elwood Brown to organize regional games in Latin

21 Andreas D. Niehaus, "'If you want to cry, cry on the green mats of Kōdōkan': expressions of Japanese cultural and national identity in the movement to include judo into the Olympic programme," *The International Journal of the History of Sport* 23/7 (2006), 1173–1192.

America. By this time football and cricket had become well-established due to the intense British commercial and naval presence since the beginning of the nineteenth century. The Fluminense Football Club had been founded in 1902 by a Brazilian of British descent, and its members were European-educated. It supported the YMCA in organizing the first Latin American Games in 1922, attended by Argentina, Brazil, Chile, Paraguay, and Uruguay. A Central American and Caribbean Games (Mexico, Cuba, and Guatemala) followed in 1926. The Pan-American Games – which include both North and South America – were established in 1951 during the postwar wave of revitalization. In the same year, the first Asian Games revived the Far Eastern Games in a new and more inclusive incarnation.

Africa

The first IOC member in Africa was actually Greek. Angelo Bolonaki, or Bolonachi (as he was known in the IOC), a member of the large Greek community in Alexandria, was the IOC member in Egypt from 1910 to 1932, when his membership was switched to Greece and he continued to serve until 1963. His fifty-three years in the IOC were the longest term of any IOC member, but his background evokes troubled national histories, with the result that he has been largely forgotten by Olympic historians. Following the success of the Latin American Games, Coubertin and Bolonaki initiated a discussion with French and Italian officials about an African Games. The first installment was planned for Algiers in 1925, but under French pressure they were not held. The date was pushed back and the site changed to Bolonaki's own Alexandria, but a few weeks before the starting date, the British blocked the plans and persuaded the French to support them. Coubertin argued that victories of the "people in bondage" over the "dominant race" would not lead to rebellion, but British, French, and Italian colonial administrators were not convinced.[22]

The debate about boxing in Salisbury, Southern Rhodesia (Zimbabwe after independence in 1980) in the late 1930s illustrates the apprehensive British attitude. Boxing had become popular around 1915 without any European encouragement, stimulated by the prestige of the British-trained police who practiced it. In the local version, bouts were short, few blows were exchanged, no one was ever knocked out, no points were awarded, there

22 Dikaia Chatziefstathiou, "The diffusion of Olympic sport through regional games: a comparison of pre and post Second War contexts," Final Research Report, Postgraduate Grant Programme, IOC Olympic Studies Centre, Lausanne, 2008, pp. 36–41 (http://doc.rero.ch/record/12567).

was no decisive result, and the boxers performed strutting dance moves when an opponent took a rest. Europeans who observed the matches were mystified. Boxing clubs were organized along tribal lines and matches often provoked inter-tribal fights between the crowds of up to two thousand spectators. After considerable debate, the authorities finally decided to regulate and control boxing so as to prevent it from serving as a vehicle for self-determined "urban tribalism."[23]

Only South Africa and Egypt competed regularly in Olympic Games until after World War II. Other outstanding African athletes represented the metropole. European IOC members observing the nationalism incited by the Far Eastern Games feared that the "spreading of the doctrine of International Sport" in Africa would be ill-advised.[24] Despite their concerns, East Asia was allowed to have its sporting nationalism, while Africa was not. Although Coubertin did hold colonialist and racist views, he seemed to believe that incorporation into the Olympic system had greater potential to ensure peace than did the colonial project founded on the hierarchical notion of white men civilizing the natives through sport:

> A structure comprising independent, interrelated segments is gradually replacing the tutorship system from which Europe has benefitted for so long. Europe itself has hastened this demise through its tactlessness in using the system.[25]

The tide of history increasingly turned toward the global segmentary system that he had engineered.

Decolonization

From the 1950s to the end of the 1970s, forty-eight new National Olympic committees were recognized in Asia and Africa (almost 25 percent of the total in 2013), initiating a shift of power in the world of sport. When Indonesia hosted the 1962 Asian Games, President Sukarno was angered by the IOC's withdrawal of its approval over Taiwan's exclusion from the games, and its threat to ban any Asian Games competitors from the 1964 Olympics. He

23 Terence Ranger, "Pugilism and pathology: African boxing and the Black urban experience in southern Rhodesia," in William J. Baker and James A. Mangan (eds.), *Sport in Africa: Essays in Social History* (New York: Holmes and Meier, 1987), pp. 196–213.

24 Letter from Franklin Brown to Baillet de Latour, August 12, 1926, in Chatziefstathiou, "Diffusion of Olympic Sport," p. 32.

25 Pierre de Coubertin, "The apotheosis of Olympism," in Norbert Müller (ed.), *Olympism, Selected Writings* (Lausanne: International Olympic Committee, 2000), pp. 517–518.

organized the Games of the New Emerging Forces (GANEFO) in the following year. The First GANEFO in Djakarta attracted 3,000 athletes from as many as 51 nations, including the Soviet Union, China, recently independent colonies, and even some individual athletes from Europe. Much of the funding came from China, which at that time was outside the Olympic system. The IOC regarded it as a serious threat because it was a rival Asian initiative on the eve of the Tokyo Olympics, which were to mark the Olympic Movement's expansion into Asia. A coup d'etat in Indonesia and the Cultural Revolution in China put an end to subsequent GANEFO.

In 1978 China led a second attempt to break the West's "death grip" over sport – the establishment of the Intergovernmental Committee for Physical Education and Sport under UNESCO. By this time it had become clear to IOC President Killanin that the IOC should not continue to exclude one quarter of the world's population. He pushed through China's readmittance into the IOC in 1979 under the "Olympic formula," which prohibits the use of the name, flag, and anthem of the Republic of China, and allows Taiwan to compete under the name "Chinese Taipei."

African nations finally began to find their voice in world sport when they unified against the apartheid system in South Africa, which was excluded from the Olympic Games and FIFA from the 1960s to the early 1990s. Twenty-five African nations boycotted the 1976 Olympics in protest over New Zealand's sporting contacts with South Africa. The anti-apartheid movement is generally considered one of the few – if not the only – successful examples of mobilizing the international sport system to help bring about major political reform. This lends a special pathos to the formation of a soccer league by anti-apartheid prisoners in Robben's Island prison, who used it to create a semblance of normal life.[26]

The global sport system: the first 150 years

Most of the sports with international scope today had already been codified in rules by 1900, and by 1914 they had been incorporated into a system of national and international governing bodies that has hardly changed in the century since then. The only periods when the momentum of the global sport system ground to a halt were during World Wars I and II. However, both wars were preceded by periods of accelerated growth due to the

26 Charles Korr and Marvin Close, *More than Just a Game: Soccer vs. Apartheid: The Most Important Soccer Story ever Told* (New York: St. Martin's Press, 2010).

escalating national rivalries, and were followed by sports events marking the victories – the 1919 Inter-Allied Games in Paris (an Olympic-style competition between the troops, organized by Elwood Brown) and the 1948 Olympic Games in London. It is often argued that the 1936 "Hitler" Games added momentum to Germany's aggression against its neighbors, but four decades later West Germany chose the hosting of a second Olympics to demonstrate its peaceful reintegration into the world community. The supremacy of the system was sealed when the People's Republic of China was readmitted to the IOC in 1979. No longer on the outside of the global sport system, China became one of its most committed members. The Beijing 2008 Olympic Games were the first truly "universal" games, with 204 teams participating, which covered every territory on the planet that could conceivably mount a team (excepting Brunei).

The nodes of the sport system multiplied and flourished even where racism, sexism, class conflict, anti-Semitism, colonialism, xenophobic nationalism, two world wars, and the Cold War worked to tear the system apart. Indeed, in important ways the sport system fed on these divisive forces, and proliferated precisely because of them. The principle of complementary opposition meant that when one group organized a sporting club, a rival group felt compelled to similarly organize in order to avoid being socially out-maneuvered. This systemic logic caused sport associations to replicate around the globe wherever local people possessed freedom of assembly, and nationalities possessed self-determination.

The modern era would not exist in its current form without sports.

Further reading

Arbena, Joseph L. *Sport and Society in Latin America: Diffusion, Dependency, and the Rise of Mass Culture*. Westport, CT: Greenwood Press, 1988.

Baker, William J. and James A. Mangan, eds. *Sport in Africa: Essays in Social History*. New York: Holmes and Meier, 1987.

Bale, John and Mike Cronin. *Sport and Postcolonialism*. Oxford: Berg, 2003.

Bottenburg, Maarten van. *Global Games*. Urbana: University of Illinois Press, 2001.

Brownell, Susan. *Beijing's Games: What the Olympics Mean to China*. Lanham, MD: Rowman and Littlefield, 2008.

ed. *The 1904 Anthropology Days: Sport, Race, and American Imperialism*. Omaha: University of Nebraska Press, 2008.

Edelman, Robert. *Serious Fun: A History of Spectator Sports in the USSR*. Oxford University Press, 1993.

Gems, Gerald R. *The Athletic Crusade: Sport and American Cultural Imperialism*. Lincoln: University of Nebraska Press, 2006.

Georgiadis, Konstantinos. *Olympic Revival: The Revival of the Olympic Games in Modern Times*. Athens: Ekdotike Athenon, 2003.

Giulianotti, Richard and Roland Robertson, eds. *Globalization and Sport*. Malden, MA: Blackwell, 2007.

Guttmann, Allen. *Games and Empires: Modern Sports and Cultural Imperialism*. New York: Columbia University Press, 1994.

Sports: The First Five Millennia. Amherst: University of Massachusetts Press, 2004.

Holt, Richard. *Sport and Society in Modern France*. London: Palgrave, 1981.

Sport and the British: A Modern History. Oxford University Press, 1989.

Journal of Global History, special issue on Sport, Transnationalism and Global History, 8/2 (July 2013).

Kelly, John D. *The American Game: Capitalism, Decolonization, World Domination, and Baseball*. Chicago: Prickly Paradigm, 2006.

Kelly, William W. and Susan Brownell, eds. *The Olympics in East Asia: The Crucible of Localism, Nationalism, Regionalism, and Globalism*. New Haven, CT: Yale Council on East Asian Studies Monograph Series, 2011.

Keys, Barbara. *Globalizing Sport: National Rivalry and International Community in the 1930s*. Cambridge, MA: Harvard University Press, 2006.

Klein, Alan M. *Baseball on the Border: A Tale of Two Laredos*. Princeton University Press, 1997.

Korr, Charles and Marvin Close. *More than Just a Game: Soccer vs. Apartheid: The Most Important Soccer Story ever Told*. New York: St. Martin's Press, 2010.

Krüger, Arnd and W. J. Murray. *The Nazi Olympics: Sport, Politics, and Appeasement in the 1930s*. Champaign, IL: University of Illinois, 2003.

Krüger, Arnd and James Riordan, eds. *The Story of Worker Sport*. Champaign, IL: Human Kinetics, 1996.

Lanfranchi, Pierre and Matthew Taylor. *Moving with the Ball: The Migration of Professional Footballers*. Oxford and New York: Berg, 2001.

MacAloon, John, ed. *Muscular Christianity in Colonial and Post-Colonial Worlds*. London: Routledge, 2007.

Maguire, John. *Global Sport: Identities, Societies, Civilizations*. Cambridge: Polity, 1999.

Power and Global Sport: Zones of Prestige, Emulation and Resistance. Abingdon: Routledge, 2005.

Mandell, Richard D. *Sport: A Cultural History*. New York: Columbia University Press, 1984.

Mangan, J.A. *The Games Ethic and Imperialism*. New York: Viking, 1985.

Morris, Andrew D. *Marrow of the Nation: A History of Sport and Physical Culture in Republican China*. Berkeley, CA: University of California Press, 2004.

Niehaus, Andreas D., ed. *Olympic Japan: Ideals and Realities of (Inter)Nationalism*. Würzburg: Ergon, 2007.

Ok, Gwang. *The Transformation of Modern Korean Sport: Imperialism, Nationalism, Globalization*. Seoul: Hollym, 2007.

Pope, S.W. and John Nauright. *Routledge Companion to Sports History*. New York: Routledge, 2009.

Riordan, James. *Sport, Politics and Communism*. Manchester University Press, 1991.

Roche, Maurice. *Mega-Events and Modernity: Olympics and Expos in the Growth of Global Culture*. London: Routledge, 2000.

Sugden, John and Alan Tomlinson. *FIFA and the Contest for World Football: Who Rules the Peoples' Game?* London: Polity, 1998.

Wagg, Stephen and David L. Andrews, eds. *East Plays West: Sport and the Cold War*. New York: Routledge, 2007.

Xu, Guoqi. *Olympic Dreams: China and Sports, 1895–2008*. Cambridge, MA: Harvard University Press, 2008.

Young, David C. *The Modern Olympics: A Struggle for Revival*. Baltimore: Johns Hopkins University Press, 1996.

11

World cinema

LALITHA GOPALAN

It is commonplace in histories of cinema to see the beginning of projected moving images as the show at Salon Indien du Grand Café in Paris, commandeered by the Lumière brothers, on December 28, 1895.[1] A line up of ten short films, which the Lumières called "actualities," comprised the show, each seventeen meters long, which when hand-cranked through a projector ran for about forty or fifty seconds.[2] They were made using the cinematograph, a machine the Lumières patented that combined camera, printer, and projector. The single film from that first projection that has long been immortalized in various histories of motion pictures is the first one, *Workers leaving a factory* (1895). We watch, from the point of view of a camera on a tripod, workers streaming out of the factory at the end of a workday. The workers' routine streaming out of the Lumières' photo-processing factory in Lyon was subsequently canonized by scholars and filmmakers, and monumentalized as an iconic image of the emerging modern labor force.[3]

With their adherence to the concept of actuality – the depiction of real places and things – the Lumières' shorts cast a long shadow over both narrative and non-narrative filmmaking worldwide for more than a hundred years. Newsreel footage would emulate the Lumières' commitment to recording what film theorists call the "pro-filmic," that is, the reality or event happening in front of the camera, and seize images of battles, events,

1 Acknowledgements: Adrian Pérez Melgosa, Alejandro Yarza, and Roberto Tejada have long offered an arm across many journeys; this essay serves as a tale of our lives in the diaspora and I hope they will detect the subterfuge undertaken here. Finally, my gratitude to Ali F. Sengul for graciously rearranging his world on short-notice.

2 For one such account of origins, see David A. Cook, *A History of Narrative Film*, 3rd edn. (New York: W.W. Norton, 1996).

3 See *Arbeiter verlassen die Fabrik in elf Jahrzehnten / Workers Leaving the Factory in Eleven Decades*. A video installation for 12 monitors, produced for the exhibition *Cinema like never before*. Idea, Realisation: Harun Farocki; collaborator: Jan Ralske; video b/w and col., sound, tot 36 min. (loop), 2006.

sports, national pageantry, and so on. In a more attenuated fashion, the documentary film tradition associated with the Scottish film critic and filmmaker John Grierson would build longer films composed of such short actualities.[4] Narrative cinema wedded to ideas of realism, including Italian realism and social realism in India, would also trace its origins to notions of the duration of various activities conjured by the Lumières.

Although their factory and home in Lyon afforded many of the scenes for the Lumières' early actualities detailing work, leisure, and domesticity, the world was very much present in their films, both literally and figuratively. The brothers traveled abroad with their camera and films; scenes from Paris, Dublin, and the Alps reveal an ethnographic interest in urban and rural life. In a DVD compilation of their films, Bertrand Tavernier comments that the brothers contracted camera operators to record scenes from places further afield to capture images for projection. And their films themselves traveled. The initial showing at the Grand Café quickly made its round to various metropolitan centers in the world, reaching Bombay in 1896. This is identified as the inaugural moment for cinema in India as well, thus stressing the simultaneous development of this art form globally.[5]

While the Lumière films tend to dominate the story of early cinema, historians and filmmakers also point to other competing modes of presenting the world onscreen that were not interested in recording reality but instead partial to fantastic and surreal narratives. This other origin of narrative cinema takes us to the French filmmaker George Méliès, whose forays into inventing cinematograph machines were abandoned when better recording instruments were patented by others including the Lumières. Méliès was an illusionist and stage magician, whose interests in magic-shows persist in his short films, which are heavy-laden theater sets with fantastical narratives such as the trip to the moon, *Voyage de la lune* (1902). In this whimsical film playing with the ruse of space travel, realistic scale is dispensed with in favor of tricks of scale in the mise-en-scene.[6] On the Moon we see outsized and

4 For a short history of documentary filmmaking, see John Grierson, *Grierson on Documentary*, revised edition, ed. Forsyth Hardy (New York: Praeger, 1966). See also Philip Rosen, "Document and Documentary," in *Change Mummified: Cinema, Historicity, Theory* (Minneapolis: University of Minnesota Press, 2001), and the book series *Visible Evidence* (University of Minnesota Press) edited by Michael Renov.

5 Erik Barnouw and S. Krishnaswamy, *Indian Film*, 2nd edn. (Oxford University Press, 1980).

6 In cinema, mise-en-scence refers to aspects of design that appear before the camera, such as sets, actors, lighting, props, composition, etc.

outlandish objects existing beside familiar human figures, and from a point of view on Earth we see the Moon in an anthropomorphic incarnation as a gigantic ball with a face, and a rocket that lands in its eye. Such trompe l'oeil style effects served as a model for later Surrealist filmmakers in many places, including Luis Bunuel, Salvador Dali, and Arturo Ripstein, who used dream states to play with size, such as the giant scissors and eyes that Dali designed in Hitchcock's *Spellbound* (1945). Méliès continues to enjoy an expanded influence in the genre of science fiction and horror films worldwide, including those of David Cronenberg, Steven Spielberg, and David Lynch, among others.

Cinema is thus an example of a cultural product that spread around the world very quickly after it was first created. As it did so, it became naturalized simultaneously in dozens of cultural traditions, as local practitioners made movies in light of their own, often national, traditions in drama, literature, music, myths, and other cultural forms. For example, the arrival of the Lumières' films and Edison's kinetoscope spurred filmmaking in Japan, where filmmakers produced silent films beginning in the late 1890s and a film magazine was first published in 1909. In a holdover from Japanese *kabuki* and Noh theater, these were narrated by *benshi*, men (and occasionally women) who stood next to the screen, narrated the film, voiced the characters, and provided commentary.[7] Japanese filmmakers and studios were adept at melding technologies from elsewhere, yet fashioning them to practices of local popular arts. As it became a global art form, film styles emerged through exchange and adaption; composite and yet distinctive, filmmaking conveyed the presence of local art forms as well as cinematic traditions of other nations and regions.

The advent of the twentieth century consolidated the medium of film in several ways: theatrical projection rather than individual viewing dominated the mode of presentation and silent film production spread across the globe. As Andre Bazin provocatively argued in his landmark essay, "The evolution of the language of cinema," and as now most critics agree, as far as narrative cinema is concerned, film style was substantially established in the era of silent movies, to the extent that

7 Jeffrey A. Dym, *Benshi, Japanese Silent Film Narrators, and their Forgotten Narrative Art of Setsumei: A History of Japanese Silent Film Narration* (Lewiston, NY: Edwin Mellen Press, 2003).

the arrival of sound in the 1920s did not provoke a substantial new language.[8]

German cinema in its silent period can provide an example of the ways in which existing cultural forms were drawn upon and became a long-lasting stylistic language. German cinema was marked by expressionism, which as J. P. Telotte notes originated in the avant-garde art movements of the 1920s, committed to "an ongoing critique of postwar German society."[9] Describing an "oppositional strategy," Telotte discusses the ways in which "stylized sets, exaggerated acting, distortions of space, heavy use of shadows, irregular compositions that emphasize oblique lines, as well as specifically filmic techniques like low-key lighting, Dutch angles, and composition in depth . . . create a vision that pointedly challenges the authority of classical representation."[10] German expressionist style has had a long and complex influence beyond its historical moment and location; imitated by countless cinematographers, eschewing over-lit sets in favor of darkness and shadows, including genre films from around the world that dealt with crime and intrigue, such as film noir.[11] For example, Ridley Scott's *Blade Runner* (1982) pays overt homage to Fritz Lang's *Metropolis* (1927) in its mise-en-scene and film noir lighting.[12]

Developments in cinema studies

Cinema clearly moved across borders, and although some treatments of world cinema view this as a sum of various national traditions, others in cinema studies have become attentive to comparative or regional currents, with discussions of Asian Cinemas, Balkan cinema, European cinema, and so forth.[13] Similarly, the study of genre films no longer focuses exclusively on

8 Andre Bazin, "The evolution of the language of cinema," in *What is Cinema?*, selected and translated by Hugh Gray (Berkeley, CA: University of California Press, 1967; rpt. 2005). For an impressive reckoning of Bazin's essays, see the collection *Opening Bazin: Postwar Film Theory and Its Afterlife*, ed. Dudley Andrew with Hervé Joubert-Laurencin (Oxford University Press, 2011).

9 J. P. Telotte, "German Expressionism: a cinematic/cultural problem," in Linda Badley, R. Barton Palmer, and Steven Jay Schneider (eds.), *Traditions in World Cinema* (New Brunswick, NJ: Rutgers University Press, 2006), pp. 15–28.

10 Telotte, "German Expressionism," p. 16.

11 See my essay "Bombay Noir," in Andrew Spicer and Helen Hanson (eds.), *A Companion to Film Noir* (Hoboken: Wiley Blackwell, 2013).

12 Guiliana Bruno, "Ramble City: Postmodernism and *Blade Runner*," *October* 41 (Summer, 1987), 61–74. See Constance Penley's reading of *The Terminator* (1984), "Time travel, primal scene and critical dystopia," *Camera Obscura* 5 (Fall 1986), 66–85.

13 See, for example, Stephen Teo, *The Asian Cinema Experience: Style, Spaces, Theory* (Hoboken: Taylor and Francis, 2012); Mark Betz, *Beyond the Subtitle: Remapping*

Hollywood films, but rather examines the global circulation of genre styles.[14] Toby Miller and many others have criticized Hollywood as an imperialist force that has strangled various national film cultures.[15] In this, they draw not only on current anti-globalization sentiments, but also on a radical call to arms in the 1960s and 1970s from Latin American filmmakers known as the Third Cinema, whose vigorous polemics about colonialism, capitalism, and the Hollywood model of movies simply as entertainment to make money inspired local cinemas worldwide and continue to do so.[16] Frederic Jameson's *The Geopolitical Aesthetic: Cinema and Space in the World System* brought world system theory to Film Studies.[17] In this, he offered a reading of a wide range of films to explore the shape of aesthetics, bringing together Hong Kong art house films such as *Wong Kar-wai*, the Filipino director Kidlat Tahmik's *Perfumed Nightmare*, the French director Jean-Luc Godard's *Passion*, the American director Alan Pakula's *Parallax View* and *All the President's Men*, and the Taiwanese director Edward Yang's *The Terrorizers*. Film is increasingly being examined transnationally, as scholars explore international financing and production, the interpretation and reworking of genres and styles, worldwide distribution, and audience reception, along with the changing sociopolitical, financial, industrial, technological, and demographic changes that underpin these cinematic developments.[18] Hamid Naficy's proposal of the category "accented cinema" has helped us read films that emerge from diasporic and exilic communities that have little or no affiliation with national cinema cultures.[19]

European Art Cinema (Minneapolis: University of Minnesot Press, 2009); Catherine Grant and Annette Kuhn, eds., *Screening World Cinema: A Screen Reader* (London and New York: Routledge, 2006).

14 See my book *Cinema of Interruptions: Action Genres in Contemporary Indian Cinema* (London: BFI Publishing, 2002).

15 See Toby Miller et al., eds., *Global Hollywood* (London: British Film Institute, 2001) and *Global Hollywood 2* (London: BFI Publishing, 2005).

16 For a representative selection of essays on Third Cinema and its long-term influence, see Jim Pines and Paul Willemen, eds., *Questions of Third Cinema* (London: BFI Publishing, 1989).

17 Frederic Jameson, *The Geopolitical Aesthetic: Cinema and Space in the World System* (Bloomington: Indiana University Press, 1996).

18 For a brilliant overview of these issues, see Kathleen Newman, "The geopolitical imaginary of cinema studies. Notes on transnational film theory: decentered subjectivity, decentered capitalism," in *World Cinemas, Transnational Perspectives*, edited by Nataša Ďurovičová and Kathleen Newman (New York: Routledge, 2010). For an innovative rethinking of film styles in transnational cinemas, see Adrian Perez Melgosa, *Cinema and Inter-American Relations: Trafficking Transnational Affect* (New York: Routledge, 2012).

19 Hamid Naficy, *An Accented Cinema: Exilic and Diasporic Filmmaking* (Princeton University Press, 2001).

Among these more global views is Robert Stam and Ella Shohat's path-breaking work on the persistence of Orientalism in European and American narrative cinema.[20] Filmmakers often inserted exotic, or allegedly exotic, themes into their works, influencing their viewers' understanding (or misunderstanding) of remote places; thus filmmakers were participants in the politics of colonialism, race, and other issues. This began with the Lumières' shorts, produced in a period characterized by narratives in other cultural forms of imperial adventures under colonialism, such as novels, travel literature, and still photographs. One shot takes advantage of the pyramids of Egypt to provide scale and frame movement; the grandeur of its geometry serves as a backdrop for a human figure riding camelback across the width of the frame. Thus the ancient monuments of Egypt not only provided scale in the composition, but portrayed an exotic and photogenic world outside Paris. Revisiting the original projection of images in Paris, one cannot help remarking on the fact that they were shown in a room called "Le Salon Indien," clearly echoing the zeitgeist of turn of the century modernity, in which, as Peter Wollen notes, exotic extravaganza with eastern themes was often emphasized.[21]

Antonio Lant has proposed that American cinema in the 1910s was gripped by "Egyptomania," a trend we can actually see in the Lumières' short film.[22] Lant recounts the rise of the female star Theda Bera in the role of Cleopatra (1917) as one of the many instances in which film mounted pharoanic culture with tombs, mummies, and pyramids in the early years of narrative cinema. Publicity agents for the film even invented an exotic family background for Bara (who was actually born Theodosia Burr Goodman in Cincinnati) and claimed she had grown up in Egypt. German expressionist cinema was also Orientalist. In *Waxworks* (1924), for example, expressionist strategies find an easy alliance with the "mysteries of the Orient," as sketched out in sets of Arabian Nights and the decorativeness associated with Russian architecture. Avant-garde arts were not immune to either fascination with or the stereotyping of cultures outside the European orbit. As Lant notes, this fascination all but faded away with the arrival of sound, shunted off to the lower rungs of B films. It does find an afterlife or rather echo, however, in the French film critic Andre

20 Ella Shohat and Robert Stam, *Unthinking Eurocentrism: Multiculturalism and the Media* (New York: Routledge, 1994). On Orientalism, see Edward Said, *Orientalism* (New York: Vintage Books, 1978).

21 On a close kinship between modernity and Orientalism, see Peter Wollen, "Out of the Past," in *Raiding the Icebox: Reflections on Twentieth-century Culture* (London: Verso, 1993).

22 Antonia Lant, "The curse of the pharaohs, or how cinema contracted Egyptomania," *October* 59 (1992): 86–112.

Bazin's remarks about the ontology of the photographic image, which he sees in part as a "mummy complex," a need to preserve life through mimesis.[23]

Lant deploys Bazin's remark to great effect to suggest a return of the repressed in film scholarship, and by highlighting a marginal film in the Lumière oeuvre, I wish to do the same, as do Stam and Shohat. Their work is a corrective to histories of cinema which evoke colonialism – and attendant Orientalism and racism – as addenda to the rise of European and American cinemas, rather than seeing how they have long insinuated their form and style, and bolstered the rise and domination of these cinemas globally.[24] Their revisionist undertaking is most instructive in the examples they draw on that respond to Orientalist gestures. The Egyptian filmmaker Abdel Salam's *The Night of Counting Years* (also called *The Mummy*) (1969), set in 1881, the year before British rule, tells the story of a clan selling artifacts from a cache of mummies on the illegal antiquities market. It offers a response to images of Pharaonic Egypt by presenting a national culture that incorporates a heterogeneous population with varied cultural practices in the contemporary world alongside and in opposition to the presence of antiquities that are the dominion of archaeological discourse worldwide.[25]

These more comparative, transnational, and global ways of evaluating films provide formative framing devices that allow us to approach films and decipher their varying articulations of the world, both literally and figuratively. This essay will use these various reading strategies in the rest of the essay not to survey all of world cinema, but instead as a method to reanimate familiar film texts, especially the canon of postwar French, German, and Italian cinema, from angles that have hitherto been underexplored, thus viewing them through a world cinema lens in which themes of colonialism, Orientalism, difference, and distance gain greater prominence.

French cinema

Among the most influential French films with a colonial setting and themes was *Pepe Le Moko* (1937) by the director Julien Duvivier, which

23 Andre Bazin, "The Ontology of the Photographic Image," in *What is Cinema?*

24 See also Gaylyn Studlar's reading of another star of early American cinema, Rudolph Valentino, whose own currency was mined in the imperial adventure pictures of the silent era set in exotic locales, such as *The Sheik*. Gaylyn Studlar, "'Out-Salomeing Salome': Dance, The New Woman, and Fan Magazine Orientalism," in Mathew Berenstein and Gaylyn Studlar (eds.), *Visions of the East: Orientalism in Film* (New Brunswick: Rutgers University Press, 1997).

25 Stam and Shohat, *Unthinking Eurocentrism*, pp. 152–156.

tells the story of a gangster, and one of France's most wanted criminals, Pepe le Moko, on the run from police, who takes refuge in the Casbah, the old city around the fortress in Algiers, but eventually leaves it to find his lover, the mistress of a rich businessman. He is pursued by the French police, and also by a native Algerian investigator, who becomes his friend. In an elegant reading of the film, Ginette Vincendeau has commented that it combines the over-laden mise-en-scene of expressionism from earlier films about crime, and over-decorated scenes of the Orient from films about imperial adventure, grafting a crime thriller onto an Orientalist fantasy film.[26] Images of Algeria were long available in painterly traditions and in the various world expositions staged in Paris, which Vincendeau sees as an influencing strand in Duvivier's film. Central to her reading is the way in which the thriller absorbs tenets of French colonialism so as to exploit the setting of the Casbah for its intrigue and beauty (an Orientalist gesture), but also allows the star-crossed inter-racial romance to reveal the thrust of colonial attitudes towards the stringent differentiation between races. Vincendeau makes a formidable case for the film's ambivalent relationship to colonialism, most prominently articulated in the figure of the white woman whose romantic desire will transgress boundaries, but will eventually be regulated by the film in its choice of an ending that returns her to France rather than to a union with her lover in Algiers or abroad.

Vincendeau's reading prepares us for Alan Williams' expansive evaluation of French cinema under German occupation, a period that commences a couple of years after the release of *Pepe Le Moko*.[27] Williams' attention to the discursive conditions of cinema does not allow a detailed reading of film style, but he mentions a distinct shift from the fluid camera movement of an earlier period to tableau compositions, which he reads as the stifling effects of the occupation. Under German occupation, French cinema was hemmed in on several fronts, including an exodus of French filmmakers to Hollywood, negotiations with censors, and an attempt by German authorities to destroy all films made before 1937. These constraints may have led to the popularity of themes and narratives that were either allegorical or turned inwards, such as ghost and fantasy films; a world outside France would only reappear in the late 1950s.

26 Ginnete Vincendeau, *Pepe Le Moko* (London: BFI Modern Classics, 1998).

27 Alan Williams, *Republic of Images: A History of French Filmmaking* (Cambridge, MA: Harvard University Press, 1992). Thanks to Elissa Marder for reminding me of *Pepe Le Moko* and for directing me to Alan Williams.

European cinema was deeply marked by the war.[28] Studios were bombed and film industries collapsed, giving way to the ascendancy of Hollywood in Western Europe. At the same time, the ruins of the war spurred filmmakers to reinvent styles that liberated them from the conventions of studio sets. Italian neo-realism, for example, became known primarily for its use of locations and non-professional actors, as will be discussed in more detail below. In France, an independent style was well underway in the 1950s, which would eventually coalesce in 1959 as the "French New Wave," although scholars have remarked that this term is insufficient to describe the varying styles and themes undertaken. While there are many ways of evaluating these films, images and concerns with spaces beyond France mark many of them, as does a fascination with American films. Many of the New Wave filmmakers were influenced by the film showings at the Cinèmatheque Français, a collection and archive founded in Paris by Henri Langlois. Its programing and the pages of the *Cahiers du Cinema*, the most important French film magazine, bear testimony to the vibrant culture of film writing and evaluation that, in turn, influenced many other filmmaking styles.[29] Francois Truffaut's *400 Blows* (1959) and Jean-Luc Godard's *Breathless* (1960) are signal points of origin, films whose influence over film culture globally continues to endure: film taste, film schools, film studies, filmmaking, and film writing are inspired deeply by the aesthetics of the French New Wave in one way or another. While engagements with Hollywood films characterize French film culture of the 1950s onwards, the postwar terrain fueled the works of other filmmakers who were coming to terms with the shock of genocide and massacre unleashed in Europe, Asia, and elsewhere. An appraisal of films by Alain Resnais, Agnes Varda, and Chris Marker reveals an interrogation of narrative form as important to all of them; both the sequencing and duration of images unfolding onscreen convey the unspeakable horrors of the war.

In Resnais' *Night and Fog* (1955), tracking shots of Nazi camps after liberation combine with the voice-over enumerating with precision the various functions of the buildings to underscore the systematic program of extermination of Jews by Nazis. In a recounting that is enhanced by the sequencing of images, the film impresses us with the horrors of record keeping, tabulations,

28 For postwar cinema, see among many, Gilles Deleuze, *Cinema 2: The Time Image* (Minneapolis: University of Minnesota Press, 1989).

29 In addition to various books on French New Wave, see the biography of Henri Langlois, Glenn Myrent, and Georges P. Langlois, *Henri Langlois, First Citizen of Cinema* (New York: Twayne Publishers, 1995).

architectural layout, and other techniques of modernization. Tracking shots will emerge as a motif in Renais' work, leading Godard to remark in a roundtable discussion of *Hiroshima Mon Amour* (1959) that "tracking shots are a mark of morality." In that film, Resnais moves beyond Europe, connecting France and Japan through the structure of a love story between Elle, a visiting French actress shooting a film about the effects of the atomic bomb over Hiroshima, and Il, a Japanese architect. Their affair develops between breaks during the film shoot, but it can barely sustain the intrusions of Elle's affair with a German soldier during the occupation in the village of Nevers in France, which is rendered as long cutaway sequences. In these evocations of Nevers rendered as elaborate flashbacks, we see a young Elle absorbed in a clandestine affair with a soldier enlisted in the German occupation. Later the condemnation of the affair by the village results in her head being shorn and her subsequent incarceration at home, where she goes crazy. Long suppressed, these memories, rendered as flashbacks, are reignited during her encounters with her lover in Hiroshima; the trauma of atomic bombing in Hiroshima evokes the trauma of Nevers, one loss relays the other and takes over the affair in Hiroshima, as the men replace each other. Written by Marguerite Duras, the dialogue plays with tense and address, enhancing the film's deployment of flashbacks and voice-overs to flatten the differences between different temporalities and persona, as Sharon Willis has proposed in a delicate reading.[30] Rather than service the images so as to produce a unity between sound and image, the voice-over issues a different temporality that shuffles any firm pairing, favoring dissonance instead. In short, Resnais' film rehearses the structuring of trauma in which one event provokes another with rank disregard for temporal and spatial continuity, as it suggests that the narration of events in Hiroshima are intimately tied to German occupation of Nevers. Although the deployment of flashbacks as memory had already been launched in *Citizen Kane* (1941) and *Rashomon* (1950), its articulation in *Hiroshima Mon Amour* anticipated the study of trauma in films.[31]

Agnes Varda's film *Cleo 5 a 7* (1962) brings in a different reckoning of the world by positing a relationship between present and future as seen through the frame of chance, diagnosis, and conscription. Cleo the eponymous

30 Sharon Willis, *Marguerite Duras: Writing on the Body* (Urbana-Champagne: University of Illinois Press, 1987).

31 On a reading of flashbacks in world cinema, see Maureen Turim, *Flashbacks in Film: Memory and History* (New York and London: Routledge, 1989). On the idea of trauma cinema, see Janet Walker, *Trauma Cinema: Documenting Incest and the Holocaust* (Berkeley, CA: University of California Press, 2005).

heroine is a pop singer waiting for a diagnosis from her doctor who suspects she has cancer. She spends the two-hour waiting period, which closely matches the length of the film, wandering through Paris letting chance dictate her hours of anticipation. The film opens with her visit to a tarot card reader who offers an ominous reading that puts her in a superstitious mood until she is distracted by her own song playing on a cab radio, by clowning friends at home, and by a short film viewed from a projection room of a movie theater. The film's focus on the superficial travails of a minor pop singer is not the entire story; rather it draws us into the ambience of Cleo's loitering through the city punctuated by various signifiers of French colonialism.[32] News of protests in Algeria against French colonialism play on the radio during Cleo's cab ride minutes before her own song; it is the latter that sparks her attention whereas our ears are tuned to both. In one of her perambulations through a neighborhood, the camera tracks her against a shop window showcasing ritual masks from Africa that are exhibited as *objets d'art* in France. Again, Cleo's lack of interest is at odds with the camera's slow recording of these objects. A racist gag is the theme of the black face comedy of the film-within-film that Cleo watches with her friends from the projection room; her laughter offers an analysis of the widespread and little questioned racism of the French. More pointedly, Algeria is presented to the oblivious Cleo as she wends her way to the hospital through the Luxembourg gardens and runs into a French solider who is headed off to Algeria to fight against the growing anti-colonial resistance. As the two stroll through the gardens with the hospital soon in clear sight, the film chooses to hold off supplying us with a final verdict on Cleo's condition. By chronicling Cleo's desultoriness as one grid, the film offers us another strategy of reading that solicits our keenness towards the visual and auditory registers of the film in which signifiers of French colonialism and news of Algeria proliferate. In its bifurcated concerns of the personal and colonial, the film undercuts the cohesiveness of either character-driven narratives or politically oriented films, a split one can detect in other films from this period as well, such as *Hiroshima Mon Amour*.

A not-so-distant comparison is Jacques Rozier's *Adieu Philippine* (1962) whose virtuosity has been evoked rather belatedly. The film presents a summer romance involving Michel, a TV technician in Paris about to be sent to Algeria in the army, who dates two best friends separately, which they eventually find out. He goes to Corsica to escape them, they follow, various

32 I hope Sharon Willis will accept my ventriloquizing of her reading of colonialism in Varda's film as a long-belated appreciation; it has indeed stayed with me.

complications ensue, and the film ends with the young women watching Michel sail away to Algiers. Despite its seeming nonchalance, the film diverges to a sympathetic engagement with the struggle for independence in Algeria; further divergence emerges from the title that offers us tropes of misrecognition, as it is Algeria and not the Philippines that offers a theater of strife. Despite the ways in which these two films shape the image of Algeria in French films, Algeria's militant struggles are best known from Gilles Pontecorvo's *Battle of Algiers* (1966) whose head-on engagement seems to have eclipsed earlier renditions of the topic. Although an Italian, Pontecorvo had only a tangential relationship to the reigning aesthetics in Italy of neo-realism; by extension, *Battle of Algiers*, his best film, crosses identification with any particular national film styles, and what emerges is a subtle balance between fact and fiction.

Chris Marker's films cast a different set of strategies to engage with the events of the world, strategies that tie him to the other filmmakers yet mark him as distinctive. As a recent documentary on his works suggests, Marker's films defy classification: elements of fact and fiction collude to produce films that are deeply personal. *Statues Also Die* (1953), which he co-directed with Alain Resnais, presents masks, sculptures, and other art forms from sub-Saharan Africa, along with a dying gorilla and people of African descent living in Europe and the United States; it suggests that colonialism is responsible for the commercialization and demystification of African culture. *Letter to Siberia* (1957) also focuses on the end of indigenous cultures, examining the modernization of Siberia in a combination of newsreel footage, stills, cartoons, and footage that Marker himself shot in Siberia. In his review, Andre Bazin notes the film's ability to embrace a personal tone within an observational mode of filmmaking, as the film takes the form of an essay, complete with Marker's commentary as a letter.[33] The concept of the essay film conjured initially by Bazin upon viewing Marker's film has had a lasting imprint on subsequent evaluations; Nora Alter's critical assessment gives further shape to this concept by reiterating that endless mutations of this genre are part and parcel of Marker's own experiments in each and every subsequent film.[34] Marker's engagements with the world as evident in *Letter to Siberia, Loin du Vietnam* (1967) – a group protest against the Vietnam War with segments from several filmmakers – and *Sans Soleil* (1983) – a montage mixing documentary, fiction, and commentary, shot in Japan, Guinea-Bissau, the United States, Iceland,

33 Andre Bazin, "Chris Marker's *Letter from Siberia*." Translated by David Kehr. *Film Comment* (July / August 2003).

34 Nora M. Alter, *Chris Marker* (Urbana and Chicago: University of Illinois Press, 2006).

and elsewhere – displays a commitment to contingency in the form of presentation about places distant yet implicated in a history that is tied to Europe either through the lens of Orientalism or through the apparatus of colonialism. Contingency in filmmaking receives further support from the travelogue genre adopted by Marker whose voice-over in first person undercuts the objective stances espoused by extant observational filmmaking practices. These are strategies that surface in *Sans Soleil* most forcefully where travel to Japan leads us to journeys elsewhere on the globe, as well as to Marker's own archive from which uncommon associations between ideas and objects are established: Iceland to Japan for instance.

As is the case with several directors of the French New Wave who were initially enamored of American films, particularly Hitchcock's Hollywood products, Marker too inserts quotations from *Vertigo* in his time travel masterpiece *La Jetée* (1962), a film composed of filmed photographs that tells of a post-nuclear war experiment. But a fascination with Hollywood soon transferred to other cinemas, and Marker's discovery of the long-forgotten Soviet director Aleksander Medvedkin is immortalized in his *The Last Bolshevik* (1992), a biopic that assumes the form of an essay film. Eclipsed in the historiography of Soviet Cinema by Eisenstein, Pudovkin, and Vertov, Medvekin's filmmaking practice receives sustained attention in Marker's film that marvels at his agility with parables and irony. Medvekin's deployment of cutouts of camels as a recurring motif in his films finds an unexpected kinship with Marker's own appearance as a cutout cat in films, thus sealing a consonance of styles between two filmmakers forged across space and time. In the case of these two films, Marker's turn is towards the cinephile's archive, which as is obvious is not limited to national cinema taste or to the dominant Hollywood but bespeaks of a fascination with world cinema. Alter's evaluation, the fullest on his work, notes Marker's definitive move towards video installation as part of his ever-shifting relationship to the moving image. *Immemory* (1998), for instance, is a vertical stacking of five video monitors that bank on simultaneity and dispersal, an arrangement that barely bears a hint of his earlier work. Marker's work truly defies a unifying style.

The essay form also flourished in Godard's work starting with his collaboration with Jean-Pierre Gorin and Anne-Marie Mievielle in the Dziga Vertov Group, a group of politically active filmmakers formed in 1968. Although the group was short-lived, there are two works worth mentioning for their stylistic innovations of the essay form: *Letter to Jane* (1972) used photographs and film stills to deconstruct a news photograph of Jane Fonda as a way of critiquing American war in Vietnam, and *Ici et Ailleurs* (Here and Elsewhere, 1976) used video and film footage of the lives of a French family and Palestinians to draw out the silences on the question of Algerian independence from French colonialism and also reflect on the process of filmmaking.

German New Cinema and its influence

Concerns with past horrors and with cultural difference also emerged as central issues in films characterized as German New Cinema, and colonialism was a theme in some of them. Accounts of German New Cinema generally begin with the Oberhausen Manifesto of 1962, a declaration by a group of young filmmakers that called for a radical break from conventional styles, along with state funding for films so that they would not be under the control of commercial stakeholders. Although one is hard pressed to describe a collective filmmaking style discernible among Rainer Fassbinder, Hans-Jürgen Syberberg, Werner Herzog, Wim Wenders, Volker Schlondorff, Helke Sanders, Margaretta Von Trotta, and other directors associated with German New Cinema, it can be said that a preoccupation with German history, particularly the postwar reckoning of the Nazi past, would characterize this movement in the 1970s and 1980s. Such a preoccupation with Germany's national past generally entailed a concomitant pulling back from international interests, but exceptions are worth noting. In Fassbinder's prolific career, the German past is evoked from the vantage point of the present, which allowed him to cast North African immigrants in *Ali Fear Eats the Soul* (1974), a Black American soldier in *Marriage of Maria Braun* (1979), and so on as outsiders whose presence relays the unspeakable horrors of Nazi governance and the unbearable military presence of Americans. Riven with dilemmas of complicities, Fassbinder's films offer a sustained computation of events and incidents that mark the practice of historiography.

As is the case with the auteurs of French New Wave, we can detect an elaborate engagement with American cinema, most visible in the genre of the road movie as embraced by Wim Wenders whose *Paris, Texas* (1984) is both a canonical film in German New Cinema and a revisionist Western given its capacious meditation on American iconography. Wenders would exploit the travel genre more widely in his exploration of the Cuban music scene in *Buena Vista Social Club* (1999), or more evocatively in his exploration of the world of the influential Japanese film director Yasujiro Ozu in *Tokyo-Ga* (1985).

In *Fitzcarraldo* (1982), Werner Herzog portrayed an Irish adventurer (played by Klaus Kinski) who dreamed of building an opera house in Peru, and sought to move a large steamship over the mountains to transport rubber down the Amazon in order to finance this. This involved enormous physical effort, and traveling in an area where the indigenous people were hostile; ultimately the local people assisted him and the ship was taken over the mountains, but their chief cut the rope and the ship floated, empty, back down the river. Herzog filmed without special effects, and the physical ordeal was tremendous; the situation was made more difficult by Kinski, who fought with Herzog, other members of the crew, and the local people hired as extras. Herzog collaborated with Les Blank in *Burden of Dreams* (1982), a documentary about the making of *Fitzcarraldo* that reanimated the ethnographic film as a personal essay film and revised the documentary mode of presentation globally. *Burden of Dreams* heralded the genre of self-reflexive films on the work of filmmaking, and also included a monologue by Herzog on the destruction of the jungle. Herzog's diaries about the difficult production were published in 2009 (2004 in German) as *Conquest of the Useless*, with many reflections on the wildlife and people of the Amazon jungle.

In a manner unprecedented in filmmaking, German New Cinema was characterized by a large contingent of women filmmakers whose association with feminism was somewhat varied. Helke Sanders organized the first feminist film conference in Germany and founded a feminist film journal, *Frauen und Film*. Her *All-Around Reduced Personality* (*Die allzeitig reduziert Persönlichkeit- Redupers*, 1977), in which she played the main character, examines three days in the life of a woman photographer in Berlin, commissioned with other women to take pictures of West Berlin. Her examination of the situation of being a woman and of the divided city itself is a meditation on the slim line between autobiography and fiction and on the construction of identity. Margarethe Von Trotta's melodrama *Marianne and Juliane* (1981) portrayed two sisters who were both involved in the women's movement, but took different paths of rebellion, with one joining a violent revolutionary terrorist group and ultimately dying in prison, supposedly by suicide. The film examined political issues, but focused more on the sisters' relationship; they barely reconcile their differences between the personal and political.

Ulrike Ottinger's inventive films moved out of Germany, in both their subjects and their filming. In *Joan of Arc of Mongolia* (1989), a cross-section of European women, including an anthropologist who speaks Mongolian, travel by train across Siberia and the steppes of Central Asia when they are taken hostage by a Mongolian princess. The moving camera on the train gives way to a large number of still shots of the striking Mongolian landscape and episodes of interactions, thus changing in style from a travel genre to an ethnographic filmmaking mode. In its novel entwining of different filmmaking styles, Ottinger's film accentuates the idea of difference, both cultural and sexual.[35] The European women are fascinated by and generally get along with their captors, a novel re-grafting of sexual difference and politics with a wide range of utopian possibilities. Ottinger returned to Mongolia to direct and photograph the eight-hour documentary *Taiga* (1992) that focuses on the lives of nomadic peoples. Many of her other films also examine interactions across cultures, and frequently across time: Through photographs, documents, and interviews, *Exil Shanghai* (1996) traces the lives of six Austrian, German, and Russian Jews in World War II Shanghai and their subsequent move to the San Francisco area, combined with scenes of Shanghai in 1996, a time when the city was being transformed into a modern megalopolis. *The Korean Wedding Chest* (2009) examines the collision of ancient tradition and modern culture in marriage practices in Korea. The visually stunning *Under Snow* (2011) combines documentary sequences of the snowy Echigo region of northwestern Japan, where distinctive religious rituals, wedding traditions, and festivals have developed, with a story of two students played by Kabuki performers, who travel through time and are transformed with the help of a vixen fox.

Both French New Wave and German New Cinema had global influence. In his canonical essay "An atlas of world cinema," Dudley Andrew remarks on the ripple effects of both as far away as Taiwan decades later.[36] Noted for a rise of auteur-based cinema, Taiwan New Wave can be scarcely united under a single aesthetic banner. Nevertheless for heuristic reasons it is possible to see the works of Hou Hsiao-hsien, Edward Yang, and Tsai Ming-liang, the chief among several others, as exploring time and space in cinema through extensive experiments of the long take. For instance, in Hou's *City of Sadness* (1989) and *Flowers of Shanghai* (1998) and in Yang's *A Brighter Summer Day* (1949), the long take allows for a radical reconsideration of the image of the historical event. Similar New Wave movements also began in Japan and in the enormous movie-making industries of various parts

35 Annette Kuhn, "Encounter between two cultures: a discussion with Ulrike Ottinger," *Screen* 28/4 (Autumn 1987), 74–79. Janet A. Kaplan, "Encounter between two cultures: interview with Ulrike Ottinger," *Screen* 61/3 (Fall 2002), 7–21.

36 Dudley Andrew, "An atlas of world cinema," in Stephanie Dennison and Song Hwee Lim (eds.), *Remapping World Cinema: Identity, Culture and Politics in Film* (London and New York: Wallflower Press, 2006), pp. 19–29. See other chapters in this volume for an appraisal of world cinema as a theoretical issue.

of India, in part influenced by European film and in part as independent developments.

In *World Cinema and the Ethics of Realism*, Lucia Nagib offers an innovative comparison, placing Francois Truffaut's *400 Blows* (1959) alongside the Canadian Inuktitut *Atanarjuat: The Fast Runner* (2001), the Burkinabe *Yaaba* (1989), the Brazilian *God and the Devil in the Land of the Sun* (1964), a cluster of films which defies conventional classifications either along national cinema boundaries or periodization.[37] Rather, she suggests the resemblance between the films lies in their status as forerunners of various film movements and the uncanny reverberation at the thematic register: protagonists literally take flight through the film. Nagib's analysis of the films is nestled in a book arguing for viewing realism as a conceptual peg that can be sustained both synchronically and diachronically to read world cinema, and as a productive lens to read a range of films that are in conversation with one another despite geographical and temporal distances. Realism is the operative word she privileges so as to sketch a productive archaeology of world cinema, an exercise that follows, according to Nagib, Stam and Shohat's directive to imagine "polycentric multiculturalism" against extant hierarchies and dichotomies, such as Hollywood and other, art and popular, first and third cinemas, national and global, and so on.

Realism in Italian, Indian, and Iranian cinema

Such claims about realism as a conceptual category have been made before, as film studies has focused on realism from its earliest moments with Lumière actualities, to early ethnographic films such as Robert Flaherty's *Nanook of the North* (1922), to the films grouped under Italian neo-realism. The received wisdom on Italian neo-realism sees this as starting with Roberto Rosellini's *Open City* (1945) – a drama set in Rome during the Nazi occupation – and lasting about a decade, spurred on by a set of material conditions that coincided with the collapse of the Italian film industry.[38] Scholars have debated whether material conditions can determine style so extensively, and in an elegant revisionist book, Noa Steimatsky has recently suggested that earlier documentary filmmaking also influenced neo-realism, a point that she makes especially in her resurrection of the scant footage of Michaelangelo Antonioni's first film *Gente del Po* (*People of Po* 1942/47). She

37 Lucia Nagib, *World Cinema and the Ethics of Realism* (London: Continuum, 2011).

38 See essays in *Springtime in Italy: A Reader on Neo-Realism*, edited by David Overbey (Hamden, CT: Archon Books, 1978).

reads this persuasively as intimations of a style that was yet to arrive: focus on a flooding river, recession from plot development, and underplaying the actions of human protagonists.[39] While this mostly lost work cannot rewrite the entire genealogy of neo-realism, we are nevertheless alerted to the force of earlier documentary footage of landscape in Italian neo-realism, a detail that is often attributed to the discovery of outdoor locations after studios were bombed. Steimatsky also considers the role of film in restoring and reinventing Italian society after the war, however. Luca's run towards a set of tall buildings in extreme long shot at the end of Luchino Visconti's *Rocco and his Brothers* (1960), for example, brings into focus a postwar nation ruined by war and committed to rebuilding in a climate of economic and political compromises.

Realism was not simply an Italian national style, but was also embraced in India coinciding with independence. Satyajit Ray founded a film society in Calcutta in 1947 that showed the canonical works of Italian neo-realism; he was also close at hand while the French director Jean Renoir was shooting *The River* (1951) in India. He directed *The Apu Trilogy* (1955–59) based on a classic Bengali novel, which won many national and international awards, despite their use of amateur cast and crew. Moinak Biswas draws our attention to the naturalism in Ray's recording of landscape, and the flow and sound of outdoor locations.[40] Reviving film director Ritwik Ghatak's admiration of rhythm in Ray's *Aparajito* (1956), Biswas sees duration in Ray's landscape as a way of presenting cinema itself; by eschewing an actor-driven narrative, the film allows the viewer to discern the aesthetic of rhythm most evident in lengthy descriptive segments, pastoral or otherwise. Ray's films show the influence of Italian neo-realism and Renoir, and yet as Biswas reveals simultaneously offer a protracted engagement with the naturalism of the Bengali novel.

Images of ruin, particularly catastrophic detritus, that are present in much Italian neo-realism, reemerged decades later in Iranian cinema as natural disaster, particularly in Abbas Kiarostami's Koker Trilogy: *Where is the Friend's Home?* (1987); *And Life Goes On* (1992); and *Through the Olive Trees* (1994). In the second two of this trilogy of films, set in the small village of Koker in northern Iran, Kiarostami is concerned with indexing the events of

39 Noa Steimatsky, *Italian Locations: Reinhabiting the Past in Postwar Cinema* (Minneapolis: University of Minnesota Press, 2008).

40 Moinak Biswas, "Introduction" and "Early films: the novel and other horizons," in Moinak Biswas (ed.), *Apu and After: Re-visiting Ray's Cinema* (Calcutta: Seagull Press, 2005).

the earthquake that struck the area in 1990, thus revealing a partiality to realism, but is equally committed to interrogating the idea of space as a compositional puzzle in cinema. For instance, *Through the Olive Trees* revolves around a film shoot in the environs of Koker, with particular focus on the rehearsal and retakes of a scene between a couple whose union in both the film and outside it is far from being decided, a hesitation that the film exploits to complicate the distinction between the actors and their real-life dilemmas. Sync sound is used to expand the space of the frame so that we hear off-screen sounds such as the film director's instructions, which remind us that a film shoot in progress. The end of the film further devolves the differences between fact and fiction. In extreme long shot we see the protagonists Tahreh and Hossein walk and briefly engage in conversation; previously we have seen them in medium long shot rehearsing a scene as newlyweds. Rather than divulging the contents of their exchange on the soundtrack, we instead hear a concerto piping as Hossien turns around to run towards the camera and the film closes. The non-diegetic music points to the device of closure in realism, which folds into the conventions of fiction. What is at stake, the film suggests, is for us to grasp the artifice of realism in narrative cinema, and the fact that its limits are set by the poetics and politics of composition, not by events triggered from the outside.

Conclusion

To end is often to return to the beginning, and when we are dealing with globes and circles the return seems inevitable. One version of the story suggested in this chapter begins in France and I want to end it in China. Despite significant differences in composition and sequencing, deep echoes of the Lumières' workers leaving the factory can be found in subsequent filmmaking; film and work would long designate one image of modernity. The film with which I wish to end, a feature length narrative, opens with a steadicam moving backwards, wending its way out of a long corridor while keeping a woman's frenetic search for a pin in focus. Starting *in media res*, its takes a few minutes for us to figure out that the Chinese-speaking woman clad in Indian costume is part of a dance troupe working in a theme park in Beijing; to be exact, in this sequence we find her performing in front of a replica of a Taj Mahal. The Chinese director Jia Zhangke's film, *The World* (2004), follows the stories of migrant workers from various parts of the world whose space of labor is an actual theme park in Beijing. In keeping with its title, Beijing World Park is dotted with scaled-down replicas of various historical monuments and famous landmarks from different countries and regions.

Jia's film rearranges the composition of actualities shot by operators retained by the Lumières, which introduced *trompe l'oeil* effects. In a manner not so dissimilar, Jia's *The World* relays the compositional ironies through reversals that abound in the park: a miniature Taj Mahal, the human size Leaning Tower of Pisa, and the monumental Eiffel Tower whose grandeur is visible in the skyline of the Beijing World Park when seen from afar, but less so up close. But in *The World* and other of his films, Jia disperses his engagement with the origins of cinema, in a multiplicity of signposts that direct us to abandoned factories, drowning villages, and theme parks. *Still Life* (2006), for example, is set in a village that is being destroyed by the building of the Three Gorges Dam, *Useless* (2007), a documentary, examines China's fashion and clothing industry, and *24 City* (2008) follows three generations as an aircraft factory is torn down and an apartment complex put up instead. In these films, images of work are vastly transformed not only from those of the Lumières' workers but also from the promised utopias of communism; in their place we witness a rapidly transforming idea of work and the workday.

The distance covered between the Lumières and Jia Zhangke is one way of narrating a story of world cinema whose varied and uneven history is hemmed in by national cinemas and studio styles, but also at other moments flung open by the promiscuous exchange of international styles at film festivals, the curriculum at film schools, and above all by the audacity of cinephiles.[41] It is in the spirit of cinephilia that I wish to end this chapter with my own 2012 submission to the Decade Poll solicited by the British film magazine *Sight and Sound*, which every decade asks an international group of film professionals to vote for the top ten films of all time. My list is a sign of my investment in the concept of world cinema. These are films that do not find a mention in my essay, but with this I hope to impress upon the reader that there are many alternative histories of world cinema, and that any single history flattens the story of world cinema.

Lalitha Gopalan's Ten Films

1. *The Man with a Camera* (1929) dir. Dziga Vertov
2. *Jeanne Dielman, 23 Quai du Commerce, 1080 Bruxelles* (1975) dir. Chantal Akerman

41 See my introduction in *Cinema of Interruptions: Action Genres in Contemporary Indian Cinema* (London: BFI Publishing, 2002). See more recent essays on cinephilia in *Framework* (Spring and Fall 2009): 50.1/2.

3. *Salò, or the 120 Days of Sodom* (1975) dir. Pier Paolo Pasolini
4. *Amor* (1980) dir. Robert Beavers
5. *Goodbye, Dragon Inn (2003)* dir. Tsai Ming-liang
6. *13 Lakes* (2004) dir. James Benning
7. *Tropical Malady* (2004) dir. Apichatpong Weerasethakul
8. *Johnny Gaddaar* (2007) dir. Sriram Raghavan
9. *The Wire* (2002–08) created by David Simon (Second season)
10. *In Camera* (2010) dir. Ranjan Palit

Time revises taste; time challenges love; time is cinephilia's muse. And time informs duration. Not all ten films from my list a decade ago have survived; they haven't lost their luster, but have been shunted to the archives awaiting exhumation at a later date.

Further reading

Andrew, Dudley with Hervé Joubert-Laurencin, eds. *Opening Bazin: Postwar Film Theory and Its Afterlife*. Oxford University Press, 2011.

Alter, Nora M. *Chris Marker*. Urbana and Chicago: University of Illinois Press, 2006.

Badley, Linda R., Barton Palmer, and Steven Jay Schneider, eds. *Traditions in World Cinema*. New Brunswick, NJ: Rutgers University Press, 2006.

Barnouw, Erik and S. Krishnaswamy. *Indian Film*. 2nd edn. Oxford University Press, 1980.

Bazin, Andre. *What is Cinema?* selected and translated by Hugh Gray. Berkeley, CA: University of California Press, 1967; rpt. 2005.

Berenstein, Mathew and Gaylyn Studlar, eds. *Visions of the East: Orientalism in Film*. New Brunswick: Rutgers University Press, 1997.

Betz, Mark. *Beyond the Subtitle: Remapping European Art Cinema*. Minneapolis: University of Minnesota Press, 2009.

Biswas, Moinak, ed. *Apu and After: Re-visiting Ray's Cinema*. Calcutta: Seagull Press, 2005.

Cook, David A. *A History of Narrative Film*. 3rd edn. New York: W.W. Norton, 1996.

Deleuze, Gilles. *Cinema 2: The Time Image*. Minneapolis: University of Minnesota Press, 1989.

Dennison, Stephanie and Song Hwee Lim, eds. *Remapping World Cinema: Identity, Culture and Politics in Film*. London and New York: Wallflower Press, 2006.

Ďurovičová, Nataša and Kathleen Newman. *World Cinemas, Transnational Perspectives*. New York: Routledge, 2010.

Dym, Jeffrey A. *Benshi, Japanese Silent Film Narrators, and their Forgotten Narrative Art of Setsumei: A History of Japanese Silent Film Narration*. Lewiston: Edwin Mellen Press, 2003.

Gopalan, Lalitha. *Cinema of Interruptions: Action Genres in Contemporary Indian Cinema*. London: BFI Publishing, 2002.

Grant, Catherine and Annette Kuhn, eds. *Screening World Cinema: A Screen Reader*. London and New York: Routledge, 2006.

Grierson, John. *Grierson on Documentary*, edited by Forsyth Hardy. Revised Edition. New York: Praeger, 1966.

Jameson, Frederic. *The Geopolitical Aesthetic: Cinema and Space in the World System*. Bloomington: Indiana University Press, 1996.

Melgosa, Adrian Perez. *Cinema and Inter-American Relations: Trafficking Transnational Affect*. New York: Routledge, 2012.

Miller, Toby et al., eds. *Global Hollywood*. London: British Film Institute, 2001.

Global Hollywood 2. London: BFI Publishing, 2005.

Myrent, Glenn and Georges P. Langlois. *Henri Langlois, First Citizen of Cinema*. New York: Twayne Publishers, 1995.

Naficy, Hamid. *An Accented Cinema: Exilic and Diasporic Filmmaking*. Princeton University Press, 2001.

Nagib, Lucia. *World Cinema and the Ethics of Realism*. London: Continuum, 2011.

Overbey, David. *Springtime in Italy: A Reader on Neo-Realism*. Hamden, CT: Archon Books, 1978.

Pines, Jim and Paul Willemen, eds. *Questions of Third Cinema*. London: BFI Publishing, 1989.

Rosen, Philip. *Change Mummified: Cinema, Historicity, Theory*. Minneapolis: University of Minnesota Press, 2001.

Shohat, Ella and Robert Stam. *Unthinking Eurocentrism: Multiculturalism and the Media*. New York: Routledge, 1994.

Steimatsky, Noa. *Italian Locations: Reinhabiting the Past in Postwar Cinema*. Minneapolis: University of Minnesota Press, 2008.

Teo, Stephen. *The Asian Cinema Experience: Style, Spaces, Theory*. Hoboken: Taylor and Francis, 2012.

Turim, Maureen. *Flashbacks in Film: Memory and History*. New York and London: Routledge, 1989.

Vincendeau, Ginnete. *Pepe Le Moko*. London: BFI Modern Classics, 1998.

Walker, Janet. *Trauma Cinema: Documenting Incest and the Holocaust*. Berkeley, CA: University of California Press, 2005.

Williams, Alan. *Republic of Images: A History of French Filmmaking*. Cambridge, MA: Harvard University Press, 1992.

Willis, Sharon. *Marguerite Duras: Writing on the Body*. Urbana-Champagne: University of Illinois Press, 1987.

PART III

⋆

MOMENTS

12

Atlantic revolutions: a reinterpretation

JAIME E. RODRÍGUEZ O.

When considering eighteenth-century political transformations, historians initially identified the American and French upheavals as the democratic revolutions of the Atlantic world. Subsequently other scholars included the Haitian and the Hispanic transformations as part of this process. Those political revolutions, however, constituted the culmination of a centuries' long process of developing representative government based on the principle of *sovereignty of the people*. Political revolutions, including an independence movement, had occurred in the sixteenth and seventeenth centuries. Because historians have concentrated on national histories, these early upheavals have not been interpreted as "Atlantic revolutions."

A shared political culture

Western Europe developed a common political culture in the Middle Ages. The works of scholars, who were creating a Western legal and political culture, circulated throughout Europe because they were written in Latin, the language of scholarship. Some of these treatises advanced the theory of a mixed government. Based upon the political cultures of ancient Greece, Rome, late medieval Europe, and the Italian Renaissance city states, mixed government was a regime in which the one, the ruler; the few, the prelates and the nobles; and the many, the people, shared sovereignty. Mixed governments were considered the best and most lasting because they established limitations upon the arbitrary or tyrannical power, of the king, the nobles, and the people.[1]

Cities rose and commerce expanded in Western Europe during the twelfth to fifteenth centuries. Urban residents, who were neither vassals nor nobles,

1 James M. Blythe, *Ideal Government and the Mixed Constitution in the Middle Ages* (Princeton University Press, 1992).

constituted a new social class. They emerged as significant political actors in twelfth-century Iberia. The cities and towns gained power and influence in León-Castilla because their financial and physical resources, particularly their militias, were crucial to the Crown during the *reconquista* (the reconquest of territory from the Muslims).[2] In 1188, King Alfonso IX convened the *Cortes*, the first parliament in Europe that included the three estates: the clergy, the nobility, and the towns. Although the Magna Carta of 1215 is often considered the "foundation of representative government," the first true English parliament, which included the representatives of cities, met in 1275; and although regions of France created *parlements* (autonomous courts), the first true French congress, the States-General, met in 1302. Subsequently, other areas of Europe also established representative assemblies. All of those bodies convened randomly when the king required counsel and, especially, when he sought tax increases.[3]

Three events in the sixteenth century contributed to a major transformation of the nature of European political thought. A great political revolution, the *Rebelión de las Comunidades de Castilla* (the Rebellion of the Cities of Castilla), erupted in the Iberian Peninsula during the years 1518 to 1521. The representatives of the cities and towns with self-government, or comunidades, of Castilla attempted to assume power and establish a new constitutional order. They formed a *Junta General* (General Committee) that insisted that the cities represented the *patria*, that the king was their servant, that they possessed the rights to convene Cortes on a regular basis and to use force, if necessary, to defend their liberties. They maintained that the ruler must recognize the will of the people and obtain the consent of the governed. They demanded not only liberty but also democracy. The movement, which has been called the first modern revolution, was ultimately defeated by the forces of the Crown in the battle of Villalar on April 23, 1521.[4]

The Protestant Reformation also contributed to the expansion of the concept of popular sovereignty among political theorists. When Martin Luther advanced the principle of the divine right of princes, in order to reject similar papal claims, the theorists of the School of Salamanca – Diego de Covarrubias, Francisco de Vitoria, Juan de Mariana, Francisco Suárez, and,

2 Joseph F. O'Callaghan, *The Cortes of Castile-León, 1188–1350* (Philadelphia: University of Pennsylvania Press, 1989).

3 Jan Luiten Van Zanden, Eltjo Buringh, and Maarten Bosker, "The rise and decline of European parliaments, 1188–1789," *The Economic History Review* (2011), 1–28.

4 José Antonio Maravall, *Las Comunidades de Castilla: Una primera revolución moderna* (Madrid: Revista de Occidente, 1963); Stephen Haliczer, *The Comuneros of Castile: The Forging of a Revolution, 1475–1521.* (Madison: University of Wisconsin Press, 1981).

the most important, Fernando Vázquez de Menchaca – responded to Luther's arguments by asserting the principle of *potestas populi* (sovereignty of the people). They "helped to lay the foundations for the so-called 'social contract' theories of the seventeenth century . . . " Moreover, "they advanced a theory of popular sovereignty which, while scholastic in origins and Calvinist in its later development, was in essence independent of either religious creed, and was thus available to be used by both parties."[5] As Quentin Skinner has shown, the Hispanic Neo-Scholastic theorists provided "a large arsenal of ideological weapons available to be exploited by the revolutionaries" of later periods.[6] Some of the Hispanic theorists' ideas, particularly those of Vázquez de Menchaca, entered English and French political thought through the works of Johannes Althusius and Hugo Grotius.[7]

Subsequently, the northern provinces, or *states*, of the Netherlands relied on these and other political theories to challenge the authority of the king of the Spanish Monarchy, Felipe II. In 1579, they signed the Union of Utrecht, which created the *united states* that agreed to cooperate with each other in their opposition to higher taxes, the persecution of Protestants, and the elimination of their medieval representative governing structures. Later, in 1581, they issued the Act of Abjuration, their declaration of independence, from Felipe II. Then, in 1588, they established the Dutch Republic. Those insurgents justified their revolt against the king, to whom they owed allegiance, in numerous treatises defending their right to self-determination, religious freedom, and representative government.[8]

During a period of conflict in the seventeenth century, particularly the French Wars of Religion and the English Civil War, political theorists continued to refine concepts about the nature of government and the rights of the people. French and English authors, who believed in the importance of a strong state, reasserted the principle of the divine rights of kings. Bishop Jacques Bossuet argued that the Scriptures demonstrated that absolute hereditary monarchies were the ideal forms of government. Jean Bodin translated the Latin concept *potestas* as sovereignty, a term subsequently

5 Quentin Skinner, *The Foundations of Modern Political Thought*, 2 vols. (Cambridge University Press, 1978), II, pp. 159, 347.

6 Skinner, *Foundations of Modern Political Thought*, II, p. 114.

7 Annabel S. Brett, *Liberty, Right and Nature: Individual Rights in Later Scholastic Thought* (Cambridge University Press, 1997).

8 Martin van Gelderen, *The Political Thought of the Dutch Revolt* (Cambridge: Cambridge University Press, 1992). See also his "'*So merely humane*': theories of resistance in early-modern Europe," in Annabel S. Brett, James Tully, and Holly Hamilton-Breakly (eds.), *Rethinking the Foundations of Modern Political Thought* (Cambridge University Press, 2006), pp. 149–170.

widely used. He also emphasized the importance of a strong state at a time when the kingdoms of Spain, France, and England were "composite monarchies," polities composed of their homelands as well as principalities in Europe and territories in the Americas and in Asia.[9] In his *Leviathan*, Thomas Hobbes also stressed the importance of a strong unified state. Unlike the French theorists, who maintained that the kings obtained the right to rule from God, he argued that such a government was the result of the evolution of society from its original state of nature. John Locke refined the arguments of the sixteenth-century Hispanic theorists of the rights of the people. He maintained that God had granted rights, such as life, liberty, equality, and property, to the people during their state of nature. They, thereafter, conferred their rights to a government that would protect them and offer them the opportunities to live well. It is important to note that Locke wrote his most significant texts, *Two Treatises on Government* and the *Letter Concerning Toleration* while in exile in the Netherlands during the period 1679 to 1681.[10]

The English endured four armed conflicts during the seventeenth century. The first three (1642–1646, 1648–1649, and 1649–1651) were known as the English Civil War and consisted of clashes between parliamentarians and supporters of the Crown. The English Parliament composed of the House of Lords and the House of Commons, like its counterparts in Spain and France, met at the monarch's wish, primarily to approve taxes. King Charles I of England believed in the divine rights of kings and governed as a tyrant in the view of many. In addition, he married a French Catholic princess, raising the possibility that an heir to the throne could be Catholic, something that English Protestants opposed.[11] Charles I, who rarely convened Parliament, and then mostly to seek taxes for his military ventures in Europe, Scotland, and Ireland, was defeated by pro-Parliament forces; tried; found guilty of tyranny, treason, murder, and being a "public enemy"; and beheaded on January 30, 1649. His son, Charles II, was recognized as the new king, but when he continued his father's policies, he was soon exiled, thus precipitating the third conflict between supporters of Parliament and the Crown. Thereafter, a body called the Commonwealth of England governed from

9 John H. Elliott, "A Europe of composite monarchies," *Past and Present*, 137 (November 1992), 48–71.

10 Skinner, *Foundations of Modern Political Thought*, II.

11 John Morrill, "The religious context of the English Civil War," *Transactions of the Royal Historical Society*, 5th. Ser., 34 (1984), 155–178.

1649 to 1653, followed by the Protectorate of Oliver Cromwell, who ruled as a dictator from 1653 to 1659, when the monarchy was restored.[12]

The fourth upheaval, called the Glorious Revolution, occurred during the reign of James II (1685–1688), a Catholic whose policies of religious tolerance and close ties with France disturbed many Protestants. Moreover, a believer in the divine right of kings, James II diminished the authority of Parliament. A crisis erupted when the birth of a son, who might become a Catholic, displaced the line of succession of his daughter Mary, a Protestant and the wife of the Dutch Stadtholder, William of Orange. Leading Protestant opponents of King James II invited William of Orange to invade England and ascend to the throne with his wife Mary as joint rulers. William crossed the English Channel in November 1688 with a large army, which together with English Protestant forces, defeated James in the Battle of Reading on December 9. William and Mary were recognized as joint rulers after they agreed to accept a limited bill of rights, which excluded Catholics from the throne. Parliament, essentially the House of Commons, who claimed to represent the sovereignty of the people, insisted on a greater role in government.[13] Great Britain, created by the union of England and Scotland in 1707, established a sort of constitutional monarchy. In that respect, Parliament achieved a portion of the demands that the Revolt of the Cities of Castile had made in 1519 to 1521. Moreover, Parliament expanded its authority over time.

Conflict among the monarchies

During the eighteenth century, the British monarchy waged war against the Spanish and French monarchies for control of the Atlantic world. The death of the childless Carlos II of Spain triggered the War of the Spanish Succession (1700–1713). The Treaty of Utrecht that ended that conflict reordered the Western European world when it recognized the grandson of Louis XIV of France, Philippe de Bourbon, as King Felipe V of the Spanish Monarchy. Thereafter, formal and informal Bourbon family pacts allied the French and Spanish monarchies against the British. The latter subsequently engaged in war with Spain and France numerous times – from 1718 to 1720, 1727 to 1729,

12 Christopher Hill, *God's Englishman: Oliver Cromwell and the English Revolution* (London: Penguin Books, 1990).

13 Steve Pincus, *1688: The First Modern Revolution* (New Haven: Yale University Press, 2009); Edmund S. Morgan, *Inventing the People: The Rise of Popular Sovereignty in England and America* (New York: W.W. Norton & Co., 1988), pp. 17–121.

1739 to 1740, and 1742 to 1748 – to defend its interests in Europe and to force the Spanish monarchy to grant Britain greater commercial privileges.[14]

The Seven Years' War (1756–1763) – a world war fought in Europe; America, both north and south; and Asia – was disastrous for the French and Spanish monarchies. The British took Canada and East and West Florida and occupied Havana and Manila. Although the Treaty of Paris of 1763 returned Havana and Manila to Spain and although France ceded Louisiana to Spain as compensation for the loss of the Floridas, the threat to the Spanish monarchy from the British in North America increased. France's withdrawal from the continent in 1763 left Spain and Britain as the principal contenders for control of North America.[15]

The American Revolution

The English had begun to colonize North America a century after the Spanish; by the end of the Seven Years' War, Great Britain had established more than twenty-six colonies stretching from present-day Canada to South America and the Caribbean.[16] The British victory over France and Spain in the Seven Years' War emphasized the Britishness of both sides of the North Atlantic. It also highlighted the Protestant nature of the empire in contrast to the Catholic religion of its enemies. Increased maritime trade and communications integrated those North American societies, which became more alike in cultural practices and political ideology. The thirteen colonies, extending from New Hampshire to Georgia along the seaboard of North America, developed a sense of unity while identifying with the motherland. Those colonies possessed extensive, fertile agricultural lands. They were united not only by easy coastal communications but also by excellent river systems. Because of the greater availability of agricultural land and of efficient low-cost water transportation, most white British Americans acquired property, and many were able to export a variety of agricultural products

14 Christon I. Archer, "Reflexiones de una edad de guerra total: El impacto de la defensa marítima de Nueva España en la época revolucionaria, 1789 a 1810," in Manuel Chust and Juan Marchena (eds.), *Por la fuerza de las armas: Ejército e independencias en Iberoamérica* (Castelló de la Plana: Publicaciones de la Universitat Jaume I, Castellón, 2008), pp. 239–275.

15 Stanley J. Stein and Barbara H. Stein, *Silver, Trade, and War: Spain and America in the Making of Modern Europe* (Baltimore: Johns Hopkins University Press, 2000).

16 Using different criteria, scholars identify twenty-six, twenty-nine or thirty-two British colonies. David Armitage, "The American Revolution in Atlantic perspective," in Nicholas Canny and Philip Morgan (eds.), *The Oxford Handbook of the Atlantic World, 1450–1850* (Oxford University Press, 2011), pp. 516–532.

to Europe and the West Indies. These conditions helped create propertied classes who would later defend their interests from royal reforms. By the end of the eighteenth century, about 5.5 million people, excluding the Indians, lived in the former British North America, the United States. Half a million of these were enslaved blacks, most of them residing in the southern colonies.

British North America, like its Spanish American counterpart, was part of "a consensual empire." The great difference, however, was that it possessed a substantially larger white settler population. They – not the Indians, the free people of color, or the slaves – are the ones US historians have in mind when they write about the rights and opportunities available in the thirteen colonies. Only if one limits consideration to that important group, and ignores all the others, is it true that the British Americans possessed greater rights and liberties than the other Americans.

The Seven Year's War increased the British monarchy's debt substantially. Moreover, royal troops now were required to protect the colonies and to police the vast territory that France had lost in North America. As a result, the royal government acted to strengthen the colonial administration, which required increasing taxes that were much lower in the colonies than in Britain. Consequently, it introduced a series of acts restricting trade and settlement in the Indian territories and introducing new taxes and regulations, such as the Sugar Act, the Currency Act, and the Quartering Acts. In 1765, Parliament extended the Stamp tax to the colonies, which provoked extensive protests. Although that body repealed it the following year, it nonetheless insisted that it retained the power to enact laws in the colonies "in all cases whatsoever." Other acts to enforce its authority continued to arouse the ire of the colonials who resorted to violence. In March 1770, frightened British soldiers fired into a violent mob, killing five persons. Subsequently, in December 1773, a group of men dressed as Indians boarded ships in the port of Boston and threw 90,000 pounds of tea into the harbor to demonstrate their rejection of the Tea tax. The government in London retaliated by closing the port and restricting local government.[17]

In an effort to resolve the conflict over the nature of the British monarchy, colonial leaders convened a Continental Congress, consisting of fifty-six delegates from twelve of the thirteen colonies, which met in Philadelphia on September 5, 1774. Most representatives were unwilling to sever relations with the British Crown. Therefore, they submitted a petition to the King

17 Pauline Maier, *From Resistance to Revolution: Colonial Radicals and the Development of American Opposition to Britain, 1765–1776* (New York: W. W. Norton, 1991).

George III, insisting that their rights and liberties as Englishmen be restored. On April 19, 1775, a British force clashed with the local militia in Concord, Massachusetts. It was the first act in a war of independence. Nevertheless, the second Continental Congress, which met on May 10, 1775, continued to pursue reconciliation. It sent to the king a "Declaration of Rights and Grievances" that requested His Majesty recognize their rights and resolve the conflict that existed. King George III refused to receive the petition and instead declared that rebellion existed in North America and that "traitors" had to be arrested.[18]

Why British Americans objected so strongly to the new measures and why the British government insisted on enforcing its authority remains not fully understood. The British monarchy clearly feared that the colonials would achieve independence if their demands were met. At the same time, the British Americans were convinced that the reforms sought to deprive them of their rights and liberties as Englishmen. Clearly, the revolution resulted from the inability of the disputants to agree upon the nature of the new British monarchy. But in addition, the British, like the Spanish subsequently, proved unwilling to accept a settlement comparable to the later British Commonwealth.

The war for US independence became an international conflict in which France and Spain, eager to avenge their defeat in the Seven Years' War, fought Britain both on land and sea. At the height of the struggle, France fielded a force of more than 10,000 men in North America while Spanish troops harassed the British along its vast border with New Spain and retook the Floridas. The combined French and Spanish navies neutralized the British fleet at sea.[19] As a result of foreign involvement, the United States obtained its independence through an international settlement, the Treaty of Paris of 1783.

Many of the founders of the new nation were members of the oligarchy. During the struggle for independence, the British American upper and upper-middle classes shared moderate goals. Although other social groups participated in the conflict, they did not seriously challenge the elites. No social revolution threatened their interests. The US war of independence, with few exceptions, was characterized by traditional military engagements. Local insurgents seeking fundamentally different goals from those of the elite are notable for their absence. No rural insurrection occurred.

18 Morgan, *Inventing the People*, pp. 239–287.

19 Thomas E. Chávez, *Spain and the Independence of the United States* (Albuquerque: University of New Mexico Press, 2002).

Most black slaves did not revolt against their masters. And the Indians did not take the opportunity to recover the lands from which they had been dispossessed. "Despite the universalistic pronouncements of the Declaration of Independence and the apparent inclusiveness of the phrase 'We the People' in the Constitution, the American Revolution was a limited revolution that really fully applied, immediately, only to adult white [property-owning] men."[20]

Although regional tensions existed, and although the first US constitution, the Articles of Confederation, was rapidly discarded in favor of the stronger Constitution of 1787, the British American elite managed to direct the new nation without serious challenges from other social groups. To a great extent, this was the result of post-independence prosperity engendered by twenty-five years of war in Europe. The French Revolution of 1789 and the wars that followed created an insatiable demand for United States' products. Therefore, the tensions that existed in the new nation were eased by the country's general prosperity. The United States emerged as an oligarchic republic that slowly incorporated other groups into full participation.[21]

The independence of the United States, moreover, did not result in the political and economic destruction of the British world. Despite brief and relatively minor conflicts, social, cultural, economic, and diplomatic relations continued between the former metropolis and the former colony. The United States prospered, in part, because Great Britain considered the country an "informal dominion."[22] Thus, during the first half of the nineteenth century, the new nation benefited from the protection, support, and assistance of Great Britain, the preeminent industrial, commercial, financial, technological, and naval power in the world. The history of the United States would have been considerably different had Spain achieved that preeminence while Britain collapsed. In a world dominated by a country with a different language, religion, and culture, the United States would have been less privileged politically, less able to exploit its rich endowment of easily available resources, and, moreover, would have had to compete

20 Jack P. Greene, "The American Revolution," *American Historical Review* 105/1 (February 2000), 93–102.

21 Jack P. Greene, *Understanding the American Revolution* (Charlottesville: University Press of Virginia, 1995), p. 72.

22 I owe this term to Anthony Hopkins, Walter Prescott Webb Professor of History at the University of Texas, Austin, who argues that the United States was an "informal dominion" of Great Britain until the 1860s.

with powerful neighbors. That situation, of course, did not occur. Instead, the United States grew territorially through conquest, expanded economically, and maintained a stable political system that became increasingly inclusive.

The French Revolution

The Kingdom of France, which experienced substantial population growth during the eighteenth century, was the most populous state in Europe, increasing from 20 million people in 1700 to 28 million in 1789. It possessed some of the most extensive and fertile agricultural lands in Europe. Although predominantly rural, some regions were industrial and engaged in commerce in the Atlantic world. However, France suffered from uneven development. Northeastern France was a prosperous area with a growing and important textile industry. The south of France, the center, and the west have been described as undeveloped areas with primitive farming and extreme poverty. Agriculture was characterized by large holdings in the hands of a few and small properties in the hands of the many, with vast disparities of wealth between these two groups. Land-tenure arrangements included sharecropping, tenant-farming, and private as well as collective ownership of land. During the second half of the eighteenth century, a growing rural population found it increasingly difficult to support itself and its families through agriculture. Moreover, France suffered from periodic crop failures that resulted in high prices, famine, epidemic disease, and the displacement of peasants. It is interesting to note, in this regard, that great crop failures preceded the French Revolution.[23]

French society consisted of three estates: the clergy, the nobility, and the third estate, which meant primarily the representatives of the cities. That traditional division, however, did not reflect reality in the second half of the eighteenth century. It neither recognized the emergence of the bourgeoisie nor the variety of wealth among peasants. It also failed to account for poor *cures* and impoverished aristocrats. Economic distinctions between the nobles and the bourgeoisie blurred in France. Both were large landowners and both engaged in business. The richest among them possessed immense fortunes. Because they shared economic interests, serious class conflict did not erupt often between the two groups during the Revolution. Indeed, the

23 C. E. Labrousse, "The crisis in the French economy at the end of the Old Regime," in Ralph Greenlaw (ed.), *The Economic Origins of the French Revolution: Poverty or Prosperity?* (Boston: D.C. Heath and Company, 1958), p. 64.

wealthy – noble and non-noble – would emerge as the notables who dominated the post-revolutionary period. The clerical hierarchy in France, particularly the episcopate, consisted mainly of nobles, but most priests were relatively poor and from other social groups. Thus, the interests of the clergy varied significantly.

In addition to the bourgeoisie, the cities contained artisans and workers of various sorts who constituted a prosperous urban class. However, late-eighteenth-century France was characterized by a large and growing urban lumpen proletariat who existed at the margins of society. The rural population was similar. Absentee landlords, many of whom resided near the seat of government or in major provincial cities, generally owned great estates. A small, but important, group of middle-sized landowners and wealthy peasants operated as linking agents in the countryside. Tenants and sharecroppers also constituted a middling group of rural society. Finally, the country possessed a large and growing landless, or almost landless, rural proletariat who had become increasingly marginalized.[24]

Although the economy in France, with regional variations, appeared to prosper during the period 1733 to 1770, economic pressures on artisans and workers increased because prices rose faster than wages. After 1770 the French economy contracted. The cost of the Seven Years War and the war for US independence contributed to large-scale financial speculation, which resulted in massive bankruptcies that exacerbated the economic downturn and led to a loss of confidence. In addition, the government's fiscal crisis, particularly the increasing reliance on loans to finance its activities, contributed to the country's economic and political instability. The economy began to recover in the mid 1780s only to fall victim in 1788 to a crop failure. In those circumstances many of the already marginal urban and rural poor faced starvation.

France experienced a constitutional crisis. The conflict centered on the question of governmental accountability, particularly with regard to finances. It focused on the role of the *parlements* and the obligation of the Crown to French society. The first crisis resulted from noble intransigence. The aristocratic revolt, as it is sometimes called, occurred because the nobility who dominated the *parlements* would not acquiesce to increased taxes. As a result, the monarchy was forced to convene an Estates General. Once that congress met, however, the traditional nobility proved unequal to

24 Peter McPhee, "The French Revolution, peasants, and capitalism," *American Historical Review* 94/5 (December 1989), 1265–1280.

the task of leadership and was forced to concede authority to a coalition of the third estate and a significant minority of liberal nobles. In the political struggle that ensued, the third estate, with the support of some clergymen and the liberal nobles, transformed the Estates General into a National Assembly in 1789. Thereafter, the Crown and the intransigent noble majority found themselves reacting to changes initiated by the third-estate-dominated coalition.

The triumph of the third estate led to a political transformation in France. Monarchical rule succumbed to representative government. The Declaration of the Rights of Man and of the Citizen, the Constitution of 1791, and other progressive acts represented the victory of the urban bourgeoisie. Men of property obtained the right to participate in government. But the Revolution heralded a political, not a social, transformation. Neither the peasants nor the workers obtained full redress of their grievances.[25] The revolution of the peasantry is instructive in this regard.

In the spring of 1789, rural people unleashed a series of jacqueries. In some instances, they attacked manor houses, destroyed the records of their traditional obligations, and demonstrated their hostility to the privileged classes, both noble and non-noble, by humiliating and sometimes harming them. In other cases, they prevented the transport of grain from their areas, often taking some for themselves and their families. But the most striking aspect of the rural uprising is the hysteria experienced by rural society. Fear of brigands, of a counter-revolutionary aristocratic plot, and of famine seems to have gripped rural people in what has been called the Great Fear. The peasant revolution in France ultimately achieved only moderate results. The dread, indeed the terror, of a rural revolt convinced urban politicians, both bourgeois and noble, to abolish privilege in the countryside. This was, no doubt, a significant achievement. But it was not a major social revolution, and it was obtained at the cost of relatively little violence. Indeed, the third estate was the chief beneficiary of the peasant revolution. Although threats to the Revolution remained, both the Crown and the aristocracy essentially conceded defeat to the bourgeoisie.

The French Revolution abolished seigniorial institutions and was characterized by mass politics. The radical politics of 1792 to 1794, however, should not be confused with the transformation of social relations. Property generally remained inviolate. Although popular groups broke into the

25 Timothy Tacket, "El proceso de la Revolución Francesa, 1789–1794," in Jaime E. Rodríguez O. (ed.), *Revolución, independencia y las nuevas naciones de América* (Madrid: Fundación MAPFRE/Tavera, 2005), pp. 21–40.

Tuileries on August 10, 1792, demanding "equality" and invoking the "nation," the Revolution of the people served the interests of the middle class. True, the *sans-culottes* were ultimately responsible for the execution of King Louis XVI and the destruction of the monarchy. But the leaders who emerged as a result of mass politics, the Jacobins, were bourgeois. While Maximilien Robespierre and the Committee of Public Safety conducted the Terror, they did not overturn the established relations of society. Neither the urban nor the rural poor obtained redress of their grievances. The Constitution of 1793 and mass politics, manipulated by members of the bourgeoisie, ultimately consolidated the political power of the middle class. The defeat and execution of Robespierre only transferred political power from one bourgeois group to another. Subsequently, the Thermidorean regime and the Directory consolidated the political gains of the middle class. Napoleon Bonaparte completed the task of political revolution. Among the achievements of the Revolution was the establishment of a strong centralized state that replaced the relatively weak ancient regime.[26] By the end of the century, revolutionary France had become an imperial nation dominating large parts of the continent. In 1804, Bonaparte became Emperor of the French.

The Haitian Revolution

France lost its thinly populated possessions in North America in 1763. As a result of the Seven Years' War, Britain obtained Canada and Spain acquired Louisiana. The extremely valuable islands in the Caribbean, however, remained French. Initially, during the late seventeenth century, *engagés* – indentured servants – were recruited in France for three-year terms in the West Indies. As the plantation economy expanded, large numbers of African slaves replaced the *engagés* because they were a cheap and reliable labor force. By the end of the eighteenth century, the planters of Saint-Domingue imported 30,000 enslaved Africans a year to meet their labor needs.

The exploited slave majority formed the base of the social pyramid. Above them were a group of free people of color, *gens de couleur*, composed primarily of racially mixed persons and a few blacks. Some of them formed a wealthy, sophisticated, and cultured elite with ties to France. The

26 François Furet, *Interpreting the French Revolution* (Cambridge University Press, 1981); John F. Bosher, *The French Revolution* (New York: W.W. Norton, 1988), pp. 6–157.

Europeans of Saint-Domingue did not constitute a socially homogeneous group. The *grands blancs,* planters, high officials, and large merchants, constituted the political, social, and economic elite of the island. In contrast, the *petits blancs*, many of them descendants of the seventeenth-century *engagés,* found themselves in an ambiguous position. They considered themselves racially superior to the *gens de coulour* elite but lacked their wealth and education.

The social structure of the French colony reflected the composition of an exploitative plantation society. People were divided by race as well as by socio-economic status: the *grands blancs* held the *petits blancs* in contempt; the latter feared and despised the free people of color who were often their economic and cultural superiors; and the *gens de couleur*, while disdainful of the *petits blancs*, feared and loathed the exploited slaves.

Saint-Domingue, although occupying only the western third of the island of Hispaniola, became, during the second half of the eighteenth century, the most productive colony in the West Indies. During the 1780s and 1790s, Saint-Domingue accounted for about 40 percent of France's foreign trade. Two-fifths of the world's sugar was grown on the coastal plains of this small colony and more than half of the world's coffee was raised in its mountainous interior. Its productivity doomed most of Saint-Domingue's inhabitants to exploitation. Approximately 25,000 whites dominated the social pyramid, almost the same number of free persons of mixed blood constituted an intermediate subordinate group, and, at the bottom, were about 500,000 slaves from Africa or of African descent.[27]

The French Revolution influenced the nature and process of the Haitian Revolution. The violence in Saint-Domingue was initiated by the whites in 1790. As the *grands blancs* and the *petits blancs* fought for control of the colony, they armed not only themselves but also their slaves. When the French National Assembly granted political rights to the free *gens de coulour*, the whites temporarily united to limit political power to their race. Naturally, the free people of color also armed their slaves to defend their interests. After two years of fighting for the liberty and equality of the free people of Haiti – white and non-white – the slaves rebelled to win their own freedom. Although Pierre-Dominique Toussaint Louverture won a temporary victory for the slaves in 1793, which the National Assembly in France appeared to ratify when it abolished slavery, the struggle continued for another decade.

27 Laurent Dubois, *Avengers of the New World: The Story of the Haitian Revolution* (Cambridge, MA: Harvard University Press, 2004).

The British and the Spanish as well as the French intervened in the conflict, but Toussaint Louverture's forces drove them from the island, controlled internal dissent, and even conquered Spanish Santo Domingo.

When Toussaint Louverture named himself governor-general for life in July 1801, however, he did not declare independence. French attempts to reassert control of Saint-Domingue caused the final rupture. Napoleon Bonaparte, who wished to restore French power in America, seized Louisiana from the Spanish and, in 1802, dispatched a massive French army to restore order in Saint-Domingue. Although Toussaint Louverture was captured and sent to prison in France, where he died, his cause survived. Jean-Jacques Dessalines, his successor, defeated the French and declared Haitian independence on January 1, 1804.[28]

Haiti began its process of independence, like the rest of America, by continuing patterns and processes that had been evolving for years, but it experienced a dramatic social as well as political revolution. At first, Saint-Domingue participated in the transformations of the French Revolution, but the slaves, who were not initially included in those changes, insisted upon freedom and equality. Bloody and destructive wars were necessary to achieve those goals. The Haitians also transformed their agriculture from large-scale plantations to small-scale, self-sufficient agriculture. While they reoriented their production away from exports to internal markets, they nonetheless retained a minor export market sector.[29] However, a revolution of former slaves – people of African ancestry – terrified the white societies of both America and of Europe. When their armies failed to subdue the Haitians, the Europeans and the United States isolated the country. Although some Haitians sought to continue sugar exports, most markets were closed to them. Instead, European nations introduced profitable tropical agriculture to other Caribbean islands. Thus, the citizens of Haiti, an isolated and impoverished land, proved unable to form an economically prosperous and politically stable nation.

The independence of Spanish America

At the end of the eighteenth century, the Spanish monarchy's possessions in America constituted one of the world's most imposing political structures.

28 David Geggus, "The Haitian Revolution in Atlantic perspective," in Canny and Morgan (eds.), *The Oxford Handbook of the Atlantic World*, pp. 533–549.

29 Franklin Knight, "The Haitian Revolution," *American Historical Review* 105/1 (February 2000), 103–115.

Its territory, which included most of the Western Hemisphere, stretched along the entire Pacific coast from Cape Horn in the south to Alaska in the north. On the east coast, it shared South America with Brazil and the Guianas, Central America with British Honduras, and North America with the United States and Canada, both of which were limited to strips of land along the Atlantic. In the Caribbean, Spain possessed the principal islands. The Spanish Indies – generally called *America* in the eighteenth century – also included the Philippines and other islands in the Pacific Ocean.

Originally consisting of two viceroyalties, New Spain and Peru, the Crown further subdivided South America when it established the viceroyalties of New Granada and the Río de la Plata in 1739 and 1776. But the most enduring territorial units were those areas administered by the *audiencias* (high courts), often referred to as *reinos* (kingdoms). With the exception of the audiencias of New Spain, these were the areas that became the new nations of Spanish America. New Spain possessed two audiencias, Mexico and Guadalajara. The other audiencias of Spanish America consisted of Guatemala (Central America), Santa Fe de Bogotá (New Granada), Caracas (Venezuela), Quito, Charcas (Alto Perú/Bolivia), Lima (Peru), Santiago (Chile), Buenos Aires (Río de la Plata), and Santo Domingo (Caribbean). Although Cuzco obtained an audiencia in 1787, that high court had not existed long enough when independence was achieved to consolidate the region's separate identity. The area subsequently formed part of the republic of Perú.

In 1800 the Spanish territories in America had a population of approximately 12.6 million people, nearly half of them residing in New Spain. Spanish America was a diverse and complex region. Not only were some kingdoms more populated, developed, and prosperous than other areas, but also within realms, some regions were more advanced than others. Although claiming the vast majority of the continent, Spanish America possessed very limited fertile agricultural land. For example, only about 15 percent of New Spain, present-day Mexico, is arable without irrigation, while the vast fertile Pampas of present-day Argentina – like the Great Plains of North America – were considered in the eighteenth century to be a desert because they could not be cultivated given the technology of the time.

The settled portions of eighteenth-century Spanish America, the region's heartland, were characterized by massive mountain ranges, jagged canyons, great deserts, and extensive rain forests, which posed formidable barriers to communication. Despite Spanish America's extensive shorelines on both sides of the continent, coastal shipping was restricted by the lack of good harbors and by the location of the major population and production centers in the highlands away from the coast. Since very few of the settled areas possessed navigable rivers, the cost and difficulty of land transportation, universally more expensive than water, limited external trade to a few tropical agricultural products and valuable exports, such as silver. Despite the geographical obstacles, the kingdoms of Spanish America engaged in extensive internal trade. During the eighteenth century, the Viceroyalty of New Spain became the most populous, richest, and most developed area in America.

Regional economic variations in Spanish America contributed to social diversity. The core areas included significant urban groups – a diverse elite of government officials, clergy, professionals, merchants, large and middle-sized landowners, miners, and other entrepreneurs – as well as a varied artisanal and working sector. Those regions possessed a complex peasantry, predominantly Indian; it was also composed of mestizos, criollos, blacks, and *castas* (people of mixed African ancestry), which included small landowners, renters, resident workers, day laborers, and corporate villagers. While "Indians" constituted the majority of the population in core areas, many were not "juridical" Indians, those living in corporate villages subject to tribute. In the urban centers, the population was increasingly defined along class rather than racial lines.

Although generally similar to the core regions, the agricultural-producing areas possessed a simpler social structure, the result of a less complex economy and a smaller population. Dominated by a significant plantation labor force, which included large groups of blacks and castas as well as a smaller contingent of Indians, mestizos, and criollos, the tropical regions contained a comparable but smaller urban component. In many respects, tropical rural society was less differentiated than its counterpart in the core areas. The peripheral, or frontier regions, were characterized by a sharp distinction between settled groups, mostly mestizo, and the generally nomadic "barbarous Indians." They also contained a much smaller population and less social differentiation than the tropical areas.

Native society, which under the Republic of Indians enjoyed rights to lands, language, culture, laws, and traditions, also possessed its own governments, popularly known as *repúblicas*. Located in the settled pre-Hispanic areas, these regional governments consisted of the *cabecera*, the principal town and seat of administration, and subordinate villages called *pueblos sujetos* (subject towns). The *repúblicas* did not exist in isolation. Even in areas of dense Indian population, those polities coexisted with Spanish cities, mestizo and mulatto towns, and rural estates of various kinds.

The Republic of Spaniards, which expanded over time not only because of population growth but also because of miscegenation and acculturation, possessed countless representative corporate bodies. *Ayuntamientos* (municipal councils that governed provinces), universities, cathedral chapters, convents, mining and merchant organizations, and numerous craft guilds elected officials who represented their constituents. All these corporate entities, as well as the *repúblicas*, enjoyed a large measure of self-government and transmitted their views to the higher authorities such as the audiencias and the viceroys or directly to the Council of the Indies and the King.

After the Seven Years' War, Spain, like Great Britain, had to reorganize its American territories during the last years of the eighteenth century. It established a small standing army and a large force of provincial militias, reorganized administrative boundaries, introduced a new system of administration – the intendancies – restricted the privileges of the clergy, restructured trade, and limited the appointment of Americans to government in their *patrias*. Although Spanish Americans objected, sometimes violently, to these reforms, they did not imitate their northern brethren by seeking independence. The Spanish monarchy was sufficiently certain of its American subjects' loyalty, that it fought Great Britain during the British American struggle and signed the Treaty of Paris of 1783, which granted independence to the United States.

Spanish Americans opposed those innovations that injured them and managed to modify many to suit their interests. Although the reforms initially harmed some areas and groups, even as they benefited others, the existing political and administrative structures appeared capable of negotiating acceptable accommodations and establishing a new equilibrium. The constitutional crisis in the Spanish Monarchy had not yet reached the breaking point. Events in Europe, however, prevented an orderly readjustment. The French Revolution, which unleashed twenty-five years of war in which Spain became an unwilling participant, further eroded stability. Thus, at the end of the eighteenth century, the Spanish Monarchy faced the greatest crisis of its history.

The collapse of the Spanish monarchy in 1808, as a result of Napoleon Bonaparte's invasion of the Iberian Peninsula and the abdication of its rulers, triggered a series of events that culminated in the establishment of representative government throughout the Spanish world. The first step in that process was the formation of local governing juntas in Spain and America, which invoked the Hispanic legal principle that, in the absence of the king, sovereignty reverted to the people.

Events in Spain profoundly affected the New World. Unwilling to accept French domination, the people of the Peninsula opposed the invader. Although initially divided, the provinces of Spain ultimately joined forces on September 25, 1808, to form a government of national defense, the *Junta Suprema Central Gubernativa del Reino* (Supreme Central Junta of the Kingdom), to wage a war of liberation. The new Spanish national government, however, could not defeat the French without the aid of its overseas territories. Therefore, the new regime recognized the equality of the American kingdoms and, in 1809, invited them to elect representatives to the Junta Central.

Although restricted to a small elite, the elections enhanced the political role of the municipalities – the ayuntamientos – and were the first of a series of elections that provided Spanish Americans with the opportunity to participate in government at various levels. When the Junta Central convened a national assembly, the Cortes, in 1810, it again invited the American kingdoms to send delegates. The elections to the Cortes extended political participation more broadly than those for the Junta Central, by including Spaniards born in America and Asia and Indians and the sons of Spaniards and Indians.

The deputies of Spain and America who enacted the Political Constitution of the Spanish Monarchy in March 1812 transformed the Hispanic world. The Constitution of Cádiz was not a Spanish document; it was as much an American charter as a Spanish one because the American deputies to the Cortes played a central role in drafting the constitution. The Charter of Cádiz abolished seigniorial institutions, the Inquisition, Indian tribute, forced labor – both in America and in the Peninsula – and asserted the state's control over the Church. It created a unitary state with equal laws for all parts of the Spanish monarchy, substantially restricted the authority of the king, and entrusted the Cortes with decisive power. When it enfranchised all adult men, except those of African ancestry, without requiring either literacy or property qualifications, the Constitution of 1812 surpassed all existing representative governments, including those of Great Britain, the United States, and France, in providing political rights to the vast majority of the male population.

The Political Constitution of the Spanish Monarchy not only expanded the electorate but also dramatically increased the scope of political activity.

The new charter established representative government at three levels: the municipality (the constitutional ayuntamiento), the province (the diputación provincial), and the monarchy (the Cortes). By permitting cities and towns with a thousand or more inhabitants to form ayuntamientos, it transferred political power to the localities as vast numbers of people were incorporated into the political process. Studies of the popular elections in Spanish America demonstrate that although the elite dominated politics, more than two million middle- and lower-class men, including Indians, mestizos, blacks, and colored castes, actively participated in politics.

Despite the unparalleled democratization of the political system, civil war erupted in Spanish America because some groups, who refused to accept the government in Spain, insisted in forming local juntas, whereas others, who recognized the new authorities in the Peninsula, opposed them. Political divisions among the elites combined with regional antipathy and social tensions to exacerbate the conflict in the New World. The struggle in Spanish America waxed and waned during the first constitutional period, 1810 to 1814, and, at times, when the authorities acted with restraint, accommodation seemed possible.

King Fernando VII's return from captivity in France in 1814 provided an opportunity to restore the unity of the Hispanic world. Although he abolished the Constitution, at first, it appeared that he might accept moderate reforms, but ultimately the king opted to rely on force to restore royal order in the New World. Free from constitutional restraints, the royal authorities in the New World crushed most autonomy movements, such as those in New Spain, Venezuela, Nueva Granada, and Chile. Only the isolated Río de la Plata remained beyond the reach of a weakened Spanish monarchy.

The Crown's repression prompted the minority of Spanish America's politically active population, who favored independence, to act decisively. In South America, self-proclaimed generals gained immense power and prestige as the leaders of the bloody struggles to win independence. Although civilian and clerical institutions – ayuntamientos, courts, parishes, cathedral chapters – continued to function, and although new governments were formed and congresses elected, military power predominated.

It was clear by 1819 that King Fernando VII would have to send more troops if he wished to retain control of America, but raising yet another expeditionary force to reconquer the New World only increased discontent in the Peninsula. The liberals, exploiting the army's disenchantment with the war in America, eventually forced the king in March 1820 to restore the constitution. The return of constitutional order transformed the Hispanic political system for the third time in a decade.[30]

The restoration of constitutional government elicited disparate responses in Spanish America. When the news arrived in May, the people of New Spain and Guatemala (Central America) enthusiastically reestablished the constitutional system. In the months that followed, they conducted elections for countless constitutional ayuntamientos, provincial deputations, and the Cortes.

Political instability in the Peninsula during the previous twelve years, however, had convinced many New Spaniards that it was prudent to seek autonomy within the Spanish Monarchy. The autonomists, the members of the national elite who ultimately gained power after independence, opted for a constitutional monarchy. They pursued two courses of action: autonomy within the Spanish Monarchy or establish an autonomous government at home.

In 1821 New Spain's deputies to the Cortes of Madrid proposed a project for New World autonomy that would create three American kingdoms governed by Spanish princes and allied with the Peninsula. The proposal would form a Spanish commonwealth similar to the later British Commonwealth. Indeed, its proponents argued that they did not wish to follow the example of the United States. Instead, like Canada, they sought to retain ties with the monarchy. The king, however, rejected the proposal that would have granted Spanish Americans the home rule they had been seeking since 1808.

At the same time, New Spain's autonomists convinced the prominent royalist Colonel Agustín de Iturbide to accept their plan for autonomy, which resembled the one presented to the Cortes. Independence was assured in 1821 when Iturbide and his supporters won the backing of the majority of the royal army. Mexico achieved its independence, not because the royal authorities had lost on the battlefield, but because New Spaniards no longer supported the Crown politically. Central America also declared independence and joined the new Mexican Empire. It seceded peacefully in 1823, after the empire was abolished, and formed a separate nation.[31]

30 Jaime E. Rodríguez O., *The Independence of Spanish America* (Cambridge University Press, 1998).

31 Jaime E. Rodríguez O., *"We are Now the True Spaniards": Sovereignty, Revolution, Independence, and the Emergence of the Federal Republic of Mexico, 1808–1824* (Stanford University Press, 2012).

The newly independent Mexicans carefully followed the precedents of the Spanish constitutional system. Although they initially established an empire, they replaced it in 1824 with a federal republic, modeling their new constitution on the Hispanic charter because it had been part of their recent political experience. In keeping with Hispanic constitutional practices, they also formed a government with a powerful legislature and a weak executive branch. Federalism in Mexico arose naturally from the earlier political experience; the provincial deputations simply converted themselves into states. Like Mexico, the new Central American republic established a federation based on Hispanic constitutional practices.

In South America, the restoration of the Spanish Constitution provided the advocates of independence with the opportunity to press their campaign to liberate the continent. In contrast with New Spain, the South American insurgents defeated the royal authorities in battle.

Two competing political traditions emerged during the independence period: one, forged during more than a decade of war, emphasized strong executive power, and the other, based on the civilian parliamentary experience, insisted upon the preeminence of the legislature. They epitomized a fundamental conflict about the nature of government. New Spain, which achieved independence through political compromise rather than by force of arms, is representative of the civil tradition. There, the Hispanic constitutional system triumphed and continued to evolve. Despite subsequent coups by military men, civilian politicians dominated Mexican politics.

Unlike Mexico, in Colombia, Peru, and Bolivia, the men of arms dominated the men of law and the Hispanic constitutional experience exerted little influence. The three newly independent South American nations established strong centralist governments with powerful chief executives and weak legislatures. In 1830, Colombia – sometimes called Gran Colombia – splintered into three countries: Venezuela, New Granada, and Ecuador.

The southern cone, which also had won independence by force, did not fall under the control of military men. There, warfare with royalist forces had been limited. Most of the fighting occurred among provinces that struggled for autonomy from their capital cities. Chile eventually established a highly centralized oligarchic republic, whereas, in the Río de la Plata, the various provinces formed a loose confederation. Despite vast differences in the nature of their regimes, civilians dominated both nations.

The independence of Spanish America did not constitute an anti-colonial movement but formed part of the *political revolution* within the Hispanic world and the *dissolution of the Spanish monarchy*. Although a very radical

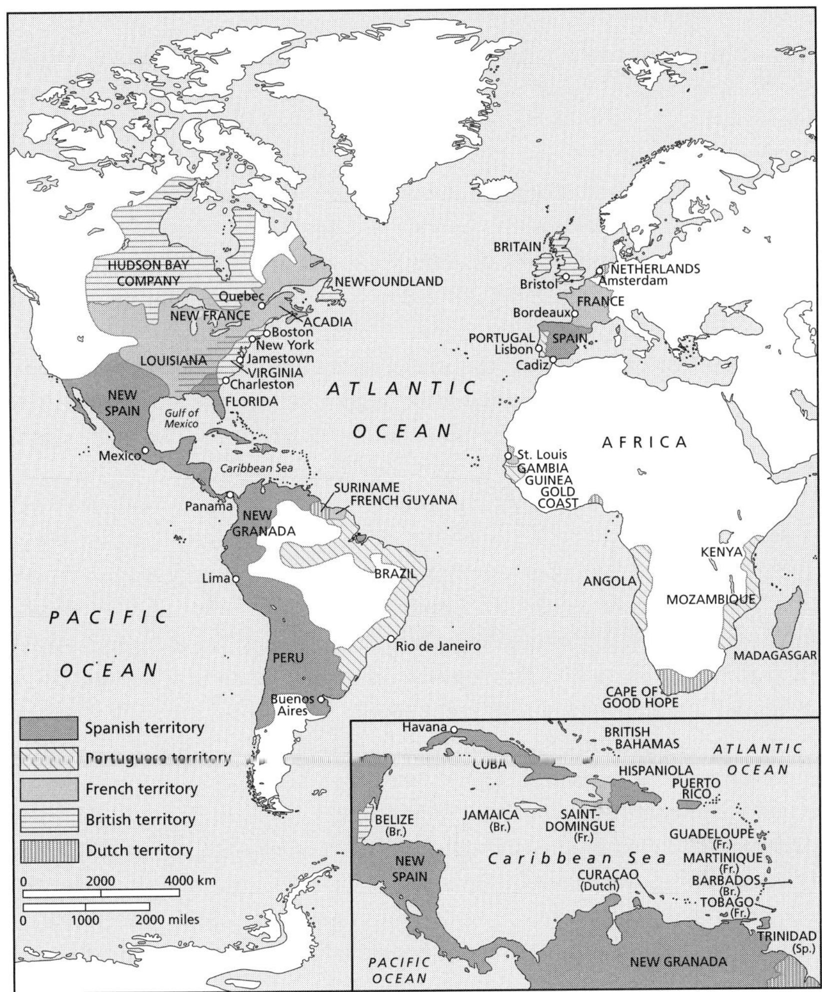

Map 12.1 Atlantic world, 1826–1830

political revolution occurred, it did not transform the social structure of Spanish America. Members of the complex socio-ethnic groups who existed in the continent based their participation in those processes on political and economic interests rather than on their membership in a particular ethnicity or race. Individuals from all groups participated on all sides of the complex struggle and were willing to modify alliances as circumstances changed. Many Indians, blacks (both enslaved and free), mulatos, mestizos, and creoles sided with the royalists, whereas some of their counterparts supported the varied insurgencies. These shifting coalitions formed to defend particular social, political, and economic interests rather than to advance the interests of these poorly defined heterogeneous socio-economic classes and racial groups.

The emancipation of Spanish America did not merely consist of separation from the mother country, as in the case of the United States; it also destroyed a vast and responsive social, political, and economic system that functioned relatively well, despite its many imperfections. For nearly three hundred years, the worldwide Spanish Monarchy had proven to be flexible and capable of accommodating social tensions and conflicting political and economic interests. After independence, the former Spanish Monarchy's separate parts functioned at a competitive disadvantage. In that regard, nineteenth-century Spain, like the American kingdoms, was just one more newly independent nation groping for a place in an uncertain and difficult world.

By 1826, the overseas possessions of the Spanish Monarchy consisted only of Cuba, Puerto Rico, the Philippines, and a few other Pacific islands. In contrast to the United States, which had obtained its independence in 1783, just in time to benefit from the insatiable demand for its products generated by the twenty-five years of war in Europe that followed the French Revolution of 1789, the Spanish world achieved emancipation after the end of the European conflicts. Not only did the new nations have to rebuild their shattered economies, but also they confronted the world's lack of demand for their products. Instead, Western Europe and the United States flooded Spanish America with their goods. Therefore, the new countries did not enjoy prosperity during their formative years as did the United States; rather, the Spanish American states had to face grave internal and external problems with diminished resources.

Spain's and Spanish America's nineteenth-century experience provides stark proof of the cost of independence. The two regions suffered political chaos, economic decline, economic imperialism, and foreign intervention. Both the Peninsula and the nations of the New World endured civil wars and military *pronunciamientos*. In their efforts to resolve their political and-economic crises, Spain and Spanish America experimented with monarchism and republicanism, centralism and federalism, and representative government and dictatorship. Unfortunately, no simple solution was found for nations whose economies had been destroyed by war and whose political systems had been shattered by revolution. Consequently, the members of the former Spanish monarchy were forced to accept a secondary role in the new world order. Although military strongmen – not a modern institutional military – frequently came to dominate their countries, they could not eliminate the liberal tradition of constitutional, representative government that had emerged in the Cortes of Cádiz. That tradition, together with the achievement of nationhood, remains the most significant heritage of Spanish American independence.

Further reading

Armitage, David. "The American Revolution in Atlantic perspective," in Nicholas Canny and Philip Morgan (eds.), *The Oxford Handbook of the Atlantic World, 1450–1850*. Oxford University Press, 2011, pp. 516–532.

Armitage, David and Sanjay Subrahmanyam, eds. *The Age of Revolutions in Global Context*. London: Palgrave Macmillan, 2010.

Bosher, John F. *The French Revolution*. New York: W.W. Norton, 1988.

Chávez, Thomas E. *Spain and the Independence of the United States: An Intrinsic Gift*. Albuquerque: University of New Mexico Press, 2002.

Chust, Manuel and Juan Marchena, eds. *Por la fuerza de las armas: Ejército e independencias en Iberoamérica*. Castelló de la Plana: Publicaciones de la Universitat Jaume I, Castellón, 2008.

Dubois, Laurent. *Avengers of the New World: The Story of the Haitian Revolution*. Cambridge, MA: Harvard University Press, 2004.

Furet, François. *Interpreting the French Revolution*. Cambridge: Cambridge University Press, 1981.

Geggus, David. "The Haitian Revolution in Atlantic perspective," in Nicholas Canny and Philip Morgan (eds.), *The Oxford Handbook of the Atlantic World, 1450–1850*. Oxford University Press, 2011, pp. 533–549.

Greene, Jack P. "The American Revolution," *American Historical Review* 105/1 (February 2000), 93–102.

Understanding the American Revolution. Charlottesville: University Press of Virginia, 1995.

Knight, Franklin. "The Haitian Revolution," *American Historical Review* 105/1 (February 2000), 103–115.

Maier, Pauline. *From Resistance to Revolution: Colonial Radicals and the Development of American Opposition to Britain, 1765–1776*. New York: W. W. Norton, 1991.

McPhee, Peter. "The French Revolution, peasants, and capitalism," *American Historical Review* 94/5 (December 1989), 1265–1280.

Morgan, Edmund S. *Inventing the People: The Rise of Popular Sovereignty in England and America*. New York: W.W. Norton & Co., 1988.

Pincus, Steve. *1688: The First Modern Revolution*. New Haven: Yale University Press, 2009.

Stein, Stanley J. and Barbara H. Stein. *Silver, Trade, and War: Spain and America in the Making of Modern Europe*. Baltimore: Johns Hopkins University Press, 2000.

Rodríguez O., Jaime E. *The Independence of Spanish America*. Cambridge University Press, 1998.

"We are Now the True Spaniards": Sovereignty, Revolution, Independence, and the Emergence of the Federal Republic of Mexico, 1808–1824. Stanford University Press, 2012.

Rodríguez O., Jaime E. ed., *Revolución, independencia y las nuevas naciones de América*. Madrid: Fundación MAPFRE/Tavera, 2005.

13

Global war 1914–45

RICHARD OVERY

The most remarkable aspect of the two global wars that dominated the thirty-year period from 1914 to 1945 was the contrast between their modest origins in political disputes in south-east and eastern Europe between just two states and the worldwide dimension that both wars quickly assumed. No-one in July 1914 could have predicted that the crisis between Serbia and the Austro-Hungarian Empire would result by 1918 in a war that embraced every continent and every ocean over its four-year course. Few people in August 1939 could have imagined that the imminent German–Polish war, ostensibly over the status of the Free City of Danzig, would by 1942 have led to a global conflict in sites as far apart as the Aleutian Islands, Madagascar and Dakar.

In the case of both World Wars there were factors that explain how local disputes became interlocked with wider conflicts, at both a regional and international level, capable of transforming local war into global war. In late-nineteenth-century Europe, the emergence of a great power system in which national identity and national interests came to supplant any wider commitment to a peaceful European order, created the circumstances in which national rivalry came to be regarded as a natural product of the modern age and warfare, either alone or in alliance, as the most likely way in which those rivalries would be expressed. The growth of large permanent armed forces, equipped with the sophisticated military products of modern science and industry, and the emergence of mass nationalism as a feature of European political culture, together created conditions in which the possibility of restraint in international crisis became progressively reduced.

National rivalry was also sustained by economic competition. In the mid nineteenth century, when British industrial and commercial strength had helped to precipitate widespread international co-operation and a reduction in economic restrictions on trade and production, market competition did not directly stimulate national rivalry. By the late nineteenth century, with widespread European industrialization and increasing pressure to secure the consumer interests of the new industrial, urban workforce and the emerging business classes, economic restrictions surfaced once again, while European states began to see wider global markets and sources of raw materials as an arena in which government protection and national self-assertion would be needed to preserve or enlarge national well-being at the possible expense of other states.

There has always been debate about whether these European historical developments explain the upsurge of the so-called 'New Imperialism' in the last third of the nineteenth century, but there is no doubt that imperialism did play a major part in turning regional European rivalries into global tensions. In 1917, Lenin famously defined World War I as the product of an imperialism which he titled 'the highest form of capitalism'.[1] Competition for markets, secure trade routes and trading bases, valuable raw materials or military outposts characterized much of the expansion of European economic and political interests between the 1870s and the outbreak of war in 1914. The link with empire became explicit as the areas of the globe not yet occupied by European powers, or brought under European suzerainty, were remorselessly eliminated, leaving Ethiopia as the only independent polity in Africa, and Siam (Thailand) the only independent state in south Asia and the South Pacific. For those states with old-established empires (Britain, France, The Netherlands, Spain, Portugal) the new wave of imperialism promised some advantages, but also compelled them to define the territories they controlled more closely, and to extend influence in areas which they regarded as strategically vulnerable, such as Egypt, or Indo-China (present-day Vietnam/Cambodia/Laos). For states now searching for empire for the first time (Germany, Italy, Belgium), or for Russia and the United States – after the Spanish–American war of 1898 – extending their influence and political control over wide areas of Asia and the Pacific, the old empires were a barrier to be challenged. The 'New Imperialism', which generated endless conflicts with indigenous societies, now assumed a more pronounced European dimension and the regular crises in the years before 1914 reflected that reality. Empire, for all its costs and problems, came to be seen as a way of protecting national interest and an expression of national vitality and economic strength.[2]

1 Vladimir Ilyich Ulyanov (Lenin), *Imperialism: The Highest Stage of Capitalism* (London: Lawrence & Wishart, 1933).

2 John Darwin, *After Tamerlane: The Global History of Empire since 1405* (London: Bloomsbury, 2008); Victor Kiernan, *European Empires from Conquest to Collapse* (London: Fontana, 1982).

The role of European imperialism (or rather of European illusions about what imperialism represented) in creating conditions for exacerbating national rivalry and the possibility of global war should not be underestimated. As the possibility of acquiring new territories disappeared, so the European states were encouraged to look to the failing empires in China or the Ottoman Middle East for possible compensation. British intervention in Egypt, occupied in 1882, French annexation of Algeria and Tunisia, and the Italian-Turkish war of 1911 brought the Ottoman Empire to crisis point, while the intervention of European and American expeditionary forces in China from the Opium Wars of the 1840s to the suppression of the 'Boxer Rebellion' in 1900 accelerated the decline of the Chinese imperial system while opening up apparently boundless commercial possibilities. The extension of European political and economic interests worldwide, part cause, part consequence of the crisis of traditional empires and political systems, not only failed to bring enhanced security for the new imperial powers, but created a web of fragile and unstable regional security zones in which it was difficult to project metropolitan power effectively. It also explains how local crises in 1914 and 1939 came immediately to have worldwide implications because the threat to the metropolitan power in Europe meant the automatic involvement of the network of dominions, settler states, protectorates and colonies that circled the entire globe.

The place of empire in explaining the origin of the World War and defining its global scale was not confined only to the coming of war in 1914. Indeed, issues of empire arguably played a larger part in the outbreak of World War II. In 1919 the Allied peacemakers created a situation in which British and French imperial interests were protected and enlarged by the peace settlement, in particular through the addition of mandated territories taken from the former German colonies and the collapsed Ottoman Empire and held loosely on behalf of the League of Nations.[3] Yet in reality the settlement after World War I created the prospect of further instabilities in the worldwide European empires with the spread of European ideas of nationalism to colonial peoples and the imagined threat from international communism, following the Bolshevik revolution in 1917 and the consolidation of Communist power in what became, in 1922, the Soviet Union. Safeguarding the security of the empire, even at its territorial zenith, permanently strained the capacity of Britain or France, as the two states dominating the League, to

3 Margaret Macmillan, *Peacemakers: The Paris Peace Conference of 1919 and the Attempt to End War* (London: John Murray, 2001).

act effectively in Europe or Asia. The post-1919 settlement at the same time created powerful national resentments among states that felt they had not received their due in 1919 or had been unfairly penalized. In the 1930s Germany, Italy and Japan each tried to extend their own imperial interests in defiance of an international system that seemed designed to benefit Britain and France and to limit their national aspirations. They were also aware that the Soviet Union and the United States, though playing little part in the League order, might soon exert their great economic and military potential at their expense unless they could secure greater regional power. The idea of a 'New Order' in which Germany, Italy and Japan would build their own regional empires defined the military and economic ambitions of all three and was agreed in the Tri-Partite Pact signed in September 1940 which divided the Old World into three new spheres of imperial influence in Europe, the Mediterranean basin and Africa, and mainland Asia. In this sense, the global competition for empire did not disappear with the end of World War I but was reconfigured as a result of the deficiencies of the post-1919 settlement and the rise of neo-imperialist and radical nationalist ideologies.

World War I and the failure of internationalism

Empire was not the only explanation for the failure of the international order to prevent the outbreak of a major European war in August 1914 and the subsequent inability to find a way to end it.[4] The pre-1914 world was, for all the confident belief in progress, a world in a state of rapid flux, in which new political and social forces were being released through mass education and economic modernization, which challenged the established order in Europe and in the wider world. The instability that these new historical forces created were evident in the Young Turk Revolution, launched in 1908 to try to modernize the ailing Ottoman Empire, or the collapse of Manchu China and the rise of a national revolutionary movement signalled by the Sun Yat Sen revolution in 1912, or the revolutionary ferment in the Russian Tsarist Empire which resulted in the 1905 revolution and a struggle for constitutional reform in the decade that followed. The other European states did not face revolution before 1914, but the rise of mass politics, both liberal and socialist, compelled regular concessions from the established ruling classes and a growing emphasis on patriotic and imperial symbolism to divert

4 Christopher Clark, *Sleepwalkers: How Europe Went to War in 1914* (London: Allen Lane, 2012); Jay Winter and Antoine Prost, *The Great War in History: Debates and Controversies 1914 to the Present* (Cambridge University Press, 2005).

some of the demand for political reform into popular nationalism. The attraction of imperial and nationalist propaganda can be explained by the search for new forms of identity by an increasingly literate and mobile population for whom the established conservative order held little appeal. The aristocratic and military elite in Europe still held on to political and social power where it could, but in 1914 part of the price to be paid for its national-imperial rhetoric was an exaggerated sense of threat and a population easily swayed by national fervour.

The crisis in 1914 exposed all these structural defects and insecurities. Otherwise it is difficult to make sense of how a minor crisis in the Balkans could spark within five weeks a conflagration involving all the major European empires. It has often been argued that the heart of the crisis lay in German ambition and insecurity, but a better case can be made for the argument that the problems confronting the ageing Habsburg Empire, and its ageing emperor, Franz Joseph, were decisive. Like the Russian and Ottoman Empires, the Habsburg Empire was faced with internal paradoxes it could not resolve. The semi-autonomy of Hungary in 1867 made it hard to justify the suppression of other national aspirations in a multi-national empire; the search for liberal constitutional reform merely fed the appetite for more radical solutions, while nationalism in Bohemia, Austrian Poland, Slovakia and among the south Slavs drove the Germans of the empire into strident Pan-German movements, with strong anti-Slav and anti-Semitic sentiments. The collapse of Ottoman power in the Balkans and the emergence of independent states created a power vacuum that both the Habsburgs and the Romanovs hoped to fill, but at the same time success here encouraged revolutionary nationalism inside the Habsburg Empire. The Balkan Wars against Turkey (and each other) in 1912–13 cemented independence and created a larger Serbia, the national representative of south Slav aspirations inside the Austrian territories. In Vienna, Serbia was seen as the principal threat and a solution to the south Slav question came to be seen as the one factor that would permit the Habsburg Empire to survive in more or less its existing form. Annexation of Bosnia and Herzegovina in 1908 was one step; extending some kind of godfatherly supervision over Serbia might be the next. When the Habsburg heir, Franz Ferdinand, and his wife Sophia were assassinated by Bosnian nationalists on 28 June 1914, the military leadership in Vienna saw this as an opportune moment to extend that supervision. When Serbia refused to allow her recently won sovereignty to be compromised by allowing Habsburg officials to monitor the murder investigation, Austria declared war.

This war might have been just another Balkan conflict had the crisis not had the unfortunate effect of immediately triggering the other insecurities of Europe. The major states were divided into loose alliance blocs, not necessarily to threaten each other, but to restrain alliance partners. There was nothing certain about how the major states would react to a crisis generated by one side or the other. Britain had an ambivalent relationship with Russia following the 1907 entente, while France was locked into a financial relationship with the burgeoning Russian economy that made support for Russia more certain. Germany was anxious that its principal ally, the Habsburg Empire, should not create major instability by an aggressive policy in south-east Europe as long as Russia, whose industrial modernization had made possible a large-scale military build-up, remained an uncertain factor.[5] Italy, an unnatural ally for Germany and Austria, remained neutral in 1914 and then switched sides in 1915 on the Allied promise of territorial gains at Austria's expense. The Serb crisis created a collective paranoia among the capitals of Europe and immediately mobilized popular patriotism, as all crises did. Germany tried to restrain Austria once the possibility of a broader crisis emerged, but the German military were worried that Russia and France would seize a sudden opportunity to stifle German power. The Tsar wanted to make a clearer statement of Russian determination to protect Serbia in order to allay domestic criticism and to divert popular feeling to a national cause. He approved a risky mobilization and when Russian leaders refused German demands to stop, Germany mobilized and launched a pre-emptive campaign against France and Russia. Britain responded to the violation of Belgian neutrality not from any great love for the Belgians but from fear that defeat of France would swing the European balance of power heavily against British interests. By 4 August a general European war had emerged from the Austro-Serb crisis and Britain and France rallied their empire populations across the globe. In October 1914, the Ottoman Empire, hoping to reverse the recent losses of territory to Serbia, Greece and Italy, joined the so-called Central Powers, Germany and Austria-Hungary, turning the Middle East into a war zone as well, where the principal Allied states, Britain and France, had further interests to defend.

Two battles ensured that the war would not be ended in a single campaign in 1914. The Battle of the Marne in September in France checked the onrushing German armies and created a long defensive front through north-eastern

5 Sean McMeekin, *The Russian Origins of the First World War* (Cambridge, MA: Harvard University Press, 2011).

France, the Western Front. In the east the Russian armies were defeated at Tannenberg in late August 1914, preventing a Russian march on Berlin. Although war was more mobile on the Eastern Front, fixed defensive lines were also built here. When Italy joined the war on the side of the Allies in May 1915, more trenches appeared on the Italian–Austrian border in north-east Italy. The stalemate that resulted on all the European fronts resulted from the development of a military technology that favoured the defence – machine-guns, heavy artillery with a sophisticated range of deadly ammunition, and poison gas. The defensive trench was protected by mine-fields and barbed wire; breaching fixed defences required heavy sacrifice of manpower. Armoured vehicles were almost unknown until the last year of war and aircraft were in their technical infancy, duelling in the sky to no very great effect.

It was nevertheless possible to restore peace by agreement. The few explorations of a possible peace broke down on the intransigence of both sides, neither willing to accept concessions or to abandon the prospect of a favourable settlement. The high casualties and the heavy industrial commitment soon required, locked the major nations into a conflict in which the sacrifices had to be justified in some way by success, however ill-defined. What began as an ill-conceived conflict fuelled by mutual distrust was soon rationalized as a struggle for survival, drawing on a generation of social-Darwinist thinking which saw human conflict as the inevitable reflection of the wider struggle for survival in nature.[6] Defeat of the Allies was seen as the precondition for the continued existence of the German, Austrian and Turkish empires, while defeat of the Central Powers was seen as the precondition for the establishment of a more stable and liberal international order. The intensity with which the war was fought and the triumph of a narrow nationalist, even racist, ideology among all the combatant powers ensured that the war would be fought to the death if it could be. The war in this sense developed its own momentum and its own bloodthirsty rationale, related to but increasingly distant from the values and interests of the pre-war world.[7]

The war was not, however, a unitary conflict. The massive bloodletting against fixed defences that characterized the war on all the major European

6 Paul Crook, *Darwinism, War and History: The Debate over the Biology of War from the 'Origin of Species' to the First World War* (Cambridge University Press, 1994); Michael Hawkins, *Social Darwinism in European and American Thought 1860–1945: Nature as Model and Nature as Threat* (Cambridge University Press, 1997).

7 Daniel Pick, *War Machine: The Rationalization of Slaughter in the Modern Age* (New Haven: Yale University Press, 1996).

fronts, or in the failed British assault on Gallipoli against Turkey from April 1915 to January 1916, was accompanied by a global conflict against Germany's overseas colonial possessions and a naval war involving Japan (Britain's ally) in the Pacific, and the British, French and Italian fleets in the Atlantic and the Mediterranean. Germany's colonies were soon overrun except in German East Africa (Tanganyika), where the garrison held out until the end of the war in 1918. Japan in 1914 seized the German colony of Jiaozhou in China and the Mariana, Marshall and Caroline Islands, giving the Japanese a foothold in the central Pacific. The most important naval theatre was the Atlantic. The German battle fleet was bottled up in the North Sea by the larger British navy, but German submarines could operate in the Atlantic against British trade. The object was to cut off British overseas supplies, on which Britain was dependent and so force Britain to withdraw from the war. In January 1917 the German Kaiser, Wilhelm II, agreed to the introduction of unrestricted submarine warfare to ensure that all vessels, even those of the neutral United States, could be sunk. In July 1917 this undersea assault was accompanied by a bombing campaign against London and coastal towns using the first heavy bombers developed in the war. The attempt to fight the war away from the European front lines proved disastrous. The bombing achieved little but prompted the British to found the Royal Air Force and to begin preparing the bombing of German industrial cities, which began in the summer of 1918. The anti-shipping campaign finally provoked the neutral United States, whose sympathies were broadly with the Western Allies, into a state of war against Germany. This decision, taken by President Woodrow Wilson in April 1917, turned the war into a truly global conflict and brought into the scales the overwhelming economic strength of the world's largest industrial and agricultural producer.

Entry of the United States did not make the defeat of the Central Powers inevitable but made it probable. Given the tight economic blockade imposed on Germany and Austria and the escalating cost of the war in men and industrial resources it is remarkable that they sustained combat for as long as they did. The war imposed severe social strains and widespread hunger, with declining health, shortages of fuel and flourishing black markets. These pressures proved too great for the Russian Empire, since its industrial base was more fragile and its organization of the war corrupt and incompetent. In February 1917 the Tsar was overthrown and a revolutionary state proclaimed, though the war continued to be fought to prevent a harsh peace. The costly war effort broke the new revolutionary state as well. The radical Marxist 'Bolsheviks' seized power from the Provisional Government in late October 1917 and sought ways to end the war. The subsequent treaty of Brest-Litovsk, signed under duress in March 1918, gave the Central Powers control of large areas of Ukraine and Belorussia and freed precious manpower to be moved to the Western and Italian Fronts. A final German fling in Operation Michael on the Western Front in March 1918 was halted after a few weeks and with the addition of fresh American troops, the German army was slowly driven back from its front lines. In Italy an Allied victory at Vittorio Veneto in late October 1918 broke the Austrians' resistance while Turkish forces were routed in Palestine and Syria. The domestic alliance that had kept the Central Powers fighting collapsed. The Habsburg Empire fragmented into its ethnic fractions while in Germany working-class militancy broke out into open confrontation with the old regime which was by now secretly negotiating a ceasefire. On 29 October mutinies began in the German fleet. On 9 November the Kaiser abdicated and a day later an armistice was agreed, to come into effect at 11 a.m. on the eleventh day of the eleventh month. Separate agreements were reached with Austria-Hungary and Turkey some weeks before.

An armistice for twenty years

The war was the central event of the twentieth century. The prolonged and savage nature of the conflict directly touched the lives of millions of men and indirectly affected tens of millions of war-workers, farmers, sailors and officials. Families across Europe bore losses exceptional even in a world where the death of children and the premature death of adults was commonplace. Some 8.4 million soldiers were killed from both sides and 22 million wounded out of the 65 million men (and some women) mobilized, a casualty rate of 47 per cent.[8] Millions of civilians – the exact number will never be known with precision – lost their lives through hunger, disease, bombing, shelling, racial violence and wartime atrocities. The dislocating effect of the conflict was evident at every level – political, social, economic, cultural and demographic.[9] Yet in 1919 the victorious Allies (now no longer including Russia, whose Communist revolutionaries rejected bourgeois peacemaking, even had they been invited) assumed that it would be possible to build a better world, based on collaboration and mutual respect, a liberal

8 H. P. Wilmot, *World War I* (London: Dorling & Kindersley, 2003), pp. 306–307.

9 Dan Todman, *The Great War: Myth and Memory* (London: Hambledon, 2005); Robert Gerwarth and John Horne, eds., *War and Peace: Paramilitary Violence in Europe after the Great War* (Oxford University Press, 2012).

internationalism that would bring to an end the domination of ethnic minorities by larger dynastic empires and encourage the democratization of politics through the principle of self-determination. These ambitions lay at the core of the so-called Fourteen Points outlined by President Wilson to the American Congress in January 1918 and reiterated in September. The better world was to be supervised by a new League of Nations, the product of British and American idealist thinking during the war about how to overcome the threat of alliance systems, economic restrictions and the wasteful expenditure on armaments.

It would be easy to dismiss these ambitions to solve the whole world's problems as deluded in the light of what subsequently happened. There were important political and geopolitical achievements made possible as a consequence of war.[10] The German, Russian, Habsburg and Ottoman empires all disappeared to be replaced by republics, though only Germany and Austria were democratic republics, and even there only for a little over a decade. In central and Eastern Europe new states were created, loosely based on self-determination and temporarily democratic – Austria, Hungary, Poland, Finland, the Baltic States, Czechoslovakia and Yugoslavia. New states were carved out of the collapsed Ottoman Empire in Palestine, Syria, Lebanon, Transjordan, Iraq and Saudi Arabia but all but Arabia were put under the control of Britain and France and none was remotely democratic (though Iraq won its independence in 1926). These rearrangements helped to shape the map of what are now modern Europe and the modern Middle East.

The effort to reach a settlement in the Allied conference at Versailles in 1919 that would confirm and support these changes resulted in the formation of a League of Nations and a notional commitment to universal disarmament, both enshrined in the Treaty of Versailles forced on Germany in June 1919. The subsequent treaties of St. Germain and Trianon with Austria, Hungary and Bulgaria, and the Treaty of Sèvres with Turkey (replaced by a new Treaty of Lausanne in 1923 confirming a new sovereign Turkish nation in Anatolia) elaborated the settlement in Eastern Europe and the Middle East. The League met for the first time in 1920 in London before moving to its permanent seat in Geneva. All disputes between member states were to be submitted for discussion with the object of arriving at a judicious settlement without resort to arms.

10 Zara Steiner, *The Lights that Failed: European International History 1919–1933* (Oxford University Press, 2005).

The long catalogue of half-resolved issues that resulted from the political and social upheaval of war shows the extent to which the peacemakers and League activists lived an illusion. The years after the war were punctured by continued violence, in Ireland (where the British government had to agree to self-determination in 1922), in a savage war between Greece and Turkey, and an equally savage and prolonged civil war in Russia which saw the mobilization of armies on the scale of the World War. The bitter war between the Red Army and the counter-revolutionary 'Whites' scarred Soviet development in the 1920s and 1930s and encouraged the development of a militaristic and terroristic dictatorship. An attempted invasion of Poland by the victorious Red Army was repulsed outside Warsaw in 1920 by the narrowest of margins. In China the collapse of imperial rule prompted the fragmentation of Chinese territory into rival warlord territories, and growing Japanese intervention in the economic development of the north. Chinese instability was exploited by European and American traders, who competed, as they had done before 1914, for special favours.

The League could do nothing about these conflicts and was weakened immediately by the failure in 1920 of the United States Congress to ratify the treaty, cutting America off from the experiment Wilson had pioneered. The League was dominated by British and French interests; Germany became a member for seven years from 1926 to 1933, and the Soviet Union for five years, from 1934 to 1939. Japan left it in March 1933, Italy in December 1937. With only two of the major powers as continuous members, the League's political ambitions were doomed. Nor were Britain and France the model liberal internationalists the system needed. The commitment to disarm was not ignored entirely, but both states remained heavily armed throughout the 1920s and 1930s, while for years denying Germany the right to rearm. Self-determination was not offered to the French and British colonies and protectorates, or to India, though they had all supplied men and resources for the World War. Imperial rule came to be seen as oppressive and unjust as nationalist ideals were imported into the empire areas and demands for independence or self-government articulated in European terms. Anti-colonial politicians could point to the paradox of a World War for liberty and their continued subjection. Although liberal trade policies were talked about in 1919, Britain and France continued to practise restrictions on trade and made little effort to reconstruct the pre-war trading and financial system on which a flourishing world economy depended. Economic stabilization in the 1920s owed much to the United States, which rescued the German and Central European currencies in 1923–4 and extended large loans to sustain growth in Europe, while not insisting on the full repayment of wartime credits.[11]

These structural economic and political defects might have been overcome if a liberal willingness to create more open trade and political partnerships had really been manifested, or the paradoxes of British and French dominance, itself the product of chance rather than intention, properly addressed. There remained, however, other legacies of war that were more damaging to the prospect of a liberal reconstruction. The revolutionary movements at the end of the war in Germany, Italy, Austria and Hungary, which drew inspiration from the Bolshevik example, provoked bitter ideological feuding. In China the warlord conflicts of the 1920s became distilled into a central and violent conflict between the Nationalists led by the young soldier Chiang Kai-shek, and the Chinese Communists. The Japanese government and military detested communism, a hatred that prompted their intervention in Siberia in 1919 against the Red Armies. The 1920s witnessed an incipient Cold War against the Soviet state and against the attempt by the Communist International, set up in Moscow in 1919, to spread the revolutionary movement worldwide. The most conspicuous reaction against the radical left was the emergence of a radical nationalism in the 1920s, led by embittered veterans of the World War who saw the struggle still in terms of national survival and self-assertion, and believed their sacrifice to be dishonoured by the internationalism and pacifism of the left. Where they could, these veterans mimicked wartime ceremonial (with all its religious overtones), adopted political uniforms and titles, engaged in routine street violence and rejected collaboration with other parties of the right. Their radical nationalism flourished best in a context where the traditional conservative forces were weakened by the war and its aftermath, as in Germany or Italy or Austria.[12] In the absence of a powerful but more moderate conservatism, the revolutionary nationalists of the trenches appealed to all those frightened of communism and still susceptible to the crude patriotic appeals of the war years. Without the conditions created by war and the embedded hatreds and fears it engendered it is unlikely that Benito Mussolini's Italian Fascist Party would have come to power

11 Patricia Clavin, *The Great Depression in Europe, 1929–1939* (Basingstoke: Macmillan Press, 2000).

12 E. R. Dickinson, 'Biopolitics, facism, democracy: some reflections on our discourse on "modernity"', *Central European History* 37 (2004), 1–48; Emilio Gentile, *The Origins of Fascist Ideology* (New York: Enigma Books, 2005).

in Italy in 1922, or Adolf Hitler's National Socialists in Germany in 1933, or the quasi-Fascist Fatherland Front of Engelbert Dollfuss in Austria in 1934.[13] Without the legacy of war and the growing resentment at Western claims on Asia that the postwar settlement prompted, it is unlikely that young Japanese militarists would have become the driving force of Japanese anti-communism and imperialism in the 1930s.

It is important to recognize that the generation that experienced the war at first hand –wounded like Mussolini, or gassed like Hitler, or a prisoner like Dollfuss – grew up by the 1930s into the politicians, officials and senior officers that ran the political and military establishment. Their reference points were the experiences of war and its aftermath and their sense of personal commitment to comrades and their shared prejudices and resentments, were the product of these years. Hitler gave speeches in 1920 on the elimination of the Jews in Europe, who he blamed for 'stabbing Germany in the back' at the end of the war, and he was making similar speeches twenty years later on the eve of launching the deliberate genocide of the Jews. Fumimaro Konoye, Japanese representative at the Versailles Conference, expressed his resentment at the treatment of Japanese interests in an essay in 1918 on rejecting the 'Anglo-American centred peace' and twenty years later as Japanese prime minister declared a 'New Order' in Asia to exclude the Western powers from Japanese affairs in China.[14] Radical nationalism, whether in Germany or Italy or Japan, was nourished on the belief that the World War had opened up opportunities to remodel domestic politics and to remodel the world system.

It was not, of course, inevitable, as the French Marshal Ferdinand Foch warned in 1919, that there would only be an armistice for twenty years and then another war.[15] But with the passage of time it is evident that no explanation for the descent into a second World War in the late 1930s can ignore the dysfunctional effects of the conflict of 1914–18 with its messy and violent aftermath and its lingering psychological and ideological legacies. Even among those who campaigned against war in the 1920s and 1930s, chiefly in Britain and France, there was a demoralizing expectation that the drift to a new war was irresistible, driven by forces that civilization

13 Roger Griffin, ed., *International Fascism: Theories, Causes and the New Consensus* (London: Arnold, 1988).

14 Aaron William Moore, *Writing War: Soldiers Record the Japanese Empire* (Cambridge, MA: Harvard University Press, 2013).

15 'This is not a peace: it is an Armistice for twenty years', cited in Leopold Schwarzschild, *World in Trance: From Versailles to Pearl Harbor* (London: Hamish Hamilton, 1944), p. 50.

could not restrain.[16] The probability of a new war was exacerbated by the economic crisis that destroyed the fragile world economy in 1929–30, itself the product of the failure to restore a more liberal trading and financial order in the 1920s, or to compensate for the economic damage sustained by the war and, in the case of Germany and Austria, a punitive peace treaty. Britain and France survived the Slump more effectively than economies that relied on favourable export markets and open trade, such as Germany and Japan. The failure of economic multilateralism resulted in as many as 40 million unemployed worldwide and crippling poverty in the weaker economies. Protectionist trade regimes in Britain, France and the United States convinced other states that the Western economic system was bankrupt and that the narrow self-interest of Britain and France, made evident by their possession of large territorial empires, was a barrier to the successful national self-expression of other states. The result was a deliberate search for a 'New Order' both economically and politically that would challenge Western dominance and create the conditions for national self-assertion stifled by the war and its aftermath.[17]

In truth the 'New Orders' were not new at all, but were rooted in old-fashioned mercantilist economics and the search for empire, connected much more with a world well before 1914 than with any new age. The ambitions formulated in Japan, Italy and Germany – the Axis states – in the 1930s were closely linked to the idea of empire. In Japan and Italy, both of which already had territorial empires, the object was to consolidate these and to expand further, using territorial conquests as a means to secure both a high degree of economic self-sufficiency (autarky) to protect military production and an exalted international status. In 1931 the Japanese army seized control of Manchuria in northern China and embarked on a course of territorial expansion that was to end with the launching of war in the Pacific and South East Asia in December 1941 in order to secure the further resources necessary to sustain a new Asian empire against Western efforts to challenge it.[18] In Italy, Mussolini had consolidated his personal dictatorship by 1926 and now looked for opportunities to exploit what he regarded as Western decadence by embarking on a programme to extend Italian imperial power in Africa and eventually in the Mediterranean basin. The war against Ethiopia, waged

16 Richard Overy, *The Inter-War Crisis 1919–1939*. 3rd edn (Harlow: Longmans, 2007).

17 Randall Schweller, *Deadly Imbalance: Tripolarity and Hitler's Strategy of World Conquest* (New York: Columbia University Press, 1998).

18 Rana Mitter, *China's War with Japan 1937–1945: The Struggle for Survival* (London: Allen Lane, 2013).

between October 1935 and May 1936, was the first step; war against Britain and France declared in June 1940 saw Italian forces threaten the Suez Canal, expel the British from Somaliland and embark in October 1940 on a war against Greece. Hitler was also obsessed with issues of empire. He could remember by heart the population size and territorial extent of the British and French Empires. His ambition to conquer Eurasia was clearly imperialist in a conventional sense: 'What India was for England, the territories of Russia will be for us', he remarked in August 1941.[19] The drive to extend German power into central Europe with the acquisition of Austria, the Czech lands, and then Poland in 1939, was to open the way to building an integrated German-dominated empire in Eastern Europe where colonial forms of government could be imposed and the economic resources exploited for a self-sufficient 'large area economy' [*Grossraumwirtschaft*].[20] Nevertheless, all three of these 'New Orders' could only be constructed at the expense of those states which wished to preserve as much of the 'Old Order' as they could. The result was a rush to rearm from the mid-1930s on a scale that dwarfed the military preparations of pre-1914.[21] In 1914 most states devoted around 3–5 per cent of the national product to military purposes; by 1939 Germany devoted 30 per cent, Britain 22 per cent and France 23 per cent of the national product. All three states began an arms race from the same point, 1936–7. Soviet military expansion followed the same trajectory; even in the neutral and isolationist United States President Roosevelt was able to persuade Congress to accept limited rearmament for defence in 1938–9.

World War II: from one New Order to another

The war that broke out on 3 September 1939 after Germany ignored British and French ultimatums to withdraw from the invasion of Poland, begun two days before, was only part of this wider project pursued, though not coordinated, by the three Axis states to overturn the existing international disorder and to impose their own version of international stability. Japan began a war against Nationalist China in July 1937 which was soon extended to the whole of northern, central and eastern China. In 1938 and again in 1939 large operations were conducted against Soviet forces on the unstable

19 Hugh Trevor-Roper, ed., *Hitler's Table Talk 1941–44* (London: Weidenfeld & Nicolson, 1973), p. 24 (entry for 8–9 August 1941).
20 Chritian Leitz, *Nazi Foreign Policy 1933–1941* (London: Routledge, 2004).
21 Joseph Maiolo, *Cry Havoc: How the Arms Race Drove the World to War* (New York: Basic Books, 2006).

border with Soviet-dominated Mongolia. Japan took advantage of the German war in Europe, which had resulted in a spectacular defeat over France and a British Expeditionary Force in May/June 1940 (what was supposed to happen in 1914), to extend influence into French Indo-China and to think about a southern campaign to seize the oil, rubber, tin and bauxite of the European empires in South East Asia. Mussolini occupied Albania in April 1939 and built up Italian forces in Libya before releasing them against a weakened British Commonwealth defence in September 1940. Hitler consolidated his hold on Eastern Europe in 1939–40, defeated France and hoped that blockade and bombing, the hope of 1917, would bring Britain to the negotiating table. On 27 September 1940 the three Axis powers signed the Tri-Partite Pact in Berlin (with another ceremony in Tokyo) declaring their intention to construct a New Order in each of their areas of imperial interest.

There was in all this much unfinished business. Indeed, the analogies between the two World Wars are striking. The German Schlieffen Plan of 1914 – to defeat France first and then turn to deal with Russia – was repeated, apparently successfully, by the autumn of 1941 when Hitler believed that Russia, invaded by four million Axis and co-belligerent forces in June, was close to imminent defeat. Once more German submarines tried to blockade Britain while the Royal Navy imposed blockade on Germany and German-occupied Europe. Once again bombing was used by the German armed forces to try to force Britain out of the war, and once again Britain responded as in 1918 by planning a large-scale bombing campaign against German industrial cities. The Middle East, because of Italian aggression this time, became a major theatre for British Commonwealth troops. Once again German unrestricted submarine warfare targeted American ships and pushed the American President, Franklin Roosevelt, to a strategy of economic and financial assistance for the Allies. For many of those involved at command and managerial level, this was the familiar architecture of world war. Only Turkey succeeded in avoiding a repetition of the conflict.

There were nevertheless important differences. The German expectation that war against the Soviet Union would resemble war against the ramshackle Tsarist empire, encouraged by German racial and ideological prejudices, proved woefully misjudged and German and Axis forces found themselves bogged down, often literally so, in a long war of savage attrition. To prepare for the new German Empire, the rear areas under German control were the site of a vast ethnic and political cleansing, predominantly of Jews (who were seen as a world enemy by Hitler and his entourage), but also of Poles and Czechs who were displaced to make way for German settlers, and Ukrainians, Belorussians and Russians who were left to starve or were deported for forced labour or killed as partisan sympathizers.[22] The Jews throughout the area of the New Order were the target from 1941 of death, deportation, ghettoization and slave labour. The genocide was an expression of the National Socialist conviction that a second war, against world Jewry, had to be fought to ensure success in the wider military conflict. The result was the murder by shooting, gassing or starvation of 5.7 million European Jews.

While this cruel colonial project was being realized, German forces found that the industrialization of the Soviet Union under Stalin had fostered the material means for an effective military revival, while the thoughtless violence meted out to the conquered peoples created just the conditions for stubborn Soviet resistance and a widespread partisan terror. Unlike the Tsarist system, the Stalin dictatorship organized a centralized military and economic effort, accepted the need for reform of Red Army operational doctrine, tactics and technology, and mobilized popular support for a crusade against the German invader. From December 1941, when the German advance on Moscow was reversed, it was evident that Hitler had miscalculated the prospects for Soviet resistance; in 1942 most of the front line in the East was static, but the one major campaign undertaken by the Axis armies to seize the Caucasus oil and cut the Volga River trade route ended in the disaster at Stalingrad. After that German forces foundered on Soviet revival and were forced into a slow but relentless retreat.

Something similar happened to the Japanese effort to conquer Asia from the east. What was viewed in Tokyo as a straightforward contest with the poorly prepared and racially inferior Chinese, turned into a long war of attrition in which Japanese soldiers, like their German counterparts, found themselves taking high losses in distant, inhospitable terrain. They were threatened by Chinese partisans, warlord armies, Chinese Communists and by the chinese Nationalist Army that refused to admit defeat, though it was too poorly resourced to imitate what the Soviet Red Army was able to do in Europe.[23] The war for Asia, from east and west was characterized by an exceptional level of military brutality, with routine atrocity committed by both sides, little respect for the status of prisoner-of-war, and the widespread targeting and killing of civilians. Millions died in the Soviet Union

22 Timothy Snyder, *Bloodlands: Europe between Hitler and Stalin* (London: Bodley Head, 2010).
23 Mitter, *China's War*; Moore, *Writing War*.

and China from starvation (and disease) brought about by the seizure of food supplies, the disruption of transport and the decline of medical facilities. An estimated 16 million civilians died in the Soviet Union, perhaps as many again in China.

Britain, the British Commonwealth, the United States and more than thirty other states that joined the United Nations (as they were known from January 1942) fought a different kind of war, reliant on weaponry and equipment that maximized the engineering, scientific and production skills of the Western Allies. The Western war effort relied on the sea above all, and the truly global dimensions of the war owed most to the worldwide network of sea communications and supply established by Allied navies in every major ocean, including essential American resources sent to China, the Soviet Union and Britain under the Lend-Lease scheme begun in March 1941. For Britain and the United States the most effective way of projecting power against all three Axis states was by sea and air, and this is where the largest portion of the Western Allied war effort was devoted. In the Pacific, Japan's weak island garrisons stretched out along the perimeter of the new Japanese empire, though they fought tenaciously and, when they had supplies, effectively, were no match for the large American naval, army and Marine Corps presence once the Japanese fleet carriers had been destroyed at the Battle of Midway in early June 1942. In the Atlantic, high-level secret intelligence, radar and long-range air-power combined to defeat the German submarine threat, which at its peak in 1942 sank 7.8 million tons of Allied shipping.[24] Britain became the base for two major air offensives against German occupied Europe, first by RAF Bomber Command by night from May 1940 to the final raids in April 1945, second by the US Eighth Air Force flying from British bases (joined later by the Fifteenth Air Force flying out of Italy), which between them destroyed German Air Force resistance and German supplies of oil in 1944, hastening German defeat in all combat theatres. Sea and air power were central to the successful amphibious operations in Sicily in July 1943, mainland Italy in autumn 1943 and the invasion of Normandy in June 1944. Defeat of German armies in France relied heavily on massive air power and the ability to bring seaborne supplies and reinforcements for Allied ground armies.[25]

As in World War I, there were no short cuts to peace. German hopes that Britain in summer 1940 or the Soviet Union in autumn 1941 would ask for an

24 Stephen Roskill, *The War at Sea 1939–1945*, 3 vols. (London: HMSO, 1961), Vol. III (Part 2), p. 479, appendix ZZ.

25 Richard Overy, *Why the Allies Won*. 2nd edn (London: Pimlico, 2006).

armistice were frustrated not only by their continued capacity to fight back in the most adverse of circumstances, but principally by the rejection of German domination, which was regarded as far worse than the high costs of continued belligerency. This meant finding ways to keep the home population committed to war and able to work in the Soviet Union, where food was scarce and death from starvation common among non-workers, a situation very different from the conditions in the United States, where incomes rose over the war and food was relatively plentiful. Forcing Axis surrender was equally difficult, except in the case of Italy, where an exasperated population protested the failures of war in 1943 and encouraged army and Fascist party leaders to get rid of Mussolini in July. An Italian surrender followed on 8 September 1943. In Germany and Japan, both fearful of what would happen if they lost, and hampered by the Allied call for 'unconditional surrender', laid down by Roosevelt at the Casablanca Conference in January 1943, fought with a savage fatalism to put off the hour of defeat. In both states the populations shared the anxieties about the cost of peace, while the security forces punished any expression of defeatism or political dissent. When a group of army officers tried to kill Hitler in July 1944, they were caught and executed. Secret police reports showed evidence of widespread relief at Hitler's survival and endorsement from the population of the punishment meted out to the conspirators. German surrender in May 1945 and Japanese surrender in August came only after the urban area had been reduced to ruins, an estimated 500,000 civilians killed by conventional bombing, 200,000 killed by the atomic attacks, the transport system wrecked and around eight million soldiers killed, five million of them German, three million of them Japanese.[26]

The aftermath of World War II did not repeat the mistakes of World War I, although violence continued long after 1945 in the messy conclusion to civil wars in Greece, Ukraine, Poland and China, and confrontations between local populations and the British, French and Dutch imperialists who tried, unsuccessfully in the end, to re-impose the imperial system in Indonesia, Indo-China, Malaya, India and Burma.[27] In 1945 all empires were either destroyed or in the

26 The 700,000 included approximately 355,000 Germans and foreign workers in Germany, 200,000 Japanese dead from firebombing and up to 200,000 from the atomic bombings. In addition in Europe there were 60,000 Britons, 54,000 French, 60,000 Italians, 10,000 Dutch, 18,000 Belgians who were killed by bombing, a global total of almost one million victims of air war.

27 Ben Shepard, *The Long Road Home: The Aftermath of the Second World War* (London: Bodley Head, 2010); William Hitchcock, *The Bitter Road to Freedom: A New History of the Liberation of Europe* (New York: Free Press, 2008).

throes of terminal dissolution. The last fling of traditional territorial imperialism tried by Germany, Italy and Japan contributed not only to their own defeat but to the unravelling of the other European empires in the twenty years that followed. The defeat of Japan was in many ways the more significant because it destroyed the old international order in the region and opened the way for different world powers, the United States, Communist China, India and a reformed Japan, to become key players in Asian, Pacific and world politics. In Europe the hatreds prompted by two World Wars did not evaporate, but after the impact of a second war even more deadly and destructive than the first, and dominated by two superpowers, the Soviet Union and the United States, European radical nationalism melted away and the circles that had sustained it became marginalized politically, most of the leaders dead or imprisoned.

The most important contribution to a more permanent global peace (local wars have remained an endemic feature of international politics ever since) was the willingness of the United States, now immensely wealthy in comparison with the stricken economies of Asia and Europe, to play a central part in constructing a new economic order in which general agreement on financial, currency and trade policies could be introduced and in which economies in crisis could be helped by the collective efforts of the others through the IMF and the World Bank. In the Communist bloc, which by 1949 stretched from the German Democratic Republic to North Korea, deep distrust of the capitalist West did not create the conditions for a third global war, partly due to the deterrent effect of nuclear weapons, partly from divisions that soon opened up between the major Communist states themselves, partly from the belief that capitalism would collapse of its own accord.

The age of global war reflected profound instabilities in the existing world order with the decline or collapse of important parts of the traditional structure, and the social and political consequences of large-scale and rapid economic modernization and urbanization. Empire and imperial competition was seen in Europe as one way of resolving the problems posed by rapid social and political change, just as the pursuit of resources and land drove Russia across Siberia and American and Canadian settlers across North America. The attempt to stave off political change but at the same time to try to keep abreast of economic and technical competition and to satisfy popular appetites for new forms of national identity created before 1914 a dangerous mix if ever a crisis occurred that could not easily be regulated by great power collaboration. The crisis in July 1914 could not be contained, and the subsequent war, on an unprecedented scale and across much of the globe, fought principally in the very part of the world that had boasted of exporting civilization to the rest, created antagonisms of a profound and dangerous kind which exploded after 1919 in irreconcilable ideological conflict between popular forces many of whose members had been through the violence and deprivation of frontline service. To many, war seemed the normal condition of modern society, both between ideological enemies and between nations or peoples. More dangerously there were political leaders who assumed that the crises generated by the distorting effects of modernization could be resolved by the very unmodern resort to empire building. The result was a second world war whose consequences brought the long age of empire to an end, but at a cost in lives now estimated as anything between 55 and 80 million.

Further reading

Bessel, Richard. *Nazism and War*. London: Weidenfeld & Nicolson, 2004.

Clark, Christopher. *Sleepwalkers: How Europe Went to War in 1914*. London: Allen Lane, 2012.

Clavin, Patricia. *The Great Depression in Europe, 1929–1939*. Basingstoke: Macmillan Press, 2000.

Crook, Paul. *Darwinism, War and History: The Debate over the Biology of War from the 'Origin of Species' to the First World War*. Cambridge University Press, 1994.

Darwin, John. *After Tamerlane: The Global History of Empire since 1405*. London: Bloomsbury, 2008.

Dickinson, E. R. 'Biopolitics, fascism, democracy: some reflections on our discourse on "modernity"', *Central European History* 37 (2004), 1–48.

Garside, W. R., ed. *Capitalism in Crisis: International Responses to the Great Depression*. New York: St. Martin's Press, 1993.

Gentile, Emilio. *The Origins of Fascist Ideology*. New York: Enigma Books, 2005.

Gerwarth, Robert and John Horne, eds. *War in Peace: Paramilitary Violence in Europe after the Great War*. Oxford University Press, 2012.

Gregory, Adrian. *The Last Great War: British Society and the First World War*. Cambridge University Press, 2008.

Griffin, Roger, ed. *International Fascism: Theories, Causes and the New Consensus*. London: Arnold, 1998.

Hawkins, Michael. *Social Darwinism in European and American Thought 1860–1945: Nature as Model and Nature as Threat*. Cambridge University Press, 1997.

Hitchcock, William. *The Bitter Road to Freedom: A New History of the Liberation of Europe*. New York: Free Press, 2008.

Imlay, Talbot. *Facing the Second World War: Strategy, Politics and Economics in Britain and France 1938–1940*. Oxford University Press, 2003.

Leitz, Christian. *Nazi Foreign Policy 1933–1941*. London: Routledge, 2004.

Kiernan, Victor. *European Empires from Conquest to Collapse, 1815–1960*. London: Fontana, 1982.

Macmillan, Margaret. *Peacemakers: The Paris Peace Conference of 1919 and the Attempt to End War*. London: John Murray, 2001.

Maiolo, Joseph. *Cry Havoc: How the Arms Race Drove the World to War*. New York: Basic Books, 2006.

McDonough, Frank, ed. *The Origins of the Second World War: An International Perspective*. London: Continuum, 2011.

McMeekin, Sean. *The Russian Origins of the First World War*. Cambridge, MA: Harvard University Press, 2011.

Mitter, Rana. *China's War with Japan 1937–1945: The Struggle for Survival*. London: Allen Lane, 2013.

Moore, Aaron William. *Writing War: Soldiers Record the Japanese Empire*. Cambridge, MA: Harvard University Press, 2013.

Overy, Richard. *The Inter-War Crisis 1919–1939*. 3rd edn. Harlow: Longmans, 2007.

Why the Allies Won. 2nd edn. London: Pimlico, 2006.

Pick, Daniel. *War Machine: The Rationalization of Slaughter in the Modern Age*. New Haven: Yale University Press, 1993.

Schweller, Randall. *Deadly Imbalances: Tripolarity and Hitler's Strategy of World Conquest*. New York: Columbia University Press, 1998.

Shephard, Ben. *The Long Road Home: The Aftermath of the Second World War*. London: Bodley Head, 2010.

Snyder, Timothy. *Bloodlands: Europe between Hitler and Stalin*. London: Bodley Head, 2010.

Steiner, Zara. *The Lights that Failed: European International History 1919–1933*. Oxford University Press, 2005.

The Triumph of the Dark: European International History 1933–1939. Oxford University Press, 2011.

Stevenson, David. *The First World War and International Politics*. Oxford University Press, 1988.

Todman, Dan. *The Great War: Myth and Memory*. London: Hambledon, 2005.

Welch, David and Jo Fox, eds. *Justifying War: Propaganda, Politics and the Modern Age*. Basingstoke: Palgrave, 2012.

Wilmot, H. P. *World War I*. London: Dorling Kindersley, 2003.

Winter, Jay and Antoine Prost. *The Great War in History: Debates and Controversies 1914 to the Present*. Cambridge University Press, 2005.

14

The Cold War

DANIEL SARGENT

The inhabitants of the Southern Hemisphere were the last to die, but their deaths were inevitable enough. After the radiation passed through the convergence zone where the winds of the hemispheres meet, it continued towards Cape Horn and the Cape of Good Hope. Who knew where the last human died? Perhaps in Patagonia? Or at a scientific base in the Antarctic? All that could be said was how history ended. Not in a thermonuclear explosion but in the radiation sickness that followed it.

This was how the Cold War ended – again and again and again. The above scenario is from *On the Beach*, a 1957 novel by Nevil Shute, but the variations were endless.[1] Nightmares of nuclear holocaust permeated the era of the Cold War. Thirty years after Shute's characters expired, Jim and Hilda Boggs, a fictional British couple, survived atomic war in the animated film "When the Wind Blows," only to succumb to the nuclear winter that followed it. How plausible were such scenarios? None occurred, but the scientists who built the atomic bomb feared the prospect. As if to forewarn, the *Bulletin of the Atomic Scientists* created a "Doomsday Clock" that estimated the probability of apocalypse; the closer to midnight the clock's hands moved, the greater its likelihood.[2] For much of the 1950s, it was two minutes to midnight; during the 1960s and 1970s, the risk of catastrophe waned, only to resurge in the early 1980s.

In reality, the finale was peaceful. When the Soviet Union abandoned Marxist-Leninism in the late 1980s, embracing political and economic reform, the Cold War ended in a fashion that few foresaw – with handshakes among leaders and the intercontinental delivery of economists, not a catastrophic

1 Nevil Shute, *On the Beach* (New York: Random House, [1957] 2010). On the genre, see Paul Brians, *Nuclear Holocausts: Atomic War in Fiction, 1895–1984* (Kent State University Press, 1987).

2 On the Doomsday Clock, see www.thebulletin.org/content/doomsday-clock (accessed February 18, 2012).

exchange of missiles. This was an ideological victory, not a military triumph. With it, Francis Fukuyama, an American political scientist, proclaimed "the end of history."[3] What had ended, in this view, was the historical credibility of a communist (or Marxist–Leninist) ideological system whose core elements included the dictatorship of the Communist Party, a self-appointed revolutionary vanguard; the public ownership of industries and far-reaching economic planning; and a commitment to the pursuit of economic egalitarianism. What remained was the liberal-capitalist synthesis for which the United States stood, comprising political pluralism and representative democracy; a capitalist economic system based on private ownership and free markets tempered by public regulation; and an overarching commitment to the defense of individual rights. Once the Soviet Union abandoned communism, history – as a struggle of ideas – was over, resolved in favor of freedom and free markets.

Insofar as endings shape meanings, historians should remember that the Cold War did not have to end as it did. Had the Cold War resulted in a fusillade of missiles, its historians might be inclined to emphasize its military aspects rather than the struggle of ideas – if any historians remained to write history, that is. Fortunately, the Cold War ended peacefully, leaving ample opportunity to debate its meanings.

What was the Cold War? Was it a geopolitical struggle between two military blocs? Or was it an ideological competition, a war of ideas more than arms? In fact, the Cold War entwined geopolitical and ideological aspects. An ideological disjuncture in the 1980s precipitated its conclusion, but it does not follow that ideas defined the Cold War from the outset. The Cold War's rationales varied, and a fluctuating combination of ideological and geopolitical elements made it a distinctive conflict.

Situating the Cold War in a world-historical context, meanwhile, opens questions of a different kind. Was the Cold War ever so encompassing as it appeared in the nightmares of atomic extinction such as Nevil Shute's? It may be tempting to conflate the Cold War with the international history of the post-World War II world, as textbooks often do. But was it really the case that "for forty five years, the world held its breath"?[4] This may have been how leaders on both sides construed the world-historical significance of their competition; whether it accurately renders the Cold War's importance in the history of the postwar world is harder to say. What can be said is that the

3 Francis Fukuyama, *The End of History and the Last Man* (New York: Free Press, 1992).

4 Jeremy Isaacs and Taylor Downing, *Cold War: For Forty-Five Years the World Held its Breath* (London: Abacus, 2008).

Cold War's intensity, like its nature, varied from place to place and from time to time.

Making the Cold War

"The principal instrument of the former is freedom; of the latter, servitude."[5] So wrote Alexis de Tocqueville of the Americans and the Russians in 1835. Besides sociological generalization, Tocqueville offered a prediction. "Each of them seems to be marked out by the will of Heaven to sway the destinies of half the globe." Oft quoted, these words seemed prophetic in the era of the Cold War. Since its end, Tocqueville has looked less prescient, but he still offers clues as to the Cold War's nature. Conflict between America and Russia, he tells us, was ordained by allocations of power in the international system and by ideological differences for which culture, institutions, and history all accounted. A combination of ideology and geopolitics, in other words, made the Cold War.

Configurations of power and the rivalry of ideas may explain "why," but are they insufficient to tell us "when" and "how"? Answering these questions require us to situate the Cold War's origins in the conjuncture that the twentieth-century's world wars and the Great Depression created. World War I exploded a system of economic globalization that took shape in the last decades of the nineteenth century. After the Great War, the European powers sought to reconstruct the old system, while the United States tried to reform it. In Russia, Vladimir Ilich Lenin seized control of the state and set out to make revolution from above, contending that political power would enable his Bolshevik Party to create the communist society that Karl Marx had foretold in social and economic conditions unfavorable to proletarian revolution. So was born the Soviet Union and Marxist-Leninism, an ideological project that took Marx's theory of history and transformed it into a tryst with history itself.

The recasting of the pre-1914 international order did not endure long. The Great Depression shattered the international economy and sent some nations scurrying for alternatives. Italy, Japan, and Germany rejected liberalism and embraced the politics of nationalism and the economics of autarky. The British and the Americans abandoned the gold standard and retreated towards protectionism. The Soviet Union, having oscillated between engagement and autarky in the 1920s, opted for autarky in the first Five Year

5 Alexis de Tocqueville, *Democracy in America* (New York: Penguin, [1835] 2003).

Plan (1928–32). German and Japanese geopolitical ambitions soon transformed the world crisis of the 1930s into World War II, a vast and violent cataclysm. Besides killing one-and-a-quarter percent of humanity, World War II left vacuums of authority at its end, as Japanese and German imperial projects crumbled. For Europe, the war marked a stunning reversal. The center of global power since the Industrial Revolution, Europe was at the war's end broken and bereft, its future uncertain.

Europe's catastrophe marked the passage from an era of great powers to the age of the superpowers. Coined in 1943–44, the term applied initially to the United States, Great Britain, and the Soviet Union.[6] Britain's claim was tenuous, which left two. It did not follow that the United States and the Soviet Union were equal. Vaster in territory, the Soviet Union lagged behind in economic might, technological prowess, and the atomic bomb, which the Americans tested in July 1945. The two had combined forces to defeat Germany in the Second World War, but their relations remained tense.

By 1945, Joseph Stalin had led the Soviet Union for two decades. The dominant figure in Soviet politics and foreign policy, Stalin viewed the capitalist world with a suspicion that Anglo-American intervention during the Russian Civil War (1917–22) had not allayed. He saw linkages between internal enemies – deviationists, Trotskyites, and saboteurs – and external foes, and these compounded his suspicions of the outside world. Still, Stalin was a nationalist and a communist, and he did not aspire to globalize his revolution by force. What he sought was security and time for the Soviet Union to recover after a war that killed 23–24 million of its citizens. His ambitions for the postwar settlement hinged upon the acquisition of a buffer zone in Eastern Europe, through which Germany had attacked in 1914 and 1941.[7]

Of the war's victors, the United States was the most victorious. Having prevailed in Europe and the Pacific, only the United States among the world's great powers was in 1945 a global military power. Moreover, Washington monopolized the atomic bomb. Still, it was in the arena of economic power that US preeminence was clearest. At the war's end, the United States alone produced 60 percent of the industrialized world's economic output. President

6 William T. R. Fox, *The Super-Powers: The United States, Britain, and the Soviet Union* (New York: Hartcourt, Brace & Co., 1944); and Nicholas Spykman, *The Geography of the Peace* (New York: Harcourt, Brace & Co., 1944).

7 On Stalin's motives, see Vladimir Pechatnov, "The Soviet Union and the world," in Melvyn Leffler and Odd Arne Westad (eds.), *The Cambridge History of the Cold War*, 3 vols. (Cambridge University Press, 2010), Vol. 1, pp. 90–111; and Vojtech Mastny, *The Cold War and Soviet Insecurity* (Oxford University Press, 1996).

Harry Truman in August 1945 anointed the United States "the most powerful nation, perhaps, in all history."[8] Few could disagree, but what did the Americans seek to accomplish from the pedestal of preeminence? During the war, policy planners under President Franklin Roosevelt prepared blueprints for the postwar world. These envisaged restoring, stabilizing, and reforming the international order that had imploded in the 1930s.[9] The American design for the postwar future reflected the lessons of the recent past. Free trade would be restored, the 1930s having exhibited the links between economic protectionism and international conflict, but new institutions, above all the IMF, would stabilize the international economy. The United Nations, a reincarnation of the failed League of Nations, would superintend collective security, but the United States and the other great powers would take special responsibility for keeping the peace. Taken as a whole, the American design revealed a liberal intent but not a doctrinaire vision. Restoring the open world economy was an overarching goal, but it was to be reconciled with national self-determination; the protection of individual human rights; and the economic needs of the welfare state, of which Roosevelt's own New Deal was a leading example.[10] This grand design would have to be constructed, however, amidst circumstances that the Second World War created.

The definition of the Cold War's frontiers did not await the war's end. When they met Stalin at Yalta in February 1945, Franklin Roosevelt and Winston Churchill conceded a Soviet sphere of influence in postwar Eastern Europe. This was a cynical gambit, and Roosevelt never reconciled it to his lofty hopes for a liberal peace in which human rights and self-determination would prevail. Roosevelt died in April 1945, and his successor Harry Truman lacked his capacity for holding contradictory ideas in suspension.[11] A straightforward Missourian who failed as a haberdasher but

8 Truman, "Radio Report to the American People on the Potsdam Conference," American Presidency Project, online at www.presidency.ucsb.edu.

9 On the American postwar concept, see G. John Ikenberry, *Liberal Leviathan: The Origins, Crisis, and Transformation of the American World Order* (Princeton University Press, 2011); and Robert Latham, *The Liberal Moment: Modernity, Security, and the Making of Postwar International Order* (New York: Columbia University Press, 1997).

10 Elizabeth Borgwardt, *A New Deal for the World: America's Vision for Human Rights* (Cambridge, MA: Harvard University Press, 2005). On the IMF's accommodation of the welfare state, see John G. Ruggie, "International regimes, transactions, and change: embedded liberalism in the postwar economic order," *International Organization* 36/2 (1982), 379–415.

11 For an authoritative and up-to-date account of the transition from world war to Cold War, see Frank Costigliola, *Roosevelt's Lost Alliances How Personal Politics Helped Start the Cold War* (Princeton University Press, 2011). But also see John L. Gaddis, *The United States*

succeeded in the US Senate, Truman hoped to sustain Soviet–American cooperation. Friction nonetheless intensified during 1945. Stalin's refusal to hold free elections in Poland, which his Red Army now occupied, outraged the United States. When the US Congress terminated wartime aid to the USSR in September 1945, Stalin sensed a hostile move. A decisive rupture came in December 1945, when the Soviet Union announced that it would not participate in the international economic institutions established during the war. The move confirmed that the Soviet Union would not participate in the liberal world order that the United States sought to build. Within months, leaders on both sides were speaking of schism. Stalin's "Election Speech" of February 1946 marked a return to the anti-capitalist dogma of the 1930s. The next month, Winston Churchill declared that an "iron curtain" had descended across Europe. It more-or-less followed the line where Soviet armies, fighting from the east, and Anglo-American forces, coming from the west, had divided Europe, atop the ruins of Hitler's fleeting empire.

Still, division did not make inevitable the consolidation of the parts into hostile blocs. This was an incremental process, and it took the rest of the 1940s to complete. Unveiled in 1947, the Marshall Plan was the foundational act in the creation of "the West" as an alliance and a category in international politics. Providing some $13 billion in American assistance, Marshall Aid served both economic and strategic purposes. The infusion of dollars bridged Europe's transatlantic trade deficits and enabled the international economy to function.[12] The Marshall Plan also clarified Europe's division. Opposition to it discredited Western Europe's communist parties, and Stalin's refusal to permit the East European countries to accept Marshall Aid confirmed Europe's division. Thereafter, the rupture widened. Where the Red Army ruled, Moscow Sovietized the East, overthrowing Czechoslovakia's coalition government in February 1948, for example, and replacing it with a Stalinist regime. The United States also worked to shape political outcomes within European nations. The CIA channeled funds to Italy's anti-communist parties, which helped to ensure the defeat of the powerful *Partito Communista Italiano* in the elections of April 1948. The Cold War thus came to define the limits of political diversity in Europe. Communist parties predominated in

and the Origins of the Cold War, 1941–1947 (Oxford University Press, 1972), an older but foundational treatment.

12 Michael Hogan, *The Marshall Plan: America, Britain, and the Reconstruction of Western Europe, 1947–1952* (Cambridge University Press, 1987). More skeptical on the economic benefits is Alan Milward, *The Reconstruction of Western Europe, 1945–1951* (Berkeley, CA: University of California, 1984).

the East, with Moscow's support. Christian Democrats and Social Democrats prevailed in the West, competing in elections but united in opposition to communism. (Left-wingers who had encountered communists were often the fiercest anti-communists of all, as the career of Britain's Foreign Secretary Ernest Bevin suggests.) The blocs were not impermeable, and defections did occur. One came in 1948 when Josip Tito, Yugoslavia's charismatic communist leader, split with Stalin and opened a dialogue with the West. For the most part, however, the Cold War's geometry remained stable.

The fulcrum of Europe's Cold War was Germany, now defeated and divided into occupation zones. From 1947, the United States and Great Britain moved to incorporate their occupation zones into the Western Alliance. Stalin retaliated in the spring of 1948 by shutting down access to West Berlin, a western enclave in the Soviet zone. The Berlin Crisis sharpened Europe's division, but it also revealed the reluctance of the superpowers to use military force. The United States did not attempt to break the blockade by force but instead airlifted supplies to West Berlin. The crisis nonetheless militarized the Cold War. Early in 1949, the Western powers created the North Atlantic Treaty Organization, a permanent military alliance. Later that year, the Federal Republic of Germany was born, its feet planted in the West. Its formal integration into NATO in 1955 prompted the creation of the Warsaw Pact, the East Bloc's military alliance, the same year. With this, Europe's division into armed and militarized Cold War blocs was completed.

Europe's division was mostly peaceful; East Asia's would not be. Here, the dynamics were different. Japan had ruled parts of East Asia for decades, and the collapse of its empire left complex struggles for power. In Southeast Asia, where Japanese imperialism had displaced European regimes, these involved not only nationalist claimants but also the Europeans – the French in Indochina and the Dutch in Indonesia both sought to reimpose colonial rule. Neither the United States nor the Soviet Union wanted East Asia to become a Cold War battleground. Both were content to neutralize flash points, and the United States in 1946 granted the Philippines independence, which struck a salutary contrast to Europe's colonial nostalgia. Still, the superpowers found themselves drawn, almost inexorably, into East Asia. To a considerable extent, however, local leaders made their own Cold War, as the experiences of China and Korea will attest.

China in 1945 exhibited manifold divisions. World War II left China between those parts that Japan had conquered – Taiwan, Manchuria, and coastal China – and the vast interior, where the Chiang Kai-shek's

Nationalists or Kuomintang (KMT) and the Chinese Communist Party (CCP) of Mao Zedong vied. These two parties fought a decade-long civil war from 1927, but they came together as the Second Sino-Japanese War (1937–45) began. Their United Front endured only as long as their common foe. With Japan's defeat, the CCP and KMT turned upon each other. Mao was a communist, and Chiang was connected in the United States, but both superpowers tried to remain aloof. The Soviet Union maintained working relations with the KMT, and the United States, while aiding Chiang, did not intervene against the CCP. Chinese protagonists resolved China's Civil War largely on their own terms. Better organized than the KMT, Mao's forces pressed forward. In 1949, the CCP secured control of China's mainland, exiling the KMT to Taiwan. That October, Mao declared the People's Republic of China. A momentous shift, Mao's triumph led to a formal alliance with the Soviet Union in February 1950 that transformed the Cold War's geopolitics.

Besides consolidating a communist bloc, the Sino-Soviet alliance encouraged Kim Il-Sung, a Korean communist, to reunify Korea by force. Neither superpower was much invested in Korea, where Japan had ruled for half a century, but they both promoted Korean clients during the years of joint occupation that followed Japan's defeat, the Soviets in the north and the Americans in the south. After securing grudging support from Stalin, Kim attacked in June 1950. The United States organized an international effort to assist South Korea. The ensuing war claimed about 2.5 million lives, most of them Korean. After several months of movement and a decisive Chinese intervention on the side of the North Koreans, the fighting settled into a stalemate. Korea's plight resembled Eurasia's division, with a great deal more blood shed. More than a microcosm, the Korean War transformed the Cold War. Korea galvanized the Sino-Soviet alliance, and it prompted Japan's rehabilitation and integration into the Western Alliance. Other American commitments were formalized, including a military guarantee to Taiwan, a pact with Australia and New Zealand (ANZUS), and the South East Asian Treaty Organization (SEATO). The Korean War, which continued until 1953, confirmed the world's division and militarized the Cold War. Still, with the Soviet Union reluctant to intervene directly and Washington deciding not to use nuclear weapons – after debating the possibility – Korea also defined the Cold War's limits.

By the end of the Korean War, the Cold War had become something more than a conflict between the superpowers and their allies: it had become a framework for organizing international relations. Bipolarity became a source of stability, at least so far as the superpowers were concerned. It was on the Cold War's periphery, in places like Korea, that instability and violence prevailed. An international system that linked internal and external politics, the Cold War became, in effect, the settlement that ended World War II. As such, it might be compared to earlier postwar orders. It was not a settlement–like those of 1815 and (less successfully) 1919 – in which shared values bound participants together.[13] American planners had attempted to build a postwar order based upon liberal commitments to economic integration and political self-determination, but what emerged instead was something quite different: a world order based upon an antagonistic equilibrium that evolved, unplanned and unintended, in the years after 1945. On this accidental equipoise, the peace of the world now depended.

Waging the Cold War

After Korea, the Soviet Union and the United States waged an arms race that made the prospect of superpower conflict steadily more atrocious. The destructiveness of nuclear weapons increased fast. It took the Soviet Union four years (and some espionage) to mimic the bomb that destroyed Hiroshima. By the mid 1950s, both superpowers were testing thermonuclear bombs far more powerful than these. Engineers were soon setting thermonuclear warheads atop intercontinental ballistic missiles (ICBMs). Such weapons could not be stopped; the only defense against them was the probability of retaliation. The logic of mutual deterrence did not emerge overnight, however. Nor was it so symmetrical as the word mutual implies. What emerged in the Cold War's first fifteen years was an asymmetric balance whereby more plentiful US nuclear (or "strategic") weapons offset the Soviet Union's abundant conventional forces but in which Soviet technical accomplishments spurred the development of US strategic weaponry. Nuclear weapons differentiated the superpowers from other powers, except for the few that tested nuclear weapons of their own: Britain in 1952, France in 1960, China in 1964, and India in 1974. So long as their arsenals far exceeded all others, nuclear weapons consecrated the special role of the superpowers in the Cold War international system.

Contrasted with earlier arms races, such as the Anglo-German naval race that prefigured the First World War, the Soviet–American estrangement was

13 On the role of shared commitments in the 1815 settlement, see Paul Schroeder, *The Transformation of European Politics, 1763–1848* (Oxford University Press, 1994).

remarkable. It did not lead to war but may have facilitated war's avoidance. The nuclear stalemate engendered what historian John Gaddis famously called the Cold War's "long peace."[14] But it did not make war impossible. The Korean War might have ended differently. Had General MacArthur continued his campaign into China, as he proposed to do, he would have invited all-out war, perhaps involving nuclear bombs. Perhaps the most dangerous crisis of all came in 1962, when the Soviet Union decided to install nuclear missiles in Cuba. Moscow's reasoning was logical enough; insofar as the United States outreached the USSR in strategic weaponry, locating medium-range missiles on Cuba closed the nuclear gap. Soviet leaders anticipated neither the strength of the American response nor the narrowness of their own options. After pondering escalatory alternatives, President John F. Kennedy opted for a compromise that drew down forces on both sides. Had he followed the advice of his more hawkish advisors, it is possible, even probable, that a nuclear exchange would have ensued. The brush with disaster was chastening. After Cuba, leaders on both sides sought stability as a shared imperative. The 1963 installation of a communications link between the Kremlin and the White House – the iconic "red telephone" that was, in fact, neither red nor a telephone – symbolized the new mood and prefigured future collaboration to control the arms race and stabilize the Cold War.

Retreating from the brink did not mean that the Cold War was passing. On the contrary, the terrible prospect of nuclear war brought other aspects of the superpower competition to the fore, including the ideological conflict between Soviet communism and American liberal capitalism and, increasingly, the struggle for the Third World.[15]

The ideological struggle proceeded at multiple scales. At the international scale, the Cold War began with the Soviet Union's repudiation of the open, liberal world order that the United States aspired to build. Over time, the war of ideas came to focus not on the international system, which was divided, but on the futures of particular societies. This Cold War would be fought within nation-states as much as between them. What defined the contending camps? Whereas American-style liberalism prioritized free markets, private property, and representative democracy, Soviet-style communism favored economic planning, party dictatorship, and a long-term commitment to the pursuit of egalitarianism. To see the ideological struggle as a conflict between

14 John Lewis Gaddis, *The Long Peace: Inquiries Into the History of the Cold War* (Oxford University Press, 1987), esp. pp. 215–246.

15 These themes receive central attention in Odd Arne Westad, *The Global Cold War: Third World Interventions and the Making of Our Times* (Cambridge University Press, 2005).

individualist and collectivist dogmas would be reductionist, but these were poles towards which the two systems gravitated. For all the differences, there were underlying similarities. Feuding children of the Enlightenment, liberalism and communism shared rationalist, secular, and materialist biases. Crucially, both camps believed history to be on their side. Heirs to Karl Marx's historical determinism, Soviet leaders presumed that history's objective forces ran in their favor. Liberals lacked a historical schema so intricate as Marx's, but their historical determinism was no less powerful for it. The future, they too believed, was theirs. Ideology thus reinforced the stabilizing implications of nuclear weapons. Why risk the future in a reckless military gamble if long-term victory was assured?

Still, the Cold War's ideological aspect was not a constant; like the nuclear arms race, it developed over time, and its implications ranged from context to context. While liberalism lacked communism's canonical coherence, the United States worked to export its ideological synthesis earlier than did the Soviet Union. Vis-à-vis Europe and Japan, the Americans propounded a triangular compromise between liberalism, capitalism, and democracy that proposed to harness the efficiencies of free markets while assuring the stabilization of democracy and the protection of individual rights. Orchestrating growth was key to the project. Drawing on the lessons of their own history, American officials proposed to transcend distributive conflicts within societies through the achievement of material abundance. In Japan and Europe, these efforts met with considerable success; by the 1960s, these core allies had rebounded from defeat to prosperity and social stability.

Elsewhere, America's ideological Cold War proved more disruptive. It began early, when President Truman debuted his Point Four Program in 1949. Truman envisaged a "bold new" effort to share "the benefits of our scientific advances and industrial progress" with the "underdeveloped" peoples of the world. Assistance programs followed, including to India, Egypt, Southeast Asia, and, on a more limited scale, Latin America. Married to the insights of economists and sociologists who discerned generalizable lessons about the historical transitions from "tradition" to "modernity" from the West's experiences, these efforts came to constitute a distinctive agenda for "modernization." Ensuring that developing countries became liberal, market-oriented societies – and did not follow the communist path – became a Cold War commitment. In practice, however, the United States ended up collaborating with a host of illiberal regimes in the developing world, and the pursuit of liberal modernization became entwined with ulterior commitments to the containment of communism.[16]

The Soviet Union, for its part, was somewhat slower to propound its ideological system as a model for emulation. China was the principal focus of Moscow's development efforts during the 1950s, and Soviet expertise and resources flooded into the People's Republic during China's first Five Year Plan (1953–1958). But if Stalin had engaged the world cautiously, his death in 1953 brought to power, after an initial phase of collective leadership, a leader as brash as he had been cagy. Nikita Khrushchev espoused a true believer's faith in the Marxist–Leninist creed, according to which the Soviet Union was constructing a "socialist" social order that would soon give way, like a caterpillar's cocoon, to reveal the "communist" utopia that Marx had predicted, in which the state would wither away and human equality and material abundance would prevail. Khrushchev's ideological commitments made him a disruptive influence on the Cold War – a hardliner in some ways, a reformer in others. To his credit, Khrushchev dismantled aspects of the Stalinist system, denouncing in his "secret speech" of February 1956 Stalin's political crimes. Khrushchev nonetheless became an outspoken booster for Marxist–Leninism on the global stage, promising that the Soviet Union would "bury" the West. He did not mean by this to intimate war. The boast was that socialism would eclipse its adversary, by its egalitarianism and by its production of material abundance. To this end Khrushchev refocused the command economy on the production of consumer goods and food. One consequence of his reformism would be to open a schism with Mao, who had fashioned his own revolution on Stalin's. Still, Khrushchev found new allies elsewhere. He embraced Cuba's Fidel Castro, who seized power in a 1959 revolution and turned towards Moscow thereafter, becoming a stalwart of Third World revolution.

In 1959, Khrushchev also met US Vice President Richard Nixon in an impromptu debate in an American model kitchen at the Moscow World's Fair. Pointing and jabbing, they debated the merits of their respective social

16 The literature on modernization, development, and the Cold War is abundant. For overviews, see David Ekbladh, *The Great American Mission: Modernization and the Construction of An American World Order* (Princeton University Press, 2010); and Michael Latham, *The Right Kind of Revolution: Modernization, Development, and U.S. Foreign Policy From the Cold War to the Present* (Ithaca, NY: Cornell University Press, 2011). For finer-grained studies of the intellectual substance, see Nils Gilman, *Mandarins of the Future: Modernization Theory in Cold War America* (Baltimore, MD: Johns Hopkins University Press, 2007); and Michael Latham, *Modernization As Ideology: American Social Science and "Nation-Building" in the Kennedy Era* (Chapel Hill: University of North Carolina Press, 2000).

systems, but they concurred that their competition should be peaceful. It was not, at least not in the developing world. Animated by a mixture of fear and opportunism, both superpowers intervened, by a variety of methods, and their interventions resembled each other. That is not to say that superpower interventions were symmetrical. The United States intervened faster and harder. In Iran in 1953 and Guatemala in 1954, it conspired with local reactionaries to orchestrate coups that overthrew democratic governments, replacing them with illiberal but pro-Western regimes. These set the pattern for future interventions, and the 1950s and 1960s marked the heyday of American interventionism. The Soviet peak came later. Still, the methods of American meddling varied from case to case. Guatemala and Iran were cynical moves, implemented by covert means. In South Vietnam, by contrast, the United States worked to help Ngo Dinh Diem build a modern society that would stand firm against communism. It was Vietnam, nonetheless, that became America's catastrophe. From the early 1960s, the United States took sides in a civil war that claimed sixty thousand American and up to one million Vietnamese lives.[17] The Vietnam War – the American War, as Vietnamese remember it – was the high-water mark of American Cold War interventionism. Thereafter, the United States retreated from direct action, relying on material aid and military assistance to anti-Communist proxies. Soviet leaders, by contrast, concluded that the developing world was going their way, and they escalated their involvement in it.[18]

Besides intervening in the developing world, both superpowers acted coercively within their own blocs. Here the Soviet Union was the more forceful of the two. After Stalin's March 1953 death, the East Bloc erupted in anti-communist strikes and protests. In East Germany, Moscow responded by sending in the Red Army. Three years later, renewed unrest followed Khrushchev's repudiation of Stalin, especially in Poland and in Hungary where demonstrators massed. Imre Nagy, a reformer, came to power in Hungary in late October 1956 and tried at first to mediate between Moscow and the anti-communist revolution building on Hungarian streets. Unsuccessful, he sided with the masses and appealed for help to the United

17 Estimates of the Vietnamese death toll range. The Vietnamese government claims 3.1 million war-related deaths for the period 1945–1975. Charles Hirschman et al. estimate 882,000, a figure derived from postwar census data. See "Vietnamese casualties during the American War: a new estimate," *Population and Development Review* 21/4 (1995), 783–812.

18 Besides Westad's *Global Cold War*, see Christopher Andrew and Vasili Mitrokhin, *The World Was Going Our Way: The KGB and the Battle for the Third World* (New York: Basic Books, 2005).

Nations. Unwilling to let Hungary defect from the East Bloc, Khrushchev sent in the Red Army. It crushed the revolution and arrested tens of thousands of Hungarians, including Nagy. By coincidence, the United States was at the same time flexing its own muscles against Great Britain, which colluded with France and Israel to invade Egypt in a bid to reverse Egypt's recent nationalization of the Suez Canal. When he learned that Anglo-French troops had landed on the canal's banks, President Eisenhower was furious. He worried that Britain's resort to naked colonial tactics would lose the Third World for the West. To force the British and the French to retreat, he ordered his Treasury Secretary to sell sterling bonds, applying financial pressure to coerce a British retreat. This was better than Khrushchev's methods, but it also betrayed inequalities of power. Still, America's predominant role owed not only to military and financial margins but also to cultural resources – from jazz to jeans – which made America's dynamic, sunbaked modernity a model to which Europeans – and others – from across the Cold War's frontiers aspired.

If the power of the superpowers defined the high Cold War that endured from the late 1940s to 1960s, the late 1960s and early 1970s were a turning point. Within the United States, Vietnam eroded the political consensus that had supported a Cold War foreign policy. With support for Cold War commitments waning, the question of how to sustain burdensome responsibilities preoccupied the Nixon Administration that took power in 1969. In Western Europe, the Vietnam War brought the legitimacy of American leadership into doubt. Here it was the student demonstrators who rallied in Paris, London, West Berlin, and elsewhere who asked the most forceful questions. Demonstrations also occurred in Eastern Europe, most notably in Czechoslovakia. Like the Hungarian events of 1956, the Prague Spring of 1968 involved popular protests and an experiment in "reformed socialism," which ended up threatening the unity of the East Bloc. Moscow again sent in the Red Army, but doing so again revealed the brittleness of Soviet power in Eastern Europe. Even more consequential was the deterioration in Sino-Soviet relations that culminated with a decisive split and the exchange of gunfire over the Ussuri River in March 1969. Historians debate whether ideological disagreements or geopolitical differences caused the Sino-Soviet split, but they agree that its consequences were momentous.[19] With the

19 Lorenz Luthi, *The Sino-Soviet Split: Cold War in the Communist World* (Princeton University Press, 2008), emphasizes ideology, while Sergey Radchenko, *Two Suns in the Heavens: The Sino-Soviet Struggle for Supremacy, 1962–1967* (Palo Alto, CA: Stanford University Press, 2009), prioritizes geopolitics.

communist world's fracturing and the slow emergence of a more cooperative Soviet–American relationship, focused upon the pursuit of nuclear arms control, the Cold War international order looked to be fragmenting.[20]

Ending the Cold War

The Cold War did not end in the late 1960s; it endured for another two decades. It was nonetheless transformed in the 1970s in ways that altered its nature and prefigured its resolution. Cold War elites on both sides sought to stabilize the Cold War system while advancing their own national interests. Recognizing that the Vietnam War was a setback for the United States, some Soviet leaders pressed for advantage in the Third World. President Nixon and his national security advisor Henry Kissinger calculated, by contrast, that opening relations with China would shift the Cold War's balance of power towards the United States and permit Washington to dial back expensive military commitments, including to the defense of South Vietnam and other Third World allies. The triangulation of Cold War geopolitics, which hinged on Nixon's May 1972 visit to China, was a major achievement. It marked the beginning of China's defection from the East Bloc, and it prefigured China's reintegration to the US-led global economy in the 1980s.

By equipping Washington with a lever against the Soviet Union, the Sino-American opening facilitated direct negotiations between the United States and the Soviet Union. The ensuring dialogue, often characterized as a détente relationship, brought important benefits. Arms control negotiations produced the Strategic Arms Limitation Treaty (SALT) in 1972. This agreement capped the size of both sides' nuclear arsenals, albeit at levels that did not reduce current arsenals. SALT nonetheless helped to control budgetary costs, a central goal for Washington. Leonid Brezhnev, who became the USSR's predominant leader after Khrushchev's 1964 ouster, sought for his part to establish through détente the USSR's status as a superpower coequal to the United States. This recognition the Basic Principles agreement of 1973 and the Conference on Security and Cooperation in Europe (CSCE) of 1975 conferred. The 1973 agreement established a code of conduct for superpower relations;

20 For example: see Kenneth Waltz, "The politics of peace," *International Studies Quarterly* 11/3 (1967), 199–211; Marshall Shulman, *Beyond the Cold War* (New Haven, CT: Yale University Press, 1966); and Paul Seabury, *The Rise and Decline of the Cold War* (New York: Basic Books, 1967). For an ingenious interpretation that describes youth's generational challenge to an entrenched Cold War order as the defining theme of the 1960s, see Jeremi Suri, *Power and Protest: Global Revolution and the Rise of Detente* (Cambridge, MA: Harvard University Press, 2003).

the 1975 conference formalized Europe's Cold War division and offered implicit Western recognition of the East Bloc's legitimacy. Between 1972 and 1975, then, a raft of negotiations and agreements stabilized the Cold War system even as the Sino-American rapprochement transformed its geopolitics. This stabilization was an impressive feat, all the more striking given how tenuous the authority of the superpowers had looked to be as the 1960s drew to a close.

Taking measure of détente's accomplishment, the *Bulletin of the Atomic Scientists* in 1972 moved the hand on the Doomsday Clock back to twelve minutes before midnight. Superpower war appeared far less likely than it had in the 1950s, when the clock had been stuck at two minutes to midnight. This was détente's achievement, but there was an ironic aspect to it. Nixon and Brezhnev stabilized the Cold War, but they also reified it at a time when its insufficiency as a framework for comprehending complex international relations was becoming manifest. There was more to world politics than could be seen through bipolar lenses: youth was revolting against adult authority, economic globalization was stirring, and decolonization was reaching its historical climax.[21] Superpower elites remained preoccupied with Cold War rivalries as a post-Cold War world was coming into being. What characteristics defined this new world? It was a postcolonial world, but it also revealed thickening interdependencies among nations, what might now taken for resurgent globalization. While the Cold War's superstructure remained stable, the substructure, as Marx might have put it, was changing. Economic, technological, social, and ideological developments were transforming international relations. These transformations, intersecting with détente's accomplishments, would define the terms on which the Cold War ended in the 1980s.

Still, the Cold War's demise was hard to foresee in the late 1970s. From this vantage, the Cold War looked to be spreading into new theaters, as if détente had achieved peace between the superpowers by transplanting Cold War tensions to the Third World. Africa became in the 1970s a theater of confrontation. When Portuguese rule in Angola ended in 1974, there began a struggle for succession in which the Soviet Union, the United States, and China took sides. The Horn of Africa became a zone of conflict when Somalia attacked Ethiopia in 1977, triggering an infusion of Soviet aid and a resurgence

21 On these themes, see Richard Cooper, *The Economics of Interdependence: Economic Policy in the Atlantic Community* (New York: Council on Foreign Relations, 1968); Daniel Philpott, *Revolutions in Sovereignty: How Ideas Shaped Modern International Relations* (Princeton University Press, 2001), esp. chapters 8–12; and Suri, *Power and Protest.*

of Cold War thinking in Washington. In both cases, Cuba eclipsed the Soviet Union as a provider of fraternal aid, sending tens of thousands of troops to Angola and Ethiopia. Violence also rent Latin America, where the Cold War's ideological struggles unfolded not between nations so much as within and across them. Coups in Brazil in 1964, Chile in 1973, Argentina in 1976 installed authoritarian regimes that collaborated, with Washington's support, to suppress not just the insurgent left but unarmed progressives too. In Nicaragua, by contrast, the tumbling of the Somoza dictatorship in 1979 enabled the left-wing Sandinistas to seize control of the state. This prompted the right to embrace paramilitary violence. After Ronald Reagan's election in 1980, the United States provided significant (and under U.S. law illicit) aid to the anti-Sandinista Contras, which turned Central America into one of the bloodiest battlegrounds of the late Cold War. The specter of the Global Cold War, as historian Arne Westad calls this struggle for the Third World, prompted some in Washington to repudiate détente, calling instead for a return to the tough-minded anti-Soviet policies of the past.[22]

While détente prevailed in the Cold War's core and conflict raged in the Third World, the idea of human rights emerged in the 1970s as a surprising – and surprisingly malleable – priority in the foreign policy of the United States and other Western powers. The origins of human rights were complex: a flourishing of NGOs brought attention to human rights abuses, and the Carter administration in the United States embraced human rights diplomacy issues in the aftermath of Vietnam. Human rights proponents assailed US foreign policy, arguing that the Soviet Union's violations of human rights made détente an amoral collaboration and rebuking alliances of convenience with oppressive anti-communist regimes in the Third World. Human rights had important consequences for the Cold War. Carter's insertion of human rights themes into Soviet–American diplomacy proved rancorous, but Western European diplomats succeeded in inserting human rights provisions into the treaty that concluded the CSCE negotiations, the so-called Helsinki Final Act of 1975. Doing so energized East European dissidents. Two years later, a group of Czechoslovakians that included the playwright Vaclav Havel constituted themselves as Charter 77. They demanded that the Communist Party honor the commitments to which it had acceded in the Final Act. Even more disruptive still was the Solidarity movement in Poland. A labor organization that drew succor from the international human rights movement and from the election in 1979 of Pope John Paul II, a Pole and an outspoken anti-communist,

22 Westad, *Global Cold War.*

Solidarity's general strikes in 1980–1981 brought Poland to a standstill, prompting the regime to declare martial law. Unlike the coups d'état that brought Communist parties to power throughout Eastern Europe, Solidarity's was a popular – if unsuccessful – revolution. Communist rule endured, but an opposition was emerging, including in the Soviet Union itself. The immediate influence of Soviet dissidents like Andrei Sakharov and Aleksandr Solzhenitsyn was limited, but their invocation of human rights against the party-state in the 1970s prefigured the legitimacy crisis of the 1980s. For those who bothered to look, the disjuncture between the emancipatory boasts that communist rulers made and the tawdry, repressive realities they had created was becoming glaring.

Human rights were not all that the socialist system struggled to produce. The leaders of the Bolshevik Revolution had staked their legitimacy not only on the advancement of social equality but also upon their ability to transform the Soviet Union into a productive, industrious society. From the 1930s to the 1960s, they looked to be succeeding. The coercive mobilization of labor and capital produced impressive industrial growth. By the late 1960s, however, the Soviet growth model was flagging. So long as basic industries predominated, the command economy proved adept at mobilizing growth. But as the opportunities for heavy industrial growth expired – as surplus labor disappeared and as citizens demanded food and high-quality consumer goods, not pig iron and coal – the planned economy struggled. Lacking market incentives, the managers of state-owned enterprises had no reason to devise new product lines or make existing products more efficiently; they had planning targets to meet, not consumer demand. With private enterprise outlawed, the opportunities for entrepreneurship were minimal. What the Soviet Union did have were natural resources, and it mined these ruthlessly. During the 1970s, it benefited from rising commodity prices, especially for oil, which it exported to world markets. These earnings masked the system's underlying failures. The East European socialist economies were less fortunate. Lacking oil wealth, they turned to debt to finance imports of consumer goods from the West. These imports helped to preserve political stability, but they came at the cost of structural deficits that left Eastern Europe's Communists in hock to the capitalists.[23]

23 For an overview of the socialist economy and a comparison to the West, see Barry Eichengreen, *The European Economy Since 1945: Coordinated Capitalism and Beyond* (Princeton University Press, 2008). Especially useful on Eastern Europe is T. Iván Berend, *From the Soviet Bloc to the European Union: The Economic and Social Transformation of Central and Eastern Europe Since 1973* (Cambridge University Press, 2009). For an illuminating study of the East German cases, which illustrates the structural failures of the command

Still, the West itself was not exactly flourishing in the 1970s. Rather, it found itself confounded by recessions, unemployment, and price inflation. The oil crisis of 1973–1974 exacerbated these difficulties but did not cause them. Much like the East, the West was reaching the limits of energy-intensive industrial growth. High growth rates in the 1950s and 1960s had been sustained not by innovation but by the proliferation of existing industrial technologies, like the mass-production automobile plant. By the late 1960s, the opportunities for extensive growth (which comes from adding new factors of production to the economy, distinct from intensive growth, which comes from making existing factors more productive) were dwindling. Unemployment surged, especially in the recessions of the mid and late 1970s. Deindustrialization scarred the industrial heartland of the United States. Invigorated growth, it appeared, would have to come from innovation and new technologies. Here, however, the West fared better than the East.

While its roots ran deeper, it was in the 1970s that a postindustrial economy emerged. Entrepreneurs founded new corporations such as Apple (1977) and Microsoft (1975). This had consequences for the Cold War. The Soviet Union's command economy had competed credibly in the age of heavy industry, but it struggled to keep up with the postindustrial technologies that Western firms were mastering. Besides propelling capitalism into a postindustrial age, 1970s era developments brought important consequences for the world economy. The adaptation of new (and not so new) technologies from communication satellites to wide-body passenger jets reduced the costs of communications and travel. These developments facilitated the integration of the world economy, pushing it forward into a new era of globalization. While Cold War divisions still endured, the capitalist world economy was transforming itself; a new system of economic globalization was emerging, and high-tech, consumer-oriented goods were circulating within it, pushing the West into a novel, postindustrial modernity.

The Cold War wore on, meanwhile, and even intensified in some places. The Middle East became a particular focus for American power, which owed to the West's dependence on the region's oil. Military alliances with Saudi Arabia and Iran aimed from the early 1970s to hold the Soviet Union at bay. This indirect strategy for regional security persevered until 1979, when Islamic fundamentalists overthrew Iran's pro-Western Shah. While radical

economy, see Charles S. Maier, *Dissolution: The Crisis of Communism and the End of East Germany* (Princeton University Press, 1997).

Islamism was a distinctive challenge, it was the prospect of Soviet encroachment into the Middle East that most troubled American leaders. The fear was exaggerated but not unfounded; the USSR had, after all, become involved in the Horn of Africa, from where oil freighters passing through the Gulf of Aden could be intercepted. Thus, when the Soviet Union invaded Afghanistan at the end of 1979, American leaders inferred an offensive thrust towards the Middle East. To thwart it, President Carter in January 1980 declared the Carter Doctrine. It held that any assault by an external power on the Persian Gulf would be repelled by force. This doctrine prefigured America's subsequent entwinement in the Middle East, but it misread Soviet intentions in Afghanistan. The Soviet invasion served no coherent purpose; much like the United States in Vietnam, the Soviet Union was drawn into Afghan politics by a spiral of instability that it helped set in motion but could not control.

The year 1979 was a transformative year in the Cold War. That January, the United States and the People's Republic of China normalized relations. Hereafter, China's reintegration to the liberal world economy accelerated; trade with the West expanded, and China's economy grew. While this reintegration built upon the opening that Mao and Nixon had forged in 1972, it was Deng Xiaoping who played the vital role. Where Mao had played a cautious, balancing game, Deng threw his lot in with the West, seeking a de facto alliance against the Soviet Union and a stage-managed economic opening that would generate trade, investment, and the transfer of technology – all on the Communist Party's terms. "To get rich," Deng is said to have explained, "is glorious." The Communist Party retained its monopoly on power, but market reforms and integration to the globalizing world-economy transformed China's Cold War, shifting the Middle Kingdom into the Cold War camp of the United States and leaving the Soviet Union isolated.

The Soviet–American Cold War, by contrast, intensified after the invasion of Afghanistan. Leaders on both sides were responsible for this. On the Soviet side, Leonid Brezhnev, his collaborators, and his immediate successors charted a conservative course. Creatures of the Cold War, they clung to its dogmas, clamped down upon their critics at home, and waged an unforgiving war in Afghanistan. Ronald Reagan, by contrast, was a different kind of Cold War president. He was among the most ideological leaders of the era; in the depth of his convictions, he resembled Khrushchev. For Reagan, it was not the USSR that was the enemy but communism itself. Here, Reagan took a hard line, supporting arms insurgents in Nicaragua and Afghanistan (he called them "freedom fighters") and proclaiming the USSR an "evil empire." Reagan also promised to build a defensive shield to protect the United States against Soviet missiles. This initiative, known as the Strategic Defense Initiative (SDI), threatened to destabilize the deterrence system that for decades made nuclear war improbable. Flaunting deterrence, Reagan rejected entrenched beliefs and frightened his critics. The *Bulletin of the Atomic Scientists* set the Doomsday Clock at four – and then three – minutes to midnight. Western Europe saw massive anti-nuclear protests, inflected by anti-American sentiment.

Reagan in fact proved flexible as well as radical. Having defined communism as the enemy, he was ready to deal with any Soviet leader who might be willing to rethink old ideological commitments. In the mid 1980s, such a leader emerged. The youngest member by far of the Soviet Politburo, Mikhail Gorbachev was convinced of the need for reform. A young man during Khrushchev's thaw, Gorbachev was convinced by the mid 1980s – as he whispered to his wife – that "we can't go on living like this."[24] After 1985, he moved to reintegrate the Soviet Union to the world economy and to build a more open relationship with the West. He was moved by developments elsewhere, especially the wave of democratization that from the mid 1970s felled authoritarian regimes from Portugal to the Philippines.[25] Spain's post-Franco transition to democracy was especially influential.[26] Committed to dismantling the machinery of repression at home, Gorbachev aimed to reengage with the world and to achieve reform at home. His achievements included the creation of an elected legislature and a Soviet presidency, to which he was himself elected in 1990. Abroad, Gorbachev worked with Reagan to end the Cold War. While the two leaders did not achieve all that they sought, they reached an agreement to abolish intermediate-range nuclear missiles in 1988. Economic reform proved harder to achieve. Unlike Deng, Gorbachev sought at first to improve the planning system through a program of "acceleration," not to replace it with the market. By the time he accepted the need for more wholesale reform, the economic, social, and international orders that the Communist Party of the Soviet Union had created would all be crumbling.

The implosion began in Eastern Europe, but the key act was Gorbachev's. In December 1988, he told the United Nations that the Soviet Union would

24 Mikhail Gorbachev, *Memoirs* (New York: Doubleday, 1996), p. 165.
25 Samuel Huntington, *The Third Wave: Democratization in the Late Twentieth Century* (Norman, OK: University of Oklahoma Press, 1991).
26 Archie Brown, *The Gorbachev Factor* (Oxford Univeristy Press, 1996), p. 116.

not intervene in Eastern Europe to prop up Communist parties. The East Europeans, as Gorbachev's press secretary put it, were free to do it their way. It did not take long for the façade of Communist Eastern Europe to fall. Before 1989 was out, Solidarity ruled in Poland after winning the free elections, and the authors of Charter 77 were taking over the government of Czechoslovakia, with Václav Havel as president. That it all happened so peacefully, apart from the troubled case of Romania, owed to good fortune and an East–West engagement that traced back to the 1970s. Economic ties between the blocs disincentivized state violence; in East Germany, the Communist Party refrained from massacring demonstrators in part because its leaders knew how dependent on Western credit they had become. Instead, they stood aside when unarmed civilians broke through the Berlin Wall on the night of November 11, 1989, and turned upon the thirty-year old barrier with shovels and sledgehammers. These events affirmed what Havel had called the "power of the powerless" against the power of the party-state.

With the collapse of the East Bloc, the Cold War ended. East Germany ceased to exist in 1990, absorbed into larger and more prosperous West Germany. Most stunning of all, the Soviet Union itself would not endure much longer. A failed coup against Gorbachev in the summer of 1991 led to the dissolution of the USSR at the year's end. In the last months of 1991, leaders of the national republics – from the Baltic Republics to Russia itself – opted to dissolve their federation and, with it, the Soviet Union itself. Having set in motion processes of state building intended to offset the power of the Communist Party, Gorbachev became a leader without a state. His attempt to reform the Soviet Union and to reincorporate it to a larger international order had led, with stunning rapidity, to the extinction of the Soviet project that he tried to salvage and redeem.

Conclusions

The Cold War, to return to its origins, began because Stalin would not participate in the open, liberal international order that the United States tried to build after World War II. It ended when Gorbachev attempted to integrate the USSR to the liberal world and, by doing so, brought down the Potemkin village of socialist modernity. The crude equipoise that existed through the intervening four decades ensured that the Soviet–American Cold War was mostly peaceful, at least in its core. There was no systemic war, although there were moments, as in 1962, when the superpowers danced upon the ledge of disaster. Instead, the Cold War's violence was borne by Africans, Latin Americans, Southeast Asians, and others – people who lived far from the initial geopolitical fault lines and who bore no responsibility for the world's division. Theirs was "the other Cold War," as Heonik Kwon calls it, a conflict that emerged from the Soviet–American confrontation but remained distinct from it.[27] Estimating the damage that this Cold War did remains a matter of conjecture. Whether the millions who died in Africa, Korea, and Vietnam, and the victims of torture chambers in Buenos Aires, Phnom Penh, and Tehran, should be counted among its victims is contestable. The Cold War made their catastrophes, but so did other struggles – postcolonial conflicts for power, efforts to make modern societies out of traditional cloth, and the eternal temptations of barbarism. Either way, one of the Cold War's ironies was this: while the struggle for control of Europe was never fought, the Third World still encountered the radioactive fallout.

The Cold War may have ended, but its effects endure, and for its historians it remains an ongoing struggle. Still a work-in-progress, Cold War historiography has become a dynamic and innovative field, whose maturation the 2010 publication of the three-volume *Cambridge History of the Cold War* confirmed.[28] For historians, the Cold War's end was a watershed. Before 1989–1991, historians fixated on the problem of origins and the ascription of blame. So-called "orthodox" historians blamed Soviet aggrandizement for the Cold War's advent; their "revisionist" critics indicted American economic ambitions.[29] This debate subsided from the 1970s, and a "post-revisionist" synthesis emerged, locating the Cold War's origins in mutual misperceptions and in incompatible strategic and ideological expectations. The revisionist synthesis prefigured the field's post-1991 development. Since then, historians have turned themselves to a diverse array of themes, which the Cambridge volumes showcase. While hundreds of historiographical flowers have bloomed, the overriding historiographical development has been the Cold War's globalization. Looking far beyond the superpowers, historians now

27 Heonik Kwon, *The Other Cold War* (New York: Columbia University Press, 2010).
28 Leffler and Westad, *Cambridge History of the Cold War.*
29 For a classic orthodox interpretation of the Cold War's origins, see Herbert Feis, *From Trust to Terror: The Onset of the Cold War, 1945–1950* (New York: W.W. Norton, 1970). Influential revisionist treatments include William Appleman Williams, *The Tragedy of American Diplomacy* (New York: W.W. Norton, 1972); and Gabriel Kolko and Joyce Kolko, *The Limits of Power: The World and United States Foreign Policy* (New York: Harper & Row, 1972). Prominent post-revisionist accounts include Gaddis, *Origins of the Cold War*; and, more recently, Melvyn Leffler, *A Preponderance of Power: National Security, the Truman Administration, and the Cold War* (Palo Alto, CA: Stanford University Press, 1992).

treat European countries as independent historical agents, probe the Cold War's diffusion into the Third World, and undertake sophisticated, multi-archival reconstructions of the East Bloc's internal politics. It has become difficult to construe the Cold War as residing exclusively – or even primarily – within the Soviet–American dyad of popular lore; instead historians now stress its global dimensions and its global consequences. At the same time, influential scholars still present the Soviet–American confrontation as the Cold War's central theme.[30] Herein may reside the field's most pressing interpretative dilemmas: how global should the Cold War be?

Mulling the question, we might beware a distinction between the history of the Cold War and the history of the Cold War's era. The two are not synonymous. Whether the twentieth century's second half should be understood as an era of Cold War is a question that bears examination and brokers no clear answers. Expanding the Cold War's purview beyond the superpower dyad has enriched our understanding, especially of the global Cold War that became so violent in the Cold War's later decades. We might nonetheless be wary of conflating the history of the Cold War with the history of the postwar world. Conflation risks an analytical flattening that accepts clichés about the world holding its breath and ignores wide differences of experience between countries and regions where the Cold War rent massive damage – from Argentina to Cambodia to Zaire – and those where its effects were relatively muted – India, West Africa, and Scandinavia all come to mind. Then, of course, there are themes that exist apart from the Cold War but that intersected with it and about which it is difficult to say what the Cold War's real influence was. The Israeli–Palestinian conflict is one example. A second risk of conflation, beyond the flattening of historical experience, is that it may explode the Cold War into a meta-historical framework for postwar history, which precludes situating it within history, where it can be usefully related to other developments of its times. Processes extraneous to the Cold War – processes that antedated and outlived it – shaped the Cold War's course. Two obvious examples are decolonization and globalization. Yet these themes may be obscured if they are treated as subthemes of Cold War history.

30 These include John Gaddis, the unofficial dean of Cold War studies. See *We Now Know: Rethinking Cold War History* (New York: Oxford University Press, 1998); and, more recently, *The Cold War: A New History* (New York: Penguin, 2005).

None of this is to say that the Cold War was smoke and mirrors, more illusion than reality. It was a deathly serious confrontation that shaped the international relations of its times, so much so that the temptation of conflation of the Cold War with its era tempts and beckons. Instead, we would do well to recall Reinhold Niebuhr's call for historical perspective. "It is easy to forget that even the most powerful nation or alliance of nations," Niebuhr wrote in 1952, "is merely one of many forces in the historical drama." Warning against determinism of all kinds, Niebuhr cautioned against the arrogance and recklessness of inscribing in history a coherent will, purpose, or logic. Instead, he insisted, history must be viewed as a "conflict of many wills and purposes," "a bizarre pattern in which it is difficult to discern a clear meaning."[31] Decades after the Cold War's ending, it would be hard to find a better epitaph on the postwar era than this.

Further reading

Andrew, Christopher and Vasili Mitrokhin. *The World Was Going Our Way: The KGB and the Battle for the Third World*. New York: Basic Books, 2005.

Berend, T. Iván. *From the Soviet Bloc to the European Union: The Economic and Social Transformation of Central and Eastern Europe Since 1973*. Cambridge University Press, 2009.

Cooper, Richard. *The Economics of Interdependence: Economic Policy in the Atlantic Community*. New York: Council on Foreign Relations, 1968.

Costigliola, Frank. *Roosevelt's Lost Alliances How Personal Politics Helped Start the Cold War*. Princeton University Press, 2011.

Eichengreen, Barry. *The European Economy Since 1945: Coordinated Capitalism and Beyond*. Princeton University Press, 2008.

Ekbladh, David. *The Great American Mission: Modernization and the Construction of An American World Order*. Princeton University Press, 2010.

Feis, Herbert. *From Trust to Terror: The Onset of the Cold War, 1945–1950*. New York: W.W. Norton, 1970.

Fink, Carole. *Cold War: An International History*. Boulder, CO: Westview Press, 2013.

Gaddis, John L. *The Cold War: A New History*. New York: Penguin, 2005.

The Long Peace: Inquiries Into the History of the Cold War. Oxford University Press, 1987.

The United States and the Origins of the Cold War, 1941–1947. Oxford University Press, 1972.

We Now Know: Rethinking Cold War History. Oxford University Press, 1998.

Gilman, Nils. *Mandarins of the Future: Modernization Theory in Cold War America*. Baltimore, MD: Johns Hopkins University Press, 2007.

Hogan, Michael. *The Marshall Plan: America, Britain, and the Reconstruction of Western Europe, 1947–1952*. Cambridge University Press, 1987.

31 Reinhold Niebuhr, *The Irony of American History* (University of Chicago Press, 2008), p. 141.

Ikenberry, G. John. *Liberal Leviathan: The Origins, Crisis, and Transformation of the American World Order*. Princeton University Press, 2011.

Kolko, Gabriel and Joyce Kolko. *The Limits of Power: The World and United States Foreign Policy*. New York: Harper & Row, 1972.

Kwon, Heonik. *The Other Cold War*. New York: Columbia University Press, 2010.

Latham, Michael. *Modernization as Ideology: American Social Science and "Nation-Building" in the Kennedy Era*. Chapel Hill: University of North Carolina Press, 2000.

The Right Kind of Revolution: Modernization, Development, and U.S. Foreign Policy From the Cold War to the Present. Ithaca, NY: Cornell University Press, 2011.

Latham, Robert. *The Liberal Moment: Modernity, Security, and the Making of Postwar International Order*. New York: Columbia University Press, 1997.

Leffler, Melvyn. *A Preponderance of Power: National Security, the Truman Administration, and the Cold War*. Palo Alto, CA: Stanford University Press, 1992.

Leffler, Melvyn and Odd Arne Westad, eds. *The Cambridge History of the Cold War*, 3 vols. Cambridge University Press, 2010.

Luthi, Lorenz. *The Sino-Soviet Split: Cold War in the Communist World*. Princeton University Press, 2008.

Mastny, Vojtech. *The Cold War and Soviet Insecurity*. Oxford University Press, 1996.

Milward, Alan. *The Reconstruction of Western Europe, 1945–1951*. Berkeley, CA: University of California Press, 1984.

Philpott, Daniel. *Revolutions in Sovereignty: How Ideas Shaped Modern International Relations*. Princeton University Press, 2001.

Radchenko, Sergey. *Two Suns in the Heavens: The Sino-Soviet Struggle for Supremacy, 1962–1967*. Palo Alto, CA: Stanford University Press, 2009.

Sargent, Daniel J. *A Superpower Transformed: The Remaking of American Foreign Relations in the 1970s*. Oxford University Press, 2015.

Seabury, Paul. *The Rise and Decline of the Cold War*. New York: Basic Books, 1967.

Suri, Jeremi. *Power and Protest: Global Revolution and the Rise of Détente*. Cambridge, MA: Harvard University Press, 2003.

Westad, Odd Arne. *The Global Cold War: Third World Interventions and the Making of Our Times*. Cambridge University Press, 2005.

Williams, William Appleman. *The Tragedy of American Diplomacy*. New York: W.W. Norton, 1972.

15

1956

CAROLE FINK

> It is impossible to reduce, or at least to hold a distant country against the wishes and efforts of its inhabitants.
>
> *Edward Gibbon,* The Decline and Fall of the Roman Empire, *Vol. 4.*

> Herein lies the tragedy of the age . . . that men know so little of men.
>
> *W. E. B. Du Bois,* The Souls of Black Folk

One date or year can never encompass the complex political, social, economic, cultural, and intellectual transformations that comprise human history or the even more intricate developments in medicine, science, technology, climate, and the environment. Nonetheless, certain dates resonate in human consciousness, signifying important moments of political disjuncture that affected large numbers of people and afterwards served as markers of their legacy. In the Cold War era 1956 was such a year, and it indeed had a global impact.[1]

Two striking events are associated with 1956: the Soviet repression of the Hungarian Revolution and the abortive Anglo-French-Israeli campaign in Suez. These nearly simultaneous episodes are also linked to other momentous developments: The upheaval in European communism was accompanied by the onset of the Sino-Soviet split and the transformation of global Marxist movements. The Suez crisis not only drew the US and the Soviet Union more deeply into the Middle East but also underlined the oil factor in international affairs and the growing nuclear danger. And the Franco-British withdrawal from Egypt accelerated the decolonization of Africa and Asia but also the decision by six West European governments to create a Common Market.

[1] *Das Internationale Krisenjahr 1956*, ed. Winfried Heinemann and Norbert Wiggershaus (Munich: Oldenbourg, 1999).

Hungary

Within six months of Joseph Stalin's death in March 1953 the Communist Party of the Soviet Union had a new leader, Nikita Khrushchev. After gaining control over the party machinery and vanquishing his political rivals, Khrushchev set a new course for the USSR in order to reduce its political, financial, and military burdens. In 1955, in spectacular displays of conciliation, he made an expiatory pilgrimage to Belgrade and reestablished relations with Yugoslavia whose leader, Josip Broz Tito, Stalin had failed to topple in 1948. That year Khrushchev also took three substantial diplomatic steps, agreeing to the withdrawal of Allied forces from Austria in return for that country's permanent neutrality, the return of Soviet captured bases to China and Finland, and the establishment of diplomatic relations with the Federal Republic of Germany, including the repatriation of the remaining 10,000 German prisoners of war still held in the Soviet Union. At the Geneva Big-Four conference, ten years after the last Allied summit in 1945, Khrushchev uttered the words "peaceful coexistence."[2]

More surprises awaited in 1956. Shortly after midnight on February 25 Khrushchev shook the communist faithful with his four-hour-long "Secret Speech" to the 20th Party Congress of the Soviet Union, the first such gathering since Stalin's death. In grim detail he denounced the dictator's crimes: the self glorification and the cult of the individual that violated Leninist principles of collective leadership; the terror tactics toward his enemies; the ruinous errors during the Great Patriotic War; the hideous postwar purges; and Stalin's "suspicion and haughtiness [toward] whole parties and nations." Circulated almost immediately, the revelations by one of Stalin's former intimates suddenly stirred hopes for greater freedom in Eastern Europe.[3]

The Soviet empire in Eastern Europe had been a prime cause of Cold War friction. During the early years the West had contested the denial of freedom to people beyond the USSR's borders, first through diplomatic means and undercover agents, then with a barrage of propaganda through Voice of America, Radio Free Europe, and the BBC.[4] But by 1953 US leaders

[2] Aleksandr Fursenko and Timothy Naftali, *Khrushchev's Cold War* (New York and London: W.W. Norton, 2006), pp. 15–82.

[3] Nikita Khrushchev, "Speech to a closed session of the CPSU Twentieth Party Congress," Feb. 25, 1956, in Thomas P. Whitney (ed.), *Khrushchev Speaks!* (Ann Arbor, MI: University of Michigan Press, 1963), pp. 259–265.

[4] Stephen A. Garrett, *From Potsdam to Poland: American Policy toward Eastern Europe* (New York: Praeger, 1986).

Figure 15.1 Arrival of Nikita Sergeyevich Khrushchev, Soviet politician and General Secretary of the Central Commitee of the Communist Party of the Soviet Union, at Schönefeld Airport on a visit to the German Democratic Republic in 1963 (© INTERFOTO / Alamy)

recognized that Moscow's possession of nuclear weapons made any change in the European status quo unlikely.

The Kremlin was the overwhelming master of Eastern Europe, with troops on the ground in Poland, Hungary, East Germany, and Romania and thousands of military and political "advisors" stationed throughout the region. Through the Cominform (The Communist Information Bureau, founded in 1947) Moscow managed the affairs of foreign fraternal parties, and through Comecon (The Council for Mutual Economic Assistance, founded in 1949) it coordinated the economies of Eastern Europe with the Soviet Union's. The 1955 Warsaw Pact (the Treaty of Friendship Cooperation, and Mutual Assistance, the Kremlin's response to West German rearmament) established tight control over its seven small dependents from the Baltic to the Black and Adriatic seas.[5]

Khrushchev's secret speech in February 1956, accompanied by a relaxation of party supervision over East European artists and intellectuals, the dissolution of the Cominform in April, and Tito's invitation to Moscow in June, hinted at an overall loosening of the Kremlin's control over its satellites. However, the Soviet leader had no intention of encouraging independent initiatives. Despite his reference in February 1956 to "many different paths to socialism," Khrushchev lectured his Yugoslav guest on the priority of Leninist principles and brandished Soviet economic power in an attempt to win Belgrade back to a "unified communist camp."[6]

The first demonstration of Khrushchev's methods occurred in Poland. In response to the massive anti-Soviet demonstrations in Poland between June and October and the return of Władisław Gomułka (whom Stalin had earlier deposed) Khrushchev initially decided on a Soviet military strike. However, he backtracked in return for Gomułka's assurances that the existing communist power structure in Warsaw would remain intact and that Poland would remain a loyal member of the Soviet bloc.[7]

The Hungarian revolution of 1956 posed an existential problem for Khrushchev by challenging the principles of Stalin *and* Lenin. By mid October Hungary's massive anti-Soviet demonstrations led by workers, students, soldiers, and writers had led to the disintegration of communist

[5] V, M. Zubok, *A Failed Empire: The Soviet Union in the Cold War from Stalin to Gorbachev* (Chapel Hill: University of North Carolina Press, 2007), pp. 94–123.

[6] Andrey Edemskiy, "Tito and Khrushchev after the 20th Party Congress: the new nature of Yugoslav-Soviet relations," in Carole Fink, Frank Hadler, Tomasz Schramm (eds.), *1956: European and Global Perspectives* (Leipziger Universitätsverlag, 2006), pp. 122–126.

[7] Pawel Machcewicz, *Rebellious Satellite: Poland, 1956*, trans. Maya Latynski (Washington, DC: Woodrow Wilson Press/Stanford University Press, 2009).

control. The newly appointed Prime Minister Imre Nagy, a moderate party man who lacked Gomułka's political agility, was swept along by the revolutionaries. At first, Khrushchev was inclined to withhold the use of force until Nagy suddenly announced a multiparty system and Hungary's withdrawal from the Warsaw Pact.[8]

The danger to Moscow was clear. A liberated Hungary, ruled by non-communists and with an independent army, threatened to create a physical wedge in the Soviet Union's East European empire, the "first domino" that could encourage imitators and even menace the homeland.[9] It would also provide the "imperialists" with a valuable propaganda victory, especially at the very moment when the Israelis, British, and French were threatening Khrushchev's client Egypt. Indeed, the Anglo-French bombardment of Egyptian air bases on October 31 provided valuable cover for Khrushchev's fateful decision.[10]

There were also strong political and personal reasons why the wavering General Secretary opted for a military intervention: Facing Khrushchev was a Politburo, KGB, and military leadership that would undoubtedly hold him responsible for the loss of Hungary because of his de-Stalinization campaign and his vacillation during the crisis.[11] Moreover, the former party chief in the Ukraine had scarcely shrunk from using force in the past. Thus, with the support of the Kremlin's hard-line majority and the assent of Mao, Tito, and even Gomułka (all recognizing the peril to communism's as well as their own future) Khrushchev decided on the night of October 31 to intervene militarily, reestablish reliable communist rule, and maintain Soviet troops in Hungary.[12]

It was a pyrrhic victory. By crushing the Hungarian revolt, the Soviet Union preserved Stalin's conquests in Eastern Europe for more than three decades, but the price was substantial. The casualties were high: some 640 Soviet soldiers were killed and 1,251 wounded. On the Hungarian side 2,000 died, tens of thousands were wounded, some 35,000 were arrested, 22,000

[8] *The Hungarian Revolution of 1956: Reform, Revolt and Repression 1953–1956*, ed. György Litván et al. (New York: Longmans, 1996).

[9] Johanna Granville, *The First Domino-International Decisionmaking during the Hungarian Crisis of 1956* (College Station, TX: Texas A & M University Press, 2004).

[10] At the crucial Presidium meeting on October 31 Khrushchev declared: "If we depart from Hungary, it will give a great boost to the Americans, English, and French – the imperialists . . . Our party will not accept it, if we do this. To Egypt they [the imperialists] will add Hungary. We have no other choice." Quoted in Fursenko and Naftali, *Khrushchev's Cold War*, p. 130.

[11] Veljko Mičunović, *Moscow Diary* (Garden City, NY: Doubleday, 1980), p, 134.

[12] Johanna Granville, *In the Line of Fire: The Soviet Crackdown on Hungary, 1956–1958* (Pittsburgh: The Carl Beck Papers in Russian & East European Studies, Vol. 1307, 1998).

incarcerated, and 200 executed (among them Imre Nagy in 1958), and over 200,000 people (2 percent of Hungary's population of 10 million) fled the country.[13] Not only was Khrushchev's stature greatly diminished at home and abroad; but he also forced his country to assume the economic and political burdens of pacifying millions of resentful Hungarian and other East European subjects through continued military occupation and the institution of "goulash communism" – a less austere, more consumer-oriented economic regime – while the USSR was embarking after 1956 on a costly nuclear and global competition with the West. In the meantime the emerging "thaw generation" in the Soviet Union – imprinted with Khrushchev's denunciation of Stalin and his "spasmodic reformism," leading to better food, housing, wages, and social services – would now express rising expectations and a diminution of their parents' Socialist fervor.[14]

The Western public reacted strongly to the news from Hungary. Eleven years after the end of World War II the images of Soviet tanks crushing a popular uprising in one of Europe's ancient cities received wide coverage in the press. (To be sure, the prevailing Cold War mindset prevented most Western observers from drawing comparisons between Soviet control over Eastern Europe and Western imperialism in North Africa, the Middle East, Asia, and Africa and the US sphere of influence in Latin America.) In Western Europe, where intellectuals decried the straitjacket of the Cold War, the nuclear threat, and the growing Americanization of their economies and culture, Khrushchev's revelations about the show trials and the gulags followed by Soviet repression in Hungary served as a reminder that the world behind the Iron Curtain was far more dismal. In a taunt to disillusioned radicals, the French political philosopher Raymond Aron declared in October 1956 that the Soviet Union was merely a "long-term despotism" that was doomed to fail.[15]

The bloodbath in Hungary ostensibly delivered a propaganda victory to the United States, which promptly admitted some 35,000 Hungarian refugees. Yet Washington, which for several years had officially preached "rollback" in

[13] Csaba Békés, "New findings on the 1956 Hungarian Revolution," *Cold War International History Project*, cwihp.si.edu; Mark Kramer, "The Soviet Union and the 1956 crisis in Hungary and Poland: reassessments and new findings," *Journal of Contemporary History* 33/2 (1998), 210.

[14] *Russia's Sputnik Generation*, ed. and trans. Donald J. Raleigh (Bloomington and Indianapolis: Indiana University Press, 2006), pp. 1–23.

[15] Tony Judt, *Postwar: A History of Europe since 1945* (London: Heinemann, 2005), p. 322; Georges Soutou, *La guerre de cinquante ans: Le conflit Est-ouest, 1943–1990* (Paris: Fayard, 2001), p. 335.

Eastern Europe and whose paid radio broadcasters in Central Europe had until the last moment imprudently encouraged the revolutionaries' belief that outside support was imminent, had also suffered a political and moral defeat.[16]

Dwight Eisenhower, the architect of D-Day in 1944, preferred peace in Europe over confrontation. In the final days of his second presidential campaign and in the midst of the agonizing Suez imbroglio involving two of his closest allies, the president made it clear that America was unwilling to risk a nuclear war over Hungary. Indeed, prior to the Soviet invasion Washington had sent reassuring signals to Moscow and declined to raise a ruckus in the UN. After the revolt was crushed and his reelection sealed, Eisenhower combined expressions of sympathy for the Hungarians' plight with an open acceptance of a divided and stable continent, thus dispelling the myth of liberation and moving toward détente in Europe.[17]

One major Cold War problem – the question of a divided Germany – remained outside the headlines in 1956. One year earlier, Khrushchev had faced the disagreeable *faits accomplis* of the Federal Republic's entry into NATO and its imminent rearmament. Cornered at the Geneva summit meeting, Soviet negotiators had rejected a US proposal for all-German national elections and NATO membership, even accompanied by security guarantees and a demilitarized zone. Confronted with the ruin of Stalin's hopes for a neutral, demilitarized Germany similar to Austria, Khrushchev at the end of 1955 made a fateful decision: impulsively, he committed the Soviet Union to preserving the independence and survival of East Germany (which Stalin had considered merely a Cold War bargaining card), thereby saddling Moscow for more than three decades with the burden of propping up a weak and unpopular but an also economically valuable regime. Moreover, the Berlin problem – the status of the divided former Reich capital lying one hundred ten miles inside the GDR – would strain East–West relations for another fifteen years.[18]

Nonetheless, after 1956, the Cold War in Europe did moderate in at least one regard. The ideological confrontation became less aggressive. The doctrine of peaceful coexistence, repeated by Khrushchev at the 20th Party Congress in February 1956, facilitated cultural exchanges between East and

[16] Charles Gati, *Failed Illusions: Moscow, Washington, Budapest, and the 1956 Hungarian Revolt* (Washington, DC: Woodrow Wilson Press/Stanford University Press, 2006), pp. 69–112 and *passim*.

[17] Jeno Györkei and Miklós Horváth, eds., *1956: Soviet Military Intervention in Hungary* (Budapest: Central European University Press, 1999), p. 114.

[18] Gerhard Wetting, *Bereitschaft zu Einheit in Freiheit? Die sowjetische Deutschland-Politik 1945–1955* (Munich: Olzog, 1999).

West.[19] Westerners gradually discovered the films, literature, music, art, and scholarship from behind the Iron Curtain, while Soviet and East European citizens, increasingly exposed to Western visitors and ideas, continued to hope for a less repressive, more humane socialism.[20]

Outside Europe Khrushchev's tumultuous 1956 had a profound effect on Sino-Soviet relations. The Chinese leader, Mao Zedong, who had chafed under Stalin's "Janus-faced" policies during the Korean War and what he considered the Soviets' ungenerous economic and military assistance afterwards, had determined to strike a more independent course. Thus, China in 1954 concluded a pact with neutral India based on "The Five Principles of Coexistence" among nations with different social systems (*Pancha Shila*),[21] and one year later secured an important invitation to the Bandung Conference, where foreign minister Zhou Enlai began wooing the nonaligned states.[22]

Sino-Soviet relations had undergone a brief rapprochement in 1954, marked by their cooperation during the July Geneva Conference on Indochina, and followed a month later by Khrushchev's visit to Beijing to celebrate the PRC's fifth anniversary bringing generous economic and political concessions. But they cooled one year later. Mao, fearful of Soviet competition in the nonaligned world, was also deeply suspicious of Khrushchev's foreign policy, fearing concessions to the West at China's expense in the name of peaceful coexistence. And Khrushchev, like Stalin, had little sympathy for Mao's obsession with "liberating" Taiwan at the risk of antagonizing Washington.[23] The leaders of the world's two communist giants were also mismatched partners. Mao in 1954 had deemed his Soviet guest boorish and unintelligent, and Khrushchev, baffled by Mao's ideological rigidity and his "oriental" court, returned to Moscow convinced that a conflict with China was "inevitable."[24]

[19] Yale Richmond, *Cultural Exchange and the Cold War: Raising the Iron Curtain* (University Park: Pennsylvania State University Press, 2003).

[20] Zubok, *Failed Empire*, pp. 167–73; James H. Satterwhite, *Varieties of Marxist Humanism: Philosophical Revision in Postwar Eastern Europe* (University of Pittsburgh Press, 1992).

[21] Mutual respect for territorial sovereignty, mutual non aggression, mutual nonintervention in internal affairs, equality and mutual benefit and peaceful coexistence.

[22] Lorenz M. Lüthi, *The Sino-Soviet Split: Cold War in the Communist World* (Princeton University Press, 2008), pp. 36–40.

[23] Odd Arne Westad,"The Sino-Soviet Alliance and the United States," in Odd Arne Westad (ed.), *Brothers in Arms: The Rise and Fall of the Sino-Soviet Alliance, 1945–1963* (Stanford University Press, 1998), pp. 170–171.

[24] William Taubman, *Khrushchev: The Man and His Era* (New York and London: Norton, 2003), p. 337. The CIA had made the same prediction a year earlier: Phillip Bridgham, Arthur Cohen, Leonard Jaffe, "Mao's road and Sino-Soviet Relations: a view from Washington, 1953," *China Quarterly* 52 (Oct. 1972), 670–698.

After February 25, 1956, the Chinese leadership carefully scrutinized Khrushchev's Secret Speech, which was surprising only in its depth and detail. As a theorist Mao was appalled by Khrushchev's tampering with the essential tenets of Marxism. Even more disturbing was his attack on Stalin's personality cult and his record of economic and military blunders. As a former target of Stalin's arrogance, Mao readily acknowledged the boss [*vozhd*]'s "big mistakes"; but he also insisted on the dictator's "meritorious achievements" and the risk of demolishing him "at one blow." Mao could well construe Khrushchev's denunciation of Stalin as handing a weapon to his Chinese Communist Party rivals who were insisting on reviving Lenin's principle of collective leadership.[25]

The uprisings in Poland and Hungary, testing Khrushchev's vow to end Stalin's domination of fraternal governments, drew Beijing into European affairs. In the case of Poland, Mao firmly opposed a Soviet invasion, although there is no hard evidence that Khrushchev's last-minute reversal was influenced by China's stance.[26] Hungary was another matter. Mao, far less informed of the situation on the ground in Budapest, apparently wavered before agreeing to the intervention. Although China's role in Soviet decision-making cannot be determined with certainty, Mao's participation underlined his influence in the communist camp.[27]

The events in Eastern Europe confirmed the Chinese leader's growing disdain for Khrushchev – for his bungled de-Stalinization campaign that had confused communists in Eastern Europe and for his erroneous assessments of events in Poland and Hungary that had intensified both crises. Although still too weak to challenge Moscow's leadership of the communist world or openly criticize its détente efforts toward the West, the Beijing government had nonetheless by the end of 1956 embarked on a road to distance itself ideologically and politically from the Soviet Union. This decision was

[25] Mao Zedong, *On Diplomacy* (Beijing: Foreign Languages Press, 1998), pp. 185–186; Lüthi, *Sino-Soviet Split*, pp. 48–53. Indeed, that year North Korean leader Kim il-Sung stifled an internal revolt against his sole rule. *North Korean Communism: A Comparative Analysis*, ed. Chong-Shik Chung, Gahb-chol Kim (Seoul: Research Center for Peace and Unification, 1980), pp. 77–78.

[26] Lüthi, *Sino-Soviet Split*, pp. 54–57. Yinghong Cheng, "Beyond a Moscow-centric interpretation: an Examination of the China connection in Eastern Europe and North Vietnam during the era of de-Stalinization," *Journal of World History* 15 (2004), 487–518.

[27] Whereas Chen Jian, *Mao's China and the Cold War* (Chapel Hill: University of North Carolina Press, 2001), pp. 156–157, considers Mao's influence decisive, János Rainer and Bernd-Rainer Barth, "Ungarische Revolution: Aufstand – Zerfall der Partei – Invasion," in B. András Hegedüs and Manfred Wilke (eds.), *Satelliten nach Stalins Tod* (Berlin: Akademie Verlag, 2000), p. 254, maintains it was one of many factors. Cf. Nikita S. Khrushchev, *Khrushchev Remembers* (Boston: Little Brown and Co., 1970), pp. 418–419.

underlined a year later when Mao abruptly cancelled the program to liberalize China's political climate under the slogan "Let one hundred flowers bloom and a hundred schools of thought contend."[28]

The year 1956 was also a tumultuous one for the world's Marxist faithful. To be sure, Khrushchev's catalogue of Stalin's crimes did not diminish the loyalty of communist parties in Japan and Mexico, but it split parties in Latin America. The eighty-eight-year-old African American political philosopher W. E. B. Du Bois remained an admirer of Stalin for having established "the world's first socialist state," for breaking "the power of the kulaks," and for "conquer[ing] Hitler." Although regretting the excesses of Stalin's last years ("He was not the first tyrant in the world and will not be the last"), Du Bois in July 1956 pronounced Khrushchev's criticisms "irresponsible and muddled," the Soviet state "great and progressing," and the upheaval in Poland due to "the old landlord and military clan bribed by the United States."[29]

Closer to home, however, European communists faced the massive negative reaction to Stalin's crimes and to the bloodbath in Hungary. The Comintern veteran Palmiro Togliatti, himself a victim of Stalin's Cold War political maneuvers and also the leader of Italy's second largest party, now coined the term "polycentrism" to characterize his virtual independence from the Kremlin, thus facilitating his party's electoral success two years later.[30] On the other hand French Communist leader Maurice Thorez, who had been closely tied to Stalin, denigrated Khrushchev's campaign but also stayed loyal to Moscow, causing a major split in the party precisely as it faced another major crisis over its stance vis-à-vis France's colonial war in Algeria.[31]

Khrushchev's call for coexistence sent shock waves everywhere, restraining communist militants in Asia, Africa, and Latin America and quenching their efforts at sabotage, subversion, and armed action. Khrushchev's endorsement of a hybrid form of "non-capitalist" development in countries such as Indonesia, India, Burma, Iran, and Egypt dispirited their struggling communist

[28] Nick Knight, "Mao Zedong and the Chinese road to socialism," in Colin Mackerras and Nick Knight, *Marxism in Asia* (New York: St. Martin's Press, 1985), pp. 94–123. Details in Lüthi, *Sino-Soviet Split*, pp. 57–70.

[29] Letter to Anna Melissa Graves, July 8, 1956, in Herbert Aptheker (ed.), *The Correspondence of W. E. B. Du Bois*, Vol. 3 (Amherst, MA: University of Massachusetts Press, 1978), pp. 402–403. Also see Du Bois' eulogy, "On Stalin," *National Guardian*, Mar. 16, 1953, reprinted in David Levering Lewis (ed.), *W. E. B. Du Bois: A Reader* (New York: Henry Holt, 1995), pp. 796–797.

[30] Aldo Agosti, *Palmiro Togliatti: A Biography* (London and New York: I. B. Tauris, 2008).

[31] Jean-François Paroz, "La Critique du PCF face au Phénomène Stalinien," *Annals of International Studies* 15 (1986), 139–169, and, esp., Aimé Césaire, *Lettre à Maurice Thorez* (Paris: Présence Africaine, 1956).

movements; his call for an alignment with bourgeois-nationalist forces in the anti-imperialist struggle eroded the independence of African communists; and the looming Sino-Soviet split forced the North Korean and North Vietnamese communists into a delicate balancing act between Moscow and Beijing.[32]

Communist movements survived the shocks of 1956 in places unanticipated by either Khrushchev or Mao, some aligning themselves with nationalist movements (Iraq) and others with rural workers (Brazil).[33] A key country was South Africa, where in 1955 the communist party had fully endorsed the Freedom Charter calling for equal rights for all races under a welfare state democracy. Nelson Mandela who, on December 5, 1956, along with one hundred fifty African National Congress leaders was arrested on charges of high treason based on allegations of a "communist conspiracy," was no left-wing radical. Yet he upheld Marxism's "sociological constructions," valued its "conceptual vocabulary," and appreciated the South African communists' collaboration in working to create a democratic non-racial South Africa.[34]

Another unforeseen development in Cold War history occurred in America's backyard, where two years earlier Washington had toppled a left-wing government in Guatemala and restored that country as a compliant neighbor. On December 2, 1956, eighty-two revolutionaries, including Fidel Castro and Che Guevara, landed on Las Coloradas Beach in Cuba and launched a military revolt against a corrupt and unpopular, US-supported dictator. Aligning themselves with students and the disgruntled middle class, tapping local nationalism and anti-imperialism, and proceeding to destabilize the Batista regime with a string of battlefield victories, Castro's July 26 Movement triumphed three years later without local or foreign communist

[32] Fritz Schatten, *Communism in Africa* (New York: Praeger, 1966), pp. 71–100; *The Communist Revolution in Asia*, ed. Robert A. Scalapino (Englewood Cliffs, NJ: Prentice-Hall, 2nd edn. 1969), *passim*; Sepehr Zabih, *The Communist Movement in Iran* (Berkeley and Los Angeles: University of California Press, 1966), pp. 213–221; Jan Pennar, *The USSR and the Arabs* (New York: Crane, Russak & Co., 1973), *passim*.

[33] Maxine Molyneux and Fred Halliday, "Marxism, the Third World, and the Middle East," *MERIP Reports*, no. 120 (Jan. 1984), pp. 18–21, www.jstor.org/stable/3011670; Bernard Kiernan, *The United States, Communism, and the Emergent World* (Bloomington, IN: Indiana University Press, 1972), pp. 150–151.

[34] Nelson Mandela, *Long Walk to Freedom: The Autobiography of Nelson Mandela* (Johannesburg: Macdonald Purnell, 1994), pp. 189–10; Tom Lodge, "Charters from the past: the African National Congress and its historiographical traditions," in Joshua Brown et al. (eds.), *History from South Africa: Alternative Visions and Practices* (Philadelphia: Temple University Press, 1991), pp. 119–144; Text of the Charter in Allison Drew (ed.), *South Africa's Radical Tradition: A Documentary History*, Vol. 2 (Cape Town: UCT Press, 1997), pp. 121–124. To be sure, by 1956 the achievements of the US Civil Rights and the Supreme Court's decisions on the desegregation of schools and public transportation also had an impact on the global struggle for racial equality.

support. Only after Washington rebuffed Castro's overtures and Khrushchev applied his Third-World ambitions to the Western Hemisphere did Cuba become a full, if also a costly and difficult Soviet satellite.[35]

The Suez crisis

In 1956, only four years after toppling the corrupt and ineffective King Farouk, Egypt's second president and virtual dictator, the thirty-six-year-old Colonel Gamal Abdel Nasser, had become a major figure in international affairs. A veteran of the disastrous 1948–49 Arab–Israeli War and the Rhodes armistice negotiations, Nasser once in power had displayed a political ruthlessness and diplomatic acumen that impressed his countrymen and foreigners alike. At home, backed by the army and bureaucracy, this charismatic leader with a gift for stirring crowds had crushed the communist and Muslim oppositions, created a new constitution for Egypt, and launched programs to expand Egypt's economic and military power. Abroad Nasser had won a string of triumphs, obtaining Britain's agreement to withdraw its 80,000 troops from the Suez Canal Zone in two years' time, playing a starring role at the Bandung conference, and defying the West with a spectacular arms deal with communist Czechoslovakia in 1955 and the establishment of diplomatic relations with the People's Republic of China in 1956.[36]

By 1956 Nasser's pan-Arab program to unite the Middle East against Western domination had raised alarm in several capitals. In neighboring Israel, Nasser's imminent acquisition of a major cache of sophisticated weapons from the Eastern bloc – coupled with its increased skirmishes over the past year with Egyptian and Palestinian troops and the rising anti-Israel propaganda from Cairo radio – caused the Ben Gurion government to contemplate a pre-emptive strike. Israel found a kindred spirit in France where the Guy Mollet government was obsessed with Nasser's support of the Algerian Revolution and intent on toppling the Egyptian leader. On June 26, 1956, representatives of the two countries signed a secret agreement in which France pledged to supply Israel with a significant number of planes and tanks and Israel to assist France in its struggle against Egypt and the Algerian rebels.[37]

[35] Fursenko and Naftali, *Khrushchev's Cold War*, p. 295. John Foran, "Theorizing the Cuban Revolution," *Latin American Perspectives* 36 (Mar. 2009), 16–30.

[36] Jean LaCouture, *Nasser*, trans. Daniel Hofstadter (New York: Knopf, 1973), pp. 59–162.

[37] Details the Vermars agreement in Motti Golani, *Israel in Search of War: The Sinai Campaign, 1955–1956* (London: Sussex Academic Press, 1998), pp. 28–29.

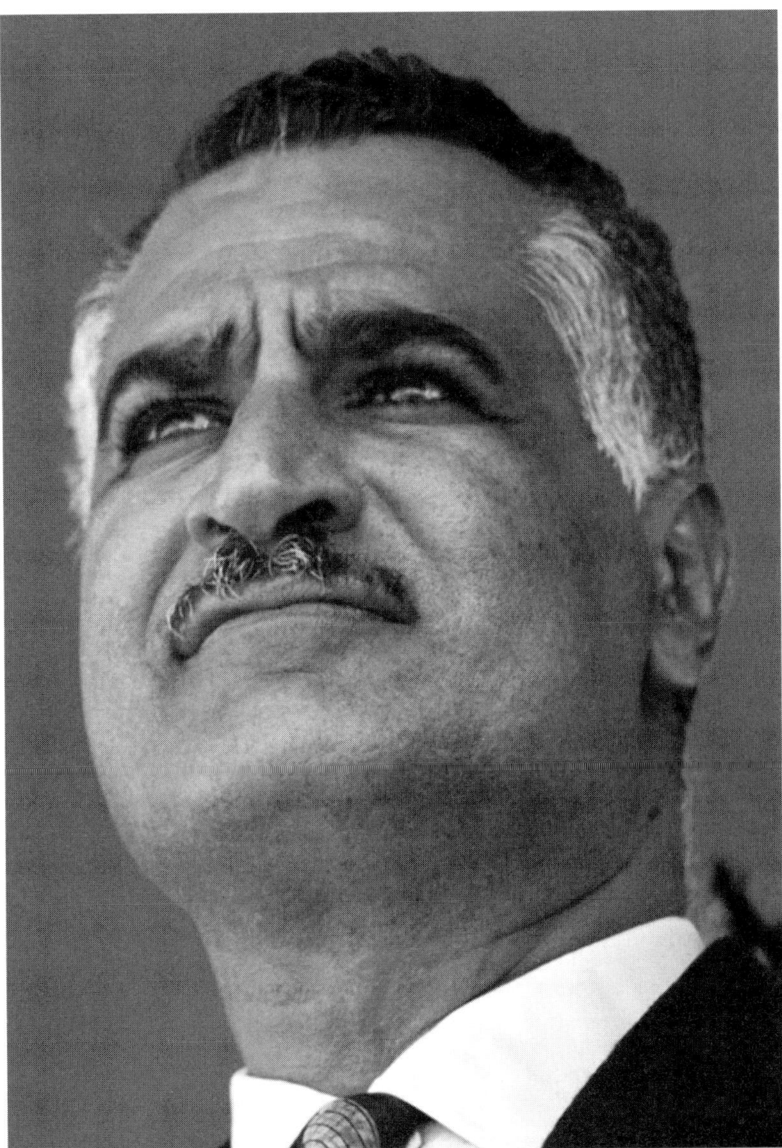

Figure 15.2 Portrait of Gamal Abdel Nasser Hussein, President of Egypt
(© World History Archive / Alamy)

British Prime Minister Anthony Eden was no less hostile toward Nasser. Eden, a decorated World War I veteran, staunch anti-appeaser in the 1930s, and newly appointed successor to Winston Churchill, viewed Nasser not only as an uncouth troublemaker who threatened Britain's leading position in Iraq and Jordan but also as an "Arab Mussolini" intent on using Soviet aid to dominate the Middle East and to threaten Western Europe's oil supplies – placing his "thumb on our windpipe."[38]

The USA and the Soviet Union were ineluctably drawn in. One year earlier, the United States, hoping to gain influence in the largest Arab state, had agreed to a $54 million dollar loan to support the building of the Aswan Dam, a major element of Nasser's campaign to raise Egypt's standard of living. This generous political gesture immediately raised objections in the US Congress and protests from Nasser's Arab rivals.

By the spring of 1956 Eisenhower had grown wary of the Egyptian leader's military dependence on the Soviet bloc, his anti-Western statements, and his hostility toward Israel. Khrushchev on the other hand – despite his nod to non-capitalist development – was absorbed in the tumult in Eastern Europe and skeptical of the dam project and therefore declined Nasser's request to enter a bidding contest with Washington.[39] Suddenly on July 19, an exasperated and suspicious Eisenhower withdrew the US loan and Eden readily vacated Britain's $14 million dollar offer as well. One week later a shocked and humiliated Nasser announced the nationalization of the Suez Canal to pay for his massive electrification and land reclamation project, stirring his compatriots, arousing the Arab world, and triggering a prolonged international crisis.[40]

The seizure of the canal, which had opened in 1869 and was administered under a ninety-nine-year lease by the Franco-British dominated Suez Canal Company, had been a longstanding goal of Nasser's.[41] In a stroke, the removal of this last vestige of Western domination placed Nasser in commanding position over the lifeline of Britain's Commonwealth and Empire as

38 Anthony Eden, *Full Circle* (Boston: Houghton Mifflin, 1960), p. 426. See also Mark Rathbone, "The Munich effect," *History Review* 64 (Mar. 2009), 21; David Carlton, *Britain and the Suez Crisis* (Oxford: Blackwell, 1988), pp. 21–34.

39 Fursenko and Naftali, *Khrushchev's Cold War*, pp. 83–84. After two years of stalling, Khrushchev in October 1958 finally agreed to fund the dam (ibid, p. 185) and in May 1964 attended the inaugural ceremony for the project (ibid, p. 531).

40 James E. Dougherty, "The Aswan decision in perspective," *Political Science Quarterly* 74/1 (Mar. 1959), 21–45.

41 D. C. Watt, *Britain and the Suez Canal* (London: Royal Institute of International Affairs, 1956); Zachary Karabell, *Parting the Desert: The Creation of the Suez Canal* (New York: Knopf, 2003), p. 269.

well as one of two principal routes of Middle Eastern oil deliveries to the West. With the closure of the Strait of Tiran, he had also gained a chokehold on Israel's maritime ties with eastern Africa and Asia.

The superpowers'[42] responses were a study in contrast. Khrushchev, caught off balance by Nasser's move, neither spread a Soviet diplomatic mantle over Egypt nor offered additional arms, expecting the United States to rein in its allies. Thus during the next three months Eisenhower took the lead, striving to prevent an attack on Egypt which, he was convinced, would destabilize the Middle East and encourage further Soviet moves into the region.[43]

Pitted against the US president were his two agitated NATO partners: France, smarting over the loss of Indochina and the Algerian uprising and with a popular opinion solidly behind punishing Nasser; and Britain, with a divided cabinet and parliament and strong Commonwealth opposition to the use of force but led by an ailing and impulsive prime minister determined to assert his nation's power and protect its oil supply. Under US pressure, France and Britain submitted to two mediating conferences in London in August and September, and in October they made a lame effort to involve the United Nations in establishing international control over the canal. During this three-month period of suspense – while Eisenhower was increasingly absorbed in the November 6 presidential election and Khrushchev in the mounting threats to Soviet control of Eastern Europe – Nasser's enemies had gained time to mobilize.[44]

Israel played a crucial role. For the hawks, Chief of Staff Moshe Dayan and Deputy Director of the Ministry of Defense Shimon Peres, the Suez Canal crisis had created an opportunity to settle scores with Nasser. Prime Minister Ben Gurion, who at first had hesitated out of fear of US or Soviet intervention, was brought over by Israel's acquisition of a long-sought Western ally and the hope of regaining navigation through the Strait of Tiran. In the summer of 1956 France delivered sixty *Mystère* jets to Israel and on September 1, Paris proposed a joint action against Egypt. In early October Eden signed on to Mollet's audacious scheme for an Israeli invasion of Egypt as a cover for an Anglo-French seizure of the canal and the toppling of Nasser, and a secret pact was concluded at Sèvres on October 24, 1956.[45]

42 "Superpower" was a term that gained currency in the 1950s to denote the nuclear-armed USA and Soviet Union, which exerted a global impact.

43 Fursenko and Naftali, *Khrushchev's Cold War*, pp. 85–86, 92–93.

44 Cole C. Kingseed, *Eisenhower and the Suez Crisis of 1956* (Baton Rouge and London: LSU Press, 1995), pp. 44–80.

45 David Tal, "Israel's road to the 1956 war," *International Journal of Middle East Studies* 28/1 (Feb. 1996), 59–81; Prina Lahav, "A small nation goes to war," *Israel Studies* 15/3 (Fall 2010), 61–68; David Rodman, "War initiation: the case of Israel," *Journal of Strategic*

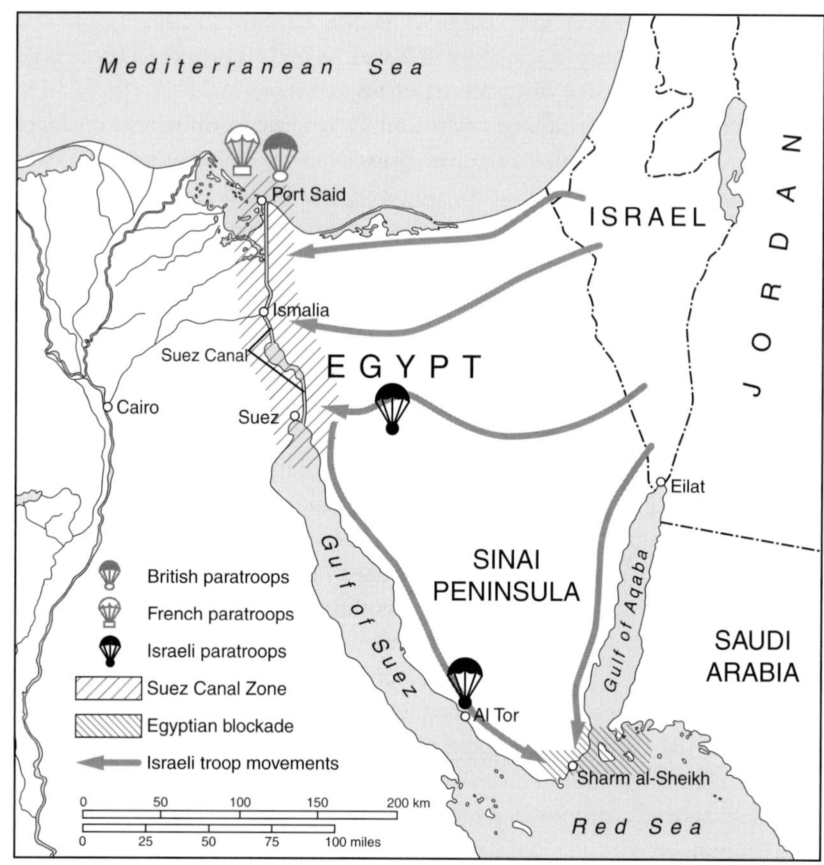

Map 15.1 Suez Crisis, 1956

"Operation Musketeer" began smoothly according to the prearranged tripartite plan: On October 29 Israeli paratroops landed in the central Sinai and quickly reached the Suez Canal. One day later Britain and France issued a 12-hour ultimatum demanding that *both* sides withdraw from the Canal Zone; and when Nasser refused, on October 31 they bombarded Egyptian airfields. After a five-day delay, British and French troops began ground operations on November 5 with the goal of occupying Port Said, Ismaila, and Suez.[46] In the

Studies 20/4 (Dec. 1997), 1–17. Avi Shlaim, "The Protocol of Sèvres, 1956: anatomy of a war plot," *International Affairs* 73/3 (July 1997), 509–530.

[46] Ben Gurion, deeply distrustful of Eden and fearing Arab retaliatory air raids, had urged his partners to reduce the delay between the Israeli attack and their intervention and fumed at the delay in Allied bombings and military action. Keith Kyle, *Suez* (London and New York: I.B. Tauris, 2011), pp. 314, 317, 319–321, 370, 382.

meantime Nasser had responded on November 1 by blocking the canal with blown-up craft and equipment. During that explosive week a wave of outrage swept the world, almost obliterating the dire news from Hungary.[47]

It was now up to the superpowers. Khrushchev was again taken unaware, having been lulled through October by Nasser's overconfidence, faulty Soviet intelligence, and his own misjudgment of Eden's resolve. Once hostilities began, Khrushchev, absorbed by Hungary, ignored Nasser's pleas for military or diplomatic support, leaving the way open for US management of the crisis.[48]

Eisenhower, far better informed, was furious over his NATO allies' actions, fearing an opening to Soviet subversion in the Middle East. Although he had acquiesced in the Soviets' use of force in Hungary, he was determined to halt the aggression against Egypt and to do so before Moscow raised its voice. The scene now shifted to the United Nations. After an Anglo-French veto blocked action by the Security Council, the USA called for an emergency session of the General Assembly which, on November 1, voted 64–5 in favor of an immediate ceasefire.[49] In an extraordinary Cold War moment, Soviet and American aims had become identical.

Both superpowers overplayed their hands. With the Hungarian uprising almost crushed, Khrushchev on November 5 suddenly sprang into action, proposing a joint US–Soviet military force to impose a ceasefire and issuing warnings to Eden, Mollet, and Ben Gurion that the Soviet Union was prepared to use its nuclear weapons to "crush the aggression and to restore peace in the Middle East." However, Moscow's threats, meant to impress the Arabs and the neutrals, were too little and too late to prevent the humiliating rout of Egypt's forces. Khrushchev's unprecedented proposal of a joint occupation force – bypassing the UN – was snubbed by Eisenhower; and his nuclear bluff compelled the three combatants to bow to Washington's wishes.[50]

Eisenhower was outwardly triumphant. On November 6 he easily won a second term, and that day the three belligerents accepted a ceasefire. The United States then took the lead in transporting a UN Emergency Force to Egypt and pressuring the three invaders to withdraw their armies. The last Anglo-French armies were gone by December 22 and the Israeli forces on March 22, 1957.[51] But Washington's victory was also questionable. Not only

[47] Kyle, *Suez*, pp. 408–438.
[48] Fursenko and Naftali, *Khrushchev's Cold War*, pp. 120–121, 126–127, 129–130.
[49] Kingseed, *Eisenhower and the Suez Crisis*, pp. 87–101.
[50] Galia Golan, *Soviet Policies in the Middle East* (Cambridge University Press, 1990), pp. 47–64.
[51] Kingseed, *Eisenhower and the Suez Crisis*, pp. 138–39.

had the USA failed to prevent bloodshed over Suez but it had also aligned itself with Egypt and the Soviet Union against its closest allies. Eisenhower's hardnosed pressure on Britain's money and oil supply had humiliated Eden and led to his replacement in January 1957 by the more pliable Harold Macmillan. However, Anglo-American relations suffered a severe shock over the president's high-handed treatment, forcing Washington to alleviate tensions with Britain and reassure other NATO members of US protection and goodwill.[52]

France was even more disaffected, furious over Eden's yielding to Washington's threats and aggrieved by Eisenhower's nonchalance over Khrushchev's saber-rattling. Musketeer's author Guy Mollet also fell from power in May 1957; and the Suez fiasco undoubtedly prepared the way for the reemergence one year later of Charles de Gaulle, a leader imbued with a profound distrust of the Anglo-Saxons and determined to ensure France's national security outside a US-dominated NATO and to build its own nuclear force.[53]

Israel, which in 1956 had taken the battle over the control of Palestine onto its neighbor's territory and demonstrated its military prowess, emerged stronger from the Suez crisis. It now had a French ally willing to supply arms and even nuclear material; and with strong French support it had secured an international guarantee of naval passage through the Strait of Tiran as well as a UN force to protect it against guerrilla raids from Egypt.[54]

Yet these gains had to be balanced against other outcomes. Given Nasser's record, Egypt's future compliance with the settlement was questionable. Moreover, the exiled Palestinian leadership in Gaza, which had observed Egypt's rout first hand, had become more determined than ever to pursue their goal of national liberation.[55] And, finally, Israel's relations with Washington had soured; following four grueling months of negotiations, Israel had been forced to relinquish the prizes of its stunning victory, Gaza

[52] Robert R. James, *Anthony Eden* (London: Weidenfeld and Nicolson, 1986), pp. 576–577; Diane B. Kunz, *The Economic Diplomacy of the Suez Crisis* (Chapel Hill: University of North Carolina Press, 1991), pp. 130–152, 193–194.

[53] Christian Pineau, *1956/Suez* (Paris: Lafont, 1976), p. 191; Maurice Vaïsse, "Post-Suez France," in William Roger Louis and Roger Owen (eds.), *Suez: The Crisis and its Consequences* (Oxford: Clarendon Press, 1991), pp. 335–340.

[54] Benny Morris, *Israel's Border Wars, 1949–1956* (Oxford: Clarendon Press, 1993), p. 428.

[55] Rashid Khalidi, "Consequences of the Suez Crisis in the Arab World," in *Suez 1956*, pp. 377–392; also Yazid Sayigh, *Armed Struggle and the Search for a State: The Palestinian National Movement, 1949–1993* (Oxford: Clarendon Press, 1997).

and the Sinai, and to recognize its minor role in Eisenhower's political calculations.[56] As events in 1967 would demonstrate, Israel was determined to avoid this fate in the future.

Eisenhower's actions in 1956 accelerated the spread of the Cold War into the Middle East. Despite Moscow's exclusion from the Suez settlement, the Soviet threat continued to haunt Washington.[57] Indeed, Khrushchev raised these fears by trumpeting the effectiveness of his nuclear threat and exaggerating his support of Nasser against Western imperialism. On January 31, 1957, he announced a multimillion arms deal with Cairo.[58]

Having dislodged Britain and France from the region, Eisenhower responded in January 1957 by introducing a new policy to "make [the US] presence more strongly felt in the Middle East." Echoing Truman's commitment to Greece and Turkey ten years earlier, the Eisenhower Doctrine pledged US military and financial aid to Arab countries threatened by the "spread of communism." Before a skeptical Congress, Eisenhower stressed the need to fill the vacuum left by the imperialists' departure from a major center of the world's oil supply. With this initiative Eisenhower continued the expansion of presidential power and also downgraded the importance of the United Nations in US policy. Implicitly, too, his administration had shifted its Middle East policy focus, abandoning its efforts to solve the seemingly intractable Arab–Israeli problem in favor of improving US relations with the oil-rich Arab countries.[59]

The local responses to the Eisenhower doctrine were predictably swift and largely negative. Israel bristled over its exclusion from the US guarantee, Syria suggested that Washington stay out of the region's problems, and Nasser dismissed it as a new version of Western penetration. Only Iraq, the sole Arab member of the increasingly hollow Baghdad pact, hailed the president's announcement; but three years later, after a military coup had

[56] "Israel is inevitably a loser in the present state of the Cold War. Unlike its Arab neighbors with their oil wells and sites for foreign bases . . . Israel has not been regarded as a prize in the maneuvers of the Great Powers. Although the United States gives Israel money and private sympathy in plenty it withholds political support. For the hard fact is that Israel is an obstacle in the way of America's fighting mission against communism." *The Economist*, Apr. 6, 1956, p. 19. Cf. Abba Eban, *An Autobiography* (New York: Random House, 1977), p. 233.

[57] Robert McMahon, "The illusion of vulnerability: American Reassessments of the Soviet Threat, 1955–1956," *International History Review* 18/3 (Aug. 1996), 591–619.

[58] Fursenko and Naftali, *Khrushchev's Cold War*, pp. 137, 162.

[59] Peter Hahn, *Caught in the Middle East: U.S. Policy Toward the Arab-Israeli Conflict, 1945–1961* (Chapel Hill: University of North Carolina Press, 2004), pp. 224–227.

toppled the pro-Western monarchy, Iraq too joined the anti-imperialist camp.[60]

Neither superpower would gain full control over the Middle East. Washington, obsessed with blocking Moscow's threat to NATO's weak southern flank, overestimated the Arabs' fear of communism and underestimated their nationalism, their regional rivalries, and their hatred of colonialism and of Israel. Moscow, fixated on securing a foothold in a strategically important region of the nonaligned world, overestimated its resources and its influence over the Arabs and underestimated the US resolve to replace Great Britain. The Suez crisis had demonstrated the readiness of Middle Eastern actors to use the superpowers but also the latter's insufficient knowledge and understanding of the region's populations and politics.[61]

The impact of Suez

Oil as a factor in international affairs

Nasser's nationalization of the Suez Canal in July 1956 raised the nightmare of a rupture in the West's oil supply. Through this waterway traveled almost 20 percent of the world's oil production from the Middle East to a Western Europe that was consuming increasing quantities of petroleum.[62]

The invasion of Egypt produced the predictable crisis. Not only was the canal abruptly closed for shipping but a day later Syria broke off diplomatic relations with Britain and France whereupon the pipeline carrying oil from Iraq to the Mediterranean was disabled when three Syrian pumping stations were blown up by the Syrians. On November 6 Saudi Arabia also broke off diplomatic relations with the aggressors and banned tankers from carrying its oil to Britain or France. Everything now depended on the United States, still a major oil producer and exporter as well as home to five of the seven multinational oil companies. An incensed Eisenhower added to the pressure on

60 Salim Yaqub, *Containing Arab Nationalism: The Eisenhower Doctrine and the Middle East* (Chapel Hill: University of North Carolina Press, 2004); Naftali and Fursenko, *Khrushchev's Cold War*, pp. 139–140, 142–143, 159–160.

61 Daniele DeLuca, "Gli Stati Uniti e i Nuovi Rapporti di Forza in Medio Oriente: La Dottrina Eisenhower, 1957–1958," *Storia delle Relazioni Internazionali* 10/2 (Oct. 1994), 117–146.

62 Two-thirds of Western Europe's oil came from the Middle East, of which two-thirds passed through the Suez Canal. The remainder was transferred via pipelines from Iraq and Saudi Arabia to the Eastern Mediterranean. James Bamberg, *British Petroleum and Global Oil, 1950–1975* (Cambridge University Press, 2000), p. 75.

Britain and France, refusing to relieve the mounting oil shortages (and currency drain) until their armies withdrew.[63]

Although the Western world's first oil scare in 1956 presaged the future crises in 1967, 1973, and 1979, it had little impact at the time. Once Britain and France had caved in, the United States helped ease the delivery problem from its own sources and from Latin America. Moreover, an unusually warm winter in Europe in 1956–57 softened the impact of reduced supplies. Higher prices reduced consumption, and the major oil companies worked cooperatively to end the crisis. By March 1957, the canal had been cleared, the pipelines repaired, and rationing ended in Western Europe. Subsequently worldwide oil production increased dramatically, and prices returned to their low, pre-crisis levels. Although Anglo-American oil cooperation had resumed, US companies were in the process of eroding British sway in much of the Middle East and North Africa.[64]

Nonetheless the specter of future oil shortages that could threaten the West's security, disrupt its economies, and bring hardship to its populations had now presented itself in 1956.[65] Moreover, although recognizing the necessity of closer collaboration among governments and the oil industry, the West made no serious preparations for future crises.

The nuclear danger

Khrushchev's nuclear threats in November 1956 against Britain, France, and Israel were the first ever issued by a Soviet leader. They occurred at a moment when both superpowers were expanding their arsenals, delivery systems, and placement of their nuclear weaponry.

Khrushchev's bluff was also the threat of an underdog. The United States still held a clear superiority in strategic weapons, its nuclear bombs and long-range bombers outnumbering the USSR by a ratio of approximately 11:1.[66] Moreover, the United States had encircled the Soviet Union with a chain of bases housing its Strategic Air Command bombers that included 1,000 B 47s, 150 B52s, and 250 B36s and were complemented by a worldwide fleet of US

[63] Kunz, *Economic Diplomacy*, p. 124; Paul Howard Frankel, "Oil supplies during the Suez Crisis – on meeting a political emergency," *Journal of Industrial Economics* 6 (Feb. 1958), 85–100.

[64] Wm. Roger Louis (with Ronald Robinson), "The imperialism of decolonization," in *Ends of British Imperialism: Collected Essays by Wm. Roger Louis* (London and New York: I.B. Tauris, 2006), p. 485.

[65] Raymond B. Stokes, "Oil as a primary source of energy," in *1956*, pp. 245–264.

[66] Robert Norris, "Global nuclear stockpiles, 1945–2002," *Bulletin of the Atomic Scientists* 58/6 (Nov./Dec. 2002), 103–104, estimated the numbers in 1956 as follows: 4,618 US bombs, 15 British, and 426 Soviet.

aircraft carriers capable of launching long-range bombers from practically everywhere. Thus in 1956 the Soviet Union was vulnerable to a massive US first strike or a retaliatory attack, while the US was still sheltered by numbers, distance, and a superior detection system.[67]

Khrushchev was determined to overcome the Soviets' inferiority. Alongside his calls for peaceful coexistence came not only a buildup in Soviet bombs and bombers but also the rapid development of intercontinental ballistic missiles. With the appearance of *Sputnik* in 1957, thrust into space by advanced long-range Soviet rocketry, the US mainland suddenly became vulnerable to attack, and America's civil defense programs were rapidly expanded.[68]

Europe stood precariously between the two superpowers; and here the Soviet Union held the decisive edge. Khrushchev's threats in November 1956 and Eisenhower's bland response had exposed the vulnerability of Western Europe. Despite the latter's growing economic strength and the turmoil in the Soviet bloc, the Warsaw Pact's ground forces – which outnumbered NATO's by a ratio of some 6:1 – could not be stopped before they reached the Rhine, even with the use of tactical nuclear weapons. Moreover, few West European leaders believed that the USA would expose itself to retaliation by launching a nuclear strike against Moscow.[69]

The crises of 1956 affected the strategic and political debate over nuclear arms. As the superpowers raced to expand their nuclear delivery systems and plant nuclear weapons throughout Europe, a backlash also developed against atomic warfare that gave rise to citizens' antinuclear movements throughout the world.[70]

By 1957 both sides had acquired enough weapons to destroy the other.[71] That year the Anglo-Australian Neville Shute's novel *On the Beach* captured world attention with its gripping portrayal of the aftermath of a nuclear apocalypse.

67 Lawrence Freedman, *The Evolution of Nuclear Strategy* (New York: Macmillan, 1989), pp. 3–119.

68 Robert J. Watson, *Into the Missile Age, 1956–1960* (Washington, DC: Historical Office, Secretary of Defense, 1997), p. 510.

69 Norbert Wiggershaus, "Elements of NATO's Nuclear War Scenario 1956," in *1956*, pp. 79–80.

70 Lawrence Wittner, *Resisting the Bomb: A History of the World Nuclear Disarmament Movement* (Stanford University Press, 1997).

71 Which became the basis of MAD (Mutual Assured Destruction) theory, which waxed and waned during the rest of the Cold War.

Decolonization, the Third World, and the Cold War

The Anglo-French debacle in Suez hastened the worldwide process of decolonization. Indeed, the British Commonwealth, a nine-member global body[72] that had been created to bolster British power by turning former colonies into strategic allies, almost collapsed during the crisis. Not only did Eden fail to convene the nine or take their leaders into his confidence, but the group itself was deeply divided. Pakistan, Australia, and New Zealand endorsed British toughness; India opposed the use of force; and Canada played the role of conciliator.[73]

Moreover, there were already cracks in European imperialism. Following World War II the French and British had withdrawn from Syria, Lebanon, Palestine, Iraq, and Jordan. In Asia, the Philippines had gained independence from the United States and India from Britain. After a bloody conflict, the Dutch left Indonesia in 1949 and the French were forced out of Vietnam in 1954. Prior to Suez, the French had granted independence to Morocco and Tunisia, and Britain had left Sudan and was preparing to grant independence to Ghana in 1957.[74]

The striking exceptions were Algeria and Kenya, two strategically important possessions and with a substantial number of European inhabitants. France was determined to crush the revolt in Algeria, which began in 1954 and two years later had spread to the entire country, including its urban areas. The Algerian struggle for independence had also gained international attention, brought before the United Nations by the Soviet bloc and Third World governments and threatening a rift in the NATO alliance. In Kenya Britain was confronted with a four-year-old uprising that it suspected had communist backing; and in 1956 it unleashed an all-out military effort to suppress the guerrilla movement. However, both countries' military campaigns, which were costly and politically divisive, ended with pullouts, the French from Algeria in 1962 and the British from Kenya in 1963.[75]

Another complex colonial site was Indochina, where France had been soundly defeated in the battle of Diên Biên Phu and was preparing to

[72] Britain, Canada, Australia, New Zealand, South Africa, India, Pakistan, Ceylon, and the Federation of Rhodesia and Nyasaland.

[73] See chapters by Sarvepalli Gopal, Peter Lyon, J. D. B. Miller, and Michael G. Fry in *Suez 1956: The Crisis and Its Consequences*, ed. Wm. Roger Louis and Roger Owen (Oxford: Clarendon Press, 1989), pp. 173–188, 257–318.

[74] Henri Grimal, *Decolonization*. Trans. Stephan De Vos (Boulder: Westview Press, 1965), pp. 295–300.

[75] Alistair Horne, *A Savage War of Peace: Algeria, 1954–1962* (New York: Penguin, 1989); Frank Füredi, *The Mau Mau War in Perspective* (London: James Currey, 1989).

withdraw. At the Geneva Conference on Indochina in 1954 Laos and Cambodia became independent.[76] But Vietnam – with Sino-Soviet acquiescence and contrary to the wishes of the nationalist leader Ho Chi Minh – was temporarily partitioned into the (communist) Democratic Republic of Vietnam in the north and a non-communist government in the south. National elections were to be held in July 1956 with the aim of unifying the country.

The elections were never held. On the eve of the Suez crisis South Vietnam's president Ngô Đình Diệm, with his US backer's compliance, refused to participate and proceeded to consolidate his regime. Three years later, when an insurgency erupted in the south (supported by North Vietnam) the Eisenhower administration sent weapons and advisors to prevent the communist domination of all of Vietnam, which ostensibly threatened the rest of Southeast Asia, thus beginning direct US involvement in the region.[77]

In the meantime, much of the Third World was attempting to escape the Cold War.[78] At the 1955 Bandung Conference the delegates had not only endorsed the goal of ending colonialism but also of resisting both US and Soviet domination. Their host, Indonesian president Sukarno, had greeted the representatives of twenty-nine states from Africa and Asia (comprising fifty-six percent of the world's population) with the announcement: "we are united by a common detestation of colonialism, in whatever forms it appears."[79]

The Bandung principles appeared to triumph in 1956. Nasser's self-proclaimed victory – three years after an Anglo-American sponsored coup had toppled Mohammad Mossadegh, who had nationalized Iran's oil industry – was heralded as an achievement of anticolonialism *and* nonalignment. The Egyptian leader had not only seized the foreign-owned Suez Canal and survived the armies of three invaders, but – ignoring the crucial role of the

[76] The Geneva Accords were signed on April 27, 1954, by Cambodia, Laos, and North Vietnam and by China, France, the Soviet Union, and the United Kingdom; the USA took note but refused to sign.

[77] Dwight David Eisenhower, *Mandate for Change: The White House Years, 1953–1956* (Garden City, NY: Doubleday, 1963), p. 337; also Franklin B. Weinstein, *Vietnam's Unheld Elections: The Failure to Carry out the 1956 Reunification Elections and the Effect on Hanoi's Present Outlook* (Ithaca, NY: Cornell University Department of Asian Studies, 1966).

[78] The term "Third World," evoking the claims of the Third Estate in 1789 on the eve of the French Revolution, was first used in 1952 by the radical French economist Alfred Sauvy to characterize the aspirations of the world's less powerful, more populous states to achieve the recognition and respect of the dominant minority.

[79] Quoted in Raymond Betts, *Decolonization*, 2nd edn. (New York and London: Routledge, 2004), p. 43.

superpowers – continued to declare his political independence.[80] The United Nations, with its growing number of African and Asian members in the General Assembly and its activist Secretary-General Dag Hammarskjöld, was also given a temporary boost in its prestige.[81] And Western European public opinion now shifted dramatically against the use of military action to hold on to empire.[82]

Nonetheless the Suez crisis presaged the future character of global decolonization: the long and costly US–Soviet competition to fill the vacuum left by the departing European powers, with each side drawn in by ideological, strategic, and economic interests. The most difficult arena would be in Africa where, by the end of 1960, twenty-five new states had joined the United Nations (representing one-quarter of its membership). The USA, although largely unprepared for the collapse of European power on that continent, was determined to shape the course of decolonization in the world's mineral-rich and strategic regions. Similarly, the Soviet Union had to scramble to win friendly governments in a largely unfamiliar terrain.[83]

The consequences in former colonial regions were devastating. After 1956 the struggle for racial equality, economic justice, cultural liberation, and self-determination were often subordinated to US or Soviet dictates. Moreover the hopes for non-alignment in the Cold War became a major casualty of the post-Suez environment. In 1957 the Tunisian leader Habib Bourguiba dourly pronounced neutralism a "precarious" stance.[84]

Building Europe

Among the most anxious witnesses to the Suez crisis was West German chancellor Konrad Adenauer. The Federal Republic, NATO's newest member, had declared its neutrality in the war against Egypt; but it had been jarred by the Soviets' brutal repression in Hungary and by Moscow's threats to London and Paris as well as by America's cavalier treatment of its principal European allies. Seizing the moment of his arrival in Paris on November 6,

80 Podeh, Elie, "Regaining lost pride: the impact of the Suez Affair on Egypt and the Arab World," in David Tal (ed.), *The 1956 War: Collusion and Rivalry in the Middle East* (London and Portland: Frank Cass, 2001), pp. 209–224.

81 Wm. Roger Louis, "The United Nations and the Suez Crisis," in *Ends of British Imperialism* (London and New York: I. B. Tauris, 2006), pp. 666–688.

82 Hélène Bracco, *Pour avoir dit non: actes de refus dans la guerre d'Algérie, 1954– 1962* (Paris: Paris-Méditerranée, 2003).

83 Odd Arne Westad, *The Global Cold War: Third World Interventions and the Making of Our Times* (Cambridge University Press, 2005), pp. 131–143.

84 Habib Bourguiba, "Nationalism: antidote to Communism," *Foreign Affairs* 35/4 (July 1957), 646–654.

just as the Suez ceasefire was announced, Adenauer was determined to "build Europe."[85]

The project of European unity had a long history, and it had gained force after World War II with the Marshall Plan and the European Coal and Steel Community as well as the abortive European Defense Community. But for more than a year the Benelux project of a "common market" – involving both economic and nuclear cooperation – had languished because of Franco-German hesitations, France over the future role of its empire and Germany caught in an internal debate over chaining itself institutionally and politically to its economically weaker neighbors.[86]

The Suez crisis was clearly the spur that brought Bonn and Paris together in 1956 in an historic gesture of real and symbolic reconciliation. Adenauer argued that Western Europe, wedged uncomfortably between the two nuclear superpowers, needed to form a counterweight to the Soviet threat and American unilateralism. Mollet, also a convinced European, readily agreed to Adenauer's suggestion of avenging the humiliation of Suez. The Treaty of Rome of March 25, 1957, which brought the European Economic Community to life, grew out of a Franco-German bargain, with substantial concessions to France's overseas territories and a major financial commitment by Bonn; but it was also a clear indication of West Germany's increased role in European affairs.[87]

Suez also cast a shadow over Britain's future role in Western Europe. Eden's successor, Harold Macmillan, was happy to shed London's ties with Paris, seek a closer relationship with Washington, and repair Britain's frayed bonds with the Commonwealth. Already a nuclear power, Britain had no need to share secrets and techniques with the continent. Moreover, it still sent 74 percent of its exports outside Europe, primarily to the Commonwealth, thus diminishing the attraction of submitting to the tariff and political and atomic controls of continental bureaucrats.[88]

With Britain outside, the EEC developed, and with Eisenhower's unwavering support. In 1959 the British created a short-lived rival, the European

[85] Christian Pineau and Christiane Rimbaud, *Le grand pari: L'aventure du traité de Rome* (Paris: Fayard, 1991), pp. 222–223.

[86] John Gillingham, *European Integration, 1950–2003* (Cambridge University Press, 2003), pp. 3–33.

[87] Hans-Jürgen Küsters, *Die Gründung der Europäischen Wirtschaftsgemeinschaft* (Baden-Baden: Nomos, 1982), pp. 390–391.

[88] Jeffrey Giauque, *Grand Designs and Visions of Unity: The Atlantic Powers and the Reorganization of Western Europe, 1955–1963* (Chapel Hill and London: University of North Carolina Press, 2002), pp. 15–17.

Free Trade Area. Subsequently, it made two abortive efforts to join the Six. For the next sixteen years Britain's isolation from Western Europe – years of unprecedented EEC prosperity – left the Franco-German duopoly in charge, much to the frustration of the smaller powers which had hoped for more robust supranational institutions.[89]

Conclusions

By the end of 1956 the Cold War had engulfed almost the entire world, pitting the United States and the Soviet Union in a long-term rivalry that outsiders found difficult to escape. But that year there were three books by Nobel-prize authors expressing a more intimate human perspective from the communist, Western, and Third World: Boris Pasternak's *Dr. Zhivago*, which depicted an idealistic physician-poet crushed by the Bolshevik Revolution (and brought severe reprisals to its author from Khrushchev), Albert Camus' *The Fall* describing an individual's search for moral responsibility within the political and material forces that dominated Western society, and Naguib Mahfouz's *Palace Walk*, recounting the erosion of an Egyptian patriarch's stature as his traditional society crumbled under foreign and domestic pressures.

The global Cold War continued for another thirty-three years. The superpowers accelerated their arms race, competed for the allegiance of peoples and governments throughout the world, and engaged in costly proxy wars. But the year 1956 had also set a pattern for the future. The Soviet Union – with Western acquiescence – was able to impose its will on its satellites but unable to prevail over China. The United States replaced Britain and France in the Middle East and thwarted Soviet claims to parity but failed to control the region. The Third World fought for independence and to resist superpower domination. And Western Europe laid the basis for economic if not political unity.

The superpowers tried to reap propaganda rewards from the other's actions in 1956. The United States long trumpeted the repression of Hungary as revealing the true nature of the Soviet regime, and the USSR castigated the Eisenhower doctrine as an expression of US imperialism. Yet despite their rhetoric both sides had exhibited remarkable caution throughout the trials of 1956. Their leaders were prudent men who had experienced two world wars, and their fear of a nuclear catastrophe far outweighed their political adventurism.

89 William I. Hitchcock, *The Struggle for Europe, 1945–2002* (New York: Doubleday, 2003), p. 438; also Paul-Henry Spaak, *Combats inachevés* (Paris: Fayard, 1969).

In the aftermath of 1956 there was thus little alteration in the US–Soviet relations. Europe remained divided by the Iron Curtain and would remain so for more than three decades, and NATO, although weakened in 1956, survived the shocks of Hungary and Suez and continues to this day. But two transformative events did occur that year: the beginning of the Sino-Soviet rivalry that would change the Cold War, and the emergence of the Middle East – a major source of the world's oil and the center of its transportation and communication networks – as a perilous arena of global politics where the local players would (and still) continue to fiercely resist outside domination.

Further reading

Bracco, Hélène. *Pour avoir dit non: actes de refus dans la guerre d'Algérie, 1954–1962*. Paris: Paris-Méditerranée, 2003.

Fink, Carole, Frank Hadler, and Tomasz Schramm, eds. *1956: European and Global Perspectives*. Leipziger Universitätsverlag, 2006.

Füredi, Frank. *The Mau Mau War in Perspective*. London: James Currey, 1989.

Fursenko, Aleksandr and Timothy Naftali. *Khrushchev's Cold War*. New York and London: W.W. Norton, 2006.

Garrett, Stephen A. *From Potsdam to Poland: American Policy toward Eastern Europe*. New York: Praeger, 1986.

Gati, Charles. *Failed Illusions: Moscow, Washington, Budapest, and the 1956 Hungarian Revolt*. Washington, DC: Woodrow Wilson Press/Stanford University Press, 2006.

Giauque, Jeffrey. *Grand Designs and Visions of Unity: The Atlantic Powers and the Reorganization of Western Europe, 1955–1963*. Chapel Hill and London: University of North Carolina Press, 2002.

Golan, Galia. *Soviet Policies in the Middle East*. Cambridge University Press, 1990.

Granville, Johanna. *In the Line of Fire: The Soviet Crackdown on Hungary, 1956–1958*. Pittsburgh: The Carl Beck Papers in Russian & East European Studies, Vol. 1307, 1998.

The First Domino – International Decisionmaking during the Hungarian Crisis of 1956. College Station, TX: Texas A & M University Press, 2004.

Györkei, Jeno and Miklós Horváth, eds. *1956: Soviet Military Intervention in Hungary*. Budapest: Central European University Press, 1999.

Hahn, Peter. *Caught in the Middle East: U.S. Policy Toward the Arab-Israeli Conflict, 1945–1961*. Chapel Hill: University of North Carolina Press, 2004.

Heinemann, Winfried and Norbert Wiggershaus, eds. *Das Internationale Krisenjahr 1956*. Munich: Oldenbourg, 1999.

Horne, Alistair. *A Savage War of Peace: Algeria, 1954–1962*. New York: Penguin, 1989.

Jian, Chen. *Mao's China and the Cold War*. Chapel Hill: University of North Carolina Press, 2001.

Kingseed, Cole C. *Eisenhower and the Suez Crisis of 1956*. Baton Rouge and London: LSU Press, 1995.

Kunz, Diane B. *The Economic Diplomacy of the Suez Crisis*. Chapel Hill: University of North Carolina Press, 1991.

Kyle, Keith. *Suez*. London and New York: I.B. Tauris, 2011.

Litván, György et al., eds. *The Hungarian Revolution of 1956: Reform, Revolt and Repression 1953–1956*. New York: Longmans, 1996.

Louis, William Roger and Roger Owen, eds. *Suez: The Crisis and its Consequences*. Oxford: Clarendon Press, 1991.

Machcewicz, Pawel. *Rebellious Satellite: Poland, 1956*. Trans. Maya Latynski. Washington, DC: Woodrow Wilson Press/Stanford University Press, 2009.

Morris, Benny. *Israel's Border Wars, 1949–1956*. Oxford: Clarendon Press, 1993.

Pineau, Christian. *1956/Suez*. Paris: Lafont, 1976.

Satterwhite, James H. *Varieties of Marxist Humanism: Philosophical Revision in Postwar Eastern Europe*. University of Pittsburgh Press, 1992.

Sayigh, Yazid. *Armed Struggle and the Search for a State: The Palestinian National Movement, 1949–1993*. Oxford: Clarendon Press, 1997.

Tal, David, ed. *The 1956 War: Collusion and Rivalry in the Middle East*. London and Portland: Frank Cass, 2001.

Taubman, William. *Khrushchev: The Man and His Era*. New York and London: Norton, 2003.

Wetting, Gerhard. *Bereitschaft zu Einheit in Freiheit? Die sowjetische Deutschland-Politik 1945–1955*. Munich: Olzog, 1999.

Wittner, Lawrence. *Resisting the Bomb: A History of the World Nuclear Disarmament Movement*. Stanford University Press, 1997.

Yaqub, Salim. *Containing Arab Nationalism: The Eisenhower Doctrine and the Middle East*. Chapel Hill: University of North Carolina Press, 2004.

Zubok, V. M. *A Failed Empire: The Soviet Union in the Cold War from Stalin to Gorbachev*. Chapel Hill: University of North Carolina Press, 2007.

16

1989 as a year of great significance

NICOLE REBEC AND JEFFREY WASSERSTROM

> The fall of communism was as decisive a turning point in modern history as the French or Russian revolutions. In 1989 the Soviet empire in Eastern Europe collapsed; the division of Europe symbolized by the Berlin Wall crumbled . . . and more pluralistic, sometimes democratic, states emerged where one-party dictatorships had dominated . . . hopes were raised, momentarily as it turned out, for a "new world order" without debilitating ideological conflicts.
>
> *Ronald Suny, "Empire falls: the Revolutions of 1989,"* The Nation, *November 16, 2009*

> Twenty years ago . . . a software consultant . . . at the European Organization for Nuclear Research (better known as CERN) hatched a plan for an open computer network to keep track of research at [a laboratory] . . . modestly titled "Information Management: A Proposal" [it] would become the blueprint for the World Wide Web.
>
> *"Remembering the day the World Wide Web was born,"* Scientific American, *March 12, 2009*

> Unsurprisingly, the twentieth anniversary of 1989 has added to an already groaning shelf of books on the year . . . [There are new] retrospective journalistic chronicles . . . spirited essays . . . and original scholarly work . . . Most add something to our knowledge . . . [And yet] I come away dreaming of another book: the global, synthetic history of 1989 that remains to be written.
>
> *Timothy Garton Ash, "1989!"* New York Review of Books, *Nov. 5, 1989*

Before 1989 had even come to a close, it was clear that it would go down in history as a special kind of year, one of significance not just for a country or two, but for the world. Thanks in part to the powerful images that flashed across front pages and television screens, from that of a lone man standing up to tanks in Beijing in June to those of crowds cheering and lending their hands to the dismantling of the Berlin Wall in November, it seemed destined to be the sort of year whose tenth and twentieth anniversaries would be marked. And this is just what happened in 1999 and again in 2009, the year when the works containing all of our opening quotations and many others reflecting on 1989 were written. Both of those anniversaries that have passed inspired backward looking books, special issues of journals, documentaries, and media commentaries in print and also, thanks in part to what was done at CERN in 1989 itself, in online venues.[1] It seemed by the time that 1989 ended that it might even join the very select ranks of years whose centennials and even bicentennials are commemorated.

If it does get commemorated in 2089 and 2189, it will not be the first year that ends with the digits 8 and 9 and is associated with revolution that gets such attention, as that distinction is already claimed by 1789. In 1889, to mark the passage of one hundred years since the French Revolution, a great World's Fair was held in Paris, at which many countries displayed their products and for which Eiffel built his famous tower.[2] In the year that interests us here, that same city hosted a lavish bicentennial parade, which again marked a national anniversary in a decidedly international way. Leaders from around the world came to France; marchers from many lands paraded. One notable thing that reinforced the idea that 1989 might join 1789 as a special sort of revolutionary year was the inclusion in that Paris march of a group of Chinese activists-in-exile who had come to France to seek refuge after the June 4th Massacre, which had put an end to the protest struggle that had brought massive crowds to Beijing's Tiananmen Square and seemed for a time to have the potential to push the Chinese Communist Party to make major political reforms.[3]

1 Most 1989 events discussed here were seen as newsworthy in the year itself, but communications technology is a different story: more was written then about developments in and the continuing spread of satellite television than about the evolution of what would become the World Wide Web. See, for example, "Murdoch gambles on satellite TV," *New York Times*, September 11, 1989, www.nytimes.com/1989/09/11/business/murdoch-gambles-on-satellite-tv.html (last accessed August 21, 2013).

2 Jill Jonnes, *Eiffel's Tower: The Thrilling Story Behind Paris's Beloved Monument and the Extraordinary World's Fair that Introduced It* (New York: Viking, 2009).

3 A first-person account of the parade, by a Chinese participant, can be found in Yan Jiaqi, *Toward a Democratic China: An Intellectual Autobiography of Yan Jiaqi* (Honolulu: University of Hawaii Press, 1992), pp. 158–159. Note that the "June 4th Massacre" rather than "Tiananmen Square Massacre" is used throughout this chapter. We do this for two reasons. First, it is the preferred term among Chinese commentators on the event. Second, few if any deaths on the night of June 3 and early morning of June 4 occurred on that famous plaza, as the main killing fields were nearby streets – a seemingly fine point, but references to "Tiananmen Square Massacre," without evidence of deaths there, allows the Chinese authorities to mistakenly suggest that Western accounts of a

It is still much too early to tell if 1989 will actually inspire important centennial let alone bicentennial rituals, but a quarter-of-a-century on, we can say that there has been no abatement of the strong initial sense that 1989 was an unusually important year. Many other late-twentieth-century years have had their champions ready to assert that they should be considered special and momentous. This is true of 1956, the subject of a chapter in this volume. It is true as well of 1968: a year that, like 1989, saw far-flung protests, including some that challenged Communist Party rule.

As if those two clear rivals were not enough, as we began preparing to write this chapter in mid 2013, we became aware of two far less obvious rivals for the distinction "biggest year in world history since 1945," to borrow a phrase that Timothy Garton Ash has employed to refer to 1989.[4] First, we came across an old newspaper article, published a full twelve months *before* the Berlin Wall fell, which argued that an epochal shift had just taken place. No less an eminence than former Carter White House National Security Advisor Zbigniew Brzezinski suggested that 1988 would "turn out to be as upsetting of the old order of things as was the year 1848." Why? Because it had witnessed a shift from a postwar era dominated by rivalry between the USA and the Soviet Union and start of a "post-postwar" period of new tensions and relationships.[5] In an article introducing and assessing Brzezinski's argument, the *Christian Science Monitor* highlighted several factors, from the rising economic clout of Japan to a China that "had become a factor in everyone's calculations," that had shifted the status quo. It was also no longer possible to take "for granted" in 1988, the article said, foreshadowing events of 1989, "that Moscow would enforce the Brezhnev doctrine (once socialist, always socialist) against any satellite which tried to break away."[6]

horrific bloody crackdown are merely propaganda without a factual basis. An early and still important discussion of the latter fact and why it matters, which also stresses that workers and members of many social groups, as opposed to mainly or exclusively students, were killed by troops is Robin Munro, "Who died in Beijing, and why," *The Nation*, June 11, 1990, 811–822.

4 Timothy Garton Ash, "1989 changed the world. But where now for Europe?" Published in the *Guardian*, November 4, 2009.

5 This was not a completely unprecedented claim in terms of an end to a world oriented around a single Moscow–Washington divide. In the 1970s, spurred by the end of Bretton Woods, the spread of atomic weaponry to more countries, and China's increased independence from the Soviet Union, some people had begun to talk of a move beyond the bipolar structures of the Cold War having taken place.

6 Joseph C. Harsch, "Welcome to the 'post-post-war' era: US-Soviet rivalry no longer dominates, as other states increase roles," *Christian Science Monitor*, October 21, 1988: www.csmonitor.com/1988/1021/opat21.html/(page)/2 (last accessed July 10, 2013).

While still digesting that counter-intuitive assertion of 1988's importance, we learned of a major just-published book that makes a comparable year-that-changed-it-all claim for 1979. Written by Christian Caryl, this revisionist text asserts that the "21st century" began a full decade before the momentous upheavals associated with Beijing's Tiananmen Square, Prague's Charles Square, the first electoral victory of Poland's Solidarity Movement, and the dismantling of the wall separating East and West Berlin. It was in 1979, Caryl notes, that a series of seemingly unrelated events occurred – from Deng Xiaoping's inaugurating reforms in China to Margaret Thatcher's election in the United Kingdom, and from the Pope's trip back to his native Poland, which helped lay the groundwork for Solidarity's eventual rise, to Iran's Islamic Revolution – that between them signaled a resurgence of free market economic strategies and the political power of religious ideas. The world, he says, would never be the same, and it seems clear that his call in raising up the importance of 1979 is in part to question the notion that the events of one decade later were as pivotal as some have imagined, particularly in the sense of curtailing socialist experiments.[7]

None of our reading has undermined our sense that 1989 can be seen as, in many ways, *the* most important single year of the past half-century if one is to choose, but we have realized it is a good deal more complicated now than it was a quarter century ago to pinpoint how exactly its significance should be described and assessed. Should it be seen as having marked the end of the Cold War era or, rather, as the year when the epoch of the World Wide Web began? Was 1989 the year when the "End of History" arrived? Was its defining image China's Tank Man or a shot of sledgehammers knocking down the Wall? Was its key figure Gorbachev (who got *TIME's* "person of the year" nod for 1989), the Dalai Lama (who won the Nobel Peace Prize, in part as a stand-in for the youthful protesters who challenged the Chinese authorities from April to June, but gained fame too late to be nominated), or Vaclav Havel (whose journey from dissident playwright to president of a the Czech Republic is tightly associated with the Velvet Revolution of that year)? Was it a year that should be remembered only for victories achieved by crowds, in Prague and East Berlin, or also for massacres, not only in China but also in Romania?

To get at these kinds of issues, and bring in less well remembered features of 1989 – which was also the year when crowds gathered in Iran to mourn

7 Christian Caryl, *Strange Rebels: 1979 and the Birth of the 21st Century* (New York: Basic Books, 2013).

Ayatollah Khomeini and some wondered if the Iranian system he did so much to create would endure, when Nelson Mandela was released from prison, and when the Exxon Valdez sank – we find it useful to consider three quite different, though sometimes overlapping ways in which any year can stand out from those near to it in the annals of history. Some do so because they can be seen as establishing a *definitive break* between eras; some do so because of their association with a *particular type of event*, such as a variety of social movement; still others do so because they were simply *unusually action-packed*, times when more than the ordinary number of perhaps largely unrelated dramatic things transpired. In the pages that follow, we will use the terms "hinge year," "movement year," and "eventful year" for heuristic purposes to differentiate between these three types of ways that a period of twelve months can stand out.

We will also suggest that in some cases, despite speaking of special "years," we may really be talking about periods quite a bit longer or quite a bit shorter than 365 days. We will thus ask which sort of special year 1989 was, and whether in categorizing it as such, we are perhaps thinking of a "long" or "short" year in the way that historians sometimes speak of a "long" eighteenth century (starting before 1700 and ending after 1800) and a "short" twentieth century (that began in the 1910s and ended with the Soviet Union's implosion). We will also consider, in the end, whether it should be seen, perhaps, as fitting into more than one category. Some years, after all, may be best thought of as hybrids, partly "hinge years" and partly "movement years" or "eventful years," or having aspects of all three sorts of years.

What exactly, then, is a "hinge year"? Our use of the term is inspired by an *Economist* review of Caryl's book on 1979, which refers to the "professional fondness" historians have for identifying "years that act as hinges of history rather than numbers in a sequence." Clear examples from the relatively distant past that came to the mind of the reviewer included, not surprisingly, 1789, as well as, a bit less obviously (except to those closely attuned to European or religious history), "1517 (when Martin Luther nailed his 95 theses on the door)." These are not just famous years, the reviewer noted, but ones whose pivotal acts "resound down the ages," dividing chronology into before and after, years when we can say that "one era ended and another was born."[8] We would add that "hinge years" are often

8 "Turning points in history: when the world changed," *The Economist*, April 13, 2013; accessed on June 18, 2013, at www.economist.com/news/books-and-arts/21576067-why-1979-was-about-so-much-more-margaret-thatchers-election-victory-when-world.

relatively easy to characterize with reference to a single act, a single date, even a single emblematic image. If 2001 deserves to be seen as a "hinge year," it is because of September 11, a single date that divides the time before the so-called "War on Terror" and the time when that undertaking was continually discussed in the English language mass media and used as a pretext for military actions across the globe. A shot of the Twin Towers collapsing works well to conjure up this hinge year's meaning in a single image.

We will devote an entire section below to exploring 1989's claim to membership in this club. For now, we will just offer one quote, from a famous essay written midway through the year itself, that speaks of it dividing time into a clear before and after. By Francis Fukayama and appearing in *The National Interest*'s Summer 1989 issue, the essay suggests to readers that the year in progress might be one that witnessed "not just the end of the Cold War, or the passing of a particular period of postwar history, but the end of history as such: that is, the end point of mankind's ideological evolution and the universalization of Western liberal democracy as the final form of human government." The essay was titled "The End of History?"[9]

Let's turn now to "movement years" – twelve-month periods that stand out because of not a single event or date but certain sorts of action and two or more related but distinctive struggles for change. Classic examples here would be 1848 and 1968, thanks to the importance of European revolutions associated with democratic causes in the first case and more globally distributed youth revolts in the second.[10] Similarly, 2011 could claim that status, due to the "Arab Spring" or "Jasmine" risings taking place in a year

9 These arguments would be expanded into a book in 1992. Despite such countervailing developments as the persistence of Communist Party rule in China and several other countries, Fukuyama did not back down on insisting on 1989's watershed status. Perhaps emboldened by the Berlin Wall's collapse and the Soviet Union's implosion in 1991, he doubled down on the notion of an epochal demise of the main competitor to liberal capitalist ways, titling his book *The End of History and the Last Man* – no question mark after "history" this time. Francis Fukuyama, "The end of history?," *The National Interest* (Summer 1989) and *The End of History and the Last Man* (New York: Free Press, 1992). Note that a similar Cheshire Cat question mark move (here and then gone) was made by Samuel Huntington in his darker ruminations on the period. His initial essay was "The clash of civilizations?" *Foreign Affairs*, Summer 1993, pp. 22–49; his book *The Clash of Civilizations and the Remaking of the World Order* (New York: Simon and Schuster, 1996).

10 Two accessible recent additions to the vast literature on these years are Mike Rapport, *1848: Year of Revolution* (New York: Basic, 2009); and Mark Kurlanksy, *1968: The Year that Rocked the World* (London: Jonathan Cape, 2004).

that also saw significant, if not system-changing, "Occupy Wall Street" demonstrations in the United States and anti-austerity demonstrations in Europe.[11]

Conceptualized in this way, 2011 can be seen, like 1848, as a year when a revolutionary tide moved through a specific region. If US and European events are brought in, though, it could qualify for a "movement year" status closer to that of more globally distributed bursts of unrest. In this sense, 1968 rather than 1848 might be the closer referent for this latest "Year of the Protester" (a term *Time* magazine employed in its annual "person of the year" decision, which especially of late has sometimes been awarded to objects, groups, and so on rather than the traditional individual).[12]

What exactly is the basis for thinking of 1989 as an important earlier "Year of the Protester"? If it qualified it did so due to struggles that were more geographically disparate than those of 1848 and yet more similar, at least in choice of target, than those of 1968. If 1989 was a "movement year," it was one characterized by upheavals in Communist Party-run states. This is what Ban Ki-Moon, the United Nations Secretary General, had in mind when making a comment about 2011 quoted in a UN report issued that spring: "The world is facing an important shift in global history, which is 'no less transformative' than the 'epochal' year of 1989, when numerous governments fell."[13]

What then of the third way that a year can stand out – as a time when a surprisingly large number of important though perhaps unrelated things took place in different parts of the world? The year 1956 might be seen as such an "eventful year," as arguably the most important developments it witnessed, the Suez Crisis and the Hungarian Uprising, were only loosely linked to one another. The eventfulness of 1989 is suggested by a 20 years on *TIME* magazine piece, "Shifting on its pivot," written by the magazine's then-editor Michael Elliott. It carried the following subheading: "From the Berlin Wall to the Web, from Tiananmen Square to a moment in South Africa, from an oil spill to a banned book – how a year of both hope and despair transformed our planet forever." And it began with Elliott reminding

11 For basic background on these events, see James Gelvin, *The Arab Uprisings: What Everyone Needs to Know* (Oxford University Press, 2012).

12 For some reflections on this designation, see Jeffrey Wasserstrom "Was 2011 really the year of the protester?" *History News Network*, January 2, 2012, http://hnn.us/articles/was-2011-really-year-protester (last accessed June 18, 2013).

13 "World faces 'epochal' change equivalent to that of 1989, UN Chief says," www.un.org/apps/news/story.asp?NewsID=37921&Cr=North±Africa&Cr1#.UcCwJOuApjh last accessed June 18, 2013; UN News Center, March 28, 2012.

readers of just how "spoiled for choice" news editors were on a singularly eventful weekend that came midway through that eventful year. In early June, they had to decide whether to lead their global coverage with reflections on Solidarity's electoral victory in Poland, the violent crackdown on protesters in Beijing, or the death of the emblematic figure of Iran's Revolution.[14]

Having laid the groundwork, let us dive in more deeply to considering each kind of special year 1989 may be said to have been, focusing especially on the "hinge year" and "movement year" categories, which seem the most compelling. In closing, we will suggest that the most useful way to approach 1989 in world-historical terms is not to choose definitively between viewing it as a Hinge Year, a Movement Year, or an Eventful Year, but rather to keep in mind the way that it was all of those things.

The hinge year

If 1989 divides the world into a time before and a time after, then it does so because it saw the end of Communist Party rule in Eastern and Central Europe. Thinking about 1989 in these terms is easily the tidiest way of approaching it. There is both an unusually close symmetry here between key developments and the passing of a period of exactly twelve months. Yes, the Soviet Union's implosion in 1991 means that one can make a case for a "Long 1989" here that took two more years to conclude, and, yes, it is possible to see the roots of the unraveling of Eastern and Central European communism going back to the early 1980s, with the initial rise of Solidarity. Still, as we will show below, events of January and December 1989 stand out as good starting and ending points for this story. There is also a sense in which this vision of 1989 picks up right where a preceding clearly dramatic year, 1968, left off – and carries forward to success some of the events that ended in tragedy then.

The easiest way to tell the tale of 1989 as a sequel to 1968 that played out over twelve months is to zero in on Prague. Some of the most gripping images of 1968 – including a famous-for-a-time but largely forgotten by 1989 shot of an unarmed man confronting a tank, which eerily presages the more enduringly famous Beijing Tank Man image to come – were photographs of protests in that city, which were eventually suppressed by Soviet forces.

14 Michael Elliott, "Shifting on its pivot," *TIME*, June 18, 2009, available online at www.time.com/time/specials/packages/article/0,28804,1902809_1902810_1905185,00.html (last accessed August 21, 2013).

The events of Prague Spring, as the 1968 protests were called, were on the minds of many Czech activists early in 1989. Some of the first important European protests of 1989, in fact, were framed as twenty-years on commemorations of the death of a Prague Spring activist, Jan Palach, who had committed suicide by self-immolation in January of 1969. Palach had performed this sacrificial act to express his frustration and anger at the 1968 struggle's failure, but by December of 1989, participants in events marking the 20th anniversary of his death were in a celebratory rather than depressed state. For while the first month of 1989 found Prague protesters invoking memories of death and failure, the last month of the year found them gathering to hail the installment of a new post-Communist government at the end of their country's Velvet Revolution.

It was not only in Prague nor only at the start and the end of the year that we see evidence to support the idea of 1989 as a crucial hinge year. Across the Soviet bloc, long-time dissidents and newly politicized youth, began to take dramatic actions and confer with and borrow tactics and slogans from one another. Some key players, such as Adam Michnik, the Polish journalist, and Miklos Haraszti, the Hungarian critic of censorship, were veterans of 1968, had been influenced by one another's writings, and had moved over the preceding decades, spent partly in prison, from thinking in terms of reforming to dismantling the status quo. They were joined by actors with very different backgrounds and motivations, including some galvanized as much by the thought of restoring control of a particular country to the people within it and freeing it from outside Soviet control as pursuing human rights, and some youth who were inspired in part simply by a desire to be part of global youth culture.

Coalitions spanning generations and linking people of varied ideological stances took shape during the opening months of the year. Sometimes, these built on old ties to traditional entities like the Catholic Church. Sometimes on linkages established through explicitly dissident networks. And sometimes they evolved out of networks created in the preceding years via new sorts of civil society organizations, such as an environmental group formed to protect the Danube River that brought together like-minded people in different nations through which that waterway flowed.[15]

15 An excellent place to go for information on this group and others like it is a George Mason University online archive, which contains primary sources and other materials, called "Making the history of 1989: the Fall of Communism in Eastern Europe"; general link http://chnm.gmu.edu/1989/ and for "The campaign to save the Danube river" http://chnm.gmu.edu/1989/items/show/315 (both last accessed August 30, 2013).

Figure 16.1 Berliners from East and West celebrating the opening of the border at the Berlin Wall, Brandenburg Gate, Berlin, 9th November 1989 / © H.P. Stiebing / Bridgeman Images

Crucial developments occurred in each month of the year in an array of Soviet bloc countries. Here are some highlights that take us through the year, with a stop in nearly every month: on February 6, in Warsaw, round table discussions began that reached a conclusion on April 4 with the legalizing of Solidarity; while those discussions were underway in Poland, massive protests on March 15 in Hungary persuaded the government in that country to begin their own round table talks with non-communist organizations; on May 2, in a precursor to the dismantling of the Berlin Wall, the Hungarian government began to take down a 150-mile barrier separating Hungary from Austria; on June 4, as noted above, Solidarity won Polish elections; on July 6, Gorbachev gave a speech signaling his unwillingness to use force against protesters in countries within the Soviet orbit; on August 24 Poland's first postwar non-communist Premier took office; in September a wave of protests in East German cities began; in October, there were massive protests in East German cities; then, in November, which is often seen as standing out as the great hinge month of this hinge year, the Berlin Wall came down.[16]

16 For a useful survey of these and other events, as covered by *New York Times* correspondents, see Bernard Gwertzman and Michael T. Kaufman, eds., *The Collapse of Communism* (New York: Times Books, 1990); for a lively overview, see Padraic Kenney, *A Carnival of Revolution: Central Europe 1989* (Princeton University Press, 2003).

As important as November events were, if there was a hinge moment within this hinge year, it may have come earlier than that, in the second week of October, when hardliners lost out to more conciliatory factions within the East German leadership, in part because Gorbachev had signaled that Moscow would not reprise the role in helping crack down on protests it had played in 1968. On October 9, the *New York Times* reported as follows:

> Protesters clashed with the police and security forces today in cities throughout East Germany as the Communist Government's efforts to celebrate its 40th anniversary ignited rallies and demonstrations . . . Spurred on in part by the presence of the Soviet President, Mikhail S. Gorbachev, who came for the celebrations, protesters took to the streets late Saturday and again today, often mingling their calls for greater freedom with chants of "Gorby! Gorby!" . . . In East Berlin, Dresden, Leipzig and elsewhere, the police beat back defiant protesters, swinging riot sticks and menacing them with water cannon.[17]

The very next day, though, the same newspaper reported that

> Tens of thousands of East Germans marched peacefully through Leipzig this evening in the largest of a wave of demonstrations for change that has swept East Germany in recent days . . . [and] in contrast to a weekend of violence and arrests, no clashes were reported, although the police presence in Leipzig and East Berlin was strong . . . [There was] a new willingness by the local authorities to consider the demands of the protesters.[18]

The following summary on George Mason's "Making the history of 1989" website sums up the shift well here:

> Some party leaders were calling for a 'Chinese Solution' to stop the growing demonstrations, a reference to the Chinese government's use of military force against pro-democracy demonstrators . . . local authorities prepared for mass arrests and even the use of deadly force – 3,000 riot police, 500 additional militia members, and 3,000 regular army soldiers were issued live ammunition and placed on alert at the outskirts of town. Faced with strong international pressure for moderation, the German authorities instead allowed the demonstration to proceed without incident. The crowds marching through Leipzig chanted "*Wir sind das Volk*" or "We are the people" . . .[19]

17 www.nytimes.com/1989/10/09/world/security-forces-storm-protesters-in-east-germany.html (last accessed August 31, 2013).

18 www.nytimes.com/1989/10/10/world/east-germans-let-largest-protest-proceed-in-peace.html (last accessed August 31, 2013).

19 http://chnm.gmu.edu/1989/exhibits/intro/gdr

By October 18, the hardliner Eric Honecker, whom Gorbachev had warned needed to adjust to the times, was out of power, replaced by the more reform-minded Egon Krenz.[20]

The movement year

The best way to begin thinking of 1989 as a movement year rather than a hinge one is to consider a dog that did not bark in the night – the Chinese Communist Party, though challenged by massive protests that brought roughly a million people to the streets of Beijing and tens or hundreds of thousands to central squares in various other cities, did not fall. It did not experience the same fate as its counterparts in Central and Eastern Europe, many of which were forced to negotiate with competing organizations in late 1988 or early 1989 and in most cases to cede power completely by the end of the latter year. Nor did it go into the spiral that year that the Soviet Union did, soon losing control of territories once under its influence. Had Beijing seen a change of government in 1989 – or even 1991 – the hinge year vision would have been complete, or at least nearly so, as there might still have been Cuba, Vietnam, and North Korea left as Communist states. And it did seem, for a time, as enormous and colorful gatherings at Tiananmen Square, the most spiritually charged political locale in the PRC, captivated the attention of audiences around the country and around the world, that the Chinese Communist Party would have to tilt in a political reformist direction, if not share power. Yet, in the end, hard-liners within the government prevailed and the most enduring Chinese image from 1989 became not the victory of protesters but a lone man standing before a line of tanks on June 5, the day after the June 4th Massacre in central Beijing, an event that saw hundreds of workers, passersby, and other urbanites as well as students slain on the streets of the capital.

In the immediate wake of the June 4th Massacre, and especially after the Berlin Wall fell a few months later, the fact that the Chinese Communist Party was still in power seemed to many an anomaly. Surely, some argued, this organization would soon follow suit and become part of what one leading political scientist would term "The Leninist Extinction," a phrase

20 One *New York Times* report dates the shift precisely to moves from October 7, when Hoeneker calling for troops to prepare to employ a "Chinese solution" to halt protests, to October 9, when Krenz "flew to Leipzig . . . and canceled Mr. Honecker's order." www.nytimes.com/1989/11/19/world/wall-was-cracked-special-report-party-coup-turned-east-german-tide-clamor-east.html?pagewanted=all&src=pm (last accessed August 31, 2013).

that took on particular force when the Soviet Union imploded in 1991.[21] Many observers took for granted that the struggles in China belonged to the same genre as those in Central and Eastern Europe, that Beijing leaders faced the same sort of threat to their legitimacy that those in cities such as Warsaw and Budapest had, and that they had merely gotten a temporary reprieve when state violence cleared the crowds from the streets. Encouraging this sense of parallels was that, during 1989, references to events in the Soviet Union and Eastern and Central Europe showed up in Chinese protests (e.g., a Beijing protest banner lamented that heaven had "given Russia a Gorbachev," but had only given China "a Deng Xiaoping"), and that well after the fact leaders in Beijing were speaking of the need to keep their country free of the "Polish disease" (a term for organizations such as Solidarity). As already noted, developments in the PRC were seen as relevant by actors in settings such as East Berlin, where some leaders used the term "Chinese solution" to refer to the possibility of using repressive tactics like those deployed in Beijing, while some demonstrators claimed to take courage from the example of the brave Chinese man who stood up to a line of tanks.[22] Further reinforcing this sense of connectedness were reports of how intensely Beijing's leaders were monitoring events in settings such as Romania and also the Soviet Union, in order to try to ensure that what had already happened in the former country and seemed on the verge of happening in the latter, did not occur in China.[23]

Over time, however, this view of China's 1989 as directly parallel to the Eastern and Central European one has become less and less tenable. Twenty-five years on, the differences between the Chinese and Central and Eastern European protests of that year loom as large to us as their similarities. There are even some ways – including the extent to which some Chinese

21 Ken Jowitt, "The Leninist extinction," in Daniel Chirot (ed.), *The Crisis of Communism and the Decline of the Left: The Revolutions of 1989* (Seattle: University of Washington Press, 1991), pp. 74–99.

22 Examples of Chinese banners and manifestos from 1989 that refer to European events and Soviet figures can be found in Han Minzhu, ed., *Cries for Democracy* (Princeton University Press, 1990); on flows in the other direction, see Diana Fong, "China's Pro-Democracy Protests Struck Hope and Fear in East Germany," www.dw.de/chinas-pro-democracy-protests-struck-hope-and-fear-in-east-germany/a-4298731-1 (last accessed July 11, 2013).

23 "Upheaval in the East: China: worried Chinese leadership says Gorbachev subverts Communism," a Reuters report run in the *New York Times*, December 28, 1989, available at www.nytimes.com/1989/12/28/world/upheaval-east-china-worried-chinese-leadership-says-gorbachev-subverts-communism.html (last accessed September 3, 2013); a good general analysis of Chinese concern over Romanian as well as Soviet events is provided in James Miles, *The Legacy of Tiananmen: China in a Disarray* (Ann Arbor: University of Michigan Press, 1997).

then placed their hopes for change in a revitalized as opposed to overturned Communist Party – in which Beijing's 1989 had more in common at times with Prague's 1968 than its Velvet Revolution.[24] Recognizing these differences, while diminishing somewhat the hold of a "hinge year" view of 1989, is not a problem for a "movement year" interpretation of it. For, after all, in the case of other "movement years," it is taken for granted that protests in different parts of the world may be both interconnected in some ways and quite dissimilar in others.

The story of China's 1989 as being of a piece with that of Eastern and Central Europe is well known, so we will focus here on offering a brief account of Chinese events that highlights contrasts. In contrast to Czech protesters who first took to the streets in 1989 to commemorate the death of a man who had self-immolated himself to express despair at Communist Party rule, Chinese youth first rallied in 1989 to express sorrow at the recent death of Hu Yaobang, who had been demoted from a high position in the official structure to a low one because of his gentle handling of student demonstrations two years earlier. Hu had come to represent hopes for the reform of the Communist Party, and throughout the Chinese struggle, many saw their goal, as was not true in most Central and Eastern European settings, as that of getting the Party and the revolution back on track, not completely jettisoning current arrangements. Though some called for systemic change, much of the focus in early wall posters and banners was on the damage to the country being done by corruption and nepotism.

A key contrast between the Chinese protests and those in other Communist Party-run countries in 1989 has to do with patriotism. Love of country was crucial in China as it was in nearly all other settings, as shown, for example, by the popularity of the anthem "Children of the Dragon" by Hou Dejian, a song infused with national pride that was part of an eclectic movement soundtrack that also included "The Internationale," the Chinese national anthem, rock songs, such as Cui Jian's "Nothing to My Name," and a reworked version of "Frere Jacques" (that included criticism of Deng Xiaoping).[25] Patriotism manifested itself quite differently in Eastern and Central Europe, where the Communist Party was seen as having been

24 For more on this notion, see Jeffrey Wasserstrom, "Chinese bridges to post-Socialist Europe," in Sorin Antohi and Vladimir Tismaneanu (eds.), *Between Past and Future: The Revolutions of 1989 and Their Aftermath* (Budapest: CEU Press, 2000), pp. 357–382.

25 On the role of songs such as these, the theme of patriotism, and the protests as a whole, see Han, *Cries for Democracy*; Craig Calhoun, *Neither Gods Nor Emperors: Students and the Struggle for Democracy in China* (Berkeley, CA: University of California, 1997); Elizabeth J. Perry and Jeffrey N. Wasserstrom, eds., *Popular Protest and Political Culture in Modern China*, 2nd edn. (Boulder, CO: Westview Press, 1994); Geremie Barmé and Linda Jaivin, eds., *New Ghosts, Old Dreams: Chinese Rebel Voices* (New York: Crown, 1992); the award-

imposed on the populace from outside, as opposed to China, where this was not the case. In places other than China, the tension between rulers and ruled often expressed itself in contestation over which symbols from the past should be valued, whereas Chinese protesters often framed their struggle as questioning the government's claim to represent national symbols both sides celebrated.[26]

This side of China's 1989 became clearest on May 4th, the anniversary of a great 1919 patriotic upsurge, which is hallowed by the Chinese Communist Party as a struggle, led by students who were joined on the streets by workers and members of other classes, that helped pave the way for the Party's eventual rise to power. The anniversary of that movement, in which many future leaders of the Communist Party took part and in which the main themes included anger at imperialism, disgust with authoritarian rule at home, and a desire to see China become a strong, modern, and open state, is often celebrated with great fanfare, especially when, as in 1989, a round number commemorative year is involved. On the 1989 anniversary, there was not just one commemoration but two battling ones in central Beijing, with officials presenting themselves, per usual, as leading the Party that had realized the dreams of May 4th activists, while student leaders insisted in a separate and larger event that in fighting for change, it was they who deserved to be seen as carrying forward the May 4th spirit. One of the most stirring manifestoes of China's 1989 was the "New May Fourth Movement" one issued on that day.

The eventful year

As attractive as it is to see 1989 as a hinge year or as a movement year, there is also a fair case to be made for viewing it simply as a year that had more than its share of disparate major events. Looked at this way, we are encouraged to frame its importance not solely in terms of a single anti-Communist storyline, or even in terms of a pair of different sorts of struggles against

winning Long Bow film "The Gate of Heavenly Peace" and the materials gathered at the associated website, www.tsquare.tv (last accessed July 11, 2013).

26 It is also worth noting, regarding patriotism, that the three other main countries in which Communist Party governments have stayed in power – Cuba, Vietnam, and North Korea – are also ones in which this organization has historic links to struggles against imperialism and foreign bullying.

authoritarian rule, with the Chinese one standing apart from the others, but rather as a time of separate and not necessarily connected or connectable developments. The "end" of communism and varied challenges to different sorts of Communist rule approaches, though valuable, simply fail to account for some important events that, in retrospect especially, stand out as having made 1989 extraordinary. Pushing this idea even further, the case could be made that the sheer variety of major events that year challenge the depiction of 1989 through the lens of *any* coherent narrative. Here, to begin this section on eventfulness, is an example of two 1989 occurrences that can be interpreted as related, though not via a through line associated with the Cold War or with movements, or completely unrelated depending on how one approaches them.

The first event we have in mind involves the tanker the *Exxon Valdez*. It left a literal mark on the Prince William Sound and a symbolic mark on the ecological conscience of Earth's inhabitants in March of 1989 after running aground and spilling approximately 10 million gallons of crude oil on the pristine coastline of Alaska. A report produced by the National Response Team in May of 1989 noted that "The lack of necessary preparedness for oil spills in Prince William Sound and the inadequate response actions that resulted mandate improvements in the way the nation plans for and reacts to oil spills of national significance."[27] The *Exxon Valdez* incident was not the first ecological disaster to make headlines, but it did so in an unusually dramatic way, and it remained for more than two decades the biggest oil spill in U.S. history, leaving an indelible mark on America's memory. The second event took place two months prior to the *Exxon Valdez* incident, on January 2, 1989: *Time Magazine* paid homage to the "Planet of the Year: endangered Earth." This was the second time – the first had come when it chose the computer in 1982 – when *Time* broke with its "Man of the Year" tradition to make a choice that was not an individual, a pair of individuals, or a group of people. Addressing human-driven ecological catastrophes like global warming, overpopulation, and looming threats to biodiversity, one article asked in its title, "What on EARTH are we doing?"[28]

27 Samuel K. Skinner Secretary and William K. Reilly, "The EXXON VALDEZ Oil Spill: A Report to the President." Environmental Protection Agency May 1989 Prepared by The National Response Team. http://docs.lib.noaa.gov/noaa_documents/NOAA_related_docs/oil_spills/ExxonValdez_NRT_1989_report_to_president.pdf (last accessed May 10th, 2013).

28 Thomas A. Sancton "Planet of the Year: what on EARTH are we doing?" Published in *Time*, January 2, 1989: www.time.com/time/magazine/article/0,9171,956627,00.html (last accessed July 17, 2013). For the cover of *Time*'s "Endangered Earth" issue from January 2,

The fact of *Time*'s 1989 selection of a "Planet of the Year" and the *Exxon Valdez* oil spill two months later evinces the complexity of how we think about a given year. *Time*'s plea for people to take a more critical look at the twentieth-century environmental impact of human civilization was published just weeks before an ecological disaster that came to symbolize the consequences of modern living. Stories about the initial devastation (and later issues of accountability and remediation) made headlines around the world; the 1989 *Exxon Valdez* spill was a major event that mattered – not because it could be worked into some sort of overarching narrative about political change but *simply because it happened.*[29]

The year 1989 could, in this sense, be a seen as a year not of coherent moves in one direction but disparate colliding impulses. It saw the Dalai Lama win the Nobel Peace Prize after Tibet had been rocked by protests the previous March, yet also was the year Khomeini not only died mid-year but months before that issued his infamous fatwa against Salman Rushdie. It was a year envisioned by some as ushering in a new era of global cooperation and peaceful cohabitation, yet many random acts of violence made headlines in that year, as in one preceding and following it. One of the most important, though hardly a singular event, was the "Stockton Massacre," a school shooting of a sort we have grown more used to since then, which resulted in the death of five children in a "random spray of gunfire," a tragic event that contributed to US President George H. W. Bush's March 1989 executive order banning the importation of semiautomatic assault weapons.[30]

Yet another key development in 1989 was the dramatic loosening if not yet complete undoing of Apartheid's grip on South Africa.[31] The year marked the beginning of the end of official, decades-old segregation policies in the country. And though Nelson Mandela would not gain his freedom until the following year and would not come to power until 1994, 1989 saw him move toward a position of centrality, as major international publications,

1989 see: www.time.com/time/covers/0,16641,19890102,00.html (last accessed July 17, 2013).

29 Ironically, while the *Exxon Valdez* had more truly global implications than most other 1989 events, commemoration of its anniversaries have largely focused on its local dimensions; see, for example, "10th anniversary of the 'Exxon Valdez' oil spill," Capital Words website http://capitolwords.org/date/1999/03/24/S3159-4_10th-anniversary-of-the-exxon-valdez-oil-spill/ (last accessed July 16, 2013).

30 Dan Morain and Stephen Braun, "The Stockton school yard massacre somber students and teachers wrestle with the horror." Published in *The Los Angeles Times*, January 19, 1989. http://articles.latimes.com/1989-01-19/news/mn-1498_1_school-custodians (last accessed May 16, 2013).

31 For an introduction to major issues and debates on Apartheid in South Africa, see Nigel Worden, *The Making of Modern South Africa: Conquest, Apartheid, Democracy* (Malden, MA: Blackwell Publishing, 2011).

such as the *New York Times* in one of its editorials, began to present him "as a legitimate leader with whom South Africans must reckon."[32]

The 1989 also saw a series of disparate political convulsions in another part of the Global South: Latin America. In Central America, under the name "Operation Just Cause," the United States invaded Panama, overthrowing General Manuel Antonio Noriega. In Nicaragua, a decade of Cold War infighting between American-backed "Contra" rebels and the Soviet-supported Sandinista government came to an end. That same year, Paraguay's Alfredo Stroessner was overthrown along with his fellow, more well-known dictator in Chile: General Augosto Pinochet. While free elections were held in Chile for the first time in nearly two decades, Brazil was holding its third free election since the end of military dictatorship. With the fall of Stroessner, Pinochet, and Noriega, 1989, for all intents and purposes, marked a watershed moment in the dissolution of Latin America's lengthy history of dictatorship.[33]

Despite major political transformations in Latin America, fear of brewing economic crises in the region dominated policy discussions: "the debt crisis gripping Latin America could lead to a political crisis and a return to authoritarian rule on the continent."[34] In 1989, economist John Williamson coined the term "Washington Consensus" to encompass requirements that highly indebted developing countries had to meet in order to continue receiving financing from global financial institutions like the International Monetary Fund (IMF) and the World Bank (WB).[35] While the Washington Consensus compelled developing countries to engage in neoliberal economic restructuring, the directives, which were blamed for intensifying economic inequality, led to outbreaks of popular discontent throughout the region – in 1989 as well as the years shortly before and after.[36] For instance, Venezuela,

32 "Just Free Nelson Mandela." Published in *The New York Times*, July 11, 1989: www.nytimes.com/1989/07/11/opinion/just-free-nelson-mandela.html (last accessed June 16, 2013).

33 For context as well as events, see Peter H. Smith, *Democracy in Latin America: Political Change in Comparative Perspective* (Oxford University Press, 2011).

34 Elaine Sciolino, "Latin debt crisis seen as threat to continent's new democracies," *New York Times*, January 17, 1989: www.nytimes.com/1989/01/17/world/latin-debt-crisis-seen-as-threat-to-continent-s-new-democracies.html (last accessed May 10, 2013).

35 On the Washington Consensus, see Joseph E. Stiglitz and Narcís Serra, eds., *The Washington Consensus Reconsidered: Towards a New Global Governance* (Oxford University Press, 2008); and John Williamson's *A Short History of the Washington Consensus* (2004): www.iie.com/publications/papers/williamson0904-2.pdf (last accessed July 16, 2013).

36 For an overview of Latin America in 1989, see Silvia Ferhmann, "Powerlessness and revolt in Latin America." Published online by the Goethe Institute at www.goethe.de/ges/pok/dos/dos/mau/ges/en4721599.htm as part of "1989/2009: the fall of the wall – new perspectives on 1989," July 2009 (last accessed May 10, 2013).

once heralded as a poster-child of liberal democracy in Latin America during the 1980s, was the site of popular revolt against President elect Carlon Andrés Pérez Rodríguez in 1989 in response to neoliberal reforms and government imposed austerity programs under his direction. In one of "Latin America's most stable democracies" in February of 1989, waves of violent protests and riots gripped the capital city of Caracas, resulting in "an estimated 300 people dead, 2,000 injured and another 2,000 in jail."[37]

While in many parts of the world people actively ushered in a new era of democratic and neoliberal economic reform measures, massive pushbacks against similar measures in countries like Venezuela complicate one of the more dominant memories of 1989 as a year of successful, nonviolent people power. And if events around the globe favor the story of 1989 as a hinge year or a movement year with narratively and thematically neat parameters, transformative events like those recounted above ask us to consider in what ways 1989 was a significant year simply because it was so filled with consequential events.

It is, of course, impossible to list every occurrence of 1989 – let alone to adequately gauge the different registers of importance on, say, a global versus a national scale. The sheer variety of events in 1989 makes the year unusually kaleidoscopic and hard to evaluate substantively. As the final year of a decade increasingly dominated by satellite television and global broadcasting, audiences around the world were unarguably privy to unparalleled coverage of major events in 1989. Perhaps 1989 continues to reverberate in memory simply because of the confluence of advancements in media during a year of major happenings without recent precedent. The proliferation of technologies to project events and news to people around the world in 1989 lends the year much significance in its own right; the level of unprecedented massive visibility served as both a medium for and a sign of an increasingly interconnected world accounts, at least in part, to the designation of 1989 as a year of events, however disparate or only tangentially connected they may be. If 1989 was a long and busy year, perhaps it is because we watched so much of it unfold live in our living rooms.

Thinking through 1989

In the end, it may be best to refuse to choose one of the three approaches to 1989 outlined above and treat it as a hybrid year. There were too many

37 Lisa Beyer, "Venezuela crackdown in Caracas," published in *Time*, March 13, 1989, www.time.com/time/magazine/article/0,9171,957236,00.html (last accessed May 10, 2013)

distinct yet iconic events to be squeezed into a single grand narrative, but this does not mean there were no recurring themes. Two that seem particularly salient to us are mobilization and spectatorship. From changes in Poland and Prague to shifts in South Africa and Venezuela, 1989 saw an uptick in popular political engagement through the mobilization of masses. These far-flung crowd-driven movements were shaped by geographical specificity – unfolding in different ways, responding to different social crises/concerns, demanding different outcomes, and achieving different levels of success. Sometimes, they even pushed in different directions: popular protest in Eastern Europe pushing through reforms toward market economics, while in many Latin American countries popular protest railed against neoliberal reforms that, on the surface, promised democracy, freedom, and rising standards of living. Still, when taken together, they suggest 1989 saw an overall uptick in popular resistance, much of which gained strength from playing out on screens around the world that made it easy for protesters in one place to know what their counterparts far away were doing in real time, something that has been important again in more recent years of the protester such as 2011, albeit with the Web joining satellite television broadcasts in this dissemination of images process.

Images of 1968's crowd actions saturated the media in a way that felt novel at the time, giving rise to phrases such as "The Revolution will be Televised" and "The Whole World is Watching," but this was taken to a new level in 1989, thanks to the rising importance of satellite television. It was not just that on a single day, June 4, Solidarity won a major election in Poland and troops massacred civilians in Beijing, but that images of these events so closely associated with crowd actions could circle the globe simultaneously, and within days compete for the attention of viewers with shots of the masses that turned out to mourn Khomeini, who had died on that most eventful day of an eventful year. One could argue that the image of the lone man staring down tanks in Beijing attained iconicity in memories of 1989 as an invocation of solitary protest made more powerful when juxtaposed to the ubiquitous television coverage of massive demonstrations of vocal discontent. And this is one way that the Exxon Valdez, which did not involve crowds, fits in, as while not the first ecological disaster to cause great damage and inspire deep concern, it was one of the first (though not the first) to get the kind of intense widespread attention that the new media technologies and new media landscape could provide – even if that one in turn did not have the intensity of the Internet-driven ones of the current moment.

Coming to terms with 1989 is more difficult than with many other big years of the past, due to its proximity to today's world, the degree to which the processes set in motion by it continue to play out. As such, there is an ongoing tension between events of immediately agreed upon import like the fall of the Berlin Wall and the early development of the Internet which, only in retrospect, become understood as critical historical turning points. Discussions of 1989's significance occurred simultaneously with the year's unfolding; more than a quarter century later the conversation continues. However one chooses to remember 1989, be it as a hinge year of before and after, a year of sequential markers fitting a mass movement narrative, or a year laying claim to a slew of major events, 1989 was a year that transformed our world, via struggles whose importance was clear at the time and phenomena from the dawn of digital media to increased awareness of climate change and other threats to the survival of our species and our planet whose significance would loom much larger by the time its tenth, twentieth, and twenty-fifth anniversaries were marked.

Further reading

Ash, Timothy Garton. "1989!" *New York Review of Books*, November 5, 2009.

Axworthy, Michael. *Revolutionary Iran: A History of the Islamic Republic*. Oxford University Press, 2013.

Barmé, Geremie and Linda Jaivin, eds. *New Ghosts, Old Dreams: Chinese Rebel Voices*. New York: Crown, 1992.

Calhoun, Craig. *Neither Gods Nor Emperors: Students and the Struggle for Democracy in China* Berkeley, CA: University of California Press, 1997.

Caryl, Christian. *Strange Rebels: 1979 and the Birth of the 21st Century*. New York: Basic Books, 2013.

Chirot, Daniel, ed. *The Crisis of Communism and the Decline of the Left: The Revolutions of 1989*. Seattle: University of Washington Press, 1991.

Day, Angela. *Red Light to Starboard: Recalling the Exxon Valdez Oil Disaster*. Pullman, WA: Washington State University Press, 2014.

Elliot, Michael, ed. *TIME 1989: The Year that Defines Today's World*. New York: Time Books, 2009.

Gwertzman, Bernard and Michael T. Kaufman, eds. *The Collapse of Communism*. New York: Times Books, 1990.

Han, Minzhu, ed. *Cries for Democracy*. Princeton University Press, 1990.

Hinton, Carma and Richard Gordon, directors. *The Gate of Heavenly Peace* (film). Long Bow Group, 1995.

Kenney, Padraic. *A Carnival of Revolution: Central Europe 1989*. Princeton University Press, 2003.

Lim, Louisa. *The People's Republic of Amnesia: Tiananmen Revisited*. Oxford University Press, 2014.

Michnik, Adam. *Letters From Freedom: Post-Cold War Realities and Perspectives*. Berkeley, CA: University of California Press, 1998.

Perry, Elizabeth J. and Jeffrey N. Wasserstrom, eds. *Popular Protest and Poltiical Culture in Modern China*. 2nd edn. Boulder, CO: Westview Press, 1994.

Picou, J. Steven, Duane A. Gill, and Maurie J. Cohen, eds. *The Exxon Valdez Oil Spill: Readings on a Modern Social Problem*. Dubuque, IA: Kendall Hunt Publishing Co., 2008.

Rushdie, Salman. *Joseph Anton: A Novel*. New York: Random House, 2012.

Smith, Peter H. *Democracy in Latin America: Political Change in Comparative Perspective*. Oxford University Press, 2011.

Suny, Ronald. *The Soviet Experiment: Russia, The U.S.S.R. and the Successor States*. 2nd edn. Oxford University Press, 2010.

Tismaneanu, Vladimir and Sorin Antohi, eds. *Between Past and Future: The Revolutions of 1989 and Their Aftermath*. Budapest: Central European University, 2000.

Worden, Nigel. *The Making of Modern South Africa: Conquest, Apartheid, Democracy*. Malden, MA: Blackwell Publishing, 2011.

Wiener, Jon. *How We Forgot the Cold War*. Berkeley, CA: University of California Press, 2013.

PART IV

⋆

LIGAMENTS OF GLOBALIZATION

17

Transportation and communication, 1750 to the present

DANIEL R. HEADRICK

The age of revolutions in transportation and communication that we live in began two and a half centuries ago. Before then, transportation relied on muscle power or the wind and communication (beyond shouting distance) meant transporting an object containing a message. Our revolutions have two causes: the application of new machines and energy sources to transportation, and the liberation of communication from the need to transport objects. The first of these revolutions has almost run its course, while the second is just beginning.

Pre-industrial forms and new organizations

In the mid eighteenth century, transportation and communication systems were still bound by traditions harking back to ancient times. On land, goods were carried on the backs of animals or humans or in carts pulled by horses, mules, or oxen. The fastest means of communication was the courier on a galloping horse, as it had been since the Persian Royal Road that Herodotus admired over two thousand years earlier. At sea, goods, persons, and letters all traveled on the same slow ships; passengers and mail traveling between London and Calcutta, for example, took five to eight months to reach their destination. If someone wrote a letter, he or she could expect an answer two years later.

Yet changes, in organization rather than in hardware, were already beginning to have an effect. During the sixteenth and seventeenth centuries, European governments eager to communicate with their distant outposts created postal systems inspired by the Roman cursus publicus. A private firm operated by the Thurn und Taxis family organized regular courier services throughout the Habsburg Empire and other parts of Western and Central Europe. Following its example, the governments of France and England also set up royal courier services. Such organizations were nothing new, for the Chinese, Mongol,

Figure 17.1 *A May Morning in the Park* (*The Fairman Rogers Four-in-Hand*) by Thomas Cowperthwait Eakins, 1879-80
(Philadelphia Museum of Art, Pennsylvania, USA / Gift of William Alexander Dick, 1930 / Bridgeman Images)

Ottoman, and Mughal empires had long had official couriers and relay stations with fresh horses placed every few miles along strategic roads. No kingdom or empire could have functioned for long without such couriers.

These systems were reserved for official messages, however. Private individuals wishing to send a letter had to find a traveler going in the right direction or bribe an official courier. When merchants established their own networks, governments, worried about subversion, often tried to forbid them. By the mid-seventeenth century, most Western European governments finally allowed private individuals to use the official courier systems, but at a cost so high it deterred all but the wealthiest patrons. Until well into the eighteenth century, mail delivery in Europe and in the great empires of Asia was slowed by obsolete rules and inefficient organizations.

By the eighteenth century, the quickening of business and political affairs in Western European nations was reflected in improvements in transportation and communication. Paper having monetary value – e.g., bills of exchange, promissory notes, and banknotes – blurred the boundary between transportation and information. Paper money, first introduced in eleventh-century China under the Song dynasty, spread to Europe in the early eighteenth century.

The eighteenth century saw governments investing in all-weather roads made of crushed stone. France, the pioneer in this field, boasted 40,000 kilometers of good roads by 1776. In England, private turnpike trusts, rather than governments, built the new roads. On them, coaches pulled by teams of horses carried mail at increasing speeds, from 6 kilometers per hour in the early eighteenth century to 10 km/h in the 1780s and to 16 km/h in the 1830s. However, the rates were still very high; both public and private mail services charged as much to carry a letter as a working man earned in a day, limiting mail service to businesses and the wealthy. This era also saw a proliferation of pamphlets, broadsheets, and newspapers, as well as books and encyclopedias. The costs of rag paper, manual typesetting, and single-sheet printing limited editions, and the high cost of transportation ensured that most printed matter remained local.

In North America, the Post Office Act of 1792 inaugurated a new era in communication. Determined to distribute knowledge of every kind to all its citizens, the US Congress had post offices built in every town. The number of post offices grew from 75 in 1790 to 13,485 in 1840, twice as many as in Great Britain and five times as many as in France. Local, state, and federal governments built roads to accommodate the stagecoaches that carried both mail and passengers. The network was designed to carry newspapers very cheaply, broadening the information available to Americans and encouraging their participation in the politics of the new democracy. Private mail continued to be very costly, however.

In Europe, the exigencies of revolution and war led to the creation of the first telegraph network. Half a century before the electric telegraph, the Frenchman Claude Chappe invented a system of horizontal and vertical boards that could be arranged in different positions corresponding to numbers in a codebook. Lines of stations installed on towers, steeples, and other high places allowed any message to be transmitted in either direction, but only on clear days. For the first time in history, a message could be sent faster than a horse could gallop. Beginning in 1794, the French government built a network that covered all French cities and even extended as far as Venice and Amsterdam. In Britain, the Admiralty built similar lines from London to a few naval bases.

After the Napoleonic Wars ended in 1815, other European governments built optical telegraph lines for official purposes. Egypt under Mehmet Ali did likewise, as did the French colonial government of Algeria. All these governments forbade the use of optical networks by businesses or private citizens, partly because such systems could carry very few signals, and partly for fear of political conspiracies. Only the United States and Great Britain allowed the construction of private lines, usually short ones between ports and nearby headlands to announce the arrival of ships.

Meanwhile, naval captains also felt the need to communicate between ships beyond shouting distance. European fleets had long used flags to convey distress signals or enemy sightings; for everything else, there was one message that commanded all captains to come to the admiral's flagship for a conference, something clearly impossible in the heat of battle. During the wars of the American and French revolutions, British naval officers devised codebooks and systems of flags that allowed any message to be transmitted in any direction, even during a battle. This gave admirals greater control over their fleets than their predecessors had ever enjoyed in earlier conflicts. Such a system was instrumental in Admiral Nelson's victory at Trafalgar over the French and Spanish fleets. When peace returned in 1815, attention turned to the needs of the merchant marine. To satisfy the demand for better communication, Captain Frederick Marryat devised a codebook for British merchant ships that was later adopted by other nations' fleets and that remained in use until the end of the nineteenth century.

Both the optical telegraphs and the naval flag signaling systems used materials available to people in ancient civilizations and ideas that had been around for centuries. Yet they did not appear until the late eighteenth and early nineteenth century because they satisfied a need that had not been felt before, namely the demand for faster communications brought on by the social and political revolutions of that era.

The industrialization of transportation and communication

The nineteenth century saw the most radical advances in transportation and communication since the domestication of the horse. They were the result of two technological innovations: the steam engine and electricity.

The steam engine that James Watt patented in 1776 was "atmospheric," meaning that the motive power that pushed the piston came from the difference between the pressure of the atmosphere and a partial vacuum created by injecting steam into a separate condenser cooled by running water. Thus it could be used only near a source of cold water. Several inventors attempted to employ one of Watt's reliable but heavy engines to propel a boat. The first successful steamboat, the North River that Robert Fulton launched on the Hudson River in 1807, was soon followed by

Figure 17.2 1909 replica of the North River Steamboat
(Detroit Publishing Company / Library of Congress)

hundreds of other steamers in North America and later in Europe. Once Watt's patents expired, inventors built high-pressure engines that were more powerful and fuel-efficient than Watt's, but were prone to bursting. European-Americans used steamboats to open up the interior of their continent. On the Mississippi River where competition between steamboats was intense, several such boats exploded, claiming many lives. Meanwhile the British, who had pioneered steamboat use on their rivers and across the Irish Sea, introduced steamboats on the rivers of India and Egypt and during their expeditions against Burma and China.

Steam power also revolutionized ocean transportation. After the transatlantic race between the steamers Sirius and Great Western in 1838, people began to consider steam power a viable alternative to sail. Beginning in the 1830s, steam-powered ships connected India with Egypt via the Red Sea, and Egypt with Europe via the Mediterranean. In the 1840s, British steamers appeared off the coast of China. The combination of iron hulls – another innovation – and ever more powerful steam engines allowed shipbuilders to build larger, faster, and more efficient ships for long oceanic voyages. In this field, Great Britain led the way and remained dominant for a hundred years.

Steamships were so complex and costly that only large companies or government agencies could finance and manage them. Shipping lines were among the largest and most complex non-governmental organizations ever created, on a par with armies and navies. Their economic impact was equally huge. For the first time, it became worthwhile to ship heavy but low-cost products over long distances, such as wheat from the Midwest of North America to Europe, coal from Britain to Australia, and wool from Australia to Britain. By the late nineteenth century, British, French, American, and German passenger and cargo lines connected all major ports of the world.

Shipbuilders built specialized ships for different purposes. Tramp steamers carried non-perishable cargo from port to port. Grain carriers carried wheat to Europe from North America. Refrigerated ships carried beef from Argentina and fruit from South Africa to Europe. Passengers, mail, and perishable freight traveled on fast ocean liners. By the early twentieth century, a voyage between England and India that once would have taken five to eight months could be accomplished in eleven days by a combination of railways and steamships. Not only was maritime travel much faster than ever before but, for the wealthy, ocean liners were safe, comfortable, and luxurious. The low cost of travel in steerage also allowed millions of poorer Europeans and Asians to emigrate to the Americas, South Africa, and Australia.

Though steamboats aroused much excitement, they were eclipsed by an even more radical technology: the railroad. Despite the dangers of derailing, collisions, and bursting boilers, public enthusiasm for fast land transportation caused a boom in railroad building, first in Britain and the United States, followed, at a more sedate pace, by the European nations. In the late nineteenth century the Latin American republics also experienced railroad-building booms and busts.

The British introduced railways to India in the 1850s. In a country where for millennia transportation had been by oxcart or by slow boats on the few navigable rivers, railways proved revolutionary. By the end of the century, India had one of the longest rail networks in the world, comparable to those of France, Germany, Russia, and Britain itself. However, these railroads were built entirely by British engineers using British equipment; while they greatly improved transportation on the sub-continent, they did little to further the technical education of Indians. In contrast, when the Japanese government decided to build a rail network in the 1870s, it employed Japanese engineers and created a Japanese industry to provide most of the equipment. In China, an impoverished state dominated by a reactionary court suspicious of all things foreign delayed the construction of a rail network until the twentieth century. The Ottoman Empire acquired its first railroad lines in the late nineteenth century; by 1914, with German help, it began construction of a line from Istanbul to Baghdad.

The revolution in transportation had an immediate impact on communications. Even the very first trains in the 1830s traveled faster than the fastest stagecoach. The year 1838 saw the first railway car devoted to carrying the mail, in which postal employees sorted the letters en route. By the 1850s, wherever there were railway tracks, stagecoaches disappeared, as passengers and mail traveled more rapidly, comfortably, and safely by train. Government postal services signed contracts with shipping lines to subsidize the carriage of mail across seas and oceans on the fastest ships available. In India, where non-governmental mail had traditionally been handled by travelers or private couriers, the British established a uniform postal system in 1837 and introduced railway mail service in the 1850s. In China and the Ottoman Empire, where mail service remained slow and unreliable, foreigners opened branches of their national postal services to serve their needs. China did not establish an Imperial Postal Service until 1897.

That left the problem of cost. Until the 1840s, governments saw private letters as a source of revenue, and charged the recipient by the number of pages and the distance covered, introducing delays and inefficiencies. In 1837 the Englishman Rowland Hill proposed charging the sender – not the recipient – one penny for any letter weighing half an ounce or less to anywhere in the British Isles. This reform, introduced in 1840, caused an upsurge in mail and was soon imitated in the United States, France, and other countries. Correspondence, once a privilege of the wealthy, was now within the means of the poor, an incentive to mass literacy.

The other revolution in communication was the electric telegraph. During the early nineteenth century, several inventors tried to use electricity to convey messages. Two practical systems emerged in 1837: that of Charles Wheatstone and William Cooke in Britain, which used five wires to move a pointer to letters of the alphabet on a dial, and that of the American Samuel Morse, which used a code of dots and dashes transmitted by a single wire with an earth return. Though the Wheatstone–Cooke system was fast and reliable, the Morse system was cheaper, and eventually prevailed worldwide.

The electric telegraph was at least ten times faster than the Chappe system and could work at night and in bad weather as well as on sunny days. Excess capacity persuaded governments to open telegraph service to the public, even in France where the government had long forbidden public access to the

Chappe network. In the United States and (until the 1870s) in Britain, the telegraphs were operated by private companies; elsewhere, they were government-run. Telegraph lines soon crisscrossed nations and continents. In Western nations, governments, newspapers, businesses, and private citizens eagerly took to the telegraph, stimulating the flow of commerce and the transmission of news. In exchange for free access to the telegraph, railways encouraged telegraph companies and administrations to erect lines along their tracks to coordinate trains and prevent accidents. Banks began to transfer funds instantaneously by telegraph, speeding up commerce.

Outside of Europe and North America, telegraph lines also spread along with the expanding European colonial empires. In India, the largest and most important of all colonial territories, the British started a telegraph network in the 1850s. Independent countries attempting to modernize, such as the Ottoman Empire, Japan, and the Latin American republics, began building telegraph lines from the 1870s on. Even China, where telegraphy at first encountered popular resistance, had the beginning of a network by the end of the nineteenth century.

Building an overland telegraph network was fairly inexpensive and could be done in stages; communicating across the sea was far more challenging. The first submarine telegraph cable was laid from England to France in 1851, setting off a scramble to lay longer cables to faraway lands. The first transatlantic cable, laid in 1858, failed almost immediately, as did several cables across the Mediterranean Sea and down the Red Sea. Finally in 1866–67, two new cables successfully linked Great Britain and the United States. In 1872, India was connected to Britain by a direct cable. These successes triggered a boom in oceanic telegraph cables that connected every continent and most islands by the beginning of the twentieth century.

Great Britain, which had pioneered the industry, dominated the intercontinental telegraph business until World War I. Only across the North Atlantic did British firms encounter competition from French, German, and American cable companies. However, the cost of intercontinental telegrams remained so high that even governments and businesses sent messages sparingly and almost always in codes that reduced the number of words. Few private individuals could afford the astronomical cost of an overseas telegram.

The mass media also changed dramatically in the nineteenth century. Two innovations – cheap wood-pulp paper and the rotary press – transformed newspapers from irregular, short, and expensive publications to the mass-circulation dailies we know today. The telegraph allowed newspapers to station correspondents in faraway places. Reuters, the Associated Press, and other news agencies provided news to papers that could not afford their own correspondents. In the late nineteenth century, photography and rotogravure allowed wide-circulation magazines and newspapers to print pictures to illustrate stories and advertisements aimed at a newly literate mass audience educated in the expanding public schools of that era. Cheap newspapers in turn contributed to mass participation in politics.

The second industrial revolution, 1876–1945

In the late nineteenth century, a series of technological and organizational innovations once again revolutionized transportation and communication. The first of these was electricity.

Decades after the telegraph had proved successful around the world, several inventors tried using an electric current to transmit the human voice. The winner in this race was the American Alexander Graham Bell, whose telephone was patented in 1876. The development of a network that allowed subscribers to communicate with one another, first in cities and later over inter-city distances, was as important as the device itself. At first, telephone companies hired young women to connect subscribers; by the 1920s, as the number of employees could not keep up with the fast-growing traffic, companies introduced the automatic switching or direct-dialing system. Meanwhile, scientists were working on relays to permit long-distance telephony. In 1915 the American Telegraph and Telephone Company inaugurated the first transcontinental line between New York and San Francisco, using vacuum tubes.

Throughout the nineteenth century, engineers and inventors had sought to apply electricity to uses other than the telegraph. The most famous breakthrough was the invention of the electric lightbulb by Thomas Edison. But Edison's more important (though less celebrated) contribution was the central power station that could supply electricity to a whole neighborhood, and later to an entire city. This allowed the development of electric vehicles that got their energy from the grid. The first practical streetcar began service in Richmond, Virginia, in 1888. After some early teething troubles, streetcars became ubiquitous in American and European cities during the 1890s and early 1900s, and were later adopted in Japan and Latin America as well. Electric traction also opened up the possibility of placing trains underground. Since the first London Underground line opened in 1890, subways and elevated urban lines have proliferated around the world. Likewise, electric power has increasingly replaced other sources of energy for railroad locomotives, especially for high-speed trains and in regions with ample hydroelectric power like Switzerland.

At the turn of the century, electromagnetic radiation or radio waves began to impact communications. In 1895 the young Italian Guglielmo Marconi succeeded in sending a message in code over a short distance. In 1899 he was able to communicate across the English Channel and, two years later, across the Atlantic Ocean. Wireless telegraphy, as it was called, interested navies and shipping companies above all, for until then a ship out of sight of land or of other ships had been incommunicado.

While Marconi's and other early systems used electric sparks to emit coded messages by electromagnetic waves, other inventors sought ways to transmit voice and music, as the telephone had done for land lines. Success came in 1906, when the Canadian Reginald Fessenden transmitted sounds accurately. In 1915, the first transatlantic telephone circuit was inaugurated, using the same vacuum tubes that had made transcontinental telephony possible. Until the 1930s, long-distance radio communication used powerful transmitters that consumed as much electricity as small towns and required antennas as large as tall buildings. The huge cost of transmission limited the spread of long-distance radio to a few dozen stations in wealthy countries and in their colonies.

This obstacle was removed in the 1930s by the introduction of shortwave radio invented by Marconi himself. Short or high-frequency radio waves did not follow the curvature of the Earth as did the long waves emitted by powerful transmitters, but bounced off the ionosphere and could thereby reach huge distances with very little power. As a result, shortwave radio allowed every town and organization, even "ham" radio operators using inexpensive equipment, to communicate with the rest of the world. During World War II, ships, tanks, airplanes, and spies were equipped with shortwave sets.

Meanwhile, radio waves had found an entirely new use in 1923 when a station in Pittsburgh, Pennsylvania, began broadcasting to the public. So successful was broadcasting that radio stations sprang up around the United States to transmit news, music, entertainment, and advertisements to owners of home radio receivers. While American radio broadcasting was purely commercial, in most other countries radio stations were owned and operated by governments that used them to influence public opinion.

Electricity had the most diverse applications to transportation and communication in this period, but in the popular mind the internal-combustion engine created even more excitement. The four-cycle gasoline engine that now powers almost all cars was invented by the German Nikolaus Otto in 1876. Ten years later, two other Germans, Karl Benz and Gottlieb Daimler, began manufacturing "horseless carriages" using these new gasoline engines. During the next twenty years, dozens of entrepreneurs in Europe and the United States used traditional handicraft techniques to build luxury automobiles for wealthy customers. In 1908, one of these craftsmen, the American Henry Ford, began building simple machines that he called the Model T. Over the next several years, he introduced the assembly line and other cost-saving methods in his factory in Detroit that lowered the price of his car. By 1927 he was producing a new car every twenty-four seconds and selling them for 300 dollars, or three months' wages for his workers. As a result, the United States became the first country in which most families could afford a car.

While mass automobility did not reach Europe until the 1950s and Asia several decades later, the internal combustion engine affected transportation in other ways. Trucks could deliver goods more rapidly and efficiently than

Figure 17.3 Model T Ford
(© Ewing Galloway / Alamy)

horse-drawn carts and reach places without access to railroads. Similarly, buses transported people in and between cities without the need for costly and complicated rails.

Roads lagged behind the rise of the automobile. For a long time, cars had to drive on cobblestone streets in cities and on dirt or gravel roads out in the country. Even before the automobile, another new machine, the bicycle, helped satisfy a demand for personal transportation. In the course of the nineteenth century, various inventors had come up with two-wheeled pedal-powered vehicles, culminating in the "penny-farthing" bicycle, a machine with a huge front and a tiny back wheel suitable only for daredevils. Two inventions in the 1880s put the bicycle within reach of ordinary people: the chain drive that allowed both wheels to be of the same size and the pneumatic tire that made riding smoother and safer. Once cycling became popular in the 1890s, cyclists demanded smooth streets and roads paved with asphalt. In the 1920s, as automobiles, buses, and trucks proliferated, such roads became standard between cities.

The most spectacular application of the internal combustion engine was aviation. Humans dreamed of flying since time of the ancient Greeks, if not before. In the 1790s the Montgolfier brothers had created the first hot-air balloon, to great acclaim. Balloons, however, drifted with the wind. In order to achieve controlled flight, inventors tried two different methods. One was the dirigible, a lighter-than-air balloon with an engine and a steering mechanism. The best of these machines, built by the German count Ferdinand von Zeppelin, were giant airships that carried a few dozen passengers in comfort across continents and oceans. Zeppelins fell out of favor in 1937 when the Hindenburg burst into flames after crossing the Atlantic Ocean, killing 35 of the 97 people on board.

The other attempt to fly was in an airplane, a heavier-than-air machine that relied on wings to hold it up. Around the turn of the nineteenth century, many inventors tried to build such a machine. Two American bicycle manufacturers, the brothers Orville and Wilbur Wright, succeeded in 1903 with their craft called Flyer I. Once they had shown it could be done, many others followed suit. The nations that went to war in 1914 sent airplanes into combat. After the war ended, daredevil pilots flying leftover fighter planes performed dangerous aerial maneuvers before huge crowds. In 1927, Charles Lindbergh demonstrated the potential of aircraft by flying across the Atlantic non-stop. By the 1930s, airlines regularly began carrying paying passengers. The Douglas DC-3, an all-metal twin-engine plane with retractible landing gear introduced in 1936, made long-distance air travel safe and popular. By the

Figure 17.4 First flight of the Wright *Flyer I*, December 17, 1903 (Library of Congress)

outbreak of World War II, hundreds of passenger planes were flying throughout the world. Since airfields or landing strips could be built very cheaply almost anywhere, aviation quickly reached remote areas not served by rail or ship, such as the interior of Africa. During the war, airplane factories poured out thousands more, many of which served to transport passengers and cargo.

Airplanes also had an impact on communication, as many former military pilots turned to carrying mail after 1918. Although airmail was expensive, it was often as fast as night-letters, the cheapest kind of telegram, and so much faster than land- and sea-mail that people and businesses gladly paid a surcharge for urgent letters.

Two other innovations in communication in this era merit mentioning. One was the phonograph, invented by Thomas Edison in 1877 as a means of recording voices on wax cylinders. By the turn of the century, cylinders were made obsolete by wax (later vinyl) disks in which a stylus followed a spiral groove, and a flourishing industry arose to produce music for home entertainment. The other innovation was the cinema or motion picture, using celluloid film originally produced for still cameras. The first halting steps toward cinematography began in the 1890s. By the early 1900s, studios were producing short movies for popular audiences. Films with synchronized sound tracks followed in the mid 1920s. Producing a realistic-looking color film was a complex challenge that occupied inventors and corporate laboratories for decades. Though a few color movies were produced in the 1920s and 1930s, most films were in black-and-white until after World War Two.

The age of globalization, 1945–2000

Before the Second World War, most innovations originated among craftsmen, businessmen, and scientists. In that war, however, the governments of the major belligerent powers invested heavily in research and development of militarily useful technologies, many of which had important applications to civilian transportation and communication after the war. Among them were radar, jet engines, computers, and guided missiles.

Radar, developed in Britain, Germany, and the United States to spot approaching enemy aircraft, made aviation and navigation safer by "seeing" through fog and darkness. With radar, ships could avoid icebergs, rocks, and other ships, and airplanes could fly at night and in bad weather.

Aviation was also greatly advanced by the development of jet engines that were more efficient and allowed greater speeds than piston engines and propellers. The British De Havilland "Comet," introduced in 1949, was the first jet-powered passenger airplane, but it suffered several accidents and ended its commercial career after a few years. The American Boeing 707 began service in 1958 and was an outstanding success, leading the way to many similar aircraft. Today, thousands of jet planes carry millions of passengers and millions of tons of freight to all parts of the world at much higher speeds and lower cost than the piston-engined planes they have replaced. So fast, comfortable, and inexpensive has air travel become that it brought mass tourism to distant destinations. In response, passenger ships have abandoned transoceanic routes and become cruise ships or floating resorts.

Despite improvements in safety, performance, comfort, and efficiency, aviation reached a plateau in the 1980s. An Anglo-French consortium tried to change commercial aviation by introducing the "Concorde" in 1976. This plane, which carried passengers at supersonic speeds and at outrageous prices, served a small but wealthy clientele until it was retired in 2003. All other attempts to carry passengers faster than the speed of sound have failed. At this time, supersonic travel is a dream that recedes further into the future every year.

Figure 17.5 Four TGV trains at Gare de l'Est station, Paris
(© imageBROKER / Alamy)

Railways also advanced dramatically when the Japanese introduced the Shinkansen or "bullet train" between Tokyo and Osaka in 1964. Such trains, which can reach a maximum speed of 300 kilometers per hour, now carry over 100 million passengers a year between all the major Japanese cities, greatly alleviating the pressure on highways and air traffic in a densely populated nation. The Japanese example was followed by the French TGV (Train à Grande Vitesse, or high-speed train) in 1981. In 2003, the TGV set a land-speed record of 575 kilometers per hour. Since then, a network of high-speed trains has spread to all major French cities and many neighboring countries as well. In the United States, however, the love of (and dependence upon) automobiles is so powerful that all proposals to improve passenger rail service have run into political roadblocks.

While American passenger rail service is now a pale shadow of its former glory, its freight service has become the most efficient in the world. Part of the reason is containerization, introduced in the 1950s and adopted by the US armed forces in the Vietnam War. While non-bulk freight was once loaded and unloaded by men, 90 percent of such freight is now shipped in sealed intermodal containers that can be transferred among trains, ships, and trucks by powerful cranes and then tracked by computers. This system not only saves a great deal of labor, it also prevents pilfering and protects the cargo from the weather.

For the same reasons, containerization has also made ocean shipping much more efficient. By the end of the twentieth century, almost all long-distance non-bulk cargo was carried in containers stacked up in the hold of specialized container ships. Bulk freight was also greatly improved in the postwar period, largely by replacing generic cargo ships with specialized vessels. The most impressive of these are the gigantic crude-oil tankers capable of carrying up to 550,000 metric tons of crude at a cost of two or three US cents per gallon. The falling cost of shipping freight by sea, air, and train and the lowering of tariffs and other trade barriers since World War II have fueled the increase in world trade, a major aspect of globalization.

Like aviation, automobile transportation improved greatly for several decades, then stalled. The improvements came at two levels. Cars themselves became more powerful, comfortable, and reliable and, especially, more affordable to masses of working people, first in North America, then in Western Europe, and more recently in Latin America and East Asia. By the early twenty-first century, there were some 800 million cars worldwide, with 250 million in the United States alone. Recently, China has surpassed the United States in the number of new automobiles purchased each year.

Governments have tried, with greater or lesser success, to cope with the flood of new vehicles. For long-distance travel, many countries, starting with Germany in the 1930s, built superhighways. The American network of limited-access interstate highways reached over 40,000 miles by the end of the century, by far the longest of any nation. Though originally designed for interstate travel, most of the traffic consists of short-distance commuting, encouraged by the construction of limited-access highways into and through cities. European nations with high automobile densities by and large have resisted the idea of destroying urban neighborhoods for the benefit of suburban commuters. Yet the result in Europe and Japan, as in the United States, has been increasingly long and frustrating rush hours, occasional gridlock (total traffic stoppage), and serious air pollution. Non-Western countries with a similar proliferation of cars but less money to spend on highway construction and pollution abatement have encountered even more serious problems; the worst traffic congestion and air pollution are now found in Mexico City, Bangkok, Cairo, and other Third-World megalopolises.

While improvements in transportation have leveled off, changes in communication have not only continued unabated, they have come at an accelerated pace. Some were improvements in pre-existing communications.

Thus radios that used large, power-hungry tubes until the 1950s were replaced by small transistor radios that people could carry in their pockets. Television, invented before the war, became an item of mass consumption. In some countries, programming is subsidized by advertisers that heavily influence popular culture toward consumerism. Most nations created government-operated television networks, as they had for radio. As with so many other innovations, radio and television found their first mass markets in the United States, then spread to Europe and Japan, and from there to the rest of the world. Today there are several hundred million television sets in the world, and countless millions of radios.

Other postwar innovations were radically different from any previous technologies. One such was satellites launched into orbit by powerful missiles, themselves the result of military research in World War II. The first satellite, called "Sputnik," was launched by the Soviet Union in 1957 for propaganda purposes. Eight years later, the United States launched Intelsat I (or "Early Bird") to retransmit telephone messages from one Earth station to another. By 1971, when Intelsat IV was launched, rapid advances in electronics increased the capacity of satellites to 2,000 simultaneous telephone conversations. While satellite transmission introduced a disconcerting delay in telephone conversations, they were perfectly suited for transmitting television programmes around the world, making global news and sports events instantaneous for the first time.

Microwave towers on land and fiber-optic cables across seas brought about an even more radical advance in communication. First manufactured into cables in 1983, glass fibers could carry light pulses produced by lasers over long distances. TAT-8, the first transatlantic fiber-optic cable laid in 1988, carried 40,000 simultaneous telephone conversations, compared to 36 for TAT-1, a copper cable laid in 1955. By the end of the century, fiber-optic cables laid across all the world's oceans could carry all telephone calls, data transmissions, and television programmes at almost zero marginal cost, with bandwidth to spare.

Microwaves, transmitted from tower to tower, began replacing copper telephone cables on land around the same time that fiber-optic cables were laid under the seas. When combined with computers, they allowed an even more astonishing new technology: mobile, or cellular, telephones. Electronic computers were invented in World War II and developed after the war for military and scientific purposes. The introduction of the transistor and, after 1958, the integrated circuit or "chip" permitted computer manufacturers to design computers that were ever more powerful even as they shrank from the size of a small house to that of a cigarette pack or less. In 1983, software engineers devised protocols that allowed computers to communicate with one another. Among the applications was a system that could switch telephone communications from one "cell" or transmitter to another as the user moved. That and advances in batteries and miniaturization led to the proliferation of pocket telephones. Japan led the way in this technology with the first urban coverage of Tokyo in 1979 and the first nationwide network in the mid 1980s. Compared to landline installations, mobile phone systems were inexpensive to install, even in poor countries with primitive infrastructures. So popular were mobile phones that they were quickly adopted around the world.

Once computers were able to talk to one another, it opened up an entirely new field of communication. Email (for "electronic mail") was introduced in the early 1970s on the first American military and scientific computer network, called ARPANET. Soon various companies introduced their own proprietary computer networks, with the digital data being transmitted via microwave towers or fiber-optic cables. In the late 1980s, new protocols were developed that allowed all these networks to interconnect, creating the Internet. In 1990, British computer scientist Tim Berners-Lee devised a method of transmitting and displaying any sort of digital data (pictures, words, music) called the World Wide Web. By the end of the century, the falling price of personal computers and easy inexpensive access to the Web turned the Internet into the most versatile and most rapidly growing communication medium in history.

Divergence, convergence, and the future

Technological revolutions do not all follow the same trajectory. At the turn of the twentieth century, the two technologies discussed in this essay clearly diverged. Transportation has stalled, while communication technologies are advancing more rapidly than ever.

Throughout the nineteenth and twentieth centuries, the revolution in transportation captured the imagination of people around the world. From sailing ship to ocean liner, from stagecoach to railroad train, from train to motorcar, from earthbound vehicles to airplanes, and from wood-and-cloth biplanes to jet airliners: these were means of travel more revolutionary than even the most inspired visionary of the eighteenth century could have dreamed of. All of these have entered the fabric of everyday life in the more developed countries, and are rapidly spreading to the less developed ones. Then, in the late twentieth century, improvements slowed down or ceased entirely. Automobiles cannot get people to their destinations any faster than forty years ago; in many cities, commuting times have even become longer. Passenger airplanes are no faster, and often less comfortable, than the jetliners of forty years ago. In some countries, high-speed trains introduced to great fanfare decades ago are now commonplace, while in other countries, such as the United States, they are still a fantasy. Only China is actively building new lines as part of its hypermodernization effort. Freight transport is now extremely efficient in the developed world, but its gains were achieved in the first decades after World War II, and have not improved much since.

Why the stagnation? One major cause is energy. Transporting physical objects, whether people or cargo, takes a great deal of energy. And increases in speed require disproportionate increases in energy consumption; this is what doomed the Concorde and other supersonic airplanes. Meanwhile the cost of energy, which declined sharply until 1973, has fluctuated since then, with a long-term upward trend.

Another cause is automobiles. Cars are not just means of transportation. They are treasured personal possessions that express their owners' taste, wealth, and status, and give drivers a sense of freedom that no train or bus or subway can approach. Unless restrained by traffic regulations, most people prefer to travel by car, almost regardless of cost or delays or inconveniences. As for improving the driving experience by building more and better roads, that hope has proved illusory, for better roads only encourage more people to drive more cars, and the result is more traffic, hence slower travel. In short, if transportation technology has reached a plateau, it is not because engineers cannot devise better systems, but because existing technologies have reached a balance between efficiency, cost, and culture.

The opposite is true of communication. Here the revolution is in full force, and innovations, driven by culture as much as by technology, are appearing faster than ever. As all kinds of information – words, data, music, pictures, motion pictures – can now be digitized and transmitted through the same computers, cables, and microwaves, the result is a convergence of media and a proliferation of new devices and organizations.

Consider the Internet. What was once conceived of as a means of transmitting data safely and rapidly from point to point has spawned several industries. Online commerce competes heavily with retail stores. Newspaper readership is declining as people turn to the Internet for their news. Movie theaters feel the competition from films streamed directly to one's home. Search engines such as Google can sort through billions of web sites in nanoseconds to find information that would once have been almost inaccessible. Wikipedia threatens to doom paper encyclopedias. Social networking sites such as Facebook and Twitter entice millions of people to display their personal information and to form instant groups of all kinds. On the Web, personal information is vulnerable to identity theft, while secret corporate and government information is subject to digital espionage, spawning an entire industry devoted to encryption and data security.

Meanwhile, mobile telephones, considered a radical breakthrough just a few years ago, have proliferated beyond all predictions. Smart phones allow users to hold a conversation, take a picture or a video, listen to music, get information from the Internet, and find a location by GPS (Global Positioning System), all in a device small enough to fit into one's pocket. Old-fashioned computers, with a keyboard, a monitor, and a mouse, are giving way to tablets the size of a magazine or paperback book that can do what computers and telephones used to do, and much more. E-books are fast replacing paper books. Long-distance telephone calls that went from outrageously expensive to very cheap are now free via the Internet.

The evolution of motorcars illustrates the divergence between communication and transportation. Although recent-model cars are no faster or more comfortable than the cars of the 1970s, they excel in information: GPS navigation systems, telephone and Internet access, satellite radio, MP3 music, and more. Drivers may not get to their destinations any faster, but while they sit in traffic, they can get work done or enjoy their choice of entertainment.

The other aspect of the revolution in communication is the worldwide diffusion of the new devices and networks. The International Telecommunication Union reported that by the end of 2011, there were 6 billion mobile phone subscribers in the world, almost as many as human beings. In 2012, China alone had 1 billion mobile phones. And the numbers are growing. Even in remote areas of less-developed countries without electricity or running water, people now have mobile phones; and these phones are used not only to converse and to send and obtain information, but also to transfer money in places without financial institutions. While translation software is still in its infancy, knowledge of English is becoming almost universal among educated youth worldwide, and international business people increasingly communicate in "global English."

The diffusion of technology is nothing new; almost all new technologies are first adopted by the well-to-do in rich countries, then by middle and working-class people, then spread to poorer countries. What is new is the speed at which the new communication technologies have spread, especially mobile phones. And that is just the beginning. Within sight are pocket-size devices that will allow anyone to view any film or television programme, talk to anyone else, access the Internet, listen to any piece of music, read any book, newspaper, or magazine, take a picture or a video, and do anything a home computer can do, from anywhere in the world, and all without being tethered to a wire. As I write this, it is still a prediction, but no doubt, by the time you read this, it will have come to pass or perhaps even seem old hat.

Further reading

Aitken, Hugh. *Syntony and Spark: The Origins of Radio*. New York: John Wiley, 1976.

The Continuous Wave: Technology and American Radio, 1900–1932. Princeton University Press, 1985.

Butrica, Andrew J. *Beyond the Ionosphere: Fifty Years of Satellite Communication*. Washington: NASA, 1997.

Castells, Manuel. *The Internet Galaxy: Reflections on the Internet, Business, and Society*. Oxford University Press, 2001.

Chandler, Alfred D. *Inventing the Electronic Century: the Epic Story of the Consumer Electronics and Computer Industries*. New York: Free Press, 2008.

Fischer, Claude. *America Calling: A Social History of the Telephone to 1940*. Berkeley, CA: University of California Press, 1992.

Flink, James J. *The Automobile Age*. Cambridge, MA: MIT Press, 1988.

Haws, Duncan. *Ships and the Sea*. New York: Thomas Y. Crowell, 1975.

Headrick, Daniel R. *Tentacles of Progress: Technology Transfer in the Age of Imperialism, 1850–1940*. Oxford University Press, 1988.

The Invisible Weapon: Telecommunications and International Politics, 1851–1945. Oxford University Press, 1991.

When Information Came of Age: Technologies of Knowledge in the Age of Reason and Revolution, 1700–1850. Oxford University Press, 2000.

Holzmann, Gerald R. and Bjorn Pehrson. *The Early History of Data Networks*. Los Alamitos, CA: IEEE Computer Society Press, 1995.

John, Richard R. *Network Nation: Inventing American Telecommunications*. Cambridge, MA: Harvard University Press, 2010.

Spreading the News: The American Postal System from Franklin to Morse. Cambridge, MA: Harvard University Press, 1996.

Levinson, Mark. *The Box: How the Shipping Container Made the World Smaller and the World Economy Bigger*. Princeton University Press, 2006.

Lubar, Steven. *InfoCulture: The Smithsonian Book of Information Age Invention*. Boston: Houghton Mifflin, 1993.

Robinson, Howard. *The British Post Office: A History*. Princeton University Press, 1948.

Sachs, Wolfgang. *For Love of the Automobile: Looking Back at the History of Our Desires*, translated by Don Reneau. Berkeley, CA: University of California Press, 1992.

Thompson, Robert L. *Wiring a Continent: The History of the Telegraph Industry in the United States, 1832–1866*. Princeton University Press, 1947.

White, Richard. *Railroaded: The Transcontinentals and the Making of Modern America*. New York: Norton, 2011.

18
Rubber

RICHARD TUCKER

In the tropical world's transformation in modern times, large-scale capital investment and consumer demand in affluent economies have displaced natural forests and small-scale farming across wide areas of the moist tropics. Single-crop export economies have displaced multi-crop food production for local consumption. Natural rubber is one of the most significant export crops from the tropics, but since the 1940s rubber has been produced from both natural latex and from petroleum. Synthetic rubber is a dimension of petroleum history; it is difficult to disentangle that from other uses of petroleum. This survey concentrates on natural rubber, considering synthetic rubber to the extent that it has limited global demand for rubber produced from the latex of tropical trees and vines.

The acreage under rubber trees would have been far greater in recent years, had not the industry developed synthetic rubber during the crisis of supplies in World War II. The technological breakthrough catalyzed by that military emergency transformed the global rubber economy. Since 1960 roughly two-thirds of global rubber production has been derived from synthetics, and the other third from trees on lands that had once sustained rain forests. In this segment of tropical forest clearance, the United States dominated market demand, through innovations in the automotive economy.

The story of industrial rubber began in the early 1800s. Rubbery substances derived from the latex of various tropical trees, bushes, and vines had long been in use. But in hot weather they tended to melt and in cold settings they became brittle. In 1837 the American Charles Goodyear invented the vulcanization process, which stabilized latex products over a wide temperature range, enabled the fabric to stretch, and made it impermeable to moisture, thus opening a wide new range of possibilities for the industrial era, and gave Goodyear's company an early lead in developing product lines and markets. At first the new product was used primarily by the clothing industry, to produce wet weather boots and clothes. Toward the end of the century this market was superseded by tires for bicycles and then automobiles, as well as a range of other commercial and industrial uses.

Searching for sources of latex, commercial adventurers from Europe and the United States scoured the world's tropical lowlands. They experimented with latex from many species; *Hevea brasiliensis*, a tree endemic to the Amazonian rain forest, proved to be the most desirable source. As world demand burgeoned, Hevea latex eliminated all others from international trade, and the tree was taken to Africa and Asia, where single-species plantations replaced rain forest over large areas.

The rubber boom and bust in Amazonia

Hevea grew naturally in wide areas of the Amazonian basin, but always scattered as one tree species among many. This prevented the parasites which had co-evolved with it from concentrating their attacks, as they could when humans planted the trees in dense groves. Beginning in the 1820s British and American explorers and speculators engaged in a strategic race in the Amazon basin, mapping the vast unknown territory and searching for any product which they could commandeer, including rubber. By the 1850s explorers probed several major tributaries of the great river.

International markets for rubber expanded rapidly after the late 1880s, led by the newly expanding tire industry. The interior of Amazonia underwent a boom in speculative land sales in the 1890s, as soon as the Brazilian government adopted simplified land registration procedures. In 1900 the Amazon basin produced 25,000 metric tons of rubber; by 1909 that figure rose to 40,000 tons. Demand rose even faster, so prices doubled in that decade. Some companies came to be controlled by foreigners, who had larger capital reserves than local people. But foreign speculations never succeeded in controlling the upriver networks, which were dominated by Brazilian land barons. Extracting the precious white liquid and shipping it out of the jungle required the skills and tenacity of people who could survive extremely difficult living conditions. Outside speculators were unable to gain direct control of forest tracts; they had no hope of participating directly in the latex extraction.

British entrepreneurs attempted to grow Hevea in dense plantations, but they never succeeded in conquering the tree's fatal disease, the South American Leaf Blight, a fungus which had coevolved with Hevea in the forest.[1] They succeeded in cultivating Hevea in concentrated plantations not in its Amazonian home but in Europe's colonies in tropical Asia, where climate conditions were favorable and leaf blight did not follow it. In the 1870s they succeeded in taking Hevea seedlings out of Brazil, first to Kew Botanical Garden in London and from there to their colonies of Ceylon and Malaya. They established their first full-scale colonial plantations in 1900, and the young trees began to produce latex in commercial amounts in 1910. Dunlop, the dominant British firm, purchased its first plantation in Malaya in 1910. Aided by intense demand during World War I, Dunlop expanded its holdings to 50,000 acres by 1920.[2]

The transformation of world rubber markets was sudden and decisive. After 1912 Brazilian rubber sales on the world market collapsed, and the entire network of Brazilian penetration into the interior of Amazonia fell to pieces. The great forest remained largely intact, though its arteries had begun to open to the world economy. In the late 1920s the American automotive magnate Henry Ford applied his massive corporate resources to another effort to grow Hevea plantations in Amazonia. Within fifteen years his Fordlandia and Belterra plantations proved to be dismal, even ludicrous failures. Monocrop rubber production was not achieved in Brazil, though portions of the deforested land were subsequently capable of producing limited tree and row crops.[3]

Colonial empires and rubber in Southeast Asia

As soon as it seemed clear that the British experiment with plantation rubber in Southeast Asia was viable, American companies joined them. Until World War II the American role in changing the face of Southeast Asia was subordinate to the colonial grip of the Dutch and British. But shortly after 1900, Southeast Asian moist forests became one of the major tropical regions which American industrial wealth helped to transform. American rubber purchasers began to fear that the British might

1 See the detailed analysis of this disease and the long history of plant pathologists' failure to defeat it, in Warren Dean, *Brazil and the Struggle for Rubber: A Study in Environmental History* (Cambridge University Press, 1987), chapter 4.

2 James McMillan, *The Dunlop Story* (London: Weidenfeld and Nicholson, 1989), pp. 37–39.

3 For details, see Greg Grandin, *Fordlandia: The Rise and Fall of Henry Ford's Forgotten Jungle City* (New York: Metropolitan Books, 2009), including the project's links to Ford's grandiose and coercive operations of his automotive production at home. For other efforts in Amazonia, see Wade Davis, *One River: Explorations and Discoveries in the Amazon Rain Forest* (New York: Simon & Schuster, 1996).

establish a monopoly of global supplies through their new colonial plantations in Ceylon and Malaya, in conjunction with Dutch interests in the East Indies.

Sumatra became the center of US operations, on the agriculture and population frontier.[4] Until the onset of plantation agriculture in the late nineteenth century, the Deli lowlands outside the coastal entrepot of Medan had supported a thin population of Muslim Malay rice farmers. In the higher reaches Batak hill tribes practiced multi-crop swidden agroforestry. Local sultans, their capital towns located near the mouths of the short rivers, skimmed tax revenues from the export of forest products, but they had little effective control over the land and its people. Dutch tobacco and rubber planters cooperated with these local rulers.

Distrusting exotic rubber species, the first Dutch planters experimented with *Ficus elastica*, but Ficus failed to fulfill their hopes. On Java they experimented successfully with Hevea, maintaining close contacts between the Dutch colonial botanical gardens at Buitenzorg (now called Bogor) and the British center at Kew.[5] The first large plantation of Hevea on Sumatra was begun in 1906. But commercially successful rubber production would need massive capital, large acreage and long leases, and a seven-year wait for the first latex. This necessitated the active support of Dutch administrators for negotiating long leases from local rajas. Over the following years virtually all land that foreign investors thought worth cultivating was leased from the rajas; very little was left to the peasant population for meeting its own subsistence needs.[6] From 435 acres under rubber in 1902, the figure grew exponentially, to over 320,000 acres planted in rubber groves by 1914.

That acreage was largely carved out of natural forest, but this was only the core of the transformation. The web of transport and settlement infrastructure which arose among the plantations, and the work force of Javanese and Chinese coolie laborers imported to clear the forest, plant the seedlings, and tend the trees, produced far more wide-ranging impacts, rippling outward from the groves across the Deli region. The population of the East Coast

4 Wolf Donner, *Land Use and Environment in Indonesia* (Honolulu: University of Hawaii Press, 1987), pp. 10–15; Anthony J. Whitten et al., *The Ecology of Sumatra* (Yokkyakarta: UGM Press, 1984), chapter 1.

5 T. A. Tengwall, "History of rubber cultivation and research in the Netherlands Indies," in Pieter Honig and Frans Verdoorn (eds.), *Science and Scientists in the Netherlands Indies* (New York: Board for the Netherlands Indies, 1945), p. 344.

6 Clark E. Cunningham, *The Postwar Migration of the Toba-Bataks to East Sumatra* (New Haven: Yale University Press, 1958), p. 11.

region rose from 568,400 in 1905 to 1,693,200 in 1930.[7] This increase was caused almost entirely by the new export agriculture.

The rubber market was greater than the Dutch planters themselves could finance, so they began searching for additional Western capital. They soon found a major American firm, the United States Rubber Company.[8] By 1913 US Rubber owned a total of 75,947 acres in Sumatra, the largest single holding in the world designated for rubber cultivation. At its greatest extent, just over 100,000 acres or 150 square miles of property were held by its new subsidiary, the Dutch American Plantation Company, HAPM or "Hoppum," as the company was referred to throughout the rubber world. In 1911 they planted 14,000 acres of trees, or 22 square miles; by 1913 the planted area was over 32,500 acres. A year later Hoppum built the world's largest rubber processing plant on the coast southeast of Medan. That year war broke out in Europe. Responding to escalating wartime prices, HAPM converted 14,200 acres more from forest to plantation in 1915. By that time 14,000 imported Chinese and Javanese indentured workers toiled under 90 European and American supervisory staff.

The first Sumatran rubber shipments to the USA were made in 1915, the year after the Panama Canal opened. Three other US companies soon joined the Sumatran adventure, led by Goodyear, the United States' largest tire producer. In 1917 Goodyear leased a 16,700 acre concession southeast of Medan that was covered almost entirely by primary forest. In three years it was cleared and planted in Hevea.[9] Unprecedented demand for rubber during World War I was a major factor in this rush to expand production.

In the immediate postwar depression, crude rubber prices collapsed. British rubber corporations in Malaya and Ceylon were faced with fiscal disaster. So Winston Churchill, then British Colonial Secretary, appointed a review commission headed by Sir James Stevenson. The resulting Stevenson Plan of 1922 restricted production on Southeast Asian rubber estates, and prohibited planting of new higher-yielding trees. But the Dutch refused to join the system of production controls, and American interests were unpredictable. American importers were determined to free themselves of European-controlled sources. In addition, American attitudes were generally

7 Cunningham, *Postwar Migration*, p. 11. For a vivid account of the Dutch plantations, see Madelon Lulofs' autobiographical novel, *Rubber* (London: Cassell, 1933). For the fullest analysis of the coolies' living conditions, see Ann Laura Stoler, *Capitalism and Confrontation in Sumatra's Plantation Belt, 1870–1979* (New Haven: Yale University Press, 1985).

8 Glenn D. Babcock, *History of the United States Rubber Company* (Bloomington: Bureau of Business Research, Indiana University, 1966).

9 Cunningham, *Postwar Migration*, p. 12.

hostile to any regulation of free markets. So the Stevenson Plan had only limited effect in its first years.

In the United States Henry Ford's new assembly lines were creating an automobile production boom. American imports of crude rubber rose from 692 million pounds in 1923 to 888 million pounds two years later.[10] By then American plantations on Sumatra were coming into full production, but American demand was expanding so rapidly in the era of the Model T that US companies had to buy most of their supplies from others.

In 1927 Goodyear leased another huge estate southeast of Medan: 28,600 acres, all virgin jungle except for a small area that had been developed by a former Japanese lessee. Goodyear mobilized 16,000 workers to clear that forest and create Wingfoot Plantation. Ultimately Wingfoot boasted 40,028 acres, all in high-yielding trees.[11] In 1933, at the height of their operations, American holdings in Sumatra totaled 218,393 acres, including 131,000 acres actually planted.[12]

From the start the Dutch and Americans in Indonesia cooperated closely in research that intensified production on the estates.[13] In a botanical breakthrough of major importance, Hoppum pioneered a new technique of budgrafting high-yielding varieties on older, hardy root stock. Planting with high-yielding clones began on a large scale in 1925. In order to approach the full productive genetic potential of the new trees, Hoppum also imported large amounts of American fertilizers. By 1925 the USA supplied 75 percent of all sulfate of ammonia imported into Sumatra. The new trees more than doubled latex yield. This was a decisive step toward the extraordinary increase in productivity that the growers ultimately achieved – more than ten times what the first trees yielded. Intensification, rather than clearing more forest, had become the corporations' major strategy.

The boom years of the 1920s also saw rapid expansion of smallholder rubber production on the periphery of the great Sumatran estates. Farmers in both Sumatra and Malaya could grow Hevea trees as their major cash crop just as competitively as the estate planters, integrating at most a few hectares of rubber into the varied subsistence production of their annual and tree crops. A census at the end of the 1930s indicated that over one million hectares had been cleared by smallholders, who tapped their own trees and processed

10 Babcock, *History of the United States Rubber Company*, pp. 176–179.

11 Tys Volker, *From Primeval Forest to Cultivation* (Medan: Deli Planters Association, 1924), p. 173.

12 James Gould, *Americans in Sumatra* (The Hague: Martinus Nijhoff, 1961), p. 95.

13 Details are in Tengwall, "History of rubber cultivation."

the latex into brown sheets of crude rubber, which they then sold to Chinese middlemen.[14]

The fourth colonial competitor in the region was France, in its colonies in Indochina. The French government and its allied corporate interests, determined to establish a production system independent of the British and Dutch, organized a Rubber Planters Syndicate in Saigon.[15] Rubber investors began penetrating the rain forest of Cochinchina and Cambodia in 1907, in a series of small plantations, supported by the first motor roads to penetrate the forests of eastern Cochinchina. By 1913 12,500 hectares were in production (in contrast with 200,000 ha in Malaya and 95,000 ha each in Ceylon and Dutch Indies). Under wartime demand, especially from the United States, by 1921 29,000 ha were planted in Cochinchina alone. By 1929 that figure rose to 90,000 ha.

In these years the Michelin firm emerged as a fully integrated production and sales organization and the leading player among the French.[16] In 1900 the brothers André and Edouard Michelin had begun looking for plantations in Brazil, West Africa, Madagascar, and Southeast Asia. They attempted two plantations in Brazil, but the first soon failed, so they left the other as forest. In 1924–25 the Michelin brothers sent agents to survey all Southeast Asian countries, setting up a trading office in Singapore, and studied the forested hinterland of Saigon, into eastern Cambodia. In 1925 Michelin launched its first Indochina plantations of 10,000 hectares, the forest cleared by coolies from the densely populated lowlands of northern Vietnam.

During the Depression rubber was as much at the mercy of collapsing demand and prices as any tropical crop. Prices on the New York market hit their lowest point in June 1932, as supplies piled up in the warehouses.[17] Faced with precipitous price drops of 90 percent and more, the corporations chose not to reduce but to increase their production, because the new production of the bud-grafted plantations which they had planted in the mid 1920s was just reaching the market. In order to meet this crisis, the major producers formed the International Rubber Regulation Commission in 1934. The IRRC allowed no new planting of any sort, and limited replanting to 20 percent of existing acreage, for bud-grafted clones. In Indochina state subsidies enabled production in the French colonies to grow six-fold by 1938, at last meeting all of

14 Tengwall, "History of rubber cultivation," pp. 349–350.

15 Margaret Slocomb, *Colons and Coolies: The Development of Cambodia's Rubber Plantations* (Bangkok: White Lotus, 2007), pp. 50–56.

16 Charles Robequain, *The Economic Development of French Indo-China* (Oxford University Press, 1944); François Graveline, *Des hévéas et des hommes: l'aventure des plantations Michelin* (Paris: Chaudin, 2006).

17 Babcock, *History of the United States Rubber Company*, p. 353.

metropolitan France's needs, plus even larger exports to the United States. This was accomplished by rapid concentration of ownership into several vertically integrated firms, which were closely linked to the major banks in France.[18]

The war in the Pacific, which began in December 1941, spread rapidly through Southeast Asia, as Japanese forces quickly took control of critical military resources, including rubber. In Indonesia Japan's conquest of the Dutch rubber plantations severely damaged production. Japanese policy encouraged peasants to occupy the tobacco and rubber estates, cut down the older rubber trees, and grow their own food. Many plantations were taken over by local warlords and workers' unions. Three years of war, followed by four years of struggle for Indonesian independence, left the plantations badly battered and their former workers in turmoil. A different era in Indonesian and global rubber production would emerge in the 1950s.

In Indochina the Japanese occupiers maintained partial production through the war. But after they were forced out in 1945, war continued there, as the Vietnamese struggled for independence from France. In 1947 Viet Minh units launched attacks on the plantations, beginning the crippling of rubber production. The situation worsened in the American phase of the war in the decade after 1965. Only after the war ended in 1975 could Vietnam begin to bring its rubber plantations back into full production: from 52,000 metric tons in 1985 it rose to 291,000 tons in 2000, the sixth largest producer in the world.

Rubber and forest clearance in tropical Africa

In the three decades before Southeast Asian plantation rubber flooded the international market, the years when global demand was rapidly rising and inadequately supplied, forcing world prices upward, the race for rubber spread throughout tropical Africa. A long history of exports from that region, primarily ivory and slaves, was transformed after 1885, when Britain, Germany, France, Belgium, and Portugal carved the map of Africa into zones of colonial control. Each European Power then launched military conquests, setting up administrations and financing the exploitation of primary products of its African lands. In one colony after another, rubber was one of the most promising products.

18 Martin J. Murray, *The Development of Capitalism in Colonial Indochina (1870–1940)* (Berkeley, CA: University of California Press, 1980), pp. 259–270.

In contrast to Amazonia, the forests of tropical Africa supported a variety of latex-bearing trees and vines. The primary tree species, *Funtumia elastica*, (most common in West Africa) could tolerate frequent tapping, but its latex would dry up for some years if it was over-tapped for about five years. Latex-producing vines, several species of *Landolphia*, were even more vulnerable to tapping. Growing high on host trees, they were the primary source of rubber in the Congo River basin, the second greatest rain forest on earth. Scoring their bark easily killed them, and the latex from the higher reaches could be collected only by cutting the vines close to the ground.[19]

From the early 1890s the European rulers attempted to increase production and export of rubber, either by encouraging pre-existing networks of small-scale free traders or by granting enormous land concessions to private companies. The initial harvest of rubber from the forest was promising: by 1900 the African continent exported over 15,000 tons, compared with over 26,000 tons from Brazil.[20]

Similar stories in numerous African colonies marked the tentative increase of rubber exports until about 1900, accompanied by rapid destruction of rubber trees and vines. In nearly every location local labor was coerced into collecting the latex, under conditions that often became notoriously violent. In German East Africa the tapping of wild rubber vines moved gradually inland from the Tanzanian coast along old trade routes, depleting the Landolphia supplies over a widening area.[21] But the most notorious case was the Belgian Congo, the personal estate of King Leopold from 1885 to 1908. The king granted private concessionaires vast regions of the Congo basin full rights to the natural resources of those lands and full power to coerce a labor force, in return for a major share of the profits. Widespread violence accompanied the almost total depletion of rubber vines, usually within five years of beginning extraction in each area.[22]

By 1907 or so two forces combined to begin reducing the African production: disastrously declining sources of wild rubber, and declining prices on the world market. From 1913 onward Southeast Asian Hevea plantation rubber dominated international markets. Only plantations could give Africa a place

19 Robert Harms, "The end of red rubber: a reassessment," *Journal of African History* 16/1 (1975), 77; Jamie Monson, "From commerce to colonization: a history of the rubber trade in the Kilombero Valley of Tanzania, 1890–1914," *African Economic History* 21 (1993), 115.

20 Kurian Abraham, ed., *Asian Rubber Handbook and Directory, 2005* (Kochi: Rubber Asia for Dhanam Publications, 2005), p. 47.

21 Monson, "From commerce to colonization," 113–130.

22 Among various accounts of this process, the most vivid and detailed is Adam Hochschild, *King Leopold's Ghost* (Boston and New York: Houghton Mifflin, 1998).

on the world rubber stage again. This ultimately happened in Liberia on the west coast, where British entrepreneurial initiative made the first attempt. In 1906 the Liberian Rubber Corporation, a subsidiary of Dunlop, opened the first rubber plantations, but they failed to prosper.

Americans entered the African competition after World War I, in Liberia, a country founded by American ex-slaves in the 1830s. This was the only African location where Americans had both major familiarity and a political foothold. Unlike any of the other primary products from tropical trees and plants, rubber came to be considered a "strategic material" in the minds of American military and foreign policy planners. The term "strategic materials" arose during World War I. It denoted those raw materials which the industrial era had made critical for military preparedness, and whose sources any powerful country had to control if it was to survive international conflict. The list was primarily metals, but it included petroleum and rubber. From World War I onwards, therefore, rubber imports assumed a strategic priority beyond any other tropical crop.[23] This was compounded by the civilian market for rubber products. By the early 1920s Americans were purchasing 85 percent of the world's cars and three-fourths of global rubber production, of which 80 percent was for automobile tires.[24]

American planners saw that since rubber was a strategic raw material, it was urgent to break out of British domination of international supplies and prices.[25] In the effort to break British domination of the world rubber economy, no one was more central than Harvey Firestone, the rubber products magnate. During the war he had presided over the Rubber Association of America, which allotted the rubber that the British allowed the USA to import.[26] Firestone was unwilling to tolerate such a situation. In 1923 he appealed to Congress for support in identifying tropical locations appropriate for growing plantation rubber outside Europe's colonies in Southeast Asia, a move which might have ecological repercussions around the tropics.

23 Mark R. Finlay, *Growing American Rubber: Strategic Plants and the Politics of National Security* (New Brunswick: Rutgers, 2009), describes the strategic policy context and the failed efforts to find a substitute for Hevea as a source, especially guayule, *Parthenium argentatum*, a drought-resistant woody shrub.

24 Alfred E. Eckes, Jr., *The United States and the Global Struggle for Minerals* (Austin: University of Texas Press, 1979), p. 46.

25 Joseph Brandes, *Herbert Hoover and Economic Diplomacy: Department of Commerce Policy, 1921–1928* (University of Pittsburgh Press, 1962), pp. 106–128.

26 Harvey S. Firestone, *Men and Rubber: The Story of Business* (Garden City: Doubleday, Page, 1926), pp. 258–259.

Liberia lay on 350 miles of Atlantic coastline.[27] The shoreline had no deep water ports. The coast was heavily forested, marked by lagoons and the tidal flats of a series of small rivers. Sandy soils supported dense mangrove forests. Inland, primary forest was dotted with many patches of "low bush," scrub secondary vegetation resulting from local villagers' shifting cultivation of crops.[28] Numerous ethnic groups had emigrated from the savannas of the continent's interior over the previous several centuries.[29] They grew upland rice, cassava, and a variety of vegetable and fruit crops, moving gradually from one location to another. In the 1920s there was no railroad to the interior and few good roads were built.

In that setting, American bankers succeeded in taking over a British loan in 1912, when the Liberian government defaulted. After that the USA effectively controlled the Liberian economy. Americans were not interested in a formal empire anywhere in Africa, but control of one area of Africa's wet tropical zone might well suit American commercial and industrial interests.

Liberia remained a backwater into the 1920s.[30] In April 1924 Firestone's team studied Liberia, focusing on the neglected rubber plantation, where they found promising conditions.[31] In 1926 the Liberian government granted Firestone an enormous concession: 1 million acres of land for 99 years. In return Firestone would build port and harbor facilities, roads, hospitals, sanitation, and hydropower. Firestone would also provide medical staff, a sanitary engineer, a mechanical engineer, an architect and builder, a soil expert, and a forester.

In order to exploit an estate of such a vast scale, Firestone projected $100 million capital costs and a work force of 350,000 laborers. In 1934 the first trees were tapped. Rubber soon produced over 50 percent of Liberia's exports in value. The scale of the rubber corporation's effort was daunting for a country of Liberia's size. Firestone's labor force was ultimately 50 percent larger than all other wage labor in the country. The main plantation, headquartered at Harbel, was 140 square miles in extent. It employed 21,000 workers by the

27 J. B. Webster and A. A. Boahen, *The Growth of African Civilisation: The Revolutionary Years, West Africa since 1800* (London: Longman, 1968).

28 Torkel Holsoe, *Third Report on Forestry Progress in Liberia, 1951–1959* (Washington: International Cooperation Administration, 1961), pp. 1–10.

29 Yekutiel Gershoni, *Black Colonialism: The Americo-Liberian Scramble for the Hinterland* (Boulder: Westview, 1985), pp. 1–6, 67–95.

30 W. W. Schmokel, "Settler and tribes: origins of the Liberian dilemma," in Daniel F. McCall, Norman R. Bennett, and Jeffrey Butler (eds.), *Western African History* (New York: Praeger, 1969), pp. 153–181.

31 Stephen D. Krasner, *Defending the National Interest: Raw Materials Investments and U.S. Foreign Policy* (Princeton University Press, 1978), pp. 104–105.

early 1960s, 3,000 of them skilled and semi-skilled, the rest tappers. Its senior staff was 180, mostly American and European. As an environmental consequence, vast acreage of the land was transformed partially from natural or second-growth forest and partially from cropped fields, to massive groves of Hevea trees.

World War II and the rise of synthetic rubber

In the late 1930s, as war loomed again in Europe and the Pacific, diversification of rubber source locations became an urgent strategic concern for the industrial powers.[32] Confrontation between the West and Japan over Southeast Asia's strategic materials accelerated. After Japan's 1937 invasion of China, Japanese leaders feared an American and British embargo, especially of aviation fuel, and looked to the Dutch Indies as a source of both petroleum and rubber.

The US government had been attempting to stockpile rubber from Southeast Asia for some time before that, but Britain had been only partially cooperative. At the end of 1939 the USA had less than a three months' supply of rubber on hand, and attempted to expand purchases from the International Rubber Regulation Committee. When Nazi Germany's invasions of adjacent countries began in late 1939, the British-controlled Committee began to loosen its restrictions. Nonetheless, by May 1940 the USA still had only three months' supply of rubber in stockpile.

In June 1940 the Reconstruction Finance Corporation created four satellite purchasing corporations for strategic materials, including the Rubber Reserve Company. But even after the Japanese attack on Pearl Harbor, it had reached only 30 percent of its target.[33] Firestone's production in Liberia was steadily accelerating, but it never accounted for more than 7 percent of the enormous American market.

Only a breakthrough in rubber production could solve the dilemma. Fortunately for the war effort – and in the longer run for the remaining rain forest reserves of the tropical world – a new source of rubber, synthetic rubber derived from petroleum, became available as the war continued, transforming the entire industry. From the 1860s onward, European chemists had been attempting to synthesize rubber from a wide variety of source

32 There was also a renewed but still unsuccessful search for plant sources other than Hevea. See Finlay, *Growing American Rubber*, and Wade Davis, *One River*.

33 Eckes, *The United States and the Global Struggle for Minerals*, pp. 80–83, 93–102; Alfred Lief, *The Firestone Story* (New York: McGraw Hill, 1951), pp. 250–251.

materials.[34] Collaboration between the British and German petrochemical industries broke down during World War I, when the Allies blockaded German imports of tropical natural rubber. In desperation Germany managed to produce 150 tons per month of methyl rubber, but automotive tires lost their shape when vehicles were parked for any length of time.[35] So postwar Germany dropped the effort to synthesize rubber from petroleum.

Meanwhile, in the USA, DuPont succeeded in polymerizing a form of rubber which it called Neoprene. German efforts revived by the late 1920s, as Germany attempted to become strategically independent of imported natural rubber. In a cooperative effort I.G. Farben and Standard Oil of New Jersey negotiated a contract to develop synthetic petrol. IG was already making synthetic rubber from acetylene. In 1930 IG produced acetylene from natural gas; in a stroke of good fortune for Standard Oil and American strategic interests, this product was covered in the basic information-sharing contract. So it was interested in IG's new Buna-S rubber, which was related to the acetylene process. After 1933 the new Nazi regime imported natural rubber from Brazil and elsewhere, but it wanted independence from tropical products. It pushed improvements of Buna, but tire treads stripped from their casings when Buna was used heavily. By 1939, at the beginning of the war, Germany had improved Buna enough to meet military requirements, and was able to use it for many wartime purposes, though the greater strength of natural rubber was indispensable for uses such as airplane tires.

As international military tensions rose during the 1930s, the Western Allies were just as vulnerable to disruption of natural rubber supplies as their potential enemies.[36] By the end of 1939 the American stockpile was only 125,800 tons, hardly three months' supply. As early as 1933–34, Harvey Firestone had attempted to use DuPont's Neoprene to supply the Army with airplane tires. In the summer of 1940 Firestone unveiled viable synthetic tires. Simultaneously Standard Oil continued improving Buna, now with financial support from Congress. At a cost of $700 million, in two years Standard and Firestone reached full-scale production of synthetic rubber based on petroleum and coal, making 1 million tons of rubber per year.

34 W. J. S. Naunton, "Synthetic rubber," in P. Schidrowitz and T. R. Dawson (eds.), *History of the Rubber Industry* (Cambridge: Heffer, 1952), pp. 100–109.

35 Firestone, *Men and Rubber*, p. 253.

36 Jonathan Marshall, *To Have and Have Not: Southeast Asian Raw Materials and the Origins of the Pacific War* (Berkeley, CA: University of California Press, 1995), pp. 33–53.

Meanwhile Britain struggled with critical shortages after the 1940–41 German air raids on British cities and industries. In tropical Asia the British and Dutch were caught by surprise in early 1942 by the sudden Japanese conquest of Malaya, Java, and Sumatra. The only natural rubber supplies left were from Ceylon and India. In desperation Britain linked with the USA for synthetic rubber. The British received their first American synthetics in late 1943; by 1944 they were using 75 percent synthetics.

At end of the war, Britain rapidly reconverted to natural rubber.[37] Until 1947 the British government purchased rubber from its Southeast Asian colonies to deliver to the United States, to pay its wartime debts and accumulate dollars for reconstruction. That flow helped stabilize rubber production there and prepare the plantations for the boom era of the 1950s.

After 1945 the global rubber economy rose steadily, with the reindustrialization of Europe and Japan, and the expansion of other industrial economies. But because of the rise of synthetic rubber, this did not result in a continuing massive removal of tropical forest. There was a rising percentage of synthetic rubber in the international economy, and particularly in the American industry, which was by far its largest component. Between 1948 and 1973 world demand for rubber rose 6 percent per year. Natural rubber production grew by 3.3 percent per year, but synthetic rubber increased nearly three times as fast, by 9.3 percent per year.[38] Synthetic rubber production surpassed natural rubber in 1962; by 1973 it reached two-thirds of total global rubber production. The global acreage under natural rubber remained roughly steady, but steadily rising global consumption had less cumulative impact on tropical land use than it would have had if synthetic rubber had not assumed its major role.

The rubber industry in the United States, with its limited supply base of natural rubber, pushed for further rapid development of synthetic rubber. Until the mid 1950s most production of petroleum-based rubber was in the United States. By 1973, when global production reached 7,295,000 tons, still 40 percent was produced in the USA and Canada.[39] Western Europe and Japan began large-scale production only after 1960. The primary market was for

37 S. A. Brazier, "The rubber industry in the 1939–1945 war," in Schidrowitz and Dawson, *History of the Rubber Industry*, pp. 316–326.

38 Colin Barlow, *The Natural Rubber Industry: Its Development, Technology and Economy in Malaysia* (Oxford University Press, 1978), p. 408.

39 Barlow, *Natural Rubber Industry*, pp. 109, 415.

the booming civilian automotive tire industry. Today two-thirds of all rubber is used by the auto industry, and no economy or consumer culture has been so gripped by that industry as the United States.[40]

Natural rubber production after 1945

Natural rubber, not its petroleum-based competitor, determines land use in the tropical lowlands. Global production, after its immediate postwar low of 851,000 tons in 1946, quickly revived to 1,890,000 tons in 1950. By 1973, at the onset of the OPEC petroleum era, the figure rose to 3,493,000 tons.[41] Much of this was produced on acreage which had already been growing rubber trees, as production became more efficient. The United States remained a major consumer, but not permanently the largest. In 1973 North America, including Canada as well as the USA, purchased 757,000 tons of natural rubber from the tropical world. By then Western Europe had surpassed it, with its far greater direct sources of postcolonial production, buying 921,000 tons. And Japan's purchases from Southeast Asia had risen to 335,000 tons, as Japan's consumer economy became a major source of pressure on tropical resource systems.[42]

The automotive industry was far and away the largest consumer of natural rubber, especially in the United States. In 1970 400,000 tons of natural rubber went into automotive tires, compared with 168,000 tons for other uses. In contrast, the European Economic Community consumed 384,000 tons of natural rubber in tires and nearly as much, 317,000 tons, for other purposes. Japan's pattern was similar to Europe's.

Since 1945 the geographical pattern of natural rubber production remained stable: over 90 percent has been produced in tropical Asia, about 6 percent in equatorial Africa, and only 1 percent in Latin America. Malaya (renamed Malaysia in 1957) became the dominant producer, its production rising from around 700,000 tons in the mid 1950s to over twice that in the mid-1970s. Indonesia, independent after 1949, produced much slower increases, only to

40 Enzo R. Grilli, Barbara Bennett Agostini, and Maria J. 'tHooft-Welvaars, *The World Rubber Economy: Structure, Changes, and Prospects* (Baltimore: Johns Hopkins University Press, 1980), p. 21. Later figures are also from this volume, pp. 16–20, 27, 48.

41 Barlow, *Natural Rubber Industry*, p. 408. Also see H. J. Stern, *Rubber, Natural and Synthetic* (New York: Maclaren and Sons, 1967); Neal Potter and Francis T. Christy, Jr., *Trends in Natural Resources Commodities, Statistics of Prices, Outputs, Consumption, Foreign Trade and Employment in the United States, 1870–1957* (Baltimore: Johns Hopkins University Press, 1962).

42 Barlow, *Natural Rubber Industry*, p. 412.

nearly 850,000 tons twenty years later. By contrast, rubber production in Liberia, the largest in Africa, remained a mere 2 percent of the global supply.

Smallholders had emerged as major rubber producers around Southeast Asia. By 1980 they worked 80 percent of the region's total rubber acreage, but production rates on their lands were significantly lower than on the corporate estates. For example, in 1960 Malaysia provided 35 percent of world total production, of which 413,200 tons were produced on estates and 292,800 tons were tapped by smallholders, though the acreage under the two cultivation systems was just about equal. Rubber continued to dominate the country's agricultural acreage, occupying two-thirds of the Federation's total cultivated land.[43]

The long-term environmental legacy for the peninsula was wide areas of lowland forest cleared for rubber groves, with an intensified population of both Malay and Chinese coolie labor on the land. The foreign corporations contributed greatly to making a small country a major player in world markets, and to strengthening the power of the Malayan aristocracy.[44] American investment in direct rubber plantation management in Malaysia ended in the 1950s, when US Rubber sold all its holdings there. By 1973 220,000 hectares were run by British firms and 48,000 run by Singaporean Chinese. The Malaysian industry was dominated by five British corporations which had been there, imbedded in colonial society, since the early 1900s.[45]

This was by no means the end of the United States' importance for Malaysian rubber, however. American rubber companies continued to buy large amounts of rubber in Singapore, the world's largest entrepot for the rubber economy, where sales from Indonesia, Malaysia, and Thailand were concentrated.[46] Chinese firms had gradually eliminated British firms by then. They dealt with Dunlop, Michelin, Goodyear, and other major Western buyers; some of them had their own agents in London and New York.[47]

43 Clifton R. Wharton, Jr., "Rubber supply conditions: some policy implications," in T. H. Silcock and E. K. Fisk (eds.), *The Political Economy of Independent Malaya: A Case-study in Development* (Berkeley, CA: University of California Press, 1963), pp. 131–132.

44 For further details, see Harold Brookfield, Lesley Potter, and Yvonne Byron, *In Place of the Forest: Environmental and Socioeconomic Transformation in Borneo and the Eastern Malay Peninsula* (Tokyo: United Nations University Press, 1995).

45 Barlow, *Natural Rubber Industry*, pp. 202, 205.

46 Most Indonesian rubber sales from the 1950s onward continued to be to the United States and West Europe. Japan purchased most of Thailand's rubber, and China purchased most of Sri Lanka's rubber exports. Barlow, *Natural Rubber Industry*, p. 414.

47 Barlow, *Natural Rubber Industry*, pp. 313–317.

Indonesia: nationalist politics and the plantations

American firms, especially Goodyear, gradually returned to their plantations on Sumatra after the war. American companies were reluctant to reopen under Dutch rule, which was tenuous at best in the fighting against Indonesian nationalists. In addition, they would have to return to over-aged stands of trees, since there had been little planting of new stock for several decades (just as everywhere else in Southeast Asia). The 1951 production figures were half of prewar totals. But there was a price boom during the Korean War between 1950 and 1954. The war caused international prices to triple in 1951, before settling back to pre-war levels three years later. American firms, seeing a major opportunity to supply their military's wartime demands, reopened their plantations on Sumatra, led by Wingfoot, in 1950–51. The Americans immediately began the major job of replanting the old groves with higher-yielding clones. The results were impressive: over 700,000 tons of rubber were exported every year through 1958. But in that year political turmoil once again determined the flow of rubber production, when Indonesia plunged into civil war. Most estates on Sumatra were seriously damaged, as rebels tried to cut off the government's income. By the early 1960s US Rubber was gone from Indonesia, and Goodyear's operations were being liquidated.

After 1965 General Suharto's new regime ushered in an era of political stability and economic growth favorable to the export sector. The rubber economy expanded steadily, largely at the expense of primary forest on the formerly undeveloped Outer Islands, especially Kalimantan, the vast Indonesian segment of Borneo. By 1973 the country's total exports were 886,000 tons, grown on 465,000 hectares of large estates, and over four times as much, 1,841,000 hectares, of smallholdings. In this system productivity was low: 382 kilograms per hectare in Indonesia in 1973, in comparison with 879 in Peninsular Malaysia.[48] This was more wasteful: more forest had to be felled and burned in order to achieve similar production.

Indonesian Chinese traders purchased semi-processed sheets of rubber from the growers and exported them to Singapore and Penang for further processing and sale to purchasers from Europe and North America. So American and European rubber buyers were ultimately partners in the global economic web which was responsible for the accelerating transformation of

48 Barlow, *Natural Rubber Industry*, pp. 106–107.

Borneo's rain forest away from a natural ecosystem teeming with diverse plant and animal life.

Liberia: Firestone's heyday and demise

One other important tropical source of natural rubber was still important for American markets: Liberia. Though Liberia's production in the 1960s was only about 2 percent of the world's natural rubber supply, it provided close to 7 percent of the United States' imports. Harvey Firestone had fared well during World War II in his Liberian venture. In 1960 Firestone had 69,000 acres of mature trees and 18,000 acres of young pre-producing trees on its estates. Together they produced 80 million tons of crude rubber per year. Their production averaged 12,000 pounds per acre, equal to the highest in the world.

Major new concessions to American firms such as B.F. Goodrich began in 1947, under President Tubman. Tubman also saw the usefulness of diversifying the countries to which it was linked through corporate contracts, and began cultivating European firms. In 1952 another enormous 600,000 acre land concession was granted to the German-owned African Fruit Company. This one was along the coastal lowlands; it was intended for banana production. But Panama Disease soon struck the German operation, so this concession was also converted to rubber. By 1963 5,000 acres were planted in rubber groves, under a manager who had worked for fourteen years for Firestone.[49]

Tubman's long run as President ended with his death in 1971. In the following years the increasing split between the Americo-Liberian elite and the vast majority of the indigenous population took Liberia into a period of instability and interethnic tensions. In 1980 a military coup led by Samuel Doe overthrew the government. Doe favored his own ethnic group, the Krahn, and unleashed a reign of terror against other segments of Liberian society. In response, American-educated Charles Taylor invaded the country from neighboring Ivory Coast with an insurgent force in 1989, launching a six-year civil war. Doe was killed in 1990, and five other armed factions emerged in the course of the war.

Until 1994 all factions tacitly agreed not to destroy Firestone or the smaller plantations, for any rubber which each faction could export would help finance its military operations. Taylor established his fortress inland from

49 Robert Clower et al., *Growth Without Development: An Economic Survey of Liberia* (Evanston: Northwestern University Press, 1966), p. 195.

Monrovia, up the road from the Firestone center at Kakata. When he finally attacked Monrovia, fighting quickly engulfed the Firestone plantations. Groves and facilities were largely destroyed. Only in 2005 was the chaos brought under control enough that orderly elections chose Ellen Johnson Sirleaf as Liberia's first woman President. By then Liberian society was shredded, the land lay in ruins, and the plantations were partially paralyzed. Liberia's rubber exports were only 2 percent of global production.

Natural rubber, natural forest and the changing global economy

By the early 1970s, less than a third of world rubber production came from natural rubber. Petroleum-based synthetics seemed destined to dominate the industry. Some proponents of synthetic rubber expected the entire natural rubber industry to be on its way to oblivion. But a major shock jolted the global rubber economy in 1973, when the OPEC countries imposed sudden steep price rises for petroleum. As a United Nations survey phrased it,

> In 1973 the world rubber economy suffered its first severe exogenous shock: the oil crisis and subsequent sharp rise in crude oil prices. For an industry whose major component – synthetic rubber – depends so heavily on petrochemical feedstocks, the sudden drastic increase in crude oil prices in 1973–74 represented a major change in cost structures and production economics. The other component of the industry – natural rubber – was less affected directly, but was still subject to all the indirect effects of the oil crisis: acceleration of world inflation, changes in consumer expectations, and rising doubts about the long-term future of world elastomer demand in the energy-intensive automotive sector.[50]

The immediate price rise of natural rubber was less than half of synthetic rubber's. OPEC had unwittingly introduced a new unpredictability into the rubber economy, and a new level of demand for Hevea rubber. In addition, its superior properties became decisive in tire markets in the 1980s, when radial tires, first created by Michelin's technicians, came to dominate the market. By placing cords at 90 degrees to the spin of the tire, then adding a steel belt beneath the tread, they produced longer life, better fuel consumption, and more effective handling.

The last decades of the twentieth century saw major shifts in the global industrial and consumer economy; natural rubber consumption was a major

50 Grilli, *World Rubber Economy*, p. 7.

element of that shift. Malaysia and Indonesia remained the two dominant producers, though Thailand and others began to challenge their share: Malaysia shifted from 39 percent of expanding world production in 1960 to 34 percent in 1985, though its production nearly doubled. Indonesia dropped from 31 percent to 26 percent, though its production more than doubled.

Consumption patterns changed more dramatically. The United States, which led global consumption until the century's end, expanded from 764,000 metric tons in 1985 to 1,150,000 in 2003. By that year China's rapidly accelerating economy, which had consumed 415,000 tons in 1985 (third in the world, behind Japan), became the world's largest rubber importer by 2003, consuming 1,455,000 tons – and one-third of that was now produced domestically, on large new plantations in the south. India's figures expanded similarly: from 233,000 tons consumed in 1985 to 714,000 tons in 2003; two-thirds of that was produced internally, from plantations in the southern hills which dated back to colonial times. Brazil, the demographic and industrial powerhouse of Latin America, was surging in similar fashion: from 98,000 tons in 1985 it grew to 227,000 tons in 2000. In contrast, in Europe in 2000 Germany and France together consumed 520,000 tons, and the shrunken Russian economy consumed only 36,000 tons.[51]

By the early 1990s natural rubber had risen again to well over one-third of global production. As Wade Davis succinctly notes, "Today the tires of every commercial and military aircraft . . . are 100 percent natural rubber. . . . The enormous tires of industrial machinery are 90 percent natural. Nearly half of the rubber in every automobile tire originates on plantations located thirteen thousand miles away."[52] Those thousands of miles represented the global ecological links of the automotive age and provided a horizon beyond which consumers saw no need to look.

Further reading

Babcock, Glenn D. *History of the United States Rubber Company*. Bloomington: Bureau of Business Research, Indiana University, 1966.

Barlow, Colin. *The Natural Rubber Industry: Its Development, Technology and Economy in Malaysia*. Oxford University Press, 1978.

Brookfield, Harold, Lesley Potter, and Yvonne Byron. *In Place of the Forest: Environmental and Socioeconomic Transformation in Borneo and the Eastern Malay Peninsula*. Tokyo: United Nations University Press, 1995.

51 For global statistics, see Abraham, *Asian Rubber Handbook*, pp. 49–50.
52 Davis, *One River*, p. 370.

Davis, Wade. *One River: Explorations and Discoveries in the Amazon Rain Forest*. New York: Simon & Schuster, 1996.

Dean, Warren. *Brazil and the Struggle for Rubber: A Study in Environmental History*. Cambridge University Press, 1987.

Eckes, Alfred E., Jr. *The United States and the Global Struggle for Minerals*. Austin: University of Texas Press, 1979.

Finlay, Mark R. *Growing American Rubber: Strategic Plants and the Politics of National Security*. New Brunswick: Rutgers, 2009.

Gershoni, Yekutiel. *Black Colonialism: The Americo-Liberian Scramble for the Hinterland*. Boulder: Westview, 1985.

Grandin, Greg. *Fordlandia: The Rise and Fall of Henry Ford's Forgotten Jungle City*. New York: Metropolitan Books, 2009.

Graveline, François. *Des hévéas et des hommes: l'aventure des plantations Michelin*. Paris: Chaudin, 2006.

Grilli, Enzo R., Barbara Bennett Agostini, and Maria J. 'tHooft-Welvaars. *The World Rubber Economy: Structure, Changes, and Prospects*. Baltimore: Johns Hopkins University Press, 1980.

Harms, Robert. "The end of red rubber: a reassessment," *Journal of African History* 16/1 (1975), 73–88.

Hochschild, Adam. *King Leopold's Ghost*. Boston and New York: Houghton Mifflin, 1998.

Krasner, Stephen D. *Defending the National Interest: Raw Materials Investments and U.S. Foreign Policy*. Princeton University Press, 1978.

Marshall, Jonathan. *To Have and Have Not: Southeast Asian Raw Materials and the Origins of the Pacific War*. Berkeley, CA: University of California Press, 1995.

McMillan, James. *The Dunlop Story*. London: Weidenfeld and Nicholson, 1989.

Monson, Jamie. "From commerce to colonization: a history of the rubber trade in the Kilombero Valley of Tanzania, 1890–1914," *African Economic History* 21 (1993), 113–130.

Schidrowitz, P. and T. R. Dawson, eds. *History of the Rubber Industry*. Cambridge: Heffer, 1952.

Slocomb, Margaret. *Colons and Coolies: The Development of Cambodia's Rubber Plantations*. Bangkok: White Lotus, 2007.

Stoler, Ann Laura. *Capitalism and Confrontation in Sumatra's Plantation Belt, 1870–1979*. New Haven: Yale University Press, 1985.

Tengwall, T. A. "History of rubber cultivation and research in the Netherlands Indies," in Pieter Honig and Frans Verdoorn (eds.), *Science and Scientists in the Netherlands Indies*. New York: Board for the Netherlands Indies, 1945.

Tucker, Richard P. *Insatiable Appetite: The United States and the Ecological Devastation of the Tropical World*. Berkeley, CA: University of California Press, 2000. Condensed and updated edition Lanham, MD: Rowman and Littlefield, 2007.

19

Drugs in the modern era

WILLIAM B. MCALLISTER[1]

Since the dawn of humanity, almost all societies have had access to locally indigenous psychoactive substances.[2] With the exception of peoples in far northern climes where no suitable plants or domesticable animals existed, cultures have enjoyed the benefits of, and encountered the problems attendant to, the use of chemicals that alter consciousness and body functioning. Often used for religious purposes, as medicinals, or to facilitate work, societies have universally imposed some sort of control or restriction on consumption of psychoactive substances. In many regions the use of such traditional drugs of local origin continues today. This chapter focuses on the period after 1500, during which the introduction of non-indigenous

1 The views expressed here are the author's and do not necessarily represent those of the US Government or the Department of State.

2 No universally agreed definition of what constitutes a "drug" exists. Functionally based characterizations divide drugs into categories of control according to their physiological effects as defined in legislation or treaties; the main classes include narcotics, central nervous system stimulants and depressants, and hallucinogens/cannabis (United Nations Office on Drugs and Crime, *Information about Drugs*, www.unodc.org/unodc/en/illicit-drugs/definitions/index.html). This chapter will combine that categorization with an adaptation of F. E. Zimring and G. Hawkins, *The Search for Rational Drug Control* (Cambridge University Press, 1992), pp. 31–32: "a psychoactive substance, often of medicinal value, capable of being used recreationally, and subject to control measures." Incorporating the notion of "addiction" raises difficulties because the conception of the term as currently used is relatively recent, and even since its modern inception, definitions of addiction changed as an increasing number of substances have proven to cause some form of physical or psychological withdrawal symptoms, or consciousness alteration. Any pharmacologically complete definition of drugs must also include alcohol and nicotine (tobacco). The subjects of alcohol and tobacco are so large that they can receive only cursory treatment. The bulk of this chapter will focus on medicinal and quasi-medicinal substances that are also susceptible to abuse, as those terms have been applied commonly, if somewhat imprecisely, over the last century. Rather than the common use of the term "narcotics" as a synonym for all psychoactive substances, this article restricts the use of "narcotics" to the family of natural and synthetic opiate substances used primarily for analgesic purposes that produces a distinct array of addictive characteristics. Following the terminology applied in international control treaties, central nervous system stimulants, depressants, as well as hallucinogens are grouped together here under the term "psychotropic" substances.

psychoactive substances across the globe caused significant changes in drug consumption, economic activity and world trade, societal functioning, behavioral norms, and political organization. For the purposes of this overview, the modern history of global drug expansion is divided into three periods: the Era of Diffusion (1500 to mid nineteenth century), the Era of Development and Control (mid nineteenth century to mid 20th century), and the Era of Globalization (later twentieth century to present). The cross-cultural interaction engendered by widespread drug use – for both medicinal and non-medicinal purposes – generated many schemes to manipulate the market for profit and power, as well as influential movements to regulate drug consumption.

The Era of Diffusion

Psychoactive substances played a crucial role in facilitating early modern global exchanges of goods, ideas, and people. When Christopher Columbus landed in the Caribbean, the indigenes offered him tobacco among their inaugural friendship gifts. Unknown previously outside the Americas, within 150 years tobacco use and cultivation spread all over the world. Beginning in the sixteenth century, coffee expanded from its Ethiopian origins, through the Ottoman Empire, and on to Europe and the eastern reaches of Asia. By the mid sixteenth century, tea, long consumed in East Asia, became an item of trade in Europe. Although many societies had long experience with wine, beer, mead, and other low-alcohol-content drinks, more potent distilled spirits gained in popularity, especially across Europe, in the seventeenth century. The "take-off" of these substances beyond their original areas of use illustrates the dynamic nature and thoroughgoing penetration of the post-Columbian upswing in world interaction.

Habit-forming substances emerged as prized items for merchants, governments, and consumers across multiple strata of society. First introduced into new environments by soldiers, missionaries, and imperial administrators, the profit potential of drugs became apparent to traders, public house proprietors, and revenue officials. Their high value and low bulk made them excellent cargo: a productive farmer distant from major markets or a merchant ship owner could reap much higher returns from a load of whiskey or tea than from a comparable weight of grain or timber. Governments monopolized or taxed substances first considered luxury goods and later mass consumption commodities. When introduced to a new region, early adopters usually viewed psychoactive substances as possessing medicinal qualities, which helped spread their use. Drugs also served as a status marker. When tobacco smoking became commonplace, for example, elites developed a preference for snuff. Over time, public establishments, especially in European countries and their settler colonies, distinguished themselves by the beverages they served – coffee for businessmen, alcohol for workers, tea for ladies. Houses of refreshment also provided venues for civic engagement, political activity, military recruitment, and sedition. The drugs trade also stimulated other key sectors of the economy. Manufacture of distilled spirits depended on cheap grain (for gin) or cheap sugar (for rum), and consumption of tea, coffee, and cacao required large amounts of sweetener, thereby fueling interoceanic exchanges of sugar, slaves, foodstuffs, and other items. By the eighteenth century, Europe, in particular, had developed a mass market in psychoactive substances, for both medicinal and recreational purposes.

The introduction of new and more concentrated drugs, however, generated significant concern that led to control initiatives. After an initial period of euphoria about the medicinal qualities of non-indigenous drugs, a backlash often occurred. The objections fell into several general categories including direct health effects, diminution of worker efficiency, diversion of resources from more laudable purposes, or threat to the established social order. Many governments across the Eurasian continent attempted to prohibit the increasingly ubiquitous use of tobacco.[3] King James I of England, for example, issued a decree in 1604 declaring smoking, "A custome loathesome to the eye, hatefull to the Nose, harmefull to the braine, and in the blacke stinking fume thereof, neerest resembling the horrible Stigian smoke of the pit that is bottomlesse."[4] Regardless of the medicinal qualities coffee might have been perceived to possess, Ottoman rulers attempted to suppress serving houses that they feared operated as sites of political dissent. The problems associated with alcohol use generated the most opprobrium. Religious leaders objected to the loss of individual moral control and the pernicious effect of drunkenness on families. Employers expressed concerns about productivity loss. Government officials feared that unruliness, especially among the lower classes, posed a challenge to state authority. Many Asians, Africans, and Native Americans, as well as a few westerners, found the role of alcohol in enslaving people distasteful. Authorities employed all manner of regulatory

3 For an illustrative list of governments that attempted to ban tobacco, see Fernand Braudel, *The Structures of Everyday Life* (New York: Harper and Row, 1979), pp. 260–265.

4 "A Counter-Blaste to Tobacco," www.gutenberg.org/files/17008/17008-h/17008-h.htm (accessed August 12, 2012).

measures, including moral suasion, extolling the virtues of sobriety, social exclusion, access restrictions, limits on sales, high taxes, consumption prohibitions, and attempts to provide substitutes perceived as less problematic (for example, promoting beer as an alternative to gin) in attempts to curb the pernicious effects of drink on society.

Despite many individually successful interventions, regulatory efforts generally failed to reduce drug consumption. One reason is the self-reinforcing nature of drug use; once habituated to psychoactive substances, humans will often go to great lengths to acquire them (a phenomenon that applies not only to "hard drugs" – every day untold numbers perceive they cannot function without their morning coffee). If the preferred substance is unavailable or too expensive, the poly-drug phenomenon occurs as habitués attempt to secure a substitute. In turn, this habit-forming character of psychoactive substances proved immensely profitable for entrepreneurs. After the introduction of vodka in Russia during the sixteenth century, the industry generated enormous profits for manufacturers and retailers, which eventually provided much of the capital for nineteenth-century industrial development.[5] The growth of Glasgow, Scotland, as an early center of international sea-borne trade rested largely on the city's reputation as a key exchange point for tobacco. Moreover, governments themselves became addicted to the revenues generated from drug consumption. State authorities taxed imports, exports, and sales, or monopolized the trade, either controlling it directly or selling concessions to the highest bidder who then charged whatever the traffic would bear. Many governments drew an increasing share of support from the trade; by the early nineteenth century vodka receipts comprised the largest single source of revenue for the Tsarist regime.[6] The government-supported cartels that played a central role in colonization, such as the East India and West India trading companies, profited handsomely from the traffic in tea, coffee, sugar, tobacco, and opium. Governments also supported agricultural experimentation stations (such as Kew Gardens in England or Buitenzorg in the Dutch East Indies) that developed more potent strains to plant in colonial holdings that could maximize profit.[7]

5 David Christian, *"Living Water": Vodka and Russian Society on the Eve of Emancipation* (Oxford: Clarendon Press, 1990), p. 376.

6 Christian, *"Living Water"*, pp. 5–7, 34, 134–135.

7 For recent descriptive and statistical analyses, see P. Wallis, "Exotic drugs and English medicine: England's drug trade, c. 1550–c. 1800," *Social History of Medicine* 25/1 (2011), 20–46; B. Forrest and T. Glick, "Cacao culture: case studies in history," Special Issue of C. Counihan and A. Grieco (eds.), *Food and Foodways: Explorations in the History and Culture of Human Nourishment* 15/1 (2007).

This combination of increasingly widespread drug use, profit potential for businesses, government revenue opportunities, and attempts to regulate consumption also spawned an impressive array of clandestine activity. Entrepreneurs willing to take risks for high returns smuggled, evaded taxes, circumvented control measures, and cut in on monopolies. Although smuggling is an ancient practice, its pace and scope accelerated with the expansion in world trade, and the concentrated value of psychoactive substances played an important role. Storing and transporting drugs illicitly created distribution systems that could carry other contraband. In some colonial settings, drug profiteering stimulated comprador relationships, which restructured power dynamics among imperial agents, local collaborators, and regimes in Africa and Asia that resisted incorporation into the global system on disadvantageous terms. Governments themselves engaged in agricultural espionage, ferreting out samples of promising substances from territory controlled by rivals and attempting to manipulate the most promising strains for cultivation in friendly possessions. The booming licit drug economy existed symbiotically alongside illicit trafficking, which produced profound effects on state capacity and societal functioning, a dynamic that continues to the present day.

The most notable manifestation of this worldwide activity in psychoactive substances developed across East and South Asia. Opium had long been employed widely as an important medicine, but usually in a relatively weak form – either eaten or dissolved into a solution and drunk. After smoking tobacco reached East Asia and Indonesia in the seventeenth century, the inevitable drug experimentation ensued. Individuals mixed tobacco with various substances, and opium produced a powerful narcotic effect. Chinese imperial attempts to restrict smoking exempted opium as a medicinal, a state policy that inadvertently stimulated development of a prepared form of opium that could be inhaled when heated, which came to be called "opium smoking." Dutch, Portuguese, and English traders supplied increasing amounts of smoking opium, primarily from India; although exact figures are impossible to calculate, by the mid eighteenth century opium imports into China alone probably exceeded 100,000 kilograms per annum. To reduce a chronic trade imbalance (created, in large measure, by imports of the popular drug-food tea) and to earn hard currency, the British East India Company created a monopoly to buy up all opium within the territory it controlled, and marketed the produce to merchants who carried the precious cargo to East Asian ports. In the Dutch East Indies and elsewhere, colonial authorities monopolized the distribution of opium, subcontracting retail operations to the highest bidder (referred to as "opium farming" because colonial authorities "farmed out" supplies to locals who paid handsomely for the right to an exclusive sales territory). By the early nineteenth century the trade exceeded 300,000 kilos per annum. The Chinese government became increasingly concerned about both problems associated with opium smoking and about the silver drain out of the country to pay for imports. Over the course of the eighteenth and early nineteenth centuries, Qing imperial authorities promulgated a series of edicts to reduce both imports and opium use, but to little avail. European traders coopted local officials in entrepots such as Macao and Hong Kong to smuggle opium into China. Eventually the tension led to hostilities. The Chinese Empire suffered a serious defeat by small but technologically superior British forces in the Opium War of 1839–1842, which ushered in an era of increasing encroachment on Chinese sovereignty. Most nineteenth-century contemporaries observed that opium use contributed significantly to a serious deterioration in Chinese society and governance, an assessment that eventually provided a geopolitical rationale for the imposition of drug control on a global scale.

By the mid nineteenth century, psychoactive substances played a key role in global exchanges of commodities, capital, people, and power. On a pound-for-pound basis, opium comprised the most profitable item traded across the planet. For example, the original "clipper ships" were designed to carry relatively small cargoes of the highly valuable drug from India to the East; well-armed and fast, the clippers featured not only quick turnaround times but also the capacity to outrun or outfight the pirates who plied the transit routes in search of doubly illicit gain.

Cumulatively, over the course of several centuries, "new" drugs (that is, not native to the local culture) spread around the globe as part of the post-Columbian increase in global trade. The European-dominated licit trade and illicit traffic in drugs contributed to major alterations in the daily lives of individuals, the structuring of trade relations, commodity preferences, and the balance of power among nations. Many embraced, for better or worse, a life featuring cheap and (relatively) unfettered access to mind-altering consumable substances. As the pace of global interaction quickened and its scope deepened after the mid nineteenth century, drugs presented both opportunities and challenges to emerging 20th century commercial, social, legal, medical, and governmental arrangements.

The Era of Development and Control

During the nineteenth century, a constellation of technological and commercial developments expanded the range of psychoactive substances available in an increasingly integrated global environment. Innovations stemming from the "second industrial revolution" spawned chemical-pharmaceutical companies that included units specializing in the research and development of mass-market medications. Through experimentation with different compounds, chemists created heroin, morphine, cocaine, and a variety of similar substances, all intended primarily for analgesic applications. This endeavor proved so profitable that pharmaceutical firms, such as Bayer, emerged as some of the first multinational corporate entities. As they became increasingly sophisticated at concocting medicinal substances for a variety of maladies, transnational pharmaceutical companies initiated major marketing programs to advertise their wares among both doctors and patients. Innovations in medical technology, especially the hypodermic needle, made it possible to administer the new drugs directly into the bloodstream in precise doses, and with more powerful effect. Mechanized transportation, especially steam-powered oceangoing vessels, enabled the fast, reliable, cheap shipping of high-value medicines. Rapid transport proved especially important to perishables, such as coca, the use of which remained restricted primarily to South America until it became possible to transport the leaves to western processing centers before they lost their potency.

The nineteenth century emergence in industrialized states of a medical profession and medicalized criteria for assessing drugs' efficacy influenced perceptions about psychoactive substances. Formal medical education and specialist periodical literature enabled verifiable information about a particular drug's effects to be disseminated among practitioners. Doctors played a gatekeeper function, deciding which substances qualified as "drugs," and dividing drug use into categories of "legitimate" (for medical purposes) and "illicit" use (for pleasure). A distinction between "patients" and "abusers" developed over time. Notions about "addiction" often drew upon stereotypical characterizations of race, class, or gender; the typical "drug addict" came to be seen as a person on the margins of society and therefore susceptible to regulatory measures.

Because they gradually shed the label of "drug" during this period, the manufacture, marketing, and consumption of the most commonly used psychoactive substances proceeded apace with little interference from medical or regulatory authorities. Coffee and tea came to be seen primarily as beverages, their purported medicinal qualities no longer a principal driver of consumption. The primary cacao derivative, chocolate, which required liberal application of (cheap) sugar to be palatable for a mass audience, became categorized as a sweet. Tobacco, especially cigarette smoking, grew into an extremely popular activity, viewed as essentially benign except when engaged in by children. Alcohol occupied an intermediate terrain. While not usually classified as a "drug," in most societies a general recognition maintained that distilled spirits, and often wine and beer as well, constituted a special case. Local, regional, or national governments imposed a variety of restrictions on who could drink alcohol, as well as when and where it could be sold or consumed.[8] Some jurisdictions prohibited drinking altogether. Yet even when proscribed entirely, alcohol use proved very difficult to eradicate. The mild stimulants (tea, coffee, cacao), tobacco, and alcohol all came to be treated as ordinary commodities in the international marketplace, subject to taxation, tariffs, and other trade policies that applied to normal items.

In the later nineteenth century, changes in perceptions about drug abuse and increases in demand, supply, potency, and availability caused governments to impose increasingly thoroughgoing control measures on opium- and coca-based substances. In a number of industrially developed countries subnational and national jurisdictions enacted measures to limit the distribution of opiates and coca products to "legitimate medical" purposes, as defined by Western medical standards. Colonial administrations shifted from concessions (farming) to government-controlled opium monopolies. Both in the dependencies and at home, governments implemented regulatory changes in large measure to placate religious organizations that objected to state-sponsored profiteering from the sale of addicting substances at the expense of ordinary citizens and subjects. It soon became evident, however, that the global nature of the drug trade required international

8 For an example of major nineteenth-century investigations, see the work of several Committees on Intemperance in the compilation of British Parliamentary Papers entitled *Social Problems: Drunkenness*, including "Report from the Select Committee on Drunkenness with minutes of evidence and appendices" (1834); "Report from the Select Committee on Habitual Drunkards with proceedings, minutes of evidence, appendix and index"(1872); "First, Second and Third Reports from the Select Committee of the House of Lords on the Prevalence of Habits of Intemperance with proceedings, minutes of evidence, appendices and index" (1877); "Reports from the Select Committee of the House of Lords on the Prevalence of Habits of Intemperance with proceedings, minutes of evidence, appendices and index" (1878–1879), (Shannon: Irish University Press, 1968–1969).

cooperation because illicit traders easily circumvented the strictures of individual states.

East Asian geopolitical calculations constituted the proximate factor driving the creation of an international drug control regime. By the later nineteenth century Chinese opium imports, domestic production, and consumption had reached unprecedented levels – in the 1880s Chinese imports from India alone (not counting rising imports from other sources such as Persia and Turkey) amounted to 6 million kilos per annum.[9] Most observers perceived that opium addiction seriously weakened China, and some worried that the country might be divided into spheres of influence not unlike the "Scramble for Africa" that took place in the mid 1880s. The strongest of the imperial powers, Great Britain, and the weakest, the United States, expressed the most interest in maintaining Chinese territorial integrity and central authority. The UK and the USA preferred a unified Chinese export market in order to sell their wares throughout the country. With rising tensions in Europe that required a greater proportion of British military forces closer to home, London favored an intact Chinese government that could fend off the advances of Russia, France, Japan, and the other middling imperial powers. After acquisition of the Philippines in 1898, the United States still possessed little capacity to project power on the Asian mainland and thus preferred stability in the region. Additionally, small but vocal domestic constituencies, especially in the United States, expressed concern about a potential plague of drug addiction threatening the homeland. The specter of Chinese immigrants to Western countries operating opium smoking dens that corrupted the nation's youth presented a powerful argument in favor of regulation. To promote national interest at home and abroad, London and Washington played leading roles in advocating a coordinated international response to counteract the opium scourge.

One of the most important developments in modern drug history, the fashioning of an international control regime, developed in stages during the

9 Presented here is the traditional historiography; contemporary observers estimated that Chinese domestic opium cultivation roughly equaled imports, so the total supply may have amounted to 12–14 million kilos per annum. For comparison's sake, present-day legitimate medicinal need for opiates does not exceed 1 million kilos per year, despite a world population approximately five times that of the late nineteenth century. For recent alternative accounts that discount the standard narrative, see David A. Bello, *Opium and the Limits of Empire: Drug Prohibition in the Chinese Interior, 1729–1850* (Cambridge, MA: Harvard University Press, 2005), and Frank Dikoetter, Lars Laamann, and Zhou Xuyn, *Narcotic Culture: A History of Drugs in China* (University of Chicago Press, 2004).

first third of the twentieth century. A conference at Shanghai in 1909 laid out principles of action. Treaties negotiated at The Hague in 1912, and under the auspices of the League of Nations at Geneva in 1925 and 1931, created the essential elements of the control system, and the majority of states adhered to the regime's strictures. The basic approach focused on restricting the supply of controlled substances to the amount necessary for legitimate medicinal use. Governments estimated their annual needs, and international supervisory bodies monitored the licit traffic, bringing attention to any discrepancies that might signal leakage of licit supplies into the illicit traffic. The treaties divided drugs into categories (called "schedules") that placed greater or lesser controls on their dissemination, according to their perceived addiction potential. However, the regime's framers also recognized the necessity of providing valuable medicines at a reasonable price, so the system did not limit manufactures to a predetermined amount. In practice, the profitability of drug sales ensured legal manufacturing routinely exceeded legitimate medical need, requiring detailed accounting procedures to regulate national and international distribution. Over time, the system succeeded in providing an affordable supply of high-quality medicines, at least to patients of sufficient means.

The international drug control system created incentives that channeled licit activities. Pharmaceutical firms that played by the rules benefited from access to worldwide markets, and began to refer to themselves as "ethical" drug companies. At the same time, those companies invested considerable pharmacological research and development into concocting a non-addicting analgesic; a drug that worked as well as morphine but did not carry addiction risks could corner the global market because it would not be regulated as a scheduled substance. In the 1930s, pharmaceutical companies began developing other classes of drugs, primarily stimulants and depressants, in part because they did not fall under international restrictions and therefore could be sold without interference. In subsequent decades, a plethora of non-narcotic psychoactive substances (psychotropics) reached the market, with little attention from regulatory officials. Although not recognized at the time, this quest for a type of *comparative regulatory advantage* in the licit marketplace actually created additional opportunities for individuals to become addicted as new classes of drugs with novel psychological or physiological effects entered the pharmacopeia.[10]

As officials succeeded in implementing effective controls over certain classes of drugs beginning in the later 1920s, the parallel universe of

10 William B. McAllister, *Drug Diplomacy in the Twentieth Century: An International History* (London and New York: Routledge, 2000), especially pp. 126 and 251.

clandestine activity burgeoned. Increased enforcement of the international drug control regime generated a corresponding reaction as illegal operators developed more sophisticated methods. Trafficking in illicit opium, opiate derivatives such as heroin, and cocaine expanded because those willing to run the risks of circumventing the system could generate enormous profits. Criminal organizations maintained a technological advantage because they could afford expensive weapons, transport, and communications equipment that enabled them to evade detection. A symbiotic relationship developed between drug smugglers and a transnational coalition of state-supported drug cops; when police armed with all the tools of law enforcement succeeded in some locale, the traffickers used their substantial monetary resources to devise effective countermeasures, co-opt officials, or relocate operations elsewhere.

Control of revenues derived from the drug industry comprised a key factor in the development of state capacities. In the second half of the nineteenth century, taxes on alcoholic beverages constituted between 15 and 40 percent of all national government revenues in the Netherlands, the United Kingdom, and the United States. That money fueled the growth of government social programs, especially in the fields of education and health care. Alcohol taxes also supported war; significant surcharges over and above the normal tax rate funded much of the Union effort during the American Civil War and were vital to many governments during World War I.[11]

The struggle over drug revenues proved crucial in internecine contests for state control, although long-term dependence on drug money usually proved detrimental to governing capacity. In China, after the collapse of Qing imperial authority in 1911–12, sundry warlords vied to capture opium revenues. Nationalist forces gained sufficient control over the traffic to defeat their rivals, but eventually the attendant corruption and rampant drug abuse weakened the government's command and control capabilities. In the 1930s, Japanese officials bought illicit opium from Iranian suppliers to fund occupation activities in Manchuria. Competing units within the Kwangtung Army attempted to control the trade, ultimately degrading their capacity to project military power and control the population. Notably, soon after establishment of the People's Republic of China, Communist officials launched a systematic anti-opium campaign. Sometimes employing harsh measures, the initiative was not only designed to reduce the nation's

11 J. W. Gerritsen, *The Control of Fuddle and Flash: A Sociological History of the Regulation of Alcohol and Opiates* (Leiden and Boston: Brill, 2000), pp. 87–116.

domestic drug problem, but also eliminate a source of revenue for regime opponents.[12] Insurgents also utilized drug money to support their attempts to overthrow established authorities. In the late 1940s, for example, Indonesian nationalists sold opium stocks captured from the Dutch and Japanese in their campaign to secure independence. After Communist forces occupied mainland China, remnant Nationalist military units retreated to Southeast Asia and maintained operations by controlling the region's illicit opium trading routes.

The money generated by illicit drug trafficking also blurred the lines demarcating the licit use of government power. The imposition of national and international control measures in the early twentieth century fostered institutionalized corruption in many states. Officials charged with enforcement efforts sometimes used their power to favor trafficking organizations that, in turn, provided the money, votes, and muscle to keep co-opted authorities in power. The dynamic influenced industrialists, landowners, and politicians as well as police. Authorities often blamed drug trafficking on minorities, dissident groups, or foreigners who, they believed, posed a threat to the state. Governments of regions that featured cultivation-for-export of the key controlled substances, opium, coca, or marihuana/hashish often undulated between compliance with the international regulatory norms and prevarication in order to reap the collateral benefits of illegal trafficking. In jurisdictions across the globe, some official could always be persuaded to take a bribe that facilitated transshipment and distribution. A shadowy world developed that featured addict-users willing to do almost anything for a "fix," apolitical criminals, undercover cops, co-opted informants with agendas of their own design, anti-government elements siphoning trafficking profits to support their objectives, interior ministries seeking to quash subversives, intelligence agencies operating with little accountability, and power brokers wielding governmental authority, all of which thrived on an economy suffused with drug money.[13]

Although ostensibly intended to eliminate abuse, national and international drug policies focused on control of supplies; regulatory officials and medical professionals paid little attention to the etiology of addiction. The system assumed that eliminating excess quantities would cause

12 In an enlightening illustration of the poly-drug phenomenon, mainland Chinese authorities eventually succeeded in reducing opiate usage significantly, but tobacco smoking became a similarly ubiquitous habit.

13 See, for example, Jonathan Marshall, *The Lebanese Connection: Corruption, Civil War, and the International Drug Traffic* (Stanford University Press, 2012).

habitués simply to stop using. Few drug treatment options existed. Doctors providing maintenance doses proved unpopular with their neighbors because of concerns about the clientele they attracted. Some clinics claimed to have developed successful curative programs, but in most cases the treatment consisted merely of substituting one addicting preparation for another. The few institutional attempts to impose forced withdrawal on incarcerated individuals experienced little long-term success. In part, treatment efforts received little support because of perceptions about drug addicts. Marginalized subgroups (for example, Mexican immigrants, Chinese laborers, inner-city minorities, prostitutes, or upland indigene Andean coca chewers) attracted little sympathy among members of mainstream society. Addicts from majority communities were often characterized as moral weaklings who exhibited some incorrigible pre-existing condition, such as "criminal tendencies" or "degenerate behavior." Because addressing the causes of demand seemed both unlikely to succeed and directed toward those unworthy of the effort, control efforts concentrated on supply restriction. That strategy resulted in significant unanticipated effects in subsequent decades.

During the first half of the twentieth century, attitudes toward psychoactive substances varied widely across the global cultural landscape. Several belligerent nations limited alcohol consumption for the duration of World War I. Czarist Russia even halted retail sales of the national drink, vodka, promoting instead a variety of theatrical and educational "counter attractions" as healthier alternatives.[14] "Care packages" sent to soldiers at the front routinely included cigarettes and sometimes opiates as well. In the postwar era, even after the demise of national alcohol prohibition in Finland, Norway, and the United States, in many local and regional jurisdictions temperance advocates expressed continued concerned about the moral and social effects of drinking sufficient to maintain restricted availability. Injunctions against alcohol use remained official policy in the Muslim world. The burgeoning motion picture industry appealed to both audiences; smoking and drinking could exemplify urbane sophistication or signify a characters' descent into disrepute. American jazz music often alluded to drug use, including the mysterious substance marihuana, which, although neither a narcotic nor a coca-like stimulant, governments voted to regulate under the international drug control treaties. The image of degenerates languishing in the opium

14 A. Sherwell, *The Russian Vodka Monopoly* (London: Temperance Legislation League, Cole & Co., 1915). www.archive.org/stream/russianvodkamonooosherrich#page/n1/mode/2up (accessed August 12, 2012).

den continued as a staple of pulp fiction and popular imagination, especially in East Asian settings. At the same time, pharmaceutical companies touted the advantages of "modern medicine," presenting an attractive portrait of white-coated doctors dispensing cures for all manner of ailments, backed by the full force of scientific research. In the 1930s, governments quietly accumulated large reserve stocks of morphine and other medicines; war planners had to assume heavy military casualties and significantly greater civilian requirements in the event of another world war entailing mobilization of whole societies and shortages of basic necessities. Yet the medical experience of many of the world's inhabitants changed little; lacking access to modern drugs or not persuaded of their efficacy, traditional cures remained commonplace across the globe.

Through World War II and the subsequent two decades, the trends established earlier in the century continued in much the same fashion. Governments provided beer and cigarettes at low or no cost to troops to boost morale and calm nerves, and those items routinely served as valuable specie in belligerent economies ravaged by wartime conditions. Opium monopolies run by the colonial powers ceased operations as World War II drew to a close. Owing largely to American pressure, Great Britain, France, and the Netherlands ended longstanding government policies that promoted, or at least permitted, sales of addicting substances to colonial subject peoples. Elements of the United Nations Organization took over administration of the international regulatory regime from the defunct League of Nations. States negotiated additional treaties that focused on supply control of the traditional drugs of abuse (narcotics, coca, and marihuana), including the advent of synthetically produced opiate equivalents (opioids) developed by pharmaceutical firms. At the same time, an explosion of drug development resulted in the large-scale introduction of stimulants and depressants for a variety of physical and psychological maladies. Because definitions of addiction remained tied primarily to symptoms experienced by opiate users, the new drugs remained largely outside the scope of control, traded across boundaries with few impediments. Tobacco usage reached all-time highs in industrialized countries, where as much as half the adult population smoked.[15]

15 For example, tobacco consumption peaked between 1959 and 1968 in the United States, averaging over 4000 cigarettes consumed per adult annually. US Centers for Disease Control and Prevention, *Smoking and Tobacco Use, Consumption Data*, www.cdc.gov/tobacco/data_statistics/tables/economics/consumption/index.htm. See also Cancer Research UK, *Smoking Statistics* (all accessed August 12, 2012) http://info.cancerresearchuk.org/cancerstats/types/lung/smoking/lung-cancer-and-smoking-statistics#history and International Smoking Statistics, Web Edition, www.pnlee.co.uk/ISS.htm

Alcohol consumption remained a normative societal activity in much of the world. Use of drugs that never expanded beyond their traditional region (khat in the Horn of Africa, coca chewing in upland South America), remained the province of local consumers. Conceptions about the difference between medicinal and non-medicinal use became entrenched in the industrialized West and among elites in other regions; that distinction mattered less in much of the developing world owing to continued lack of affordable "modern" alternatives.

At the dawn of the 1960s, then, psychoactive substances were fully integrated (on both the licit and illicit sides of the ledger) into the continuing worldwide exchange of goods, peoples, ideas, rules, and conceptual paradigms. Consumption of the mild stimulants, alcohol, and tobacco were commonplace, as reflected in the popular culture of the day. An alliance of medical gatekeepers and government regulatory officials defined the boundaries between licit and illicit drug use. Pharmaceutical companies played by the rules that applied to scheduled drugs, while engaging in considerable entrepreneurial activity regarding unscheduled substances. The advent of numerous synthetic opioid and psychotropic substances also created a wider gap between the relative few who could afford them and the majority who continued to rely on traditional medicines and less expensive preparations long in circulation. Insofar as the future appeared predictable, few anticipated major changes in the realm of drug use. Beginning in the mid 1960s, however, an unprecedented series of events fundamentally altered the socio-pharmacological landscape.

The Era of Globalized Interdependency

Responses to revelations about tobacco demonstrate the complexity of interactions generated by a ubiquitous psychoactive substance fully integrated into global society. A groundswell of concern emanating from the medical community about the hazards of tobacco smoking came to public consciousness in first half of the 1960s. In 1962, the British Royal College of Physicians issued an assessment critical of tobacco use, drawing on a large collection of scientific studies dating back several decades. The breakthrough moment came in 1964, when the United States Surgeon General released a major report that outlined numerous deleterious effects of tobacco use. The report immediately became front-page news, indicating the power of health officials imbued with the imprimatur of modern medical science to dramatically impact the public sphere. Nevertheless, indicating the centrality of tobacco to the world economy, the US Surgeon General announced his findings on a Saturday in hopes of lessening the impact on stock markets. The report declined to declare nicotine an addicting substance because conceptions about addiction at that time remained wedded to the opiate model. Tobacco usage in the United States and other industrialized countries began a gradual but continuous decline as millions of individuals heeded warnings about the danger of smoking. Local and national governments passed legislation limiting advertising of tobacco products and restricting access, especially to young people. But tobacco companies and their agricultural suppliers, enjoying government crop subsidies and marketing support, accelerated sales of cigarettes overseas. They directed their efforts largely toward lower- and middle-income countries that taxed tobacco imports as a source of revenue; neither farmers nor governments wished to forego the income from this profitable crop. Of course, if tariffs were raised too much, smugglers moved in to undercut the licit suppliers. In subsequent decades, prevalence of tobacco use receded to approximately half its post-1945 highs in most industrialized countries, indicating the efficacy of programs to reduce consumption that featured a mixture of public health-oriented policies and educational initiatives. Tobacco consumption increased in other parts of the world, and remains today a leading cause of preventable death, with a growing percentage of those fatalities occurring in poorer countries.[16]

In the later 1960s, consumption of controlled substances erupted into mainstream societies across the globe. Non-medical drug use, primarily among the young, served as a cultural marker signifying resistance to authority, the exercise of personal independence, the search for enlightenment, or pursuit of pleasure. Heroin use escaped the confines of inner city subcultures where it had long resided; particular concerns arose about addiction among American soldiers serving in Southeast Asia. Marihuana smoking became a common activity among young people in the industrialized West. Some leaders of an emerging "counterculture" advocated use of psychedelic drugs (primarily LSD, a substance of no medicinal value

16 U.S. National Library of Medicine, *The Reports of the Surgeon General, The 1964 Report on Smoking and Health*, http://profiles.nlm.nih.gov/ps/retrieve/Narrative/NN/p-nid/60; World Health Organization, *Prevalence of Tobacco Use Among Adults and Adolescents*, http://gamapserver.who.int/gho/interactive_charts/tobacco/use/atlas.html; World Health Organization, *WHO Report on the Global Tobacco Epidemic, 2011: Warning About the Dangers of Tobacco*, www.who.int/tobacco/global_report/2011/en/ (all accessed August 12, 2012).

inadvertently invented by a Swiss chemist decades earlier), the effects of which remained almost entirely unknown. Recreational use of non-narcotic stimulants and depressants developed by the pharmaceutical industry skyrocketed into notoriety. Cocaine made a comeback that far exceeded earlier short bursts of popularity between the 1880s and 1920s. In addition to unprecedented activity in North America and Western Europe, reports of increased indiscriminate use of drugs came from locales across Latin America, Africa, and South Asia, including societies as diverse as Japan, Israel, and Yemen, and even behind the Iron Curtain. This dramatic transformation propelled drug-related issues to headline news status, engendering an array of consequences of fundamental import in world affairs.

One reaction focused on engineering adjustments to regulatory and ameliorative measures. States negotiated additional treaties that tightened strictures on narcotics, and brought psychotropic drugs under control (although the regulatory structure created featured less rigorous strictures than those imposed on narcotics). Although the enhanced control initiatives produced scattered governmental resistance, most notably the somewhat more tolerant attitude toward personal use of certain "soft drugs" by Dutch authorities, the majority of national and local governments strengthened drug regulations, increased penalties, and enhanced the capacities of law enforcement agencies. Extreme examples include the imposition of death penalties for users and individuals caught smuggling small amounts, which in turn generated concerns about the institutionalized violation of human rights inherent in draconian enforcement policies.[17] The widespread explosion of drug use also caused many to question the primacy of supply control as the only appropriate policy option. The advent of highly publicized recreational drug use among middle-class youth generated support for alternatives to punitive enforcement policies. The United States, Great Britain, and other industrialized states initiated significant public funding and programmatic efforts to provide treatment for drug addicts, study the causes of drug abuse, and examine the psychological and physiological effects of addicting substances.

The late-1960s explosion of non-medical drug consumption also ushered in an era of heightened international enforcement activity generally referred to as the "war on drugs." The United States championed a series of assaults

17 See, for example, International Harm Reduction Association, report entitled "Partners in Crime: International Funding for Drug Control and Gross Violations of Human Rights," June 2012. www.ihra.net/files/2012/06/20/Partners_in_Crime_web1.pdf (accessed June 13, 2013).

on supply "at the source" by focusing on eliminating excess production in agricultural regions responsible for most of the world's opium, coca, and marihuana/hashish supplies. The US government first targeted, in turn, Turkey, Southeast Asia, Mexico, and upland South America as sources of the illicit trade. American drug control efforts became intertwined with counterinsurgency programs and modernization projects aimed primarily at achieving Cold War objectives. To fight communism, US officials supported national governments that wished to extend their authority to the hinterlands by defeating insurgencies and creating economies integrated into the capitalist world market. Eradicating illicit crops was subordinated to those larger goals. The USA sent technical advisers, provided military aid to bolster internal state-building capacity, supplied airplanes for spraying herbicides and transport of personnel, and attempted to "export" the American approach to drug control by encouraging other countries to amend their law enforcement statues. Although sometimes a particular center of illicit activity might be eliminated, suppression initiatives ultimately achieved little long-term success. The inhabitants of targeted regions often resisted integration into larger polities and markets, using the profits from drug running to maintain their autonomy. The dilemmas posed by the drug question could not be contained within the parameters of anticommunist or anti-insurgent campaigns.

Responding to the array of heightened control efforts, illicit drug trafficking organizations enhanced their capacities during this period of increasing interdependency. The narco-industry rose to rank among the most impressive transnational business operations in the age of globalization. Without benefit of legal status, traffickers engaged in vertical and horizontal integration, enforced contracts, developed multiple sources of supply, generated manufacturing capacity, organized extensive transportation networks, created distribution outlets, incorporated protection costs into their business model, engineered international monetary transfers and currency exchanges, and reinvested profit, all on a massive scale. In some regions drug organizations came to rival or supplant local and national governments as the arbiters of power. "Narco-states" funded entire economies that depended on illicit revenues to support schools, hospitals, municipal services, businesses engaged in ordinary (licit) activities, security forces, and even sports teams.[18] Beginning in the 1970s, Colombian drug traffickers took over many such basic

18 See special issue on drugs on Colombia, *Journal of Drug Issues* 35/1 (Winter 2005), and Francisco Thoumi, *Illegal Drugs, Economy, and Society in the Andes* (Washington, DC: Woodrow Wilson Center, 2003).

elements of state capacity, engendering societal changes of fundamental importance. In the early twenty-first century narco-organizations took advantage of the collapse of state authority in Guinea-Bissau to create a haven for global transshipment of illicit psychoactives, in turn affecting all aspects of governance.[19] Narco-regimes proved unstable and prone to violence, retarding integration of legitimate economic and social activities into global networks. Nevertheless, whenever a kingpin fell or a cartel collapsed, the profit potential ensured that others took over the business. This long-extant dynamic of heightened control enforcement followed by trafficker countermeasures, which produced additional government regulatory efforts that in turn spurred further adjustments by illicit actors, spiraled to unprecedented levels beginning in the 1970s. Having outlived the Cold War, the Drug War contributed to terrorist coffers, fueled insurgencies around the world, disrupted state governance capabilities, facilitated other disfavored activities, and redistributed wealth to actors with little stake in the functionality of the international system.

The control impetus, however, proved not only resilient, but expansive and inventive. Beginning in the 1970s, an unprecedented coalition of non-state actors combined to generate a new international agreement intended to curb tobacco consumption. A series of initiatives launched first by the World Health Organization and subsequently supported by the European Union, the World Bank, the United Nations Children's Fund, the International Civil Aviation Organization, professional medical associations, local jurisdictions, and national governments eventually resulted in creation of the 2003 Framework Convention on Tobacco Control. It represented a comprehensive approach, encouraging a variety of measures to reduce demand, support cessation programs, limit tobacco industry lobbying of politicians, pursue research about tobacco's effects, and develop programs to substitute other crops for tobacco in order to lessen the economic impact of control on farmers. This agreement differed from earlier drug treaties in that it treated tobacco usage as a public health problem. Unlike previous control agreements that often languished for lack of support, the Framework Convention quickly gained wide adherence. Whether this alternative approach proves

19 See, for example, Adam Nossiter, "Leader ousted, nation is now a drug haven," *New York Times*, November 1, 2012, and "Cocaine-related graft erodes Guinea-Bissau governance," IRIN news (UN Office for the Coordination of Humanitarian Affairs), www.irinnews.org/report/98202/cocaine-related-graft-erodes-guinea-bissau-governance (accessed June 18, 2013).

attractive for the regulation of other psychoactive substances will be an important issue over the course of the twenty-first century.[20]

On the legal side of the licit/illicit divide, multinational pharmaceutical companies developed an ever-wider array of psychoactives designed to alleviate all manner of complaints. Although often claimed to be non-addicting, subsequent experience demonstrated that many of those substances could also produce physical or psychological dependence. As in the case of earlier generations of drugs, medical professionals wrestled with expanding the definition of "addiction." Many researchers, armed with neuroscientific insights into the brain's shared pathways of pleasure, motivation, and learning, advocated including compulsive behaviors like gambling or overeating as well as use of psychoactive drugs under the heading of addictive disorders. The debate over whether the concept of addiction should be applied to new products and introduced into new realms of behavior may prove to be an important development in coming decades.[21]

Despite all the pharmaceutical developments of the modern era, the importance of traditional medicine continued unabated for many, in large measure because access to modern (licit) drugs proved elusive for the majority of the world's people. Expenditures on medicines, including controlled substances, varied widely across the globe. In poor countries, annual per capita consumption totaled as little as US$10, while in wealthy countries the average person spent as much as US$400 on medicines. At least one third of the world's population had no reliable access to modern drugs, and 70–90 percent of people in developing countries still depended on traditional medicine. With regard to morphine, a century after its debut still the most essential analgesic, a few developed states used most of the world's licit stocks; the middle- and lower-income countries that comprised 80 percent of the world's population consumed less than 10 percent of medicinal morphine. In the case of controlled substances, the World Health Organization attributed this consumption disparity to a combination of factors stemming primarily from the global supply-control regime: overzealous access limitations imposed by regulatory strictures, the complexities of complying with the import–export accounting requirements of the

20 World Health Organization, Framework Convention on Tobacco Control, www.who.int/fctc/en/ (accessed August 12, 2012); D. T. Studlar, *Tobacco Control: Comparative Politics in the United States and Canada* (Peterborough, Ontario: Broadview Press, 2002), chapter 7; A. L. Holm and R. M. Davis, "Clearing the airways: advocacy and regulation for smoke-free airlines," *Tobacco Control* 13, Supplement I (2004), 30–36.

21 I am indebted to Dr. David Courtwright for his guidance on this point.

international treaties, high retail (not wholesale) costs in some regions, and concerns about iatrogenic addiction that hinder physicians' prescribing options. The very same farmers who supplied narcotics for the impressively globalized drug trafficking business were unlikely to have access to the pharmaceutically produced medicinal form of those same substances.[22]

Conclusion

The story of human-drug interaction in the modern era includes elements of both change and continuity. The drug-use phenomenon grew to unprecedented proportions, touching every inhabited portion of the globe. As the range of substances available expanded, the prospects for addiction increased. Government attempts to regulate drug-related exchanges, and the activities of those who attempted to avoid control, produced far-reaching effects. But the underlying dynamics of human desire remained little changed. Access to modern psychoactive substances highlighted the question of pleasure in human life, a topic fully familiar to the ancients. How does one calculate the value of self-control, the benefits of delayed gratification, the definition of health, the attractions of indulgence, or what constitutes responsible behavior toward oneself and others? The modern pharmaco-universe provided a variety of new lenses through which to examine multiple facets of the human condition.

Further reading

Andreas, Peter and Ethan Nadelmann. *Policing the Globe: Criminalization and Crime Control in International Relations*. Oxford University Press, 2006.

Bello, David A. *Opium and the Limits of Empire: Drug Prohibition in the Chinese Interior, 1729–1850*. Cambridge, MA: Harvard University Press, 2005.

Berridge, Virginia and Griffith Edwards. *Opium and the People: Opiate Use in Nineteenth Century England*. London: St. Martin's Press, 1981.

Blocker, Jack S., David M. Fahey, and Ian R. Tyrrell, eds. *Alcohol and Temperance in Modern History: An International Encyclopedia*. Santa Barbara, CA: ABC CLIO, 2003.

Brook, Timothy and Bob Tadashi Wakabayashi, eds. *Opium in East Asian History*. Berkeley, CA: University of California Press, 2000.

Christian, David. *"Living Water": Vodka and Russian Society on the Eve of Emancipation*. Oxford: Clarendon Press, 1990.

22 Statistics drawn from various sections of World Health Organization, *The World Medicines Situation Report*, www.who.int/medicines/areas/policy/world_medicines_situation/en/index.html.

Courtwright, David T. *Forces of Habit: Drugs and the Making of the Modern World*. Cambridge, MA: Harvard University Press, 2002.

Dikoetter, Frank, Lars Laamann, and Zhou Xuyn. *Narcotic Culture: A History of Drugs in China*. University of Chicago Press, 2004.

Forrest, Beth M. and Thomas F. Glick, eds. "Cacao culture: case studies in history," Special Issue of Carol Counihan and Allen Grieco, eds. *Food and Foodways: Explorations in the History and Culture of Human Nourishment* 15/1 (2007).

Gerritsen, J. W. *The Control of Fuddle and Flash: A Sociological History of the Regulation of Alcohol and Opiates*. Leiden and Boston: Brill, 2000.

Goodman, Jordan, Paul E. Lovejoy, and Andrew Sherratt, eds. *Consuming Habits: Drugs in History and Anthropology*. London: Routledge, 1995.

Grivetti, Louis E. and Howard Shapiro, eds. *Chocolate: History, Culture and Heritage*. Hoboken, NJ: Wiley, 2009.

Gootenberg, Paul, ed. *Cocaine: Global Histories*. London: Routledge, 1999.

International Harm Reduction Association, report entitled "Partners in Crime: International Funding for Drug Control and Gross Violations of Human Rights," June 2012, www.ihra.net/files/2012/06/20/Partners_in_Crime_web1.pdf (accessed June 13, 2013).

International Smoking Statistics, Web Edition, www.pnlee.co.uk/ISS.htm

Journal of Drug Issues, special issue on drugs on Colombia 35/1 (Winter 2005).

Kleiman, Mark A. R. and James E. Hawdon, eds. *Encyclopedia of Drug Policy*. Los Angeles and Washington: Sage, 2011.

Korsmeyer, Pamela and Henry R. Kranzler, eds. *Encyclopedia of Drugs, Alcohol, and Addictive Behavior*. Detroit, Michigan: Macmillan, 2008.

Marshall, Jonathan. *The Lebanese Connection: Corruption, Civil War, and the International Drug Traffic*. Stanford University Press, 2012.

McAllister, William B. *Drug Diplomacy in the Twentieth Century: An International History*. London and New York: Routledge, 2000.

McCoy, Alfred W. *The Politics of Heroin: CIA Complicity in the Global Drug Trade*. Chicago: Lawrence Hill, 2003.

Matthee, Rudi. *The Pursuit of Pleasure: Drugs and Stimulants in Iranian History, 1500–1900*. Princeton University Press, 2005.

Mills, James H. *Cannabis Britannica: Empire, Trade, and Prohibition 1800–1928*. Oxford University Press, 2003.

Nadelmann, Ethan. *Cops Across Borders: The Internationalization of U.S. Criminal Law Enforcement*. University Park: Penn State University Press, 1993.

Parssinen, Terry and Katherine Meyer. *Webs of Smoke: Smugglers, Warlords, Spies, and the History of the International Drug Trade*. Lanham, MD: Rowman and Littlefield, 1998.

Porter, Roy and Mikulas Teich. *Drugs and Narcotics in History*. Cambridge University Press, 1995.

Proctor, Robert N. *Golden Holocaust: Origins of Cigarette Catastrophe and the Case for Abolition*. Berkeley, CA: University of California Press, 2012.

Rush, James. *Opium to Java: Revenue Farming and Chinese Enterprise in Colonial Indonesia, 1860–1910*. Ithaca: Cornell University Press, 1990.

Spillane, Joseph. *Cocaine: From Medical Marvel to Modern Menace in the United States, 1884–1920*. Baltimore: Johns Hopkins University Press, 2000.

Studlar, Donley T. *Tobacco Control: Comparative Politics in the United States and Canada.* Peterborough, Ontario: Broadview Press, 2002.

Thoumi, Francisco. *Illegal Drugs, Economy, and Society in the Andes.* Washington, DC: Woodrow Wilson Center, 2003.

Trocki, Carl. *Opium and Empire: Chinese Society in Colonial Singapore, 1800–1910.* Ithaca: Cornell University Press, 1990.

United States, Centers for Disease Control and Prevention, *Smoking and Tobacco Use, Consumption Data,* www.cdc.gov/tobacco/data_statistics/tables/economics/consumption/index.htm.

Wallis, Patrick. "Exotic drugs and English medicine: England's drug trade, c. 1550–c. 1800," *Social History of Medicine* 25/1 (2011), 20–46.

Walker, William O. *Opium and Foreign Policy: The Anglo-American Search for Order in East Asia.* Chapel Hill: University of North Carolina Press, 1991.

Wiemer, Daniel. *Seeing Drugs: Modernization, Counterinsurgency, and U.S. Narcotics Control in the Third World, 1969–1976.* Kent State University Press, 2011.

World Health Organization, *Prevalence of Tobacco Use Among Adults and Adolescents,* http://gamapserver.who.int/gho/interactive_charts/tobacco/use/atlas.html.

Zheng, Yangwen. *The Social Life of Opium in China.* Cambridge University Press, 2005.

Zimring, Franklin E. and Gordon Hawkins. *The Search for Rational Drug Control.* Cambridge University Press, 1992.

20

The automobile

BERNHARD RIEGER

"I think that cars today are almost the exact equivalent of the great Gothic cathedrals: I mean the supreme creation of an era, conceived with passion by unknown artists and consumed in image if not in usage by a whole population which appropriates them as a purely magical object." It was the presentation of the new Citroën DS 19 at the Paris Motor Show in October 1955 that led French intellectual Roland Barthes to compare automobiles to the religious edifices that undisputedly tower at the apex of medieval sacral culture. With its sleek elongated body, its large windows, and its air suspension, the DS – pronounced "déesse" meaning "goddess" – appeared to have "fallen from the sky" like an alien and immediately became the show's unparalleled star. On the first day, Citroën received no fewer than 12,000 orders. Still ranking among the world's iconic classical cars, the hype surrounding DS 19 highlights the fascination the automobile exerted throughout the twentieth century, and beyond.[1]

The pioneers experimenting with road vehicles powered by internal combustion engines in the late nineteenth century could not possibly have foreseen the developments they were about to set in motion. After all, the contraptions Wilhelm Maybach, Gottlieb Daimler, Carl Benz, Armand Peugeot, Emile Levassor, and others designed were modest and challenging affairs, hampered by unreliable, smelly engines, low horsepower, and average speeds below 20 mph. At the time, it was by no means a foregone conclusion that the internal combustion engine would rule the road. Buyers in search of power and speed turned to automobiles propelled by steam engines, trusting a tried and tested technological alternative to produce kinetic energy. As late as 1906, a so-called "steamer" held the speed record for cars at 128 mph. But while "steam carriages" delivered good performance, the time it took to fire them up before each journey limited their appeal.

1 Roland Barthes, "The new Citroën," in *Mythologies* (London: Virago, 2009), pp. 101–103.

They did not lend themselves to spontaneous use. This disadvantage did not affect the electric cars that proved popular in urban areas on both sides of the Atlantic well into the first decade of the twentieth century. Pleasantly silent, devoid of emissions, offering smooth acceleration, and easy to handle since they required no gearshifts, electric cars had many virtues but could not extend their range beyond 50 to 80 miles per battery charge. Rather than dramatic breakthroughs in engine design per se, advances in making the gasoline car more user-friendly, for instance by fitting electric starters, and the discovery of large oil reserves in the United States gradually tipped the balance in favor of internal combustion towards the end of the first decade of the twentieth century. The ready availability of a comparatively cheap, liquid, flammable energy source provided powerful stimuli to turn gasoline cars into devices that drivers could confidently take on short and long trips whenever they desired.

Over the next century, the impact of the automobile has been dramatic. By 2008, 850 million passenger cars were in operation around the globe, a figure projected to almost double to over 1.6 billion by 2035. These vehicles owed their existence to an international automobile industry employing 50 million people to produce almost 60 million passenger cars and 20 million trucks and buses in 2011. Although the automobile ranks as a solidly established technology, carmakers invested close to US$ 90 billion in research and development in 2010 to improve their products and production facilities. In a global league table of research-intensive sectors, this figure placed the auto industry third behind pharmaceuticals and "technology hardware" and well ahead of computer companies as well as electrical firms widely associated with innovation. At the same time, the automobile displayed an unquenchable thirst for oil as cars and trucks guzzled up over 40 percent of the roughly 85 million barrels consumed per day in 2010. In light of seemingly inexhaustible demand for cars, it comes as no surprise that in 2010 one fifth of the twenty-five largest corporations in terms of revenue were auto manufacturers.[2]

The automobile's proliferation and its manifold consequences cannot be reduced to a history of technical progress. To be sure, since 1900 the motorcar has undergone significant changes in body design, engine power, speed, fuel efficiency, suspension systems, safety engineering, accessories, and more.

2 For the figures, see OPEC, *World Oil Outlook 2011* (Vienna: OPEC, 2011), pp. 77–84; International Organization of Vehicle Manufacturers, "Production statistics," http://oica.net, last accessed August 9, 2012; Department of Business, Industry and Skills, *R and D Scoreboard 2010: Summary of G 1000*, http://webarchive.nationalarchives.gov.uk/ (last accessed August 9, 2012).

Yet these engineering features constituted incremental modifications that enhanced the performance and appeal of a device whose basic features (a combustion engine, four inflated wheels, driver behind a steering wheel, electric starter) were already in place by the early 1920s. Rather than exclusively focus on the material object, social scientists have viewed cars as elements in systems of "automobility" that encompass – beyond automobiles – "car-drivers, roads, petroleum supplies and many novel objects, technologies and signs."[3] This approach, which situates the car within a wide web of political, social, and economic relations, has proved useful for analyzing how larger frameworks have shaped specific forms of car use while highlighting how automobiles have helped transform numerous societies in multifarious ways. Unlike many social scientists interested in "systems," scholars engaged with automobility have emphasized the importance of the individual by devoting considerable attention to drivers and their behavior. Their findings thus closely intersect with historical and anthropological inquiries into the automobile's lasting fascination irrespective of its financial, social, ecological, and public-health costs. Indeed, expanding global demand for cars has been underpinned by a deeply emotional devotion to cars as personal and collective icons. Nevertheless, studies of both automobility and of cars as consumer fetishes tend to neglect the capital-intensive systems of production that, while bringing hundreds of millions of automobiles into existence since the early twentieth century, have proven of colossal economic and cultural importance beyond the industry itself. Combining studies of automobility with inquiries into the car's cultural resonance and economic impact allows us to move towards a multi-layered global history of the automobile. Focusing on the changing regimes of car production and consumption, this chapter explores the worldwide fascination with automobiles as well as their wider significance.

Regimes of production

Composed of thousands of intricate, often fragile parts automobiles are highly complicated mechanical artifacts whose production and maintenance has always posed major challenges. Manufacturing these sophisticated devices on a mass scale required novel forms of industrial organization that played key roles in reshaping labor practices all over the world.

3 John Urry, "The 'system' of automobility," *Theory, Culture & Society* 21:4/5 (2004), 27.

Making cars – as much as using them – has left an indelible imprint on many societies in the twentieth century and beyond.

Around 1900, automobiles were socially exclusive and expensive items whose high price derived in part from a mode of production that saw integrated teams of highly skilled workers and artisans assemble vehicles in their entirety. While allowing companies to accommodate individual wishes of wealthy clients and incorporate custom-made elements in early cars, labor-intensive production procedures limited the potential for price cuts that would have extended the car market. At the turn of the century, cars epitomized the luxury good not only due to their purchase price but because their maintenance and handling entailed considerable costs. Since early cars were difficult to drive, many early owners hired chauffeurs. It is no coincidence that the French moniker for these novel contraptions – "automobile" – entered into many languages: after all, with its long-standing tradition in the luxury trades, Paris figured prominently among the centers of early auto manufacturing.

This situation changed fundamentally when Henry Ford implemented his ambition to build a "universal car" for the "wants of the multitudes." Soon famed for its versatility and rugged performance, the legendary Model T provided a basic means of individual transport and generated unprecedented demand far beyond elite circles when launched in 1908 with a price tag under US$ 1,000. Beyond its pared-down engineering features, new forms of labor organization allowed Ford to satisfy a surge in annual orders from 35,000 to 533,706 and cut the car's price from $825 to $450 between 1911 and 1919. By 1921, two-thirds of all cars on America's roads and more than half world-wide were Model Ts. Ford had successfully tapped into the world's first mass market for automobiles that stemmed from the USA's rapid economic expansion in the late nineteenth century. This commercial triumph turned Ford's name into a byword for a new regime of production and consumption that observers across the globe saw as exemplary. Substantially higher than in any other country well into the 1960s, the United States' levels of individual car ownership provided a potent symbol of the country's exalted economic position at home and abroad. Only after World War II did a boom create the conditions for mass motorization in Western Europe and Japan.[4]

Exceptional productivity gains stood at the heart of Ford's corporate ascent. Ford increased the workforce at his factory in Highland Park,

4 Henry Ford with Samuel Crowther, *My Life and Work* (Garden City: Doubleday, 1922), p. 67; Douglas Brinkley, *Wheels for the World: Henry Ford, His Company, and a Century of Progress, 1903–2003* (New York: Penguin, 2003), pp. 113–160.

Michigan, from 7,000 to 30,000 as he expanded production during the 1910s, but the over fifteen-fold jump in output derived primarily from advanced forms of labor division. Drawing on examples set by precision-engineering companies manufacturing guns, sewing machines, and bicycles, the management at Ford separated assembly processes into thousands of specialized tasks. At the same time, the company designed specialized machine tools on an unprecedented scale to manufacture standardized components. The most important and best-known element in Ford's manufacturing regime was the logistical measure that maintained a steady flow between thousands of distinct work stations, where workers either produced components or assembled them into the Model T. Inspired by Chicago's slaughterhouses where hundreds of thousands of carcasses were dressed at great speed at specialized work stations as they moved along ceiling rails at a set pace, the management transferred the principle behind these gory "disassembly lines" to the car factory. After 1913, the assembly line became rapidly a central feature of a production system that turned out growing numbers of highly standardized Model Ts at ever cheaper prices.

The workforce experienced this new type of factory as a profoundly alienating environment. The blend of advanced labor division, mechanization, and a work pace set by the assembly line resulted in monotonous, deskilled, and stressful jobs that granted employees virtually no control over their daily lives on the line. In 1913, staff turnover rates at Highland Park shot up to 370 per cent and seriously disrupted production. To reverse this trend, Ford doubled wages to $5 a day in January 1914 and subsequently launched a range of welfare measures for employees that included sports facilities, hospitals, and night schools. Generous remuneration practices and a savings and loan association added to Ford's growing mystique because employment in his plant offered prospects of prosperity that workers in other industrial sectors could only dream of.[5]

Behind Ford's comparative largesse stood a deep-seated paternalist desire for comprehensive and unchallenged authority in his company. Ford forcefully quashed all attempts at unionization into the 1930s and subjected workers to eagle-eyed supervision in the workplace as well as initially in the private sphere, where investigators from the company's "sociological department" policed employees' domestic cleanliness, family life, and sexual mores between 1913 and 1920. Retaining control over all aspects of

5 Stephen Meyer III, *The Five Dollar Day: Labor Management and Social Control at Ford Motor Company, 1908–1921* (Albany: SUNY Press, 1981), pp. 123–148.

manufacturing also motivated Ford's drive towards vertical integration. To insulate itself from market swings and the vicissitudes of outside suppliers, the corporation strove to stamp its authority on all production steps from the extraction of raw materials to the manufacture of components to the finished car. By the mid-1920s, Ford Motor Company owned and operated mines, forests, saw mills, steel works, forges, tool shops, railroads, and more in addition to its assembly facilities. In an effort to gain independence from latex imports, Ford even launched an ill-fated attempt to run its own rubber plantation deep in the Brazilian rain forest.

Occasional setbacks did not diminish the international celebrity status Ford had attained by the mid-1920s. Built between 1917 and 1928, the company's gigantic new River Rouge factory attracted a steady stream of tourists, journalists, and engineers who subsequently spread tales of the daily miracle of auto production across the world. *My Life and Work* (1922), a bestselling summary of Ford's convictions and prejudices (including his notorious anti-Semitism), reinforced his stardom in many countries. Foreign observers studied what soon came to be known as "Fordism," a set of business principles that resonated far beyond the world of auto making and pointed the way to highly productive enterprises paying good wages on the basis of standardized mass manufacturing. Ford, many contemporaries were convinced, had hit on the formula for mass production and mass consumption alike. This scenario possessed great appeal across the political spectrum, allowing business circles to emphasize the importance of mechanization, standardization, as well as productivity and the Left to draw attention to the importance of generous remuneration. Indicatively, Fordism was championed by both Stalin and Hitler; indeed, the latter decorated Ford with the Third Reich's most prestigious medal for offering advice on the dictator's altogether unrealistic mass motorization program.

Ironically, however, at the very moment Ford's reputation peaked abroad, his company lost its dominant position at home. As a result of its owner's highly personalized management style, his focus on standardization, his commitment to vertical integration, and his aversion to updating the Model T, Ford Motor Company ceded market share to General Motors after 1925. Under Alfred Sloan's leadership, GM pioneered strategies for car markets that had already passed through the initial phase of mass motorization. New forms of consumer credit and marketing played a role in propelling GM to prominence as did a greater emphasis on styling and the annual introduction of re-designed models from 1923 on. Moreover, GM targeted a broad spectrum of an increasingly differentiated auto market by offering "a car for every purse and purpose," allowing drivers to switch among various GM brands. Sloan thus pursued a more flexible variant of mass production than Ford who had famously quipped that "any customer can have a car painted any color that he wants so long as it is black."[6] After 1945, General Motors consolidated its commercial lead by embracing new forms of labor-saving automation and adopting machine tools to perform several manufacturing processes under the supervision of a single worker. In the 1950s and 1960s, this colossus towered as the world's largest corporation by a wide margin.

The postwar boom accelerated the proliferation of Fordist production regimes in the international car industry as well as other sectors. In the 1950s, Western European auto manufacturers gradually gained the capital for comprehensive mechanization and automation that embedded manufacturing procedures that by and large resembled American examples. Japan, meanwhile, followed a different path. In a drawn-out process, Japanese carmakers transformed Fordism and developed a novel mass production regime that ultimately proved superior to the American original. Boomeranging back to United States and beyond in the 1980s, methods developed in Japan helped to radically change auto making and, like Fordism before, came to be seen as a new benchmark of economic efficiency across numerous industrial sectors.

Japanese executives who visited Detroit soon after World War II recognized the central importance of Fordism's labor-saving arrangements for lowering car prices. Postwar Japan, however, provided a fundamentally different economic environment than the USA in the early twentieth century. If American Fordism was born from comparative abundance that allowed vast production runs of individual models, the Japanese way of producing cars had its roots in postwar scarcity and reconstruction. As a society recovering from wartime devastation, the country suffered from capital shortages that severely restricted investment in high-priced machinery. Car executives also anticipated comparatively small production runs for individual models due to limited demand. In consequence, Japanese automakers embarked on a search for a flexible, yet highly productive mass manufacturing system that permitted the assembly of several models on the same line without lengthy interruptions for retooling when production switched between models. Flexibility and cost-efficiency were thus central to Japanese auto-making from early on.

6 Alfred Sloan, *My Years with General Motors* (Garden City: Doubleday, 1964), pp. 65–70, 155–160; Ford, *My Life*, p. 72.

Among the highly productive Japanese systems of car manufacturing, the one Toyota – a producer of looms and other equipment for textile production that had moved into truck production in the Thirties – developed between the 1950s and 1970s provides the best-known example. From 1953, shopfloor manager Taiichi Ohno gradually deployed machinery that could be easily retooled to accommodate the production of several car models and thus limited investment in expensive labor-saving hardware. As a result, Toyota workers had to become adept at operating a machine that performed more than one function – unlike the typical Fordist worker who operated a single-purpose machine. Ohno also identified the large quantities of parts American auto manufacturers stocked as a source of major and unnecessary outlay. Detroit employed so-called "buffer inventories" so as not to run out of components and suffer production delays. Ohno, by contrast, developed an ingenious system of "just-in-time" (or *kanban*) production that permitted the assembly line to flow on the basis of the exact number of parts required to fulfill the daily quota.

Although numerous bottlenecks initially hampered the "Ohno line," it subsequently became a defining feature of Japanese flow production that ran without large, expensive inventories. To ensure a steady supply of components, Toyota established long-standing relationships with small- and medium-sized companies. While Toyota developed engines and auto bodies in-house, it delegated the design and production of components such as suspensions, brakes, exhaust systems, and more to specialized contractors. Closely consulting with its suppliers and acquiring stakes in them, Toyota never aspired to the vertical integration characteristic of American auto manufacturing. As Japanese car producers came to sit at the center of networks of components producers that delivered auto parts in agreed qualities and quantities, they pioneered what has subsequently been called "outsourcing."

In addition to market forces and growing demand, an ethos of improvement (*kaizen*) galvanized auto production in Japan. Through a system of incentives and pay increases, Toyota encouraged workers to suggest how productivity and quality could be raised. The management also pooled employees in groups that were collectively responsible for the work performed at a particular section of the assembly line. While a worker's task within a group could shift from day to day, each group's duties reached from a specific manufacturing task to checking its work pieces for faults to prevent deficient components from travelling down the line. Rather than leave the detection of defects and imprecisions to an inspection department at the end of the production process as was customary in Western European and America, Japanese corporations strove to integrate quality control into manufacturing routines.[7]

Outsourcing, just-in-time assembly, group work, and quality management resulted in a vertically disintegrated, lean form of mass production that lent Japanese manufacturers a significant edge by the 1980s. Japanese automobiles made significant international inroads, when global demand for smaller cars increased during the oil crises of the 1970s. In 1983, almost a quarter of the new cars bought in the United States were made in Japan.[8] Faced with the new Asian competitors, Western European and North American automakers reexamined their Fordist principles and successfully adapted just-in-time procedures, group work, and outsourcing into their production routines. In conjunction with industrial robots and digital data processing, the impulse from Japan turned flexible mass production into the new industry standard in the 1990s. Indeed, Toyota's success gained appeal far beyond the auto sector. As business schools and management gurus extolled forms of labor organization pioneered in Japan, leanness and flexibility rested alongside neo-liberal free-market ideas as economic mantras of the early twenty-first century.

The international proliferation of Japanese production principles is indicative of broader dynamics of globalization that internationalized the auto sector in the late twentieth century. Beyond seeking to boost exports, car managers have long attempted to establish international production networks. In the first half of the twentieth century, these efforts met with limited success due to trade barriers, restricted global demand, and a lack of investment capital. Only the American giants had the financial resources to maintain international subsidiaries during the interwar years, a strategy primarily adopted to circumvent contemporary protectionist trade barriers in foreign markets. After 1945, they were joined by Western European and Japanese manufacturers including FIAT, Volkswagen, Nissan, and Toyota. While most companies focused their operations on domestic markets in the 1950s and 1960s, expanding corporations also opened plants in economically promising Latin American and African countries. As they secured footholds

7 Eisuke Daito, "Automation and the organization of production in the Japanese automobile industry: Nissan and Toyota in the 1950s," *Enterprise & Society* 1 (2000), 145–156; James P. Womack, Daniel T. Jones, and Daniel Ross, *The Machine that Changed the World: How Lean Production Revolutionized the Global Car Wars* (London: Simon & Schuster, 2007 [1990]), pp. 47–69.

8 US Bureau of the Census, *Statistical Abstract of the United States 1985* (Washington, DC: US Government Printing Office, 1984), p. 595.

in future markets, auto manufacturers became multinational corporations that tended to assign secondary importance to the developing world, employing their subsidiaries to produce dated models with aging equipment. Volkswagen's presence in Mexico provides a case in point. The country's stable growth during the 1950s and 1960s prompted VW to erect a comprehensive production facility in Puebla in 1967; there, recycled machinery initially used in West Germany produced the VW Beetle beyond the turn of the millennium.[9]

Like many other sectors, auto manufacturing displays the hallmarks of globalization's acceleration since the 1980s. The expansion of the European Union (EU), the foundation of the North American Free Trade Area (NAFTA), and the treaties brokered by the World Trade Organization removed a plethora of trade obstacles and thus substantially facilitated the international exchange of commodities, including cars. These developments encouraged carmakers to increase their stakes in low-cost countries in the vicinity of lucrative markets. Mexico, for instance, attracted sizeable investments in the 1990s due to its proximity to the United States and Canada. Volkswagen, beyond continuing Beetle production, upgraded its plant in Puebla in the 1990s for the manufacture of mid-size models destined for the USA.

Rapid growth in populous nations such as Brazil, Russia, India, and China further stoked the sector's globalization. Establishing plants in these new mass markets not only met demands by local political elites, who, most notably in China's and India's cases, insisted on foreign companies entering into joint ventures with emergent local firms. A direct presence also reduced the risks associated with currency volatility and put manufacturers in a position to design cars in accordance with local preferences and tastes. After the turn of the millennium, some firms began to morph from multinational into transnational corporations. Rather than uphold hierarchical distinctions between primary and secondary markets across the world, headquarters flexibly coordinated far-flung production networks that responded to specific regional demand patterns.[10] As the largest global manufacturer in 2011, Volkswagen exemplified these trends. Volkswagen maintained factories in twenty-six countries to produce dozens of auto models for various markets

9 Bernhard Rieger, *The People's Car: A Global History of the Volkswagen Beetle* (Cambridge, MA: Harvard University Press, 2013), pp. 256–291.

10 Michel Freyssenet, "Wrong forecasts and unexpected changes: the world that changed the machine," in Michel Freyssenet (ed.), *The Second Automobile Revolution: Trajectories of the World Car Makers in the 21st Century* (Houndmills: Palgrave Macmillan, 2009), pp. 17–22.

and employed 280,000 of its 500,000-strong workforce outside Germany. Of the 8.5 million vehicles it sold that year, VW delivered 2.25 million in China, 1.98 million in Western Europe, and 1.15 million in Germany.[11]

While carmakers have long commanded prominence in the corporate world, workers have experienced auto production as a mixed blessing. Since the early days of mass production in Michigan, auto plants have habitually attracted manual laborers from near and far, offering employment to men and women with different skill levels as well as regional, national, and ethnic backgrounds. Recent immigrants from Southern and Eastern Europe overwhelmingly staffed Ford's assembly lines in Highland Park in 1914. In the 1930s and 1940s, they were joined by a sizeable contingent of African Americans from the Deep South. During the postwar boom, West German manufacturers hired large numbers of Southern Europeans and Turks while Renault operated its plant in the Parisian suburb of Billancourt overwhelmingly with Algerian laborers. Mostly filling low-skilled, repetitive, and onerous jobs, these migrants were attracted by advantageous pay and benefits. The auto industry's comparatively high wages came largely thanks to union representation, unlike the early example of generous remuneration set by Ford. In the United States of the 1930s, the United Auto Workers union drew on Federal legislation to overcome employers' violent resistance to worker representatives and established itself as a powerful guardian of labor rights in Detroit. In postwar Western Europe, line workers also owed improving remuneration and legal protection to union lobbying. As a result, jobs in American and Western European car factories counted among the world's best-paid blue-collar positions between the 1950s and the 1970s.

Since the 1980s, however, corporate globalization strategies have weakened unions' bargaining positions. Beyond the corporate strategy of moving production to low-cost locations, labor activists identified post-Fordist manufacturing routines as a threat to the workforce. While employers praised Japanese-style group work and flexibility as a remedy to workplace alienation resulting from monotony, unions vehemently contested this rosy reading. They pointed to the lower remuneration levels, longer working hours, and higher stress levels frequently encountered in post-Fordist factories. Indeed, flexible mass production met with resistance among auto workers from the outset. In the early 1950s, Toyota and Nissan could only implement their organizational schemes after breaking up the unions that

11 *The Economist*, July 7, 2012, 63–64.

staged several strikes against the management. Over the ensuing two boom decades, Japanese car workers possessed safe jobs but earned less, worked longer, and enjoyed fewer vacations than their counterparts in North America and Western Europe.[12] As the car industry expanded into countries with weak labor laws in the new millennium, the affluent, union-backed autoworker who had been prominent in the postwar United States and Europe progressively looked like a temporary Western anomaly. To be sure, the international proliferation of auto plants contributed to boosts in income levels in low-wage regions, but numerous workers' legal position remained precarious in many countries that car executives targeted as future markets. From the workers' perspective, the advances in productivity and globalization cannot be narrated as a straightforward success story. Although critics of globalization's social inequities arising from changes in the international division of labor have primarily trained their aim at low-pay sectors such as textile production and the assembly of electronics, the auto industry has displayed similar socio-economic dynamics. Indeed, auto manufacturing inspired many of the management concepts that have transformed global production regimes with decided mixed results for line workers since the late twentieth century.

Regimes of consumption

The auto industry's growth and prominence testifies to the seemingly unceasing and unlimited appeal of the automobile. Casting a spell on millions of people in different parts of the world, cars have figured as far more than prosaic devices that allow drivers and passengers to move from A to B. As they developed tremendous individual and collective resonance, automobiles came to rank among the twentieth century's undisputed icons.

Since cars are expensive to purchase and maintain, mass markets for automobiles have been consistently predicated on rising incomes. The USA remained the only mass motorized nation for the first half of the twentieth century. In the late 1920s, 80 percent of the world's 32 million cars were registered in the United States, turning more than half of all American families into car owners. Since World War II, mass motorization has become a regular consequence of sustained economic growth, be it in Western Europe, Japan, Latin America, India, and China. Those who can

12 Steve Babson, "Lean production and labor: empowerment and exploitation," in Steve Babson (ed.), *Lean Work: Empowerment and Exploitation in the Global Auto Industry* (Detroit: Wayne State University Press, 1995), pp. 14–21.

afford it buy a car to extend their physical mobility and give them greater control over the speed, route, and timing of particular journeys. Economic motivations have long underpinned car purchases, not least mobility's ability to boost individual earning power. In the early-twentieth-century USA, farmers bought Model Ts to overcome rural isolation, to employ the sturdy vehicle for chores around the farm, and to take produce to market. The urban middle class also recognized the car's economic advantages as professionals and entrepreneurs used them to call on clients and customers.

While eminently practical considerations prompted many purchases during early stages of mass motorization, the automobile soon developed into a deeply emotive possession. Countless owners have established exceptionally close relationships with their cars, regarding them as badges of personal identity and treating them as objects of affection. Beyond its economic roles, the motorcar owes its elevated personal status to its potential to enrich free time through evening trips, weekend excursions, and extended holidays. Moreover, cars have long functioned as complex status symbols whose acquisition not only testifies to owners' socio-economic success but projects their cultural preferences and affinities. A vast number of customizing "scenes" have sprung up around certain models and styles, all obeying specific rules, rituals, and carnivalesque cultures of display. These range from Chicano men and their spectacular "low riders" with improbable suspension systems to young Asian Americans who modify import cars from Japan and Korea to countless individuals dedicating time and money to restoring and maintaining old vehicles including Rolls Royces, VW Beetles, Morris Minors, 2CVs, Fiat Cinquecentos, and Ladas.

Above all, however, the act of driving establishes an intimate bond between car and owner. In many mass-motorized societies regarded as a major rite of passage into adulthood, learning to drive amounts to a drawn-out process in the course of which a person ideally acquires – or not! – a complex set of coordinated skills involving multiple senses. Over time, habituation transforms what are initially distinct actions required to steer a vehicle into an intuitive, flowing performance that leaves many a driver with the impression of feeling at one with an automobile. Put differently, learning to drive adds a new facet to individual identity. As an anthropologist has noted, driving reveals "the individuating potential . . . of machines that empower the mundane self to expand into new domains of action and imagination." Throughout the twentieth century, the automobile's capacity to heighten an individual's sense of self manifested itself in the West and beyond. When postwar Japan underwent mass motorization, Japanese society employed a new word imported from English to label the novel sense of personhood drivers derived from handling their automobile. It became known as their "*maika*," a phonetic adaptation of the English "my car."[13]

Car owners have experienced driving as a profoundly liberating act. From the outset, observers linked the motorcar with freedom. Henry Ford received numerous letters from American farmers in the 1910s that thanked him for helping them overcome rural isolation: "Your car lifted us out of the mud. It brought joy into our lives," wrote an early fan of the Tin Lizzie.[14] At the height of the Cold War in the 1950s, Americans, Eric Foner has stated, "were constantly reminded in advertising, television shows, and popular songs" that it was while driving that "they were truly free." Praise for the car's liberating properties was by no means the preserve of political liberals. In a speech in 1933, Adolf Hitler commended the car because "it obeyed human will" rather than "the time table" that "hemmed in" the railway traveller.[15]

The automobile's emancipatory and empowering potential has stoked numerous conflicts – and not just within families when teenage offspring wished to use the family vehicle as an escape tool from parental oversight. Due to the car's association with liberty, disputes surrounding auto ownership have often revolved around the question of whose claims to freedom were recognized as legitimate in a given society. Driving and car ownership frequently gained political dimensions, highlighting the fault lines of social and political exclusion. Throughout the twentieth century, cars have served not only to advance claims to full citizenship but also to carve out autonomous niches in authoritarian environments.

Women repeatedly struggled to assert their right to drive due to notions stipulating the domestic sphere as their realm alongside a widespread equation of mechanical competence with masculinity. In the early twentieth century, numerous American female drivers confronted misogynistic charges that their presence on the road represented a public danger as well as an affront to the supposedly natural hierarchy between the sexes. American feminists countered these attacks by pointing out that driving put women in a position to fulfill their domestic tasks with greater efficiency. They gained further ammunition as growing numbers of female drivers proved their skill behind the wheel, not least by causing fewer accidents than their male counterparts. Squarely contradicting a core notion underpinning

13 David D. Plath, "My-car-isma: motorizing the showa self," *Daedalus* 119/3 (1990), 231.

14 Brinkley, *Wheels for the World*, p. 118.

15 Eric Foner, *The Story of American Freedom* (New York: W.W. Norton, 1999), p. 265; *Parole Motorisierung: Ein Jahr nationalsozialistische Kraftverkehrsförderung* (Berlin: n.p., 1934), p. 7.

contemporary gender hierarchies, displays of female automotive competence allowed American feminists to advance claims for gender equality including calls for full political rights for women. In this context, the car developed emancipatory qualities in the most literal sense. These mechanisms retained potency in the early twenty-first century when Saudi Arabian feminists demonstratively got behind the wheel to defy legal bans on female driving.[16]

In addition to gender, race has figured prominently in regimes of automotive inclusion and exclusion. The Nazi dictatorship's ban of all Jewish Germans from car ownership in 1938 provides a particularly stark example of how automotive regulations correspond with wider policies of racial marginalization. Racial discrimination against drivers also manifested itself in liberal nations. For much of the twentieth century, "driving while black" was considered a provocation among significant sections of the white population in the USA – unless African Americans behind the wheel could easily be identified as chauffeurs in a white person's employ. Indeed, in 1948 a mob in Georgia attacked and murdered an African American out on a drive with his family because his car signaled to the perpetrators that he was '"too prosperous" and hence "not the right kind of negro."'[17] Racial discrimination persisted in liberal-democratic countries including the USA and Great Britain throughout the twentieth century, irrespective of their constitutional commitment to legal equality, manifesting itself not least in disproportionately high rates of roadside traffic checks on non-white drivers. At the same time, civil rights legislation increasingly lent members of racial minorities tools to challenge these discriminatory practices and assert their legitimate right to use the road.

In the Soviet Union, the state found it difficult to position itself *vis-à-vis* the automobile. Despite casting itself as a champion of technological innovation in the quest for Socialism, the Soviet state hesitated to promote individual car ownership. Given their commitment to collectivist forms of social and political organization, Soviet officials favored investment in public transport in the form of trains, buses, and the metro system in Moscow. In the 1930s, the only way ordinary Soviet citizens could acquire an automobile was by winning one in the lottery. At the time, automobiles were the preserve of politically privileged circles to such an extent that

16 Tracey McVeigh, "Saudi Arabian women risk arrest as they defy ban on driving," *The Observer*, June 19, 2012.

17 Cotten Seiler, *Republic of Drivers: A Cultural History of Automobility in America* (University of Chicago Press, 2008), pp. 114–115.

"the appearance of a car signified an official on the road," as Lewis Siegelbaum has observed. At the height of the purges that cost hundreds of thousands of lives, their mere sight of an automobile could instill fear in bystanders because of the regular use of motorcars in arrests. The car's intimate association with state power, however, did little to undermine the desire for automobiles among the Soviet population. One concession the authorities offered to deflect popular discontent at a chronic lack of consumer goods came in the 1966 decision to quadruple car production. While motorization levels remained low in comparison with the West and delivery periods ranged between four and ten years, many owners – mostly university-trained members of the intelligentsia – devoted considerable time and energy to maintaining their treasures. Persistent shortages of spare parts and services gave rise to a black market that "guaranteed that millions of . . . citizens would become entangled in webs of essentially private relations that were ideologically alien" to the Soviet Union. Although they gave up their early fundamental opposition to privately owned cars, Soviet authorities regarded the automobile with profound ambivalence for offering citizens "a degree of privacy and personal autonomy" that stood in tension with official ideologies of collectivism, public ownership, and state control.[18]

As the Soviet example illustrates, the state has played prominent roles in the auto's history. On the one hand, state agencies adopted and adapted supervisory and regulatory frameworks to maintain public order on the road. Many initiatives not only sought to keep traffic flowing smoothly as mass motorization progressed; they also minimized dangers and disruptions arising from the presence of a powerful machine in public space. Prussia was the first state to introduce driving tests in 1903, a regulation extended to all of Germany in 1909 and subsequently implemented by state governments in the USA after 1910, albeit in a very gradual manner. Over the years, state agencies have passed a host of regulations including mandatory vehicle inspections, speed and alcohol limits, educational initiatives to encourage civil driving, and the installation of road signs. While many rules (including whether one drives on the left or the right) vary among nations, they display a considerable degree of international similarity across the world. The automobile therefore counts among the examples of globalization that have advanced comparatively uniform everyday rules and

18 Lewis Siegelbaum, *Cars for Comrades: The Life of the Soviet Automobile* (Ithaca: Cornell University Press, 2008), pp. 189, 213, 248.

routines across different continents, incomplete as this standardization undoubtedly has been given local variations.

The state has played an active role in promoting the automobile beyond regulation. Ever since Henry Ford established his global business empire and demonstrated the auto industry's economic potential, governments have vied with each other to attract carmakers. Among policymakers, the car industry has widely been viewed as a key sector furthering national economic growth by bringing investment, skills, and jobs into countries. In the 1950s and 1960s, Latin American nations including Brazil, Mexico, and Argentina permitted only the sale of cars whose parts and components were predominantly manufactured domestically. More recently, China and India have made access to their expanding auto markets conditional upon firms from North America, Europe, and Japan forming joint ventures with local firms, a strategy designed to nurture domestic manufacturers. Governments have not only encouraged the growth of the car industry so to boost a country's manufacturing base; they have also portrayed these policies as a commitment to their nations' general welfare by bringing car ownership within the reach of ordinary people.

Road projects to strengthen the national infrastructure have provided another priority for governments of many political stripes. By enhancing mobility, roads facilitated the exchange of commodities and stimulated economic growth, a conventional line of reasoning has maintained. Long before the advent of the automobile, political leaders had viewed road-building as a catalyst for nation-building. Hitler and Mussolini took up this theme and launched highways with the argument that these new arteries would allow Germans and Italians to visit distant parts of their countries and thus develop a stronger sense of national belonging. Similar arguments underpinned the program for interstate highways initiated in the USA in the second half of the Fifties. While roads complemented nation-building processes dating back to the nineteenth century in Germany, Italy, and the United States, they played a central role in creating a sense of national togetherness among the Brazilian population in the twentieth century. In the early twentieth century, Brazil possessed only a thin and patchy railway network that ran between port cities and inland areas producing cash crops including coffee, sugar, and rubber. Financed by foreign investors and designed to help connect agricultural regions to the world market, the railway network primarily complemented river navigation and did little to facilitate communication within Brazil's vast territory because no lines linked its central regions. To enhance domestic trade and communication, the government began an effective road construction scheme in the 1950s that joined previously isolated interior parts. In Brazil's case, the highway rather than the railway was the transport technology that helped transform far-flung and ethnically diverse regions into a national entity.[19]

In addition to underlining the automobile's political and economic significance, infrastructure projects draw attention to the ecological complexities of mass motorization. Only pervasive interventions could render the environment suitable for cars, buses, and trucks, whose operation subsequently threw up numerous unintended consequences. In ecological terms, automobiles have had the most palpable local and regional impact in urban areas where, among other things, they stoked suburbanization. Leaving aside the fact that extensive car use has regularly resulted in urban and exurban gridlock, cities around the world paid a high ecological price for auto-friendly traffic policies. Built-up areas with large surfaces sealed by tarmac have suffered increasing flood risks; exposure to constant noise has had adverse effects on the health of urban residents living along busy roads and highways; and between the 1960s and 1980s, North American and Western European societies banned lead additives from gasoline because of the public-health costs of cumulative poisoning and as a response to campaigns against acid rain.

Air pollution provides the most dramatic examples of the environmental damage resulting from car use. In the early 1950s, Californian scientists uncovered the photochemical reactions that transformed auto exhausts into ozone, which in high concentrations stunts plant growth, acts as an irritant to eyes, and aggravates respiratory problems. Sunny and highly motorized conurbations prone to temperature inversions proved particularly at risk to developing the brownish smoky fog that gained notoriety as "smog." First observed in Los Angeles during the 1940s, smog repeatedly became the subject of apocalyptic media reports on Mexico City between 1970 and 1990, where rapid population and economic growth underpinned an increase in the number of vehicles from around 100,000 in 1950 to 2 million in 1980. Automobiles were responsible for 85 percent of the pollutants that turned the Mexican capital into the globe's smog capital. Cheap gas from Mexico's state-controlled oil company fueled the car boom as did a social stigma surrounding the use of public transport including the city's metro system. In 1970, a Mexican doctor joined a swelling chorus deploring

19 Joel Wolfe, *Autos and Progress: The Search for Brazilian Modernity* (Oxford University Press, 2010), pp. 91–112.

that his city – previously known as the "the region with the most luminous air" – resembled a gigantic "garage with closed doors in which the driver never turned off the engine."[20] Schools habitually shut during the summer months; the population was told not to leave the house; birds fell out of the sky in mid-flight. As late as the early 1990s, an estimate put the annual death toll due to air pollution at 12,500. Since then, the city's air has improved substantially. Reforestation, initiatives to relocate industries to other parts of the country, mandatory vehicle inspections, the introduction of catalytic converters, and a scheme that bans owners from using their cars once a week have made Mexico City, like many a car city, a far less toxic place.

Given its character as a readily identifiable source of pollution, the automobile acted as an important spur of public environmental awareness during the second half of the twentieth century. Indeed, in the United States public frustration about smog and air pollution stood behind the 1970 Clean Air Act that stipulated the foundation of the Environmental Protection Agency. Since the late 1980s, ecological debates about cars have often revolved around the themes of energy use and impending climate change, thus shifting the focus from local and regional to global ecological concerns. Motor vehicles accounted for about 12 percent of the world's greenhouse gases in the 1990s. Despite a dramatic increase in vehicle registrations from 1990 to 2010, direct emissions from cars did not rise proportionately due to improved catalytic converters and more fuel-efficient engine designs. While industry-friendly circles viewed this trend as a source of optimism, restricting ecological assessments of the automobile's energy consumption to driving-related emissions provides an incomplete picture. In addition to driving them, the production of cars requires copious amounts of energy. As an environmental historian has observed of Germany, making a car in the early 1990s "emitted as much air pollution as did driving a car for ten years."[21] Residential sprawl enabled by the automobile has also added to emissions not only by increasing car use but due to the growing size of suburban homes, which, in turn, consume more energy. Satisfying the world's desire for individual mobility in an ecologically responsible fashion thus confronts humankind with an unsolved challenge. Frequently touted as a low-emission alternative after the turn of the millennium,

20 Abelardo Arriago, "Smog, desafio de la decada," *Automundo*, October 1970, 15.

21 John McNeill, *Something New Under the Sun: An Environmental History of the Twentieth Century* (London: Penguin Books, 2000), p. 311.

the electrical car continued to suffer from limited travel ranges due to available battery technology. What is more, even a practical electrical automobile fails to address the question of environmentally friendly energy generation.

While mass motorization persistently posed perplexing environmental problems, affluent societies gradually reined in the automobile's immediate physical risks. Before World War I, concern about the appearance of highly powered, fast-moving contraptions with the capacity to maim and kill road users contributed to vocal and at times violent opposition to the automobile on both sides of the Atlantic. Public animosity soon gave way to fascination, but the motorcar provided ample confirmation of initial concerns about its physical dangers. As the number of automobiles in the United States rose from 73 to 118 million between 1960 and 1972, the annual death toll on the nation's roads increased from 38,000 to 56,000. During West Germany's mass motorization in the Fifties, yearly traffic-related fatalities increased from 8,800 to 14,400. Car crashes aroused considerable attention, especially if their victims were celebrities like Isadora Duncan, James Dean, Grace Kelly, Albert Camus, and Princess Diana. Since the 1970s, however, fewer people have died in auto accidents in well-off societies despite a continuing expansion of vehicle ownership. In 2011, American and German annual road deaths stood at around 32,310 and 4,009 respectively. Public lobbying, advances in road construction, speed limits, intensive driver education, the development of seat belts, airbags, and efficient braking systems, better passive safety through sturdy auto bodies, investment in emergency services, and the enforcement of legal regulations (not least against drunk-driving): all have played important parts in reducing the physical risks of car traffic in North America and Western Europe.

Yet when placed in global perspective, the car remained replete with dangers. In 2009, the World Health Organization noted that 1.2 million people died annually in traffic-related accidents, with a disproportionate share of these fatalities occurring in poor countries. India alone registered over 105,000 road deaths in 2007. Aging cars, inadequate road maintenance, weak enforcement of safety regulations, patchy health services, and risky driving styles render the road a lethal space for drivers, bus passengers, pedestrians, bicyclists, and motorcyclists in large parts of Africa, Asia, and Latin America. It is thus not only in the worldwide distribution of automobiles but in the uneven spread of physical risks that global social inequality remained manifest in the early twenty-first century.

Table 20.1 Estimated road deaths per 100,000 inhabitants (2006/7)

Netherlands	4.8
United Kingdom	5.2
Germany	6
USA	13.7
China	16.5
India	16.8
Brazil	18.3
Pakistan	25.3
Senegal	32.5
Eritrea	48.4

Source: Global Status Report on Road Safety: Time for Action (Geneva: World Health Organization, 2009)

Conclusions

The physical and environmental risks of driving have done little to undermine the fascination that has swept the globe since the early twentieth century. Beyond serving as a convenient source of transport, a status symbol, and a badge of identity, the automobile has embodied the promise of liberty like no other object. While its association with freedom immersed the car frequently in conflicts of social and political exclusion, liberal and authoritarian political regimes alike sought to promote the automobile. At various times, governments adopted auto-friendly policies to demonstrate their commitment to popular welfare, to forging and enhancing a sense of nation belonging, and to boosting key industries. Meanwhile, auto manufacturing emerged as a catalyst of globalization processes that left as deep an imprint on the twentieth century as driving. The organizational principles of mass production pioneered in the United States and subsequently transformed in Japan reshaped labor practices not just in the car industry but proved influential across a wide range of sectors. The attempts of individual firms to turn themselves from multinational into transnational corporations in the late twentieth century provided another instance of the auto sector as a force of globalization. Although the car industry achieved staggering advances in productivity, its multinational and multiethnic workforce owed its generous wages and benefits of the postwar period mostly to forms of union representation that came under increasing pressure in the late twentieth century. Spawning new forms of production and consumption with yet unforeseeable ecological and physical consequences, the automobile has played a major part in recasting the meanings of work and leisure across the globe in a process that inadvertently began when Carl Benz and his contemporaries first took to the road.

Further reading

Babson, Steve, ed. *Lean Work: Empowerment and Exploitation in the Global Auto Industry*. Detroit: Wayne State University Press, 1995.

Brinkley, Douglas. *Wheels for the World: Henry Ford, His Company, and a Century of Progress, 1903–2003*. New York: Penguin, 2003.

Bruegmann, Robert. *Sprawl: A Compact History*. Chicago University Press, 2005.

Clarke, Sally H. *Trust and Power: Consumers, the Modern Corporation, and the Making of the United States Automobile Market*. Cambridge University Press, 2007.

Daito, Eisuke. "Automation and the organization of production in the Japanese automobile industry: Nissan and Toyota in the 1950s," *Enterprise & Society* 1 (2000), 139–178.

Dreyfus-Armand, Geneviève, Jacqueline Costa-Lascoux, and Emile Témime, eds. *Renault sur Seine: Hommes et lieux mémoires de l'industrie automobile*. Paris: La Découverte, 2007.

Flink, James J. *The Automobile Age*. Cambridge, MA: MIT Press, 1988.

Ford, Henry with Samuel Crowther. *My Life and Work*. Garden City: Doubleday, 1922.

Freyssenet, Michel, ed. *The Second Automobile Revolution: Trajectories of the World Car Makers in the 21st Century*. Houndmills: Palgrave Macmillan, 2009.

Grandin, Greg. *Fordlandia: The Rise and Fall of Henry Ford's Forgotten Jungle City*. New York: Metropolitan Books, 2009.

Johnson, Amy. *Hitting the Brakes: Engineering Design and the Production of Knowledge*. Durham, NC: Duke University Press, 2009.

Huberto Juáez Nuñez, Arturo Angel Lara Rivero, and Carmen Bueno, eds. *El auto global: desarollo, competencia y cooperación en la industria del automóvil*. Puebla: Consejo Nacional de Ciencia y Tecnología, 2005.

Ladd, Brian. *Autophobia: Love and Hate in the Automotive Age*. University of Chicago Press, 2008.

McCarthy, Tom. *Auto Mania: Cars, Consumers, and the Environment*. New Haven: Yale University Press, 2007.

McNeill, John. *Something New Under the Sun: An Environmental History of the Twentieth Cenutry*. London: Penguin Books, 2000.

Meyer, Stephen III. *The Five Dollar Day: Labor Management and Social Control in the Ford Motor Company, 1908–1921*. Albany: SUNY Press, 1981.

Miller, Daniel, ed. *Car Cultures*. Oxford: Berg, 2001.

Mom, Gijs. *The Electric Vehicle: Technology and Expectations in the Automobile Age*. Baltimore: The Johns Hopkins University Press, 2004.

Moran, Joe. *On Roads: A Hidden History*. London: Profile, 2009.

O'Connnell, Sean. *The Car in British Society: Class, Gender and Motoring, 1896–1939*. Manchester University Press, 1998.

Ohno, Taiichi. *Toyota Production System: Beyond Large-Scale Production*. Boca Raton: CRC Press, 1988.

Plath, David D. "My-car-isma: motorizing the showa self," *Daedalus* 119/3 (1990), 229–244.

Rieger, Bernhard. *The People's Car: A Global History of the Volkswagen Beetle*. Cambridge, MA: Harvard University Press, 2013.

Rinehart, James, Christopher Huxley, and David Robertson. *Just Another Car Factory? Lean Production and Its Discontents*. Ithaca: Cornell University Press, 1997.

Sachs, Wolfgang. *For Love of the Automobile: Looking Back into the History of Our Desires*. Berkeley, CA: University of California Press, 1992.

Scharff, Virginia. *Taking the Wheel: Women and the Coming of the Motor Age*. New York: Free Press, 1991.

Seiler, Cotton. *Republic of Drivers: A Cultural History of Automobility in America*. Chicago University Press, 2008.

Siegelbaum, Lewis. *Cars for Comrades: The Life of the Soviet Automobile*. Ithaca: Cornell University Press, 2008.

ed. *The Socialist Car: Automobility in the Eastern Block*. Ithaca: Cornell University Press, 2011.

Sloan, Alfred P. *My Years With General Motors*. Garden City: Doubleday, 1964.

Sperling, Daniel and Deborah Gordon. *Two Billion Cars: Driving Towards Sustainability*. Oxford University Press, 2009.

Theory, Culture & Society 21:4/5 (2004), special issue on "Automobilities."

Vanderbilt, Tom. *Traffic: Why We Drive the Way We Do (and What It Says About Us)*. London: Penguin, 2009.

Volti, Rudy. *Cars and Culture: The Story of a Technology*. Baltimore: The Johns Hopkins University Press, 2004.

Wolfe, Joel. *Autos and Progress: The Search for Brazilian Modernity*. Oxford University Press, 2010.

Womack, James P., Daniel T. Jones, and Daniel Ross. *The Machine That Changed the World: How Lean Production Revolutionized the Global Car Wars*. New York: Scribner, 1990.

21

Globalization, Anglo-American style

THOMAS W. ZEILER

Globalization, a term popularized after the Cold War, has a history, or perhaps a pre-history, stretching back to the beginning of human settlement. States and empires deepened societal interaction, achieving larger, denser, faster, and more intimate levels of communication, migration, trade, and exchange of ideas. Such integration took place almost everywhere, and in that sense was a global process. But it rarely achieved a global scale before 1800. Unified markets existed for very few products; political leaders, while they might know about counterparts on the other side of the world, almost never had to take them into account in their decision-making; and while infections might leap oceans and epidemics rage, true pandemics (such as the 1918 flu) not only did not yet occur, but could not yet occur. By the late nineteenth century, however, decades of conflict and worldwide exploration, joined with the germination of new expansionist ideologies, the development of industrial capitalism, and modernization of production, transport, and communication wrought by technology, reconfigured global space in ways that penetrated (and in many senses, erased) political boundaries and geographic distance.

The nineteenth century brought something new and different: a genuine globalization that included not only growing integration of localities and regions everywhere, but also linkages that enrolled, for better and for worse, people, states, and institutions on every continent in ways that changed their conduct and outlook, and arguably narrowed the differences among them. Change brought by truly global interconnections, whether those of finance, trade, war, or what have you, added a distinctive feature to the history of the world after 1800, and helped make what is conventionally called the modern world modern.

Different people (and firms and governments too) experienced globalization differently, and propelled it forward, or held it back, with different power. Sometimes, indeed, the same actors promoted one kind of globalization while resisting another – by, for instance, promoting free trade but not free migration, or welcoming foreign engineers but not missionaries.

Modern globalization took place at a time when first Great Britain and then the United States enjoyed unusual power – economic, political, and naval or military – in the international system, and wielded cultural influence to match; modern globalization has therefore had an Anglo-American style. To some extent globalization fed their power, but even more so their power fed globalization. Thus the modern globalizing process came to feature free trade as an economic ideal and frequent practice; parliamentary or presidential democracy as a political ideal and increasingly frequent practice; soccer as the world's sport; English as the global language; rock and its descendants as the world's most popular music; and baseball caps as the near-global (male) fashion accoutrement. Had Britain and the United States not been so powerful, all these features would have been different. This is not to say all these features were purely British or American – rock music has West African roots for example – but they all became primarily British or American before becoming part of the globalizing process. Accordingly, this chapter, while recognizing that globalization emanated from many places, focuses on its Anglo-American dimensions.

More than any other power, the British Empire predominated over the beginnings of this transformation in the nineteenth century, but power spread to other industrial behemoths such as Germany and ultimately, the United States. With a common system of laws, shared values, and dynamic capitalist histories, Great Britain and the United States together engaged in late-nineteenth century globalization – a wave that in some respects stalled in the killing fields of the First World War in Europe, but resumed later. After 1945, the United States, more than any other power, led globalization, expanding global capitalism through trade and investment, circulating money and goods under a Pax Americana that further tightened the bonds of culture, business, and ideologies.

By the latter stages of the Cold War, globalization became a buzzword, as the United States – in a politically conservative era shaped by the policies of Ronald Reagan – privileged free enterprise, open markets, and high technology as the ideal principles and forces in the world economy. Theodore Levitt, a marketing professor at Harvard Business School, popularized the word in a 1983 article, "Globalization of Markets," in the *Harvard Business Review*. By the early 1990s, globalization also became a subject of debate in the United States and elsewhere between those free-marketeers who saw globalization as America's or the world's salvation, and dissenters who perceived dark sides to the phenomenon. The argument hinged in part on how one defined globalization. Thus, before tracing the history of modern-day globalization, it is helpful to investigate the term itself, and especially its conceptualization by thinkers, business elites, and policymakers.

Conceptualizing globalization

It is useful to distinguish between globalization's consequences and the process, or, better, the processes, of globalization itself. The consequences were and remain controversial, often lauded and often decried. For its supporters, globalization promised to perfect market capitalism, boost prosperity and access to modern life, and help in making politics transparent and democratic for billions of people. But detractors blame it for the homogenization of economic and cultural practices, the disintegration of indigenous cultures, concentrations of power and losses of sovereignty, the destabilization of several capitalist economies through currency crises from the 1990s onward, harm to the environment, dangers to public safety and health, a "race to the bottom" in the conditions of labor, and a loss of accountability and transparency in government.

A complex and controversial process, globalization combined improvements in technology (especially in communications and transportation) with the ideas and practice of the deregulation of markets and open borders to expand, on a massive scale, flows of people, money, goods, services, and information, along with cultural ties. One manifestation in recent times has been the tremendous growth of the Internet; the online global flow of goods, services, and investments amounted to many trillions of dollars today, and is still growing fast. Transborder internet traffic shot up eighteen times between 2005 and 2012, and with it, jobs, profits, and boundary-free contacts among people and organizations expanded as well.[1] In this new digital domain of the world economy, all actors have to consider other actors everywhere on the globe.

The form and character of globalization today has its roots in the processes of globalization of the last 200 years. Britain and the United States played the largest role in setting globalization on its historical course. Principles of the free market, technology, and economic practices (and the legal structures of rules and standards to support them) were building blocks of modern globalization. The transatlantic economy was the most dynamic, and

[1] See Gordon M. Goldstein, "The end of the Internet?," *The Atlantic* (July / August 2014), 24.

eventually prolific, part of the British imperial system. Theoretically committed to free trade, but also locked in inter-dependence with its dominions and colonial possessions, Great Britain created networks of trade and investment that globalized the world economy. The United States plugged into this regime as it rose to world power and eventually supplanted Britain, particularly once World War I had eroded European economic strength.

British dominance to 1914

Nineteenth-century globalization was not as extensive as that of the post-Cold War years in terms of reaching the masses. Yet after the American Civil War, Anglo-American elites drove international production to new heights. Improvements in technology and an expansion of global economic connections gathered steam. New business networks sprang up, even if US (especially) and British policymakers remained burdened with protectionist political pressures and failed to recognize the global changes underway. Still, change there was. As one historian has written, by the 1870s, the "civilized" world "had been transformed – not by revolution, but by strong leaders, realists who believed in railroads, property, economic development, and national power, and the inevitability of conflict and competition." In Britain and the United States, and also in Brazil, Canada, Italy, Portugal, and Japan, states warred and took territory as they always had, but power also grew "in the hands of men of science, expertise, and property."[2]

These leaders and men of science imagined their tasks to be such things as nation-building, social improvement, and so forth, but among the consequences of their actions were several steps towards a more global world. Nineteenth-century globalization involved substantial transborder flows of capital, commodities, and people that simultaneously served liberal state-building projects and national interests. British investment (and migrants) helped build the infrastructure and economy of the USA, Argentina, and several other states. Foreign investors' efforts, for instance, helped solidify national states, which in turn (usually) protected the property of these investors in a largely symbiotic relationship. (In the late twentieth century, it has been much more difficult for political leaders to bend transborder flows to specifically national projects.)

[2] Charles S. Maier, "Leviathan 2.0: inventing modern statehood," in Emily S. Rosenberg (ed.), *A World Connecting, 1870–1945* (Cambridge, MA: Belknap Press, 2012), pp. 148–149.

At the same time, the USA began to rival Britain as an economic power, surpassing it in GDP by about 1870, and joined it in propelling processes of globalization. Private enterprise was significant as well, led by firms whose desires to turn a profit sometimes outweighed their loyalties to their governments, or by multinational firms that were not linked to any single national interest. Such multinational or transnational businesses were helped by policies that facilitated access to foreign markets, inventions, immigration, and a partial standardization of relevant legal norms and practices promoted by both diplomats and private citizens, many of them British or American. US exports and multinational enterprises began to flourish, abetted by an emerging US edge in some key technologies, and an outward push of informal imperialism led by missionaries, merchants, and, on occasion, the military. Foreign investment reached unprecedented levels between 1870 and 1929. Britain remained the world's banker until World War I, but the United States, already an important source of finance in Mexico and the Caribbean, extended its geographical reach after 1914 so as to rival Britain in global finance by the 1920s.

Migration – a key element of globalization – was also prevalent. The world from *c.* 1830–1914 witnessed vast migrations of peoples, the majority of them driven to move by the Atlantic world's industrial growth and inviting labor markets. North and South America attracted great migration inflows from Europe. Simultaneously, development of plantations, mines, and railroads drove large-scale movements of Chinese and Indians to Southeast Asia, the Pacific islands, the Caribbean, and South America. Cheaper transportation costs made year-round employment feasible for harvest laborers shuttling with the seasons between northern and southern hemispheres. The British Empire itself witnessed substantial intercolonial movement of the work force (some of it barely concealed forced labor) for plantations, as well as for mineral extractive industries, rubber, and forestry in the Caribbean and in Asia.

Migration had its limits of course. Many people were too poor to move, or were deeply attached to their homes. Many did not know enough of distant places to consider moving. And by the 1870s exclusionary laws, for instance those enacted in the USA and Canada against East Asians, began to dampen some of the flows. Nonetheless, the fact remains that in the late nineteenth century tens of millions of people crossed the oceans, responding to information from afar and adjusting their plans in life, thanks to a more global awareness.

Technology was critical to globalization and the roles of both Britain and the United States in it. European empires were responsible for building and maintaining dense commercial, communication, and transportation connections. The Suez and Panama Canals both sped up commerce around the world – and certainly between Europe and Asia – as ever-faster steamships transferred goods from ocean to ocean. As scholars have noted, the Suez Canal (built by France, but later taken over by Britain before coming under Egyptian control in the mid twentieth century) actually created new travel patterns and greatly reduced travel time from Europe and the US east coast to South, Southeast and East Asia. France, and other countries as well, established additional shipping companies and routes. Europeans and Americans were not alone: The Japanese made a major push in shipping after 1900 and undertook railway and telegraph expansion, as did the Russians, and a network of ports and rail hubs joined modern communications to connect East and South Asian regions which, in turn, linked across the Pacific and to Europe. Great powers and rising powers sought to ensure their interests by building transport links, but in the process also built a more globally connected world.

New communications technology helped US businesses to sell other US technologies around the world. American investors benefited from undersea telegraph cables into Latin America, and connected to Asia through British cable networks. The upshot was quicker communications, and thus more timely and effective marketing of products abroad. Baldwin Locomotive Works of Philadelphia, for instance, manufactured powerful and speedy train locomotives, exporting on average one a day beginning in 1900, with customers on every continent. The locomotives climbed Pike's Peak, and also crossed Siberia and the Argentine Pampas. American agricultural machinery provided another case of globalization underway. Expositions in Chicago, Omaha, Buffalo, and St. Louis – and later fairs on the US west coast – from 1893 to 1904 displayed U.S. technological prowess but just as importantly, exposed people to the notion that expansion overseas had shrunk the world into a global marketplace.

Cultural affinities followed the economic connections that were promoted by new industrial age technology. The Olympic Games, for example, which began in the 1890s, were based on competitions between athletes representing their nations, but also fostered international understanding and the transcending of national differences. Athletes were transnationals who universalized sporting values even as they carried with them their national banners. British residents brought soccer to Argentina where it gradually became the national game. Students and teachers transported baseball from the United States to Japan, where it acquired its own cultural meaning, and from there was carried to Taiwan and Korea. International tourism, entertainment (such as Buffalo Bill's Wild West Show or baseball world tours by American and Japanese clubs), and even international marriages resulted from the ease of exchange that technology brought.

Philanthropy and social activism also acquired a globalizing dimension. For example, Andrew Carnegie and John D. Rockefeller both turned to overseas giving to counter their reputations as cold, cutthroat industrialists, and to cure social ills they identified as critical. Carnegie libraries, eventually numbering more than 2,500, combated illiteracy in the Anglophone world, while Rockefeller and his son personally donated over $1 billion dollars toward scientific and medical research, as well as public health causes, in such diverse places as China, the US South, and Latin America. Rockefeller's foundations financed numerous international conferences and scientific exchanges, prompting a flow of transnational figures around the world. Other famous bankers funded human rights causes; among these was Jacob Schiff, who made efforts to alleviate the persecution of Jews at home and abroad. In related moves, politicians, civic associations, and jurists created the first international arbitration structures and legal norms to alleviate misery. Merchant banking, mining, and export firms, as well as wealthy individuals, poured money into saving victims of natural disasters (such as the 1906 Valparaiso earthquake), responding to social needs they perceived needed addressing, and shaping policies. Christian missionaries, temperance activists, and promoters of women's rights all sought to do the same thing, albeit with less ready money than Carnegie or Rockefeller, reaching beyond their borders and using the new technologies of communication and transport in an effort to change the world. This ambition was not novel, and its success was limited, but the ease with which such measures might be undertaken brought forth more effort, more activists, and more sponsorship than ever before.

At the same time as private philanthropists were extending their reach, states began to take up human rights causes in new ways. While popes and caliphs had for centuries often sought to protect Christians and Muslims in faraway lands, nineteenth-century states, or coalitions of states, sometimes responding to pressure groups at home, found it congenial to intervene abroad on behalf of religious brethren. Orthodox and Armenian Christians in the Ottoman Empire, for example, aroused the sympathy of Christians (and their governments) in Britain, America, and Russia, inspiring diplomatic initiatives and occasionally heavy pressure.

War, peace, and disrupted globalization to 1950

While some integrative and expansionist elements of globalization persisted from World War I through the Great Depression and World War II to the Korean War of 1950, this was actually a period of deglobalization. World War I splintered the international economy and divided the international system, and in its aftermath communism and fascism in Russia, Italy, and then Germany took root as ideologies opposed to liberal democratic capitalism. Powerful policy currents in these countries, and in others less definitively communist or fascist, promoted autarky rather than international trade, and vehemently opposed emigration in the 1920s and 1930s. The economic collapse of 1929 provoked further trade restrictions, even in countries that had formerly been sympathetic to free trade, such as Britain. Then, after World War II, the world divided along ideological lines in the early Cold War.

In short, states prevailed in slowing the globalization process in the economy, although some cultural ties persisted, even in wartime, and probably strengthened over the 1910s to 1940s as a whole. Today, many commentators believe that globalization is inevitable, but that is not necessarily true. Political and economic decisions and patterns can intervene to stymie that course. Such was the case during the volatile era that witnessed two world wars, the worst economic crisis to hit the capitalist world in modern history, and the advent of the divisive Cold War.

Clearly, World War I and the 1920s era of business expansion accelerated the American presence overseas, particularly as US financial institutions and firms replaced British ones in Latin American markets and began to seriously challenge them in Asia. Americans acquired key sources of raw materials, such as rubber plantations in Sumatra, and enlarged their presence in sugar, tobacco, and meat-packing in Latin America. A host of mining operations – copper, iron, nitrate, and oil – saw US entrepreneurs and corporations setting down roots in China, the Dutch East Indies, and Mexico. But in the vast British and French empires, and the growing Japanese one, US investment remained marginal, while revolution in Mexico and Russia, and world war, on occasion interrupted, and certainly further slowed, US efforts at economic expansion.

The plans that Woodrow Wilson and others made during World War I to encourage internationalism, boost self-determination for colonies in the hopes of making them independent nations, and promote collective security to end militarism, were not realized because of political instability, ideological differences, and isolationism, including powerful isolationist sentiments in the United States itself. The USA set stringent restrictions on immigration in the early 1920s with quotas based on nation of origin, and the US Senate refused to approve joining the League of Nations. The rise of Soviet communism also countered the global expansion of capitalism with the idea, articulated by Joseph Stalin and later made state policy, of "socialism in one country," which aimed to develop the USSR internally and cut it off from market forces. Meanwhile communism had its own globalizing impulse, flowing from Moscow, to spread Marxism–Leninism around the world.

Even though Wilsonianism did not reach its full fruition, transnational business leaders and some policymakers did embrace globalization, especially as the United States continued its rise to dominance over the world economy. Although it did not join the League of Nations, the US government involved itself to some degree in efforts to stabilize Europe's economy in the 1920s through efforts such as the Dawes Plan of 1924, and political leaders maintained an interest in global disarmament. Pan American World Airways, founded in 1927 to counter a German-owned firm, gained the rights to transport mail and passengers from the United States to Latin America, and in the 1930s to Europe and Asia, launching the age of international air passenger travel.

As many Americans came to believe that peace and prosperity depended on global contacts, cultural ties grew stronger. Film came of age as a worldwide phenomenon, and American stars – such as Douglas Fairbanks and Mary Pickford – became household names the world over. International societies and organizations proliferated for museums, musicians, academics, and many others. The Institute of Pacific Relations, for example, founded in 1925, was a multinational association of journalists, scholars, and businessmen designed to promote greater knowledge of the issues facing the nations of the Pacific Rim. Foundations such as the Guggenheim and the Institute of International Education funded international research and the enrollment of foreign students in American universities. Asian, Latin American, and European youth continued to migrate to the United States, creating a transnational exchange of students who often returned home to propagate American values.

Despite the efforts of many business leaders, policymakers, and philanthropists, ideology and political forces grounded globalization when the Depression hit. Domestic economies took precedence over the international system. Protectionism took hold, as the USA imposed high tariffs on foreign goods and the British Commonwealth instigated an imperial trade preference regime that reserved some Empire markets for member states and discriminated against outsiders. The Soviet Union turned to building socialism in one country while Nazi Germany strove for autarky, as did Japan in its East Asian Co-Prosperity Sphere. World War I debts continued to plague the global financial system, and as the Great Depression ravaged economies, the lack of leadership in solving the war debt problem as well as protectionist measures meant not only distress for people but a curbing of globalization. Technological improvements in travel and mass communications, and cultural products with a global audience such as movies, kept alive the process of globalization on some levels. A few political and business leaders continued to speak up for integration and internationalism. US Secretary of State Cordell Hull, for example, pushed for liberalizing trade and lowering barriers, while Thomas J. Watson, head of International Business Machines and the International Chamber of Commerce, echoed Hull in claiming that an open and freer world economy would bring world peace as well. Dictators defied their desires, however, and the outbreak of World War II, in 1937 in Asia and two years later in Europe, further threatened globalization.

While the Axis powers of Germany, Italy, and Japan used military force to destroy internationalism and set up closed, autarchic regional economic systems, the Allied powers ostensibly fought for a new world of openness, stability, and growth. However, each had its own particular interests – the Soviets to expand into Eastern Europe, the British, French, and Dutch to protect their empires, Jiang Jeshi (Chiang Kai-shek) to consolidate China under his rule, and the United States to find new markets so as to avoid falling back into economic crisis when wartime stimulus ceased. In wartime even those Allied powers with traditions of free enterprise turned to compulsion to coordinate industries and services and mobilize their armies. Regimentation became the norm, as market mechanisms gave way to government allocation, although such statism was a necessity to win the war.

During World War II globalization flew metaphorically under the radar, but radar can also serve as an example of one process of globalization that was stimulated rather than restricted by the war: the expansion of science and the development of new inventions. Medical advances such as mass-produced penicillin spread around the globe. Computers emerged in World War II, first to break enemy codes. Because vacuum tubes were bulky, these computers were too large for consumers, but research on silicon and germanium at Bell Telephone Laboratories during the war led to the invention of the transistor in 1947. This revolutionized electronics, and made possible smaller and cheaper radios, calculators, and eventually computers, which in turn gave rise to the globalized information age. Aviation developed during the war as well, as Britain and the United States turned to big bombers and then used the B-29 as a foundation for luxurious airliners. By 1954, the Boeing-707 passenger jet was launched; its roots lay in the Second World War jet tankers and experiments with jet engines. Douglas, Boeing, and Lockheed, all US companies, joined Pan Am in seizing the expanding world market for aviation in the postwar decades.

Other drivers of globalization were present as well during World War II. The presence of GIs in Europe and Asia helped spread the taste for certain American consumer items, such as Coca-cola. The war, and the redrawing of borders in its aftermath, generated huge flows of refugees, who carried ideas, skills, and labor around regions and around the world. Roughly a quarter million women, mainly from Europe, Australia, and the Philippines, married US and Canadian servicemen whom they met during (or just after) the war, creating international families. Canada sent special "war bride ships" to Europe, and in the USA the 1945 War Brides Act and its extensions offered free transport. The Act allowed most spouses, natural children, and adopted children of US military personnel to enter the USA without reference to immigration quotas, although Asians other than Filipinos were specifically excluded.[3] In ways large and small, the world war nudged ordinary people toward more globalized lives.

The Cold War, like World War II, divided the world politically and thus undermined dreams of a more unified world. Yet even those states preparing to destroy one another found arenas where they could cooperate and make strides toward introducing rules and laws to oversee the international system. At the top was the United Nations, and a host of agencies followed. The International Civil Aviation Organization, founded in 1947, established rules to govern air transport and travel, including safety and efficient routes. Within two decades, its 116 members connected markets around the world by integrating navigation codes and resolving disputes. Organizations for world health, agriculture, labor, and other sectors harmonized policies – the essence of globalization – though not without conflict and divergences throughout the years.

Other organizations, though they failed to bridge the two emerging blocs, furthered integration within one or the other of them. The International Monetary Fund (IMF) and World Bank, both established at Bretton Woods, New Hampshire, in 1944, built a structure of international finance that stabilized exchange rates throughout the Western bloc and provided aid to

[3] Susan Zeiger, *Entangling Alliances: Foreign War Brides and American Soldiers in the Twentieth Century* (New York University Press, 2010).

deal with currency crises. (The Soviet Union originally agreed to join the Bretton Woods organizations, but then changed its mind.) Vigorous American aid to allies helped them recover from the war; the Marshall Plan and the American occupations of Germany and Japan instilled liberal ideals as they rebuilt cities and economies. The occupations linked "the two greatest industrial complexes of East [Japan] and West [Germany]," wrote State Department official (and father of the Cold War containment doctrine) George Kennan, so they could "both serve as regional bases of the anti-communist coalition."[4] Money flowed more easily around the capitalist world than it had in the interwar years. In 1947, a forum for trade liberalization and rules, the General Agreement on Tariffs and Trade (GATT), oversaw tariff negotiations among two dozen countries. Successive rounds over the next five decades, until the GATT was replaced in 1995 by a more comprehensive trade agency, the World Trade Organization, reduced barriers that freed up commerce and tightened the bonds of the capitalist nations.

As part of its containment agenda the United States imposed a strategic trade embargo on the Soviet bloc, although its allies did not always comply. The sanctions did not so much hurt the communists as confirm the division of Europe, and with it, the separation of East and West – socialism and capitalism. Moscow engineered the creation of its own communist economic bloc, COMECON, that stretched from Berlin to Vladivostok, to counter the Western integration under the Marshall Plan and trade embargo regime. It certainly worked to integrate these economies in a socialist version of globalization and endured until 1991, eventually including China, Cuba, and Vietnam as observers, as well as Iraq, Nicaragua, Finland, and Mozambique as indirect participants. Thus, Cold War containment policies and responses to them stood in the way of unifying the globe, but also proved to be dynamic builders of processes of integration.

The economic segregation of the Cold War years in some ways prepared the ground for a later surge of globalization. The United States, determined to prosecute the Cold War by every means, geared up for a "superpower" conflict with the Soviet Union. US advantages were immense, including a technological edge in just about every sphere, a headstart in communications and transportation, plus a system of values, including individualism, democracy, free enterprise, and a lifestyle full of consumer goods, that were attractive to many people around the world who had some exposure to

[4] Thomas W. Zeiler, "Opening doors in the world economy," in Akira Iriye (ed.), *Global Interdependence: The World After 1945* (Cambridge, MA: Belknap Press, 2014), p. 231.

them. The Soviets could never appeal to the masses in the way the USA did, and US measures prepared the way for the dynamic era of post-Cold War globalization.

Undercurrents, 1951–1989

Throughout the Cold War, globalization germinated underneath the national security structures set up by the superpowers and their allies. For instance, the Korean War (1950–1953) stimulated producers in Japan, such as Toyota, and in Taiwan; industries in those countries, plus those in South Korea, would benefit still more from the huge surge of US purchases to fight the Vietnam War. Japanese steel products were also used to make military communications equipment. Once the Korean War ended, these producers crossed over into making consumer goods, particularly transistor radios and cameras. The consumer electronics industry in Japan, therefore, arose from the Cold War, and came to dominate the world economy in that sector. Research and development in the sciences and engineering grew from intelligence-gathering efforts, weaponry, and electronics used in the Cold War, and here the USA led the way. Contracts with the National Science Foundation, Department of Defense, and other government agencies in the 1960s expanded laboratories and projects at or near major research universities, creating a synergistic relationship that spurred growth in higher education and readied the workforce for the modern, globalized marketplace. US firms, drawing on five times as many patents as those held by foreign corporations, stimulated research as well. IBM, for example, dominated the information processing market. All of this R&D, geared toward helping the Free World meet the challenges of the communist bloc, planted the seeds of the information age that followed the Cold War.

Transportation, another driver of globalization, more than survived the Cold War conflict – it flourished because of it. Technology derived from World War II and Cold War military planning, coupled with the economic and demographic expansion of the southwestern United States known as the "sun belt" that enlisted millions of Americans in the defense effort, spilled over into the blossoming of commercial air travel, which replaced sea voyages as the main way of transiting the globe. The rise in both domestic and international air travel rose dramatically; for the latter, the increase from 1945 to 1957 was tenfold, to 4.5 million passengers, and by 1970, had quadrupled again. Boeing's gamble on developing long-range passenger jets in the late 1950s paid off, as flying time across the Atlantic dropped by half and civilians benefited from low-cost air travel in tourist class, introduced in 1973. The wide-body Boeing 747, launched in 1969, further expanded capacity and cheapened passenger tickets. Charter flights followed. Flights from New York to London (briefly) plummeted below $200, boosting tourism among college students in particular. They learned about foreign affairs, or at least certain aspects of life in other countries, as transnational travelers, and some became instilled with a culture of globalization. Jets could also accommodate freight and containers, and soon joined container ships in speeding and enlarging world commerce. Air cargo rose by 866 percent between 1957 and 1973, and by the 1980s, the impact of this tremendous transformation in shipping had worked its way through the marketplace. Engine improvements and weight reduction led to a Boeing airliner in 1989 that could carry 412 passengers for up to twenty hours.

Improvements in maritime shipping, especially containerization, complemented these developments in the air. The process of using truck-trailers with standard-sized containers that could be loaded on to or off of a ship raised the productivity of a longshoreman from 15 tons of cargo per hour in 1956 to 700 tons in 1973. The results were faster ship turnaround, efficient coordination, and lower transportation costs. Throughout the 1960s, containerization skyrocketed, aided by shipping needs associated with the Vietnam War (another Cold War conflict that spurred globalization). After the Yom Kippur War of 1973 raised the costs of petroleum, the international shipping industry then designed special ships for automobiles and liquefied natural gas.

Developments in communications during the Cold War era also boosted the globalization process. The number of transatlantic calls in 1927 had numbered about 10,000; thirty years later, they had soared to 250,000. The era of noisy and impractical radio telephones, which only elites could afford, ended in 1956 with American Telephone and Telegraph opening the first transatlantic telephone cable by using microwave amplification techniques. Soon big companies, such as Ford, laid their own telephone cables to coordinate business operations overseas. By the late 1980s, most parts of the world could take advantage of long-range telephone communications, as satellite coverage ended isolation and created a truly global village of contact. The next step, to the Internet and the information age in communications, was not far off.

In the general political economy, globalization also moved forward despite crises and regionalization. The establishment of the European Common Market in 1957 helped lure massive US investment, as well as turning

Western Europe into a powerful and consolidated trade entity. By the 1980s, the Common Market had added several new members, and planned for a single currency to integrate the region further and compete with outsiders.

Such regionalization shaped the globalization process. It created certain regions that integrated more fully than others intramurally, even while they erected barriers (usually to trade) against interaction with other regions. In this respect, as in others, globalization was patchy. During the Cold War years, Europe's Common Market was perhaps the most integrated area outside of the close integration of the USA and Canada, but regional trade agreements, defense accords, and other forms of integration contributed to the mosaic.

As noted by the Canadian social theorist Marshall McLuhan, the culture of a global village emerged in the Cold War decades. This was not just a one-way street from the United States to points overseas. The Beatles, for example, epitomized cultural globalization. Capitalizing on the new era of communication and travel, they adapted African-American rock n' roll in Liverpool to launch Beatlemania around the globe by the early 1960s. Their hits swept through the English-speaking world, and then many non-English-speaking cultures. The Beatles took America by storm, gluing 60 percent of viewers to the Ed Sullivan show when they appeared on television in 1964. They were the first band to sell out sports stadiums worldwide and were so successful that they affected the British balance of trade, for which they were honored by the Queen in 1965. Youth across the planet went wild over them, and they took part in the first global satellite broadcast in a music special in 1967. The Beatles unified pop culture, at least for a moment, and they did so as a British export flowing across borders commercially and culturally.

From the late 1970s, Anglo-American globalization acquired a new momentum. As usual, new communications and transport technology played a role. But added to this came a wave of deregulation spearheaded in the USA and UK, one that in some respects merged with an East Asian wave of economic and political liberalization. For myriad reasons, most of them deriving from domestic politics, the regulatory structures put in place over decades by Labor governments in the UK and by the New Deal in the US began to wane. The regime of fixed exchange rates ended, and flexible rates gave greater power to transnational investors. Meanwhile, an era of "financialization" took root, in which financial instruments became increasingly important to the way that other goods and services were produced and consumed, allowing financiers to influence and profit from sectors in which they had not been deeply involved before. While most "financialization" happened within countries, such as the US boom in student loans as a way to finance higher education and in home equity loans as a way to finance consumption amidst stagnant per hour earnings, capital markets were, in the last instance, trans-national. Thus even a local bank lending against the value of a house down the street was ultimately connected to global institutions, and "financialization" meant that more and more spheres of everyday activity could potentially influence, and be influenced by, credit conditions thousands of miles away. In the United States once stable industries such as automobiles, steel, and machine tools lost market shares to new entrants, at first often manufacturers from Japan. In other sectors, US firms took advantage of the decentralized markets that opened at home and abroad. The more open climate for international business of the 1980s created winners and losers alike, reshuffling the fortunes of various sectors in all those countries enmeshed in this decentralization trend. Like other surges in global integration, this one conferred advantages on those people best informed about the wider world, and upon those people and firms whose assets were most mobile, and who were best able to seek the highest returns wherever they might be had.

The world of ideas fomented this political push for market liberalism, providing intellectual support. Nationalism, though critical to foreign policy and domestic politics, gave way somewhat to a more global view of money, in some respects a return to laissez-faire doctrines formalized in the nineteenth century, now championed by economists such as Milton Friedman. In the 1970s, the Trilateral Commission of business, political, legal, and academic members from the United States, Western Europe, and Japan convened to facilitate cooperation outside the purview of government supervision. In Davos, Switzerland, business leaders met starting in 1982, and soon expanded their networks to bring together world leaders to discuss public policy issues in an annual World Economic Conference. In the United States, business lobbying accelerated against unions, taxes, and regulations and in favor of more free enterprise. What had once been a "Washington Consensus" of an activist and expansive role for government evolved into a consensus in favor of neoclassical economics, and an attack on Keynesianism. Entrepreneurship, competition, free trade, and labor competition were the cardinal features of the era. President Reagan extolled these principles and, when he could, enacted them by privatizing government services and liberalizing trade.

American globalization, 1990 to now

As Reagan left office in 1989, he bequeathed to his successors major changes in the economy, politics, and culture that reflected the rising era of globalization. New institutions accompanied the freer exchanges of goods, capital, and culture that quickened and enlarged state and transnational contacts. Among these were the North American Free Trade Agreement (NAFTA) and the World Trade Organization (WTO) of the mid 1990s, both of which liberalized commerce, integrated business practices and methods, and stressed a rules-based economic system. The administration of President Bill Clinton even made globalization its foreign policy mantra, as it perceived the potential of prosperity by harmonizing world economic behavior, customs, development, and democracy. America stood at the helm, in this view of the situation, guiding all who would embrace it to a new Washington Consensus of universalist and integrative market-based globalization. But while the benefits were many, and the process seemingly inevitable due to new technologies abetted by a free-market ideology, the costs were also significant and debates raged over the desirability of globalization. At the center of the argument in the USA was the issue of how far the government should go toward promoting market-based capitalism throughout the world. Business was generally in favor, but the labor movement, many academics, environmentalists, and several members of Clinton's own Democratic Party – who favored traditional big government policies – were not. A rebounding American economy in the mid 1990s persuaded people across the political spectrum that globalization had advantages, however, and with the advent of widespread use of the Internet – with 304 million users worldwide by 2000 – it even had a certain cachet.

The Anglo-American push towards economic liberalization and greater global engagement dovetailed with similar trends in East Asia. Taiwan, Singapore, South Korea, and Japan moved dynamically toward the world market model by liberalizing their economies and embracing more open competition at home and abroad. To some extent these liberalizations drew inspiration from the Anglo-American examples, but each had its own internal drivers as well. East Asian businesses found many opportunities in a rapidly globalizing world.

Among the beneficiaries of late-twentieth-century globalization were Japanese businesses. In the 1990s, children around the world were gripped by the Pokemon game fad, and the Japanese dominated other forms of media and electronic culture. Japan tended to play by its own variant of the rules of capitalism, through industrial planning and protectionism, rather than by market-driven, free-trade capitalism. Japanese producers also beat the United States at its own game of innovation, at least until the 1990s, when a housing bubble in Japan destroyed the stock market and hamstrung their economy for well over a decade. In the meantime, while Disneyland opened in Tokyo, Japanese investors invaded sanctums of American culture and business, as its auto companies seized a third of the US market and its investors bought up icons such as Universal Studios, MCA Entertainment, Rockefeller Center, and Columbia Pictures.

India served notice that it, too, would engage in the process of globalization. Although it experienced slower growth than China – and, indeed, had some of the poorest people on the planet – India experienced great growth once the government removed many of its myriad internal controls in the 1990s. The dynamism was led by information technology. Software designers and engineers – the brightest young minds of the information technology revolution – found homes in the southern city of Bangalore, the birthplace of IT giant Infosys in 1981. By 2008, Infosys had 100,000 employees worldwide, and revenues topping $4 billion. Call centers served international clients seeking assistance for phone use, household appliances, and computers, while research and development facilities cropped up where English was spoken and labor cheap, places such as Bangalore. Overseas business identified India as a prime place to outsource engineering, research, and manufacturing operations to cut costs. Deutsche Bank, Citigroup, Goldman Sachs, Barclays, and other foreign investment banks poured money into the country. Consumption boomed; in the telecom sector, for instance, India added 7 million mobile phone subscribers every month in 2006, surpassing even the explosion in China. Bollywood began to globalize too, producing films and music videos that found audiences throughout the Indian diaspora and beyond. Familiarity with English among educated Indians made it easier for India to find rewarding niches in the global economy.

But China was in many ways the poster child for post-1990 globalization. China had been a bastion of hostility to market economics in the 1950s to the 1970s, but this began to change in 1978. In the course of the 1980s, China started to welcome foreign investment, which came mainly from nearby Asian economies, especially those with many ethnic Chinese in their populations. As China cautiously opened its market to foreign participation, it in effect brought a large pool of underemployed labor together with the world's underemployed capital in a profitable mix. That fusion yielded a quarter century of rapid economic growth – and new linkages between China and the world. Through inducements such as tax breaks and guarantees of profit repatriation, Beijing encouraged foreign investment and joint ventures with the capitalist world by creating 124 special economic zones around the country, particularly in coastal cities. Wholly Foreign Owned Enterprises (limited-liability corporations organized and capitalized by foreign investors), other types of foreign companies, and contractual ventures invested in market-oriented "micro climates" that quadrupled foreign investment in the 1990s. Although bureaucratic, trade, and financial obstacles remained – and job-creation by rural Township and Village Enterprises (TVEs) far outpaced that in special economic zones – direct investment in export-oriented goods poured into coastal areas from overseas Chinese and multinational corporations.

Suzhou Industrial Park illustrates this penetration by global capitalism. Founded in 1994 by Singapore and China, the Park hosted 103 foreign-invested enterprises capitalized at over $16 billion by 2002. An efficient service-oriented staff attracted overseas investors by minimizing state interference and pursuing a pro-business agenda. Companies flocked to do business there; the Dutch multinational Philips Semiconductor chose the Park as its site for a new factory. It was a model of transnational financial strategies and regional business networks: Singapore shipping and engineering behemoth Keppel and United Industrial Suzhou, both controlled by the Salim group, Indonesia's largest transnational corporation, operated in alliances with state and private capital.

Globalization, rather than outright Americanization, quickened among the world's cosmopolitan elites, in business and finance, government, academia, media, and sports. Convergence was clear, as English increasingly became the language of international commerce. Leaders in government, business, and the media flew in the same airplanes, wore the same business suits, stayed in the same hotels, and read the *Wall Street Journal* and *Financial Times*.

The middle class and the poor joined the process of globalization as well. Increasingly, like elites, average educated people in the middle class around the world took part in the global revolution delivered by technology. They communicated by fax, cellphone, and email, then through such social media networks as Twitter and Facebook. By 2000, one million conversations occurred simultaneously through satellite; by 2010, that technology allowed 4.6 billion of the world's nearly 7 billion people to talk and do business through cellphones. To be sure, not all of this communication was global, as Facebook friends oftentimes lived in the same neighborhood, but some of it was.

In transportation, ship tonnage rose six-fold from the mid 1950s, but air freight grew even faster (albeit from a much smaller base), and costs plummeted. By 2000, two million people a day crossed a border somewhere in the world. Some 2.5 percent of the world's population lived outside of their country of birth in 2000, slightly exceeding the former high water mark of 2.3 percent in 1913. Immigrant numbers tripled in the United States between 1970 and 1998.

Some 7,000 transnational companies existed in 1970; thirty years later, there were 63,000 parent firms with nearly 700,000 foreign affiliates, with a substantial number of inter-company arrangements. The production of these transnationals exceeded that of many nations, and certainly increased faster than the gross domestic products of many countries. Branding worldwide led to a tremendous expansion in profits. Marlboro cigarettes, Nike shoes, and a host of other companies gained global market shares. Sports teams, such as the Chicago Bulls in basketball and soccer's Manchester United, appealed to world audiences, and American professional basketball, hockey, and baseball leagues actively recruited foreign players. This led to broadcasting in hundreds of countries, and further branding of these sports, especially for the National Basketball Association. In baseball, nearly one-quarter of the players in the Major Leagues of the USA came from outside the country, while the Seattle Mariners club was owned by Nintendo's president Hiroshi Yamauchi, and then by the Nintendo Corporation itself.

The integration of equity and bond markets, or financial globalization, was another hallmark of the post-1990 surge in globalization. The middle and upper classes invested savings overseas at ever greater rates, with US-based global mutual funds climbing from $16 billion in 1986 to $321 billion by 1997. The velocity of foreign exchange was staggering; in 1973, the average daily turnover in the global exchange market was $15 billion, but by 1998, some $1.5 trillion passed through the markets every day, and about $5 trillion in 2013. Thanks to electronic trading, billions of dollars could be invested into markets in a flash, and just as quickly removed. When home prices in the USA began to fall in 2006, a rash of home mortgage defaults, especially among borrowers with subprime loans ensued and triggered a massive number of foreclosures across the country. Loans and securities backed by subprime mortgages lost their value, straining the banking and insurance systems in the United States – and then worldwide. A global credit crunch followed. Major risk-taking players in investment markets – Bear Stearns,

American International Group, Lehman Brothers, Merrill Lynch, and Citigroup – went out of business or were acquired by competitors for a fraction of their previous value. In the UK and Ireland, the state acquired large shares of formerly private banks to keep them solvent. As central banks scrambled to pump liquidity into frozen money markets, the International Monetary Fund warned that the housing slump in the USA, Spain, and elsewhere would not only hurt the North; developing nations would also suffer from slackening demand.

By March 2009, the economic news was bleak around the world. Some observers even foresaw a complete failure of capitalism, as the United States and the world descended into a prolonged depression. The process of globalization appeared to be a dangerous phenomenon. As American economist and Nobel Prize winner Paul Krugman noted, the need for international cooperation was imperative "[b]ecause we have a globalized financial system in which a crisis that began with a bubble in Florida condos and California McMansions has caused monetary catastrophe in Iceland. We're all in this together, and need a shared solution."[5]

The world economy eventually stabilized, due to massive intervention by governments, but recovery was spotty, incomplete, and slow – providing fodder for a renewed round of critiques of globalization. Clearly, the rapidity and scope of economic integration had led to great volatility that prompted repeated crises in the world economy. Before the crash of 2008, international markets had been instrumental in a run on the Mexican peso in 1995, the Asian financial contagion in 1997–1998, and the dot.com bubble burst of 2001. Developing and poor countries played vocal parts in the new round of criticism, as the United States, multinational corporations, and private investors had encouraged them to deregulate their capital markets and open their economies to foreign investment. This made them susceptible to outside pressures from institutions, nations, and world economic fluctuations. Changes in one country could affect entire regions, as in 1997 when the Thai baht plummeted in value, setting off a currency "flu" that sickened other nations. Those favoring the Washington Consensus of liberalization and globalization, however, blamed such crises on the host countries' corrupt practices, inefficiencies, and lack of oversight. Optimists argued that not only did globalization help these emerging countries, but it was an irrevocable

[5] Paul Krugman, "Moment of truth," *New York Times*, October 10, 2007, www.nytimes.com/2008/10/10/opinion/10krugman.html?scp=1&sq=Moment%20of%20Truth&st=cse.

phenomenon that could not be halted. And why should it, since it brought such great rewards?

Critics of globalization countered with additional concerns over labor, environment, and national sovereignty. The world's biggest retailer, Walmart, came under fire for low pay and insurance benefits, as did many other corporations. Globalization, critics contended, gave rise to sweatshop conditions around the world as capitalist firms competed to find the cheapest labor anywhere. In the environmental arena, globalization came under attack for promoting a "race to the bottom," among countries seeking foreign investment, each trying to outdo the others in rolling back environmental protections in the competition to woo firms. To many critics, the international organizations and agreements dedicated to liberalizing trade, such as the WTO and NAFTA, elevated the principle of deregulation at the expense of adequate labor or environmental standards. A backlash against the power of bureaucrats in the WTO and IMF arose, as concerns about the role of government oversight called into question the power of a handful of unelected individuals immune to democratic pressures. Opponents of globalization also pointed to the growing power of transnational corporations and financiers to destabilize nations and markets and undermine democratically achieved labor and environmental regulations.

The protest movement against globalization exploded at the turn of the millennium. Anti-globalization forces first took to the streets of the United States in 1999, when the WTO was meeting in Seattle to plan a new round of trade negotiations. Demonstrations followed over the next several years at gatherings of the United Nations, the IMF and World Bank, the Davos World Economic Forum, Summit of the Americas, and Group of Seven industrial powers' meetings. In the period from 2008 to 2010, economic depression, national protests under the banner of the Occupy Wall Street movement, and other protests in Spain, Greece, and elsewhere over austerity programs, fueled resentment against seemingly market-oriented, pro-globalization governments and regional organizations such as the European Union. Even the Arab Spring movement of 2010–2011, though a protest against local and national authorities, was shaped in part by a critique of a global capitalist system which was skewed against the masses but had been very lucrative for cooperative authoritarian leaders like the ones protestors were trying to oust.

New voices from the corridors of power soon harmonized with the chorus of popular protest against globalization. Government officials preoccupied with security issues worried about globalization's effects, noting that the 9/11 terrorists used Internet communications, easy entry requirements into the

United States, and a relatively open financial system to plan and fund their horrendous mission. Chinese, Iranian, and other authorities worried about the Internet access of ordinary citizens, fearing what they regarded as contamination by foreign, excessively democratic, ideas. Authorities everywhere worried about the movement across borders of illicit drugs and food, disease, and criminals, which seemed easier than ever before. Moral critiques about fairness from people as prominent as popes and UN General Secretaries added to the assault on globalization.

Conclusions

Governments enabled globalization. But, in so doing, they also unleashed the power of transnational flows of individuals, ideas, and innovation that networked billions of people together around the world, thereby rendering the state more of an umpire than a gatekeeper to the global economy and culture. Some observers reveled in the thought that globalization meant the end of history, and the triumph of liberal democracy based on open-door capitalism. Others cringed at the loss of control to market factors and worried about the replacement of local music, art, literature, food, clothing, and everything else by a flattened and uniform global culture. Since the more modern era of globalization, beginning in the nineteenth century, the process has emerged, waned, and flourished, largely in response to the behavior of governments and the uneven march of technology. But the long-term trend is now clear: the world has become more unified, and people from prime ministers to peasants have learned to take into account global conditions when making their decisions. Globalization is now among the defining trends in world history, and will likely remain so in the future.

Further reading

Appelbaum, Richard and Nelson Lichtenstein. "A new world of retail supremacy: supply chains and workers' chains in the age of Wal-Mart," *International Labor and Working-Class History* 70 (2006), 106–125.

Arrighi, Giovanni. "The World Economy and the Cold War, 1970–1990," in Melvyn P. Leffler and Odd Arne Westad (eds.), *The Cambridge History of the Cold War*, Vol. 2, *Endings*. Cambridge University Press, 2010.

Barber, Benjamin R. *Jihad and McWorld: How Globalism and Tribalism are Reshaping the World*. New York: Ballantine Books, 1996.

Beck, Ulrich. *What Is Globalization?* Cambridge: Polity, 2000.

Becker, William H. and Samuel F. Wells, Jr., eds. *Economics and World Power: An Assessment of American Diplomacy Since 1789*. New York: Columbia University Press, 1984.

Bhagwati, Jagdish. *In Defense of Globalization*. Oxford University Press, 2007.

Chanda, Nayan. *Bound Together: How Traders, Preachers, Adventurers, and Warriors Shaped Globalization*. Yale University Press, 2007.

Eckes, Alfred E., Jr. *Opening America's Market: U.S. Foreign Trade Policy Since 1776*. Chapel Hill: University of North Carolina Press, 1995.

Eckes, Alfred E., Jr. and Thomas W. Zeiler. *Globalization and the American Century*. Cambridge University Press, 2003.

Ferguson, Niall, Charles Maier, Erez Manela, and Daniel J. Sargent, eds. *The Shock of the Global: The 1970s in Perspective*. Cambridge, MA: Belknap Press, 2010.

Frieden, Jeffry A. *Global Capitalism: Its and Rise in the Twentieth Century*. New York: W.W. Norton and Company, 2006.

Friedman, Thomas. *The Lexus and the Olive Tree*, rev. edn. New York: Picador, 2012.

The World Is Flat: A Brief History of the Twenty-First Century. New York: Picador, 2007.

Greider, William. *One World, Ready or Not: The Manic Logic of Global Capitalism*. New York: Simon and Schuster, 1997.

Hay, Colin and David Marsh, eds. *Demystifying Globalization*. Houndsmill: Macmillan Press, 2000.

Held, David and Anthony McGrew, eds. *Governing Globalization: Power, Authority and Global Governance*. Cambridge: Polity Press, 2002.

Hoganson, Kristin. "Stuff it: domestic consumption and the Americanization of the world paradigm," *Diplomatic History* 30/4 (September 2006), 571–594.

Hopkins, A. G., ed. *Globalization in World History*. New York: W.W. Norton & Company, 2002.

Jones, Geoffrey. *Multinationals and Global Capitalism: From the Nineteenth to the Twenty-First Century*. Oxford University Press, 2005.

Lang, Michael. "Globalization and its history," *Journal of Modern History* 78/4 (2006), 899–931.

LaFeber, Walter. *Michael Jordan and the New Global Capitalism*. New York: W.W. Norton, 1999.

Lechner, Frank J. and John Boli, eds. *The Globalization Reader*, 4th edn. Malden, MA: Wiley-Blackwell, 2011.

Levitt, Theodore. "The globalization of markets," *Harvard Business Review* 61/3 (May-June 1983), 92–102.

Levinson, Marc. *The Box: How the Shipping Container Made the World Smaller and the World Economy Bigger*. Princeton University Press, 2006.

Lynch, Katherine L. *The Forces of Economic Globalization: Challenges to the Regime of International Commercial Arbitration*. The Hague: Kluwer Law Internationa, 2003.

McKevitt, Andrew C. "'You Are Not Alone!' Anime and the globalizing of America," *Diplomatic History* 34/5 (November 2010), 893–921.

Mittelman, James H. *The Globalization Syndrome: Transformation and Resistance*. Princeton University Press, 2000.

Narlikar, Amrita, Martin Daunton, and Robert M. Stern, eds. *The Oxford Handbook on the World Trade Organization*. Oxford University Press, 2012.

O'Rourke, Kevin H. and Jeffrey G. Williamson. *Globalization and History: The Evolution of a Nineteenth-Century Atlantic Economy*. Cambridge, MA: MIT Press, 2001.

Rhode, Paul W. and Gianni Toniolo, eds. *The Global Economy in the 1990s: A Long-Run Perspective*. Cambridge University Press, 2006.

Rosenberg, Emily S. *A World Connecting, 1870–1945*. Cambridge, MA: Belknap Press, 2012.

Sassen, Sakia. *Globalization and Its Discontents: Essays on the New Mobility of People and Money*. New York: The New Press, 1998.

Steger, Manfred B. *Globalization: A Very Short Introduction*. Oxford University Press, 2003.

Stiglitz, Joseph E. *Globalization and Its Discontents*. New York: W.W. Norton, 2002.

Williamson, Jeffrey G. "Globalization, convergence, and history," *Journal of Economic History* 56/2 (1996), 277–306.

Wolf, Martin. *Why Globalization Works*, 2nd edn. Yale University Press, 2005.

Yergin, Daniel and Joseph Stanislaw. *The Commanding Heights: The Battle Between Government and the Marketplace That is Remaking the Modern World*. New York: Touchstone, 1998.

Zachary, G. Pascal. *The Global Me: New Cosmopolitans and the Competitive Edge: Picking Globalism's Winners and Losers*. New York: PublicAffairs, 2000.

Zeiler, Thomas W. "Opening doors in the world economy," in Akira Iriye (ed.), *Global Interdependence: The World After 1945*. Cambridge, MA: Belknap Press, 2014.

Index